Mastering

Philosophy

Palgrave Master Series

Accounting
Accounting Skills
Advanced English Language
Advanced English Literature
Advanced Pure Mathematics
Arabic
Basic Management
Biology
British Politics
Business Communication
Business Environment
C Programming
C++ Programming
Chemistry
COBOL Programming
Communication
Computing
Counselling Skills
Counselling Theory
Customer Relations
Database Design
Delphi Programming
Desktop Publishing
Economic and Social History
Economics
Electrical Engineering
Electronic and Electrical Calculations
Electronics
Employee Development
English Grammar
English Language
English Literature
Fashion Buying and Merchandising
  Management
Fashion Styling
French

Geography
German
Global Information Systems
Human Resource Managemer
Information Technology
Internet
Italian
Java
Management Skills
Marketing Management
Mathematics
Microsoft Office
Microsoft Windows, Novell
  NetWare and UNIX
Modern British History
Modern European History
Modern United States History
Modern World History
Networks
Organisational Behaviour
Pascal and Delphi Programmi
Philosophy
Physics
Practical Criticism
Psychology
Shakespeare
Social Welfare
Sociology
Spanish
Statistics
Strategic Management
Systems Analysis and Design
Team Leadership
Theology
Twentieth Century Russian H
Visual Basic
World Religions

www.palgravemasterseries.com

Palgrave Master Series

Series Standing Order ISBN 0–333–69343–4
(outside North America only)

You can receive future titles in this series as they are published by placing a standin;
Please contact your bookseller or, in case of difficulty, write to us at the address bel
your name and address, the title of the series and the ISBN quoted above.

Customer Services Department, Macmillan Distribution Ltd
Houndmills, Basingstoke, Hampshire RG21 6XS, England

Mastering
Philosophy
Second edition

Anthony Harrison-Barbet

palgrave

First edition 1990
Second edition 2001
Published by
PALGRAVE
Houndmills, Basingstoke, Hampshire RG21 6XS and
175 Fifth Avenue, New York, N.Y. 10010
Companies and representatives throughout the world

PALGRAVE is the new global academic imprint of
St. Martin's Press LLC Scholarly and Reference Division and
Palgrave Publishers Ltd (formerly Macmillan Press Ltd).

ISBN 0–333–79384–6

This book is printed on paper suitable for recycling and
made from fully managed and sustained forest sources.

A catalogue record for this book is available
from the British Library.

10   9   8   7   6   5   4   3   2
10   09 08 07 06 05 04 03 02

Printed in Great Britain by
Creative Print & Design Ltd (Wales), Ebbw Vale

For Clíona and Morwenna

Contents

Preface to the second edition

What do you do for a living? If you can say you are a 'bus conductor, plumber, engineer, or secretary, for example, you will be on safe ground. But to call oneself a philosopher, or even a philosophy teacher, is to run the risk of eliciting a variety of uncomplimentary responses. To some people of a conservative, traditionalist, no-nonsense, or down-to-earth disposition, philosophers are often seen as the supreme exemplars of intellectualism – the term being used pejoratively – and are thus objects of suspicion and distrust: they are regarded as subversives, corruptors of the social order, liable to undermine the moral standards of the nation. To many other people the philosopher is an eccentric, unworldly figure, the epitomy of the absent-minded professor, but for the most part harmless. To some 'hard-headed' scientists philosophers are people who ask funny sorts of questions and come up with many different answers – or none at all. Critics of all three kinds tend to concur in the judgement that philosophers are not particularly useful members of society – or are even parasitic on it.

Such extreme and prejudiced views are of course stereotypes and are, fortunately, representative of a minority. Moreover, as the extract from *The Times* leader article that follows this Preface shows, philosophers are now getting a 'better press'. Nevertheless, there is still wide-spread ignorance as to what philosophy is all about and why its pursuit may be worthwhile. This is understandable; you no doubt studied maths and English at school, and perhaps some history and science, but it is unlikely that any philosophy would have been included in the curriculum. Your first acquaintance with the subject would usually have been at a university, where you would be studying for a degree, or you might have been following a general studies course in a local college, with philosophy as a component. The situation in Britain is thus different from that existing in, say, France, where large numbers of secondary school pupils study philosophy as one of many subjects in preparation for the Baccalaureate. However, philosophy has been available for a good many years to students as an option at 'A' level and in the International Baccalaureate – both of which are now becoming increasingly popular.

Many people, while recognizing they know little about the nature and value of philosophy, would admit to being curious. It is perhaps such curiosity that has led you to purchase or borrow this book. Or perhaps you have already embarked on a formal course of study and would welcome further guidance. It is for such individuals as yourself, people with a questioning approach to life and a genuine interest in intellectual problems, that *Mastering Philosophy* has been written. There are, of course, already many excellent introductory text-books of philosophy in print. *Mastering Philosophy*, however, has been designed to cater for a wide readership with varying requirements. Attention has been paid both to the texts of a number of major philosophers and to many of the central problems of philosophy. It is hoped therefore that the book will be of benefit to students preparing for 'A' level or the International Baccalaureate, as well as to beginners with no particular examination objective in mind. It should prove useful also as a first introductory text for students working externally for the London University B.A. in philosophy.

Comprehensive Reading lists and a wide range of Questions have been included with each chapter (except the first). To assist you further, 'Guided' answer notes to selected questions are provided at the end of the book, together with a Glossary of technical terms. You should find you are able to tackle most of the questions successfully provided you have studied the relevant sections of the text and the set books, and have thought hard about the issues. Some questions, however, are more testing and presuppose an acquaintance with some of the books or essays included in the Reading lists under 'Supplementary reading'.

For this second edition I have revised all the chapters, in some cases extensively. More attention has been paid to recent developments in 'continental' philosophy, and new chapters – on logic and critical thinking, and Chinese and Indian Philosophy – have been added. Necessarily they can do no more than provide a vary basic introduction to these fields: but I hope they will add to the general appeal of the book.

Inevitably there are weaknesses. Some critics may feel that the ground covered is too wide. Others may regret that this or that philosopher has not gained a mention. But I have endeavoured to achieve a balance between depth and breadth, and I have tried to integrate a 'problems' approach to philosophy with the recognition that it has a historical dimension. Students who are required to study set authors for examination purposes have thus also been catered for.

I am grateful to the two (anonymous) publisher's reviewers for their constructive criticisms of the first edition, though I have not been willing or able to implement all their suggestions. I alone of course take sole responsibility for the text as it stands. I should also like to express my appreciation to Suzannah Tipple, Publisher, for her support and encouragement.

The Verulam Institute of Human Studies
May 2000

Acknowledgements

The author and publishers wish to thank the following for permission to use copyright material:

Lawrence & Wishart Ltd for extracts from *The German Ideology* by Karl Marx, ed. C.J. Arthur, 1970; Oxford University Press for extracts from *Republic* by Plato, trans. Robin Waterfield, The World's Classics, 1994, © 1993 by Robin Waterfield; Times Newspapers Ltd for leading article, 'Think on', *The Times*, 15.8.98, Copyright © Times Newspapers Ltd 1998; and the International Baccalaureate for questions from past and current specimen examination papers. Examination questions marked AQA or AQA (AEB) are reproduced by permission of the Assessment and Qualification Alliance.

Every effort has been made to trace all the copyright-holders, but if any have been inadvertently overlooked the publishers will be pleased to make the necessary arrangement at the first opportunity.

▪▼ Think on

Philosophy is a quintessentially modern discipline

For Immanuel Kant, the Enlightenment could be captured in two small words: *sapere aude* – 'dare to think' . . .

. . . [I]n this age of uncertainty, when today's vocational training may be tomorrow's passport to redundancy, 'dare to think' should be the motto pinned on the wall of every undergraduate room and recruitment agency. Philosophy is making a modest comeback in British universities, and not before time.

The great virtue of philosophy is that it teaches not what to think, but how to think. It is the study of meaning, of the principles underlying conduct, thought and knowledge. The skills it hones are the ability to analyse, to question orthodoxies and to express things clearly. However arcane some philosophical texts may be . . . . the ability to formulate questions and follow arguments is the essence of education.

It can be studied at many levels. In the US, where the number of philosophy graduates has increased by 5 per cent a year during the 1990s, only a very few go on to become philosophers. Their employability, at 98.9 per cent, is impressive by any standard. Philosophy has always been a good training for the law; but it is equally useful for computer scientists. In this country, the Higher Education Statistics Survey puts philosophy of science right up with medicine in its employment record for graduates.

Philosophy is, in commercial jargon, the ultimate 'transferable work skill'. That is not the only argument for expanding philosophy departments, and encouraging sixth-formers to read Plato, or John Stuart Mill on liberty. Chris Woodhead, the Chief Inspector of schools, has cautioned against an obsession with the narrowly vocational. Lecturing the Confederation of British Industry on the 'sly utilitarianism' of employers, he defends a liberal education as needing 'no justification beyond the satisfaction and enjoyment it brings'. Teenagers waiting for their 'A' level results and pondering degree courses should consider philosophy. It is rewarding in itself; and it could nowadays be the passport to a successful, varied career.

[From *The Times*, 15th August 1998]

▣ M ▮ Introduction

1.1 What is philosophy?

The question 'What is philosophy?', unlike the apparently similar questions 'What is history?' and 'What is science?', does not admit of a straightforward answer. Indeed it would not be too much of an exaggeration to say, paradoxically, that the question is itself a philosophical one – in so far as different philosophers tend to have different conceptions as to the nature of their chosen discipline. Perhaps the best way of finding out what the various answers are is to plunge straight in and to 'do' philosophy by studying this book. Nevertheless, we shall first provide you with a number of general accounts which will help you to find your bearings before you set out on your journey of intellectual discovery.

(1) The word 'philosophy' is derived from two Greek words, *philos* ('lover') and *sophia* ('wisdom'). The first thinker to describe himself as a philosopher may well have been Pythagoras (born *c.* 570 BC), but it is with Plato (born *c.* 428 BC) that the term in its original and primary sense is most closely identified. For him wisdom is a condition or state which gifted individuals seek to attain as a result of many years of education culminating in 'dialectic'. Having achieved wisdom they are enabled to apprehend Truth or Reality and thereby to acquire virtue – the knowledge of how to live rightly. Philosophy thus comes to be **the study of ultimate reality**, the fundamental principles of existence which in some sense both unify and transcend the insights offered us through both religious faith and the scientific knowledge we gain as a result of observation and experiment.

The possibility that such 'ultimate' knowledge might be achieved through the exercise of pure reason was the motivation which lay behind attempts made by many later philosophers to construct all-embracing metaphysical systems. Spinoza, Leibniz, Hegel and Bradley are good examples of this kind of thinker. A major criticism which has been levelled against these representatives of **'rationalist'** and **'idealist'** traditions is that they ignore or pay insufficient attention to the claims of sense-experience. In any case, it is argued, 'pure' reason on its own can give us no knowledge of the world. Accordingly we find a number of major philosophers – Locke, Berkeley and Hume, and later still Russell and Ayer, to name but a few – starting out not from pure reason but from the data of our everyday senses. (This is not to say, of course, that the philosophical premises of such **'empiricist'** thinkers do not involve any metaphysical presuppositions of their own.) A recognition of the legitimate clams of both reason and experience was the achievement of the eminent eighteenth century German philosopher, Kant: for him philosophy was essentially **an investigation into the preconditions**

and limits of human knowledge. He rejected rationalist metaphysics yet argued against any philosophy which failed to take account of the role played by reason in giving sense-experience its structure and coherence.

(2) P.F. Strawson has made a fruitful distinction between 'descriptive' metaphysics, which 'describes the actual structure of our thought about the world', and 'revisionary' metaphysics, which is 'concerned to produce a better structure'. Descartes, Leibniz and Berkeley, he says, are revisionary, while Aristotle and Kant are descriptive. The philosophy of Hume is in part descriptive and in part revisionary. Strawson is to some extent influenced by Kant, but his writings also exhibit an important characteristic of much twentieth century British philosophy: the turning away from any attempt to discover fundamental features of the 'world' or 'reality' toward **a systematic investigation of the language** we use to describe it. Associated with this concern for language, two contrasting approaches are discernible: there are those who set out to discover a 'perfect' language which will accurately 'picture' the world, while other philosophers seek to uncover and describe the *variety* of ways in which, they believe, language may be used for different purposes – each being entirely appropriate within its own sphere and conforming to its own criteria. The movement from the first approach to the second is identified particularly with Ludwig Wittgenstein. Representatives of both positions tend to agree, however, that the primary task of the philosopher should be to show that the traditional problems of 'metaphysically-minded' thinkers are as often as not pseudo-questions which have arisen through their disregard of the rules or 'logical grammar' underlying the correct use of the language they use. The philosopher's role thus becomes both analytical and therapeutic.

(3) This concern with language is closely linked with another interpretation of the nature of philosophy, which has gained currency during this century – again particularly in Britain and America – the view that philosophy is a **'second-order' discipline**. Whereas earlier philosophers were concerned with system-building, with an examination of the basic data and structure of experience, or with investigations into the scope and limits of human reason, the job of philosophy, according to this third account, is to analyse not only its own concepts, principles and methods (as in epistemology, that is, the theory of knowledge), but also those specific to other disciplines. This approach therefore gives rise to 'philosophies' of science, religion, history, mathematics and so on.

(4) Some mention should also be made of several developments this century in Germany and France. Philosophy there has been dominated by three, often overlapping movements. (a) **Marxism**, originating in the nineteenth century, rejects Hegel's idealism but applies his dialectic method to the 'material' world, claiming that human actions and institutions are determined by the laws of economics, and that change is brought about by class struggle. (b) **Phenomenology**, associated in particular with Husserl, attempts through a process of 'intuition' or 'grasping', followed by the method of 'transcendental reduction', to uncover acts of experiencing and then to analyse the structure of experiences as such, without admitting any of the metaphysical or other explanatory presuppositions of traditional philosophy. (c) **Existentialism** emphasizes personal experience – freedom, moral conflict, commitment – in

what is seen by many to be a meaningless and deterministic universe. Existentialists, however, eschew all metaphysical systems and moral codes which are imposed on the individual from outside; each person is ultimately responsible to himself alone for making his own being, his own 'world' and his own values.

More recently, the writings of the German philosophers Gadamer and Habermas have attracted wider interest outside their own country. Drawing on phenomenology, Gadamer has made a major contribution to **hermeneutics** – a philosophical movement concerned with the interpretation of texts and indeed of culture in general. Habermas is a representative of the so-called 'Frankfurt School' of **critical theory**. He is influenced by Marxism and attempts to develop a systematic theory of the social sciences with a view to showing how 'distortion of communication' by ideologies can be eliminated. The debate between these two thinkers concerning the attainability of truth and the role of critical reason is of considerable importance. It is interesting also to note that the work of Gadamer and especially Habermas typifies the willingness of many contemporary 'continental' philosophers to make use of the resources of Anglo-American linguistic philosophy to develop their own philosophies.

Despite their differences these various movements have at least two features in common. (i) Philosophy is seen neither as an arid obsession with the dissection of language, nor as a futile search for 'metaphysical' explanations of reality, but primarily as a response to the human condition resulting in *action*. (ii) Philosophy tends to be integrated with human culture in general – with art, religion, literature, the natural and social sciences, and politics. These characteristics can be clearly seen in the work of Sartre, perhaps the most typical of recent 'continental' thinkers, and certainly the most widely known in this country by philosophers and non-philosophers alike. A novelist of repute and a political activist, as well as a philosopher, he brings together in his writings elements drawn from both phenomenology and existentialism, while his last published work before his death shows a commitment to Marxist dialectical materialism. Breadth and insight are also features of Ricoeur, whose writings span phenomenology, critical theory and methodology, hermeneutics and literary theory, language, religion and ethics, and who may well prove in retrospect to be a major figure in the philosophy of the late twentieth century.

It must be stressed that the four accounts we have given of philosophy are themselves generalized and are over-simplified. To gain an adequate understanding of these, and other interpretations of the nature and methods of the subject, you would have at the very least to embark on a thorough and systematic study of its history. Our intention here is no more than to help you appreciate that there is no *single* description which may be regarded as uniquely definitive of philosophy. This should become clearer as you work through the book. If one *had* to pick out some lowest common denominator of all philosophical schools or traditions, all one could say, perhaps, is that philosophy deals with certain sorts of problems which cannot be solved by, or are no longer regarded as the proper concern of, other disciplines, especially the natural sciences. A more cynical commentator might be inclined to think of the philosopher as the refuse-collector of the intellectual world, picking up the many problems discarded by workers in other fields. But think what would happen to a civilized society, as ours purports to be, if there were no dustmen!

1.2 Is there progress in philosophy?

A scientist may justly claim that over the past five hundred years or so we have steadily gained a more complete understanding of the nature and structure of the universe. Likewise it may be said that today's historians are able to provide a more accurate and truthful account of the past than ever before. In both historical research and the natural sciences there has been substantial progress. Can philosophers make such a claim for their discipline? At first sight an affirmative answer seems unlikely. In the last section it was stated that much contemporary philosophy is concerned with problems which have ceased to be of interest to workers in other fields; to them such problems have become redundant. At one time physics (the study of *ta phusika*, 'the things of Nature') was bound up with metaphysical disputes about 'qualities', 'essences' and 'substances', which were believed to lie behind or to be manifested in natural phenomena. But from the sixteenth century onwards, with the development of systematic experimental techniques designed to test hypotheses, '*natural* philosophy' gradually dissociated itself from philosophy as such and later came to be known as physical science. Chemistry emerged as a second major science in its own right in the eighteenth century. The development of the atomic theory provides us with an excellent illustration of progress in science. The idea that the universe might be composed of small indivisible particles or 'atoms' (Greek *atomos*, 'that which cannot be divided') was first suggested in the fifth century BC by a 'school' of Greek philosophers known as the Atomists and developed by Epicurus two hundred years later. This essentially philosophical theory was, however, largely ignored for more than two thousand years until it was revived by the French Epicurean thinker Gassendi in the seventeenth century and adopted about 1800 by the English scientist John Dalton, who subjected it to experimental testing. Today we no longer think of atoms as hard, impenetrable, indivisible corpuscles but as energetic clouds of still smaller particles orbiting a central nucleus which under certain conditions can be split. Still more fundamental particles have also been postulated, for the existence of which there is some experimental support. A philosophy of qualities and essences seems to have become superfluous. In much the same way, attempts have been made to substitute the methodological procedures of experimental psychology and neurology for speculation about the mind or soul and its relationship to the body, which has been at the centre of philosophical thinking since at least the time of Plato.

Philosophers are notorious for their persistence. They refuse to admit there is nothing left for them to do – and quite rightly; for the emergence of new and autonomous disciplines continually throws up further intellectual problems. The concept of God, which first appeared in the writings of Plato, has been central to the 'science' of theology since the early years of Christianity. But questions about the existence and nature of such a being, the problem of reconciling God's omniscience and omnipotence with human freedom and the seeming presence of evil in the world, and the analysis of such terms as 'belief' and 'faith', keep contemporary philosophers of religion fully occupied. As for the particles of the physicist, it is legitimate to question their ontological status. Are atoms, electrons and quarks equally real? Are they real in the sense that tables and horses are said to be real? What is meant by 'reality' in such cases? And what of the explanations of 'mental' activity put forward by psychologists and neurobiologists? *Is* mind reducible to or equivalent to the behaviour of the brain? *Has* modern science ruled out the possibility of a 'soul' acting in, but separable from, the body? If not, the problem of the relationship between these two entities remains to be solved. Of course philosophers belonging to different 'schools' will try to deal with such questions in different ways. That they are continuing to make the attempt is indisputable. In other fields too, philosophical argument is as lively as ever it was. In ethics, for example, there are many important issues. What makes certain actions good or bad, right or wrong? Are motives important? Should the *results* of human actions be regarded as relevant to their goodness or badness? In a complex society there are also likely to be conflicting views concerning such matters as euthanasia, contraception, divorce and nuclear war (on all of which the theologian has something to say). The philosopher too must have a role to play here – if not in providing final and incontrovertible solutions, then at least in clarifying the issues and terms used. Is there then progress in philosophy? The answer is surely, yes. To make clear what was previously unclear must count as an advance. Moreover, a careful study of the history of philosophy shows that some of even the greatest philosophers have made fundamental mistakes, and it has been to the credit of their successors that these errors have been discovered and satisfactory explanations put forward to account for them. As J.L. Austin once wrote: 'In philosophy, there are many mistakes that it is no disgrace to have made: to make a first-water, ground-floor mistake, so far from being easy, takes *one* form of philosophical genius.' And, one might add, to discover such a mistake takes another form of philosophical genius. Therein also lies progress in philosophy. (Reference to some examples will be made in the course of the book.)

But even if there were no progress at all in either of the two respects just mentioned, the cultural value of philosophy cannot easily be denied. Concern for the validity of arguments, precision in use of language, imaginative insight, bold speculations, close examination of the principles and concepts of other disciplines, clarification of controversial issues, especially in ethics, law and politics – all of these, which have at one time or another been grist to the philosopher's mill, are essential for the well-being of a liberal democracy. Moreover, many instances can be cited of the profound effect philosophical writings have had on the political, social and wider cultural development of nations. The influence of Plato's *Republic* on St Augustine and through him on the religious and political 'world-view' of early Christian Europe, the relevance of Rousseau's *Social Contract* to the French Revolution, and the significance of the philosophical works of Hegel for an understanding of Karl Marx and the emergence of Communism are particularly good examples. Whether such influences should themselves be regarded as 'good' or 'bad' is of course itself a suitable question for philosophers and historians of ideas to argue about!

1.3 Plan of the book

The approach we have adopted is to present philosophy to you in such a way as to take account of the various interpretations discussed in the previous section. Our aim also is to acquaint you with the main themes and arguments of a number of major philosophers within a broadly historical perspective, as well as to help you get to grips with many of the fundamental problems occupying the attention of philosophers today.

Chapter 2 offers firstly an introduction to formal logic. Most university courses in philosophy include the study of logic. There are two reasons for this: (1) it encourages clear reasoning and helps in the detection of invalid arguments; (2) some grasp of formal logic is needed for an understanding of certain problems in a field of philosophy known as philosophical logic – which overlaps with both epistemology and metaphysics. A second aim of the chapter is to introduce you to some aspects of what is often called 'critical thinking'. Unfortunately, despite the seeming clarity of this phrase, it is not easy to define precisely what it means. If you are able to reason clearly and can identify invalid arguments in formal logic then you will already have achieved some competence as a 'critical thinker'. Critical thinking may also be said to be exhibited in the capacity to understand and analyse different kinds of discourse, and as such it has much in common with 'informal logic' and the 'language analysis' characteristic of much of the philosophy practised in the English-speaking world in the last century. An account of informal logic is therefore also included in Chapter 2. However, critical thinking, as it is taught in many schools and colleges, particularly in the United States of America, extends beyond philosophy as such and moves into the realm of literary criticism. This of course is not our concern in this book. However, the chapter will end with a brief look at some of the rhetorical devices and informal fallacies frequently used in persuasive arguments.

In Chapters 3 and 4 we shall guide you through Plato's *Republic* and Aristotle's *Nicomachean Ethics*. This will not only enable you to learn something about the ethics and political philosophy of two of the greatest philosophers of all time, but will also introduce you to some of the principal presuppositions of their thought as contained in their theories of knowledge, metaphysics and 'psychology'.

Chapter 5 will be concerned with a more extensive and critical investigation into the problem of knowledge, with reference in particular to the philosophies of Descartes, Hume, Kant, Husserl, Russell, Ayer and Ryle.

Chapters 6 and 7 will deal with some central issues in ethics and political philosophy. Again the discussion will relate to the writings of a number of major philosophers including Hume, Kant, Rousseau, Mill, Nietzsche, Marx and Sartre.

If Chapters 5 to 7 are concerned with the 'hard-core' of philosophy – epistemology and ethics – Chapters 8 to 10 consist of introductions to several important fields of philosophy in which it can be seen as acting in its role as a 'second-order' discipline. Thus Chapter 8 will introduce you to some of the main issues in the philosophy of science; Chapter 9 covers the philosophy of religion; and Chapter 10 is about aesthetics (roughly, the philosophy of art or beauty).

Chapter 11 includes an examination of four important metaphysical problems – mind, causation, freedom and reality. We shall also refer to the wider problems of the legitimacy or otherwise of metaphysics in general; and you will learn something of the different views held by, among others, Kant, Ayer, Wittgenstein and Heidegger.

In Chapter 12 we shall investigate a number of interconnected fields which have to some extent begun to provide a bridge between the 'linguistic' philosophy which has characterized much British and American philosophy during the twentieth century and so-called 'Continental' philosophy. These subject areas are the philosophy of the social sciences, the philosophy of man and culture, the hermeneutics of Gadamer, and Habermas's 'critical theory'.

Mastering Philosophy ends with a – necessarily brief and incomplete – survey of several non-Western philosophical traditions. This has been included partly to counter the impression that the reader might understandably have been given that philosophy is a uniquely Western cultural enterprise. It should be recognized, on the contrary, that India and China, for example, have also nurtured philosophical speculation and analysis of the highest quality for over two thousand years. It is of course also broadly accurate to say that, for much of this time, oriental philosophy was closely bound up with religious systems or ways of life such as Taoism, Confucianism, Hinduism and Buddhism. Nevertheless, it is instructive to discover that despite the considerable differences between the assumptions and methods employed within Eastern and Western philosophical traditions, there are also many parallels and similarities. One might also add that some appreciation of these traditions is surely desirable in a multi-racial and pluralistic society and could contribute to greater understanding and tolerance of other cultures. It is no doubt on the basis of such considerations that 'World Philosophical Traditions' has been included as an 'optional theme' in the International Baccalaureate curriculum; and it is hoped that Chapter 13 will go some way towards meeting the requirements of students who have chosen this topic.

1.4 How to use this book

Earlier we suggested that the best way to learn about philosophy is to 'do' it, and it was stated, perhaps rather boldly, that the purpose of this book was to show you how. We should be severely at fault, however, if we were to give you the impression that *all* you need to do is to read through the next twelve chapters and that you would then have become an expert. Philosophy is not a soft option. While a good case can be made out for the view that most of us do 'philosophize' unawares some of the time, to articulate our arguments, to make our premises explicit and to subject them to sustained critical analysis does require determination and a willingness to think deeply and intensively. All a book such as this can do is to set out some of the problems for you, draw your attention to the several ways in which they have been tackled by different philosophers, and suggest how *you* might approach and respond to them. In this way you will acquire some mastery of the subject. We hope the following suggestions will be found helpful.

(1) Most chapters are largely self-contained, but numerous cross-references have been included. They can therefore be studied in any order. However, you will probably find it more convenient to read through the book systematically, though do not feel you have to work your way through the chapter on logic and critical thinking; you can dip into this while studying other topics. Note that if you are preparing for the 'A' level or the IB examinations you do not have to tackle any formal logic, but you should study the other sections in Chapter 2. To assist you we have also provided, at the beginning of each relevant section, references to the appropriate parts of the prescribed texts and, in some instances, to other texts which, although not 'set' books, will, we hope, be found useful. We suggest you read through the relevant texts before studying the material of each chapter. You can then go back to the text with greater understanding and in a better position to acquire a firmer grasp of the problems by tackling some of the books and essays suggested in the reading lists. Do not be alarmed about the length of some of these lists. Examiners will certainly not be expecting you to have read more than a small selection. (We have indicated the books which we think you should look at first.) If, however, you want to extend your knowledge and understanding of philosophical problems – perhaps you are contemplating taking a degree course – then you can always explore some of the many other listed titles at your leisure. By the way, in case you want to get some idea of the historical development of philosophy, so as to acquire a broader perspective or for general reference, a short list of suitable books has been provided at the end of this section.

(2) Make you own notes and summaries. Be ready always to *question* the arguments put forward not only in each chapter but also in other commentaries or articles you choose to study. As you read through *Mastering Philosophy* you will find interspersed throughout the text numerous hints or references (they are marked with an asterisk *) which are designed to help you think critically abut the various issues. More extensive 'comments and criticisms' are to be found at the end of many sections. You might also try to find someone with an interest in the subject with whom you can discuss your reading. Philosophy is not the easiest subject to study in isolation. If you intend to study externally for the London University B.A., you may like to know that the author offers a comprehensive distance learning programme. Details are provided at the end of the 'guided' answers section.

(3) If you decide to attempt some of the essay questions listed at the end of each chapter, whether or not you have an opportunity of submitting your answers to an experienced philosophy teacher, remember these four requirements for good writing: (a) conciseness – be *economical* in your use of words; (b) comprehensiveness – make sure you have covered *all* the main points; (c) relevance – take care that you are answering the question *actually asked*; (d) avoid florid or excessively 'literary' language. (This is not to say that there is no place for 'style'; many of the great English-speaking philosophers, from Hobbes in the seventeenth century to, say, Ryle in the twentieth, have been superb

writers. Just remember when preparing tutorial essays or examination answers that you are not writing a novel or an article for a popular newspaper.)

So now to work. Good luck!

Note: To avoid confusion with other books mentioned in the course of the text, when referring to particular chapters or sections of *Mastering Philosophy* we shall use the following conventions: 'Chapter' will be denoted by 'Ch.' (with the first letter an upper-case (capital) 'C'); '2.6' (for example) will denote Chapter 2, section 6, and so on. In general, cross-references to *Mastering Philosophy* are in 'round' brackets. Cross-references to other books are denoted by 'ch.' (with the first letter a lower-case (small) 'c'); other cross-references are generally in 'square' brackets.

GENERAL READING

(For details of editions and publishers, see the comprehensive Bibliography at the end of the book.)

Copleston, F.C., *A History of Philosophy*, 9 vols.
Hamlyn, D.W., *A History of Western Philosophy*.
O'Connor, D.J. (ed.), *A Critical History of Western Philosophy*.
Russell, B., *History of Western Philosophy and its Connection with Political and Social Circumstances from the Earliest Times to the Present Day.*

■ ⌄ **2** Critical thinking

2.1 Introduction

Each one of us is an individual, having his or her own unique personality. There is not much difference between one amoeba and another, or between bees belonging to a particular species but, in the later stages of evolution, individuality – as expressed through appearance and 'character' – becomes increasingly evident. We can perhaps reasonably talk of cats, dogs, horses and especially apes as having their own personalities, though in attributing personality to them we run the risk of anthropomorphism, and in a strict sense we should perhaps confine this term to ourselves alone. Why are we so different? Individuality seems to be a function of both biology and culture. None of us has the same genetic make-up (except for identical twins), and while we have much in common with each other at the level of instincts and emotional responses to certain kinds of stimuli, these – together with our intellectual and physical capacities, our potential for, say, music, languages, philosophy and sport – are shaped and channelled by our various family backgrounds, environment, education, relationships with others, and so on. These biological and cultural factors would seem also to account for the fact that we often differ so greatly in our religious beliefs, ethical principles, political affiliations and economic theories – even within a particular cultural milieu. Looked at from another point of view, this is surprising. After all, we inhabit the same planet in the same universe, have similar sense organs, and similar brain structures and nervous systems. If there are 'absolute' truths and moral standards (and this is of course questionable), then it might be expected that we should all have recognized and acknowledged them. Arguably there is a 'lowest common denominator' of ethical standards which cut across cultural divisions (see 6.8). At least there should be a broad consensus about 'empirical' and 'historical' facts: but even here we often find disagreement. These many differences should not really matter. It would be a dull world if we all agreed about everything. In itself, variety is probably a good thing; arguably, without it there could be no progress. Unfortunately, as we all know, there is a negative aspect. For all our individuality there seems to be a deep need in most of us to identify with the group, especially in religion and politics; and as the history of civilization has shown this has often led to disputes, wars and genocide. There have been, and still are, very many unpleasant representatives of our species. As the eighteenth century German scientist, philosopher and critic Georg Lichtenberg wrote: 'Perhaps man is a bastard creature, a hybrid product of the ape and a now extinct higher being: and is derided by both apes and angel.'

However, we do possess the capacity to reason, to think critically. We can assess the evidence and seek to find weaknesses in the arguments of those whose views differ from ours and who often seek to convert us to their positions. But at the same time it is incumbent on us to justify our own beliefs and commitments while remaining open to the possibility that we may be in error. Such openness is the mark of balanced and intellectually healthy individuals – people who, arguably, have a role to play in eliminating tensions and conflicts in human society at both the local and global levels. Perhaps this is over-optimistic. At the beginning of this new millennium disputes proliferate. Science continues to raise serious ethical issues such as genetic engineering, and radical techniques for reproduction. There is much disagreement about how we should treat our environment or about how much funding should be devoted to space exploration while so many are dying from malnutrition on Earth. Resurgent nationalism often breeds violence. But is there any alternative to critical thinking? Without it there can be no consensus, and we then run the risk of either succumbing to totalitarianism or sinking into chaos.

How is this 'critical thinking' to be cultivated? What does it involve? Some attempt will be made in this chapter to answer these questions. Critical thinking is not of course a twentieth century phenomenon. It may be said to have originated with the early Greek philosophers and in particular with Plato and Aristotle. In the case of Plato it corresponds approximately to what he called **dialectic**, which encompassed a variety of methods to be employed by the philosopher to refute false doctrines and discover truth. In his lectures Aristotle set out to examine systematically the whole range of human reasoning and logical disputation. He termed this investigation the 'analytics' [see his *Prior Analytics*]. He distinguished between four types of argument: 'scientific', dialectical, inductive and rhetorical. As for the first [see *Posterior Analytics*] he is not using the term 'scientific' in its modern sense; rather, it refers to arguments whose premises are primary, true and provide 'causal' explanations of their conclusions and thereby knowledge. Dialectical arguments, on the other hand, start from 'opinions' and cannot lead to knowledge. However, such arguments are like 'scientific' ones in that they involve inferences from universal premises to particular conclusions. This is contrasted with inductive arguments which start from particulars and lead to universal conclusions. Lastly, rhetorical arguments essentially utilize a variety of techniques of persuasion. Dialectical, inductive and rhetorical arguments are all subsumed by Aristotle under a more general concept of dialectic argumentation – as the body of 'popular' reasoning [*Topics* and *Sophistic Elenchi*]. However, he also sets out to show that all modes of argument, 'scientific' or 'popular', share a common structure – the **syllogism**. And he sees this as the basis of his formal logic – a system which remained influential until the nineteenth century. Although a magnificent achievement, it is now recognized as at once too wide-ranging (Aristotle was mistaken in supposing all modes of argument are syllogistic) and too narrow (it is inadequate and indeed incorrect in its analysis of many kinds of linguistic patterns). These shortcomings will become apparent later in the chapter. Nevertheless, it is convenient to take some of Aristotle's distinctions as a starting-point for our examination of critical thinking; and we are going to consider some of the issues under three headings: (1) *formal* *logic*; (2) *informal logic* (including induction and 'conceptual analysis'); and (3) *rhetoric* – the study of each of which can be regarded as making a contribution to critical thinking.

FORMAL LOGIC

Note: Necessarily only a relatively brief survey is possible in a book of this size, but enough detail has been provided to give you a fair understanding of some of the main concepts and techniques. Should you want to study formal logic in greater depth you are directed to the Reading list at the end of the chapter.

I. Aristotelian logic

As much of this section is primarily of historical interest you may prefer to omit it altogether and move on directly to the next section. However, a basic knowledge of 'traditional' or 'classical' Aristotelian logic is recommended if you are to appreciate fully the power and scope of 'modern' symbolic logic.

2.2 Terminology

Formal logic is, we may say, concerned with the consistency of our beliefs, or with the correctness of our reasoning. This was Aristotle's view although he also supposed it at the same time to be about the thoughts which language signifies and which enable us to grasp reality. Some later logicians, following Aristotle, have as a result tended to obscure the differences between logic and on the one hand psychology and on the other epistemology (the theory of knowledge). Moreover, we should note that not all thinking is reasoning. So it is best to concentrate on language as such.

We shall start by introducing a few technical terms. In an argument we pass from one or more **propositions** to another. By 'proposition' is meant anything that can be said to be true or false. Propositions are generally distinguished from sentences and statements. Consider, for example, these three sentences: 'It is raining'; 'Il pleut'; 'Es regnet'. These are different sentences in so far as they belong respectively to English, French and German. Yet they have the same meaning, that is, they express the same proposition and can be used to make the same assertion.

*Comment

It should be mentioned here that the notion of a proposition is a controversial one, and much has been written about how it should be understood – what propositions are. Some philosophers have thought of them variously as the 'intentions of propositional attitudes', as meanings of sentences, or referents of what sentences are 'about'. Others have been more inclined to eliminate the term altogether. We shall not enter into the debate here and will in general use the terms 'statement' and 'proposition' synonymously. Note that the branch of philosophy which is concerned with such matters as the nature of propositions, sense and reference, the nature of truth and many others is called **philosophical logic**. It should not be confused with the **philosophy of logic** which deals with the methods of logic and the symbols employed (what we shall be covering in the next few sections) – though there is some overlap between the two fields.

In an argument we pass from one or more propositions called **premisses** to another proposition called the **conclusion**. This combination of premisses and conclusions constitutes the argument's **structure**. We usually identify arguments by such link words as 'because', 'since', 'therefore' and the like. A distinction is usually made by logicians between the mental process which allegedly occurs when we reason and the actual relationship between premisses and conclusions. The former is termed **inference**, the latter **implication**. These terms are often confused in everyday speech. As logicians we should say '*A* implies *B*' but '*We infer B from A*'. This notion of implication is central in logic. When we say *A* implies *B* we mean that *A* follows from *B* conclusively; the premisses provide **conclusive evidence** for *B*. Such a relationship is called **deductive**. Propositions, whether premisses or conclusions, are said to be **true** or **false**, but deductive arguments are said to be **valid** or **invalid**. This distinction is important. As you will see later, it is possible for an argument to be valid even though both premisses are false; and some arguments with true premisses and a true conclusion may be invalid. Validity or invalidity is a characteristic of the relationship between premisses and conclusion and not dependent on their **material** truth or falsity. Another way of putting this is to say that the logician is concerned with **logical form**, for it is on this that the validity of an argument can be seen to depend. Consider the following:

(1) All cats are black; Tom is a cat; therefore Tom is black.
(2) All schoolmasters are impecunious; Mr Squeers is a schoolmaster; therefore Mr Squeers is impecunious.

These two arguments, although their 'material' contents are different, have the same (valid) logical form in virtue of which they are valid instances: 'All *A*s are *B*s; *x* is an *A*; therefore *x* is a *B*'.

The phrase 'the **logic of terms**' is often used to describe 'traditional' Aristotelian logic. This is because it was based on the four standard forms of **categorical** propositions, that is, propositions which deny or affirm a predicate term of a subject term. For example:

All *S* is *P*	All cats are black,
No *S* is *P*	No Englishmen are Chinese,
Some *S* is *P*	Some politicians are plausible,
Some *S* is not *P*	Some students are not hard-working.

These forms are called respectively universal affirmative [A], universal negative [E], particular affirmative [I] and particular negative [O]. A and E propositions are said to differ in **quantity** from I and O propositions, and A and I propositions differ in **quality** from E and O propositions. Note that it is only propositions themselves that can be true or false; propositional forms do not assert anything, and become propositions only when terms are substituted for S and P (in the example of All S is P above, 'cats' is the subject term and 'black [things]' the predicate term). The connecting verb 'is' (or 'are') is called the **copula**. When terms designate *every* member of the classes of things they characterize ('Englishmen', for example) they are said to be **distributed**. On the other hand, 'politicians' and 'students' refer only to some members of the classes of things referred to by these terms. The terms are then said to be **undistributed**. Predicate terms likewise may be distributed or undistributed. Thus if we say 'No Englishmen are Chinese', we thereby exclude from the class of Englishmen the whole class of Chinese. However, if we say 'All cats are black', we state nothing about black objects which are not cats. The distribution of terms can be summarized thus: in universal propositions the subject is distributed; in negative propositions the predicated is distributed.

*Comment

Propositions in everyday language do not often come 'ready-made', as it were, and expressed in any of the four propositional forms. And often the traditional logicians had to reformulate sentences radically to force them into the supposedly standard S–P pattern. Moreover, in so doing – and this is one of the criticisms made today of traditional logic – they thereby obscured the true logical structure of the sentences. A distinction is thus made between grammatical form and logical form. There has been much debate between philosophers of logic as to whether there are in fact 'ideal' logical structures underlying everyday discourse, or whether 'natural' languages have their own 'logic'. (More will be said about this in 2.10.)

2.3 Immediate inference

A distinction is made between **immediate** and **mediate** inferences. Immediate inference is made from one proposition directly to another, whereas in mediate inference the transition is effected via a third proposition. This is the basis of the **syllogism**. We shall look briefly at immediate inference first. Seven fundamental relations have been identified:

(1) **Equivalence** (or Co-implication). Two propositions are equivalent if they are either both true or both false. Example: 'Students always pass their examinations', 'Students never fail their examinations'.

(2) **Superalternation** (Superimplication). In this case two propositions can be true together, but the second can be true while the first is false. Example: 'All

students always pass their examinations', 'Some students always pass their examinations'.

(3) **Subalternation** (Subimplication). This is the converse of (2); the truth of the first is compatible with the truth or falsity of the second. Example: 'Some students always pass their examinations', 'All students always pass their examinations'.

(4) **Independence**. Two propositions are said to be independent of each other when they can be true together, false together, or when one is true and the other false. Example: 'Students always pass their examinations', 'Students demonstrate'.

(5) **Subcontrariety**. Both propositions may be true, or one may be true while the other is false. But we cannot assert the falsity of both at the same time. Example: 'Some students pass their examinations', 'Some students do not pass their examinations'.

(6) **Contrariety**. Two propositions are contraries of each other if one is true while the other is false, or if both are false together. They cannot both be true. Example: 'All students pass their examinations', 'No students pass their examinations'.

(7) **Contradiction**. Here the situation is similar to that of contrariety, but now the possibility of two propositions being false together is also ruled out. If one proposition is false, the other must be true. Examples: 'All students pass their examinations', 'Some students do not pass their examinations'; 'No students pass their examinations'. 'Some students pass their examinations'.

Moves from premises to conclusions in immediate inference are made in accordance with rules. Traditional logic distinguished between two kinds: **Opposition** and **Eduction**. Opposition is a relationship between propositions which have the same subject and predicate. This is exemplified in Contrariety, Subcontrariety, Subalternation and Contradiction. In these cases propositions have the same subjects and predicates but differ in quantity, quality, or both. The various relationships are illustrated in the **Square of Opposition**:

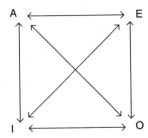

A and E are contraries.
I and O are subcontraries.
A and O, and E and I are contradictories.
A and I, and E and O represent subalternation (the universals are usually called superalterns, while the particulars are called subalterns).

In eduction we pass from one proposition to another which differs from it in its subject or predicate. The two fundamental forms are **Obversion** and **Conversion**. In the former, a proposition is derived from another by contradicting its predicate. Thus, for example, 'All cats are black' (A) becomes 'No cats are non-black' (E). In the latter, one proposition is converted to another by the interchanging of subject and predicate (transposition). A and O propositions do not convert since this would break the rule concerning the distribution of terms. But A does convert 'by limitation' (*per accidens*): 'All cats are black' becomes 'Some black things are cats' (I). By successively obverting a converse or converting an obverse, two other important eductions are possible: Contraposition and Inversion. In **contraposition** we obtain propositions which have in them as subjects the contradictory of the respective predicates in the original propositions. Example: 'All cats are black' (A) becomes 'No non-black things are cats' (E). (Note that, because O has no converse and because I obverts to O, I has no contrapositive; and that, because the converse of A is a subimplicant and not an equivalence and because E obverts to A, the contrapositive of E is not an equivalent.) A contrapositive is a converted obverse. With **inversion** a proposition is obtained which has as its subject the contradictory of the subject in the original proposition. Example: 'All cats are black' becomes 'Some non-cats are non-black' (O).

2.4 Mediate inference: the syllogism

All cats are black;
All black things are colour-blind;
therefore: All cats are colour-blind.

This is an example of a valid syllogism. One of the terms, 'black (things)', occurs in both premisses. This is called the **Middle Term**. The predicate of the conclusion ('colour-blind') is the **Major Term**, and the proposition containing it the **Major Premiss**. The subject of the conclusion ('cats') is called the **Minor Term**, and the proposition containing it the **Minor Premiss**. The order of the premisses is normally shown as in the example, but it would make no difference to the logical relationship between premisses and conclusion if the order were reversed.

Aristotle thought of the syllogism as 'discourse in which, certain things being stated, something other than what is stated follows of necessity from their being so.' But in time the syllogism came to be defined more narrowly. Every syllogism contains three propositions (they need not be explicitly stated); each proposition must be expressed in one of the four categorical forms, A, E, I or O; and the syllogism must contain three and only three terms.

In logic we are concerned with **proof**, and this requires consideration of further **Rules** or **Axioms**. These will be summarized briefly:

(1) The middle term must be distributed in at least one of the premisses. (Violation of this axiom is called committing the fallacy of the **Undistributed Middle Term**. Example: All cats have four legs; all dogs have four legs therefore: all cats are dogs.)
(2) A term distributed in the conclusion must be distributed in its corresponding premiss. (The fallacy here is called **Illicit Process of the Middle Term**. Examples: [**Illicit Minor**] All hard-working people are happy; some students

are hard-working people; therefore: all students are happy. [**Illicit Major**] All cats are mammals; all dangerous things are cats; therefore: no dangerous things are animals.)

(3) At least one premiss must be affirmative; a syllogism containing two negative premisses is invalid. Example: From the premisses 'no politicians are popular' and 'some popular people are not trustworthy' we cannot infer the affirmative conclusions 'some politicians are trustworthy' and 'all politicians are trustworthy'. The fallacy committed in such cases is called the fallacy of **Exclusive Premisses**.

(4) If one premiss is negative, the conclusion must be negative. We cannot infer, for example, 'all politicians are trustworthy' or 'some politicians are trustworthy' from the premisses 'no politicians are popular' and 'some popular people are trustworthy'. A breach of this rule is called committing the fallacy of **Drawing a Conclusion**.

(5) If both premisses are affirmative, the conclusion must also be affirmative. Thus the premisses 'all bread-eaters are mice' and 'some bread-eaters are hungry' do not permit us to infer that the class of mice is wholly or partly excluded from the class of hungry creatures; and any conclusion must therefore be affirmative, such as, 'some mice are hungry'.

Now it is clear that if a syllogism contains three propositions each of which can be one of four forms, A, E, I, or O, then 64 (4 × 4 × 4) combinations are possible: AAA, AAE, and so on. Each of these is called a syllogistic **Mood**; and they differ in the quantity and quality of their constituent propositions. Further syllogisms are possible if we alter the position of the middle term. For example:

(a) All **cats** are black;
    Some **cats** are merry;
    therefore: Some black things
        are merry.

(b) All black things are **cats**;
    Some **cats** are merry;
    therefore: Some merry things
        are black things.

Both syllogisms are of Mood AII, but they differ in that the middle term of (a) is the subject of both premisses, whereas in (b) the middle term is subject in the minor but predicate in the major premiss. Such syllogisms are said to be in different **Figures**. Four figures are possible:

I. M	P		II. P	M		III. M	P		IV. P	M
S	M		S	M		M	S		M	S
S	P		S	P		S	P		S	P

Our total of possible syllogisms thus rises to 256 (64 × 4). Now to discover the invalid syllogisms we apply the General Rules (the Axioms) to the four figures, and thereby obtain a number of Special Rules applicable to each. The derivation of the special rules for the First Figure is given as an example:

(i) The minor premiss must be affirmative. Assume the minor premisses to be negative. The conclusion must therefore be negative (Axiom (3)). The Major term will then be undistributed in the major premiss but distributed in the conclusion. This violates Axiom (2). So the conclusion cannot be negative and must be affirmative.

(ii) The major premiss must be universal. By (i) the minor premiss is affirmative. Its predicate (the middle term) is therefore undistributed, and the middle term must be distributed in the major premiss (Axiom (1)). It is the subject in the major premiss. Therefore the major premiss must be universal.

By applying these rules it can be shown that only nineteen of the 256 possible syllogisms are left. (As universal conclusions also allow particular conclusions some moods, called weakened moods, are superfluous and can be ignored.) Medieval logicians made up a nice Latin mnemonic which covers all these valid moods:

> Barbara, Celarent, Darii, Ferioque prioris;
> Cesare, Camestres, Festino, Baroco secundae;
> Tertia Darapti, Disamis, Datisi, Felapton,
> Bocardo, Ferison habet; quarta insuper addit
> Bramantip, Camenes, Dimaris, Fesapo, Fresison.

You will notice that the vowels of each name stand for the moods (thus, **B**a**rb**a**r**a: **AAA**).

To show that the majority of the possible syllogistic moods conflict with the rules is not of course to demonstrate that the nineteen remaining ones are valid. To prove these syllogisms Aristotle used a process called **Reduction** by means of which the moods could be transposed, directly or indirectly, into syllogisms of the first figure, which he supposed to be logically more fundamental then the others on the grounds that what can be predicated affirmatively or negatively of a class can be predicated similarly of everything else in that class. In general, *if* every *M* is *P* (or not) *and* all (or some) *S* is *M, then* all (or some) *S* is *P* (or not). This axiom is usually called the **Dictum de Omni et Nullo**. Then since the syllogism of Figure I are valid, and the others can be reduced to them, they too must be valid. (Space does not allow an account of reduction here.)

II. Modern logic

Modern logic, which we owe largely to the eminent German mathematician and philosopher Gottlob Frege (1848–1925), is sometimes called symbolic logic. This is perhaps misleading, in that symbols were also used in Aristotelian or 'classical' logic. However, in modern logic symbolism plays a much greater and central role. This will become clear in the following short survey of the **Logic of Propositions**, **Propositional Functions** and the **Logic of Classes**.

2.5 The logic of propositions

In the logic of propositions – often called 'truth-functional logic' – propositions are usually symbolized by the logical **variables** *p*, *q* and *r*. **Simple** propositions can be linked together to form **compound** propositions, and in truth-functional logic these links are symbolized by connectives or '**operators**' – so-called because they have functions or 'jobs', rather as such mathematical symbols as '+', '×', and '=' do. We shall look at these in turn.

Negation. Consider the proposition 'All horses are brown'. This is of course false. We can say 'It is false that all horses are brown'. To express this symbolically we write '$-H$', where 'H' is a shorthand symbol for 'All horses are brown' and '$-$' is the logical **constant** to indicate negation. (In some books '~' or '¬' are used.) Negation can then be defined by means of a **Truth-Table** or **Matrix**. For any proposition p, if 'p' is true, '$-p$' is false; and if 'p' is false, '$-p$' is true ('p' and '$-p$' are contradictories):

p	$-p$
T	F
F	T

Conjunction. Consider now the compound proposition 'All horses are brown and cows eat grass'. This could be symbolized as 'p', but to bring out the logical structure it is preferable to symbolize it as '$H \& C$', where '&' is the constant used to denote conjunction. (Alternatives often used are '•' and '∧'.) The operation of conjunction may be defined as follows:

p	q	$p \& q$
T	T	T
T	F	F
F	T	F
F	F	F

This truth-table stipulates that the conjunction '$p \& q$' shall have the truth-value 'true' only when its constituent propositions p and q are both true together. In all other cases '$p \& q$' shall have the truth-value 'false'.

Disjunction. Suppose we change the 'and' in the compound proposition to 'or'. This gives us a disjunction. The symbol generally used is 'v' (from Latin *vel*), and it is defined by another truth-table:

p	q	$p \lor q$
T	T	T
T	F	T
F	T	T
F	F	F

Implication. This is a logical relationship that underlies compound conditional or hypothetical propositions – characterized by the form 'If . . . then . . .' (for example, 'If it rains tomorrow, the garden will get wet'). Such propositions assert that from the truth of the 'if' sentence (the **antecedent** or **protasis**) the truth of the 'then' sentence (**consequent** or **apodosis**) follows, but that the falsity of the consequent is incompatible with the truth of the antecedent. In terms of our symbolism this can be expressed thus: $-(p \& -q)$. We call this relation **Material implication** and symbolize it by the constant '$\rightarrow$' (alternatively '$\supset$'). '$p \rightarrow q$' may thus be defined as: '$-(p \& -q)$', as shown in the truth-table:

p	q	$-q$	$p \& -q$	$-(p \& -q)$	$p \rightarrow q$
T	T	F	F	T	T
T	F	T	T	F	F
F	T	F	F	T	T
F	F	T	F	T	T

Material equivalence. p is said to be materially equivalent to q if and only if it is the case both that p materially implies q and q materially implies p. Expressed symbolically the definition becomes: '$(p \leftrightarrow q)$' = '$(p \rightarrow q) \& (q \rightarrow p)$', where the 'meaning' of the logical constant '$\leftrightarrow$' (alternatively '$\equiv$') is given by the truth-table:

p	q	$p \leftrightarrow q$
T	T	T
T	F	F
F	T	F
F	F	T

Propositional forms. From the various logical constants we have defined we have obtained corresponding propositional forms (or statement forms): $-p$, $p \& q$, $p \vee q$, $p \rightarrow q$ and $p \leftrightarrow q$. Whatever propositions are substituted for the variables p and q, the forms retain their relevant logical features in virtue of these definitions. Now let us look at some combinations and compare the truth-values of the compound propositions we obtain:

(1) $(p \vee -p)$ (2) $(p \& -p)$

p	$-p$	$(p \vee -p)$	$(p \& -p)$
T	F	T	F
F	T	T	F

You can see that in the first case only Ts are obtained, whereas in the second case we get only Fs. Thus, regardless of the truth-values of p and $-p$, the propositional form $(p \vee -p)$ always has true substitution instances. If we substitute a proposition, say A, into the schema, the resulting compound proposition $(A \vee -A)$ is always true. Such a proposition is called a **tautology**, and its truth follows from the definition or 'meaning' of the operator and the constituent terms. Tautologies are often said to be **logically necessary**. On the other hand, $(p \& -p)$ is a propositional form that gives rise only to false substitution instances, and is called a **self-contradictory** or logically impossible propositional form. And $(A \& -A)$ is a self-contradictory proposition. Both tautologies and self-contradictory propositions are non-factual in that their truth or falsity follows from or is exemplified by their form. (Note that although tautologies are logically necessary, not all logically necessary propositions are tautologies. This is because the notion of tautology is understood in terms of truth values and the 'meanings' of the logical connectives. Individual *simple* propositions, such as 'This red rose is red' and '2 + 2 = 4' are symbolized in the logic of propositions as, say, '*p*'; no operator ('&', '∨' and so on) is involved. Certainly it would be self-contradictory to deny these propositions, and so they are logically necessary. But they are not strictly tautological – in the way that the compound 'It is *not* the case *both* that roses are red *and* that roses are *not* red' *is*.] If on substituting truth-values in a propositional form, a mixture of true *and* false instances is obtained, we then have a **contingent** propositional form. Propositions exemplifying such forms are contingent propositions', the truth or falsity of which depends in some way on 'facts' in the world and are often said to be **empirical** propositions. Two propositions are said to be **logically equivalent** when the proposition asserting their equivalence is itslf tautologous. Thus $(p \rightarrow q) \leftrightarrow -(p \ \& \ -q) \leftrightarrow (-p \lor q)$. Tautology, self-contradiction, contingency and logical equivalence can all be demonstrated by the construction of truth-tables. Finally, it should be mentioned that logically necessary propositions are sometimes called **analytic** propositions. An analytic proposition is one whose negation is self-contradictory, or one whose truth can be determined by an analysis of the meaning of the terms constituting the sentence used to express the proposition. The eighteenth century German philosopher Kant thought of an analytic proposition (though he talked of 'judgements') as one in which the predicate is in some sense contained in or connected with the subject. Those in which the predicates are not so contained are termed **synthetic**. His definition does of course presuppose the traditional subject–predicate logic, and as we have seen S–P formulations do not always bring out the true logical nature of propositions. His definitions are therefore of limited value. (See further 5.9.)

*Logic and language I

(This section is perhaps rather more demanding. You may prefer to move on to **Extended arguments** and come back to this later.)

We referred earlier to the problem of expressing some sentences in the S–P 'standard' form, There is, however, also in modern logic often some disparity between words in our everyday language and the formulations which make use of the truth-functional logical operators. 'Not', for example, does not always denote contradiction as symbolized by '–'. 'Some cats are not black' is not the contradictory of 'Some cats are black'. There is also an ambiguity in use of 'and'. In 'Jack and Jill went up the hill', for example, '&' as defined earlier cannot be used to stand for 'and'. We could reformulate it as the compound proposition 'Jack went up the hill and Jill went up the hill' ('$p \ \& \ q$'), but arguably this is not the intended meaning of the original, suggesting instead that Jack and Jill went up the hill separately. In the case of disjunction a distinction should be made between inclusive (or weak) and exclusive (strong) alternatives. If you are asked whether you would like tea or coffee after your meal, this is generally understood as suggesting you may have one or the other but not both. The truth-table definition is designed to cover both.

Ambiguity is perhaps most apparent in conditionals. Consider these examples:

(1) 'If all cats are black and Tibby is a cat, then Tibby is black'. (2) 'If a man is a bachelor, then he is unmarried'. In both cases there is a necessary connection between the antecedent and the consequent. The first is a deductive argument, valid 'in virtue of form', while in the second the consequent follows from the antecedent in virtue of the definition or meaning of the terms 'bachelor' and 'unmarried'. Thus the truth of these compound propositions does not depend on 'the world of facts'. But now look at (3): 'If he is a philosopher, then I am a Dutchman'. Here there is no logically necessary connection between antecedent and consequent. The truth of the component propositions, and hence of the compound, does in some sense depend on 'facts'. The consequent is normally taken to be false, and the point of the statement would seem to be to deny the truth of the antecedent. This is usually called **material implication**, and it is this which is defined in the truth-table above. Examples (1) and (2) also satisfy the minimum requirements of material implication, but they are regarded as examples of a stronger kind which we call **entailment**. This gives rise to some interesting problems – called the **paradoxes of material implication**.

If you apply a truth-table analysis to the propositional forms (1) $p \to (q \to p)$ and (2) $-p \to (p \to q)$, you will find them to be tautologies. But, then, is there not something odd about them? They would seem to suggest that any proposition at all may be implied by any other proposition, whether the latter be true or false! Thus, if we substitute specific sentences into these propositional forms, we can get:

(1) Because it is true that pigs can fly it follows that 'mermaids live on the moon implies that pigs can fly';
(2) Because it is false that pigs can fly it follows that 'pigs can fly implies that mermaids live on the moon'.

Moreover, the falsity of 'pigs can fly' also implies that 'pigs can fly does *not* imply that mermaids live on the moon'. Surely something is wrong here? The point, of course, is that we are confusing **material implication** with **entailment**. Let us consider this more closely.

In material implication, as mentioned earlier, we are concerned solely with the truth relations of the constituent propositions of a compound. What the propositions are about is of no interest to us. We may need to know the meaning of the propositions – incidentally as it were – simply to establish whether the constituents are materially true or false; that is, we need to look at the facts. But once the truth values are known the truth conditions of a material implication can be stated. It is for this reason that material implication is called a truth-function. We are here said to be considering the proposition **extensionally**. The relationship of entailment, on the other hand, is a **necessary** logical relation. For one proposition to entail another there must be an essential connection between them – a relation of **meaning**. Thus, 'If John is a bachelor, he is unmarried' is a necessarily true implication. And this would be the case even if there were no bachelors in the world. Similarly, 'If the animal is a unicorn, it has only one horn' is a necessarily true implication, unless, of course, the unicorn meets with an accident – but then we would say that being that kind of creature it *should* have one horn; and the truth of the proposition is unaffected. In these cases we are said to be interpreting propositions **intensionally** (not to be confused with intentionally). All these terms – 'analytic', 'synthetic', 'logically necessary', 'contingent' – have given rise to a great deal of discussion among philosophers in recent years, particular concerning their scope and whether such distinctions are clear-cut or even legitimate.

Extended arguments

So far we have been concerned with simple propositions and their inter-relationships via logical connectives. Arguments, of course, usually involve a number of propositions. The standard syllogisms of classical logic, as we have seen, require three – two premisses and a conclusion. In this section we shall explore such compound arguments further and examine methods for testing their validity and invalidity in the context of the Logic of Propositions.

Consider these four arguments:

(1) If Plato was a philosopher, then he must have been a wise man; Plato was a philosopher; therefore: he was a wise man.
(2) If Fido is a dog, then he has four legs; he does not have four legs; therefore: Fido is not a dog.
(3) Either the thief was in Ireland or he was in England; he was in Ireland; therefore: he was not in England.
(4) Either logic is easy, or Bill is a hard worker; Bill is not a hard worker; therefore: logic is easy.

Each of these arguments is valid. Traditionally they were given the Latin names *ponendo ponens, tollendo ponens, ponendo tollens* and *tollendo tollens,* respectively. ('*Ponere*' means 'to affirm', '*tollere*' means 'to deny'.) Corresponding to these modes of argument are four invalid arguments. Thus, for example:

(5) If politicians are wise, then democracy is desirable; democracy is desirable; therefore: politicians are wise.

It should be clear that here the conclusion does not follow logically from the premisses. The truth of the consequent certainly follows from the truth of the antecedent, but not vice versa; the truth of the consequent is consistent with the falsity of the antecedent. Likewise the argument would also be invalid if we denied the conclusion, on the grounds that the antecedent were false. These two fallacies are termed, respectively, **Affirming the Consequent** and **Denying the antecedent**. Examples can easily be found to illustrate the invalid arguments corresponding to (3) and (4).

Let us return briefly to the notion of **form**. In traditional syllogistic logic, form was made explicit through the use of symbols standing for the three terms of the syllogism, and we came to speak of, for example, the valid syllogism

M	a	P
S	a	M
S	a	P

as typifying the Form AAA-1.

We can now consider logical form by using the truth-functional or propositional variables *p, q, r*, etc. An **argument form** can be defined as a series of symbols containing propositional variables such that when they are replaced by propositions (consistently throughout) the result is an argument. Such an argument is called a **substitution instance** of the argument form. Thus the invalid arguments:

(a) If politicians are wise, they should be applauded; politicians should be applauded; therefore: politicians are wise
(b) If Socrates died of old age, he was a great thinker; Socrates was a great thinker; therefore: Socrates died of old age

which may be symbolized respectively as:

P → A   D → G
A   G
     ∴ P   ∴ D

both exemplify the same argument form, namely:

p → q
q
     ∴ *p*

In fact, for any given argument there is a unique argument form which is *the* form of that argument and results from the replacement of each propositional form by a different simple proposition. (It is important to realise this, for both the above arguments are also substitution instances of the argument form '*p, q,* ∴ *r*'. *The* form of both, however, is *p → q, q,* ∴ *r.*) It follows that if we can see that a given argument exhibits a valid (or an invalid) argument form then it must correspondingly be valid (or invalid) as the case may be. But it is not always easy to recognize the validity or invalidity of argument forms. So we must have recourse to a more mechanical method for testing arguments; and this is where truth-tables become useful. Suppose we want to test the validity of argument (5) above. It exhibits the form *p → q, q,* ∴ *p*. Constructing a truth-table we get:

1	2	3	4	5	1
p	*q*	*p → q*	[(*p → q*) & *q*]	→	*p*
T	T	T	T	T	T
T	F	F	F	T	T
F	T	T	T	F	F
F	F	T	F	T	F

You can see from this that the truth-values in column 4 represent the conjunction of the values in columns 2 and 3. You will note also that in line 3 we have a T in column 4 and an F in column 5. This shows the argument form is invalid (it commits the fallacy of Affirming the Consequent). The two arguments above, which exemplify this argument form, are therefore also invalid; and their refutation is said to be by **logical analogy**. In a similar fashion, arguments exemplifying the form '$p \lor q, -p, \therefore q$' can be shown to be valid.

Note the importance of brackets when you are setting out sequences of truth-functional formulae; their use will enable you to avoid ambiguity. Consider, for example, the difference between, say, '$p \lor q \to r$' and '$(p \lor q) \to r$'. (If you are in doubt, try a truth-functional analysis of each.) In the absence of brackets, the constants (the operators) are taken as following a rule of **scope-precedence**: '$\leftrightarrow$', '$\to$', '$\lor$', '&', '$-$'.

The weakness of the truth-table method of testing the validity of arguments is that we end up with a large number of lines in the matrix for relatively few constituent propositions. (An extended argument containing five component propositions will require $2^5 = 32$ lines.) For this reason, **formal proofs** have been developed. A formal proof is a sequence of propositions, each of which is a premiss of that argument or which follows from preceding propositions through elementary valid arguments, the last proposition in the sequence being the conclusion of the argument whose validity is being proved. A formal proof makes use of **Rules of Inference** or Derivation. These are either (1) **Elementary Argument Forms**, or (2) **Logical Equivalences**; and both of these can themselves be shown by standard truth-table techniques to be respectively valid arguments or tautologies. There is of course a large number of possible rules of inference, and not all will be required to develop a formal proof of a given argument. Two well-known equivalences are called De Morgan's Theorems: '$-(p \mathbin{\&} q) \leftrightarrow (-p \mathbin{\&} -q)$' and '$-(p \lor q) \leftrightarrow (-p \mathbin{\&} -q)$'. To illustrate the method we shall just consider a simple example which makes use of Constructive Dilemma (CD) (a rule of inference) and Transposition (Trans.) (a logical equivalence):

If the rate of taxation is increased, then wages will rise. But wages will not rise unless exports improve. Wages either will rise or will not rise. Therefore, either the rate of taxation will not be increased or exports will improve.

First we symbolize these three premisses and conclusion:

(1) R → W
(2) −E → −W
(3) W ∨ −W
∴ −R ∨ E

where R stands for 'Rate of taxation is increased', W for 'Wages will rise' and E for 'Exports will improve'. Now we consider the inference from the premisses to the conclusion by referring to the sequence of valid steps – the formal proof:

(4) W → E   from (2) by Transposition
(5) −W → −R   from (1) by Transposition
(6) (W → E) & (−W → −R)   from (4) and (5) by Conjunction
(7) −R ∨ E   from (3) and (6) by Constructive Dilemma.

(7) is of course the conclusion; and we have thereby shown the argument to be valid.

Some of the most common Rules of Inference can now be listed:

- Addition (Add.): p; $\therefore$ $p \lor q$. (Sometimes called $\lor$-Introduction.)
- Assumption (A): Any proposition (usually a premiss) may be introduced into a proof.
- Conditional Proof (CP): allows the derivation of a conclusion $p \rightarrow q$, where p is an assumption on which q depends, sometimes on the basis of other assumptions which can then be 'discharged'. Example: given $p \rightarrow q$ and $-q$ as assumptions, $-p$ follows (MT), and hence the conclusion $-q \rightarrow -p$.
- Conjunction (Conj.): p, q; $\therefore$ $p \& q$. (Sometimes called &-Introduction.)
- Constructive Dilemma (CD): $(p \rightarrow q) \& (r \rightarrow s)$, $p \lor r$; $\therefore$ $q \lor s$.
- *Modus Ponens* (MP): $p \rightarrow q$, p; $\therefore$ q.
- *Modus Tollens* (MT): $p \rightarrow q$, $-q$; $\therefore$ $-p$.
- Simplification (Simp.): $p \& q$; $\therefore$ p. (Sometimes called &-Elimination.)

In addition to the logical equivalences mentioned above, the following should be noted:

- Commutation (Com.): $(p \lor q) \leftrightarrow (q \lor p)$ and $(p \& q) \leftrightarrow (q \& p)$.
- Double Negation (DN): $p \leftrightarrow --p$.
- Exportation (Exp.): $[p \rightarrow (q \rightarrow r)] \leftrightarrow [(p \& q) \rightarrow r]$
- Material Implication (MI): $(p \rightarrow q) \leftrightarrow (-p \lor q)$

(You will find other rules of inference and logical equivalences in standard text-books of logic.)

Although formal proof has advantages, it is inferior to the mechanical truth-table method in that we have no specific procedure to follow that enables us to pass rapidly from premisses to conclusion; demands are made on our imagination and insight to determine precisely which and how the various primitive argument forms and replacement formulae are to be employed most economically and effectively. Inability to construct a formal proof does not mean that an argument is invalid; it may merely testify to a lack of insight or skill – and of course this can be developed through practice and experience. However, we can prove invalidity if we can single out one row of the truth-table matrix such that by assigning the truth value True to the premisses we get a false conclusion.

From what has been said it follows that if in an argument *no* assignment of truth values produces a line of the truth-table in which the premisses are true and the conclusion false, then the argument must be valid. However, it may happen that in a particular argument it is not even possible to assign values such that the premisses are all true – regardless of the truth or falsity of the conclusion. This would occur if the premisses were self-contradictory – substitution instances of a self-contradictory propositional form, that is, if the premisses were inconsistent. To put the matter in another way, we can say that from false premisses anything follows. But such an argument is still valid, and a formal proof could still be constructed. The argument exemplifies material implication, which, as can be seen from the truth-functional matrix defining the material implication constant, preserves the technical meaning of 'validity'; we do not have in our argument a state of affairs in which the premisses are true while the conclusion is false. From the standpoint of ordinary language, an argument whose premisses are false but whose conclusion is true might seem odd. But any objection based on such a consideration can be dismissed once it is realized that a technical term of logic ('validity') should not be confused with a term of everyday discourse ('inference'). An argument may be unsound yet logically valid.

2.6 Predicate logic (the logic of propositional functions)

So far we have examined two main kinds of logic: 'traditional' or classical syllogistic logic (the logic of terms) and 'modern' truth-functional logic (the logic of propositions). In both cases validity of arguments has been understood in terms of the idea of form. This can be seem from these examples:

(1) Categorical syllogism	(2) Truth-functional argument
All M is P	$p \rightarrow q$
All S is M	p
$\therefore$ All S is P	$\therefore q$

It must be made clear, however, that these two types of argument differ radically. In the logic of propositions we are concerned with the way in which simple propositions (p, q) are combined truth-functionally to form compound propositions ($[(p \rightarrow q) \mathbin{\&} p] \rightarrow q$). But in the case of the syllogism we find that the inner logical structure of the proposition is relevant. The categorical syllogism containing only simple propositions cannot therefore be expressed in truth-functional terms. Conversely, the *Modus Ponens* valid argument form (containing the compound proposition '$p \rightarrow q$') can be expressed in such terms but cannot be easily formulated as a syllogism. (This was first noticed by the Stoic logicians in the third century BC.) Moreover, there are many arguments which are neither syllogistic nor can be expressed truth-functionally. We therefore need a logic of greater generality and power. Predicate logic satisfies these criteria.

We start with the notion of a **propositional function**. This is an expression which contains an individual variable and which can become a proposition. Propositions may be obtained from a function in two ways, Instantiation and Quantification.

Instantiation

Consider this example of a singular proposition: (i) 'Wittgenstein is a philosopher'. Here a property (being a philosopher) is predicated of the individual (Wittgenstein). (Note that 'individuals' need not be persons.) This may be written as Pw, where 'P' is a constant symbolizing the property of being a philosopher, while 'w' is the individual constant. In the same way we can symbolize (ii) 'Fred is a human' as *Hf*. The common pattern should be obvious. We can represent it as Φx, where 'Φ' stands for any predicate at all and '*x*' for any individual. 'Φ' is not a proposition but becomes one when we substitute 'values' for these variables, that is, when the propositional function Φx is given substitution instances. Logicians often refer to propositional functions as 'empty schemata'. That which 'satisfies' the function is called an **argument** (in a narrow sense – not to be confused with the meaning it has in the previous discussion), and the class of all possible arguments of the function is termed its **domain**. The significant propositions produced by substitution constitute the **range of significance** of the propositional function.

Quantification

Consider now the general proposition 'All things are holy'. This can be rephrased as 'Given any thing in the universe, then it is holy'; or, by using the notation mentioned above, we get 'Given any thing in the universe, then *Hx*'. For 'Given any *x* in the universe' we may write '(x)'. This is called the **Universal Quantifier**, and we obtain: (x) (Hx). This is a proposition – though the *Hx* included in it is not. Placing the universal quantifier before a propositional function has thus given us a second way of obtaining a proposition. Similar considerations apply to the **Existential Quantifier**. Take this example: 'Something is good'. We can rephrase this as 'There exists at least one thing which is good; or as 'There exists at least one *x* such that *Gx*'. The phrase 'There exists at least one *x* such that' is symbolized as '$(\exists x)$ (Gx)'. $\exists x$ is what we mean by the existential quantifier, and this too turns the propositional function *Gx* into a proposition. It should be noted, lastly, that it is possible to relate the two quantifiers to each other. Thus, to say 'something is not a Φ', that is, '$\exists x$ $(-\Phi x)$' is to deny the universal 'Everything is Φ', that is, '$-(x)$ (Φx)'. Similarly it can be shown that '(x) (Φx)' = '$-(\exists x)$ $(-\Phi x)$'; that '$(\exists x)$ (Φx)' = '$-(x)$ $(-\Phi x)$'; and '(x) $(-\Phi x)$' = '$-(\exists x)$ (Φx)'.

Note that when a variable occurs as part of a quantifier or lies within its scope it is said to be **bound**, but otherwise it is **free**. Thus in '$(\exists x)$ $(Sx \rightarrow Px)$ & Px' '*x*' is a free variable only in its last occurrence.

We now have a means of making explicit the inner logical structure of the four categorical forms of traditional logic. 'All *S* is *P*' [A], for example, is translated as follows:

Given any thing in the universe of discourse, if it is *S* then it is *P*; given any *x* in the universe of discourse, if *x* is an *S* then *x* is a *P* hence (x) $(Sx \rightarrow Px)$, or more generally, (x) $(\Phi x \rightarrow \Psi x)$.

And 'Some *S* is not *P*' [O] becomes:

There exists some entity *x* such that *x* has the property *S* and *x* has the property *P*: $(\exists x)$ $(Sx$ & $Px)$.

The introduction of these notions of instantiation and quantification (sometimes called generalization) in the predicate calculus extends the analytical power of logic. They also provide us with further Rules of Inference which we can use, together with those from propositional logic, for testing the validity of arguments. These rules are Universal Instantiation (or Elimination): from (x) $(Fa \rightarrow Ha)$ we may derive Gm, where 'm' is the name of some arbitrary object; Universal Generalization (Introduction): from $Fa \rightarrow Ha$ we obtain (x) $(Fx \rightarrow Gx)$; Existential Instantiation: Ga gives us $(\exists x)$ Gx; and Existential Generalization: from $(\exists x)Fx$ we get Fa. (Similarly, invalidity can be proved if we can show that in an argument involving quantifiers there is at least one instance in which the conclusion is false when the premisses are true.) The logical justification for these rules cannot be dealt with here.

2.7 The logic of classes

Class logic, as a system, resulting from the application of mathematical formulae to logic, was worked out in the nineteenth century by George Boole.

If we talk about all the instances (possible or actual) of a characteristic or property of an individual we are referring to a **class**. These instances are called its **members** or **elements**; the class contains its members. The individuals which constitute the membership of a class are picked out by **enumeration** (thus we might enumerate the individuals Balliol, Magdalen, Wadham, etc. – these constituting the class whose members are these individuals); or by the **selection** of a characteristic, for example, being a college of Oxford University. The second method is applicable to both finite and infinite classes. A characteristic **determines** the class whose members exemplify the characteristic; such a characteristic is called a **class-property**. Note that we use class-symbols even if we do not know whether a given class has or does not have members. Class-symbols are descriptive. When there *are* members and when we refer to all of them we must distinguish between two uses of 'all': the **distributive** use when each member is signified individually, and the **collective** use as in 'All the King's men could not put Humpty Dumpty together again', that is, all of them working together.

Consider the two propositions 'All philosophers are wise' and 'Socrates is a philosopher'. It should be clear that the first proposition asserts that the class of philosophers is included in the class of wise people. The latter could conceivably be included in the former, though the proposition does not itself assert this. (In any case 'All wise people are philosophers' is no doubt factually false – as indeed is the assertion that all philosophers are wise!) It would not make sense, however, to say that the class of philosophers could be included in Socrates; the second of the pair of propositions is a singular proposition and asserts class-**membership**, whereas 'All philosophers are wise' exemplifies class-**inclusion**. (From this we can see that the traditional logicians were mistaken when they classified singular propositions as universal. Logically the two kinds of propositions are distinct, an individual and a class being of different logical **types**.)

Emphasis on the class aspects of propositions provides us with another method of testing for validity and invalidity of categorical syllogisms – a method aided by a scheme of diagrammatic representation developed by John Venn, a contemporary of Boole:

To indicate that a class *S* is empty, a circle is shaded out This symbolizes the proposition 'There are No *Ss*' (*S* is an empty class: *S* = 0).

To indicate that a class *S* has members a cross is placed inside the circle. This symbolizes 'There are *Ss*' (*S* is not an empty class: *S* ≠ 0).

The four standard form categorical syllogisms may then be presented iconically:

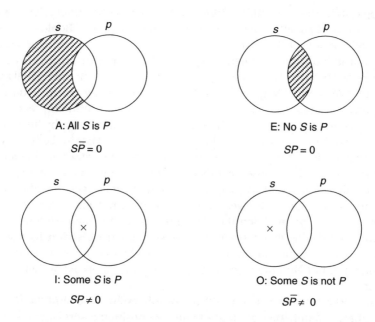

A: All *S* is *P*	E: No *S* is *P*
$S\bar{P} = 0$	$SP = 0$
I: Some *S* is *P*	O: Some *S* is not *P*
$SP \neq 0$	$S\bar{P} \neq 0$

'*P̄*' in these formulae stands for 'the class of things which are not-*P*'.

Venn Diagrams are particularly useful in that they can be used to test the validity of categorical syllogisms directly – by-passing the laborious application of the rules outlined earlier. The method is as follows:

(1) Label three circles representing the three terms of the syllogism.
(2) Diagram the premisses. Note (a) if there is a universal and a particular premiss, diagram the universal first; (b) if it is unclear which side of the line the 'x' should go, place it *on* the line.
(3) Examine the diagram of the premisses to see whether the diagram of the conclusion is also included. If it is not, the syllogism is invalid.

The following example should make this clear:

All bookworms are vegetarians;
$P\overline{M} = 0$

Some philosophers are vegetarians;
$SM \neq 0$

Some philosophers are bookworms.
$SP \neq 0$

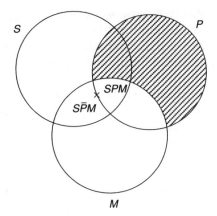

The important point to notice here is that no information is provided by the premisses which will enable us to decide whether the '×' should be placed in $S\overline{P}M$ or SPM. So we place it on the line. The conclusion is *not* diagrammed; so the syllogism is invalid.

Boole was not of course primarily concerned with reformulating traditional syllogistic logic, and he devoted a great deal of his energy to developing his class logic systematically, introducing definitions, axioms, rules of inference, and so on, using what is called Boolean algebra.

*Logic and language 2

Boolean logic raises another important issue in relation to the distinction between the apparent 'surface' meaning of some propositions and their 'underlying' logic. This is the issue of **existential import**. A proposition is said to have existential import (EI) if it asserts the existence of some object or other. Thus 'There are cats on our planet' has EI, whereas 'There are no green-eyed monsters on Pluto' does not; the class of green-eyed Pluto monsters is empty (so far as we know!).

We have seen that the four categorical propositions of traditional logic – A, E, I and O – can be interpreted as being assertions about classes. Do these propositions have EI? Consider the universal sentence 'All cats are black'. If this is to be used meaningfully so as to make a true or false proposition, we must usually presuppose that there do exist such things as cats. Ordinary usage would not normally require us to say that such a proposition is false if there were *no* cats, but that we were mistaken in thinking that the proposition had EI at all. But not all propositions carry this presupposition of existence. 'All people who break the law will be punished', for example, is asserted specifically to dissuade people from following a life of crime – in fact to *keep* the class of law-breakers empty. And in some cases the question of existence is not even relevant, as in 'The angles in any (Euclidean) triangle add up to 180 degrees'. What of particular propositions? Here the existential reference is clear, as when we say 'Some snakes are poisonous' we mean to affirm the existence of certain kinds of snakes. A difficulty is encountered when we come across propositions in novels or plays. Talking of

H.G. Wells's *War of the Worlds*, for example, we might say 'Some Martians look like squids'. But here there is a context, albeit fictional; and within this sub-set of discourse the proposition can be said to be true. Otherwise it would be false. Thus we can say that I and O propositions do have EI while A and E propositions do not.

But now this brings us into conflict with the assumptions of the traditional Square of Opposition. If I and O propositions have EI, the corresponding A and E propositions also have EI, since they are held to follow validly from them (by subalternation). And if both the universal and particular propositions have EI they can both be false ('All green-eyed monsters live on Pluto' and 'Some green-eyed monsters live on Pluto' are both false if there exist no such green-eyed monsters), and they cannot therefore be contradictories! The Square of Opposition thus breaks down. Similarly A and E propositions are not contraries, I and O are not subcontraries, and so on. Thus, if we are to preserve the relationships of traditional logic intact, we must limit the assertive power of categorical propositions: they can no longer be allowed to deny the existence of the classes designated by their terms. We should in fact be contradicting ourselves if we said that all cats are black but that there are no cats. Modern logic, however, is content to restrict the scope of the traditional Square of Opposition in such ways. In Boolean logic I and O propositions do have EI while A and E propositions do not. Thus, if we say that all cats are black, we imply that there are no objects which are cats and not black. The class of things which are both cats and non-black is empty. We are not committed to affirming that the class of cats has members, only to saying that *if* there are any cats they are black things. Other inferences from the Square of Opposition are of course affected by this concept of EI. To preserve the validity of, for example, the inversions from A and E (see above), we must stipulate that the classes symbolized by S, non-S, P and non-P must have members.

2.8 The logic of relations

The discussion so far has by no means covered all the possible areas of logic which have been developed during the twentieth century. For example, there has been great interest in 'many-valued logic' and in so-called 'fuzzy logic' which attempts to fit standard logic to what is perceived to be the vagueness and ambiguity of informal argument. (See 2.10 below.) A great deal of work has also been done on systematizing modal logic, which is concerned with such concepts as necessity and possibility, and on relations. (Both of these areas were anticipated by Aristotle, and he wrote extensively on the former.) Space will allow only a brief account to be given of the logic of relations. But if you would like to learn something about these other branches of the subject you are directed to the Reading list at the end of the chapter.

Individuals, characteristics, and indeed all objects in the universe, are not completely isolated entities but are interrelated. Terms denoting such entities are likewise related. Precisely how the interrelatedness of things is to be understood is of course a contentious issue among philosophers, as is also the question of how language and its supposed underlying logical structure relate to the world. We shall not address these metaphysical problems here but will confine our attention to the *logic* of relations. Relations between terms may be **dyadic** (two terms related), for example, '*Mary* is the **mother of** *Julie*', or **triadic** (three terms related), as in '*John* **lent** *Bill* a *book*. Such propositions may be symbolized as '$R(x,y)$' or 'xRy', $R(x,y,z)$', and so on. The term from which the relation comes is called the **referent**, while the term to which it goes is called the **relatum**. If R holds (as opposed to 'fails') from x to y, a relation holding from y to x is said to be the **converse** of the original relation. The totality of possible referents of R is called the **domain** of the relation, and of possible relata the converse domain. The domain and its converse together constitute the **field** of the relation. There are a number of logical properties that relations can have:

(1) **Symmetry**. A relation R is symmetrical when xRy is equivalent to yRx: if xRy, then yRx; if yRx, then xRy. Examples: equal to, sibling of. A relation is asymmetrical when xRy is incompatible with yRx: if xRy, then never yRx. Examples: mother of, smaller than. The relation is said to be non-symmetrical when xRy is neither equivalent to nor incompatible with yRx: xRy may or may not be yRx. Examples: brother of, implication.

(2) **Transitivity**. A relation is transitive when if it holds from x to y and from y to z, it must then hold from x to z: if xRy and yRz, then xRz. Examples: older than, above. A relation is intransitive when, if xRy and yRz, then never xRz. Examples: by the side of, twice as big as. A relation is non-transitive when, if xRy and yRz, then maybe or maybe not xRz. Examples: brother of, similar to.

These properties of symmetry and transitivity can be combined in four ways. In the case of symmetrically transitive relations they also have the properties of **equality** and **reflexivity** – a relation being reflexive if it holds between x and itself, xRx, for example, as big as. Symmetry, transitivity and reflexivity together characterize **identity**. In contrast to reflexive relations, asymmetrical and some symmetrical relations are said to be **aliorelative**, that is, x cannot have this relation to itself, for example, ancestor of.

(3) **Connexity**. For a given field and a relation R two terms need not necessarily be related by R. Connexity occurs when the terms *are* related in this way: for two terms x and y in the field, xRy or yRx. Relations which are transitive, asymmetrical and connected are called **serial** relations. Example: (in the field of natural numbers) smaller than.

(4) **Correlation**. Here we are concerned with the number of terms the relatum or referent may be related to in the relation R. There are four possibilities: (a) **many–many** relations – the domain and converse domain both contain more than one member, and the selection of a term from the one is independent of the selection of the term from the other, for example, brother of; (b) **many–one** relations – the selection of a term from the domain determines the selection of the term from the converse domain, for example, son of;

(c) **one–many** relations – selection of a term from the converse domain determines selection of the term from the domain, for example, father of; (d) **one–one** relations – selection of a given referent determines selection of the relatum, and reversely, for example, eldest daughter of a mother.

(5) **Relative product**. Relations can be combined. Thus, from xRy and ySz we obtain a new relation between x and z, which may be symbolized as R/S. This is the relative product. Example: the relative product of 'son of' and 'brother of' is '(fraternal) nephew'. Note that the relation may be different if the order of the constituent relations is reversed. The relative product of 'brother of' and 'son of' is 'son of'. The converse of the relative product is obtained by reversing the order of the relations and substituting their converses. The relative product of a relation with itself is called the **square**. R/R can be symbolized as R^2. Example: the relative product of 'son' and 'son' is 'grandson'. Note that in some cases the square of a relation may be the relation itself, as with 'descendent'.

The above summary does of course only scratch the surface of the logic of relations. As with other kinds of logic, attempts have been made to present it as an axiomatic system. You can learn about such systems in advanced text-books of logic. We shall finish this brief survey by showing the relevance of relations to the validity of inferences and to the categorical syllogism.

Immediate inferences

Not all conclusions are logically equivalent to the premises from which they are derived (for example, the converse of an *A* proposition is subimplicant to it). Now *A* propositions are statements of class-inclusion. As this is a non-symmetrical relation we cannot argue from '*X* is included in *Y*' to its converse '*Y* is included in *X*'. This from *SaP* we can infer only *SiP*. But I and E propositions are respectively statements of partial inclusion and total exclusion, both of which are symmetrical relations and which therefore license inference from *SiP* to *PiS* and from *SeP* to *PeS*. We can see that the possibility of conversion is dependent on the type of relation holding between the classes designated by the terms of a proposition. This takes the question of validity much further than its treatment in traditional logic.

Categorical syllogisms

Consider the Barbara Syllogism. It can be formulated thus:

If	*a* is included in *b*,
and	*b* is included in *c*,
then	*a* is included in *c*.

'Included in' here is clearly a transitive relation, and the conclusion can be seen to follow from the two premises. The inference

a is the father of *b*,
b is the father of *c*,
∴ *a* is the father of *c*,

is, however, invalid, and we note that 'father of' is an *in*transitive relation.

To call an argument transitively relational is thus to draw attention to its validity. The valid syllogism can now be regarded as a special case of a transitively relational inference. Failure to realize the importance of relations is another weakness of traditional logic and led logicians into difficulties when they tried to force arguments into the limiting syllogistic mould.

INFORMAL LOGIC

There is a certain ambiguity about the phrase 'informal logic'. In an obvious sense it refers to logic which is not formal. But within this description we can distinguish two broad senses to be found in contemporary philosophical literature:

(1) Informal logic is logic which is not deductive: it is in fact inductive.
(2) It is a logic that is concerned with the variety of arguments we encounter in different fields of discourse – everyday language, scientific reports, religious tracts, history essays and so on – rather than with the argument forms, symbolism and formulae which we have seen to be the stock in trade of the formal logician, whether 'traditional' or modern. More particularly, for many philosophers it has come to be seen as a study of the ways in which philosophical confusion can be engendered through a misunderstanding of the ways 'ordinary', that is, non-formal language actually works or should be used in the various domains. Informal logic, according to this view, becomes an investigation of methods of argument and a kind of language analysis, as a result of which, it is claimed, philosophical problems are dispelled. We shall try to make this clearer in 2.10. But first let us look at inductive arguments.

2.9 Induction

Consider the following arguments:

(a) All philosophers are eccentric;
   Eccentric people are anti-social;
   ∴ Philosophers are anti-social.
(b) Tom, Dick and Harry were all born under the sign of Pisces, are 34, and have had an unpleasant experience on the thirteenth day of June;
   Mary is also 34, and had an unpleasant experience on 13th June;
   ∴ Mary is a Piscean.
(c) I have observed the Sun to rise every day for the last fifty years;
   ∴ It will rise tomorrow.

(a) is of course an example of a deductive inference. Provided the premises are true, the conclusion follows with logical necessity; it would be self-contradictory to accept the truth of the premises while denying the truth of the conclusion. (b) and (c) are quite different. They are both examples of inductive arguments. (b) is an argument from **analogy.** Essentially it involves an inference from premises stating that a group of things share a number of features to a conclusion which affirms that another member of the group known to possess all but one of the given features must possess that one as well. (c) is an example of **simple enumeration**, in which we move from a statement about past instances of a thing or event possessing a number of characteristics to a statement affirming a future occurrence. Now clearly (b) and (c) cannot be said to be valid in the sense of the term as used in formal deductive logic. The conclusions go beyond what is given in the premises and as such can be regarded as only *probably* true, that is, it would not be self-contradictory to affirm the premises and yet deny the truth of the conclusion. Indeed a conclusion of an inductive argument could well be false – though how this could be ascertained is a question which itself gives rise to many difficulties.

(1) To consider arguments from analogy, can we be sure which characteristics are **relevant** or what constitutes **similarity**? Thus, in the case of the Pisceans discussed above, it might be queried whether the *place* of birth is relevant. To determine this we should have to have more information to decide how significant such a detail is. It is, for example, just possible that three people born in the same place, and in the same month and year, might find themselves in circumstances on the 13th of June (in a given year) which led to their undergoing the same unpleasant experience; and from this is might be reasonable to infer that Mary was indeed born in March and therefore a Piscean. But the acceptability of such an argument then depends on many factors, not least that the experience should have been the same by virtue of the fact that they were in the same circumstances on the stated occasion and that their date and place of birth was in some sense the reason for their being together. Moreover, it is doubtful whether the argument can now be said to be from analogy. Of course it can be further objected that having an unpleasant experience is in any case irrelevant to whether one is born under a particular star sign. (A great deal has been written about the 'scientific' credentials of astrology; and what little statistical evidence there is is not convincing.)

The question of similarity is also a tricky one. We might say, for example (perhaps in support of animal 'rights' – see 6.8) that humans are living and can feel pain; cats/mice/fish are living, and therefore also feel pain (hence they should not be maltreated). The characteristic of similarity here is 'being a living thing'. But then trees are also living. Does it follow that they too experience pain? Perhaps it is the possession of a nervous system that consitutes a more important similarity in such an argument. On the other hand, if the conclusion of the argument is to be that a plant is edible then its being a living thing might be regarded as a resemblance of greater significance.

It is of course sometimes not easy to establish precisely in what respects two or more things resemble each other. Both relevance and similarity can well be matters of a subjective judgement which varies from person to person. You can be left to make up your own examples.

(2) Is there a genuine 'causal' connection between characteristics or events, or is the possession in common of a given feature nothing more than coincidence? To deal with this problem John Stuart **Mill** (1806–73) formulated a number of methodological procedures, namely, the method of **Agreement**, the Method of **Difference**, the Joint Method of **Agreement and Difference**, the Method of **Concomitant Variations**, and the Method of **Residues**. Thus, to illustrate the Method of Agreement, we might take the case of a group of people suffering from a particular disease. It is found that although they differ in many respects (age, race, home environment and so on) they all have one factor in common. This is then taken to be the cause of the disease. This still does not rule out the possibility of coincidence of course. But if it could then be shown that people *lacking* that factor had not contracted the illness, whereas those possessing the factor were showing the symptoms, then the case would be stronger for identifying it as the cause of the disease. (More will be said about 'causation' in 11.3.)

(3) It is often claimed (see 5.4, for example, where we refer to Russell's discussion of induction in his *Problems of Philosophy*) that the greater the number of observed instances, the more certainty we can place in the conclusion. While this may be so in some situations, there are many counter-examples. A tossed coin may have landed 'heads' up on ten successive occasions, but the probability of a 'heads' on the eleventh toss is still 50 per cent. Even in the case of our expectations about the Sun's rising tomorrow, which Russell deals with, it can be argued that given an understanding of gravitation, the orbiting of planets, Newton's laws and so on, we are no more or less certain about the possibility that it will rise tomorrow than we were when we made our prediction yesterday than we were today (unless we become aware of some special circumstance, for example that another massive body was on course to collide with the Sun).

(4) For our present purposes the most interesting issue concerns the logical 'status' and 'justification' of inductive arguments. This was a particular problem for the Scottish philosopher David **Hume** (1711–76). (Hume's philosophy is treated in detail in 5.4.) As we have seen, there is no logical contradiction involved in a denial of the conclusion of a simple enumerative inductive argument. For Hume, only 'relations of ideas', that is, statements of (deductive) logic and mathematics can be said to be 'certain'; 'matters of fact', which are ultimately grounded in what he called our impressions (roughly, sense-experiences) and on the relation of cause and effect, are only 'probable'. However, Hume regarded this as an unsatisfactory state of affairs, in so far as all or knowledge, including the natural sciences, would seem to be built on shaky foundations. Can we therefore find some justification for our inductive procedures?

One approach is to say that inductive arguments have been successful or reliable in the past, so we can be confident that they will continue to be so. But this proposed solution does not assist us at all; for it is circular, relying as it does on the very principle of induction we are trying to justify. Inductive arguments may not be reliable in the future. Indeed many generalizations made in the past and based on a set of observation statements have since been shown often not to hold. John Stuart Mill suggested that inductive arguments were really deductive ones, conclusions such as 'All *As* are *Bs*' being validly inferred from a true premiss, 'Nature is uniform', and observed instances. Clearly, however, we cannot know Nature is uniform without already assuming the correctness of the inductive principle. Mill tried to answer this by saying that the circularity was not vicious. More recently a similar view was proposed by R.B. Braithwaite (1900–90). He argued that the claim to 'validity' of induction (implicit in the appeal to the uniformity of nature) is not itself a premiss of the argument, but rather is used as a rule of inference which cannot be denied and which can license the inference. This approach seems inadequate. If such a principle were to be undeniable it would have to be either analytic, and therefore tell us nothing about the world at all, or be itself grounded in incontrovertible evidence. But how could any such evidence be incontrovertible? Quite apart from the possibility of errors of identification, we cannot rule out the possibility that future observations might conflict with observations made so far; and again the support is inductive. There are also still problems about the nature of the evidence – whether or not it is actually relevant, or whether *sufficient* evidence has been provided. Are all the *As* typical? Are the *Bs'* characteristics incidental such as to allow that the link between themselves and *As* to be broken? How can we know what constitutes relevance? At best induction must be probable; it could never be certain.

Some philosophers have accepted this last view and have tried to develop a probability 'calculus' in terms of 'long-run' frequencies. Hans Reichenbach (1891–1953), for example, attempted to justify induction on pragmatic grounds, arguing that if there are any true laws of nature (by which is meant certain kinds of universal or statistical statements) then they can be discovered only be enumerative procedures. Reichenbach referred to what he called 'the straight rule' which licences the move from '*n* per cent of observed *As* are *B*' to '*n* per cent of all *As* are *B*'. It is then claimed that because such inductive methods have been frequently successful we have good reason for placing our trust in them. It has been argued against this theory that continued use of the straight rule can never tell us when we have actually discovered a law of nature. Reichenbach has said that a 'limiting frequency' can be found from a finite but undetermined sample of *As*. But what we do not know is how large such a sample must be before we are in a position to make a reliable prediction of this limiting frequency of *As* that are *Bs*. Moreover, we have no reason to suppose that, even if continued use of the 'straight rule' does enable us to discover laws of nature, the use of many other kinds of inductive rules (these are usually called 'asymptotic rules') will not be equally successful in leading us to the limiting frequency; and our initial choice of one type of rule in preference to another would seem to have been made for arbitrary reasons. Finally, it has to be said that Reichenbach's attempt to deal with induction does not solve the problems of typicality or relevance.

So what alternative accounts can be offered? Some philosophers have suggested that it is sufficient to say that inductive arguments in some sense work, that is, they enable us to make successful predictions which are useful to us in our dealings with the world. We can of course *define* inductive arguments in such a way that those that do not work are ones which do not lead to true conclusions and are therefore invalid. The problem here is that in some if not all situations we can never be sure that the inference has 'worked' or has been successful because there is always the possibility that subsequent events may prove to be contrary to our expectations and needs. We can also point to scientific progress. Science, it would seem, has enabled us to attain to ever wider or more complete explanations of phenomena. So our confidence in scientific method, and *a fortiori* the inductive procedures it employs, is fully justified. Some philosophers of science (for example, Thomas Kuhn and Paul Feyerabend) would dispute that science progresses in this sense. Karl **Popper** (1902–94), on the other hand, while subscribing to the notion of scientific progress and gradual approximation to the 'truth', in effect by-passes the problem of induction altogether in so far as he supposed inference in scientific procedures to be not primarily inductive at all but, rather, deductive. However, it can be argued that some criterion is still required in accordance with which the approach to truth can be determined – 'correspondence' to the world, predictive power, testability by reference to appropriate evidence, for example, in which case it can still be questioned whether future evidence will continue to be adequate or relevant. And there is no guarantee that because scientific methodology, however, understood, has proved effective in the relevant respects in the past it will continue to 'deliver the goods' in the future. (See Ch. 8 for a fuller discussion of scientific methodology.)

A different kind of answer has been proposed by Peter **Strawson** (b. 1919). He says that it is superfluous to seek for a justification of inductive arguments, because (i) it is reasonable or rational to accept them, and (ii) such notions belong to the very contexts in which inductive arguments are deployed. To deny that it is reasonable to expect a specific conclusion to follow from the premises of an inductive argument would be to contradict oneself, because the statement of reasonable expectation is analytically true by virtue of its constituent terms. In answer to this we may say that inductive arguments themselves are certainly reasonable and rational, and that it would be odd to deny this in that they involve reasoning. But clearly the terms 'reasonable' and 'rational' do not suggest the certainty one associates with deductive inferences. Moreover, such reasonableness is not inconsistent with the supposition that the future in a particular respect may *not* be like the past; and it is equally reasonable to expect this to be so. As for providing a firm epistemological foundation for induction we are no further on. It might also be argued that though the meanings of 'rational' and 'reasonable' are drawn from the context in which they function we can still legitimately ask what it *is* about such situations which determines our correct usage of the terms. Suppose we say an inference is reliable, and that from a given context of observation and inference we can account for our usage 'rational'. We can still enquire as to what makes the inference reliable. Clearly we cannot appeal to rationality or reasonableness without circularity. So again we seem forced back to an implicit appeal to the fact that such an inference has always been reliable in the past. Nevertheless we should not underestimate the importance of Strawson's approach. In stressing context and reasonableness he is drawing attention to the fact stressed by many contemporary 'ordinary language' philosophers, that inductive arguments should be assessed in accordance with their own criteria and the role they play in our everyday discourse rather than by the stringent standards of 'certainty' which are properly applicable only to formal deductive logic.

A similar but more radical approach proposed by another British 'linguistic' philosopher, Stephen **Toulmin** (b. 1922), and influenced by Gilbert **Ryle** (1900–76) is of particular interest. It is a mistake, he argues (in *The Uses of Argument*), to take a pure or 'idealized', that is, formal logic as a paradigm or standard against which all other argument forms should be judged. Arguments in the many fields of 'applied' or 'working' logic (such as the sciences and jurisprudence) have their own criteria for validity. However, he starts by suggesting that arguments of all kinds conform to a particular pattern:

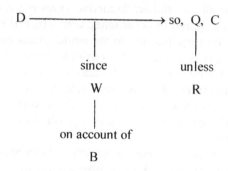

W is the warrant or inference licence which allows us to pass from data (D) to conclusion (C). B stands for the backing for our warrant and is variable and field-dependent, although it need not be made explicit. W is hypothetical; B and D are categorical. Q is a modal qualifier, warrants being of different kinds and conferring different degrees of force on the data. Such qualifiers are 'necessarily', 'probably' and the like. R stands for conditions of exception or rebuttal. Toulmin then introduces a distinction between analytic arguments and what he terms substantial arguments. Analytic arguments are those in which the backing for their authorizing warrants include, explicitly or implicitly, the information conveyed in the conclusions; substantial arguments are those in whose conclusions the information is not so conveyed. The analytical–substantial pair is then compared and contrasted with other types of argument pairs: (1) formally valid arguments and arguments which may be valid but not in virtue of form; (2) warrant-using and warrant-establishing arguments; (3) necessary or conclusive arguments and probable or tentative ones; and (4) deductive and inductive arguments. Space precludes a detailed account of these. (You are recommended to read his book in full.) Suffice it to say that Toulmin sets out to show that the distinction between analytic and substantial arguments does not correspond precisely to any of these pairs. His general thesis is that formal logicians have regimented these various divisions of arguments into a single distinction, and have moreover attached the terms 'inductive' and 'deductive' equally to all four distinctions, whereas in practice (in 'working' logic – 'outside the study', as he puts it) the deductive–inductive pairing is used to mark only the warrant-using and warrant-establishing distinction. It is thus entirely reasonable for Sherlock Holmes to talk of having made 'deductions' from observations, and for Sir Isaac Newton to have spoken of 'rendering a proposition general by induction', that is 'using our observations of regularities and correlations as the backing for a novel warrant'. Thus customary usage, Toulmin says, tends to deviate from the professional usage of logicians.

Perhaps then we should deny there is a 'problem of induction' at all. Induction is induction: deduction is deduction. Induction is just the procedure which licences us to move from particulars to principles which although having general application are neither certain nor immune from exceptions. Why should we have to 'justify' it? It works well enough in everyday life – provided we recognize that it is not infallible. Unfortunately this seemingly innocuous and common-sense view has given rise to paradoxes, in particular, Hempel's 'paradox of confirmation'. This involves an apparent inconsistency between a logical requirement and an empirical requirement of confirmation of general laws (see 8.3).

2.10 Conceptual analysis

It is in its manifestation as 'conceptual analysis' that informal logic is most relevant to critical thinking. But before we examine this something should be said about the genesis of philosophical 'analysis'.

Modern symbolic logic not only introduced a radical change within the sphere of logic itself but also brought about a revolution in twentieth century philosophy. Language can be misleading (you will remember the discussions earlier about language and the logical constants, the paradoxes of material implication, and existential import). And many thinkers, especially Bertrand **Russell** (1872–1970) and **Wittgenstein** (1889–1951), were struck by the clarity, order and precision of logical systems – in contrast to the ambiguity of 'natural' language and its potential for leading us astray, philosophically speaking, that is, giving rise to seemingly insoluble puzzles, or *aporiai*, as Aristotle had called them. Perhaps then such problems could be avoided or overcome if we looked to logic rather than to everyday language? To illustrate the possibilities we shall look at a famous example – Russell's *Theory of Descriptions*. Again this is rather technical, but if you have worked through the section on formal logic you should be able to follow the theory without too much difficulty.

We shall start by saying something about the notions of 'sense' and 'reference' – a distinction we owe to the famous German logician and philosopher Gottlob **Frege** (1848–1925). According to Frege, all terms of a natural language are 'about' something. Proper names ('Louis', 'Venus', for example) and 'denoting' phrases, what Russell later called 'descriptions' ('a man', 'the King of France', 'the morning star'), refer to things in the world. **Reference** (*Bedeutung*), we can say, is a relationship between the word and the object picked out by the word. But proper names and descriptions (which together are usually called singular terms) also have a **sense** (*Sinn*). The sense is 'out there' in the public domain, 'fixed' or determined, as it were, by the reference. This should become clear if you consider the names 'Phosphorus' and 'Hesperus'. These names have the same reference (the planet Venus) but have different senses – given by the meanings of their corresponding descriptive phrases, 'the morning star' and 'the evening star'. (Frege goes on to argue that the senses and references of predicates are respectively the meanings of predicate expressions and concepts, and in the case of complete sentences are propositions (*qua* thoughts – *Gedanken*) and 'truth-values': but we cannot deal with these distinctions here.)

Now Russell tended to think of 'sense' as 'meaning'; and he held the view that the meaning of a name or description is the object denoted, that is, referred to by them (the so-called 'denotation theory of meaning'). This gives rise to a serious difficulty. Consider the name 'Louis XVI' and the phrase 'The King of France'. While there was towards the end of the eighteenth century an entity denoted by this name and phrase (until Madame Guillotine intervened), there is no such object at present (and no doubt for the foreseeable future). So what are we to say about such a sentence as 'The present King of France is bald'? Russell's solution was not to resort to postulating special sorts of unreal but 'ideal' subsistent entities to act as the denotata of singular terms (as did the philosopher Meinong). Rather he made three claims. (1) Only *logically* proper names could be supposed to refer (for example, 'this', which might be used to denote things we are directly 'acquainted' with, such as 'sense-data' and universal concepts). (You will find some discussion of Russell's account of knowledge by acquaintance and knowledge by description in 5.5.) 'Ordinary' proper names are to be understood as definite descriptions, and descriptions themselves could not be said to be denoting phrases at all but are what he called 'incomplete symbols'. (2) He argued that sentences like 'The King of France is bald' are not, logically, of the subject–predicate form but are to be understood as existential sentences. (3) Such sentences could then be restructured and represented in terms of logical symbolism in such a way that supposedly denoting phrases are eliminated without any change in truth-values from the original to the new formulations. This can be illustrated as follows. When I say 'The King of France is bald' I am supposing three things:

(1) There is a King of France.
(2) There is only one King of France.
(3) Anything which is King of France is bald.

Expressed in terms of a logical structure this becomes: There is an entity x such that x is King of France; and, for all values of y, if y is King of France, then y is identical to x; and x is bald. And this can be symbolized as $(\exists x)\,[Fx\ \&\ (y)\,(Fy \to y = x)\ \&\ Gx]$. It is clear that if there is no King of France then the first of the three statements is false, and this falsifies the complex statement as a whole. In this way a philosophical problem which, according to Russell, has arisen because we have attended to a grammatical structure in a natural language, has been resolved by the simple device of reformulating the sentence so as to bring out its 'true' but equivalent logical structure. Russell and others came to regard this as a paradigm of philosophical method.

Russell's Theory of Descriptions has engendered a great deal of critical discussion, particularly among those philosophers influenced by the later philosophy of Wittgenstein. You will find an account of his ideas in Ch. 11. For present purposes we need note only that when he returned to philosophy in the thirties after a gap of some fifteen years he came to change the views he had held in his *Tractatus Logico-Philosophicus*. In particular he now rejected the idea that philosophers should seek to uncover an ideal or perfect logical language underlying natural language. Rather language, he argued (in a variety of notebooks culminating in his influential *Philosophical Investigations*), functions in a variety of ways – it has many uses. Consequently it is mistaken, for example, to think of the meaning of expressions in terms of denotation, as Russell had done, or indeed to look for *the* meaning of a word at all. This radical approach to language is reflected in Strawson's criticisms of Russell's theory. He argues firstly that if Russell's view of meaning is mistaken then there is no need for the Theory of Descriptions. Secondly, Strawson claims that when we use an expression such as 'the so and so' we are not committed to asserting that the entity exists. Rather, the presupposition that there is such an object is tied up with the conventional 'proper' or correct use of the phrase. It is, as it were, a condition of its correct use in our normal discourse that we intend that the phrase should be about some existing thing. If there is no such thing then the use of the phrase is inappropriate. What Russell has failed to do, argues Strawson, is to distinguish referential and assertive usages of an expression.

Now it is important to note here that the kind of philosophy that Strawson is 'doing' in his critique of Russell is also 'linguistic analysis'. But whereas Russell and the early Wittgenstein were dedicated to resolving philosophical problems by restructuring normal language into a supposedly ideal logical language, the later Wittgenstein and other philosophers such as Strawson and Ryle sought to eliminate philosophical errors by working within 'informal' or 'ordinary' language itself. Another very clear example of this is afforded by Ryle's famous concept of the **category mistake**. In his book *The Concept of Mind* he set out to destroy the 'myth' of what he called the dogma of the 'Ghost in the Machine'. According to this myth, words like 'knowing', 'believing', 'imagining', 'sensing' and so on are supposed to refer to a private non-spatial 'mind' which we can know only by 'looking within' ourselves. Philosophers who have been seduced by this dogma, Ryle argues, have committed a category mistake. To explain this he gives the example of a visitor to Oxford who, having seen all the colleges, then asks where the university is. The university is of course not an entity which exists or can be looked at in the way that its constituent colleges can. Ryle goes on to suggest that, in the same way, when we look at human bodies we must not suppose there is inside some entity which controls the body; there is no need to postulate a 'ghost' to account for its workings. The 'mind' is not a thing of which we can say it is 'there' in space and time in the way that we talk of a body's existence. (You will find a fuller discussion of this in 5.6 below.) This identification of and elimination of category mistakes – what Toulmin calls crude muddles – illustrates philosophy in action. As Ryle puts it, its job is 'to determine and rectify the logical geography of our concepts'.

2.11 Conclusion

We can now see that whether we think of informal logic as characterized by inductive arguments (as opposed to formal deductive argumentation) or by the arguments we employ in the 'ordinary' discourse of natural language (as against a putative underlying logical structure), philosophers working within the later 'linguistic analysis' tradition regard it positively and reject the claims made for formalism by many previous philosophers and logicians. Philosophy, for such practitioners as Wittgenstein, Austin, Ryle, Strawson and Toulmin – to name but a few, has thus become variously the study of fields of discourse, a close investigation into the workings of natural language, an examination of methods of argument, and so on, the consequence of which is the uncovering of supposed philosophical errors. Perhaps the clearest, and most entertaining, account of this view of philosophy is provided by Ryle in his *Dilemmas*. The greater part of the book is concerned to resolve quarrels which often break about between what he calls one team of ideas and another. An example is the conflict which can arise between our everyday experience of perception and the account the scientist gives us in terms of light and neuro-chemical processes. Another is the seemingly incompatibility of our feeling that we are at liberty to make free and responsible choices in our actions and the view that we cannot help behaving in this or that way because of our genetic make-up, or because of our upbringing, and so on. Ryle argues that these disputes cannot be resolved by a reduction to standard problems of formal logic but by an uncovering of conceptual confusion. Certainly a training in formal logic can be useful in providing us with the discipline to tackle the difficulties. Parade-ground drill can certainly make soldiers efficient but more than stereotyped movements are needed to cope with nasty situations in irregular and unfamiliar country, to make on-the-spot decisions, and thereby to win battles. Or, to change the analogy, formal logic is to informal logic, Ryle says, as geometry is to the cartographer, or as accountancy is to the merchant. Formal logic employs such semi-technical, 'meatless', 'conscript' terms as 'and', 'not', 'all', 'some' and so on. But it is the philosopher who looks at how they are actually used in our 'civilian' life when he investigates 'full-blooded' concepts such as 'pleasure', 'seeing', 'memory' and the like. They are both doing logic, but their aims and methods are different. Interestingly, this approach receives support from current research in cognitive psychology. Steven Pinker writes in his *How the Mind Works* [p.338]:

> Logic by itself can spin off trivial truths and miss consequential ones. The mind does seem to use logical rules, but they are recruited by the processes of language understanding, mixed with world knowledge, and supplemented or superseded by *special inference rules appropriate to the content* [my italics].

In the light of the above account we can reasonably say that to do philosophy in this way is thus to think critically. And you will find many discussions in this book which illustrate this approach. However, there is more to critical thinking than 'linguistic analysis'. Moreover, it should be stressed that many philosophers, and not only those working in the so-called 'continental' tradition, are deeply suspicious and often overtly critical of what they see as an arid obsession with linguistic minutiae, which has little to do with the 'real' problems of the human condition. (You will be able to weigh up the pluses and minuses of these two seemingly opposing positions after you have finished the book.) So what else might critical thinking involve? To answer this a short account will be given of rhetoric.

RHETORIC

2.12 General survey

'Rhetoric' is a word which nowadays tends to carry a somewhat pejorative connotation. We normally use it to refer to empty, bombastic discourse, contrived or excessively ornamented language. We talk of rhetorical flourishes and rhetorical questions – which do not require answers. We often associate it with politicians seeking our vote at election times. The concern to persuade or convert others is of course not unique to politicians. Campaigners against, say, hunting, abortion, vivisection and the like often use rhetorical language, believing it to be more effective in winning converts to their cause than calm and non-emotive rational debate. Neither is rhetoric a recent phenomenon. The Greek Sophists of fifth century Greece were notable for their deliberate cultivation of 'eristic' techniques for using language to win arguments without regard for 'truth' and were perhaps the earliest rhetoricians in Western culture. (*Rhetor* in Greek meant 'orator'.)

One of the earliest academic studies of rhetoric was undertaken by Aristotle. Like his teacher Plato, he was critical of the Sophists' emphasis on the emotive aspect of oratory and their neglect of the argumentative; and in his book *Rhetoric* he attempted to provide a thorough account of what it involves as a practical 'science'. He considered rhetoric to be a branch of dialectic concerned with the 'probable' but as closely linked with 'politics' – this being understood in a broad sense as having to do with human character. (Man for Aristotle was a 'political animal', *zoon politikon*, able to realize or fulfil himself only as a member of the '*polis*', the Greek city state (see 4.9).). Rhetoric, he says, is 'the power to see the possible ways of persuading people about any given subject.' Accordingly he examines arguments appropriate to the varieties of oratory employed by different types of speakers: the political, the judicial ('forensic') and the declamatory – for show or exhibition. He also distinguished three aspects of discourse: the ethical relates to the character of the speaker; the emotional is (obviously) concerned with the arousing of emotion; and the logical, which relates to the force of the argument. Associated with the last is rhetorical induction and the rhetorical syllogism (the enthymeme), which is a syllogism with one of its constituent propositions omitted. In the third part of the *Rhetoric*, Aristotle examines such matters as style and arrangement of language, arguing for clarity, 'naturalness', the avoidance of excess and ornamentation in vocabulary, and for a fixed structure (to state one's position and then to give one's proof).

Although not of major philosophical importance, the *Rhetoric* influenced many writers from Roman times onwards, though its importance declined during the nineteenth century. Aristotelian principles were revived, albeit in modified form, early in the twentieth century in new cultural contexts, particularly in America. However, what is characteristic of the so-called 'new' rhetoric is an interest not so much in the speaker as on the effect of both the spoken and the written word on the audience or reader. Much recent work has been influenced by the 'linguistic analysis' philosophy outlined in 2.9; and it can reasonably be claimed that there is some overlap between the two disciplines in so far as rhetoric can be in part regarded as an investigation of practical reasoning. In this context mention should be made of J.L. Austin's (1911–60) ground-breaking theory of 'illocutionary forces'. He distinguished a number of kinds of 'speech-acts' as characterizing our utterances. Take, for example, the sentence 'The cat is on the mat'. When I utter this sentence I am of course making a sequence of noises. This is a phonetic act. As an utterance made in conformity with appropriate rules of grammar it is said to be a 'phatic' act. The utterance considered as having a specific sense and referring to a particular object is called by Austin a **'locutionary'** act. However, in saying 'The cat is on the mat' it may be the speaker's aim to get someone in the room to shoo the cat out; or perhaps it is being suggested or hinted that the children might like to stroke it; or maybe it is an expression of amazement. In this respect the utterance is called an **'illocutionary'** act. If the speaker through the utterance actually brings it about that the cat is stroked or put out of the room, this consequence is called the **'perlocutionary'** act. It is understandable that this kind of analysis of language use, speaker's intention and consequences should have been discussed by contemporary writers on rhetoric. (Austin's work has also been utilized by the 'continental' philosophers Habermas and Ricoeur (see Ch. 12).)

The boundaries of rhetoric are not sharp. Certainly it does not coincide completely with linguistic analysis, which has a narrower focus and is more specifically philosophical. And there are two other disciplines which rhetoric has much in common with:

(1) With its concern for style, structure and figures of speech – especially metaphor, in which there has been a resurgence of interest in recent years – rhetoric overlaps with literary criticism. Indeed one of the major figures in twentieth century literary criticism, I.A. Richards (1893–1979), was the author of an influential text *The Philosophy of Rhetoric*.

(2) Of considerable importance too is the use made of rhetorical themes by philosophers working in the field of hermeneutics or the theory of interpretation – of literature, art, religion and indeed culture in general. How are books and works of art to be understood? What is meant by the 'truth' of a

work? Can the intentions of their creators be ascertained retrospectively? Is understanding of their intentions relevant to the appreciation of 'truth'? Can, and should, the individual and cultural prejudices of the interpreter be eliminated so that an 'objective' interpretation be achieved? (These issues will be examined in Ch. 12.)

2.13 Informal fallacies

We end this wide-ranging chapter with a summary of some of the common informal fallacies employed by many politicians, priests and ideologues, advertisers, lawyers and so on, perhaps even philosophers, when attempting to convert us to a particular cause, or to accept a particular agenda. Quite often, and more seriously, this can involve deliberate attempts to distort the truth. Being aware of some of these tricks can help to make us more critical and sensitive individuals, and less susceptible to the wiles of demagogues and those who would seek to control our lives – more often than not for their own selfish ends.

To talk of informal fallacies is perhaps not quite accurate in so far as a fallacy is in a strict sense an invalid argument which, as we have seen, is in breach of the rules of formal logic. Invalid arguments, however, can often seem acceptable or plausible as a result of either inadvertent error or through deliberate subterfuge; and this can lead – or rather mislead – the hearer or reader to agree with conclusions which do not strictly follow from the premises. For the sake of convenience we shall continue to refer to these errors, most of which relate to the rhetorical aspects of language use, as fallacies. They fall broadly into two main groups: (1) fallacies of ambiguity; (2) conceptual fallacies and fallacies of irrelevance.

Fallacies of ambiguity

(1) **Equivocation**. Consider this argument:
Heidegger joined the Nazi Party and after the war failed to condemn their treatment of the Jews, so he could not have been a good man. Therefore he could not have been a good philosopher.

What constitutes the goodness of a person is an important issue in ethics. Heidegger was no doubt a good father and husband (though he did have an affair with the philosopher Hannah Arendt). But the suggestion that he could not have been a good philosopher does not follow. It is debatable, to say the least, whether there is any connection between moral goodness and being a good philosopher (or poet, plumber, or politician). 'Good' is an ambiguous term (see, for example, Aristotle's account in 4.5). The criteria by which a philosopher is judge to be 'good' in his or her professional capcity are different from those by which we judge a person's moral goodness. (This is not to say of course that one's life-style can be entirely divorced from what and how one thinks about the human condition. But that is a wider issue.)

(2) **Amphiboly**. This is an error that arises through a misunderstanding of the grammatical structure of a sentence:

> Mary: 'John, I have just heard that your car has been reported as having been stolen by a police sergeant.'
> John: 'Thanks for telling me. Crime in the police force seems to be on the increase. I'll have to see my solicitor.'

Not surprisingly, John did not proceed when he realized what Mary really meant. This is of course a trivial example. But it is easy to see how poor sentence structure can mislead.

(3) **Accent**. Errors can arise in conversation if stress is put on the wrong word:

> 'You should not tell lies to your *mother* [stressed]', said the Vicar to Henry.

Henry therefore supposed it would be all right to lie to everybody else – the vicar included. The vicar had not of course intended to suggest that the seventh commandment should be broken at all.

(4) **Composition and Division**. These fallacies involve the error of confusing attributes of the part with those of the whole (or vice versa). Here are two examples.

(a) Hydrogen and oxygen are component elements of water and are gases at room temperatures; so water must be a gas at 20 degrees Celsius.

The inference here is mistaken, because the physical nature of water depends primarily on structure.

(b) The Conservative Party has always been concerned with the people's welfare (or so it might be claimed). Mr X is the MP for Barsetshire, and Miss Smith lives in that county. So Mr X is concerned with her welfare.

Comment here is superfluous.

Conceptual fallacies

(5) **Accident**. This fallacy occurs when a general rule is applied to a particular case but no note is taken of any specific, 'accidental' circumstances which could well count against the application of the rule. It is often encountered in ethics. For example, take the general rule 'Thou shalt not kill' or 'it is wrong to kill'. Here it is arguable that if one killed a person attacking oneself or a close relative, then this accidental factor of defensive action might be sufficient to justify a breach of the rule. Thus, special circumstances ought to be taken into consideration, and to ignore these could be to commit the fallacy. Converse fallacy or hasty generalization involves argument from particular cases to a rule alleged to apply to all cases regardless of context. As an example we may cite the claim that

because some people are worried or offended by pornographic books or books which promote violence, nobody should be allowed to read them. This is not to say that censorship can never be justified: but clearly this raises wider issues about the relationship of the individual to society and the nature of society itself. (See Chs 6 and 7.)

(6) **Ignoratio Elenchi** ('ignoring of proof'). This fallacy is committed when an argument, allegedly presented to establish a specific conclusion, is in fact used to support a different and therefore irrelevant conclusion. Thus, in arguing against (or in favour of) the theological doctrines of the Roman Catholic Church or the economic and historical dialectic of Marxism, someone might, rather, be attempting to show that the effects of these institutions on many people are in some sense bad (or good). If it is then claimed on these grounds, implicitly or explicitly, that the relevant doctrines are therefore incorrect (or correct), the reasoning is fallacious.

(7) **Post hoc ergo propter hoc** ('after this, therefore on account of this'). This is sometimes called 'false cause'. A good example is that of the witch doctor who casts a magic spell whenever there is an eclipse of the Sun or Moon and claims his spell had been effective in bringing back the heavenly body. There is a problem here, however: how to distinguish genuine causal connections from coincidences. This is particularly difficult for empiricist philosophers. (See the discussions in 5.4 and 11.3.)

(8) **Complex (or Many) Questions.** The standard example of this is the remark made by the lawyer cross-examining the innocent defendant. 'Have you stopped beating your wife?', he asks, thereby giving the false impression that the poor man has been systematically maltreating his spouse. This is of course not a fallacy in the strict sense so much as a trick or ploy, and in itself is not even an argument. Similarly an opposition politician might ask a government minister to state how many people had become ill as a result of eating genetically modified cornflakes, knowing full well that nobody had. But by raising the matter he supposed he might sow doubt in the minds of many voters before the important by-election.

(9) **Argumentum ad Baculum** (appeal to force – 'baculum' in Latin means 'stick'). Thrasymachus, in Plato's Republic (see the next chapter), argues that morality is nothing other than the advantage of the stronger party, in other words, that 'might is right'. This claim has frequently been made by tyrants and autocrats throughout history, but is of course fallacious. The 'rightness' of a cause is not to be measured by the numbers of its proponents, still less by the forces at the command of a ruler. Plato devotes much space to showing the incoherence of Thrasymachus's position.

(10) **Argumentum ad Hominem** (appeal to the 'man'). This fallacy comes in two varieties: abusive and circumstantial. In the former, a person seeks to gain acceptance for or to reject an assertion by directing attention to the special characteristics or qualities of those who make the assertion. Thus, it has been said that the doctrines of the Catholic Church, or of socialism, or what have you, must be false because some popes or prime ministers have been lazy or immoral. More specifically, the Church's teaching on, say, the family must be wrong because some popes had mistresses. Closely connected with this is the second

kind of *ad hominem* argument, which involves appeal to special circumstances. One might say, for example, that a priest (or politician, as the case may be) ought to accept a particular view because of his position in the institution. This may be justified, but it would be fallacious to argue from these special circumstances to the truth (or falsity) of the doctrine or dogma in question.

(11) **Argumentum ad Ignorantiam** (argument from ignorance). 'There are more things in heaven and earth, Horatio, Than are dreamt of in your philosophy', said Shakespeare's Hamlet. Indeed, but we may know nothing about them. Perhaps there is intelligent life on other planets somewhere in our galaxy. But to say there cannot be because we have no evidence would be to commit the fallacy of the argument from ignorance. Positive claims to the existence of other beings must, however, in general be supported. Often, even when there is substantial evidence in favour of a claim, there are those who will reject it. So-called 'creationists' argue that there is no evidence for neo-Darwinism, or that it cannot be tested in nature, or that there are serious flaws in the theory. Such people, however, are guilty of ignorance or irrationality. The evidence is over-whelming, and what flaws there are are incidental and not a feature of the over-arching theory as a whole. Ironically, there seems to be even less evidence for the creationist 'theory'. To accept it one would have to jettison over five hundred years' of scientific progress. This is not to say that everything science tells us is 'true' – or that religion is 'false'. It can indeed be reasonably argued that there is no inherent incompatibility between theism as such and modern science, though there are serious philosophical problems generated by the former. To deal with these issues requires a careful investigation of the nature of evidence and the concept of explanation (see Chs 5, 8 and 9). But the general point to be made here is that just because we do not know about something, it cannot be dismissed out of hand.

(12) **Argumentum ad Misericordiam** (appeal to pity or other emotions). This error is encountered particularly in courts of law. The defendant cannot be guilty, it is implied, because of the way he was brought up by a drunken father and an impoverished mother, thrown out of his home when he was only fourteen, the victim of a serious assault soon after which led to the loss of both legs, and so on. The aim of the defence lawyer is to make the jury feel sorry for him and thereby to cloud their judgement. Such experiences could well be taken into consideration by the judge as mitigating factors when passing sentence. But they are irrelevant to the central issue – whether or not he actually committed the crime for which he was charged. Whether or not such a person can be said to be fully responsible and culpable for his actions is of course an interesting but different question. (See 4.7 and 11.4.)

(13) **Argumentum ad Populum** (appeal to the multitude). This is an argument favoured by dictators and other infamous figures who seek to persuade or manipulate the 'masses' (us!). They appeal not to reason, evidence, or facts, but to the feelings or emotions. (There is obviously some overlap between this argument and the last two. The difference here lies in the intention to influence the people as a whole.) Thus the Nazi propagandists in Germany aroused hatred of a racial minority or of other persons who did not accept the philosophy and methods of the National Socialist movement. Less insidious but equally

fallacious are the 'arguments' *ad populum* employed in television advertisements. 'Everybody', it is claimed, is using this or that product; so it must be worth having. The appeal here is usually to ambition, vanity, envy, greed and other similar human characteristics.

(14) **Argumentum ad Verecundiam** (appeal to authority). This is perhaps one of the most common tricks of argument. While it is reasonable to appeal to the views of Stephen Hawking when one is making assertions about the cosmos (though even he is not infallible!), what he has to say about, say, Manchester United, the performance of the government in improving the National Health service, or the morality of NATO's involvement in Kosova is probably no more reliable than anybody else's opinions. He is an authority only in his own field. Advertisers also use this kind of argument when they portray famous people (usually glamorous stars of stage or screen, or photogenic footballers) to promote the sales of a particular brand of drink, washing powder, motor-car, or whatever. The probability is that such individuals do not use those products anyway!

(15) Finally, something should be said about **Petitio Principii** (begging the question), which is not really a fallacy at all. It is in fact a *valid* argument but one which does not take us anywhere in so far as it involves arguing in a circle: what is claimed to have been proved in the conclusion is already implicitly assumed in one or other of the premisses or appealed to in the course of the argument. Here is a fairly transparent example. John wonders what is the right thing to in a given situation and is told that the right action will be that one which has good consequences for him. Little the wiser, John makes his choice but is unsure how the result should be assessed. Unfazed, his mentor tells him that what happened must have been good because John did the right thing.

Interestingly, J.S. Mill contended that there is a *petitio principii* in every syllogism, considered as an argument to prove the conclusion. In the argument 'Every X is a Y; this is an X; therefore this is a Y' we cannot know that every X is Y unless we have already taken account of the truth of the conclusion that this A is a Y. Here the conclusion provides part of the evidence for us to accept the truth of the universal premiss. The main question perhaps is whether the argument provides us with new knowledge. Two points may be made. (1) If we learn that this A is an X, then we can argue to the conclusion by appealing to the premiss that every A is a Y, that is, we *assume* that there is a good reason for accepting the truth of the premiss without actually having ascertained its truth for ourselves, in which case it is unlikely that there has been any circularity. Nevertheless, the question may then be raised how the truth was established, since we have after all accepted its truth and must therefore have had a reason for doing so. (See the earlier discussion about induction.) The premiss may result from definition or from enumeration of all the instances. If the person who had made the enumeration or definition had used the argument to derive the conclusion, then Mill's contention may well have been correct. (2) The truth for such a major premiss, however, may well be in doubt; the evidence is often inconclusive. But to the extent that we are prepared to accept the premiss the conclusion can be said to have been validly derived without circularity. Much more can be said about this problem; and many philosophical articles have been published on the subject.

QUESTIONS

1 Explain the distinction between *truth* and *validity*, and to illustrate this give examples of invalid arguments with (a) true premisses, (b) false premisses; and of a valid argument with a false conclusion.

*2 Put each of the following into logical form and state the ('traditional') logical relations which exist between them:
(a) All that glitters is not gold.
(b) Gold glitters.
(c) Only gold glitters.
(d) Nothing both glitters and is not gold.

*3 Translate the following argument into standard form, name the Figure and Mood of the syllogism obtained, and test its validity by drawing a Venn Diagram:
Some syllogisms aren't syllogisms at all, because some arguments have five terms and there aren't any syllogisms which contain more than three terms.

*4 Write down the smallest set of axioms required for the demonstration of the validity of any syllogism, and from these axioms prove that, in any syllogism, if the major premiss is particular, the minor premiss must be affirmative.

*5 Use the truth-table method to determine which of the following formulae are tautologies:
(a) $(P \rightarrow Q) \rightarrow (Q \rightarrow P)$.
(b) $(P \rightarrow Q) \leftrightarrow (-P \vee Q)$.
(c) $(P \vee Q) \vee R \rightarrow (P \& Q) \& R$.
(d) $P \rightarrow -Q \leftrightarrow (P \& Q)$.

6 Explain the difference between '*entailment*' and '*material implication*' and discuss the 'paradoxes' of material implication.

*7 Construct a formal proof for each of the following:
(a) If scientists are right, then there is an alternative explanation if different phenomena have been observed. If there is an alternative explanation, then this would suggest a more complex situation than had previously been supposed. However, if there is an alternative explanation, this would have been indicated already in the relevant experimental data. No such data have been found. So if different phenomena have been observed, the scientists cannot be right.
(b) It is either the case that all things are composed of water, or it is the case that all things are made of earth; therefore all things are made of either water or earth.

*8 Do inductive arguments need to be 'justified'? (See also questions **22** and **23** in Ch. 5, and the discussion of Popper's philosophy in Ch. 8.)

*9 Read the following (fictional) address, comment on its style, and identify as many informal fallacies as you can:
The indisputable decline in moral and religious standards in recent years is a matter of profound concern to those of us who have been given the responsibility of preparing the youth of this community to meet the challenges of the new millennium. How are they to stand firm against the forces of secularism, materialism and relativism now ranged against them? They are as in a leaking vessel tossed by the raging waters, rudderless, seemingly destined to

destruction upon the rocks. How can we guide and save them? We must defeat their scepticism and encourage them to return to the core beliefs of our order, and we must set an example by our own behaviour. Consider the facts. History testifies to the countless holy men and women whose lives demonstrate the truth of our Founder's teaching. Many suffered cruel martyrdom in defence of their religion. Would he have permitted this had the truth not been revealed to him in that first wondrous experience? Consider the good works millions of our brethren have performed in foreign climes, often enduring great hardship to bring light into pagan darkness. Many of you here today may fear that we shall see that darkness soon descend upon our own land. But I say to you that a faith that has survived a thousand years, a faith that is affirmed by some ten million people, has all the marks of truth. Many of the great philosophers and scientists are believers, and it is a source of joy to us that our great president has renewed her commitment to the Truth. I have no doubt that the coming generations will respond to the call and return our country to the path of contentment and eternal salvation. But we must be vigilant. We have seen the effects of false doctrines and immoral behaviour in the twenty per cent rise last year in the crime figures. Stricter controls on the publishing houses will be essential if this trend is to be reversed. And of course we must look to dedicated teachers and parents to lead our youth along the true path. May the Founder be with you.

*Notes/guided answers have been provided for questions **2**, **3**, **4**, **5**, **7**, **8** and **9** (at end of book).

READING LIST

1. Formal logic
Hodges, W., *Logic*.
Lemmon, E.J., *Beginning Logic*.

2. Historical background
Passmore, J.A., *A Hundred Years of Philosophy*.
Pears, D.F., *Bertrand Russell and the British Tradition in Philosophy*.
Ryle, G. (ed.), *The Revolution in Philosophy*.

3. Informal logic (induction and 'conceptual analysis'); philosophical logic/philosophy of language
Grayling, A.C., *Introduction to Philosophical Logic*.
Haack, S., *Philosophy of Logics*.
Lycan, W., *Philosophy of Language: A Contemporary Introduction*.
Moore, A.W. (ed.), *Meaning and Reference*.
Parkinson, G.H.R. (ed.), *The Theory of Meaning*.
Russell, B., *Human Knowledge: Its Scope and Limits*.
Ryle, G., *Dilemmas*.
Strawson, P.F., *Introduction to Logical Theory*.
Strawson, P.F. (ed.), *Philosophical Logic*.

Swinburne, R. (ed.), *Justification of Induction*.

Toulmin, S.E., *The Uses of Argument*.

Wittgenstein, L., *Tractatus Logico-Philosophicus; Blue and Brown Books; Philosophical Investigations*.

[See also Reading lists for Ch. 5 (Hume) and Ch. 8 (Philosophy of Science).]

4. Rhetoric

Richards, I.A., *The Philosophy of Rhetoric*.

Ricoeur, P., *The Rule of Metaphor*. (Not for the beginner: come back to this after you have studied Ch. 12.)

■ ⊻ 3 The philosophy of Plato

3.1 The historical background

No philosopher can be viewed in total isolation from the cultural milieu in which he was reared. To understand fully the arguments of a great thinker, his prejudices, and the presuppositions underlying his doctrines, we must have some appreciation of the main ideas of his predecessors – even if his own position develops through an explicit rejection of them. This is especially true of Plato, who sought to reconcile and systematize ideas which over a period of some two hundred years had been articulated and developed for the first time in the West by a remarkable succession of Greek philosophers. It is of course not possible here to provide a complete history of Greek thought. (Suggestions for further reading will be found in the book list at the end of the chapter.) But some account must be given of the main themes which played a part in the development of Plato's philosophy.

(1) **Reality and change.** The earliest Greek philosophers, from about 600–450 BC, were concerned primarily with the search for a unifying principle in terms of which the richness and diversity of the world might be understood. The problems they tackled included the nature of the 'real', the opposition of change and permanence, and the conflict between unity and multiplicity. Thus the Milesians (from Miletus in Ionia) sought to pass beyond the appearances of the sensory world and to penetrate to a postulated unchanging and underlying reality, and thereby were the first thinkers to begin to disengage themselves from a mythological framework and to show a determination to enquire into the nature of things, freely and without regard for religious dogma or prejudiced opinion. Thales (*c.* 640–550 BC), for example, is alleged to have said that the 'material cause' of all things is water. For Anaximander (*c.* 610–547 BC) the ultimate principle (*arche*) was not any particular 'element' but rather an indeterminate potentiality (*to apeiron*); and he suggested that natural processes are due to the encroachment of 'opposites' on each other, thereby producing an 'injustice' which can be restored only when the opposites are reabsorbed into the eternal and unlimited totality. According to the third member of the Milesian School, Anaximenes (*fl. c.* 550 BC), the basic principle was air, which is subjected to a process of alternate condensation and rarefaction. In this way qualitative changes are made to depend on changes in quantity.

A later thinker, Heraclitus of Ephesus (*c.* 500 BC), attempted to deal with the problem of permanence and change by rejecting the idea of permanence altogether. He identified the One with change or becoming: reality *is* a plurality of conflicting opposites in continual flux. The essence of all things is fire – which by its very nature is continually being changed into something else. All things are in a state of constant strife or tension.

Later still, Parmenides of Elea (c. 515–480 BC) rejected both change and multiplicity as illusions. Being is One, not a many. It is a self-complete, finite, solid sphere; there is no such thing as empty space; it is Not-Being. There is disagreement over the significance of Parmenides' philosophy. Some scholars argue that although he does distinguish between reason and sense, his 'Being' is to be interpreted 'materialistically'. The 'Atomists' of the next century (who believed the world is made up of an infinite number of immutable and indivisible particles, identical in essence but differing in shape, size, weight and position) understood his doctrine in this way. But it can be argued that an 'idealist' position is also implicit in his system, in so far as he rejected change and multiplicity as unreal and stressed the immutability of Being. It is this aspect of his philosophy that was later to be taken up and used by Plato. And this interpretation helps us to understand Plato as attempting to reconcile Parmenides' world of permanent Being with the changeable plurality of the Heraclitan flux. Plato was also influenced by another Eleatic philosopher, Zeno (b. c. 490 BC), who is famous for a number of dialectic arguments (including the well-known 'Achilles and the Tortoise' paradox) designed to show that common-sense opinions about motion and plurality are mistaken. Plato's interest in logical puzzles raised by the Eleatics is evident in many of his writings, in particular the *Parmenides* and the *Theaetetus*.

(2) **Mind.** Another central concept in Plato's philosophy is that of 'mind' or 'soul'. His interest in the problem may have been due in part to the belief in transmigration of souls held by the Pythagoreans (and before them by adherents of the religious cult called Orphism). The Pythagorean 'brotherhood', founded by Pythagoras (c. 570–500 BC), was a religious community which subscribed to rigid rules and ascetic practices as a means of purification and liberation from bodily distractions. (They believed further that 'the essence of all things is number' – another doctrine which finds an echo in Plato's thought.) The possibility that the philosopher Anaxagoras (c. 500–428 BC) may have given him the idea of looking to 'mind' (*nous*) as the primary cause of change in the world should also be considered – though, like his teacher Socrates, Plato was severely critical of the lack of use to which Anaxagoras had put this concept. In Plato's *Phaedo*, Socrates says: 'From this wonderful hope, my friend, I was at once cast down; as I went ahead and read the book I found a man who made no use at all of Mind, nor invoked any other real causes to arrange the world, but explained things by airs and aethers and waters and many other absurdities.'

(3) **Ethics.** After about 450 BC Greek philosophy underwent a change. Philosophers turned away from speculations about the physical world (change, multiplicity, appearances and so on) to consider man himself and his relationships with others in society. Greeks, in particular the Athenians, were becoming increasingly interested in culture and art, and in the benefits of knowledge when applied to the running of a more complex society. Philosophers were therefore now much in demand as educators, with the responsibility of providing their pupils with the practical skills (especially rhetoric and dialectic)

necessary for success in public life. This led to the emergence of a class of itinerant teachers, called Sophists by the best-known of them, Protagoras (*c.* 490–420 BC). He is famous for his dictum, 'Man is the measure of all things', which was interpreted by Plato to mean that each individual's sense-experience is true for him: what one person feels is hot is hot, but for another that same thing might be cold. Extended to the sphere of ethics (or behaviour) the doctrine might be taken to assert that the laws of different societies are likewise relative: no set of laws is 'truer' than another – though they may be more 'useful' or effective in their results. And although Protagoras believed that law in general was based on an innate ethical tendency common to all men, each individual could be virtuous only by conforming to the authoritative conventions of the society of which he was a member. Protagoras was undoubtedly a man of integrity: but this cannot be said of later Sophists, in whose hands Sophism degenerated into a political movement characterized by superficiality and expediency. It was against such tendencies that Plato reacted strongly. He regarded the Sophists as teachers for whom the search for truth and virtue had become subordinate to their desire for making money and winning arguments by whatever means: they were 'illusionists' and no more than masters of 'the art of making clever speakers [*Protagoras*, 312]. Aristotle defined a Sophist as 'one who makes money by sham wisdom'. (It is to Plato and Aristotle that we owe today's meaning of the term as one who uses 'clever' but basically unsound arguments.)

(4) The most significant influence on Plato's life and philosophy, however, was undoubtedly **Socrates** – who deserves to be examined in a separate section.

3.2 Socrates

At the time of Socrates' birth in Athens in 470 BC, Greece was in decline: the city states were at war with each other, while civil and political authority was under attack from an extreme individualism which stressed the supremacy of private judgement, denied objective truth, and claimed that the test of virtue lay in the satisfaction of the senses. Not surprisingly, the teachings of the Sophists were seen by many Athenians to be undermining the security and cohesion of the state. It is against this background that we can appreciate the contribution of Socrates to Greek philosophy and in particular his influence on Plato.

Socrates spent his whole life in Athens apart from several occasions when he fought in the Peloponnesian war, distinguishing himself by his bravery and fortitude. He was also noted for his exceptional powers of concentration. According to some accounts he was introduced to cosmology by Archelaus who had been a pupil of Anxagoras. However, he soon rejected natural philosophy as incapable of leading to knowledge and turned his attention to a consideration of man and his conduct in society. This change in direction is associated with his so-called 'conversion', as recorded so graphically by Plato in his dialogue, the *Apology*. Socrates' friend Chaerephon had apparently paid a visit to the famous oracle at Delphi and had asked whether there was anyone wiser than Socrates. The priestess replied that there was not. Puzzled by this, Socrates consulted wise men, politicians, poets and craftsmen, and came to the conclusion that being expert in a particular field did not give one the right to claim a perfect understanding of all other subjects; and that in reality the truly wise man is he who has recognized his own ignorance – 'real wisdom is the property of God'. He thereupon decided to make it his life's work to seek for truth or wisdom, hoping to persuade as many as would listen to him to join in his quest.

What Socrates actually taught is a matter for dispute; he left no writings of his own, and we have to rely on conflicting accounts for an understanding of his philosophy. The historian Xenophon thought of him largely as a successful teacher of ethics with no interest in problems of logic and metaphysics. But according to A.E. Taylor and J. Burnet, Socrates was responsible for all the theories developed by him in Plato's dialogues. It is not possible to enter into this controversy here. For the purposes of our later examination of Plato's philosophy we shall adopt the middle view put forward by Aristotle, which suggests that Socrates was indeed concerned with logical and metaphysical issues, but that the doctrines expounded in the dialogues, in particular those relating to the '**Forms**' or '**Ideas**' as subsisting apart from individual things, are essentially to be attributed to Plato, as a development of Socratic teaching. As Aristotle wrote, 'Socrates, whose interest lay in character-building, was the first to raise the question of universal definitions; but he never treated universals or definitions as existing separately. It was his successors who did that; they called them 'Ideas' and involved themselves in the recognition of an Idea for every universal.' (Whether Plato himself actually held this view of 'universals', or whether it was a theory adopted by 'Platonists' in his Academy, is a question to be discussed later in section 3.5.) On this interpretation, therefore, Socrates looked for **universal definitions**, particularly in the sphere of ethics, but did not concern himself with their ontological status (that is, with the question of their 'being' or 'nature'). Thus, while we may talk of different objects as being beautiful to a greater or lesser extent, Socrates would argue that this implies there is an absolute standard or Beauty to which the beautiful qualities of the various things approximate. What Beauty 'is', and whether it exists independently of beautiful things or only 'in' them in some sense, are matters taken up by Plato but not considered by Socrates. In the same way he argued that while ethical systems and accounts of justice might vary from society to society, underlying them is a universal Justice which is an absolute standard, however much individual states may fail to realize or incorporate that definition in their moral codes.

To determine what the absolute standard or definition is, Socrates employed what he called the method of the 'midwife' (his mother's profession), helping others to 'give birth to the truth' [*Theaetetus*, 150]. He would engage in conversation men who claimed to know what is meant by, for example, courage. In the course of the discussion Socrates would lead his companions to make explicit the underlying difficulties in their definitions, thereby causing them to be modified. The modified definition would in turn be shown to be inadequate. And so the 'dialectical' process would continue, each successive definition approximating more closely to the universal. Aristotle commended Socrates for introducing this '**inductive**' method – so termed because it involves a search for **general** definitions but with **particular** instances as the starting-point. It should be stressed, however, that for Socrates this was no more than a *practical* method: he was not formulating a theory of induction as a logician.

In his overall approach – his rejection of traditional beliefs, his use of a conversational technique and his concern for ethical issues – Socrates clearly had much in common with the Sophists. However, there are fundamental differences. In his search for the universal definition, an absolute standard of Truth and Justice, and in his unshakeable conviction in the power of human reason, he cuts through Sophistic relativism and pragmatism. To discover the truth is to *know* what the good life is and how to act justly. Unlike the Sophists, Socrates recognized his own ignorance – though this characteristic irony should not be overlooked – and believed *real* knowledge was possible. The pronouncement of the Delphic Oracle, 'Know thyself', Socrates placed at the centre of his philosophy. Self-knowledge is both the beginning and the end of morality and must necessarily lead to happiness or well-being. For Socrates, 'virtue is knowledge, vice is ignorance'.

In view of these differences between Sophism and Socrates' teachings, it is tragically ironical that he should have been regarded as a dangerous Sophist by the more conservative of his fellow Athenians and accused of perverting the minds of the young. Condemned to death, he refused to follow the usual course of proposing an alternative punishment such as exile (which would most probably have been accepted) and, determined to remain true to his obligations as a good citizen, he rejected offers made by his friends to help him escape. He spent his last day discussing the concept of immortality with his companions. His final words after drinking the appointed cup of hemlock were: 'Crito, we ought to offer a cock to Asclepius. See to it and don't forget'.

3.3 Plato's life and writings

Plato was born in Athens *c.* 428 BC of a noble family, and received a good all-round education. He seems to have come under the influence of Socrates quite early, and was already becoming critical of Athenian politics by the time of Socrates' trial. The death of his teacher in 399 affected him profoundly. When he was about forty he visited Italy and Sicily and was invited to the court of Dionysius I, the tyrannical ruler of Syracuse, before returning to Athens to establish his famous Academy as a centre for the training of statesmen. The curriculum, however, not only covered rhetoric and politics, but also ranged over mathematics, the physical sciences and philosophy. Pupils came from many parts of Greece and from abroad to attend his lectures. In 367 Dionysius died, and his brother-in-law Dion, who had befriended Plato during his visit to Syracuse, asked him to return to take on the responsibility for the education of Dionysius' successor along 'Platonic' lines. Unfortunately, owing to a breach between Dionysius II and Dion, the venture was unsuccessful, and Plato returned once more to Athens. A third visit occurred in 361, but this too ended in failure. Plato thereupon devoted the remaining years of his life to the work of the Academy, where he died in 348 BC.

Plato's lectures, unfortunately, were not published, but his 'popular' writings, the so-called **dialogues**, do survive. There has been much argument among scholars as to the order in which the thirty or so dialogues were written. This is not a debate we shall be entering into here; and we shall adopt the widely accepted view that of the dialogues to which some reference will be made in this chapter the *Apology, Crito, Protagoras, Republic* (Part I), *Gorgias* and *Meno* belong to an 'early' period (to about 390 BC); the *Phaedo* and the rest of the *Republic* belong to a 'middle' period (to *c.* 375 BC); while the *Theaetetus, Parmenides* and *Sophist* may be attributed to the period of Plato's 'old age' (*c.* 368 to his death). Some writers also include the *Timaeus* in this final group: but Gilbert Ryle argues for an earlier date, placing it in the middle period.

We are going to concentrate primarily on the *Republic*. But if you have the books readily available you may like to start by reading through the *Apology*, in which Plato describes the trial of Socrates; the *Crito*, in which he treats of Socrates' attitude while in prison towards the idea of escape, and his views on obedience to lawful authority; and the final part of the *Phaedo*, which is an account of Socrates' last day. These dialogues will give you an insight into the character of Socrates and will also enable you to experience something of the flavour of Plato's techniques and philosophical thinking.

The *Republic* is a particularly good choice as an introductory text. It is intellectually stimulating, controversial and entertaining; and although Plato is trying to come to terms with some quite difficult problems, his style is lively and his arguments are developed in such a way as to make the various issues readily accessible to the beginner. And of course the dialogue as a piece of literature is worthy of acclaim in its own right. (You should note that the traditional numbering of the *Republic* into 'books' does not correspond to any clear division of subject-matter, but was dependent on the size of a papyrus roll. While mention will be made to these books throughout this chapter, standard references will also be supplied to facilitate use of a variety of editions. Quotations will, however, be from the recent translation by Waterfield, who divides the text into sections which pay close attention to the actual organization of Plato's arguments.)

3.4 The *Republic*: outline of the main themes

The *Republic* is essentially Plato's statement of the aims of his Academy. His major concern is to define **Justice** and to answer the question why the just life is preferable to the unjust one. Part I is devoted to an attack on the 'might-is-right' theories of some Sophists. This leads on in Parts II and III to an examination of the nature and structure of an 'ideal' state and the kind of education necessary for its future rules if they are to rule wisely. In Part IV he sets out his views on the tripartite state and discusses the relationships between the three classes. His theory of the 'cardinal virtues' is introduced in Part V. He there argues that in order to consider the nature of Justice in the individual it would be helpful first to examine how it is manifested in the wider context of the State. This is followed by an investigation into the nature of the soul and his definition of justice. Part VI deals with a number of difficulties which must be overcome if the scheme is to be implemented. Part VII is concerned with Plato's distinction between the Ideal and the Actual, and with his definition of the philosopher; for he argues that the rulers of the ideal state be 'true lovers of wisdom'. He discusses further the characteristics required of the philosopher-ruler; analyses the concept of the Good as the ultimate object of knowledge; and then returns to the question of education first raised in Part III. Education of the philosopher, culminating in dialectic – necessary if he is to aspire to knowledge of the good – is examined in detail in Part VIII. Part IX treats of the various forms of 'imperfect' societies and the different kinds of imperfect individuals corresponding to them. In Part X he expounds his theory of art, with reference to (a) the metaphysical theories discussed in Part VII, and (b) its effects on the individual soul and hence on society. In the final Part of the dialogue Plato returns to a discussion of the soul – this time to offer a proof of its immortality; and he completes the *Republic* by considering the question of the good man's rewards in this life and the next.

You will have seen from this outline that although the *Republic* is primarily about ethics and politics, much of the discussion relates to Plato's psychology, epistemology and metaphysics. It is important to note that for the most part his use of ideas drawn from these areas of philosophy is uncritical. Certain assumptions have been made about the mind–body distinction, the nature of knowledge and the existence of the Forms, but he neither indicates how he came to adopt these views nor attempts to deal with any difficulties associated with them. This is left to his other writings. Thus several of his earlier dialogues (for example, the *Meno* and the *Phaedo*) deal with the acquisition of knowledge and the immortality of the soul; what he regards as false theories of knowledge are investigated in the *Theaetetus*, while some basis for his own theory is sought in the *Sophist*; and problems concerning the relationship of individual things to the Forms and to the One are tackled in the *Parmenides*. Reference to these issues will be made in the course of this chapter. This will not only help you to gain a better understanding of Plato's thought but will also serve as an introduction to some of the main areas of the philosophy to be investigated later in this book. In general, however, our discussion will be confined to an exposition of the central themes of the *Republic* itself.

* **Note**: Before moving on to the next section, which will examine Plato's views on knowledge and his theory of Forms, you should settle down to read through the *Republic* from cover to cover. This is desirable even if you are working for the 'A' level or the IB examinations, which require you to study only parts of the book. Plato's arguments about Justice and the Good are closely connected with what he has to say about knowledge, the Forms and the soul; and what he says in one place often throws much light on his views as set out elsewhere in the *Republic*. Having read the complete dialogue you will be in a much better position to follow the analysis we shall be providing in this chapter.

3.5 Knowledge and the Forms

Reading: *Republic*, 472–480; 509–511; 423–524; and 595–602

A characteristic feature of Plato's philosophy that you should take note at the beginning of your study of the *Republic* is his **dualism**. This shows itself most obviously in his psychology, where he distinguishes sharply between body and soul, and in his metaphysics, where he contrasts the world of appearances with an underlying reality which consists essentially of what he calls the Forms. These Forms are the proper objects of definitions. It is clear then that some understanding of this theory is relevant to his primary aim in the *Republic* – the search for a definition of 'Justice' [see 472–474].

The **Theory of Forms** may be seen as a development of Socrates' doctrine of absolute standards – of Justice and Goodness, for example. Plato's account at first sight seems to differ in two respects. (1) He maintains that there are such 'absolutes' or 'Forms' not only in the sphere of Ethics but also as patterns or models for things belonging to the physical world. As he says in 596, '. . . we always assume that there is a single essential Form corresponding to each class of particular things to which we apply the same name'; and he goes on to refer to the Forms of Bed and of Table. (2) The Forms should be understood as existing in some sense independently of the individual physical or moral things or qualities for which they are the absolute models. We shall approach this issue of the Forms first of all by considering what he has to say about knowledge and belief [474–480].

Plato first points to a distinction between pairs of opposites such as beauty and ugliness, justice and injustice, good and evil, and the actions and material objects which each member of these pairs is seen in combination with. Now consider, for example, beauty. Many of us, if we are lovers of the arts, may see and appreciate beautiful things and yet be unable to *see* the essential nature of Beauty itself: indeed, we may not accept that there *is* an Absolute Beauty. We are then said to be 'dreaming' – in the state of **belief**. In contrast, the man who *can* see both Absolute Beauty and the things which share its character, and who therefore does not confuse the particular with the universal, is, says Plato, in the state of **knowledge**. Only the Forms may properly be said to 'exist'. Knowledge is thus of something **existent**, that is, of something **real**. Objects of ignorance – the opposite state to knowledge – must therefore necessarily be **non-existent**.

Plato goes on to examine more closely the nature of belief. Belief and knowledge, he says, are both 'powers in us and in other things that enable us to perform our various functions'. (By 'functions' he means, for example, sight and hearing.) Each faculty has its own special function and object. Belief cannot therefore be of something which exists; for that properly is the object of knowledge. But equally it cannot be of what is non-existent; it must be directed to something. Belief is therefore neither ignorance nor knowledge. It is, however, clearer than ignorance and more obscure than knowledge, and so is regarded by Plato as an intermediate state. What, then, can have the characteristics both of existence and non-existence? Plato's answer is: individual things, which may be seen as being, for example, both beautiful and ugly, large and small – depending on the point of view. Of such things we can no more say that they *are* than that they *are not*. They therefore occupy the intermediate realm between non-existence and full existence: they are *partially* existent in so far as they manifest the eternal unchanging realities. The man who sees beauty, justice and so on *in* individual things but is unable to reach *Absolute* Beauty or Justice is therefore said to be in a state of belief. The man whose heart is 'fixed on Reality', who sees – has knowledge of – the eternal, unchanging Forms, is he who properly deserves the title of Philosopher.

These two related distinctions – between knowledge and belief, and between appearance (partial reality) and full Reality – are illustrated in greater detail by means of the famous simile of the Divided Line (Figure 3.1) [see 509–511]. By giving a summary of the various kinds of objects we apprehend through knowledge and belief, Plato hopes to provide us with a better understanding of the two states of mind and of the degrees of truth about the world we are able to achieve through them. He distinguishes between the intelligible world (*noeta*) and the physical world (*doxasta*). The first world consists of (a) the objects of pure thought (*archai*), and (b) physical objects 'used' for the purposes of mathematical reasoning (*mathematika*). Thus we may observe a triangle drawn on a page and consider it not as a series of drawn lines but as an exemplar of the mathematical concept of triangularity in general. The physical world is likewise subdivided into (a) physical things (animals, tables, etc.), and (b) shadows and images (*eikones*) of physical things. Corresponding to these four classes of objects are four 'levels' of apprehension, as it were. Thus, knowledge (*episteme* or *gnosis*) may be either (a) pure thought or dialectic (*noesis*), or (b) the abstract reasoning (*dianoia*) of mathematics; while belief (*doxa*) includes (a) opinion or belief in a narrower sense (*pistis*), whose proper objects are physical things, and (b) illusion (*eikasia*),

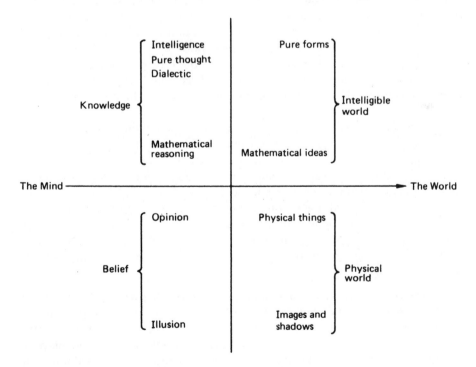

Figure 3.1 Plato's 'Divided Line'

which characterizes our experience of shadows and images – mere copies of physical things.

What Plato is setting out, therefore, is a progression from illusion to pure thought, an ascent from the less real to the truly real. Whatever reality may be possessed by images is derivative in so far as they are reflections of physical objects. The reality of the latter is likewise only partial (though more complete than that of their images), and is attributable to the Absolute Reality whose qualities they partake of. As for the mathematical ideas, they are transitional as between the two realms: they constitute the means by which the philosopher may pass from the world of changing sensible objects to the immutable eternal forms.

Plato's support for the theory

(1) **Negative support.** As was mentioned above, in the *Republic* Plato supplies little in the way of backing for his views on knowledge and the existence of the Forms. A negative approach is to be found in the *Theaetetus*, an account of a discussion between Socrates and Theaetetus, a student of mathematics who is trying to provide a definition of knowledge. The first theory is the Protagorean thesis that knowledge is sense-perception. To refute this Plato gets Theaetetus to admit that knowledge must have an object of some kind and must be infallible. He then argues that there must be a clear difference between knowledge and perception because we can know we have seen something in the past (we remember) without actually perceiving it now. Further, when we compare different colours or sounds, for example, we must make use of a thought process. To know that one thing is similar to another cannot therefore be equated with perception. Moreover, if knowledge and perception were identical then no man could be wiser than another. He also criticizes the Protagorean dictum, 'Man is the measure of all things' (in perception as well as ethics) on the grounds that it leads to absurdity, since in claiming it to be false one is thereby making a true statement.

The second theory, that knowledge is 'true judgement', raises problems concerning the possibility of false judgement. (This was later to be taken up in the *Sophist*.) Plato also shows that a judgement may be true without its truth being known by the person who makes it. The judgement may therefore be no more than true *belief* and not true knowledge.

This leads to the third suggestion of Theaetetus, that by adding an explanation or account (*logos*) of some kind, one *could* convert true belief into knowledge. Plato's criticism of this view centres on the difficulty of understanding what is meant by the giving of an account. (We shall refer to this again in 'Comments and criticisms' below.)

(2) **Positive support.** This is to be found in Plato's earlier writings, in particular the *Meno, Phaedrus* and *Phaedo*. The central themes of these dialogues are the nature of learning and the immortality of the soul (see 3.7). In the *Meno*, Socrates claims to have shown that it is possible for a skilled teacher to elicit from his pupil a truth, for example, of geometry, by means of a process of questioning but without actually revealing that truth to him directly. This proves, says Socrates,

that there must have been a pre-natal state of existence in which we were all in possession of truths. These were then forgotten when our souls passed from that 'other' world to reside in our material bodies. This doctrine is taken up in the *Phaedo* and *Phaedrus* (written about the same time as Book I of the *Republic*) to support the view that knowledge must be of a timeless world which is in some sense beyond or behind the world of everyday experience. The *educated* soul can reach out towards this ideal world from which it came and to which it will once more return after death.

*Comments and criticisms

(1) It is difficult to be sure how far Plato intended his doctrine of the Forms, as set out in the *Phaedo* and *Republic*, to be dependent on the correctness of his assertion that the soul is immortal. Some of the other arguments for the soul's pre-existence and its survival after death will be referred to later. But the proof in the *Meno* is questionable and does seem to be at variance with what is known today about the learning process and the acquisition of truth. Dialectical disputation may reveal what is implicit in the premises of an argument or in the hints proffered by a teacher. It does not, however, support the claim that we have pre-natal or even innate knowledge, or the view that knowledge is of an intellectual realm divorced from sense experience. Nevertheless, Plato's failure to establish the immortality of the soul in this way would not of itself invalidate his theory of Forms, though he might have to admit that human access to it is something restricted – and, of course, he would be left with fewer arguments to support it.

(2) A more important problem concerns the range of his Forms. From what Plato has said about the Forms in 596 (see above) it would be reasonable to assume that there is a Form not only for every common noun (for example, for man, animal and earth) but also for things named by words referring to qualities (for example, red and sweet). (This is sometimes referred to as the 'One over Many argument'.) Plato's Theory of Forms is thus sometimes seen to be a theory about universals, that is, what can be **predicated** of a number of things. This can be understood in the following way: if we say 'this book is red' and 'that apple is red', both the book and the apple may be thought of as sharing a common quality of redness. 'Apple' and 'book' are called **subjects**; while 'red' is termed the **predicate**. According to the Platonic theory we apprehend things denoted by predicates as Forms. In other words, things (apples and books) *are* red because they in some way derive their red appearance from the *real* Form of Redness – just as these objects *are* apples or books because they derive their 'appleness' or 'bookness' from Forms of Apple or Book.

This interpretation seems plausible. There are, however, difficulties; and scholars disagree as to what Plato's view actually was. We shall make two points here. (a) It is clear from what Plato says in other dialogues that he was himself uncertain as to what things could be said to have Forms corresponding to them. In the *Parmenides* [130], for example, he says that such things as dirt, mud and hair do not have Forms. But in the *Timaeus* [52], he argues that the four basic elements or qualities out of which all physical objects are allegedly made (this derives from a theory first put forward by the philosopher Empedocles) are modelled on original Forms, which are 'things-in-themselves'. But within the *Republic* itself there is the suggestion of a different account. (*Read again 523–524 carefully, where Plato discusses the sizes of the three fingers.) He seems to be making a distinction here between direct perceptions of things that do not require 'thought' and perceptions that involve intellectual 'judgement' of some kind. Thus if we look at our fingers, it is immediately clear to us that the reports of our senses are adequate: we *see* that they are fingers. But if we hold up three fingers with a view to determining their size, we are obliged to reflect on what we perceive; when we assert that the middle finger is small (that is, in relation to the forefinger) this is not to rule out the possibility that it is not also at the same time large (that is, in comparison with the little finger). In such cases there is a 'contradiction' which is not apparent in the instances of direct perception. In this way Plato distinguishes between the intelligible realm and the visible realm. Size belongs to the former, because it might be both Large and Small: but other qualities belong to the latter, because, for example, red could not at the same time be not-red. On this interpretation, therefore, only some qualities derive from Forms. (b) A more telling objection, however, is that the 'subject–predicate' distinction was not formally articulated before the development of Aristotelian Logic; and it is unlikely that Plato was fully aware of it until his later dialogues (for example, the *Sophist*), that is, *after* he had worked out the essentials of his Theory of Forms in the *Phaedo* and *Republic*. It is therefore doubtful that the 596 quotation can be used to support the identifying of Forms with 'universals'.

We cannot discuss this alternative account further here, beyond making the general point that any kind of *perception* would seem to involve some degree of reflection or judgement – though this would not necessarily overturn Plato's distinction between the cases which involve 'contradiction' and those which do not. It does, however, lead to a further issue, namely that concerning knowledge and belief.

(3) Plato's distinction between *episteme* and *doxa* is by no means clear. His account in the *Republic* [474–480 and 509–511] might suggest there is a radical difference in kind between them, and that they constitute two contrasting states of mind. Thus we have infallible knowledge of the unchanging world of pure thought which we acquire through a process of reasoning (as in mathematics): but *doxa* is of the changing physical world of things, perceptions and images, and is uncertain. However, towards the end of the dialogue Plato seems to provide an alternative interpretation of the Divided Line distinction. In 601–602, he argues that a flute-player has *knowledge* of his instrument (how well it performs), but that the manufacturer needs to rely on this knowledge if he is to come to a correct *opinion* about its merits and defects. Some scholars have suggested that this shows that knowledge and opinion both involve acquaintance with the *same* objects (facts, including Forms and mathematical truths), and that the difference between them lies in the way that we support our claim to this knowledge or opinion. Thus we *believe* a fact or truth when we have read about it or have been told something about it by another person: belief is 'second-hand'. But we have *knowledge* when we are able to explain, define, or account for the fact or truth (for

example, what Justice is, or why a theorem is true), thus giving us 'first-hand' or direct acquaintance. If this is so, then *doxa* must have a rather different meaning in 474–480 from the meaning it has in 601–602: in the former, perhaps something like 'having an immediate awareness of a changing object'; in the latter, perhaps 'true belief based on second-hand accounts'. In the *Theaetetus*, Plato showed that neither of these constitutes knowledge. We are then left with two contrasting views in the *Republic* as to the nature of knowledge: (a) it is a different faculty from belief and has *different* objects; (b) it has the *same* objects and differs only in that our acquaintance with those objects is accompanied by an intellectual process of 'proof' or 'explanation'. It is possible to see in the following extract from the *Timaeus* (which was written almost certainly after both the *Theaetetus* and those parts of the *Republic* we have been examining) some attempt to reconcile these two positions:

> If intelligence and true opinion are different in kind, then these 'things-in-themselves' certainly exist, forms imperceptible to our senses, but apprehended by thought; but if, as some think, there is no difference between true opinion and intelligence, what we perceive through our physical senses must be taken as the most certain reality. Now there is no doubt that the two are different because they differ in origin and nature. One is produced by teaching, the other by persuasion; one always involves truth and rational argument, the other is irrational; one cannot be moved by persuasion, the other can; true opinion is a faculty shared, it must be admitted, by all men, intelligence by the gods and only a small number of men.   [*Timaeus*, Sec. 19]

Plato seems here to be saying *both* that Forms are known (apprehended) by thought and not through the physical senses *and* that knowledge presupposes rational argument. We might then suppose Plato's 'final' account to be this: 'true opinion' is confined to physical objects – though we may have been persuaded to accept that a relationship to a Form is involved (so that we are enabled to state correctly, for example, that 'the tree is large'); whereas when we have knowledge we have direct acquaintance with the Forms themselves, acquired through teaching and following through of the appropriate intellectual procedures. The difference is between *accepting* that an object exemplifies a Form and '*seeing*' (apprehending) the Form itself. This is not inconsistent with the view that knowledge and belief are two different states of mind.

(4) The precise nature of the relationship between the Forms and the physical objects by means of which they are 'manifested' is another issue which has led to much debate. Some scholars argue that Plato did not really claim that the Forms are *literally* apart from and existing in total independence of sensible things. Nevertheless, whatever status he intended to attribute to the Ideas, there is still a problem about the dualism referred to at the beginning of this section, and the so-called 'separation' (*chorismos*) of the Forms. If particular things are only partially real, how exactly *do* they acquire their limited degree of reality? How do they *relate* to the Forms? Plato himself recognized the difficulty and devoted

much space to a consideration of Eleatic objections to the solutions put into the mouth of Socrates in the *Parmenides*: namely, that particular things might be thought of (a) as **participating** in them, or (b) in terms of some kind of **imitation**. One such (mentioned also by Aristotle in his *Metaphysics*) is the so-called 'Third Man' argument. According to this, if there is a Form of, say, Man or Largeness, corresponding to a feature shared by a number of objects having the same name ('man', 'large'), then there must be a yet 'higher' Form corresponding to the property belonging to Man and the various individual men; and so on *ad infinitum*. (*Do you think there is any way Plato could have avoided this difficulty while retaining the notions of 'resemblance', 'imitation', or 'participation'? **Note**: Plato did *not* think of Forms as *things*, so does it make sense to talk of a Form and its particulars as sharing a property?)

There are of course many difficulties with Plato's account in the *Parmenides*, which we cannot deal with here. And it is clear, from his later writings (especially the *Sophist*) that Plato himself was not entirely satisfied with his earlier arguments. Neither was Aristotle, who set out in the *Metaphysics* some powerful critical arguments directed against both the *chorismos* and the alleged 'hypostatization' of the Forms.

You will most probably have found this section quite testing. Do not be disheartened; you should find much of what follows more straightforward. Plato's Theory of the Forms is, however, of central importance in his philosophy. Moreover, the discussion should have given you some idea of how professional philosophers tackle the work of a great thinker such as Plato. To examine his theories adequately would of course require detailed study of the dialogues and a fair degree of critical expertise. If you would like to follow up some of the issues we have raised, you should refer to the Reading list at the end of the chapter – particularly to the book by Julia Annas.

3.6 The Idea of the Good and Plato's later views

Reading: *Republic*, 503–509

It is suggested in the *Republic* [see 502–509] that the Forms themselves are not *isolated* essences but are linked by virtue of their common origin in the Absolute Idea of the One, which Plato identifies with the Good and (in the *Symposium*) with Beauty. It is knowledge of this ultimate unifying principle that is so necessary if the philosopher is to rule wisely. But what is this Idea of the Good? Some of Plato's contemporaries argued that the Good *is* knowledge. Such people, however, says Plato, are forced to concede that this knowledge must itself be *of* the Good and hence argue in a circle. Others maintain that pleasure is the Good. They have to admit that there are both good and bad pleasures and are thus led into contradiction.

Plato's own conception of the Idea of the Good is illustrated by his simile of the Sun. Just as the Sun is the source of the light necessary for an object to be seen by the eye, so is the Idea of the Good the source of the intellectual relationship which makes possible the knowledge of an intelligible object by the mind. The Good is thus the ultimate source both of the **existence** of all Forms (and hence of the physical things in which they are manifested) and of their **value**. Their Reality and Goodness are determined by their place in the hierarchy. Goodness is equated by Plato with 'function'. His ethics and metaphysics are 'teleological' (from the Greek word *telos*, 'end'); each Form and hence every individual thing has an end or purpose. The Absolute Idea of the Good is the ultimate end both of human knowledge and conduct, and indeed is the 'final cause' of the cosmos itself.

What precisely is the relationship between the Forms and the One and between each other? A possible solution to this question is provided in the *Sophist*. This later dialogue is concerned primarily with the nature of definition as such – rather than with the quest for the definition of a particular term such as 'Justice' (as in the *Republic*). Plato approaches the problem from the standpoint of logic: he shows that to arrive at a definition one must follow through a process of 'division' (*diairesis*) by which the term to be defined is brought under a wider class or 'genus', other members of the same class being distinguished by their possession of appropriate 'differences'.

The dialogue opens with a discussion about the definition of the Sophist and, on the assumption that the Sophist is a kind of hunter, Plato illustrates his method by taking the angler as a model; for both classes of person are possessed of the 'acquisitive art'. After applying his analytical technique he arrives at his conclusion, and has Socrates say to the student Theaetetus:

> So you and I are not only agreed as to the word 'angling'; we have also given a satisfactory account of the thing itself. Taking Art as a whole, we found one half of it to be the acquisitive branch. One half of the latter we named 'capture', with the following as one line of its derivatives; hunting; animal hunting; water-animal hunting; fishing; striking; barb-fishing; and angling. This last, the object of our search, in which the stroke is directed upwards *at an angle*, is named accordingly. [221]

In like manner he reaches the definition of the Sophist:

> It would seem then, according to our present line of argument, that sophistic is a form of hunting, which is itself a branch of acquisitive art employing the method of capture. It is a mode of animal-hunting; its quarry is tame land-animals of the species Man; and it operates privately, offering rich and likely young men a so-called education in return for cash payment. [223]

Plato claims that his account:

(1) Provides an answer to the question raised in the *Theaetetus* – 'What is knowledge?' – for it can now be seen to consist in the intellectual apprehension of class-concepts through the application of **definition** by genus and difference.

(2) Explains the relationship between the Forms (or 'Kinds', as he calls them in

the *Sophist*); for now we can see that to say (at the level of logic or discourse) 'for example' 'a fish is an animal' is equivalent to saying that the Form Fish **'blends'** with the Form Animal (which is an ontological statement, that is, about what according to Plato is 'real'). Some Kinds blend with others, he says, while others do not. Thus, Motion partakes both of Sameness and of Difference (it is the same as itself but is different from the other kinds): but it does not partake of Rest (the two Kinds are mutually exclusive). *All* Kinds blend with Existence. The inseparability of discourse from the Forms is central to Plato's position:

> To isolate every single thing from everything else is to do away with discourse lock, stock and barrel; for all discourse originates in the weaving together of Forms . . . Observe then how timely was our struggle with the isolationists, when we compelled them to recognize that one Form blends with another.
>
> [259–260]

(3) Bridges the gap between the Forms and individual things. If analysis is complete we reach what he calls 'lowest species' (*atoma eide*) – Forms which cannot be subdivided further. The Form of Man, for example, includes *individual* men but does not itself contain any other *sub-classes*. The Individuals belong to the realm of sense. Plato therefore sees himself as having brought together the two realms. Likewise he has reconciled the One and the Many; for the Form of Man is 'Many' in so far as it contains the common genus and the specific differences, but yet it is One because it is an *atomon eidos*. (*Do you find this convincing? Do you think Plato *has* overcome the *chorismos* and reconciled the Many with the One?)

(4) Makes possible a solution to the problem of false judgement raised in the *Theaetetus*. The discussion is complex and technical, but Plato's argument is essentially as follows. If we make the statement 'Theaetetus is not Flying', then on *Parmenidean* premises we would appear to be talking about something that does not 'exist' (not-Flying). Plato's answer is in effect to detach the 'not' from the 'Flying' and attach it to the 'is'. The original statement is thus reformulated as 'It is not the case that Theaetetus is flying' – or, at the 'ontological' level, 'Theaetetus does not blend with the Form Flying' (or, in the case of an individual, does not participate in it). (Whether or not Plato's solution is adequate, it is significant in that he has recognized the ambiguity in the verb 'to be': it may be used to assert an identity, as in, for example, 'London is the capital city of England'; or to predicate some quality of a subject, as in 'London is a city'.)

A further step was taken by Plato in the *Timaeus*, where he sets out his 'physical' theories. Concerned to account for the origin of the sensible world, he introduces the idea of a good and rational 'Demiurge' which imposes order on primitive raw matter or qualities, so as to bring them into 'conformity' with the Forms. This matter is found in a condition of disordered motion in the Receptacle of Space. Plato describes the Receptacle as the 'nurse of all Becoming', and the material world as being fashioned into 'a living creature with soul and reason patterned after the supreme One Living Being'. This latter reference might suggest that Plato is identifying the One with God. There is certainly some support for this in the *Republic* where he talks of the absolute Form of Good as

> responsible for everything that is right and fine, whatever the circumstances, and that in the visible realm it is the progenitor of light and of the source of light, and in the intelligible realm it is the source and provider or truth and knowledge. [517]

and of God as the author of the nature of things, his creations being ultimate realities [597]. It would, however, be mistaken to interpret this 'God' in a conventional religious sense as a person and creator. More probably Plato thought of God as the supreme principle of Being from which proceeds (i) the Forms, and (ii) the Demiurge (equated with Reason and the 'World-Soul'), responsible for ordering (iii) matter. He describes the generation of the cosmos as being a 'mixed result of the combination of Necessity and Reason'.

*Comments and criticisms

Much can be written about Plato's doctrine of the One. You might like to consider the following two points:

(1) **Change and the One**. Plato's account of this problem is not entirely coherent. If matter-in-motion is co-eternal with the Forms and the demiurge, then motion itself and hence change must presumably be attributed to the Absolute One from which all things proceed. This would not be consistent with the theory of blending discussed in the *Sophist*, according to which various Forms (and hence individual things participating in them) blend with the Form of Motion (the efficient cause being the Demiurge of the *Timaeus*). There are, moreover, difficulties with both positions. On the first account, change or Becoming has not really been explained at all; rather it is accepted as a cosmic fact (a 'necessity'). If it is proceeding eternally from the Supreme Principle, does this mean that the One itself is constantly changing? If not, then how does the static One give rise to motion? A similar difficulty arises with the second account. How does change occur as the result of a blending or participation of a Form or thing in another Form which is essentially immutable and timeless?

(2) **The One and the Good**. It is debatable whether the One can be identified with the Good at all; what is allegedly 'factual', or at least an 'ontological' statement ('The Supreme Principle is One') is being equated with what is essentially a 'value' judgement. By way of example we can consider the two judgements: 'The man is tall' and 'The man is good'. The terms 'tall' and 'good' belong to two different categories. We may of course want to say that being tall is a good thing in certain circumstances (for example, if one wished to join the police force); but is it legitimate to say that tallness is in itself good, that is, has *intrinsic* value? Likewise can one claim that the One is intrinsically good, such that all things which flow from it are good in proportion to the degree of reality they possess – as Plato

seems to hold? If it is not, then what is the *justification* for the statement that the One is good? (Compare the reference above to the two functions of 'is' which Plato himself distinguished.)

Further discussion of the problem of God and the Good will be found in Ch. 9.

3.7 'Psychology' or philosophy of mind

Reading: *Republic*, 435–445; 608–621

Just as Plato was not concerned to set out a detailed theory of knowledge in the *Republic*, so neither does he offer a philosophical or 'scientific' account of the 'soul'. That man does possess a soul or mind (for the time being we shall use the terms interchangeably) is accepted by Plato without question. And he does discuss two characteristics of the soul to the extent that they are relevant to his ethics and political philosophy, namely, (1) its so-called '**tripartite**' nature, and (2) its **immortality**.

Arguments in support of the soul's tripartite nature
[see 436–441]

Plato's first 'argument' is that since there are certain qualities in city states these same qualities must exist in individuals, for where else could they have come from? (This will be dealt with later.) His main argument, however, is built on evidence drawn from introspection. It falls into two stages.

(a) 'Desire' is a correlative term and may be qualified or unqualified. Thus, when we are thirsty we desire drink without qualification; drink is the 'natural object' of our thirst. Likewise we may talk of knowledge as unqualified – as knowledge of an 'object'. But just as knowledge of a *particular* kind of object (for example, of disease) must itself be of a special type (medical knowledge), so desire too may be qualified in the same way: we may have a *great* thirst (we desire a *lot* to drink), or we may desire a particular kind of drink, in which case we experience a particular type of thirst. These examples suggest that there is something in the mind other than desire which must *assess* the object and ascertain its qualities, thereby resulting in a qualification of the desire. As he says:

> It's clear that one and the same thing cannot simultaneously either act or be acted on in opposite ways in the same respect and in the same context. And consequently, if we find this happening in the case of these aspects of ourselves, we'll know that there are more than one of them. [436]

Plato is thus led to distinguish between an 'irrational' element (*to epithumetikon*), which desires the drink, and a 'reflective' element (*to logistikon*), which categorizes it as little or much, sweet or bitter, and so on. Our urges and impulses are attributed to the former ('appetite'), while the reason also exercises control.

(b) He now isolates a third element, which he calls 'spirit' or 'indignation' (*to thumoiedes*). This 'part' of the soul normally comes to the aid of the reason when it is struggling against desire. He tells the story of Leontion, who wanted to look at some corpses. For a time he struggled with himself but in the end his desire got the better of him and opening his eyes wide he said, 'There you are, curse you – a lovely sight! Have a real good look!' Another well-known analogy is found in the *Phaedrus*. The rational element is compared to a charioteer trying to control two horses, one good (the spirited element), the other bad (the appetitive element). The former is obedient to the charioteer's instructions, but the latter is given to passion and has to be restrained by the whip. Indignation is thus different from appetite and has a natural affinity with reason – though it may be corrupted by a bad upbringing. The distinctness of indignation from the other two elements is, says Plato, seen clearly in children, who possess it before they become reasonable.

The soul's immortality [608–620]

Plato deals with the question of the soul's immortality at the end of the *Republic*. Although goodness for Plato is to be understood without reference to the consequences of our actions ('goodness is its own reward'), he argues nevertheless that the just man is rewarded not only in his lifetime (by his society) but to an even greater extent after death. Now Plato does not claim to know this: rather his belief in such an afterlife takes on something of a *religious* conviction, and his doctrine is presented in his 'Myth of Er', the story of a brave man killed in battle who is commanded by the Judges of the dead to observe the fate of other souls and then to return to Earth as a messenger. But before Plato outlines the myth he does offer some sort of 'proof'. The soul, he says, is fundamentally pure but becomes deformed through its association with the body. Nevertheless it retains something of its true nature – and shows this through its longing for wisdom. Now each individual thing has its own particular evil (as well as good) which will cause it to deteriorate and eventually to be destroyed. Thus the body is prone to disease, and the soul is open to injustice and ignorance. If, however, the body were killed after the ingestion of bad food, we should not say the badness of the food was the *cause* of death; rather we should attribute it to one of the body's own characteristic illnesses of which the bad food was the *occasion*. Plato's point is that if anything is destroyed it can be only through its own specific evil. So, unless bodily evil can produce in the soul the soul's own evil, we must conclude that it is only through its own inner weaknesses that the soul can be destroyed. We have no proof that the soul is made worse morally by the death of the body. Neither is it extinguished by its own injustice and ignorance. It must therefore be immortal.

*Criticisms

(1) It should be noted that this 'proof' of immortality is rooted in Plato's unexamined dualist assumption of a soul and a body, each possessing its own specific form of evil.

(2) But if we leave this problem on one side we must still be doubtful about the argument itself. It is taken for granted that the soul is neither destroyed nor weakened by the presence in it of injustice and 'other forms of evil', and it is left as an open question whether the soul remains unaffected by the destruction of the body; for this depends on an assumption which has not been established, namely, that the specific evil of one thing cannot destroy quite another thing. Plato says it would be *illogical* to suppose that it could. It is not clear though where the implied inconsistency lies. The central idea of a 'specific evil' is also altogether too vague to bear the weight of his argument.

(3) There is, however, a third difficulty. In the *Republic*, as we have seen, Plato claims that the soul has three parts (*mere*). Now, it is doubtful if he means by this that the individual soul is actually composed of three distinct elements: rather he may be understood as holding the view that the soul has three **functions** (*eide*). As Lee points out in his commentary [between 434 and 435], Plato has warned us that he is not speaking with scientific precision, and, writes Lee, 'he is concerned with morals and not with psychology, with a general classification of the main motives or impulses to action, rather than of a scientific analysis of the mind'. Necessarily then there is some ambiguity and lack of clarity in Plato's account of the tripartite nature of the soul or mind; and what he says in 611–612 shows that for him we cannot hope to understand what the mind is like when it is 'deformed by its association with the body', the result of 'countless malign influences'. What we have to do is 'to look in a different direction':

> We should take note of the fact that it is attracted towards wisdom, and consider what it is related to and the affiliations it desires, given that it is of the same order as the divine, immortal and eternal realm. And we should consider what would happen to the mind if the *whole* of it allowed this realm to dictate its direction . . . Then we'd be able to see what it's really like – whether it is manifold or uniform, or what its true nature and condition is.

Either way there does seem to be a difficulty raised by the doctrine of immortality. Once the soul has completely separated from the body, does it retain its *functions*? Perhaps the rational part survives actively, while the 'spirited' and 'appetitive' parts remain only potentially – dormant without the body to act on and through?

Other arguments for immortality

Plato's main arguments for immortality of the soul (and its existence before birth) are to be found in several other dialogues, particularly in the *Phaedo*, which was probably written about the same time as or just before the bulk of the *Republic*. Brief summaries are provided here:

(1) The first argument recalls the ancient religious tradition of reincarnation, which in Greek culture is particularly associated with Pythagoras. Socrates also assumes as a universal law of nature that all things are involved in an eternal

cyclical process. Contraries, he says, come from contraries (for example, we awake from sleep and then pass from the waking state into sleep once more). Likewise just as death comes from life, so must death return to life again.

(2) This argument involves in part a more elaborate restatement of the notion of recollection discussed in the *Meno*. Socrates maintains that our knowledge of comparisons (for example, equality) and the failure of individual things fully to exemplify absolute limits implies a previous knowledge of an ideal standard. Similarly while knowledge of particulars is achieved through sense-perception, recognition of their incompleteness also points to pre-natal knowledge which is forgotten at birth and has to be recollected with the help of a skilled teacher.

(3) Socrates distinguishes between the two worlds – of Becoming or change, and of Being (the Forms) – and argues that the soul is akin to the latter; for it is invisible, achieves tranquillity when contemplating the Ideas (whereas it is confused in sense-perception), and naturally rules the body. The Forms are immutable; so therefore must the soul be.

(4) Two contrary Forms, for example, Tallness and Smallness, cannot simultaneously exist in an object. In the same way 'essential attributes' such as heat and coldness are incompatible. Confronted by fire, snow will either melt or will extinguish it. The soul derives its life through participation in the Form of life, and so cannot admit Death. But unlike snow the soul cannot perish (it is by its nature or 'definition' imperishable), and therefore withdraws to another world.

These short statements do of course fail to do full justice to Plato's arguments, which are developed in the *Phaedo* in the face of some sustained criticism by Socrates' hearers Cebes and Simmias. But they should give you some idea of his approach. You are strongly recommended to study this famous dialogue at length.

3.8 Justice: preliminary suggestions and Plato's criticisms

Reading: *Republic*, 327–367; see also *Gorgias*, 453–end

The discussion so far should have given you a fair understanding of Plato's account of knowledge, his theory of Forms and his doctrine of the soul as presented in the *Republic* and several other dialogues. We can now examine the central concern of the *Republic* itself: the definition of 'Justice'.

The dialogue opens with an account of a conversation between Socrates (the narrator) and some of his friends: the wise old man Cephalus and his son Polemarchus, both of whom represent the conventional views of the 'ordinary' man; Thrasymachus, a Sophist of the less reputable kind; and Plato's two brothers, Glaucon and Adeimantus, who for the purposes of the argument develop the sophistic account of justice.

The first answer [331–336]

(1) Cephalus equates justice with rectitude but, although an upright and honest man all his life, cannot say what doing right means except that it consists in being truthful and returning what one has borrowed. Socrates shows the weakness of this account by pointing out that it would not be the right thing to return a weapon to a madman.

(2) The problem is taken up by Polemarchus: he argues that to be just is 'to give every man his due'. Given the reply made to Cephalus, Polemarchus is persuaded to modify his position. He now argues that to do right is to give everyone what is 'appropriate', that is, to do good to a friend but harm to an enemy.

To refute Polemarchus, Socrates appeals to several analogies. In matters of health, he says, a doctor is the person best able to benefit his friend and harm his enemies; on a sea-voyage it would be a navigator. Likewise the just man will be of value in time of war; he will be able to fight for his friends. But healthy people, and those who remain on land, will have no need of doctors or navigators. So what use will the just man be in peacetime? Socrates forces Polemarchus to admit that his various suggestions as to the use of justice – in situations where some sort of transaction between people is involved (for example, chess-playing, building, buying and selling) – are untenable. A useful partner in chess is a chess player; and in music a musician is needed, not a just man. It would seem that it is only when things are *not* being used that justice may have a role to play (as in the banking of money or the storing of objects). He then goes on to argue that just as skill in defence goes with skill in attack, so we should expect a man good at storing things to be good at stealing them. So justice is a kind of stealing – but to help a friend or to harm an enemy.

Polemarchus is not convinced. Socrates therefore follows a new line of attack. We may be mistaken in believing a person to be a friend (or enemy), in which case would justice involve doing harm to a friend or good to an enemy? Polemarchus rephrases his definition. A friend is no longer someone who *seems* good and honest, but is now *identified* with someone who *is* good, and an enemy with someone who *is* bad. Justice is then to do good to someone who is a friend (that is, a good person). But, says Socrates, if we harm someone, he actually becomes *worse* 'by the standards of human excellence' (that is, justice), in which case the use of justice must make others *unjust*. This, however, is surely contrary to the function of the good or just man, which must be to do good to others and not harm – in the same way as it is the function of heat to make things hot. So the definition of justice as the giving to every man his due – harming his enemies and helping his friends – cannot be acceptable: it is *never* right to harm anyone. The doctrine is self-contradictory.

The second answer [336–353]

(1) The argument presented by Thrasymachus is essentially based on the doctrine 'might is right'; he defines justice or right as 'what is in the interest of the stronger party'. Asked to explain more clearly what he means, he says [338]:

Now, each government passes laws with a view to its own advantage: a democracy makes democratic laws, a dictatorship makes dictatorial laws, and so on and so forth. In so doing, each government makes it clear that what is right and moral for its subjects is what is to its own advantage; and each government punishes anyone who deviates from what is advantageous to itself as if he were a criminal and a wrongdoer. So, Socrates, this is what I claim morality is: it is the same in every country, and it is what is to the advantage of the current government. Now, of course, it's the current government which has power, and the consequence of this, as anyone who thinks about the matter correctly can work out, is that morality is everywhere the same – the advantage of the stronger party.   [339]

Socrates agrees that what is right is an 'interest', but he is not sure that it is of the stronger party. He gets Thrasymachus to accept that it is possible to conceive of a ruler giving an order which will be obeyed by his subjects but which will yet *harm* him. To avoid that contradiction, Thrasymachus argues that when making a mistake a ruler is not then a ruler as such (just as when a skilled craftsman is said to have 'made a mistake' he is then, strictly speaking, not a skilled craftsman, because his skill has momentarily failed him). So Socrates tries a new tack. Each group of individuals (doctor–patient, ship's captain–crew) has its own particular interest, the furtherance of which is the object of the relevant profession. That object is something *other* than the profession itself. Thus, the interest of medicine is the body, not medicine; the doctor is concerned with the health of his patient. In the same way, concludes Socrates, a ruler in the precise sense must be concerned with the welfare of his subjects and not with his own interest.

(2) Undaunted, Thrasymachus now [343] appeals to the actual condition of Greek states. Rulers are like shepherds who fatten their animals solely for profit. It is a fact of social and political life that the simple and 'just' promote not their own happiness but that of their rulers. The acquiescence of the ruled in their masters' laws gives rise to 'conventional' morality. Socrates' so-called 'just' man comes off worse than his 'unjust' ruler. 'Injustice' actually pays; when given full scope (as in a tyranny) it has greater strength, freedom and power than 'justice'. An individual caught out in petty crime will be punished: but the man who 'succeeds in robbing the whole body of citizens and reducing them to slavery' is called happy and fortunate.

In answer to Thrasymachus' first and more political point about the nature of society, Socrates returns to his earlier argument concerning the true aims of various professions. The doctor tends to his patient in order to restore him to health. Getting a fee is not the *primary* object; the gaining of wages derives from the exercise of a separate 'profession', namely that of wage-earning. To refute Thrasymachus' second point – that the pursuit of injustice brings greater rewards than conventional justice – Socrates develops a three-stage argument: (i) [349] The unjust man, he says, will compete with others, just or unjust, to get a greater share of anything. Just men, however, do not compete with each other any more than a musician or doctor will compete with another member of his profession when engaged in his own appropriate activity: rather, each strives to achieve the same highest standard. The man with professional knowledge is wise and therefore good. So the good man will not compete with his like. Only the ignorant and therefore bad man will try to compete both with his like and his opposite. According to Thrasymachus, the unjust man is like and hence is the man of good sense: but now it appears that the unjust man is bad and ignorant. Once again Thrasymachus seems to have been led into contradiction. (ii) [352] Thrasymachus believes that injustice has greater strength and power than justice. But, argues Socrates, on the contrary, injustice breeds dissent whether in society or in the individual. (iii) [352–354] What of Thrasymachus' claim that the unjust man is happier than the just man? Socrates introduces yet another analogy. Each thing has a function – that which only it can do or that which it does best. It also has a characteristic virtue which enables it to perform its function and a characteristic defect which makes it perform badly. (In the case of the eye, for example, if it possesses such a defect it will be unable to see.) Now there is no function we can perform without the mind – even life itself. It is goodness that enables the mind to perform its functions (for example, control and attention) well, and badness the reverse. The peculiar virtue of the mind has already been identified with justice [see 350] and its defect with injustice. So the just-minded man will have a good life and hence will be happy and prosperous. Justice therefore pays better than injustice.

The third answer [357–367]

Glaucon and Adeimantus now take up the cudgels on behalf of Thrasymachus (though they do not accept all his arguments themselves). Glaucon says that our natural instinct is to inflict injury and to avoid suffering it. To avoid chaos men therefore enter into mutual agreements to establish laws and obey them – a kind of **social contract** (compare Ch. 7). Justice is then a compromise between what is most desirable (doing wrong and avoiding punishment) and what is most undesirable (suffering wrong without redress). Men practise it against their will but only because of the forcible restraints sanctioned by the 'contract'. But this is conventional justice – the justice of the common herd. The perfectly unjust man who rejects the constraints of law and conventional morality actually comes off best in the long run. (Glaucon illustrates what he means by telling the story of Gyges, a Lydian shepherd, who discovered a ring which made him invisible. With its aid he got into the royal palace, seduced the queen, murdered the king and seized the throne. If the just man and the unjust man had such a ring, both would follow the same course.) Adeimantus agrees with what Glaucon has said and argues that, whether people seek justice or injustice, the test lies in material rewards, in this life or in the next; and he claims that contemporary religious beliefs and educational theory support this view. They now ask Socrates to prove that justice *is* preferable not because of any material consequences but because it is good in itself, whereas injustice is intrinsically evil and destructive of the soul of its possessor.

*Comments

These opening arguments have been summarized extensively because they do show clearly Plato's characteristic question-and-answer technique, whereby he seems to draw his interlocutors as if inevitably to the conclusion he wishes to reach, and secondly his frequent recourse to analogy – a recurrent feature in most of his dialogues. Do you find this convincing? In particular, note his move from 'functions' and 'actions' associated with a professional person such as a doctor to those appropriate to the good or just man. It is certainly questionable whether it is legitimate to make use of analogies drawn from non-ethical contexts to illustrate specifically ethical terms such as 'good' and 'just'. You should examine Socrates' answers to the arguments of Thrasymachus, Glaucon and Adeimantus critically. Is he at any time devious? Can you discover any *non sequiturs*, or any hidden premises?

3.9 Plato's own account of justice

Reading: *Republic*, 369–375; 427–444

From now on the *Republic* is designed to answer the challenge thrown down by the two brothers in Part I. Justice, whatever it may be, can be a characteristic of both a community and an individual. It is easier to read a notice when it is in large letters; in the same way, says Socrates, it may be easier to recognize justice in the larger entity. He therefore proposes to examine the community first. Sections 369–372 deal with the origins and nature of a 'simple' society and hence with the emergence of justice.

No man can live in isolation. Society therefore evolves as the means by which men can satisfy their mutual needs. A simple society, that is, a 'city-state' (*polis*), makes use of the various skills exercised by different individuals: some people are good at farming, others at building, weaving and so on. Plato thinks the 'minimum state' would consist of four or five men. Now the best results are obtained when each man does his own job. This gives rise to a fundamental harmony, and it may be that it is in the relationship between the various elements of the community that justice originates. Such a society is of course primitive (Glaucon remarks that the diet Plato is proposing for his citizens is exactly the fodder that would be supplied for a community of pigs); and if a society is to enjoy the luxuries of civilization it must be enlarged. Plato therefore goes on [373–375] to expand the list of occupations necessary for its smooth functioning: artists, poets, tutors, barbers, cooks, doctors, and many others, are all needed. Moreover, since an expanding city-state will require more territory, it will soon come into conflict with other states. A 'Guardian' class, distinct from the 'workers', will therefore be needed to fight for the community. (Later in the dialogue [412–414] this Guardian class is subdivided into two separate categories: (1) the Auxiliaries, who include soldiers, law enforcers and 'civil servants'; (2) superior Guardians or Rulers.) Thus the ideal state consists of three distinct but interdependent classes. Plato is now in a position to present his account of justice [427–444].

If the state as outlined by Socrates is perfect then it must exhibit four **virtues**: wisdom, courage, discipline and justice. The first three are easily identified. **Wisdom** (*sophia*): each citizen possesses his own peculiar skill (carpentry, farming and so on). The skill of the Rulers is exercised on behalf of the city as a whole, not in favour of any particular interest; and it benefits the state both internally and externally. It is through the Guardians therefore that the city may be said to have judgement and wisdom. **Courage** (*andreia*) [see also 375–376]: this is the skill appropriate to the Auxiliaries. To possess courage (roughly, 'mettle' or 'spirit') is to have 'the ability to retain under all circumstances a true and lawful notion about what is and what is not to be feared'. Through it the Auxiliaries are able to fight bravely, and it is this that makes us call the state brave. **Discipline** or **temperance** (*sophrosune*): whereas wisdom and courage are possessed by the Guardians (more especially the Rulers), discipline is characteristic of *all* the members of the state and is diffused throughout the community. It is, he says, a kind of natural order and harmony (or attunement) between the 'higher' and 'lower' elements about which of them is to rule in both state and individual. Through temperance 'the desires of the common majority are controlled by the desires and the intelligence of the minority of better men'. In the disciplined society the workers are obedient, while their rulers govern wisely and moderately. The fourth quality, **Justice** (*dikaiosune*), remains to be explained. [**Note**: Waterfield interprets this term as being often used by Plato in a wide sense and translates it as 'morality'; see the explanation on p. xii of his edition.] Socrates says this has been the subject of the discussion all along but that they did not appreciate that they were already in a sense talking about it. Justice is in fact the principle laid down at the beginning of the discussion and followed in the outline of the ideal state: it consists in the minding by each individual of his own business and the getting on with the job he is most suited to. It must be the virtue that makes possible and preserves the existence of wisdom, courage and discipline. It is thus present in the perfect state when the rulers are governing wisely, the auxiliaries are fighting bravely, and all the 'artisans' are doing their own jobs efficiently and energetically. For justice to be exhibited in the state its existence is presupposed in the individual, who *sees* that to get on with his or her own work without interfering with others *is* just. The way is therefore now open for Plato to define justice in the individual. Given that the tripartite structure of the state is paralleled by a three-part division within the individual soul (see 3.7), justice can be seen to be present when each 'part' performs its own special function properly: wisdom being the virtue of the rational part, courage the virtue of the 'spirited' element, and temperance consisting in the subordination of desires and feelings to the reason.

*Criticisms

Plato's account of the relationship of citizens to the state and of the cardinal virtues is undoubtedly plausible. It may well have been necessary if he was to be sure of avoiding unrestrained individualism and anarchy. Nevertheless there are difficulties:

(1) To consider first the role of the 'working' class. For them, as we have seen, justice consists in their placing themselves under the direction of wise Rulers (aided by the law-enforcing Auxiliaries) and the performing of their own special skills efficiently. Likewise, at the level of the soul, the individual's many desires are controlled by reason and encouraged to achieve their legitimate ends (the satisfaction of hunger, for example). But (a), we may ask, is it entirely acceptable to compare the performing of a job or the exercise of a skill with the satisfying of a desire or appetite – at least so far as the end product is concerned? Certainly the *means* may be directed in both cases (by the Ruler and by reason respectively), but whereas the *product* of a skill admits of description in terms of a criterion, a standard of perfection, a desire is either fully satisfied or not. (b) In any case a strict conformity to the analogy would relate the desires in the soul to the *individuals* of the third of the state's classes rather than to their functions or skills. Given this interpretation, however, one problem is that individuals can act and choose, whereas *within* the individual his desires are usually *occasions* or provide *motivations* for the rational part of the soul to institute action. (c) Moreover, an individual can have many skills, but a desire is single (though it may admit of being satisfied in different ways); and while it may well be that an uncontrolled quest for the satisfaction of basic desires can lead to disharmony in the soul (intemperance), there is no reason to suppose that the performance by individuals of several different jobs would necessarily bring about an imbalance in the state. (d) It might also be questioned whether Plato is right to allocate all occupations, other than those of guardianship, to the third class. The kinds of skill required for the successful performance of a variety of tasks may well be different from that exercised by the Rulers: but many professions surely demand a high level of rationality if not wisdom in Plato's strictly philosophical sense.

(2) (a) Plato's ethics and political philosophy are based on the supposition that there are *four* Cardinal Virtues. However, the assumption of just four virtues does seem to be somewhat arbitrary and is not backed by any substantial arguments. Should not a place be found for other virtues, such as benevolence or altruism for example? Or would Plato have regarded these as aspects of justice? (b) His uncritical adoption of this doctrine of four virtues gives the impression that his account of the three classes has been developed so that it *will* relate to the doctrine of the tripartite soul which he has accepted on other grounds. So it would not be surprising that justice in the latter should be understood in terms of a parallel or analogy with the former. Does he therefore beg the question?

(3) More seriously, his account of justice is inadequately supported by argument. It is *assumed* that it consists in the right performance of function. As the subsequent history of political philosophy has shown, the concept of justice is much more complex and controversial than Plato could have imagined (see Ch. 7).

3.10 The ideal state

Reading: *Republic*, 376–327; 449–502; 514–541

You will already have realized that the lines of demarcation between the various fields of philosophy are not clear in Plato's writings. His theory of knowledge, metaphysics and ethics interrelate and shade into each other; and you have seen how closely his theory of the state and account of justice are linked to his views on the mind or soul. Something more can now be said about his political philosophy.

Plato's ideal society is, as has been made clear, composed of three classes of citizens. In Books III–IV [412–427] he sets out details of the kind of life the Rulers and Auxiliaries are required to follow if they are to be of service to the state. They should have no private property except for the basic essentials, for personal possessions are a source of envy and temptation. Houses, money, food and so on should therefore be provided by citizens. Guardians will derive their happiness from a realization that they are serving the community as a whole. They must also be responsible for controlling the size of the state, for ensuring that workers do not enjoy extremes of wealth, and for maintaining the education system which trains future leaders.

Between 449 and 502 Plato considers three 'waves' of difficulty which might be thought to arise in any attempt to establish his ideal society. They relate to (a) the role of women, (b) the elimination of the family, and (c) the concentration of political power in the hands of philosophers. As to the first [449–457], Plato declares that apart from the difference in biological function, no distinction is to be made between the two sexes. Women would be expected to participate fully in the work of society. They should receive the same education as men, and the most intellectually gifted would be fitted for the role of Guardian. The elimination of the family [457–466] necessarily follows – at least so far as the Guardians are concerned; family ties would distract them from their primary concern, the welfare of the community as a whole. Plato therefore proposes that there should be mating festivals to ensure the production of the best 'stock'. All children resulting from such unions would be reared in state nurseries to prevent them from identifying with a family group and to ensure that their loyalty is given to the state.

The requirement that the Rulers be philosophers is central to Plato's scheme [474–502]; only the genuine philosopher is devoted to the search for truth and knowledge and committed to a virtuous life. As he says [473]:

Unless communities have philosophers as kings, . . . or the people who are currently called kings and rulers practise philosophy with enough integrity – in other words, unless political power and philosophy coincide, and all the people with their diversity of talents who currently head in different directions towards either government or philosophy have those doors firmly shut in their faces – there can be no end to political troubles, my dear Glaucon, or even to human troubles in general, I'd say, and our theoretical constitution will be stillborn and will never see the light of day. Now you can appreciate what made me hesitate to speak before: I saw how very paradoxical it would sound, since it is difficult to realize that there is no other way for an individual or a community to achieve happiness.   [473]

After Plato has defined the philosopher and discussed the qualities required in him [474–487] Adeimantus points out [487] that many who claim to be philosophers are in fact rogues or poseurs, and that in fact the genuine philosophers are usually so disgusted with political life that they as far as possible avoid any involvement with it. This is of course, says Plato, a criticism of the state of contemporary Athenian politics; and he goes on [497–502] to discuss how through appropriate selection and training the best elements in society might in due course take over its organization and running, so that the ideal state could eventually be realized notwithstanding the difficulties.

Plato's **educational scheme** for potential Guardians consists of two stages. The first stage [376–412] starts when they are very young, and should be concerned with the development of mind and character through **literary** education. This is to be achieved by telling children stories. Whether they are true or fictional is less important than that they should have the right moral content. Such stories should teach them about the goodness and unchangeability of God (compare section 3.6). Evil cannot be attributed to God but must be explained in terms of his punishment of the wicked – which actually does them good. The literature children are allowed to read must also inculcate the virtues of courage, truthfulness and temperance. All literature which encourages moral weakness must be censored or banned altogether (even if it is about the behaviour of the gods themselves). By literary education Plato means not only 'simple' and 'imitative' poetry, or their combination, but also music and other creative arts. The state must ensure that all such activity be directed solely towards the perception of beauty – which will in turn encourage right thinking and right behaviour. (*It is worth noting that the imitative arts relate to the lowest levels in Plato's hierarchy of things and ideas (see section 3.5), which are at two removes from 'reality'. This explains his concern that literature and art should be vetted to ensure that they point potential Guardians on the upward path towards Truth, Goodness and Beauty. You will find a fuller account of his theory of art in Book X of the *Republic*, 595–608. Further reference to this will be made in Ch. 10; and you may wish to postpone a more detailed examination of Plato's arguments until then.)

Training is not just of the mind and character: literary education must be followed by **physical** education consisting of gymnastics. This will ensure that courage is added to the temperance imparted to the soul by music and that the Guardians will develop a strong constitution (especially useful to the Auxiliaries):

So in my opinion what we find is that, since we have a dual nature, God gave us two corresponding areas of expertise – culture and physical exercise – for our passionate and our philosophical aspects. He didn't give them for the mind and body, except incidentally; the purpose was for those two aspects of our nature to fit harmoniously together by being stretched and relaxed as much as is appropriate . . . Therefore, it isn't the person who attunes the strings of a lyre to one another, it's the person who makes the best blend of physical exercise and culture, and who applies them to the mind in the right proportions, whom we should really describe as a virtuoso and as having the most harmony in his life.   [411–412]

The second stage, which involves essentially a training in **science** and **philosophy**, is described in Book VII [521–541]. The central purpose of such education is the *conversion* of the mind or soul towards knowledge of the Good. What is meant by this conversion is made clear a little earlier [514–521] in Plato's famous **simile of the cave**, which incorporates the truths he was trying to present in his simile of the Sun and the Divided Line analogy (see 3.5). [**Note**: As both Lee and Waterfield point out, it would be a mistake to attempt to find direct one-to-one correlations between the Cave and the Line.] Plato has Socrates asking his listeners to imagine a group of prisoners tied down in a cave. Behind them is a fire which casts moving shadows on the wall in front of them. They cannot turn their heads and therefore have no knowledge of the entrance to the cave. Suppose one of them were released from his bonds and could turn round. He would be dazzled by the fire and would be unable to see the objects which had cast the shadows. Suppose, further, that he could make his way to the cave entrance and was told that outside were objects still more real than those by the fire. Initially he would not be able to see these either; his eyes would be so dazzled by the Sun: but after a while he would become accustomed to the brightness and would come to recognize the reality of the world outside. As he is now the only person able to compare the real objects with both the things in the cave and their shadows on the wall, it must be his responsibility to return to the cave and enlighten the other prisoners. He must 'turn their minds round'.

(*We may assume, with Lee, the following correspondences: the tied prisoners represent Illusion, the freed prisoner Belief; looking at the shadows may be compared to the use of Reason; looking at the real things outside involves Intelligence; while looking at the sun is analogous to having a vision of the Form of the Good.)

> An implication of what we're saying at the moment . . . is that the capacity for knowledge is present in everyone's mind. If you can imagine an eye that can turn from darkness to brightness only if the body as a whole turns, then our organ of understanding is like that. Its orientation has to be accompanied by turning the mind as a whole away from the world of becoming, until it becomes capable of bearing the sight of real being and reality at its most bright, which we're saying is goodness.   [518]

To bring this conversion about, Plato says, trainees should first study mathematics and science (arithmetic, geometry, astronomy and harmonics); these disciplines will encourage judgement and abstract thinking, the apprehension of concepts rather than perception of individual things, and will thereby direct their attention towards knowledge and away from belief. The educational process is completed at about the age of thirty with the study of Dialectic, which starts from the hypotheses of science and passes to ultimate truths. What precisely is meant by 'Dialectic' has been much discussed. It is of course implicit in the question-and-answer techniques employed by Socrates throughout the dialogue, which we have referred to earlier. Plato himself says:

It may be an intelligible theme [which dialectic develops], but sight can be said to reflect it, when . . . it sets about looking at actual creatures, at the heavenly bodies themselves, and finally at the Sun itself. Just as, in this case, a person ends up at the supreme point of the visible realm, so the summit of the intelligible realm is reached when, by means of dialectic and without relying on anything perceptible, a person perseveres in using rational argument to approach the true reality of things until he has grasped with his intellect the reality of goodness itself. [532]

Dialectic is thus a philosophical activity through which an individual can develop insight into the reality of things in themselves, but part of the earlier training in rational argument involves the study of mathematics, and of course it is also fundamental to the formation of character. Perhaps we can say dialectic promotes the integration of man's intellectual and moral life and culminates ideally in a vision of Truth and Goodness – as the ultimate Reality.

The completion of the five-year stage of Dialectic is to be followed by a fifteen-year period of practical experience in various minor offices before a candidate is regarded as properly qualified to take on the supreme task as Ruler.

One question that might be raised about Plato's views on education in the ideal state concerns the apparent inflexibility of his scheme: each individual, whether worker or Guardian, has his own special task for which he is best fitted, but there does not seem to be scope for change. Can workers move to a different job, take on new tasks? More importantly, how is it possible when children are so young to determine that they are suited to the education which will eventually enable them to rule? Plato does in fact deal with this problem in his so-called 'Foundation Myth' [414–415] which he hopes later generations of citizens might come to believe:

Although all of you citizens are brothers . . . nevertheless during the kneading phase, God included gold in the mixture when he was forming those of you who have what it takes to be rulers (which is why rulers have the greatest privileges), silver when he was forming the auxiliaries, and iron and copper when he was forming the farmers and other workers. Now, despite the fact that in general your offspring will be similar in kind to yourselves, nevertheless, because you're all related, sometimes a silver child might be born to a gold parent, a gold one to a silver parent, and so on: any of them might be produced by any one of others. Therefore, of all of his instructions to the rulers, there is none that God stresses more than this: there is no aspect of their work as guardians which they shall be so good at or dedicated to as watching over the admixture of elements in the minds of the children of the community. If one of their own children is born with a nature tinged with copper or iron, they shall at all costs avoid feeling sorry for it: they shall assign it the status appropriate to its nature and banish it to the workers or farmers. On the other hand, if a child born to a worker or a farmer has a nature tinged with gold or silver, they shall honour it and elevate it to the rank of either guardian or auxiliary, because of an oracle which states that the community will be destroyed when it has a copper or iron guardian. [415]

The primary purpose of the 'myth' is to encourage loyalty among all members of the community – though it is clear also that Plato does envisage that citizens will be moved from class to class according to their abilities as revealed in the course of the educational process. For Plato, then, individuals are, in modern terms, born with a particular genetic 'make-up', but it is the responsibility of the Guardians to ensure that their skills are made use of to benefit the State as a whole.

*Criticism

It does not matter, says Socrates [592], whether the ideal state exists or ever will exist; it is the only state in whose politics the intelligent man can take part. Whether you share this belief or not, many of you will have doubts about some aspects of the Republic as described by Plato. You might like to think about one particular issue: can the limiting of individual freedom (as suggested by the censorship of literature and the abolition of the family) be justified on the ground that it is in the interest of the community as a whole? Are the Rulers 'paternalistic'? These issues will be referred to again in Chs 7 and 10. But for the time being it is worth recognizing that while Plato's ideal society has been attacked as being totalitarian and illiberal by political philosophers of a variety of persuasions, his scheme is firmly rooted in a vision of goodness and a genuine concern for the physical, moral and spiritual well-being of all citizens (though he seemed unable to emancipate himself from the contemporary Greek attitude to slavery!).

3.11 Imperfect societies

Reading: *Republic*, 543–576

Plato seemed to believe that his ideal state, which is an **aristocracy** (*aristokratia* – 'rule by the best-born'), could evolve from the Athenian society in which he lived – though he recognized that it would be difficult [see 502]. At the least it could stand as an ideal, 'a pattern in heaven, where those who wish can see it and found it in their own hearts' [592], against which the quality of other societies might be judged; and he devotes much of Book VII [543–576] to an examination of 'imperfect' societies and the characteristic types of individuals generally admired in each one. Four such societies are discussed in order of the degree to which they may be said to have fallen away from the ideal.

(1) **Timocracy** (rule by men of honour – though Plato uses the term to refer to rule by the ambitious). This kind of society comes into existence when, largely as a result of excessive emphasis being placed on gymnastic, the 'spirited' element takes control of reason. Young trainee Guardians become ambitious, and disputes arise between those wishing to preserve traditional values and those who now seek after personal profit. The Auxiliaries come to dominate; genuine rulers are displaced. War will be the constant occupation of such a society. The timarchic character is identified by his self-assertiveness and personal ambition.

(2) **Oligarchy** (government by the rich). The oligarchic society devolves from timocracy as a result of greed and the accumulation of wealth in the hands of a small group. Political power depends entirely on money. Society now consists of only two classes, rich and poor, many of the latter becoming criminals. Oligarchy also suffers from the inability to wage war. The oligarchic man, similarly, devotes his whole life to the getting of money. He has the appearance of being virtuous but is not in so far as he is not ruled by reason.

(3) **Democracy** (rule by the people). Such a society is not democratic in the sense we understand today in Britain or the United States. Democracy in Greece, Plato believes, arises when the rich fail to notice the growth in power of the poor class and are eventually overthrown. It is a society in which all citizens have equal political opportunity to hold public office – regardless of their 'fitness' for it – and have the freedom to do as they wish. Pleasure becomes the 'test' which determines what each man is to do. There is thus a lack of respect for authority and the rule of law, and as a result a democracy lacks cohesion and tends to anarchy. The democratic man is a kind of hedonist, believing himself to be free but totally at the mercy of his ephemeral impulses.

(4) **Tyranny**. The descent from oligarchy into democracy is marked by conflict between rich and poor. In the free-for-all which obtains in a democracy the talkers and doers gradually squeeze the money-makers and distribute their wealth to the largely unpolitical masses. The rich, in defending themselves, are then accused of being reactionaries and of plotting against the people. In the ensuing struggle the ordinary citizens look for a popular leader. In due course he comes to gain absolute power and can be removed only by assassination. The tyrant is a man who, starting out as a democrat, falls totally into the grip of a 'master passion' – lust, drink, crime, absolute power: he becomes a megalomaniac.

*Comment

Consider carefully Plato's criticisms of these several kinds of 'imperfect' states in the light of his own positive views about the 'ideal' society. You will be in a better position to assess his political philosophy after you have read through Ch. 7.

3.12 Virtue and happiness

Reading: *Republic*, 576–592; 612–620; also *Gorgias*, 466–end

The last point brings us back to a central issue in Plato's ethics. In Book II [352–354] (see 3.8), when disputing with Thrasymachus, Glaucon and Adeimantus, Socrates argued that the just man is happier than the unjust. In 420 he makes it clear that the objective of the perfect just state is the satisfaction of the whole community; each class finds its own happiness in performing its proper function as well as possible. Now, in 576–592, he shows that conversely the unjust life (for example, of the tyrant) leads to misery. Three proofs are put forward:

(1) [576–580] The tyrant, who represents the extreme type of individual, just as the tyrannical state is the worst of the four imperfect societies, is the most unhappy because he is himself in a condition of slavery and has no real freedom. Not only is he ruled by passion but is surrounded by enemies and lives in constant fear of his life. Moreover, having rejected all normal standards he is likely to become even worse.

(2) [580–583] The second proof arises out of an analysis of pleasure. (This is examined further in the *Philebus*.) Plato argues that to each of the three parts of the soul (see 3.7) there correspond three different 'objects' and three kinds of pleasure. Thus the third or lowest (appetitive) element looks for satisfaction of the senses through food, drink, sex and so on, and also the wealth which will help his desires to be fulfilled. The second (spirited) element seeks for ambition or honour. The third (rational) part thirsts after truth. One or other of these three motivating factors must predominate, says Plato; and this gives rise to three kinds of men – the oligarch, the timocrat and aristocratic philosopher respectively (as summarized in the previous section). Each would think his own life the most pleasant, but only the philosopher's claim can be accepted; he alone of all the three types has experienced the three kinds of pleasure. He is therefore in the best position to judge.

(3) [583–587] Given that pleasure is the opposite of pain and that there is an intermediate state in which we feel neither, Plato suggests that people often say that relief is pleasurable and that the cessation of enjoyment is painful. Rest, which was accepted as an intermediate state and neither pain nor pleasure, thus seems to be both. This is absurd. So Plato concludes:

> Inactivity merely appears pleasant and painful on those occasions, because it's being contrasted respectively with pain and with pleasure. These appearances aren't reliable in the slightest: they're a kind of deception. [584]

An analogy follows. Anyone in the world who has risen from the bottom to the middle thinks, as he looks down, that he is at the top – never having seen the real summit. Likewise the man who is ignorant of true pleasure may be led to make a false contrast between pain and its absence, just as someone who had never seen white might similarly contrast grey with black. Now qualities of mind such as judgement, knowledge and understanding are more real than food and drink. Further, the less real the means of satisfaction and the thing satisfied, the smaller the reality of the satisfaction. It follows that the old man who has no experience of wisdom and goodness cannot be completely satisfied. Similar considerations apply to those who, governed by the spirited element, seek after success. In conclusion, then, says Plato:

> when the whole mind accepts the leadership of the philosophical part, and there's no internal conflict, then each part can do its own job and be moral in everything it does, and in particular can enjoy its own pleasures, and thus reap as much benefit and truth from pleasure as is possible for it.   [586]

But if the mind is under the control of either the spirited or appetitive element, it cannot achieve its own proper pleasure and forces the other two elements to pursue a false pleasure. In so far as passionate desires are farthest removed from reason and hence from law and order, the tyrant is furthest removed from man's true and proper pleasure and therefore leads the most unpleasant of lives.

In the final sections of the book [612–616] Plato suggests that although he has tried to show in the course of the discussion that virtue is its own reward quite apart from any consequences, the good man does in fact receive some benefits – from society in this life and from the heavenly gods after his death. Plato's vision of the next world is communicated in the 'Myth of Er' (compare 3.7 of this book and the myth in the *Gorgias*, 523–527).

*Criticisms

(1) Two points might be made against Plato's appeal to pleasure as a criterion. (a) The term 'pleasure' is ambiguous: he uses it to refer both to an acceptable or enjoyable condition of 'feeling' and to satisfaction or happiness of the self as a whole. Is the move from the one meaning to the other legitimate? (To answer this you will also have to consider Plato's assumption that there can be degrees of 'reality' in satisfactions.) (b) Is he in any case justified in appealing to pleasure as a criterion at all? What I find pleasurable or what gives me happiness may be different from what is satisying to you. But can one say that my pleasure is in any sense *morally* superior to yours? (Again you would probably have to take into consideration the apparent inseparability of Plato's ethics from his theory of Forms; and it must be recognized that he relates the moral worth of an individual to the degree to which an ideal of 'wholeness' is realized in his apprehension of 'reality' and in his total behaviour.)

(2) Another difficulty with Plato's account of virtue and happiness concerns the problem of suffering. The just man may have the satisfaction of knowing that he

is just and behaves justly, and of believing that he will be rewarded, if not in this life, then at least in the next. He may, however, have first to endure misery and hardship, perhaps even to undergo mental and physical torture. Can this be regarded as only partly real and therefore discounted in anticipation of the delights of heaven (about which of course he cannot be certain)?

(3) A more serious criticism of Plato's ethics concerns the problem of weakness of the will (later to be taken up by Aristotle). If an individual does come to recognize the 'good' and therefore knows how he *ought* to conduct himself in a given situation, how can he fail to do the right thing? Yet that such failures occur is surely a commonplace. Plato would say that the reason in such cases is temporarily obscured, perhaps because one has given way to the appetites. But does this not seem to beg the question? How can he allow this to happen? Why has the 'spirited' element failed to give support to the reason? Wherein lies the individual's free-will? (This is another issue which will be examined at greater length in Ch. 11.)

QUESTIONS

1 By what arguments did Socrates convince Polemarchus of the falsity of his belief concerning the nature of justice?
2 Glaucon argues that justice is convenience. Explain what he means by this and assess his argument critically.
*3 Discuss why, according to Socrates in the **Gorgias**, it is better to suffer injustice than to commit it.
*4 How does Plato refute the doctrine that justice is 'in the interest of the stronger'?
5 Explain carefully the methods of Socrates in dealing with the question of Justice in the 'larger letters' of the state.
6 'We . . . are pretty well agreed that there are the same three elements in the individual as in the state.' Do you agree?
7 Critically examine Plato's fourfold division of Virtue.
*8 Explain Plato's simile of the line. What is its significance for his theory of knowledge?
9 Give a clear account of Plato's 'parable' of the cave. What exactly did he intend to teach by it?
10 Discuss Plato's concept of 'the Good'.
*11 It was Socrates' belief that the genuine philosopher will not only love the truth but will also possess wisdom. Why did he believe this? Examine the connection between these two concepts in Plato's philosophy.
12 Examine why Plato, in the **Republic**, is critical of democracy.
13 (a) What reasons does Plato give for the bad reputation which philosophy has in existing societies?
(b) Discuss critically his views as to how the reputation of philosophy may be improved.
14 Why did Plato think there are Forms?
15 How did Plato think that knowledge of the Forms was to be regained by the philosopher?

16 Explain the contrast Plato makes in the **Republic** between examples of visible beauty and the beautiful itself. Why does he believe true knowledge must relate to the latter and not to the former? (IB, specimen, 2000)

17 Examine Plato's attempts in the **Theaetetus** to deal with the problem of false belief.

18 Examine critically Plato's distinction between **episteme** and **doxa**, and his claim that knowledge is 'true belief plus an account'.

19 Explain what Plato means by the 'separation' of the Forms.

20 Do Plato's arguments in the **Sophist** enable him to deal satisfactorily (a) with the problem of knowledge (raised in the **Theaetetus**), and (b) the problem of the 'separation' of the Forms?

21 Expound and discuss any two of Plato's arguments for the immortality of the soul.

22 What is meant by 'dialectic' as used by Plato in the **Republic** and the **Sophist**?

*Notes/guided answers have been provided for questions **3**, **4**, **8** and **11** (at end of book).

READING LIST

A. Prescribed text
Plato, *Republic*. [AEB, IB]

B. Other texts
Plato, *Apology, Crito, Gorgias, Meno, Parmenides, Protagoras, Sophist, Theaetetus, Timaeus.*
As mentioned earlier, quotations from the *Republic* are taken from R. Waterfield's translation. There are of course many other editions of the *Republic* and Plato's other dialogues. A convenient single volume containing all the dialogues is that of Hamilton and Cairns. (References to 'Lee' are to the Penguin edition.)

C. Supplementary reading
(If you are a beginner, you are recommended to start with the titles marked with an asterisk.)

1. Historical background
Armstrong, A.M., *An Introduction to Ancient Philosophy.*
Burnet, J., *Greek Philosophy: Thales to Plato.**
Frankfort, H., Frankfort, H.A., Wilson, J.A. and Jacobson, Th., *Before Philosophy.**
Guthrie, W.K.C., *Greek Philosphers from Thales to Aristotle.* (Best for general reference.)
McKirahan, R.D., *Philosophy before Socrates.*

2. Plato
Annas, J., *An Introduction to Plato's 'Republic'.*
Crombie, I.M., *An Examination of Plato's Doctrines.*
Field, G.C., *The Philosophy of Plato.**

Gosling, J.C.B., *Plato.*
Hare, R.M., *Plato.**
Irwin, T., *Plato's Moral Theory.*
Popper, K.R., *The Open Society and its Enemies.**

Collections of essays
Allen, R.E. (ed.), *Studies in Plato's Metaphysics.*
Kraut, R. (ed.), *The Cambridge Companion to Plato.*
Vlastos, G. (ed.), *Platonic Studies*, Vol. 1 (*Metaphysics and Epistemology*); Vol. ii (*Ethics, Politics, and Philosophy of Art and Religion*).

■ ☑ **4** The philosophy of Aristotle

4.1 Life and writings

The movement towards greater systematization and unification within Greek philosophy evident in the writings of Plato achieved its highest expression in the work of his successor Aristotle, perhaps the greatest philosopher of the ancient world and one of the finest speculative and analytical thinkers of all time. He was described by Dante as 'the master of them that know'.

Aristotle was born at Stagira in Thrace in 384 BC. When he was eighteen he enrolled in the Academy at Athens. He remained there for some twenty years, initially as a pupil of Plato but in later years he became more of a colleague and fellow lecturer. His earliest writings were also composed during this period. When Plato died in 347, Aristotle, possibly because he felt himself at odds with the ideas of Plato's successor Speusippus, left Athens and spent three years in Mysia, where he joined a discussion group and also married Pythias, the daughter of a former student of the Academy. (After his wife's death he took as a companion Herpyllis of Stagira, who bore him a son, Nicomachus.) From there he went to Mitylene on the island of Lesbos and then to Macedonia to act as Tutor to the thirteen-year-old future Alexander the Great. In Mitylene he developed his interest in natural history; and it is probable that his discussions with his young royal pupil led to Aristotle's interest in political philosophy. He returned to Athens in 334 soon after Alexander succeeded his father to the throne, and founded the Lyceum as a rival school to the Academy, which became known as the Peripatetic school from the fact that he 'walked around' every morning with his pupils discussing logic, physics and metaphysics. In the afternoon and evenings he lectured to larger audiences on less difficult subjects. When Alexander the Great died in 323 he found himself under suspicion from the anti-Macedonians in Athens, and he therefore withdrew to Chalcis where he died a year later.

Aristotle's writings are encyclopaedic in their range of subjects – covering logic, metaphysics, psychology, ethics, political philosophy, as well as physics and natural history. There has been much discussion about the development of his thought. Some scholars have distinguished three distinct periods: a broadly Platonic period, followed by a stage during which he worked out his criticisms of the Theory of Forms, and finally a period when he was anti-metaphysical, basing his philosophy on empirical science. It is now accepted, however, that although he did indeed come to reject what he believed to be the 'transcendentalism' of Plato's philosophy, he never abandoned his own metaphysical interests and throughout his life sought to systematize his doctrines. While he himself did not feel that he had actually ever achieved a complete synthesis, you should recognize when studying the following sections that the various 'branches' of his philosophy are closely interconnected. It is not easy to separate his metaphysics from his 'physics' or from his account of knowledge; and his theories of ethics and politics cannot be properly understood without some appreciation of his metaphysics and 'psychology'. But before we move on to an examination of some of the key concepts and arguments in his philosophy, a brief account of Aristotle's classification of the sciences will be given to help you get your bearings.

Aristotle distinguishes three kinds of 'science', that is, fields of human knowledge: (1) **productive** science, which involves the 'making' of things (for example, art and farming) – we might perhaps call it 'technology' (though not quite in the sense that we use the term today; *techne* in Greek means 'skill'); rhetoric, which we said something about in Ch. 2, is also included under this heading; (2) **practical** science (for example, ethics and politics); and (3) **theoretical** science, whose goal is truth. The theoretical sciences are subdivided into natural philosophy, mathematics and 'theology'. Natural philosophy is concerned with nature (*phusis*) – material objects which are subject to change and motion, and thus includes physics, chemistry and biology, as well as astronomy, which for Aristotle deals with unchanging and material objects. None of these sciences is to be understood precisely in the modern sense of the term. The objects of mathematics are inseparable from matter but are themselves immaterial and not subject to change. As for metaphysics, this is concerned generally with objects which are 'transcendent', that is, in some sense separate from matter, and unchanging. The supreme example of transcendent being or 'pure substance' for Aristotle is 'God'. His 'special' metaphysics is therefore called theology. (This is of course not to be understood in the standard, that is, Christian religious sense, though Aristotle's concept came to be adapted for this purpose by medieval philosophers.) While many of his discussions of metaphysical problems are found in his treatise called *Metaphysics*, many issues we would regard as metaphysical are considered implicitly or explicitly in other works. Thus he examines substance and predication in the *Categories*; and his treatment of change and causation is to be found particularly in his *Physics*. Indeed it would seem that the *Metaphysics* was so called by commentators on Aristotle simply because it dealt with certain philosophical problems arising out of previous discussions; 'metaphysics' comes from the Greek for 'after the physics' (*ta meta ta physika*). In so far as it is concerned with being in general, metaphysics for Aristotle is the primary science; whereas the 'natural' or demonstrative sciences, which deal with facts and principles derived from fundamental axioms, are 'lesser' sciences – though he accorded them a more important role than did Plato.

4.2 Philosophy of nature

Reading: *Physics*, Books I and II

In Book I [chs 1–13] Aristotle seeks to provide a proper explanation of nature and to account for change. He says that the aim of empirical science is to discover the clear first principles (*archai*) underlying what we are already acquainted with. He devotes the first four chapters to a critique of the views of the early Greek philosophers such as Parmenides, who was a monist and argued for a single unchanging principle, and pluralists such as Empedocles, who held that there were many principles (see 3.1):

Aristotle's problem is to account for becoming – a problem which had perplexed the Presocratics: how could something have arisen either from that which is or from that which is not? To solve this he introduced [5–9] three 'principles' or factors which he supposed to be involved in any change: (1) **material substratum** (*hyle*), (2) **privation**, and (3) **form** (*morphe*). He discusses first what he calls change as alteration. Suppose we say of a man who acquires musical skills, 'The unmusical becomes musical'. This seems to be a case of being coming from non-being. However, if we reformulate the assertion as 'A man becomes musical', we can see that a man as a persisting entity – a primary substance (we shall examine this concept in the next section) – who previously *lacked* (the 'form' of) musicality has now acquired it. In the case of substantial change, say, when a statue is created from a piece of stone or bronze, what persists is the *matter* (the stone or bronze), the statue being the primary substance which has come into being by virtue of the imposition of the form on the material substratum – a form which it previously lacked.

In Book II [chs 3, 7 and 12] Aristotle links these notions of matter and form to two other concepts he uses in his natural philosophy, namely **nature** and '**cause**' (*aition*). By 'nature' he means that feature of a primary substance which gives it its special character and which governs its behaviour. This nature is at once active and passive in that it both acts on itself and is acted on by itself. As for the *aitia*, these are factors which enable us to account for, and make sense of things and events. Thus they have an explanatory role. Aristotle lists four. (1) The constituent cause (traditionally called the **material** cause). Bronze can be regarded as such a cause in so far as it accounts for various qualities a bronze statue may have, such as colour and heaviness. (2) The essential (or **formal**) cause. This explains in some sense why a thing is the kind of thing it is, and why it functions in a particular way as that thing. Thus we might refer to the formal cause of an eye as that which accounts for its shape and its capacity to receive images. (3) This is usually called the **efficient** cause – 'initiatory cause' might be a better term. The creator of the statue, the sculptor, is such a creative cause; using appropriate tools and applying skill, he or she starts the process and can change it. (4) The **final** cause. This relates to the end or goal of a thing or process. Thus the sculptor has an idea or intention of what he or she wants to achieve and aims at bringing into being.

*Comments

(1) Note that the translation of *aition* as 'cause' is not really accurate. Aristotle uses the term in a wide sense – to cover both the dependence of one event on another and explanations which may involve intentions or motives. 'Explanatory

factor' may therefore be a better translation. The distinction can be made clear from an example. Suppose I am asked why my curtains faded. I can say it is because they were exposed to strong sunlight. The sunlight 'caused' the change. (In modern science we would refer to light waves and chemical changes.) But in answer to the question why I took the curtains down, I might say that I did not wish them to be damaged further; this is my 'reason' or 'motive'. In both cases I am providing an explanation, but most philosophers would say they are of different types. Aristotle would seem to be saying that a complete account of, say, the statue must involve both 'causal' and 'intentional' explanations. His account is thus more sophisticated than Plato's and, arguably, superior – showing a greater awareness of the different kinds of language patterns to be found in our everyday discourse. (The concept of explanation is examined further in Chs 8 and 12.)

(2) Aristotle's terminology can also be misleading in other respects. For example, he talks of the premises of an argument as a 'material' cause, in so far as they can be regarded as the 'constituents' from which the conclusion is derived; and in such a case there is clearly no suggestion that 'matter' is involved. Furthermore it should be recognized that final causes cover not only 'goals' in the sense already referred to but to 'ends' or 'purposes' in nature. Thus he denies that, say, the formation of rain in the clouds and its falling onto crops is a matter of chance and lacking regularity. The process seems to be 'purposive', for some end – its final cause. (Such explanations are often called **teleological**; both '*finis*' in Latin and '*telos*' in Greek mean 'end' or 'goal'.) 'Nature', Aristotle says in his *On the Heavens*, 'does nothing in vain, nothing superfluous.' But this need not imply some deliberate intention or will in a stronger sense, for example, of Nature itself or of 'God'. His point is that, although not designed or intended, such events may still have a function. By 'function' of an item or event, he means that it is to be understood in terms of the role it plays in the larger whole. For example, today we know that the 'job' of the heart – the end towards which it is 'directed' – is to pump blood around the body and thus sustain the life of the organism by distributing oxygen to and removing carbon dioxide from the cells. The organism itself might also be said to have a function in relation to the wider environment (see 4.6 below). Thus, for Aristotle, things and events can be accommodated within an explanatory framework which is both mechanical (material 'cause' – how the rain comes into being) and teleological (efficient → formal → final 'cause' – how it serves some 'end', namely, to make the corn grow). It would seem therefore that he may well have admitted different 'levels' of explanation appropriate to different kinds of situations or objects.

(3) Note also that there is some flexibility in his application of the four causes: a formal cause in one context might be an efficient cause in another situation. (You might like to try to think up suitable examples for yourself.) Aristotle in fact tends often to reduce the four *aitia* to just two. His references to material causes reflect the way he sees the natural world as governed by mechanical necessity. The final cause can be assimilated to the formal cause, the two together pointing to emergent or teleological processes in things, which are not necessitated by external causes but are internally self-determining. The efficient cause seems to

have a role to play in relation to both the material and formal-final 'dimensions', and thus in effect connects the two.

4.3 Metaphysics

Reading: *Categories*, chs 2–4; *Metaphysics*. **Note**: The *Metaphysics* is particularly difficult for beginners. If you want to study this work, the relevant 'Books' for the topics of this section are VII–X (Zeta, Eta, Theta and Iota) and XIII (Mu).

A central concept in Aristotle's metaphysics is that of **substance** (*ousia*). His initial treatment of it is found in his *Categories*. After examining different sorts of linguistic expressions [ch. 2], he divides reality (things in the world and the words we use to talk about them) into four groups depending on the ways in which terms can be regarded as predicable (that is, asserted of) or as being 'in' things (inseparable from them). He then [ch. 4] sets out a list of ten ways in which something can be said of a subject. These **categories** or 'predicables' relate to different sorts of question one can ask. Consider Socrates. We can say he is a man (and hence an animal, since all men are animals). The individual Socrates is a particular and 'separable' thing who is neither 'in' nor predicable of any other thing. He therefore belongs to the class **primary substance**. Man and animal are said to be **secondary substances**. 'Manness' is not 'in' Socrates, but it is in the species that Socrates is a member of, just as the species itself is included in the genus animal. The other nine types of predicables are qualities which are both in other things, that is, substances, and can be asserted of them. They are: quantity (for example, 1.5 metres tall); quality (white); relation (double, larger than); place (in Athens); time (yesterday); position (seated); possession (wearing shoes); activity (is cutting); and passivity (is being cut). The category of substance for Aristotle has primary being; the other categories possess being derivatively.

It is in the *Metaphysics* that Aristotle sets out to examine the concept of substance in depth and considered as 'being *qua* being' [see Book Zeta, chs 1–3]. He regards it as special because all other modes of being are dependent on it. It is prior in definition, time and knowledge. So many thinkers in the past, he says, have proposed as substances either 'sensible' things (animals and their parts, or the elements, for example) or non-sensible things (Plato's Forms, or mathematical objects). How are we to decide? What we need to find is some 'mark' or test by which we can identify substantiality; and he examines three possibilities. (We consider them here in a different order from Aristotle's.)

(1) Substance cannot be simply a bare unqualified 'subject', that is, a material substratum or support for properties; for then it would be unknowable. So what is wanted is a way of pinning down the 'thisness' or individuality of a thing – that which makes it a 'this so-and-so' (*tode ti*).

(2) Aristotle [ch. 13] also considers and rejects the view that substances are universals (including genera), both being interpreted by him as Platonic separable forms. The basis of his objection is that if this universal were to be a

substance, it would have to be the substance either of all individuals or of none – both of which options he disallows. He also points out that, while substance is not predicable of a subject, the universal always occurs as the predicate term and indicates a 'such' and not a 'this'. Aristotle suggests other arguments and later [14 and 15] sets out some more criticisms of Plato's doctrine of the Forms and its absurd consequences. He draws attention particularly to the problems arising from the supposition that Forms are separable. If this were so, then each 'part' of an individual man would have to have a substantial Form corresponding to it. Moreover, how could we *know* anything about a separate Form? In Book Mu [Seventh Objection] Aristotle makes another telling point: separate Forms could have any role to play as 'causes' of our sensible world; they could not initiate motion. He writes:

> In the *Phaedo* it is put in this way: Forms are causes both of being and of coming into being. Yet even if Forms exist there is still no coming into being unless there is something to start things moving; and many other things come into being, like a house or ring, of which they say there are no Forms. So clearly those things of which they do say there are Forms can also be and come into being because of causes like those of things just mentioned, and not because of Form. [108a 1–8]

So Aristotle's general conclusion is that there can be no separable Forms and that universals cannot be substances.

*Comment

In 3.5 we pointed out that there is some dispute about what Plato's theory actually was. It is likewise, and for similar reasons, uncertain whether Aristotle is criticizing the theory of Plato himself or the 'Platonic theory' as developed and modified by other members of the Academy. Although this is obviously an important matter, it is one we need not concern ourselves greatly with here, as this section is intended to provide an introduction to Aristotle's own position, and we need only be clear about some of the ideas he was reacting against without regard to their origin. A number of criticisms are made in *Metaphysics* Zeta. Twenty-three objections are raised in Book Alpha; in Book Mu the number has been reduced to seven. You can of course read this up for yourself. As for the issue of the *chorismos*, there is little doubt that Plato did indeed think of the Forms as separate from individual things but this could mean either that, despite their being instantiated in physical objects, they possess a reality of their own, or that they can genuinely 'exist' transcendentally and literally *apart* from such objects ('subsist' would be a better term because they could not be supposed to 'exist' in space and time, for this would make them like the things which share in them). Many passages in the *Phaedo*, *Republic* and *Timaeus* support the second alternative; and he writes of Beauty in the *Symposium* as 'existing alone with itself, unique, eternal, and all other beautiful things as partaking of it, yet in such a manner that, while they come into being and pass away, it neither undergoes any increase or diminution nor suffers any change'. He seems also to have believed that he had solved the problem of the *chorismos* by means of the method of *diairesis* described in the *Sophist* (see 3.6 above). But whether or not this is so, Aristotle clearly rejected the notion of an Idea existing apart from things of which it is the substance.

(3) Could it then be 'essence' (*ti en einai* – 'what it is said to be in virtue of itself' [1029b 13] – what it is to be something)? Now, being musical, say, or even having bones and flesh is not essential to one's being what one is. In fact the only things which have their own properties essentially are species; and they are things whose 'formula of their meaning' [1030c 16] is given by a real definition. So when we refer to Socrates as being a man, this is to talk of him as having an essential property by virtue of his belonging to the *species* man; whereas as an individual he may be supposed also to possess accidental properties (such as being pale). Thus it would seem that the species is a substance because of the essentiality criterion. Aristotle takes the discussion further [chs 7–9] by considering the possibility that form has substantiality (and interestingly he now uses the same term *eidos* for both 'species' and 'form' – previously *morphe*). He reintroduces [ch. 7] the distinction he had made in the *Physics* [I, 7] between immanent form and matter, and argues that it is the form in the composite nature (*phusis*) of form and matter which constitutes its primary substantiality – makes it what it is. This is the so-called doctrine of **hylomorphism**.

Aristotle's thesis in the *Metaphysics* can be summarized as follows. An individual, say Socrates, is a composite of matter and form. It is this 'essential' or 'species form' of 'humanness' which determines that Socrates belongs to the species (or kind) of human being, that is, makes him a man. Such 'species forms' are thus substances in the primary sense. Being a man is Socrates' essential property – the 'formula' given by the real definition, 'the formula of its meaning' [1030a 16]. And as Aristotle says, 'There is an essence only of those things whose formula is a definition' [1030a 5]. But there is now a problem. In the *Categories* he had argued that it is individual things, that is, things which in the *Metaphysics* are called composites of matter and form, that are primary substances, species such as man being substantial only in a secondary derived sense. He does point out [1030a 18–20] that the notion of definition is ambiguous: in one sense it means substance and a 'this', whereas in another sense it means one or other of the predicates. Nevertheless it is questionable whether the *Categories* account can be reconciled with that presented in the *Metaphysics*. Some Aristotle scholars have suggested that a solution may lie in his use [*Metaphysics* Theta, 7] of the concepts of **potentiality** and **actuality** introduced in his *Physics* [Book I, 8]. In *Metaphysics* Zeta, 17 he argues that there must be some principle of unity – over and above form and matter – which keeps these two components together. Take the example of the bronze sphere [see Eta, 6]. This is not a single definable unity; and this is because the matter of the bronze is only a *potential* existent. Before being made into a sphere, or a statue, the bronze had certain non-substantial properties, and it is these that now exist in *actuality* in the sphere. The bronze itself, however, is not actually present and does not therefore break up the unity of the form and matter of the sphere. Thus Aristotle can now clam that both the unitary composite and the 'species form' are substantial entities, the latter giving substantiality to the former. So we can say that for him an individual thing is a composite of matter, the physical stuff (as potentiality), and form, the individual's essence (as actuality). [See especially Lear, Ch. 1.] Individuals belonging to the same species possess the same form or essence, but this form is *numerically* different: it is not *one* (Platonic) Form instantiated in different individuals. Now, because the formal aspect is the same in all individuals belonging to a given species (for example, man), it must be the material aspect which makes the individuals (Socrates, Callicles) different. It is therefore the matter that is said to be the principle of factor of **individuation**. At the same time, Aristotle says, it is the form which *actually* makes the material aspect into an individual thing. In conclusion then, it is form, primary substance in the (metaphysical) sense, that makes a unitary composite of form and matter into a primary substance in the 'everyday' and 'scientific' sense of individual things.

4.4 Knowledge

Reading: There is no one single text dealing with Aristotle's account of knowledge. The *Posterior Analytics* and *On the Soul* contain most of the relevant material.

Aristotle opens his *Metaphysics* with the famous statement: 'All men by nature desire to know'. What then is knowledge? For Aristotle it is, in a strict sense, apprehension of the universal and of what is 'necessary' or 'essential'. It can be acquired, he claims [*Post. Anal.*, I, 2] only through application of 'demonstration', that is, scientific deduction, and this must involve the quest for 'explanatory factors':

We think we understand a thing *simpliciter* (and not in the sophistic fashion accidentally) whenever we think we are aware both that the explanation because of which the object is is its explanation, and that it is not possible for this to be otherwise.

In other words, we can be said to know a fact when we can (a) trace it back to its cause, and (b) show that the fact is 'necessary'. To trace the fact back to its cause is to explain it in the sense discussed earlier; and this means in effect to relate the fact to the 'self-explanatory definition' – which states the 'essence' of the thing that the fact is about. As for the 'necessity' ('it is not possible for it to be other than it is'), this means that the fact is 'eternal' in so far as it is derived from 'eternal' universal axioms (primary definitions). This seems to rule out knowledge of facts about everyday 'particular' events (such as London is the capital of England), which *could* conceivably have been otherwise. Aristotle does, however, also talk of knowing and knowledge (*episteme*) as being of two kinds – potential (of the universal and 'indefinite') and actual (of 'definite' particulars) [*Metaphysics*, 1087a]. Such particulars are either the individual things we are aware of through the senses, or contingent facts which we have acquired or been taught and which are grounded in sense perception. This raises two issues: (1) how knowledge in the strict sense is achieved from sense perception as the starting point; and (2) how Aristotle distinguishes between knowledge and belief (or opinion – *doxa*).

(1) **Sense perception** [*On the Soul*, II, 5–11; III, 1; *On the Senses*, 7]. To account for sense perception, Aristotle introduces the idea of a general faculty of 'common sense'. This manifests itself through specialized faculties corresponding to the various sense organs. Thus the eye perceives colour, the hand feels heat. Several organs may be involved in instances of 'unspecialized' or common perceptions, as when, for example, size, shape, or movement are perceived by both sight and touch. Common sense is required for distinguishing between the objects of different senses and for simultaneous perceptions. Aristotle also refers to 'incidental' perceptions. We may see a white object (to see a colour is 'essential') but also see it as the son of Cleon (this is incidental, not essential). Sense perception for Aristotle is not a purely passive process. He regards it as an actualizing of potentiality (this being the faculty possessed by the sense organ): the eye itself becomes white when it sees the white object, the hand becomes hot. This actualizing involves a 'reception of form' without the matter of the perceived object [*On the Soul*, II, 12]. How then does sense perception lead to knowledge? The key points are that when we perceive a particular object, we are perceiving characteristics which it possesses in common with other things, and that it is the intellect that is involved when form is received from the perceived object. He sets out the process by which we ascend from sense to knowledge in the *Posterior Analytics*, II, 19. Perceiving an object leaves an image in the soul through the operation of the faculty of imagination (*phantasia*) [see *On the Soul*, III, 3]. In memory we become aware of this image as relating to something past [see *On Memory*, 1 and 2]. With repetition of memory images or impressions we acquire 'experience' through universal concepts of objects, and it is from these universal concepts that we can move to the highest unanalysable universals or definitions, which are apprehended or intuited by *nous* (reason) Herein lies genuine knowledge.

(2) **Knowledge and belief** [*Post. Anal.*, I, 33]. In a general or loose sense we do of course have knowledge (*gnosis*) of particular things. When we perceive a cloud, say, are we not certain that we are seeing something white? Do we not know that man is an animal? However, perception must involve judgement, and this opens up the possibility of error, of contingency. Two people may judge that man is an animal, but while the one may regard this as an incidental attribute, the other has identified animality as man's essence. The mental state of the former is that of opinion; only the latter can be said to truly know. Even to say an object is seen to be white involves the fallible judgement that there is a real thing of some sort, not just a chimera or illusion. Perhaps there is little or no chance of error if we confine ourselves to the bare seeing of white as such; but Aristotle seems to suggest that this is a purely passive state that involves no judgement. Such limiting particularity cannot therefore provide us with knowledge in the strict sense.

*Comments

You may not have found this too easy to follow. Your immediate reaction may well have been to say how similar Aristotle's position is to Plato's, for whom to have certain knowledge is to have recognized a Form and to have worked through a proof or deductive process leading to an 'account' or 'explanation'. And indeed they both distinguish between knowledge and belief (or opinion) as representing different states of mind. When we believe something to be true, it may happen to be so. But if we are to know something, that is, to state its definition (essence, or cause), it *must* be true and be seen to be true (or so it is claimed). There are, however, two significant differences between these two great thinkers. (1) Plato, dismissing our sense-experience as changeable and open to error, seeks for the 'universal' or the general through Reason, and only then admits a measure of reality to those particular experiences. Aristotle, on the other hand, while not denying the centrality of the formal aspect, argues that it can be apprehended only *in* the particular thing. (2) Both philosophers accept that to gain knowledge we must start out from sense-perception of individual things. But while Aristotle argues that knowledge, although it is of the formal and universal aspect in the particular, must still be grounded in sense-experience, for Plato sense-experience is regarded more as concealing or distorting a knowledge already possessed by the soul before it was embodied at birth. Knowledge has to be recollected in all its purity through dialectic, reasoning and intellectual endeavour; the sensory factor is incidental and can ultimately be transcended. Knowledge for Plato can thus be said to be **a priori**, that is, existing prior to our experience; whereas for Aristotle it is **a posteriori**, coming after experience. (These notions will be referred to again in Ch. 5.) Aristotle's account of knowledge can thus be not unfairly described as much more 'down to earth' than that of his teacher – and this can be said also of his ethics. But before moving on to our study of his moral philosophy we shall sketch out some of his views about the 'soul', an understanding of which will help you to gain maximum benefit from your reading of the *Nicomachean Ethics*.

4.5 Psychology

Reading: *On the Soul (Peri Psuche* – usually known by its Latin title, *De Anima*). As with the other texts mentioned so far, this is not a 'set' book, but it is one of Aristotle's most influential writings and is well worth reading.

When studying Aristotle's account of the 'soul' you should bear in mind that he was not only a metaphysician but also a biologist; his psychology is also very much part of his physics or 'science of nature' and thus belongs to the sphere of 'theoretical' knowledge. In *On the Soul*, Book II, 1 he describes the *psuche* as 'the first actuality (*entelecheia*) of a natural body which has life potentially' [412a 27]; and as 'the cause and first principle of the living body' [415b 9]. We shall try to unpack what he means by this.

Consider 'entelechy'. There is some controversy about the precise interpretation of this technical term, but most commentators are of the opinion that, according to Aristotle, the soul is the form of the material body: that is to say, the soul is that which empowers the body to function as an active living thing. The soul is at once the efficient cause (it initiates change or movement), the final cause (as the body's 'goal') and the formal cause (as the integrating or organizing principle). The soul must therefore be the formal aspect of a living organism and be inseparable from it. What then is it for a body to 'function as an active living thing'? Aristotle in fact distinguishes different functions appropriate to the level of complexity of 'a natural body which has organs' [412b 4]:

> Plants have the nutritive faculty only; other creatures have both this and the faculty of sense-perception. And if that of sense-perception, then that of desire also; for desire comprises wanting, passion and wishing: all animals have at least one of the senses, touch, and for that which has sense-perception there is both pleasure and pain and both the pleasant and the painful: and where there are these, there is also wanting; for this is a desire for that which is pleasant   [414a 34–414b 5]

Some things have in addition the faculty of movement in respect of place, and others, such as men and anything else which is similar or superior to man, have that of thought and intellect. [414b 18–20]

There are thus three 'kinds' of soul in Aristotle's 'hierarchy' of living things: the 'vegetative' soul of plants; the 'sensitive' soul of animals, which adds to the nutritional and reproductive faculties of the vegetative soul sense-perception (upon which imagination and memory depend), appetite or desire, and the capacity to move around; and the 'rational' soul of humans, which adds to all these powers of the lower souls the ability to reason 'theoretically' and 'practically' in so far as it possesses '*nous*'. Man's 'purpose' or 'goal' (*telos*) can now be seen to be **truth** both for its own sake and as a matter of 'prudence' – which leads us naturally to a study of Aristotle's ethics.

*Comments and criticisms

Reference was made above to the generally accepted view that the soul for Aristotle is the 'entelechy' of the material body, so that form and matter together constitute two 'aspects' of the living organism. It is important to appreciate the contrast between his view and that of Plato. The soul for Plato is an entity which in some sense exists before birth, enters the body and then survives corporal decay after death. (This 'dualist' position was revised by Descartes in the sixteenth century; it will be examined in Ch. 5.) However, you should note that some scholars have suggested that the account in De Anima does not seem to be consistent with the doctrine of substance as set out in Aristotle's Metaphysics. At the beginning of Book II of De Anima [412a 5 ff.], for example, he seems to reject the account of substance as form plus matter and argues that the soul must be substance 'as the *form* of a natural body which potentially has life', identifying it with 'actuality'. In the same way, he says [412b 16 ff.], if an axe were a natural body, its substance would be being an axe, which would then be its soul; without it, it would not continue to be an axe. Aristotle may well be using 'substance' in a different sense here.

His account is further complicated by another distinction he makes in *On the Soul*, namely that between the 'active intellect' (*to poioun*) and the 'passive intellect' (*nous pathetikos*). The former is described as being productive 'by becoming all things', and as 'distinct, unaffected and unmixed, being in essence activity' [430a 15 ff.]. Aristotle goes on to say that in its separated state, the active intellect is 'just what it is, and this alone is immortal and eternal. But we do not remember because this is unaffected, whereas the passive intellect is perishable, and without this [that is, the active intellect] nothing thinks.' This raises a dilemma. If the soul is the 'entelechy' of the material body, then on the basis of Aristotle's general doctrine of substance one would expect the soul to perish with the body. But if, as now seems to be the case, *part* of it is separable from and survives the body's disintegration at death, how are we to account for the *relationship* between the active and passive intellects? If not, how can a substance (in the sense of form) have parts? Moreover, if it has no memory, can we talk of an active intellect in individualist terms? Or is it perhaps a principle which is identical in all human beings? If it has no content, is Aristotle right to call it thought at all? (These and other related issues were to lead to much intense debate and 'soul-searching' among medieval philosophers. Note also that in his *On the Heavens*, Aristotle holds the view that the only pure separate form is the prime and unmoved mover – 'God'.)

One possible way of resolving the dilemma would be to regard the soul as a substance which has a potential to become actualized, that is, a capacity for development (for example, the acquisition of knowledge). Both the passive potentiality and the active actuality thus share the soul's substantiality. But in so far as knowledge for Aristotle is grounded in sense-perception, the movement of the soul from potentiality to actuality can be achieved only when the active intellect 'informs' the body which is thereby at the same time given the potentiality to develop (that is, the passive intellect). His comparison of the active intellect with light is revealing and should be considered carefully: 'for in a way light too makes colours which are potential into actual colours' [430a]. This is clearly a difficult issue and, however one looks at it, Aristotle does seem to be attributing separability to one aspect of the soul – though it is probably still correct to say that he is not reverting to the altogether more rigid dualism of Plato. We cannot discuss the problem further here. If you would like to follow it up, you should consult some of the books on Aristotle listed at the end of the chapter.

4.6 Aristotle's moral philosophy: the good and happiness

Reading: *Nicomachean Ethics*, Book I

We shall now examine some of the main arguments of Aristotle's ethics, starting with his views on the Good and Happiness. The *Nicomachean Ethics* is, like Plato's

Republic, one of the most famous treatises ever written. It was originally a series of lectures which were subsequently edited, it is believed, by his son, Nicomachus (hence the name).

The first three chapters of the *Ethics* are introductory. Aristotle holds the characteristically Greek view that the individual and society are inseparable. Ethics, the 'science' of morals, must apply to men as members of the *polis* or community (that is, the city-state). It is thus subordinate to political science, which may be thought of as applied ethics [ch. 3]. Ethics is primarily about 'goodness'; and Aristotle's initial concern is to determine what 'the good' is. His position is stated at the very beginning of ch. 1:

> Every art and every inquiry, and similarly every action and choice, is thought to aim at some good; and for this reason the good has rightly been declared to be that at which all things aim. [1094a]

The problem here is that there are many different ends – corresponding to different activities. The absolutely good must therefore be the end which as moral agents we seek for its own sake [ch. 2]. In ch. 4 this end is identified as 'happiness' or 'well-being' (*eudaimonia*). But while there is general agreement about this, people dispute about what happiness actually consists of: some say it is pleasure, some find it in honour, while for others it is to be located in virtue. Aristotle is dismissive of the life of sensuality [ch. 5]. As for honour, this is too superficial and men active in public life prefer virtue to honours. But even virtue itself cannot be identified with happiness as the end towards which we aim; virtuous people often meet with misfortune.

Before embarking on a more detailed analysis, Aristotle devotes some space to an attack on the Platonic theory of a 'universal' good [ch. 6]. (*You should study this carefully, relating it to the discussion in 3.6. Note the typical Aristotelian approach to which much recent 'linguistic' philosophy bears some similarity):

> Things are called good both in the category of substance and in that of quality and in that of relation, and that which is *per se*, i.e. substance, is prior in nature to the relative (for the latter is like an off-shoot and accident of what is); so that there could not be a common Idea set over all these goods. [1096a 19–23]

Likewise he states that 'things are said to be good in as many ways as they are said to be'. The word 'good' may be used to describe a person or a thing; it may refer to the qualities or excellences of things; we may use it to mean 'useful', that is, as a means to an end; and so on. In terms of Aristotle's categories we may predicate 'good' of substances, qualities, quantities, relation, time and space:

> Clearly the good cannot be something universally present in all cases and single; for then it would not have been predicated in all the categories but in one only. [1096a 28–30]

Aristotle now presents his examination of 'happiness' [chs 7–12]. In our various activities we aim at more than one end, but some (for example, wealth, tools and instruments) are means to something else. The good we are searching for must be the most 'complete' of all possible ends: it must have the highest degree of finality (see also 4.2) and will thus be pursued for its own sake and never for the sake of something else. The final good must also be self-sufficient, that is, one which in itself tends to make man's life in society desirable and lacking in nothing. The only candidate which is both self-sufficient and chosen for its own sake is happiness. (We may choose other good qualities such as pleasure and intelligence for their own sake in the sense that we may like to possess them, but in seeking them we also believe, says Aristotle, that they are means to achieving happiness [ch. 7].) A clearer definition of '*eudaimonia*' is then developed, based on the concept of 'function' (see 4.2). When we are engaged in a special job or profession we may be said to exercise an appropriate talent or excellence – this exercising of skill is our 'function'. Aristotle goes on to argue that there must also be a function we exercise *as* human beings, that is as beings having the capacity to reason. (In his discussion he refers to distinctions we have already examined in his theory of the soul – see 4.5.) On the basis of a number of assumptions, Aristotle then draws the conclusion that the good for man is

---

activity of the soul in accordance with excellence, and if there are more than one excellence, in conformity with the best and most complete.
[1098a 16 ff.]

The assumptions incorporate the following points: (1) that man's function is a certain form of life characterized by the activity of his soul in accordance with a rational principle or 'ground' of action; (2) that the function of a *good* man is to perform this function *well* (compare, a good harpist); and (3) that this function is exercised well when 'performed in accordance with the excellence proper to it' [ch. 7]. Such a definition, he says [ch. 8], is consistent with various common views about the nature of the good. Life for the 'actively good', the 'virtuous soul', is inherently pleasant – though happiness does seem to require a degree of external prosperity. But he mentions two caveats (*again note Aristotle's realism in contrast to the view of Plato): (a) whatever good fortune we may possess through birth and upbringing, or as a divine gift, happiness in the last analysis depends on ourselves – on our performance of virtuous actions [ch. 9], (b) given the possibility of frequent *mis*fortune, the well-being of an individual should be judged only in the context of his life as a whole [chs 7 and 9]. Happiness as a kind of permanent condition is thus thought of by Aristotle as being independent of the 'vicissitudes of fortune'. If the soul's energies are directed on the basis of sound moral principles, we shall achieve well-being: it is their direction towards evil that makes us unhappy. The degree of permanence of the state of happiness is proportional to the 'intrinsic value' of our virtuous activities [ch. 10].

In ch. 12 Aristotle seeks to support his argument by drawing attention to the fact that we do not *praise* or *value* happiness in the way that we do justice or pleasure; and this is because happiness is itself the 'standard' to which all other goods are referred – it is one of those things that are perfect and beyond praise.

In ch. 14 he discusses again the irrational and the rational parts of the soul (compare 4.5) and introduces an important distinction between the **intellectual virtues** and the **moral virtues**, which we shall look at in the next section.

*Comments and criticisms

(1) It is important to consider what Aristotle means by '*eudaimonia*'. It is usually translated as 'happiness' or 'well-being' but these terms are rather general and often have connotations in English which can lead to a misunderstanding of Aristotle's theory. '*Eudaimonia*' is essentially an *activity* but, more importantly, it is that activity which is unique to man, namely the activity of the soul in accordance with reason and thereby with virtue. Of course such activity may well lead to or be accompanied by happiness (including contentment and pleasure). But strictly speaking it is not happiness as such which the rational man aims at but the proper functioning of himself as a human being. This should become clearer after you have considered what Aristotle has to say about the virtues.

(2) Note also Aristotle's astute psychological analysis in recognizing that it would not be inconsistent with his general account of *eudaimonia* if a man were unhappy or discontented on particular occasions. As humans most of us are prey to anxieties or to the vagaries of fortune. We have experienced moments of grief as well as of great pleasure. What matters, says Aristotle, is the general quality of the *complete* life. Despite 'ups and downs' the truly contented man can remain serene; and it is this serenity which characterizes the man who consistently acts in accordance with excellence or virtue.

(3) One point of criticism that needs to be made is that Aristotle has perhaps tended to accept without demur what is in fact little more than an assumption. 'Every art and every inquiry, and similarly every action and choice, *is thought* to aim at some good; and for this reason the good has rightly been declared to be that at which *all things* aim,' he writes at the beginning of ch. 1. 'Verbally there is *very general agreement*; for both the general run of men and people of superior refinement say that it is happiness, and identify living well and faring well with being happy' [ch. 4] [my italics]. He does of course allow that people differ as to what happiness is, and that many do not give the same account as the wise. However, the philosopher should examine not just what happiness is but also whether the 'end' of all human activity is in fact happiness at all. There is by no means general agreement about this among all philosophers from the time of Aristotle to the present day. The only support he seems to provide for his view is [ch. 12] that we do not praise happiness, so it must be, like God, 'the standard to which all other goods are referred'. You should consider this claim critically while at the same time giving him credit for his careful analysis of what it means to be 'happy'. The metaphysical presuppositions of his account of man (see 4.2 above) should also be examined carefully. His ethics is grounded in the assumption, that man has a 'proper end' or 'function'.

(4) Following on (3), it should be mentioned that Aristotle's ethical theory lacks any reference to the concepts of 'obligation' or 'duty', His ethics is 'naturalistic' and 'teleological' rather than 'deontological', to use the technical vocabulary. He does not tell us how we *ought* to behave so much as suggest that a certain kind of behaviour is conducive to our well-being. Some philosophers, notably Kant, would see this as a major weakness in his philosophy. It is an issue you will be able to take up after you have read Ch. 5.

4.7 Virtue and justice

Reading: Books II, III [chs 6–12], IV, V and VI

The 'moral' virtues [Book II]

Moral virtue or 'excellence of character' is a condition which develops as a result of habit. Moral goodness is not in us by 'Nature', Aristotle says [ch. 1]; if it were then we should be able to train the virtues. Rather, we are born with a capacity to acquire them, which can be encouraged by appropriate education. 'Like activities produce like dispositions.' Aristotle's theory is worked out in chs 2–6. Given that virtues may be engendered by virtuous action and are expressed in subsequent similar action, any immoderacy (deficiency or excess) in the agent must affect his moral qualities [ch. 2]. And in ch. 3 he suggests that our experience of pleasure and pain provides us with an 'index' by means of which we may determine how far our moral dispositions have become established in us. In ch. 4 he anticipates an objection which is often made against his account: how can a man perform just actions unless he be just already? To answer this he points out that strictly speaking an action is not just or temperate in itself (though it may be so called when it is the kind of action we would expect a just man to perform), but its justness consists in the way it is done. The agent, he says, must be fully conscious of what he is doing, must will his action for its own sake, and the act must proceed from an unchangeable disposition. If he performs such actions in this 'frame of mind' he will experience a strengthening of this disposition. The main thesis is now presented [chs 5 and 6]. The *genus* of moral virtue is that it is a disposition or 'state': but the sort of state it is, its *species*, may be identified as that state which makes man good and enables him to perform his function well; therein lies his excellence. And this is made possible when in his actions he avoids excess. Excellence may therefore be defined as:

> a state concerned with choice, lying in a mean relative to us, this being determined by reason and in the way in which the man of practical wisdom would determine it. [1106b 36–1107a]

Note that Aristotle makes it clear that he is not talking of an absolute mean (as 6 is the mean between 2 and 10), but rather a *relative* mean which is considered to be the right amount in the circumstances. Ten pounds of food may be a large amount for an athlete, two pounds small. It does not follow that a trainer will prescribe six pounds. Similarly in matters of morality the right measure of action or feeling must depend on the rightness of the occasion, time, motive, and must be directed towards the right people [ch. 6]. (*We see here again Aristotle's sensitivity to the 'concrete' instance [in contrast to Plato]. This forms the basis of what has been called 'situation ethics'. You should study carefully the many examples of specific virtues he examines throughout the remaining chapters of Book II and Books III [chs 6–12] and IV in order to show how his general definition may be applied in particular cases.)

*Comment

Aristotle has argued that an action is just if the agent performs it in the right 'frame of mind', that is, with the right motive. But how is this disposition to be acquired? Aristotle's answer is that from early childhood the right behaviour patterns are to be imposed on us by parents or teachers. By acting rightly (in this objective sense) we will progressively develop the appropriate dispositions within ourselves to act justly (that is, in a subjective sense). We do not therefore need to be just in the first instance to perform just actions. Virtue, he says, is to be acquired by habit or training, because if we were virtuous by nature no amount of habituation could alter the direction of its development. But is this entirely satisfactory? Is this view consistent with his theory of man as having a proper and 'natural' purpose? It is almost as if he were saying that it is natural to an acorn to become an oak but given the wrong kind of tending it might turn into a fungus. If virtue or goodness were entirely a matter of following social conventions, there would be no problem. Aristotle does, however, explicitly reject this sophistic view. Perhaps the way to avoid the paradox would be to admit that certain actions are (objectively) right in that they are conducive to human well-being, but that the right motive or intention is necessary if an individual is to appropriate that action to himself so as to achieve that condition. It is debatable how far this *is* Aristotle's own position as set out in ch. 5. Certainly he does not attempt to examine the problem of how intentions or motives are to be wedded to 'objective' standards.

Justice. Lack of space precludes a discussion of Aristotle's numerous illustrations of the mean, but something must be said about his treatment of Justice in Book V, as it is of central importance in his ethics.

He in fact distinguishes [chs 1 and 2] two senses of the term: (1) **Universal** Justice, which is equated with virtue itself in its social context. He quotes the proverb: 'in justice is every excellence comprehended'. In this first sense 'justice' means obeying the law; the man who is not law-abiding is unjust. (2) **Particular** Justice, which Aristotle considers to be *a* virtue; and it is with justice in this sense that he is primarily concerned. It is subdivided into two kinds: **distributive** and **remedial** or **corrective** justice. How do these two concepts of justice differ? Both are concerned with 'proportionality' but in different ways. The essential difference is that in distributive justice the proportion is **geometrical**, while in corrective justice it is **arithmetical**.

He examines distributive justice in ch. 3. His account is not too easy to understand, but essentially what he is saying is that distributive justice is concerned with 'fairness' or 'equality' of shares (honour, money, possessions, etc.) as between two persons. It is an equality and hence a mean between a greater and a lesser inequality. But justice, says Aristotle, depends as much on the character of the two people involved as on their two shares: '. . . when quarrels and complaints arise it is when people who are equal have not got equal shares, or vice versa.' It is for this reason that he calls distributive justice 'geometrical'. It is a *relative* proportion; it is right in the *circumstances* – regard being given both to the transactors and to their properties. What is unjust is either too much or too little; it is 'a violation of proportion'.

Corrective justice (chs 4 and 5), on the other hand, is independent of character; the law treats as equals the parties involved in a dispute whether they are good men or bad. Moreover it arises from an equality which is the mean between loss and gain ('more good and less evil being gain, and more evil and less good being loss'). In corrective justice the proportion is arithmetical. Aristotle points out that judges are 'mediators' (*medismoi*) and that the Greek word for 'just' (*dikaior*) derives from the word *dicha* which means 'in half'. Hence the word for 'judge' (*dikastes*).

He goes on [ch. 5] to argue that justice (in either sense) is not, as the Pythagoreans maintained, 'reciprocity' (to have done to oneself what one has done to another). Certainly reciprocity may involve justice (*study his examples here), but the ground of justice is to be found in proportion not in equality as such. And he is able to conclude:

> Just action is intermediate between acting unjustly and being justly treated; for the one is to have too much and the other to have too little. Justice is a kind of mean, but not in the same way as the other excellences, but because it relates to an intermediate amount, while injustice relates to the extremes.
>
> [1133b 30–34]

Mention should be made of two further important points that Aristotle draws our attention to. (1) Justice has to be applied in society (the *polis*). Political justice is certainly 'conventional' (when rules are decided upon by agreement and can be modified), but there is also such a thing as 'natural' justice – though it is not easy to establish whether a rule of justice is of one kind rather than the other. In both cases, however, the universal law relates to the many particular actions [ch. 7]. (2) Actions can be regarded as just or unjust only when the agent acts voluntarily.(Aristotle's treatment of the will and moral responsibility is covered in Books III and VII. We shall be looking at this in 4.8.)

*Criticisms

Aristotle's distinction between geometric and arithmetic proportionality, as characteristic of distributive and remedial justice respectively, seems a little artificial. Discussion of it is, however, best subordinated to that of the more important question of whether Justice is really to be conceived of as a mean in the way that other virtues are. Let us consider some examples. If you invest in a business, then 'justice' would dictate that you receive back profits in proportion to the amount of money you have put in. In the same way, Aristotle argued that the 'goods' of the State should be distributed on the basis of merit. In the case of corrective justice, merit or 'investment' are not relevant; the aim is to redress an injury (for example, theft) by giving back to the injured party what he has lost so that he 'gains', while the transgressor loses what he had illicitly gained. Now how does this fit in with Aristotle's assertion that justice is a mean between acting unjustly and suffering injustice? If a person distributes goods fairly or imposes damages justly then obviously he is not acting *un*justly. But how could it be ever supposed that he thereby also avoids being unjustly treated? And what if he were to give *more* than was appropriate in the circumstances? Would this always be regarded as an example of injustice? Would we necessarily think that the recipients were being treated unjustly? It is from considerations such as these that Aristotle concluded that justice was not a mean between 'absolute' injustices but, rather, a mean between two excesses, that is, between one person having too much and another person having too much. Nevertheless, the question remains whether justice should be thought of at all as a mean between extremes and measurable in mathematical and commercial terms. Justice and injustice, it might be argued, are diametrically opposed; they are contradictories.

The 'intellectual' virtues [Book VI]

It may be thought surprising that 'intellectual' qualities are discussed in a book on ethics. But it has to be remembered that for Aristotle, as for Plato, what is right or good is to be ascertained by the reason. Aristotle's first concern in Book VI is to examine what is meant by 'right reason' (*logos*) [see Book II, ch. 2], which enables us to determine the mean. In ch. 1 he distinguishes between the 'scientific' and the 'calculative' faculties of the rational soul as being concerned respectively with 'things whose first principles admit of no variation' and those 'which do admit of change'. But both parts are involved in decision-making:

> The origin of action – its efficient, not its final cause – is choice, and that of choice is desire and reasoning with a view to an end. This is why choice cannot exist without thought and intellect or without a moral state; for good action and its opposite cannot exist without a combination of intellect and character. Intellect itself, however, moves nothing, but only the intellect which aims at an end and is practical; for this rules the productive intellect as well, since every one makes for an end, and that which is made is not an end in the unqualified sense (but only relative to something, i.e. of something) – only that which is *done* is that; for good action is an end, and desire aims at this. Hence choice is either desiderative thought or intellectual desire, and such an origin of action is man. [1139a 32–1139b 5]

In subsequent chapters Aristotle postulates and discusses five 'modes', or 'expressions' by which the soul attains truth:

(1) **Knowledge** (*episteme*). This is defined as 'a state of capacity to demonstrate'. The claim to knowledge or 'science' presupposes that it has been derived in accordance with valid deductive procedures from first principles which are given to us by the method of induction and are known with certainty [ch. 3].

(2) **Art** (*techne*): 'a reasoned state of capacity to make' [ch. 4].

(3) **Practical wisdom**, or prudence (*phronesis*). This is the 'calculative' faculty. It is 'a true and reasoned state of capacity to act with regard to the things that are good or bad for man' [ch. 5].

(4) **Comprehension** (*nous*) – sometimes translated as 'intuitive reason'. This is the activity or state by means of which we grasp the truth of first principles and truth in reasoning generally [ch. 6].

(5) The union of (1) and (4) gives rise to **wisdom** (*sophia*), which Aristotle says must be the most finished of the forms of knowledge [ch. 7]. For action, both wisdom in this sense and practical wisdom are required.

The remaining chapters of Book VI are devoted to an analysis of the relationships between these various faculties or dispositions. This is fairly straightforward, and you can be left to read these chapters on your own. Note in particular his examination of the *uses* of wisdom in ch. 12 and his discussion in ch. 13 of the parallels between (a) cleverness and practical wisdom in that part of us which forms opinions, and (b) natural excellence and excellence in the strict sense (which involves practical wisdom) in the moral part of us. It is clear, he concludes, that while prudence ensures we perform our proper function as human beings efficiently, it is through the exercise of wisdom, as part of virtue as a whole, that we are made happy; prudence and moral goodness are inseparable.

4.8 Responsibility and weakness of will

Reading: *Nicomachean Ethics*, Books III [chs 1–5] and VII [chs 1–10]

We are here concerned essentially with the problem of **moral responsibility**. Starting from the assumption that only *voluntary* actions can be held to be virtuous, Aristotle devotes the first half of Book III to an important analysis of voluntariness and choice; while in Book VII he tackles the problem (never satisfactorily resolved by Plato) of how humans can often fail to act virtuously when they know what the good is.

Responsibility and willing [III, ch. 1]

Praise or blame should be assigned only to voluntary actions. But what constitutes 'voluntariness'? Aristotle tackles the problem in ch. 1 by examining actions commonly regarded as involuntary, namely those performed (a) under compulsion, and (b) as a result of ignorance. Now compulsion seems a straightforward concept. A sea-captain, for example, would be thought of as acting involuntarily if forced to change course by mutineers. But other cases are less clear-cut. What if one were faced with alternatives – say, to act dishonourably in order to save the lives of one's family held captive by a tyrant? Such an action, involving deliberate choice, must be voluntary: but, says Aristotle, they are voluntary only in the special circumstances; nobody would choose to perform a disgraceful act for its own sake. He also rejects the view that the motive for an action might be thought to compel us; all actions involve some pleasurable or honourable motive, and it would be easy for us to blame external influences instead of ourselves. The compulsory, he says, 'seems to be that whose moving principle is outside, the person compelled contributing nothing' [1110b 15].

What of ignorance as a justification for non-culpability? Aristotle distinguishes between (i) acting *in consequence of*, that is through ignorance, and (ii) *in* or *with* ignorance. Ignorance in the first sense is *general* ignorance; and it is in such cases that a man is held to be responsible for his actions and liable to censure. The second, however, involves ignorance of the particular circumstances in which an action is performed. The agent does not know what is for his own good and is said to act involuntarily. He should not therefore be blamed but, rather, pardoned or accorded pity. Aristotle goes on to list six kinds of particular circumstances, the agent and the act being the most important, and then concludes that a *voluntary* act would seem to be 'that of which the moving principle is in the agent himself, he being aware of the particular circumstances of the action' [111a 23]. (*Note that Aristotle includes as voluntary actions those occasioned by anger and desire. You might be inclined to criticize him here in so far as he cites the example of a man acting under the influence of drink. But he does make it clear later [ch. 5] that a drunkard can be blamed for allowing himself to get into such a state. Nevertheless, it remains an open question for you to think about whether the distinction between acting through and acting in ignorance can be maintained.)

Choice and deliberation [Book III, chs 2–5]

'Moral choice' (*proairesis*) for Aristotle has a narrower connotation than willingness. The concept is discussed in ch. 2. The actions of children and animals are voluntary, but they do not have the same capacity for deliberate choice. Choice is not to be identified with desire, passion, wish, or opinion. It presupposes prior reasoning, and is therefore defined as 'what has been decided on by previous deliberation'. So what is deliberation? Deliberation, argues Aristotle [ch. 3], is about means and not ends, and is confined to 'things that are in our power and can be done'. We do not deliberate about 'eternal things', irregularities in nature, the results of chance, or about matters in which knowledge is detailed and complete (as in a science). Deliberation is appropriate only where there is uncertainty and where we are ourselves involved as agents. 'The end cannot be a subject of deliberation, but only what contributes to the ends; . . . If we are to be always deliberating, we shall have to go on to infinity.' He concludes that the object of deliberation and the object of choice are one and the same. (*Aristotle's account gives rise to at least one difficulty: is not some 'deliberation' required to establish in the first place whether an event *does* really result from chance, whether knowledge *is* complete, and so on? Indeed, can deliberation establish its own limits?)

After a further discussion of 'wishing' [ch. 4], Aristotle finishes his analysis of deliberation by considering whether we do at all times have the power to perform the right action and to refrain from performing the wrong one. Note two important points he makes. (1) The fact that fine actions are rewarded while misbehaviour is punished suggests that we do have this capacity. (Even ignorance is punished when it is held that the offender was responsible for it – see above.) (2) Responsibility for virtuous action is inseparable from responsibility for vice. If one claims that one should not be blamed for doing something wrong, then it would be illogical to commend him for doing something good. (*His detailed argument [1114b 1–25] should be studied carefully; it is particularly characteristic of Aristotle's way of doing philosophy. Note also his summary in the penultimate paragraph.)

Weakness of will [Book VII]

In ch. 1 Aristotle sets out six general beliefs about 'incontinence' (*akrasia*). We shall confine our discussion to his account of the third, namely: '. . . the incontinent man, knowing that what he does is bad, does it as a result of passion, while the continent man, knowing that his appetites are bad, does not follow them because of his reason' [1145b 13 ff.]. It is this, of course, that Socrates (and Plato) denied. According to Aristotle this is contrary to the facts; and he sets out to refute the Socratic position.

He tackles the problem first of all [ch. 3] by examining the term 'knowledge'. It can be used in two senses: (a) a man can have knowledge in an 'active' form – he acts on it, in which case we should be surprised if he did wrong; (b) he can have knowledge but is not using it; it just 'happens' to him: it may be latent or subconscious (he might even be asleep, drunk, or insane), and in this case wrong-doing would occasion no surprise; the incontinent man has knowledge but only in a limited sense. Aristotle develops his argument by considering a 'practical syllogism'. A man may know a universal premiss ('Dry food is good for all men') and a particular premiss ('I am a man') but may not know or be able to act on the knowledge that a particular food belongs to the class 'dry'. Incontinence can also be accounted for in terms of *opinion*. A person may believe, for example, that 'All sweet things ought to be tasted' and 'That thing is sweet'. The latter is a particular statement about sense-perception. But at the same time he may believe two further universal premisses: 'Every sweet thing is pleasant' and 'You must not taste'. Despite the injunction that he should not taste, his desire, following his perception of the sweet object, leads him to act in contradiction to the 'right principle'.

His second approach is to examine what incontinence (and continence) actually mean [ch. 4]. Can they be 'absolute' or must they be manifested only in particular actions? Like intemperance, incontinence is concerned with pleasure and pain. In the strict sense its application should be confined to the necessary pleasures and pains of the body (for example, eating, drinking and sex). The incontinent man, although acting against the 'right reason' and against his better judgement, is unable to help himself; he is in the grip of his passions. (We do, however, talk of incontinence in a qualified and analogical sense, as when in the deliberate pursuit of such ends as honour and riches we give way to emotions such as anger. It is less disgraceful, Aristotle argues [ch. 6], because although an angry man may be justly blamed for acting to excess he does not entirely ignore the dictates of reason, and the ends pursued are desirable in themselves.) Incontinence in the 'strict' sense, although reprehensible, differs from intemperance (as a 'vice', that is, profligacy or total lack of self-control) in that, whereas the incontinent man can be encouraged to change his mode of behaviour and can feel remorse, intemperance is incurable: 'for excellence and vice respectively preserve and destroy the first principle, and in actions that for the sake of which is the first principle' [1151a 14]. An incontinent man (whether 'impulsive' or 'weak' – ch. 7) is not bad (unjust), but he acts badly. He is morally superior to the vicious man because he is aware of his incontinence, while the vicious man does not know he is vicious [ch. 8]. (*Whether the man whose will is weak does in fact act on latent knowledge, opinion, awareness and so on is debatable. The important issue here, however, is whether a man who in a fundamental sense knows or claims to know can act wrongly; and it can be argued that Aristotle has not really taken the discussion much further than Plato. *Why* does the incontinent person ignore the dictates of reason? If he or she genuinely *cannot* help giving in to the passions, should we not offer him or her pity rather than blame? We shall look at this issue again in 6.7.)

4.9 Pleasure

Reading: *Nicomachean Ethics*, Book VII [chs 11–14]; Book X

We shall not consider Aristotle's treatment of friendship in Books VIII and IX but will conclude this short survey of the *Nicomachean Ethics* by looking at what he has to say about pleasure and happiness (following on his arguments of Book I).

Book VII [chs 11–14] are devoted largely to a refutation of a number of views about pleasure current in Aristotle's day. It had been claimed that no pleasure is a good thing; or that only some pleasures are good; or that even if all pleasures are good, pleasure cannot be the supreme good. (The last two views are to be found in Plato's dialogue the *Philebus*.) After setting out the arguments presented by the supporters of such theories [ch. 11] he puts forward his own detailed objections in ch. 12. (1) 'Good' and 'bad' are ambiguous terms; they can be applied both absolutely and relatively. What may seem to be a bad pleasure may well be good for a particular person at a particular time. (2) We must distinguish between good as an activity and good as a state. The kinds of pleasures which gratify us when our natural state is being restored to its normal condition are different from those we enjoy when already in the state of normality (for example, the pleasure of philosophic reflection). The former are pleasant only 'accidentally': the latter are pleasant in themselves. (3) It is a bad definition of pleasure to call it a 'perceptible process'. Pleasure is in fact 'unimpeded activity of our natural state'. And not all pleasures have some end other than themselves. Those that do are merely incidental to the activity we are engaged in when advancing towards the perfection of our nature. (4) To argue that pleasures are bad because some pleasant things damage our health is like saying that health is bad because some healthy things affect our bank balance. Both healthy things and pleasant things can be bad relatively, but that does not make them bad in themselves. (5) Qualities such as prudence are not hindered by their own pleasures (though they may be by pleasures from another source). On the contrary, the pleasure we experience in learning reinforces our pursuit of it. (6) Most of the remaining arguments of Aristotle's opponents are refuted by reference to a distinction between bodily pleasures that involve desire and pain, and pleasures which are good without qualification. Thus in ch. 13 Aristotle makes four points. (a) Pleasure must be a good, he says, since its opposite – pain – is generally admitted to be an evil. (b) Even if some pleasures *were* bad, this would not prove that a particular pleasure cannot be the supreme good. Indeed, true happiness consists in the unimpeded exercise of some or all of our faculties, and this exercise is a pleasure; so the *summum bonum* must at the least involve pleasure as a component. (c) The fact that all men and animals seek pleasure suggests that pleasure must in some way be the highest good, for there is a divine element in all things. (They may not of course be aware of this when they confine themselves to the pleasures of the body.) (d) Finally, if pleasure is not a good and activity not a pleasure, then a happy man's life is not bound to be pleasant. And if pleasure is neither good nor bad, then neither is pain, in which case why should he seek the one and shun the other?

Point (c) is taken up in ch. 14, where Aristotle examines the status of the bodily pleasures. The truth of the matter, he says, is that bodily pleasures are certainly good in so far as pains are bad. What makes the bad man is not the pursuit of such pleasures but experiencing them to excess. They may often seem more desirable than other kinds, but this is because they drive out pain and are irresistible to people who find no pleasure in any other sort either because of their youth or their constitution. But such 'anodynes' are pleasant only 'accidentally'. They are therefore to be contrasted with naturally pleasant things which 'stimulate the action of a healthy nature' and thus encourage enjoyment for its own sake rather than as a relief from, say, boredom or anxiety.

There is clearly much of interest and value in Aristotle's careful and detailed analysis of pleasure. Many of his arguments are repeated in Book X, and we shall leave you to read through chs 1–5 yourself. But you should note that he now directs his attack not only against the view current in Plato's Academy that pleasure is not a good at all but against the doctrine of Eudoxus, who held that pleasure *is* the supreme good (on the grounds that all creatures seek it and that what is desirable is always good, the most desirable being the best). Aristotle makes three important points. (1) Pleasure is not a 'process'; at all times it is complete in its nature at any moment: it is never in transition from one state to another. (2) It is certainly a good but in the sense that it accompanies and perfects our activities when they are directed to their proper ends. Pleasure completes our activities, brings them to 'precision'. A musician, for example, makes progress as a musician if he enjoys his work. (3) Pleasures are of different kinds and differ in value – corresponding to the different kinds of activity which they complete. The pleasures which are distinctively human must be those which accompany characteristically human activities; and pleasures in the fullest sense of the word must be those which accompany the activities of the perfect and perfectly happy man.

Book X [chs 6–8] are devoted essentially to a recapitulation of Aristotle's account of happiness (*eudaimonia*) first set out in Book I and to a summary of his reasons for supposing that happiness, as 'an activity in accordance with virtue', must lie in the exercise of the highest virtue, that is of excellence, and is to be found in the speculative or contemplative life. The moral life will be happy too, but only in a secondary sense, for moral qualities are specifically human and not divine. But

> the life according to intellect is best and pleasantest, since intellect more than anything else *is* man. This life is therefore the happiest. [1178a 7]

It remains only to consider how Aristotle's theories are to be put into practice. 'With regard to excellence, then, it is not enough to know, but we must try to have and use it, or try any other way there may be of becoming good' [1179b 2 ff.]. There are three different views, he says, as to how goodness might be achieved through nature or training. The first is rejected on the ground that it is beyond our control; while teaching is not always effective unless it is preceded by appropriate training. And training, which involves the regulation by law of 'the nurture and pursuits of young persons', is best undertaken by the state (as in Sparta). Most states, however, tend to neglect such matters, so responsibility for legislation as it affects the day-to-day life of the community must be shouldered by individuals willing to learn the art of politics – not from the Sophists who profess to teach it, but from expert and practising politicians. Aristotle's *Ethics* thus leads naturally on to his *Politics* (compare 4.6 above).

*Comment

Refer back again to the points made at the end of 4.6. Note also that in his treatment of pleasure in Books VII and X, although he again shows a great deal of psychological insight and analytical skill in the distinctions he makes, Aristotle is not always entirely consistent. Sometimes he seems to be suggesting that pleasure *is* well-being and therefore the supreme good, rather than that which accompanies and completes or perfects an activity – different kinds of pleasure being appropriate to different activities. However, it is reasonable to accept the arguments and balanced conclusions of Book X as representing his final position. (You will find a further discussion of the relationship of happiness to the good in 6.4 below.)

4.10 Political philosophy

Reading: *The Politics*

Aristotle's broadly 'empirical' approach to philosophical issues, in contrast to what we have loosely termed Plato's 'idealism', is apparent also in his treatment of politics. Whereas Plato, at least in the *Republic*, was concerned primarily with establishing the 'perfect' society – a society which would reflect his metaphysical presuppositions – Aristotle tended to confine himself to a constructive examination of actual Greek states with a view to discovering what might be the 'best' or most balanced form of government. Before outlining Aristotle's positive views, it will therefore probably be helpful to indicate briefly two main areas of disagreement between himself and his teacher:

(1) He rejected Plato's 'communism' – which entailed the virtual abolition of family life and of private property. The family for Aristotle was the basic biological unit of the state. The possession of property is desirable, indeed essential, for the 'good', that is, the moral or virtuous life – provided it is not excessive or accumulated for its own sake.
(2) The law as conceived by Plato has a negative function in that it is the means by which the rulers impose order on the other classes. Aristotle tended rather to encourage citizens (or at least the leisured classes) to play an active role in the running of the state. Indeed he defined the citizen in terms of his 'participation in judicial functions and political office'. Both rulers and rules submit willingly to the law, recognizing it as necessary for good government.

In order to develop his own account of political science Aristotle undertook a wide-ranging investigation of no less than 158 different constitutions. He divided them into two groups: states whose aim is to achieve the good of all their citizens, and those in which power is concentrated in the hands of a single class concerned with its own private interest. The first group consists of three types: monarchy, aristocracy and 'polity'; and corresponding to these there are three types in the second group: tyranny (rule by one man), oligarchy (rule by a few) and democracy (rule by many). In subsequent sections of the *Politics* Aristotle examines different kinds of democracies and oligarchies, the conflicting claims of such states, and monarchy. He argues that the last is theoretically the ideal form of government on the grounds that the ruler in such a constitution would be superior in wisdom and virtue to all other citizens – a 'god among men'. Unfortunately there is no such individual to be found. Even rule by a group of 'good' men is considered to be difficult to achieve. So Aristotle has to settle for what is practical; and this means in effect a constitution which combines the best elements of democracy and oligarchy, namely 'polity'. A polity is democratic in so far as *many* citizens participate in running the affairs of the state (as opposed to the 'few' of an oligarchy). But, as in an oligarchy, the politically active citizens (who are heads of families) possess the leisure, wealth and property which are necessary if they are to be free to make their contribution. They take it in turn to occupy the various judicial and administrative offices of state. Rule in the polity is thus rule by a 'middle-class' of equals who in their treatment of each other exemplify the Aristotelian principle of justice.

*Comments and criticisms

Whatever advance we may think Aristotle made on Plato's political philosophy, it must be remembered that his proposals for the best form of government were designed to be put into practice in a Greek city-state – in no way comparable in size to today's states which number their populations in millions. Note also that he shared with Plato the view that the *polis* is 'natural' in the sense that it is only in the *polis* that individuals can realize their own potential as human beings. Both tended therefore to hand over to the state responsibility for each citizen's moral and intellectual education to an extent that many of us today might feel to constitute excessive interference and infringement of personal liberty. We might also be critical of Aristotle for denying citizenship to women and to slaves – that is to persons who *by nature* belong not to themselves but to someone else (though he did insist that slaves be treated properly by their masters and that they be given the hope that they might eventually be free).

Having worked systematically through Chs 3 and 4 you should have gained a fair understanding of some of the problems which have interested philosophers for over two thousand years. The rest of the book will be devoted to a more specialized examination of these and other issues considered in the context of the various branches of philosophy to which they belong and with reference to the writings of many of the major post-Greek thinkers. After you have completed this book, in particular Chs 5 and 6, you should be in a better position to appreciate the significance of the contribution made to the subject by Plato and Aristotle.

QUESTIONS

  *1 Discuss critically Aristotle's view that happiness is the supreme end of man.
  2 What does Aristotle mean by the claim that 'well-being' (**eudaimonia**) is an activity of the soul in accordance with virtue (or excellence)?
  3 Discuss critically Aristotle's definition of virtue in relation to 'habituation'.
  *4 Examine critically Aristotle's doctrine of the mean.
  5 Why does Aristotle maintain that happiness ('well-being') consists in contemplation?
  6 According to Aristotle, for human beings to have a good life it has to be rich enough to include everything that is of value, for example, personal love and friendship. This makes people vulnerable to many factors they cannot always control. Can people limit their vulnerability, and what would be the consequences of doing so?   [IB, specimen, 2000]
  7 Examine Aristotle's distinction between corrective and distributive justice. Can this distinction be maintained?
  8 Examine Aristotle's application of his doctrine of the mean to the concepts of justice and injustice.

9 Discuss Aristotle's division of the virtues into moral and intellectual.

10 According to Aristotle, can a man treat himself unjustly?

11 Examine Aristotle's doctrine of pleasure.

12 What does Aristotle mean when he refers to man as a 'political' animal? Why does he?

13 For Aristotle, ethics is a branch of politics. How does he reconcile his concern for individual well-being with the general good?

14 Examine Aristotle's criticisms of Plato's ideal state.

15 How does Aristotle's theory of 'form' differ from Plato's doctrine of the 'Forms'? Are his criticisms sound?

16 Discuss Aristotle's distinction between 'primary' substance and 'secondary' substance.

17 Examine Aristotle's doctrine of the four 'causes'.

18 As the formal aspect of a living organism, the soul, according to Aristotle, is inseparable from the body. Is his account of the 'active' intellect consistent with this theory?

19 Aristotle classifies 'subjects' in terms of 'categories'. Explain what he means by this.

20 What does Aristotle mean by 'explaining' a fact? (You will be in a better position to deal critically with this question after you have studied Chs 5, 8 and 12.)

*Notes/guided answers have been provided for questions **1** and **4** (at end of book).

READING LIST

A. Prescribed text
Aristotle, *Nicomachean Ethics*. [AEB, IB]

B. Other texts
Aristotle, *Categories, Metaphysics, Physics, On the Soul, Politics*.
There are numerous translations of Aristotle's works. Perhaps the most convenient is the single volume edition edited by J.L. Ackrill, *A New Aristotle Reader* (from which most of the quotations in this chapter have been selected). However, this edition does not include all the chapters from the *Nicomachean Ethics*. The Penguin Classics edition (translation by H. Tredennick) is recommended, if you want to read the whole book.

C. Supplementary reading
(If you are a beginner, you are recommended to start with titles marked with an asterisk.)

1. Historical background
Armstrong, A.H., *An Introduction to Ancient Philosophy*.
Guthrie, W.K.C., *Greek Philosophers from Thales to Aristotle*. (Best for general reference.)

2. Aristotle
Ackrill, J.L., *Aristotle the Philosopher*.*

Allen, D.J., *The Philosophy of Aristotle.**
Barnes, J., *Aristotle.**
Evans, J.D.G., *Aristotle.*
Hardie, W.F.R., *Aristotle's Ethical Theory.*
Lawson-Tancred, H., the Introduction to his edition of *De Anima.*
Lear, J., *Aristotle: The Desire to Understand.*
Ross, W.D., *Aristotle* (introduction by Ackrill).*

Collections of essays
Barnes, J. (ed.), *The Cambridge Companion to Aristotle.*
Barnes, J., Sorabji, R. and Schofield, M. (eds), *Articles on Aristotle.*
Moravcsik, J.M.E. (ed.), *Aristotle.*

■ ⅴ 5 Knowledge and truth

5.1 Introduction

Reading: Start with Ayer, *The Problem of Knowledge*, ch. 1

In 4.4 we quoted Aristotle's well-known observation that all men by their nature have the desire to know. This is surely true. Throughout recorded history we have sought to understand ourselves and the universe from which we have so mysteriously emerged. Through myths, religion, natural science, or philosophy we have striven to gain knowledge – about the nature, origin and purpose of the cosmos, the evolution of life, and of course ourselves and our behaviour. Indeed the need to know has most probably been a human characteristic ever since our ancestors first came to articulate through symbolic language a dim awareness of themselves as existent beings – as part of and yet in some sense separate, even alienated from the external world. But what *is* knowledge? How do we acquire it? What is its scope – how far does it extend? Can we distinguish between knowledge and belief? Questions such as these belong to the branch of philosophy termed **epistemology**. In this chapter we shall be considering some of the answers which have been proposed by philosophers past and present.

Firstly, it will be useful to note that we use the word 'know' in a variety of ways. We can know something – an object, place, or person – directly, in which case we have what is called knowledge by acquaintance. We can also talk of knowing *how* – how to ride a bicycle, get from London to Brighton, and so on. This is an ability or skill. Or we can talk of 'propositional knowledge' – knowing *that* something is the case – that 2 + 2 = 4, that London is the capital of the UK, and the like. Whether these three types of knowledge are related to each other is itself an interesting philosophical question. Both Plato and Russell argued that propositional knowledge is dependent on knowledge by acquaintance. And certainly to know that something is the case requires minimally that we know how to use the words of the proposition correctly. We shall be looking at Russell's account later, and also how Ryle sought to assimilate knowledge 'that' to knowledge 'how'. But the greater part of our discussion in this chapter will be concerned with propositional knowledge.

The key issues to start with concern knowledge and belief. If they can be distinguished, can criteria be provided? What constitutes knowing as opposed to believing? Some more recent philosophers, for example, H.A. Prichard (1871–1947) have claimed that knowledge is essentially indefinable and is quite different from believing. Knowledge, they say, cannot be the same as believing, because the latter depends on knowledge for the evidence which supports it. To know something is to be in a special state of mind which is infallible. Such a position, however, is difficult to maintain. It raises the question of whether we could ever recognize such a mental state. How could we describe it? One characteristic we might be said to possess when in a state of 'knowing' is a feeling of certainty. But it is clear that this is inadequate. Most of us can recall occasions when we have felt convinced of our knowledge only to discover later, as new facts emerged, that we had been mistaken. It would then seem odd to have to say that we could not therefore have been in that self-certifying state after all. Perhaps we should just say that such a state was not really self-certifying; we could not rely on it. It might then be argued that what seems to be required is that the supposed certainty of knowledge should be grounded not in a subjective 'mental state' but in an 'object' of some kind. Does this mean then that knowledge and belief have different 'objects'? As you will remember from Ch. 3, Plato, at least in Book V of the *Republic*, held a view something like this. To have knowledge is to be directly acquainted with the Forms, whereas in believing we are acquainted with the semi-real changing objects of sensory-experience, the instantiations of the Forms, as it were. However, Plato's general and more developed view (for example, in Book X and some other dialogues) was that to *know* something is to believe it and to provide some adequate 'account', that is, to provide an analysis or definition of its essential features. Knowledge is therefore belief plus 'understanding'; and this understanding can perhaps be regarded as a kind of 'justification' of one's claim to knowledge. As for Aristotle, he recognized, perhaps uncritically, both the 'given' of experience (immediate perceptual data) and first principles or causes as being in some sense certain. At the same time he regarded knowledge of a particular thing as presupposing a quest for an explanation or 'ultimate' cause, which is perhaps to look for some kind of justification.

These views can be seen as anticipating an account of knowledge and belief which is widely accepted today, namely that they have the same objects but that knowledge is **justified true belief**. Thus we may be said to believe that, say, London is the capital of the UK, but we can be said to know it only if (i) the statement 'London is the capital of the UK' is true, and (ii) that this claim can be justified. The British empiricist philosopher A.J. Ayer (1910–89), who argued for such an account of knowledge, said that one must be sure of it and must have the right to be sure. Clearly this raises further questions. What constitutes 'truth'? What does justification involve? What is meant by 'sure' and 'the right' to be sure? What criteria should we appeal to? Can certainty be achieved? Many philosophers in the past have supposed that it can and have set out to discover propositions that, in their view, satisfy conditions for certainty and which can therefore provide a foundation for an indisputably true philosophical world-view. We shall look first at the philosophy of Descartes. The problem of 'truth' we shall leave until later in the chapter.

5.2 The certainty of Descartes

Reading: *Discourse on Method*; *Meditations*, I and II

René Descartes (1596–1650) lived in an age of great intellectual turmoil. The rise of experimental science was tending to undermine the theology and authority of a Church which was wedded to an anachronistic Aristotelian teleology. At the same time, particularly in France, a number of writers such as Montaigne were reviving the arguments of the Greek sceptics. This scepticism was not what today is called 'global'. (This is the view that knowledge is impossible. Cratylus, for example, having made up his mind about what he was absolutely certain about, said nothing and instead just wagged his finger. Perhaps in doing this even he had 'said' too much?) Rather the prevailing scepticism was of the Pyrrhonic kind – the writings of Pyrrho's commentator, Sextus Empiricus (*c.* 200 AD) having been republished in France in the 1560s. In order to achieve in their lives a state of what they called unperturbedness (*ataraxia*) philosophers in this tradition tended to go along with sense-experience and the customs of their society without giving their assent to their absolute truth. As for the claims made by dogmatic philosophers, who claimed to have certain knowledge about what lies beyond phenomena, the sceptics argued for a suspension of judgement (the *epoché*) and for maintaining an open-minded attitude. Now Descartes was both a devout Catholic and a mathematician and scientist of some distinction. Rejecting medieval scholasticism as failing to discover new truths and certain knowledge (although in his writings, especially those on God's existence, he continued to use scholastic concepts and arguments, albeit modified), he sought to place knowledge on an unshakeable foundation by out-doubting the sceptics. It is this radicalism that marks Descartes as one of the great figures of modern philosophy.

In his *Rules for the Direction of the Mind* he identifies two fundamental operations of the mind by which, he believes, we are enabled to arrive at the knowledge of things: intuition (roughly intellectual vision) and deduction (the logical derivation of conclusions from first principles given to use in intuition). To ensure the correct use of these mental capacities he sets out a number of rules [*Discourse*, Part II]. The first of these is:

> to accept nothing as true which I did not clearly recognize to be so: that is to say, carefully to avoid precipitation and prejudice in judgements, and to accept in them nothing more than was presented to my mind so clearly and distinctly that I could have no occasion to doubt it.

The second rule is:

> to divide up each of the difficulties which I examined into as many parts as possible, and as seemed requisite in order that it might be resolved in the best manner possible.

The remaining rules relate to starting from the most simple objects and rising to knowledge of the most complex; and to a checking procedure to ensure that nothing has been omitted. (You can read these for yourself.)

Descartes' 'method of analysis' can be seen at work particularly in his *Meditations*. In *Meditations* I and II he says that much of what he had believed to be true when he was young has been proved to be false. So he determines to reject everything that he has been taught about the world and to regard all his own experience as erroneous. Accordingly he places no confidence in the evidence of his senses; he may be dreaming. Even the apparently certain propositions of mathematics are rejected. He has a firm belief in an all-powerful God, but perhaps this too is an illusion. Maybe there is an 'evil genius' who causes him to be deceived in everything he believes. Can then nothing be known? There is indeed one thing, he argues, which *is* indubitable. In so far as he is doubting, he must be conscious, for to be doubting is to be thinking; and in that thinking consciousness (*cogitatio*) lies an awareness that he is something. He therefore concludes that the proposition 'I am, I exist' is necessarily true each time he conceives or expresses it. An alternative formulation is given in Part IV of the *Discourse*:

> I observed that, whilst I thus wished to think that all was false, it was absolutely necessary that I, who thus thought, should be somewhat; and as I observed that this truth, *I think, hence I am* (*cogito, ergo sum*), was so certain and of such evidence, that no ground of doubt, however extravagant, could be alleged by the sceptics capable of shaking it, I concluded that I might, without scruple, accept it as the first principle of the philosophy of which I was in search.

By the use of his 'analytical' method he has thus discovered the primary proposition or foundation on which he might rebuild his edifice of knowledge. The recognition or intuition (*inspectio*) of himself as a thinking thing is characterized by clarity and distinctness. What is meant by 'clear' and 'distinct' is explained in his *Principles of Philosophy* [45, 46]. We may have clear knowledge of having a pain, for example, but it may not be distinct in the sense that we may be confused about its nature or location. 'The distinct is that which is so precise and different from all other objects as to comprehend in itself only what is clear.' His account, however, does not seem to be entirely satisfactory (see the Comments at the end of this section). It should also be noted that by 'thinking', Descartes includes doubting, understanding, willing, imagining and perceiving, that is the sum total of 'mental' activity. In *Meditation* II he adopts, as a general rule, that all that is very clearly and distinctly apprehended is true – and is thus in accord with the first of the Rules set out in the *Discourse*.

It remains now for Descartes to reconstruct his philosophy and in particular to reinstate the external world, the existence of which he had for the purposes of his method doubted. He cannot rely on the evidence of his senses alone, for although he perceives clearly that he has various ideas (that is, sense-experiences, images and so on), in his mind they still do not possess the clarity necessary to guarantee the existence of the objects he believes them to resemble.

Moreover, while he thinks there can be no dispute about the certainty of the *cogito, ergo sum,* for his existence as a thinking thing is presupposed in the very act of doubting, it is still possible that he may be mistaken about the truth of other propositions, such as those of mathematics, which he claims to perceive clearly and distinctly. His next move therefore is to prove the existence of a benevolent God who, he thinks, would not permit him to be deceived in such matters. Any 'proof' could not of course presuppose the existence of the external world without circularity. So Descartes appeals to the clear and distinct idea of a perfect being, which he finds within himself. Unlike ideas of external things, this idea does not come from outside (it is not 'adventitious'); neither is it 'factitious', that is, the product of his imagination. It is therefore 'innate' in that he seems to have been born with the capacity to form this concept from within, just as he is able to form the idea of himself. From his possession of this idea Descartes argues to the actual existence of the Perfect Being or God who, he says, must have implanted it within him. (Descartes' 'proofs' for the existence of God will be referred to again in Ch. 9.)

*Comments and criticisms

Descartes' approach to the problem of certainty and knowledge is characteristic of **rationalism**. Rationalist philosophers are not of course all of one type. There are important differences between the philosophies of Plato, Descartes and Hegel, for example. But rationalists are agreed that sense-experience is untrustworthy and that certain knowledge is to be obtained only through the exercise of pure reason. This is strongly disputed by the **empiricists**. We shall set out the arguments of an empiricist philosopher (Hume) in the next section. There are however several weaknesses in the Cartesian philosophy itself which you might like to think about here.

(1) Descartes seems to be claiming to have discovered certainty in both an 'objective' and a 'subjective' sense. The equating of existence with thinking is alleged to be certain in the former sense, while the criterion of 'clarity and distinctness' may be thought of as exemplifying subjective certainty. To consider the '*cogito, ergo sum*' first. Why is it so certain? What is its status? Unfortunately Descartes' own interpretation is ambiguous. Is the '*cogito*' an inference of some kind? If it is, then it can be argued that it commits the error of circular reasoning; for the 'I' of 'I am' is already presupposed in the 'I' of 'I think', and any necessity it possesses is a matter of logic which has nothing to say about actual existent things, be they 'minds' or 'material' things. Perhaps then the '*cogito*' is to be understood as referring to some form of intuition – of himself as an existing thinking being? If so, then Descartes must contend with more serious difficulties.

(a) He says that so long as he is doubting (thinking) the certainty of the 'Cogito' is assured. Now there are certainly occasions when he is not thinking. Does he have any guarantee that he continues to exist as a potentially thinking thing? The possibility that Descartes may have direct access to a continuous 'Self' (though he does not seem actually to have made this claim himself) has been ruled out by many philosophers. If we introspect, do we find anything other than thoughts, ideas and feelings? Hume, for example, in his *Treatise of Human Nature* [Book I, Part IV, vi], describes how when he turns his reflection on himself he can never perceive a *self* without one or more perceptions; nor 'can I perceive any thing but the perceptions'. The eighteenth century German philosopher Lichtenberg suggested that the most Descartes could claim was *cogitatur* – 'there is thinking going on':

> The only thing we know is the existence of our sensations, ideas and thoughts. We should say 'it thinks', just as we say [of lightning], 'It flashes'. To say 'cogito' is already to have gone too far if we translate it as 'I think'. To assume the 'I', to postulate it, is a practical need.   [*Sudelbücher*, K 76]

(*Do you agree with this view? Read what Russell has to say about the Self in chs II and V of *The Problems of Philosophy* – but note that in his later book, *The Analysis of Mind*, he developed the theory of 'logical constructionism', according to which the conscious mind is constructed out of images and sensations; compare Ayer's 'phenomenalism' discussed in 5.11 below. See also Locke's *Essay*, Book I and Book IV, ix.)

(b) If he is to ground 'objective' certainty in the '*cogito*' (or for that matter if he is to use language at all) he has to appeal to his memory. Now leaving aside the question of his possible or actual views about a 'Self' (in which perhaps the memory might be 'located'), we can legitimately ask what justification Descartes has for believing his memory reports to be reliable? Without this assurance his 'mental' life would seem to fragment into a series of intermittent and disconnected episodes – hardly a sound basis on which to construct a philosophical system.

(2) As we have seen, Descartes' answer to the latter point would seem to be that, in the last analysis, both the 'veridicality' of sense perception and the reliability of memory depend on the validity of his proofs of God's existence. But does this not render the '*cogito*' argument redundant? Why could he not simply have *started* with his allegedly innate idea of a Perfect Being? [*Read and think about Hume's comments in section 120 of the *Enquiry*.]

(3) To turn again briefly to 'subjective' certainty, his criterion of 'clarity and distinctness' is not very helpful. Firstly, while these concepts can well be used to describe, say, a pain in one's leg (as Descartes does), to apply them to an intuition of a 'truth' in such terms is, arguably, to use them in an extended sense which lessens whatever value they may possess in providing the criterion Descartes seeks. Secondly, and more importantly, although he has asserted that mathematical propositions (for example, '2 + 2 = 4') are perceived clearly and distinctly, Descartes is still prepared to sacrifice his certainty of their truth to the hypothetical evil genie until he has proved the existence of a God who can act as the final guarantor of indubitability.

(4) A more general criticism relates to his methodology. Hume [*Enquiry*, XI, 117] rejected the very possibility both of universal doubt and of finding an original principle. If there were such a principle, he says, we should not be able to pass

beyond it without using those very faculties about which we are sceptical (*Do you agree?) An alternative but in some ways similar criticism, which owes much to the later philosophy of the Austrian born Ludwig Wittgenstein (1889–1951), concerns the question of 'privacy'. Given his sceptical premises, Descartes' experiences – perceptions, thoughts and so on – must remain private to himself (at least until the external world has been reinstated). But he has to use language to refer to them, and language is 'public': it can function only in a common world of things and persons. So in the very act of describing his 'inner' experience, Descartes is letting in at the back door the external world he had thrown out through the front. His methodological scepticism cannot therefore be sustained. This is a powerful objection. (The question of whether a '*private*' language is possible, which would not commit Descartes to presupposing the existence of things external to his 'self', will be referred to again in 5.4 and 5.6.)

5.3 Hume's scepticism

Reading: Hume, *An Enquiry Concerning Human Understanding*, Secs I–VII; Ayer, *The Problem of Knowledge*, ch. 2

In the previous section you saw how Descartes attempted to rebut scepticism and to find an indubitable principle from which to construct his philosophy. His assumption of the primacy of reason as a source of certainty and knowledge was questioned by the English philosopher, John Locke (1632–1704). According to Locke [see *Essay*, Book I, i and Book II, i], there are no 'innate ideas'; all our ideas are derived from **sensation** or **reflection**. Ideas of sensation come to us through our sense organs and are representations of external things. When we are born our mind is a *tabula rasa*, a blank tablet, on which these sensations are imprinted. Ideas of reflection, however, 'represent' inner or 'subjective' processes such as perceiving, comparing and abstracting, and are stored in the memory. David Hume (1711–76) likewise started out from sense-experience. In Sec. II, 12 he distinguishes between **impressions** and **ideas**:

By the term *impression* . . . I mean all our more lively perceptions, when we hear, or see, or feel, or love, or hate, or desire, or will. And impressions are distinguished from ideas, which are the less lively perceptions, of which we are conscious, when we reflect on any of these sensations of movements above mentioned.

Sensations, perceptions, feelings and so on are thus more 'forcible and lively' than the thoughts and images we have of them. 'All our ideas or more feeble perceptions are copies of our impressions or more lively ones' [II, 13]. His 'impressions' thus include Locke's ideas of both sensation and reflection, while he uses the term 'idea' to refer to mental images and thoughts. Hume goes on to argue that we cannot have an idea unless it has first been derived from an impression. Firstly, when we analyse our thoughts, however complex they may be, we always find that 'they resolve themselves into such simple ideas as were copies from a precedent feeling or sentiment' [II, 14]. Secondly, we note that a person deprived of a sensory organ cannot form the appropriate ideas. A blind man can have no notion of colour; a deaf man of sounds [II, 15]. This is in effect Hume's answer to the rationalists' assertion of innate ideas. [*Read carefully his footnote at the end of Section II.] In Section III Hume suggests that ideas are **associated** in accordance with three principles of connexion, namely, **resemblance**, **contiguity** in time or place (in other words, physically adjacent), and **cause and effect**. By his doctrine of association Hume tries to provide an alternative to the Lockean view that we derive 'general' ideas, such as 'man', 'triangle', or 'red' by a process of abstraction from particular ideas of sensation. (See also 5.5, 5.9 and 11.5.) [Causation is examined by Hume in Section IV of the *Enquiry*, while the first two principles are discussed in Section V.]

Leaving aside for the time being the question of whether Hume's analysis is adequate, we must now consider its relevance to the quest for certainty and knowledge. [See Secs IV–VII and XII.] Since the time of Descartes, most philosophers have distinguished in one way or another between propositions of mathematics and statements about the empirical world. Hume [IV, 20 and 21] refers to these propositions respectively as **Relations of Ideas** and **Matters of Fact**. The first kind (for example, 'three times five is equal to the half of thirty') expresses a relation between numbers or geometrical figures. They are, he says, intuitively or demonstratively certain. Their truth can be discovered by the mere operation of thought; it does not depend on anything in the world. 'Though there never were a circle or triangle in nature, the truths demonstrated by Euclid would for ever retain their certainty.' Matters of fact, however, are quite different. Firstly, we can deny them without contradiction (whereas we could not deny the truth of, say, 'two and two make four'). Secondly, support for their truth, says Hume [22], seems to be founded on the relation of cause and effect. But how do we arrive at knowledge of cause and effect? Hume's answer [see 23–33] is that we attain it not through *a priori* reasoning but from nothing other than experience itself. Now we may well be able to trace particular effects back to general causes, such as elasticity or gravity, but 'these ultimate springs and principles are totally shut up from human curiosity and enquiry' [26]. What then is the foundation of all conclusions from experience? What justifies the inference from a past conjunction of cause and effect to a similar conjunction in the future? The reasoning we engage in is not 'demonstrative' (that is, involving logic); neither is the inference 'intuitive'. The only alternative is that the justification lies in the supposition that the future will resemble the past. But how can we know this without arguing in a circle? Consider a concrete example. Let us assume that an object such as bread, exhibiting sensible qualities (colour, weight and so on), possesses 'secret powers' which nourish us. Because a cause (secret power) has always been followed by a particular effect (nourishment) in the past, we argue that the eating of bread will likewise nourish us on future occasions. There would be no contradiction in denying this; no 'relation of ideas' is involved, and no chain of deductive reasoning. Now if we are to claim that we *know* that the bread will nourish us when next we eat it, it can only be because we are assuming the truth of the general proposition 'All future conjunctions of cause and effect will resemble past conjunctions of similar causes and effects'. But how can *this* be known without begging the question?

It is clear, then, for Hume that we do not *know* that the future will resemble the past. 'All inferences from experience,' he argues [Sec. V], 'are effects of custom, not of reasoning.' By **custom** or **habit** he means 'a certain instinct of our nature' which, like other instincts, may be fallacious and deceitful' [127]. It is not knowledge that we have but *belief*. Belief is 'nothing but a conception more intense and steady than what attends the mere fictions of the imagination' [40]. It arises not only from the relation of cause and effect but also from the other principles of association (resemblance and contiguity). The *degree* of our belief or expectation of an event depends on the **probability** of causes [Sec. VI]. Thus, some causes are entirely uniform and constant in producing an effect. Fire has always burned, and 'the production of motion by impulse and gravity' is a universal law. On the other hand, rhubarb has not always proved a purge! Hume therefore concludes that in such cases as the former we expect the event with the greatest assurance: but where different effects have been found to follow from causes which *appear* to be exactly similar, we must assign to each of these effects 'a particular weight and authority, in proportion as we have found it to be more or less frequent'.

In Secs VII and VIII Hume shows that we have no direct intuition of a power or necessary connection between cause and effect; the idea we have of a necessary connection derives from the imagination and our experience of uniformity in sequences of events:

> Every idea is copied from some preceding impression or sentiment; and where we cannot find any impression, we may be certain that there is no idea. In all single instances of the operation of bodies or minds, there is nothing that produces any impression, nor consequently can suggest any idea, of power or necessary connexion. But when many uniform instances appear, and the same object is always followed by the same event; we then begin to entertain the notion of cause and connexion. We then *feel* a new sentiment or impression, to wit, a customary connexion in the thought of imagination between one object and its usual attendant; and this sentiment is the original of that idea which we seek for. For as this idea arises from a number of similar instances, and not from any single instance, it must arise from that circumstance, in which the number of instances differ from every individual instance. But the customary connexion or transition of the imagination is the only circumstance in which they differ. In every other particular they are alike. [61]

It follows then that although Hume has rejected the Cartesian methodology of universal doubt, he is forced to adopt an attenuated scepticism of his own. We can have *knowledge* of mathematical propositions or of statements derived from them by means of deductive inference. We can also be said to 'know' existences such as impressions and the ideas derived from them. But we seem doomed to be cut off from the external world or from our 'mind'. Philosophy, he says, teaches us that nothing can ever be present to the mind but an image or perception, and that the senses are only the inlets through which these images are conveyed, without being able to produce any immediate intercourse between the mind and the object. The table, which we see, seems to diminish, as we remove farther from it; but the real table, which exists independent of us, suffers no alteration; it was, therefore, nothing but its image, which was present to the mind.   [118]

The mind has never anything present to it but the perceptions, and cannot possibly reach any experience of their connexion with objects. The supposition of such a connexion is, therefore, without any foundation in reasoning.   [119]

Hume's conclusion is that what we can know is limited to mathematics and the sciences, which deal with general facts. This seems to rule out theology, ethics, aesthetics and metaphysics as constituting legitimate fields of human knowledge:

When we run over libraries, persuaded of these principles, what havoc must we make? If we take in our hand any volume; of divinity or school metaphysics, for instance; let us ask, *Does it contain any abstract reasoning concerning quantity or number?* No. *Does it contain any experimental reasoning concerning matter of fact and existence?* No. Commit it then to the flames: for it can contain nothing but sophistry and illusion.   [132]

*Comments and criticisms

Despite the vigour of his writings and his apparent self-confidence, Hume was dissatisfied with the intellectual cul-de-sac into which his arguments had led him. Certainly in his earlier *Treatise on Human Nature* he had been critical of Descartes' scepticism, in so far as this entailed the wholesale rejection (albeit 'hyperbolically') of both sense-experience and the truths of mathematics; and of his grounding of knowledge and certainty in an intellectual 'intuition' of the self as the thinking substance. Why then should Hume's scepticism be supposed to be epistemologically superior? His position is perhaps more subtle than has been suggested so far; and some further comment is needed.

Hume in fact distinguished firstly between 'antecedent' and 'consequent' scepticism. In the former, we start by doubting everything and then look for some certain, infallible criterion to provide the basis for knowledge – in Descartes' case this was the '*cogito*'. Hume's position was one of consequent scepticism, which involved essentially a thorough-going examination of the reliability of our human faculties. But whether one's scepticism is of the antecedent or consequent variety, Hume rejected extremism, which he regarded as self-destructive. It is clear from the *Treatise* that he was well aware of the consequences for the philosopher if his assumptions and arguments were followed through to their logical conclusion. As an ordinary man he dines, plays a game of backgammon, converses and is merry with his friends. But when, after these amusements, he returns to his philosophical speculations, 'they appear so cold and strained, and ridiculous, that I cannot find in my heart to enter into them any further'.

> Where am I, or what? From what causes do I derive my existence, and to what condition shall I return? Whose favour shall I court, and whose anger must I dread? What beings surround me? and on whom have I any influence, or who have any influence on me? I am confounded with all these questions, and begin to fancy myself in the most deplorable conditions imaginable, environed with the deepest darkness and utterly deprived of the use of every member and faculty.
>
> [Treatise, I, Part IV, Conclusion]

However, in *An Enquiry Concerning Human Understanding*, we find more emphasis on our natural or instinctive belief in the existence of external bodies, continuous selves and real causal connections in nature. We have to believe in such entities for our daily living. But it is clear that for Hume we are dealing here with probabilities: we do not have knowledge in any strict sense. The value of a more 'mitigated' scepticism lies in its propensity to encourage in us the development of a critical, anti-dogmatic stance, which cautions us against irrationalism of metaphysics and superstition. Let us accept this. But even if we allow that Hume is not wedded to an 'extreme' sceptical position, there are still serious difficulties with his philosophical assumptions which should be noted:

(1) **Impressions and ideas**. (a) Hume claims that a simple idea is derived from a single impression (complex ideas are to be analysed into simples). But there is a problem here. The distinction between images and thoughts or concepts has been obscured: they are all mental 'contents'. (Critics often argue that he has failed to differentiate between a **psychological** and a **logical** approach.) But if this is so, it is difficult to see how we can identify or recognize impressions if the concepts we require for the purpose must first be derived from those raw impressions. There seems to be an element of circularity in Hume's analysis. (b) Closely connected with this difficulty is the issue of 'privacy' which we first raised in 5.2. Hume has cut himself off from the world. His experiences must be private; on his own theory, we cannot know for certain that there are other objects in the world (we are aware only of impressions). How then can we refer to or talk about our experiences at all? Does not the language we use depend on a *public* context in which it functions? Language, after all, is used primarily for communication and presupposes the existence of other people and a world of publicly-observable objects. (We might say that an 'impression' or 'sense-experience' language is, as it were, parasitic on an 'object' language.) It is because we learn a language in our infancy that we *are* able to pick out features of our sensory field. And, according to some philosophers, to 'have' a concept is to know how to use a word meaningfully. [See Ayer, *The Problem of Knowledge*, ch. 2(v) and (vi) for an important discussion of the problem of 'public' versus 'private' language, in which Ayer sets out a position less sympathetic to the view discussed here.]

(2) **Cause and effect**. As with his account of impressions and ideas, Hume's analysis of causation reflects his concern to reject the rationalist notions of 'powers' and necessity. And here too his excessive empiricism seems to have led him astray. Certainly when we reflect on our experience of fire, for example, we remember that it has always burnt us. And of course Hume is right when he argues that we do not *perceive* any necessary connection or 'power' between the fire and the burning sensation in our hand. But does it follow that we must reject the possibility of a necessary link between the cause and the effect? It is a contingent fact – perhaps dependent on the properties of chemicals in the universe – that fire burns: but given the nature of fire and our bodies, is it not at least arguable that within defined limits there is a necessary causal relationship between the putting of my hand in the fire and my experiencing a burning sensation? This does not commit us to rationalist talk of 'secret powers'. Some philosophers would approach the question from a different direction and would say that the necessity lies not in the nature of 'things' but in the language we use to talk about our experiences. If 'fire' and 'burning' are used in a particular way in the context of normal discourse, it would be inconsistent to deny the truth of the statement 'fire causes a person to experience a burning sensation when his hand is put into it'. (This might be contrasted with a statement such as 'Bill lives in London' – here there does not seem to be any such necessary connection between the meanings of the terms 'Bill' and 'London'.) (We shall refer to the problem of causation again in 11.3 where a different solution will be proposed.)

(3) **Induction**. While following on from the cause–effect relationship, the problem of induction is a wider issue. (See the discussion in 2.9.) Hume is right to point out that the principle of induction is non-demonstrative; we clearly could not be expected to 'prove' it by *deductive* methods. Nor do we in some sense 'intuit' the principle. He is also correct in his recognition that any attempt to justify it *inductively* would be circular (that is to say, to accept the statement 'we can be sure the Sun will rise tomorrow because it has done so on all previous occasions' on the grounds that similar arguments from past to future events have proved to be reliable; for this would be to beg the question at issue). Hume's response to this impasse, however, seems to be too pessimistic. What we should be considering is not whether induction can in some sense be 'justified' but what part inductive arguments play in our daily lives (and in science), and in what sense we can be said to *know* that, for example, the Sun will rise tomorrow (given the facts we have about the Earth's rotation around the Sun, gravitational force and so on). In other words, we should consider the *context* in which such arguments are deployed. [See also Ayer on induction in *The Problem of Knowledge*, 2(viii).]

5.4 Kant and the *a priori*

Reading: Russell, *The Problems of Philosophy*, chs VII–XI; Ayer, *Language, Truth and Logic*, ch. IV; Kant, *Prolegomena*; *Critique of Pure Reason*, Introduction.

As you have learned so far, a distinction is made between rationalist and empiricist philosophers. The former (Descartes and Leibniz, for example) argued that knowledge can be attained only through the exercise of the reason independently of sense-experience – which they regarded as unreliable and the source of error. Reason gives us access to innate ideas and ultimate truths. Knowledge in the rationalist sense is often referred to as *a priori*, because it is logically 'prior' to and not dependent on experience. Empiricists, on the other hand (Hume and, to some extent, Locke) rejected these claims, maintaining that it is through the senses that we acquire our knowledge and that we cannot strictly know anything beyond what our senses tell us. For them knowledge is *a posteriori*, that is, roughly derived 'afterwards' from the 'particulars' given in experience. Thus, both rationalists and empiricists claim to have discovered a foundation for our knowledge, respectively, in an innate 'intuition' (for example, of the thinking self) characterized by clarity and distinctness (as Descartes put it) and in 'impressions' (Hume).

Now, as Ayer points out, the empiricists are faced with a problem. Hume had argued that no general propositions with a factual content, that is, propositions which purport to be about our actual sense-experience, could be logically certain. 'Universal' statements (based on induction), for example, might be shown to have held up to the present, but there is always the possibility that future events might refute them. Logical certainty must likewise be denied to particular statements based on experience. Hume's position is thus diametrically opposed to that of Aristotle or Descartes. If their 'ultimate' causes or principles genuinely relate to or describe the world, then they cannot be logically necessary. What then is the attitude of an empiricist philosopher towards the propositions of logic and mathematics? Either they have factual content or they are necessary or certain: they cannot be both. If they are not necessary, then why do we think of them as being so? If they are not factual, how can we attribute 'truth' to them? Are they propositions or statements at all? Hume's answer (compare 5.3 above) was to say that such propositions are not factual but are 'relations between ideas' which we can discover by intuition or by a reasoning process called demonstration. Now ideas for Hume are, roughly, 'images', and relationships between them are, for example, 'resemblance' and 'contrariety'. The necessity of relations of ideas would therefore seem to consist in the impossibility of denying them without bringing about some kind of contradiction. Thus we might have images of two things juxtaposed with two other things, the two sets being further linked by a set of four things. In 'seeing' the numerical resemblance between the sets we recognize the necessity of the proposition asserting the relationship. The images or ideas are of course derived from impressions, but the truth of the proposition itself does not depend on experience as such for its verification. Hume thus tries to be true to his empiricist premises while preserving the necessity of mathematics and logic.

Hume's solution (which he never really discussed in any detail) is not satisfactory. So far as he confines his analysis to ideas or images, the notion of a necessary proposition remains confused. The mere *incompatibility* which arise through the juxtaposition of 'opposing' images cannot add up to a *contradiction* in any strict logical sense. It was left to the eminent German philosopher

Immanuel Kant (1724–1804) to put forward a much more radical account of *a priori* knowledge and the nature of necessity. [See Russell, ch. VIII and Ayer, ch. IV.) Kant distinguished between two types of proposition (or judgement). An **analytic** judgement is one in which the predicate is in some way included in the subject. Thus, in 'all bodies are extended' the notion of extension is implicit in the concept of 'body'. A predicate can be discovered through an 'analysis' of the subject. In a **synthetic** judgement, however, no amount of analysis of subject terms can reveal any predicate. Kant gives as an example the proposition 'all bodies are heavy'. He also regards the statement '7 + 5 = 12' as synthetic, though, as Ayer points out, he seems in the case of such mathematical propositions to employ a 'psychological' criterion in addition to the 'logical' test of contradiction. To understand his position something must be said about his central philosophical aims. (A detailed account of his philosophy lies beyond the scope of this book.) He accepted Hume's important view that there is no logically necessary connection between causes and effects, and he agreed with his generally empiricist and 'anti-metaphysical' conclusions. At the same time he was convinced that there must be a way round a scepticism which seemingly denies us access to and knowledge of the world. So how is knowledge possible?

Kant first of all distinguishes between what he calls **phenomena** and **noumena**. These two Greek words mean for him, roughly, objects which we actually have in our experience, and 'things in themselves' (which correspond to Russell's 'physical objects'). Now whereas most previous philosophers had tended to think of man as a *passive* receiver of impressions, Kant argued that our experience includes a contribution which is attributable to our own nature. This contribution may be thought of as operating on two levels as it were. Firstly, we do not receive the raw data of sense (colours, hardnesses and so on) in other than an already organized or unified manner. This is because we 'intuit' them under the two **forms** of space and time. Secondly, the organized data are then 'structured' as a result of the 'imposition' of **categories** of the 'understanding' (an aspect of reason when applied to sensory experience) such as substance and causality. Neither the intuition of data under the forms of space and time, nor the imposition of the categories is a conscious process; it follows necessarily from what we are. Kant concludes (thus aligning himself with empiricists) that we cannot have knowledge of noumena, but he admits *a priori* knowledge into his scheme in so far as the raw data of sense *conform* to the 'prior' demands of our own nature (and in this respect his position is 'rationalist'). The *a priori–a posteriori* distinction in knowledge can now be combined with the distinction between analytic and synthetic judgements to give four kinds of statement: (a) **Synthetic *a posteriori*.** These are clearly possible because they refer to our experiences but are not necessarily true; predicates of such statements are not 'part of' their subjects. (b) **Analytic *a posteriori*.** These are not possible; they are analytic because the predicates are included in the subjects, in which case they cannot describe experience and must be (c) **analytic *a priori*** statements. (d) **Synthetic *a priori*.** This is the controversial class. Class (a) judgements correspond broadly to Hume's 'matters of fact', while class (c) are roughly equivalent to his 'relations between ideas'. But what are synthetic *a priori* judgements? How are *they* possible? In contrast to Hume, Kant includes in class

(d) judgements of arithmetic and geometry. He argued that 7 and 5 have to be put together to give us 12: the idea of 12 is *not* contained in the ideas of 7 and 5, nor is it thought of in the idea of their being added together. The judgement '7 + 5 = 12' must therefore be synthetic. Nevertheless although not *logically* necessary (because it is not analytic), the statement is still necessary because, according to Kant, the propositions of mathematics are grounded in spatial intuition: we *have* to 'see' the world in that way. (Kant was of course writing before it was realized that the universe might be describable in terms of non-Euclidean geometries.) Similarly we have *a priori* knowledge of causes, because events which we designate as 'cause' and 'effect' are necessarily linked in that way by virtue of their conformity to that category of the understanding.

We can now see that, if Kant is right, there are at least three significant results that he may be supposed to have achieved:

(1) Knowledge, although starting from experience, does not arise out of it alone, in that it is dependent on what is given 'prior' to it. He thus harmonizes, and indeed in a sense goes beyond both 'extreme' rationalism and empiricism.
(2) He has shown the *limits* of our knowledge and thereby the untenability of traditional metaphysics.
(3) He has produced a response to Humean scepticism, and by the same token has provided a *foundation* for knowledge. Knowledge claims, we may say, can now be justified by referring them to the way our experience is constituted and structured by the forms of intuition and the categories of the understanding.

*Comments

Even if we reject Kant's claims (and of course his assumptions and arguments have engendered an enormous number of books and articles), he remains as one of the greatest Western philosophers. Further reference will be made to him in 5.10 and 11.1. General criticisms are not appropriate here, as only a brief sketch of his epistemology has been presented. But two points should be made about the specific issue of *a priori* knowledge and his account of mathematical and scientific judgements.

(1) Most philosophers are agreed that he was wrong in regarding mathematical propositions as synthetic. 12 is known to be the sum of 7 and 5 because – on one view at least – it follows from the definitions of '7', '5' and '12' and from the function we attribute to 'operators' such as '+' and '='. Propositions of mathematics are therefore akin rather to Kant's analytic judgements. As to judgements about causal connections, it is still very much an open question as to whether our knowledge contains an *a priori* element.

(2) Although many philosophers would accept that some distinction between two kinds of propositions is tenable, they are critical of Kant's actual formulation – being based as it is on a limited Aristotelian interpretation of a judgement as consisting always of a 'subject' + 'is' + 'predicate'. Moreover, it is not altogether

clear in what sense predicates *do* belong to or are contained in subjects, or (and more importantly) how we *know* that they are.

It would seem then that the necessity of mathematical propositions and our *a priori* knowledge of them does not after all derive from the way we 'see' the world in a Kantian sense. So we must give further attention to the problem by considering what views are held by Russell and Ayer.

Russell's account in *The Problems of Philosophy* [ch. X] can be dismissed summarily. 'All *a priori* knowledge,' he says, 'deals exclusively with the relations of universals.' Thus 'two and two are four' is a relation between the universal two and the universal four (the relation itself also being a universal). But, as we shall see, Russell's account of knowledge is open to question; and it is doubtful whether the suggestion that we can 'know' the relation between 'two' and 'four' can account for the necessity associated with the propositions of mathematics and logic.

Ayer makes use of what is often called the **conventionalist** theory of *a priori* necessity. He takes over the Kantian distinction between analytic and synthetic propositions but reformulates Kant's analysis. A proposition is now regarded as analytic 'when its validity depends solely on the definitions of the symbols it contains', but synthetic 'when its validity is determined by the facts of experience'. Thus, to use Ayer's example, 'There are ants which have established a system of slavery' is a synthetic proposition, because we have to observe ant behaviour to determine whether it is true or false. 'Either some ants are parasitic or none are' is, however, analytic, because it can be seen by an examination of the function of the words 'either', 'or' and 'not' that any proposition of the form 'Either *p* is true or *p* is not true' must be valid independently of experience. In the same way we can see that the certainty of a proposition such as '7 + 5 = 12' lies in the fact that the symbolic expression '7 + 5' is **synonymous** with '12'; for that is how we have agreed by convention to use the terms in our language. Analytic propositions therefore give us no information at all about matters of fact and cannot be confuted by experience. Nevertheless, says Ayer, they are not senseless and can give us new knowledge in so far as 'they call attention to linguistic usages, of which we might otherwise not be conscious, and they reveal unsuspected implications in our assertions and beliefs'.

*Comments and criticisms

Ayer's account is attractive, but the principal objection to it lies in its very generality. In seeking to develop a theory of *all* analytic propositions he has failed to note that propositions may be of many different kinds, and that his definitions of analytic and synthetic may not therefore be always easy to apply. Consider the following examples:

(a) 'All bachelors are unmarried.' This is a so-called 'truth of language'; the conventionalist says that it is necessarily true because we have agreed to use the term 'bachelor' to mean the same as 'unmarried man' and to deny this would be contradictory.

(b) But what of the statement 'Nothing can be coloured in different ways at the same time with respect to the same part of itself'? This too seems to be a 'truth of language': but objections have been made to its categorization as an analytic statement on the grounds that some reference to experience is implicit in the attempt to validate it. Thus, when we assert, say, that 'Nothing is green and red all over at the same time' [an example from Wittgenstein's *Philosophical Observations* 78], we are really talking about the incompatibility of the two colour qualities in 'nature' referred to by the colour terms. So is the statement really empirical rather than analytic? The conventionalist might answer that whether something is green or red is to be ascertained by observation, and it cannot be both (a scientific analysis could show why perhaps). But once we have decided that the word 'green' should designate a particular colour experience, the use of the world 'red' to describe the same experience is ruled out as a matter of logic. It seems then that experience must play a part in our choice of the conventions we wish to follow, but within those conventions specific statements are logically necessary. This does, however, seem to rule out a universal necessity possessed by propositions which are true in 'all possible worlds', thus somewhat weakening the conventionalist's case.

(c) 'P and not-P cannot both be true at the same time', or, as Russell puts it [ch. VI], 'Nothing can both be and not be'. This is the 'law of non-contradiction' and one of three traditional 'Laws of Thought'. Both Russell and Ayer deny that there is anything special about these laws. They are self-evident logical principles, but are not more fundamental than other analytic propositions. However, it is debatable whether Russell and Ayer are correct here. As a conventionalist, Ayer would say that the necessity of the law of non-contradiction follows from the conventional definition of 'not'. 'Not' could therefore presumably have been defined differently. Now it is quite true that different logical systems can be set up, starting from different 'axioms' and conforming to a variety of 'rules of inference'. But surely the laws of thought, or at least the law of non-contradiction, are special in so far as *no* discourse can be possible without the assumption that 'p' and 'not-p' are mutually exclusive? Even if the term 'law' is a misnomer, it is a *presupposition* of all logic.

(d) '$7 + 5 = 12$'. There is continuing debate among philosophers about the status of mathematical propositions, and it is not possible to enter into a lengthy discussion here. But it can be pointed out that such propositions do seem to be different from the cases referred to in (a)–(c). It would be difficult to believe that there has been some sort of agreement that '12' shall be synonymous with '$7 + 5$'; for if that were so then '12' would have an infinite number of synonyms ('$1 + 11$', '$1\frac{1}{2} + 10\frac{1}{2}$', and so on). Neither does it have the special status of (c). This is not to rule out a conventionalist interpretation completely. We might think of each of the terms '7', '5' and '12' as representing successive additions of unities ('7' = '$1 + 1 + 1 + 1 + 1 + 1 + 1$', for example), the operators '+' and '=' also being defined by 'convention'. But it remains an open question as to what status should be accorded to the unit term. Is it itself defined? Or is it a primitive and fundamental concept rooted in the way we look at the world? Moreover, it might also be objected that the concept of seven must already be known if that particular succession of '1's is to be designated as '7' – unless they are made to correspond to physical points. In this case the proposition would seem to be similar to (b).

What conclusion can be drawn? There does not seem to be any good reason for supposing that we do not have some knowledge *a priori*: that is to say, there are circumstances in which we are willing to affirm the truth of a given proposition without having to refer to any observation of material facts. What we may be prepared to cite in support, so as to justify our claim to *know* the proposition is true, will depend on the context and what is acceptable within that context as appropriate backing. But there still remains the problem of what constitutes justification of our empirical beliefs about the world – Hume's 'matters of fact'. His construction of a theory of knowledge on the foundation of impressions has cut him off from this external world. (And, on one interpretation of Kant's philosophy, so does his building of epistemology on phenomena, albeit structured by the understanding – 'things in themselves' being unknowable.) Let us consider the matter further by having a look at Russell's treatment of the quest for certainty and knowledge, which in many ways can be seen as another (but non-Kantian) attempt to reconcile the sceptical empiricism of Hume with the more dogmatic philosophy of the rationalist tradition.

5.5 Russell's theory of knowledge

Reading: Russell, *The Problems of Philosophy*

A brief reference has already been made to Russell on *a priori* knowledge. We now go back to the beginning of his book. In chs I–IV he distinguishes between and examines two senses of the word 'know'. It can apply (a) to our knowledge *of* **truths**, and (b) to our knowledge *of* **things**. In the first case its objects are **judgements** – beliefs and convictions *that* something is the case. Knowledge is here opposed to error. In the second usage, the objects are **particulars**, such as **sense-data** and possibly oneself, and **universals**. Knowledge of things he calls knowledge by **acquaintance**. From knowledge of truths and knowledge of things by acquaintance we can then derive knowledge of things by **description**. We shall consider first Russell's knowledge of **things by acquaintance**.

If we look at a table it usually appears, say, oblong, brown and shiny. Likewise it feels smooth and cool, and gives out a wooden sound when tapped. Yet a change in the point of view of the observer may result in the table looking different – to other people, for example, or when viewed in artificial light. Its texture too will have a different appearance when seen under a microscope. Even its shape seems to change as we move around [compare Hume's *Enquiry*, 118]. It is these colours, smells, hardnesses and so on that Russell refers to as **sense-data**. Unlike the real table (the **physical object**), if there is one, these sense-data are known *immediately* to us. Sense-data also include things of the 'inner sense', that is, thoughts, feelings and desires. As for knowledge of the 'self', he is less certain.

Again, like Hume, he says: 'when we try to look into ourselves we always seem to come upon some particular thought or feelings, and not upon the "I" which has the thought or feelings' [ch. V]. Nevertheless, he believes that we must in some sense also be acquainted with 'that thing, whatever its nature, which sees the Sun and has acquaintance with sense-data'. Here he shows himself to be closer to the position adopted by Descartes. The seeing of a brown colour, he says [ch. II], involves a seer, but that something or somebody which is seeing is quite momentary so far as immediate certainty goes. The Cartesian intuition does not give us access to a permanent self. But it does seem, argues Russell [ch. V], that when he sees the Sun, the whole fact he is acquainted with is 'Self-acquainted-with-sense-datum', and that acquaintance with a Self, as that which is aware of things or has desires towards them, *probably* occurs. He also believes that we have acquaintance by **memory**. This immediate knowledge by memory is the source of all our knowledge of the past.

[chs IX and X]. In addition to our knowledge of particulars, Russell claims we are acquainted with **universals**. Universals for him are general ideas, 'entities' which are shared by many particulars. He distinguishes between **qualities**, which are universals represented by adjectives and nouns, and those universals represented by verbs and prepositions, which he calls **relations**. As examples of the former he gives 'whiteness', 'diversity' and 'brotherhood'. As for relations, in a proposition such as 'Edinburgh is north of London' 'north of' is a universal which 'subsists' independently of our knowledge of it. Russell uses the term 'subsist' because although 'north of', like 'Edinburgh' and 'London', 'belongs to the independent world which thought apprehends but does not create', yet it does not *exist* in space and time, and is neither material nor mental, thus differing radically from the term to which it relates. Finally, under the heading of universals which we may be said to be acquainted with, Russell also includes abstract universals of logic and arithmetic, such as 'two' and 'four', and the relations implicit in the proposition 'two and two are four'. (*That Russell's strongly 'realist' account of universals has much in common with the views of Plato summarized in Ch. 2 should be readily apparent to you. It should be contrasted with Hume's 'associationist' theory referred to in the previous section.)

When we turn to knowledge of **truths** we find that Russell differentiates between **self-evident** truths, knowledge of which is **intuitive**, and truths which are **deduced** from self-evident truths by the use of equally self-evident principles of deduction. Such knowledge is then said to be **derivative**. The kinds of truths he is thinking of as being known intuitively are general principles of logic and arithmetic, truths of perception, truths of immediate memory and perhaps some ethical principles. (*How does his distinction between intuitive and derivative truths compare with Hume's 'relations' between 'ideas' and 'matters of fact'?) This raises the important question as to what constitutes 'self-evidence', which we shall now consider.

[chs VI, VII, XI and XIII]. In ch. XI Russell comes to the conclusion that self-evidence admits of degrees: 'It is not a quality which is simply present or absent, but a quality which may be more or less present, in gradations ranging from absolute certainty down to an almost imperceptible faintness.' But he goes on further to suggest that within this idea of self-evidence are combined two different notions: the one, corresponding to the highest degree of self-evidence, being an infallible guide to truth; the other, corresponding to all other degrees, providing only a greater or lesser presumption. Self-evidence in the strong sense is a characteristic of principles of logic. Thus an argument may take the form: 'If p is true, then q is true; p is true (and suppose the evidence can be supplied to support this); therefore, q is true'. This argument (which may be symbolized as '$p \rightarrow q$') is easily seen to be valid. Russell says the truth of the principle is impossible to doubt. In the same way we can *see* the general principle that '$2 + 2 = 4$'. In both cases our knowledge can also be seen to be independent of experience, though sense-experience may initially be required if we are to become aware of the general laws of which, say, 'two and two are four' is an instance. (We have already referred to such knowledge as being '*a priori*'.) But according to Russell such self-evidence is not confined to *a priori* principles [see ch. XIII]. In perception we may be acquainted with the 'complex fact' (for example, the shining of the Sun) corresponding to a truth ('the Sun is shining'). Such a truth does no more than assert the *existence* of the sense-datum. The fact that the Sun is shining is self-evident in the sense of providing an absolute guarantee of truth – though Russell admits that error is still possible once we start to analyse the constituents of the fact and separate them. We may believe a judgement corresponds to the fact, but it is only when we know it really does correspond that we can claim knowledge. As for self-evidence in the weaker sense, which provides us with only a partial guarantee of truth, this belongs to empirical judgements themselves and is not derived from direct perception of facts. Thus, if we hear a horse trotting along the road, we may at first be certain that we are hearing its hoofs, but may then think we imagined the sound, or even come to doubt whether we heard it at all. Eventually we *know* we no longer hear anything. There is, Russell says, a continual gradation of self-evidence. Similar considerations apply to judgements of memory, which is 'trustworthy in proportion to the vividness of the experience and its nearness in time'.

The '**principle of induction**' [ch. VI; see further 2.9 above] is another example of a truth which, according to Russell, is self-evident but to a lesser degree than the principles of logic and mathematics (which underlie **deduction**). It is by an implicit appeal to the inductive principle, he says, that we are justified in claiming to know that the Sun will rise tomorrow – given that it has done so in similar circumstances on so many occasions in the past.

Lastly, derivative knowledge can now be admitted in so far as it consists of 'everything that we can deduce from self-evident truths by the use of self-evident principles of deduction' [ch. X]. In ch. XIII Russell argues, however, that such a definition of derivative knowledge is too limiting. We may well be justified in believing that the king is dead from our reading of the headlines in the newspaper. The intuitive knowledge our belief is based on is knowledge of the existence of sense-data which we are aware of when looking at the print on the page. The inference we draw from the letters to their meaning *could be* an inference of logic, but in practice, says Russell, it is 'psychological' inference. Derivative knowledge is therefore redefined as 'whatever is the result of intuitive knowledge even if by mere association, provided there *is* a valid logical connexion, and the person in question could become aware of his connexion by reflection'.

We can now return briefly to Russell's second kind of knowledge of things, namely knowledge by **description** [ch. V; see the fuller discussion in 2.10 above]. While knowledge by acquaintance is simpler than any knowledge of truths, and logically independent of them, knowledge of things by description, he says, always involves some knowledge of truths as its source and ground. Among things known in this way he includes 'physical' objects (for example, the 'real' table of ch. I), individuals and places he has not seen, and other people's minds. A description has the form '*a* so-and-so' (**ambiguous** description) or '*the* so-and-so' (**definite** description, for example, 'the man with the iron mask'):

> We shall say that an object is 'known by description' when we know that it is 'the so-and-so', i.e., when we know that there is one object, and no more, having a certain property; and it will generally be implied that we do not have knowledge of the same object by acquaintance.

Russell was led to develop this theory because of the apparent difficulty of referring to objects (especially persons) with which we are not directly acquainted. If we are to speak significantly, he says, we have to attach *some* meaning to the words we use, and this must be something we are acquainted with. Now we are not acquainted with Bismarck or Julius Caesar (how could we be, as both are dead!); so his aim is to replace common nouns and proper names by definite descriptions composed only of particulars and universals with which we *do* have some acquaintance. His fundamental principle is summarized thus:

> Every proposition which we can understand must be composed of constituents with which we are acquainted.

The chief importance of knowledge by description, he concludes, is that it enables us to pass beyond the limits of private experience.

We can now try to pull together the various threads of Russell's argument. The search for knowledge is in effect a quest for objective certainty. This is achieved, he claims, by virtue of a **relationship** between a knower (the subject) and various kinds of objects. The latter are particulars (for example, sense-data) and universals (general ideas and relations), with which we are directly acquainted; or truths known either intuitively or derivatively. Intuitively known truths include, firstly, principles of logic and mathematics which we know to be true in so far as we 'see' that there is a necessary relationship between the universals of which they are composed; secondly, general principles such as the principle of induction; and thirdly, truths which 'correspond' to a 'complex fact'. Intuitive knowledge may be regarded as reliable in proportion to the degree of its self-evidence. Thus, knowledge of the existence of sense-data and of simple truths of logic and arithmetic can be accepted as quite certain. Other judgements, however, are less reliable. We may be certain of our perception of a complex fact (the shining of the Sun), and yet may fall into error when we pass from the perception to the judgement 'the Sun is shining', because the judgement may not really correspond to the fact. Belief, then, for Russell, becomes knowledge only when what we believe is *true*, that is, when a judgement corresponds to a fact. In-between the two poles of knowledge and error lies 'probable opinion' – which we have when what we firmly believe is or is derived from something which does not possess the highest degree of self-evidence. Much of what we call knowledge is more or less probable opinion, a test for which is coherence. In conclusion, then, we may say that for Russell, too, knowledge is true belief, and that the 'justification' of knowledge in the strict or narrowest sense in effect lies in direct acquaintance of special sorts of what he calls 'hard data' – sense-data, logical truths and complex facts, or in the beliefs logically or psychologically inferred from such objects. His 'foundations' thus are more broad-based than Hume's.

*Comments and criticisms

There are many difficulties in Russell's theory of knowledge. You might like to consider the following objections:

(1) Russell seems to regard knowledge 'of' as in some sense prior to or more 'basic' than knowledge 'that'. It is difficult to maintain such a position. Is it meaningful to talk of an immediate sensation, an awareness, an intuition of something without in some way identifying it or describing it as being of a particular kind? Put more concretely, when we say we are aware *of* the colour or shape of the table, do we not at the same time affirm *that* it is brown or round? Underlying Russell's tendency to accord logical and empirical priority to knowledge 'of' is a mistaken view about the way words 'signify' or have 'meaning'. Like Plato, he seemed to believe that for a word to mean something there must be an object of some kind for it to refer to or 'denote'. (This also accounts for his theory of universals and for his theory of descriptions. We have words in our language such as 'whiteness' or 'Caesar'; they appear to mean something; we must therefore either introduce entities such as the 'universal' whiteness, or try to translate names into descriptions which can then be shown to be constructed out of particulars and universals.)

(2) Russell's use of the term 'sense-datum' is open to the same objection we made against Descartes' methodological scepticism and Hume's 'impressions'. Remember that sense-data are for Russell the ultimate source of certainty and hence of knowledge. We cannot be sure, he says, there is a real table: yet there is no doubt that we are aware of colours, shapes and so on. He admits [ch. XIII] that facts concerning sense-data (indeed all 'mental facts') are private. Yet he is using a 'public' language to talk about those experiences. (*Note Russell's claim that although facts concerning sense-data are private, universals and relations between them – which give rise to 'complex facts' – may be known by acquaintance to many people. Is his assumption that other people exist acceptable here?)

(3) Both the above criticisms relate to Russell's knowledge of 'things' (sense-data, universals and complex facts) by acquaintance (intuition or perception). But if

they are sound they must undermine Russell's theory of knowledge as a whole. This is because the other kind of knowledge – knowledge by description – depends not only on direct acquaintance with 'objects' (which are now suspect) but also on 'truths' which on Russell's own admission are liable to error. We may have a firm belief that the table is brown, but we cannot determine whether the belief is true (in which case we should have knowledge) because there is no way we can know whether there *is* a 'complex fact' corresponding to our private experience of brownness and roundness. (Indeed, if there were, what sense could be given to the notion of 'knowing' such a correspondence? Would this involve circularity?) Russell's theory thus seems to lead back to scepticism.

(4) Finally, consider what Russell has said about intuitive knowledge of *truths*. This seems to cover a wide range: (a) principles of logic and mathematics; (b) general principles such as that of induction; and (c) truths 'corresponding' to 'complex facts'. It is, however, open to question whether it is particularly helpful to include our 'knowledge' of each of these different kinds of 'truths' under a common heading of 'intuition'. We may well know intuitively that '2 + 2 = 4' is true. But can we really be said to 'know' this in the same way that Russell claims to know the Sun will rise tomorrow? (Refer back to the brief discussion of induction in the previous section and consider whether his arguments are sound.) What can be meant by 'intuiting' a truth? Russell does of course talk of *degrees* of self-evidence. But it is difficult to understand how the degree might be ascertained or assessed. We can see trees more or less clearly depending on weather conditions, the acuity of our vision, our state of health and so on. But can we 'intuit' more or less clearly, accurately and certainly? (For Descartes, an intuition carries with it the qualities of clarity and distinctness.) *Is* intuition akin to seeing? Should we not say that a truth is either self-evident or it is not? If we have to introduce the idea of degrees of self-evidence, is this not because we are appealing to different kinds of tests or criteria which in some cases might be empirical, in other cases *a priori*? If so, then are we not grounding *self*-evidence in evidence lying 'outside' those truths which are claimed to be 'seen' as self-evident?

There is also a problem with the notion of a 'correspondence' of a truth to a 'complex fact'. But we shall leave this to be considered in 5.7 on Truth.

5.6 Dispositions and performances

In previous sections we examined several accounts of knowledge and justification, and suggested possible difficulties associated with them. It would seem that if to know something is to be certain, then that certainty lies neither in a 'subjective' feeling of assurance nor in any 'objective' certainty which might be located in our acquaintance with such entities as minds, sense-data, universals, or relations between universals. The solution to the 'problem' of knowledge seems to be found neither in sceptical empiricism nor in an 'intuition' of some kind. Perhaps the most fruitful approach so far is that of Kant. However, his critical idealism does give rise to serious problems concerning causation and 'objective' scientific law, and the status of the extra-mental world (as we shall see in Ch. 11). In this section we shall turn our attention to the 'public world' in which language operates and shall consider two more recent contributions to epistemology which in different ways appeal to this common framework.

The dispositional theory

Reading: Ryle, *The Concept of Mind*, Introduction, chs I, II and V; see also Ayer, *The Problem of Knowledge*, ch. 1(ii) and (iii)

Plato may be regarded as having assimilated knowledge 'that' to knowledge 'of'. Russell, while maintaining the distinction, nevertheless gave logical and epistemological priority to knowledge 'of'. A radically different account is offered by Gilbert Ryle. His major work is – as the title suggests – about the philosophy of mind rather than epistemology as such. But the philosophical position he adopts leads him to attempt to assimilate knowledge 'that' to knowledge 'how'. This can be seen in the following way [*Concept of Mind*, ch. I]. Ryle is concerned to reject the dualist view, attributable in particular to Descartes, that man consists of a mind and a body. (*You might like to check over what you learned in 5.2 about the Cartesian view.) What occurs 'inside' ourselves is essentially non-spatial and private. Bodily occurrences and states, however, exist in space and are public and observable. Consequently while we can know with certainty what is going on in our own minds, the minds of others are inaccessible to us; we can only make problematic inferences from another person's observed behaviour to the states of mind which, by analogy, we suppose them to have. This 'official doctrine' Ryle calls 'the dogma of the Ghost in the Machine'. It is false, he argues, because it is a '**category mistake**', that is, 'it represents the facts of mental life as if they belonged to one logical type or category (or range of types or categories), when they actually belong to another'. He provides several illustrations to make clear what he means by this. One concerns a foreigner watching his first game of cricket. He sees what the bowlers, batsmen, the umpire and so on do – what their functions are – but he cannot discover whose role it is to exercise team-spirit. Ryle says that such a mistake has arisen because of the person's inability to use the term 'team-spirit' correctly. Team-spirit is not a *task* like batting or bowling: it is rather something like the keenness with which the various special tasks are performed. In the same way, mind is not an object, a complex organized unit, like the body. When we describe people as exercising qualities of mind, we are not referring to hidden 'episodes' inside their heads which are the causes of external, publicly-observable acts and utterances; we are referring to those overt acts and utterances themselves when performed in an 'intelligent' way [ch. II].

What is the relevance of his account to the problem of knowledge? Early thinkers, Ryle claims [ch. II], held the view that the defining property of a mind was the capacity to attain knowledge of truths. An *intelligent* action thus comes to be regarded as an action which is preceded by some kind of 'inner' or 'mental' process, a 'cognitive act', thinking, imagining and so on. But consider the antics of a circus clown. After much rehearsal he trips and tumbles on purpose. The spectators do not applaud some hidden performance which takes place 'in his head', but for his exercise of a skill. And a skill is a **disposition**, or complex of dispositions, not something which can be seen or not seen:

> The clown's trippings and tumblings are the workings of his mind, for they are his jokes; but the visibly similar trippings and tumblings of a clumsy man are not the workings of that man's mind. For he does not trip on purpose. Tripping on purpose is both a bodily and a mental process, but it is not two processes, such as one process of purposing to trip and, as an effect, another process of tripping.

What Ryle calls the 'intellectualist legend' – that knowing *how* is to be assimilated to knowing *that*, on the grounds that intelligent performance involves the prior observance of rules or the application of criteria – is thus quite mistaken and leads, he argues, to an infinite regress. On the contrary, one's knowledge is to be described in terms of capacities or dispositions. This is not to say that one cannot talk of doing things in one's head in an everyday sense. But Ryle claims that this is a metaphorical usage, and that 'mental' activity, as in mental arithmetic or reciting to oneself, is but a 'technical trick' whereby we can think in auditory word-images instead of in spoken words. Moreover, such activity is itself just as careful an intellectual operation as recitation or calculation aloud or on paper, and as such can be done intelligently or otherwise. It cannot therefore be used as evidence for the 'Ghost in the Machine' dogma.

How then on Ryle's thesis can knowledge 'that' be distinguished from belief 'that'? He deals with this in ch. V. To 'know', he says, is a **capacity** verb which signifies that the person described can 'bring things off' or 'get things right'. To 'believe', however, is a **tendency** verb which 'does not connote that anything is brought off or got right'. 'Belief' is a **motive** word, whereas 'knowledge' is a **skill** word. We ask *why* a person believes something, but *how* a person knows. 'Skills have methods, where habits or inclinations have sources.' The external, observable behaviour of a person who believes ice on a pond is dangerously thin may well be the same as a person who knows it is. But the latter has good reason. He has found out the wet way! To keep to the edge because one knows the ice is thin is 'to employ quite a different sense of "because" , or to give quite a different sort of "explanation", from that conveyed by saying that he keeps to the edge because he believes it to be thin'.

*Comments and criticisms

Ryle's notion of the 'category mistake' has much in common with Wittgenstein's thesis [*Philosophical Investigations*] that philosophical problems arise because we misinterpret our forms of language and try to use words outside their proper contexts (see 11.1). This approach to philosophy has undoubtedly been influential, and there is much to be said for it. But Ryle's commitment to what seems to be a quasi-behaviourist or reductionist approach to mind and knowledge is not free of difficulties. You should be in a better position to appreciate the limitations of his theory after you have studied 5.11, 11.2–11.4 and

Ch. 12. It is sufficient to suggest here that it is possible to accept his rejection of Cartesian dualism without committing oneself to the reductionist programme he seems to subscribe to. And we shall confine ourselves to making two particular points about his argument in relation to 'thinking':

(1) When the clown first starts to prepare a new routine it surely makes sense for us to describe him as thinking about what he will do. While he may not have to recite rules to himself, he would be expected to attend to certain descriptions of possible actions; and when engaged in actual training or practice for his performance he would no doubt be attentive – concentrating on what he is doing – until his routine has been perfected and he performs 'without thinking', by 'second nature'. Thus in the early stages of training he can be said to be knowing 'that' something is (or should be) the case. There is no reason to accept Ryle's claim that such 'intellectual' behaviour (which distinguishes us from robots) leads to an infinite regress. Paying attention and thinking 'intelligently' means in part conforming to certain criteria: it does not require any prior mental process – even on the 'Ghost in the Machine' legend.

(2) The examples Ryle tends to cite are special cases which do relate to publicly observable behaviour. Even if it were the case that such behaviour is never preceded by recitation or rules or something like this, it would not follow that attention to statements (knowledge 'that') must always be translatable into appropriate action. How, for example, could my knowledge that two and two make four, or that London is the capital of the UK, be understood in terms of capacities or dispositions? Certainly, my behaviour in a specific context might be accepted as *evidence* for my knowledge, but this is not the same thing as saying that such knowledge is dispositional. Even if it were dispositional, the number of possible actions into which my knowledge 'that' might be 'translated' could be very large; and this in itself makes the reductionist programme suspect.

These criticisms raise a further question – about Ryle's views on belief and knowledge. As we have seen, while he regards both as dispositional, he makes a clear distinction between them – the former being a 'tendency', the latter a 'capacity' word. Moreover, his anti-intellectualist position rules out private 'sense-data' and the like as a possible foundation for an account of knowledge as justified true belief. Any justification of knowledge for him (although he does not discuss this explicitly in such terms) would seem to lie in overt behaviour of the individual claiming to know. But it is here that more problems lie. Given that the external behaviour of a person who believes something to be the case is the same as a person who (supposedly) knows, then for an observer to be sure of the agent's disposition he would have to rely on verbal or written utterances (and would have to take on trust their veracity). Without such assurances the agent's behaviour must remain ambiguous. A person may well venture on to thin ice even though he knows it to be thin. Perhaps he is an exhibitionist, or wants to make us laugh; or it may be he is courting danger because he wants to elicit our sympathy. Is he carrying out an experiment? Careful observation may help the observer to understand the behaviour, but in the last analysis to make sense of it he needs to know something of the agent's motives and intentions, and the wider framework of his life in which his decisions and actions operate. And it could well be argued that this brings us back to something like the 'intellectualist' position of which Ryle is so critical.

The performatory theory

Reading: See Ayer, *The Problem of Knowledge*, ch. 2(iii)

This theory can be seen as a logical development of the others we have examined so far. From a view of knowledge as linked with 'subjective' certainty, we moved to theories which required knowledge to be validated by some form of 'objective' certainty. Such certainty might initially be thought to be attainable through a relationship between knower and certain kinds of objects (knowledge 'of'), but we suggested that knowledge is primarily about statements which belong to a public framework of discourse (knowledge 'that'). With Ryle we move away from statements of knowledge or belief to human *behaviour* (also assessable in the public domain); knowledge is to be understood in terms of capacities or dispositions manifested in actions. The performatory theory, developed by another Oxford philosopher, J.L. Austin (1911–60), makes the final break: knowledge is now not *about* anything at all. It has no descriptive content; to say that one knows something is to declare one's intentions. Thus, when we say we know that London is the capital of the UK, we are not uttering something that admits of truth or falsity but saying something akin to making a promise: we are in some sense guaranteeing our *acceptance* of the statement about London as being true.

*Comments

Such a theory has the merit of avoiding the difficulty we are faced with when, after we have claimed to know something, the statement in question turns out to be false, and we must then admit that we could not really have had that knowledge. Knowledge cannot therefore differ from belief. On a performative theory, however, one's authorization for the acceptance might later prove to have been unwise, based on insufficient evidence, for example, but there would be no question of any contradiction having been made. Nevertheless, there are problems with the theory. A full account would be too technical for discussion here. You would also have to read a number of major articles written by Austin to understand his analysis fully – and the changes he made to his theory. But one important point can be made. It can be argued that 'I know that London is the capital of the UK' is not entirely devoid of descriptive content. One reason for this depends on the very fact that 'I know' is held not to add anything to the statement 'London is the capital of the UK'. Now the latter is certainly descriptive. Moreover, when I say 'I know', I am saying something about myself (intention, self-confidence) which cannot be completely divorced from the content of the statement I am affirming. This is not to deny that 'I know' may well have an 'authorizing' function, but it is certainly a matter for further discussion as to whether it possesses this function alone.

5.7 Truth

Reading: Russell, *The Problems of Philosophy*, ch. XII; James, *Pragmatism*; Putnam, *Reason, Truth and History*

Before we attempt to bring together some of the threads of our discussion and present a conclusion, something needs to be said about truth as one of the conditions for knowledge. We will leave aside here the problem arising out of knowledge claims about statements that prove subsequently to be false and consider the concept of truth itself. ' "What is Truth?" said jesting Pilate, and would not stay for an answer' [Bacon, *Essays*]. Unlike Pilate, we philosophers must look for one. As you will by now have expected, there are in fact many answers which have been proposed, a number of which we shall now examine.

The coherence theory

According to this view, which was espoused by, among others, a number of 'idealist' philosophers in the eighteenth and nineteenth centuries, for example, G.W.F. Hegel (1770–1831) and F.H. Bradley (1846–1924), a statement is true if it 'coheres' or 'fits in' with other statements thereby forming a complete system. Russell [ch. XII] objects: (1) because it might be possible to devise more than one set of coherent beliefs (just as in science more than one hypothesis might account for the same set of facts on a given subject); and (2) because the theory assumes that the meaning of 'coherence' is known, whereas it presupposes the truth of the laws of logic.

*Comments

This second criticism does seem to be fatal. Certainly coherence is generally understood minimally in terms of consistency – the absence of contradiction within the system ('p' and 'not-p' cannot both be true) – as a necessary requirement. Now, if coherence is understood not only as presupposing consistency but also in terms of it (by definition), then to say 'p is true' if it coheres (= is consistent with) q, r, etc. would seem to imply that p can only be true if all other propositions in the system are also true. Thus truth becomes a property of the system as a whole rather than of its individual propositions. (Or alternatively we might say the truth of an individual proposition is inextricably linked with that of the totality or propositions: truth is relational.) This would suggest further that a true system must be all-inclusive. And this might perhaps provide an answer to Russell's first criticism; for the coherence theorist might invoke the idea of 'degrees' of truth and maintain that in a still more widely embracing system the two sets might be reconciled. This is broadly Bradley's view: Truth is to be found only in the Absolute System, which incorporates or assimilates the infinite totality of all possible but partially true statements. But then how can we know that the system is complete, that the 'Absolute' has been attained? And there is another problem here. Could there not be another viable system which consists of the negations of all the propositions of the one just discussed? How then could we decide between them if no 'external' rational or empirical verification is possible?

Is there an alternative account of coherence as involving more than just consistency? Some philosophers have suggested entailment. But this would make all propositions equivalent to every other (each would now be an instantiation of the 'Absolute'). Others have proposed dependence (as perhaps in a scientific 'system' of theories, principles and laws). However, here the question arises about the alethic (truth) status of the different levels. *A* may 'depend' on *B* in an explanatory framework. But how is *B* 'justified'? An appeal to coherence might now seem to be circular. So there has to be some reference 'outside' the system (some form of experimental tests, correspondence, etc.). An exception to this may perhaps be seen in mathematical systems, where the primitive terms and operators are defined and the rules of inference agreed upon, but these systems as such do not purport to give us information about the world in the way that empirical propositions do. As Russell says, coherence may well be a *test* of truth after a certain amount of truth has become known, but it cannot give the *meaning* of truth. For him, truth is to be understood in terms of the notion of 'correspondence'.

The correspondence theory

According to Russell [*Problems of Philosophy*, ch. XII] any theory of truth must satisfy three requirements: (1) it must admit of its opposite, falsehood; (2) truth and falsehood must be properties of beliefs and statements; and (3) these properties must depend on the relations of beliefs to something lying outside those beliefs and not on any internal quality they may possess. In an attempt to meet these conditions he therefore developed the Correspondence Theory, an early form of which was introduced in Plato's *Sophist* (see 3.6). On this view, if a belief is to be true it must correspond to a **fact** of some kind which 'exists' in the world. This 'theory' has the advantage of conforming to our 'common sense' understanding of what it is to say that something is true: but common sense is not always a good guide in philosophy, and the correspondence theory too has to answer a number of objections.

*Criticisms and comments

(1) Russell regards truth and falsity as properties of beliefs and statements. The things we believe, the opinions we hold, are generally articulated by means of language: we express and communicate them using sentences. Now consider the sentences 'It is raining', 'Il pleut' and 'Es regnet'. They are clearly different, yet

people in England, France and Germany respectively use them to make the same statement, namely that it is raining. The common content or **meaning** of these three utterances, and thus of the relevant statements and beliefs, is often called a **proposition**; and arguably it is more accurate to regard propositions rather than beliefs as carriers of truth or falsehood. Thus ' "my belief that x" is true' is better formulated as ' "x is true" and I believe it, that is, am prepared to accept it' (where x stands for a proposition). On this view, we could then say that a proposition is true if it corresponds to some fact but false if it does not. But if this is so, then we are faced with further difficulties relating to the nature of propositions. (a) How can the suggestion that truth and falsehood are actual properties of propositions be reconciled with the fact that the same proposition can sometimes be true and sometimes false (given that states of affairs in the world change; for example, it might be raining on Monday but not on Tuesday)? (b) Can propositions actually be distinguished from the facts they are meant to correspond to? In answer to the first point, it might be said that the two propositions are not the same in so far as the utterances were made on different occasions. Perhaps then we should want to say that the 'content' which makes up the true proposition is not simply 'It is raining' but 'It is raining today, Saturday, 21st April, 2001. But is even this sufficient? Should not the time and place be specified? It is clear that we could be forced into a degree of precision which would make communication difficult if not impossible. To deal with the second point, we must discuss briefly what facts actually are.

When we use the term 'fact' in everyday conversation we usually mean something like 'a state of affairs' or 'what is the case'. We say, 'It is a fact that two and two make four', or 'It is a fact that, at least at the moment of writing, the book in front of me is red and black'. For Russell [second half of ch. XII] a fact is a 'complex unity', for example, 'Desdemona's love for Cassio', in which 'object-terms' (Desdemona, Cassio) are united by an 'object-relation' (loving). But what kind of status do these facts have? Most people would agree that such facts are in some sense objective in so far as they do not depend on a particular thinker or observer. We should also recognize that the way we apprehend facts depends to some extent on the language we use and on our individual sense experience. Yet they still seem to retain some sort of objective 'existence' as intermediary entities between ourselves as observers and the actual 'real' world outside. But is not this description suspiciously like the account we have given of propositions? If so, then it would be difficult to provide an account of truth and falsity in terms of correspondence; a true proposition would now be an actual fact, while a false proposition would be understood as a 'non-fact'. (It is significant that to illustrate what he means by a fact Russell draws on the world of Shakespearian *fiction* in which the notion of 'existence' must be regarded as somewhat tenuous!)

(2) But let us suppose for the moment that a distinction *can* be made between facts and propositions. We then have to make sense of the notion of 'objective existence'. Does the fact 'London is the capital of the UK' *exist*? If London is no longer the capital of the UK in, say, a thousand years' time, do we then have to say that the fact has somehow ceased to exist? Perhaps we should therefore

introduce a more specific formulation: 'London is the capital of the UK in 2001' and regard it as a fact which (presumably like '2 + 2 = 4') has always existed and will continue to do so. But this really won't do at all. If they come in and go out of existence, facts after all would seem to be not very different from ordinary objects. However, whereas we can talk (admittedly in a loose sense) of London, capital and so on as being objects, it is difficult to think of 'London is the capital of the UK' (in 2001 or any other year) as an object. So either facts seem to be rather queer entities, or 'objective' is being used in a peculiar 'metaphysical' sense (see Ch. 11).

(3) Perhaps the central question is how we can account for the notion of 'correspondence' itself. According to Russell there is correspondence between a belief and a fact when: (a) there is a complex unity of object terms and an object-relation; and (b) when the order of these terms and relations is 'in the same order as they have in the belief', this 'order' in the objects of the belief being put there by what he calls a 'sense' or 'direction' in the relation of judgement, and indicated by the order of words in a sentence (or by word-endings in an inflected language). The act of believing (or judging – as in 'Othello believes that Desdemona loves Cassio' – is itself another complex unity in which one constituent is a mind while the others are the object-terms *and* the object-relation. This correspondence, he claims, ensures truth, and its absence entails falsehood.

(4) Russell's theory has been criticized on the grounds that his account of belief as a relation is inadequate. This cannot be examined here. But one point in particular should be made about his interpretation of correspondence, and this is best formulated in terms of a dilemma. If Russell's facts as 'complex unities' are 'meanings' comparable to propositions as discussed above, then there would seem to be a fact corresponding to any belief whatsoever as soon as it is articulated in a language, particularly as the 'order' of its terms is attributable to the act of believing. How, then, could we get 'outside' our language to check whether these *facts* correspond to the 'external' world of things and events? If, however, Russell's facts themselves *constitute* that external reality, then it is difficult to make sense of 'order'. *We* may wish to say, for example, that Mount Everest is higher than Snowdon, but considered objectively the two mountains are but two things existing in the world, and *apart* from our belief there is no 'direction' of one towards the other. To say that A is higher than B is equivalent to saying that B is lower than A. No correspondence of 'order' can therefore be claimed.

In the light of these – and many other – problems associated with beliefs, facts and correspondence, some later thinkers have tried to refine and improve the correspondence theory. The Polish logician Alfred Tarski (1902–83), for example, developed the 'semantic' theory of truth. Tarski was concerned primarily to find a definition of truth which would avoid certain paradoxes inherent in natural languages. To the extent that his analysis is confined to 'formalized' languages of logic, it has been questioned whether his theory can be regarded as a genuine correspondence theory. An attempt to apply Tarski's work to natural languages (in the context of a search for a truth-conditional theory of meaning) has been made by the influential American philosopher Donald Davidson (b. 1917). These theories, however, are too technical to be considered in this book.

The pragmatic theory

This theory is associated particularly with the American philosophers, Charles Peirce (1839–1914), William James (1842–1910) and John Dewey (1859–1952). According to Peirce, the founder of pragmatism, truth lies in the 'fixity of belief', beliefs being acquired and sustained by the verificatory methods of science. In so far as beliefs are for him (as for Ryle) dispositions to action, what we do is in some sense a test of truth. At the same time Peirce does seem to think of scientific investigations as constrained by the 'real' world, and thus his pragmatic account of truth seems to involve also a 'correspondence with reality' element. It is with **James**, however, that we associate such notions as 'workability' or 'effectiveness' as definitive of 'truth'. Following Peirce, he says that 'True ideas are those we can assimilate, validate, corroborate and verify. False ideas are those we cannot' [*Pragmatism*, Lecture V]. But by 'validation', 'verification' and so on he means that the ideas can be made to 'work' for us in the sense that they meet our expectations and can lead to the success of our chosen actions. As he says:

> The practical value of true ideas is . . . primarily derived from the practical importance of their objects to us . . . You can say of an extra truth [that is, an 'idea that shall be true of merely possible situations'] . . . either that 'it is useful because it is true' or that 'it is true because it is useful'. Both these phrases mean exactly the same thing, namely that here is an idea that gets fulfilled and can be verified. True is the name for whatever idea starts the verification-process, useful is the name for its completed function in experience. True ideas would never have been singled out as such, would never have acquired a class-name, least of all a name suggesting value, unless they had been useful from the outset in this way.
>
> [*Pragmatism*, Lecture VI]

But, unlike Peirce, James, faced with recalcitrant experiences, tends to attempt to fit them internally to his system of beliefs, to make them cohere, as it were, rather than to refer them to external reality as in correspondence theories. He is critical of the notion of beliefs corresponding to 'facts' regarded as 'truths' existing timelessly and objectively (in roughly a Platonic sense; compare also Russell's account in ch. IX of *Problems*, which we looked at in the previous section). Truth, James says, is indeed a relation between ideas and the 'world', but for him both sides of the relation of aspects of *experience* – subjective and objective respectively. The idea for James is a kind of plan which is to be tried out or tested. If it leads to the objective 'reality' then it may be said to have been verified or validated; and it is this sense that the 'true' idea can be said to relate to the world. What then of such ideas as 'God' or metaphysical beliefs about, say, 'absolute' reality? In what sense can the assertion 'God exists' be verified? These propositions, James says, may be regarded as true in so far as they provide the individual with 'vital benefits', that is, they may satisfy our religious or spiritual needs. 'If the hypothesis of God works satisfactorily in the widest sense of the word, it is "true".'

Several objections have been raised against at least James's version of the pragmatic theory by Russell ['Pragmatism' and 'William James' Conception of Truth', both in *Philosophical Essays*]:

(1) The notion of 'working' is ambiguous; a scientist may understand this to mean that a number of verifiable propositions can be derived from a hypothesis without also believing the effects of accepting the hypothesis to be good for him (*Against this, it might be argued that 'good' for the scientist consists precisely in the fact that predictions *have been* fulfilled in the context of experimental procedures; without such verifiability the scientist would have no grounds for belief. Where scientific tests are inappropriate, that is, for example, where a hypothesis such as 'God exists' cannot be falsified, then truth can only be assessed in terms of a wider sense of 'good' or 'well-being'. (The question of truth in relation to scientific hypotheses will be considered in Ch. 8.)

(2) James's notion of 'truth' is equated with 'useful', whereas in everyday discourse we distinguish between these two terms as having a different meaning. (*Does this criticism not beg the question? James is implicitly rejecting other theories of truth and is *redefining* the concept so as to avoid difficulties associated with such theories.)

(3) A more serious objection is that it is difficult if not impossible to determine the consequences of holding to a belief. What are to count as consequences? How many months or years must I wait to find out? Perhaps the effects may not become apparent long after my death. (*Can you think of an answer to this criticism?)

A more sophisticated pragmatic theory was worked out by Dewey. He agreed with Peirce that truth is absolute fixity of belief and that some of our ideas can be seen to work – they can solve problems. His major contribution, however, was to introduce the notion of 'warranted assertibility'. The confirmation of our ideas in their practical application warrants us to accept them and assert them. It is in this sense that they may be said to be true. Arguably Dewey's approach, with his emphasis on confirmation as providing the test for truth and the meaning of the word 'true', may avoid Russell's criticisms of the notion of truth as that which 'works'.

The redundancy theory

Given the difficulties engendered by these various theories of truth, some philosophers in recent years have proposed more radical approaches. F.P. Ramsey (1903–30) argued that the sentence 'It is true' is redundant in that to say 'It is true [or it is a fact] that Caesar was murdered' is to say no more than 'Caesar was murdered'. Truth is thus no longer regarded as a property of statements. For P.F. Strawson, who developed Ramsey's theory, while part of what one is doing in saying that a statement is true is to describe it in some sense (for example, to attribute the property 'true' to it), the primary role of the word 'true' is to perform an act (for example, of agreement, acceptance, endorsement). When I say ' "It is raining" is true' or 'It is true that it is raining' – I mean, I agree or I accept that it is raining. 'True', it is claimed, has thus been eliminated, and has been redefined and translated into a 'performatory' act or linguistic usage. (Compare the discussion of Austin's performatory account of knowledge in 5.6.) Discussion of this theory has turned on the question of whether complete elimination is possible. It has been pointed out that 'true' plays a variety of roles and that the redundancy theory cannot cope with the use of 'true' in formal logic. A further objection that may be raised concerns the criteria we may appeal to in order to decide whether or not to endorse or to agree to a given statement. We should want to say that it is correct to use a statement in one context rather than another. 'Today is Sunday' is true only when it is uttered on one particular day of each week. And it is always correct to assert 'The Battle of Hastings took place in 1066'. Is it not the case then that truth must be in some sense 'about' the world; and it is this which (to use Dewey's term) warrants our agreeing to the statement?

The normative rationality theory

Another significant contribution to truth theory has been made by the American philosopher Hilary **Putnam** (b. 1926). Like many other philosophers he rejects the correspondence theory. The notion of an 'objective' world consisting of the totality of all mind-independent objects, for which there is but one absolute 'corresponding' description is for him untenable. Rather, there are many possible conceptual or cultural schemes; and it is the functioning of statements within such contexts that gives a purchase on the notion of truth – and indeed also of justification, truth and warranted assertibility. Putnam's claim essentially is that when we say that a given statement is true we are pointing to its acceptability by a linguistic community; and this acceptability in turn is grounded in the possibility of the assertion's being judged *rationally* under what he says are sufficiently good epistemic conditions. 'Truth', however, is not to be defined or reduced to epistemic notions. Together with justifiability and warranted assertibility, it belongs to a *normative* conception of rationality. Indeed (as he says, in *Reason and Representation*) truth and rational acceptability are *interdependent* notions. This might seem to suggest a form of relativism. But Putnam is as equally dismissive of such a position as he is of 'metaphysical' realism. He regards reason not only as embedded or immanent in conceptual schemes but also as transcendentally normative. This is why he talks of truth as *idealized* rational acceptability – under epistemically ideal conditions. Acceptability and warranted assertibility are thus in a sense provisional, in that he allows for epistemic and alethic openness, development and 'better' conceptual schemes. He in fact goes further and argues that our conception and standards of rationality presuppose our values – and thus a theory of the good which is 'itself dependent upon assumptions about human nature, about society, about the universe (including theological and metaphysical assumptions)' [*Reason, Truth, and Rationality*, p.215]. And as our knowledge has increased and our world-view has changed, we have to revise continually our theory of the good. (You will find further discussion of the basis of Putnam's 'internal' realism and his philosophy of mind in 11.2 and 11.3.)

5.8 The Gettier problem

Reading: Gettier, 'Is justified true belief knowledge?'

So far throughout this chapter we have been concerned with a view of knowledge as justified true belief. We have seen that there are difficulties associated with this concept of justification and with the various claims made by different philosophers to have identified 'foundations' which might underpin justification and give us knowledge in some strong sense. Some other philosophers have rejected this account of knowledge and have argued for a difference not just of degree but of kind between knowledge and belief. We have also found the concept of truth to be equally controversial.

Let us suppose, for the sake of argument, that the account of knowledge as justified true belief is the correct one, and that in a given instance the conditions are satisfied – that we have, as Ayer puts it, the right to be sure. We have already mentioned the problem concerning knowledge claims about statements which turn out subsequently to be false (and that therefore one at least of the conditions could not have been satisfied although we had supposed it was). But there is now a further difficulty. Even if a statement *is* true, and even if we have the justificatory evidence to support a knowledge claim, Edmund Gettier has argued that there are circumstances in which it would still be wrong for us to say we know that such and such is the case. We can put this succinctly by saying that justification, while a necessary condition, is not a sufficient one.

In his essay Gettier presented two cases as examples. Here is the second. Smith has strong evidence for the proposition: (a) 'Jones owns a Ford'. (We need not concern ourselves here with the nature of the evidence.) Smith now infers correctly from this proposition the further propositions: 'Either Jones owns a Ford, or Brown is in (b) Boston, or (c) Barcelona, or (d) Brest-Litovsk', because each of these is entailed by (a) (see Ch. 2 for the logic of this). Smith does not *know* where Brown is. Now suppose further that Jones does not own the Ford car he is driving, and by coincidence he happens to be in Barcelona. Gettier argues that (c) is true, Smith believes (c) is true, and is justified in believing it (by virtue of the logical entailment): but yet these conditions are not sufficient to constitute knowledge.

A great deal has been written about Gettier's article. Some philosophers have argued that Smith's belief in Brown's location is not justified (so of course he could not know this), because there is no connection of relevance, no causal link, between his belief and what makes it true that Brown is in Barcelona. Attempts to establish such a link generally fail. In fact all that Smith can justifiably claim to know is not a material fact but a logical one, namely, that it is an elementary law of logic (see 2.5) that a proposition p entails the conclusion $p \vee q$, where q can be any proposition at all.

We can now see that both difficulties – (1) the emergence of evidence at some time in the future which defeats a claim to knowledge, and (2) the Gettier problem – seem to arise because there is a disconnection between truth and the justification required to guarantee the success of the claim. This seems to be inherent in standard accounts of justification, 'foundationalist' or otherwise. So perhaps resolution of the problems of knowledge and truth lies after all in some kind of performatory theory? A few suggestions will be made in the next section.

5.9 Conclusion

It is unlikely that any theory of knowledge or of truth has been proposed which is not open to some objection: such is the nature of philosophy! However, it is worth while to make some attempt to reconcile some of the views set out in this chapter in the hope of achieving a satisfactory account. It certainly seems as if we can take something from each of the theories we have been surveying:

(1) It would be generally accepted that truth and knowledge are in some sense 'about the world'. We do not of course have to think in terms of a crude 'correspondence' of beliefs and language to 'facts'. But clearly there would seem to be some link between the 'world', or sensory experience, and the language we use to articulate and describe that experience. And we can assume that the way we use language is constrained by 'reality'. (Even this is contentious. We shall be referring to some rather radical 'post-modernist' anti-realist views in Ch. 11.)

(2) Our statements about the world must be coherent in the minimal sense of being logically consistent. This is of course a requirement for all discourse. Perhaps here we should make a distinction between logical and material truth. What makes 'It is raining' true are experiences such as feeling, seeing and hearing drops of water falling on us from dark clouds in the sky. This materially true statement can then become a true statement 'p' in a logical inference such that it entails '$p \vee q$', or that it would be contradictory to assert 'not-p'. The point here is that '$p \rightarrow (p \vee q)$' is logically necessary, regardless of the material truth of 'p' or 'q'; and that '$p \,\&\, -p$' is always a logically contradictory form. Having committed ourselves to the material truth of 'p' we cannot then coherently go on to assert 'not-p'. Nevertheless it may be the case that what we took to be materially true may in fact be materially false (it is not raining, but I got wet because somebody was throwing water out of a window) – in which case it would then be logically inconsistent to assert 'It is raining'.

(3) As for 'utility', if our statements about the world are in some sense materially true, then they can facilitate our achieving of ends, the solving of problems. If scientific statements were not true, science would not 'work', and we would

have no technology – no television sets, computers or motor-cars. However, 'workability' does not give us the meaning of truth; indeed materially false statements could lead to beneficial results.

(4) While we can accept that a statement is made true by virtue of being 'about the world' in some sense, Strawson's view that the primary role of the term is performatory is a compelling one that can help us deal with the various difficulties we have been considering.

(5) As for Putnam's theory, this has the merit of seeming to accommodate changing truth conditions as our knowledge increases and our world-views are modified, while at the same time truth is taken to be inseparable from an idealized rational acceptability, a norm, to which all conceptual schemes must be subordinate.

Let us now set out the main points of our conclusions. The following points can be made:

(1) When I say I believe or know that something is the case I am making an assertion about the truth of a circumstance, situation, or event. Correspondingly, when I say 'p' is true I presuppose either that I believe p is the case or that I know it. The notions of belief, knowledge and truth are inextricably interrelated. The attribution of truth is being made on the basis of available evidence; and I am in effect setting myself up, as it were, for interrogation. To say I believe that p is true is tacitly to affirm my recognition of the possibility that appropriate evidence in support of the statement is available, but that I do not have it all or I have accepted it uncritically (or alternatively that I have taken the belief on trust, perhaps on the authority of someone else). But when I say I know that p is true, I am declaring: (i) that I am in possession of what I (in most cases articulating a community consensus) deem to be appropriate evidence to support my assertion of 'p'; (ii) that if challenged I am willing to identify or produce that evidence, make it explicit; and (iii) that I have good reasons for supposing that the evidence is adequate, that is, I am affirming my willingness to have it subjected to rigorous scrutiny. Generally we should say that the distinction between belief and knowledge claims is one of degree only, assertions of both being performatives. Perhaps in claiming to know rather than to believe I am making a stronger public commitment. I may of course still be mistaken, but if I am there is no inconsistency between my original claim to knowledge and any subsequent denial made in the light of new evidence. It is in this respect that we must have regard to the consensus of a community utilizing a conceptual scheme (be it general or specialist), under 'ideal epistemic conditions', while at the same time allowing for change and development and subject to a normative concept of rationality (as Putnam argues). It might be argued that this account of 'knowledge' and 'truth' runs counter to ordinary usage. But for a satisfactory theory of knowledge we must jettison the rather narrow usage of 'know' as *entailing* that we cannot be wrong. It is only on the basis of this new kind of approach that we can make sense of, say, both the medieval monk's claim to know that the Sun goes round the Earth and of our post-Copernican assertion that we know the Earth revolves around the Sun

(contrary to superficial appearances). We do, however, want to say our evidence is better. Criteria for being 'better' here might relate to experimental data, coherence with other aspects of our epistemological and conceptual scheme, scope, simplicity and so on. This raises further issues about science: how evidence changes and is to be assessed, whether there is progress, and whether scientific knowledge is always provisional. (Many of these points will be looked at in Ch. 9). So we can now say that, while we may have adopted a different 'stance' when we assert our knowledge rather than our belief, we have avoided both mental state theories and the tying of belief and knowledge to evidence rather than to performances.

(2) The notion of certainty can be re-admitted – but as a necessary not a sufficient condition. By this we mean: (a) that our feeling of certainty about the truth of a proposition (or statement) does not by itself justify our claim to knowledge (we can be mistaken); and (b) that the claim should not be made unless that feeling be present, for certainty would naturally be expected to arise from a judicious consideration of the evidence and from the recognition that it conforms to conventionally accepted criteria.

(3) This latter point raises a further issue – and this brings us back to the problem of 'local' scepticism. We are not committed to providing evidence of one particular kind or to meeting one specific criterion. What is appropriate will vary with context. Different standards will apply when we are claiming to know that '2 + 2 = 4', that there is a brown table in the room, or that God exists. Standards may change in the course of time. Moreover, these standards must be decided through a 'public' consensus (of scientists, historians, 'everyday' persons and so on, as the case may be). If I were to invoke a new criterion unilaterally, I should then be operating with a 'private' sense of 'knowledge' and would experience difficulty in convincing others of the acceptability of my claims. This is not to say that criteria cannot be made less stringent but that this can only be done through agreement and convention. If we changed the rules on our own, the situation would be rather like an examination candidate who, on being told that she has failed, says 'No, I haven't; I have decided that the pass mark should be 20 per cent, and I have 25 per cent'. To go to the other extreme, by making a criterion more stringent we could equally decide that knowledge is not possible at all. But in the social context, this would clearly be unreasonable if not self-refuting. [Compare Ayer, *Problem of Knowledge*, ch. I(v).] 'Global' scepticism is untenable. As Wittgenstein argues [*On Certainty*], there has to be a framework which is indubitable (albeit temporarily – he is not subscribing to 'foundationalism') for there to be doubt at all [519]. Wittgenstein also uses the metaphors of the river bed along which our thoughts flow [99] and of the unchanging scaffolding of our thoughts [211]. What is permanent may change, but for there to be change there has to be permanence. Be that as it may, we have not yet dealt adequately with 'local' scepticism. So now in the remaining two sections of this chapter we shall examine further the problem of local scepticism and look at the scope of knowledge in relation firstly to our perception of the external world, and secondly to our knowledge of the 'self'.

5.10 Knowledge of the external world

Reading: Russell, *The Problems of Philosophy*, chs I–IV; Ayer, *The Problem of Knowledge*, ch. 3; Ryle, *The Concept of Mind*, ch. VII. You will also find it useful to have some first-hand acquaintance with the works of Locke, *Essay Concerning Human Understanding*; Berkeley, *Three Dialogues* and *Principles of Human Knowledge*; Hume, *Treatise of Human Nature* and *An Enquiry Concerning Human Understanding*; and Kant, *Prolegomena* and *Critique of Pure Reason* (Transcendental Aesthetic, and Transcendental Analytic – (I) Analytic of Concepts, (II) Analytic of Principles)

'Naïve' realism

As 'ordinary' people in our everyday lives (that is, when we are not wearing our philosophical hats) we usually accept without question: (a) that there is a world outside (of which our bodies are part), and (b) that the world is pretty much as we experience it through our senses. This is sometimes called the Naïve Realist view. But a moment's reflection should make us pause and be more critical. Things often seem different from what we 'know' them to be really like. For example, railway lines appear to be converging to a point in the distance. How do we know that they are really parallel all the time? We could of course walk along them and see for ourselves. A sceptically-minded critic, however, might point out that the convergence is still there further along the line. To refute him we might then suggest he travel in a train. If the lines are really converging, then the train would have to become thinner and thinner and so would the passengers! This is clearly absurd. We have strong evidence, therefore, to support our claim to knowledge, and we could invoke theories of perspective to account for the **illusion**. Similarly we might say that a stick looks bent under the water but we know it is really straight (dive under the surface and have a look). We can explain the refraction in terms of a theory about the behaviour of light passing from one medium (air) to another (water). There are also other circumstances when we have an experience that does not seem to correspond to anything real at all. We may have hallucinations if we have drunk too much. It is possible, moreover, for neurosurgeons to stimulate parts of the brain which causes us to have similar experiences. It is clear that a 'naïve' realist position is difficult to maintain.

The causal theory

Consider once more Russell's description of the table [*Problems*, ch. I; compare 5.5 above], or of the coin [ch. III]. The table appears to have a different shape or colour according to the standpoint of the observer. A coin may now look circular, now elliptical. Is one of these shapes or colours the 'true' or 'real' shape (in the sense that a stick is really straight but appears bent when put under the water surface)? Russell's answer is that none of the appearances is the real one; the appearances are but a sign of the 'reality' lying behind them. To take another example, when we look up at the sky at night we see a multitude of twinkling lights. Scientists (especially philosophically-minded ones) will tell us that what we are actually seeing is not the stars themselves but the light produced by them hundreds, even millions of years ago. This is because light takes time to travel, and although it moves very fast (300,000 kilometres per second!) the distances of many stars to the Earth are so vast that the travelling time becomes quite considerable. Thus we are no more acquainted directly with the actual stars than we are with the 'real' table or coin. As you have already seen [*Problems of Philosophy*, chs II and III], for Russell these real things are called 'physical objects', existing in a real and public space, as opposed to the 'sense-data', which constitute the immediate experience of the percipients and exist in their apparent and private spaces. We do not have direct acquaintance with these physical objects; we know them only through inference and by description (knowledge of truths). But although physical objects are unknown to us in their intrinsic nature, we have good reason to suppose, says Russell, that there are correspondences between the spatial relations of physical objects and the sense-data. If we have two sets of sense-data which we identify as two houses, and one set is on our left while the other set is on our right, we may assume that the physical objects themselves are similarly located in the public space. Likewise we may presume that if one object looks blue and another object looks red, there is some corresponding difference between the physical objects themselves; or if two objects both look blue, then there is most probably a corresponding similarity in the objects themselves, in some cases at least. His position is summarized in ch. III:

> We can know the properties of the relations required to preserve the correspondence with sense-data but we cannot know the nature of the terms between which the relations hold.

The representative theory

Russell's conclusions are on the whole cautious. The representative theory, proposed by Locke, is an important earlier form of the causal theory and is more dogmatic. [See his *Essay Concerning Human Understanding*, Book II, especially ch. VIII; and read again the brief summary of his account of knowledge given in 5.3 above] Locke made use of a distinction between **primary** and **secondary qualities** which can be traced back to the Greek Atomists and was revived by scientists such as Galileo and Boyle. It was used also by Descartes. [Read again his discussion on the wax in *Meditation* II.] Primary qualities, according to Locke, are inherent in physical objects themselves (he talks of physical objects as 'real essences'). They are permanent and cannot themselves be perceived, only inferred. But they do cause ideas in the mind of the perceiver which resemble or represent the objects. As examples of primary qualities Locke cites shape, extension and motion. Secondary qualities, which are appearances such as colour, taste, warmth and coldness, on the other hand, are no more than *powers* of objects to produce ideas in us. They do not exist in the objects, but only in perception itself. Such qualities vary with the location and circumstances of the observer. The ideas which secondary qualities (powers) give rise to do not therefore resemble anything in the objects themselves. (The similarities between Locke's account and Russell's, as well as the differences, should be apparent to you.)

There is no doubt that there is some support for such a theory in the findings of science. Classical or Newtonian science, for example, is concerned with what can be measured; and this has tended to result in the dissolution of our world of colours and sounds, scents and tastes, into a world of molecular structures which are in themselves devoid of all such secondary qualities. (Compare Russell's analysis of the table.) But there are serious difficulties with a causal theory of this kind. These are best considered by examining the theory put forward by Locke's successor, the Irish philosopher George **Berkeley** (1685–1753).

The idealist theory

The term idealism is perhaps a little misleading. [See Russell, ch. IV, and Ayer, *Language, Truth and Logic*, ch. VII, 'Realism and Idealism'.] In its widest sense it is used to refer to the doctrine 'that whatever exists, or at any rate whatever can be known to exist, must be in some sense mental' [Russell, ch. IV]. Despite their differing premises, the philosophers Leibniz, Berkeley and Hegel would thus all be regarded as idealists. (Some commentators, most notably H. Bracken, however, have interpreted Berkeley as an 'Irish Cartesian'. You might bear this in mind as you read through the next paragraph. Refer back also to 5.2.)

Berkeley's position can be summarized as follows: (1) Everything we are aware of is an 'idea'. Ideas include sensations, perceptions, images, concepts and thoughts. But he rejects Locke's 'abstract general ideas'; we perceive only particulars or 'sensibles'. The notion of an abstract general idea, he says, is incoherent, because it would either have to contain incompatible qualities belonging to a variety of particulars or would be devoid of characteristics altogether. (*Note that Berkeley's criticisms of Locke have been widely discussed and their acceptability questioned.) (2) Locke's distinction between primary and secondary qualities cannot be maintained; primary qualities vary in much the same way as secondary qualities (great and small, swift and slow, for example, are relative). Moreover, the two 'types' of ideas are inseparable from each other (we cannot conceive of an extended body which is not coloured or possessed of some sensible quality). (3) We have no means of getting outside our experiences to check whether primary qualities are inherent in a material substance. Furthermore, the notion of a 'material substance' is incoherent, as it corresponds to no perceivable idea. Underlying these objections is Berkeley's positive doctrine that the only entites we may admit as existing are (a) active minds or spirits, and (b) the ideas contained in those minds. The 'being' of ideas thus consists in their being perceived. As he puts it himself in Latin: '*esse est percipi*'. According to Berkeley's philosophy, Russell's table would therefore be understood as being a 'collection of ideas' in the mind. This immediately raises the question: in whose mind? And closely associated with this is the problem of what happens when the person perceiving the table leaves the room: does the table thereby cease to exist? Berkeley's answer is that it does not, because the world is perceived continually by God. We cannot discuss his arguments for God's existence here, but what Berkeley seems to be saying is that the collection of ideas constituting a particular object exists in the mind of God, and that each individual human mind is vouchsafed an experience of this collection under the appropriate spatial and temporal conditions. Thus, when I walk into the room God 'excites' into my mind the relevant ideas, and I see the table. In this way Berkeley claimed to have overcome the scepticism implicit in Locke's representative theory and to have put forward an account of perception in accord with common sense.

*Comments

Berkeley's conviction that he had set out a common-sense view of the world and our experience of it is, to say the least, dubious. The redoubtable Dr Samuel Johnson kicked a stone and declared, 'I refute him thus'. To be fair to Berkeley, one must say that Johnson's reaction, although understandable, shows an ignorance of Berkeley's conclusion. Nevertheless there does seem to be something odd about it. What then should be said about his 'idealism'?

(1) It is clear that his account of perception stands or falls with the tenability of his assumption that God exists. If there is no Divine mind or spirit there can be no ideas or sensible things. (We shall consider the question of God's existence in ch. 9.)

(2) Given that there is a God, Berkeley is still faced with a difficulty concerning the relationship between my ideas and the ideas in God's mind. God, he says, has implanted or 'excited' them in my mind. Are they then unique to me? Or am I in some sense participating in the Divine vision? If God implants similar ideas (for example, of the table) in the minds of other people, but differing slightly (and thus defining their respective standpoints), is His idea of the table the sum total of all these particular sets of ideas; or if not, then in what respects does His idea differ from ours? It would seem that Berkeley must either commit himself to some form of Platonism or fall back on an idealist version of Locke's scepticism: the table in itself is mental rather than material but we are ignorant of its true nature.

(3) Perhaps the main weakness in Berkeley's 'immaterialism' is his terminology. It has been argued with justification that his use of the term 'idea' is much too wide, and that the phrase 'in the mind' is ambiguous. When I look at the table what I actually see is certainly in some sense *dependent* on me – on my 'mind' or sense organs, as well as on such factors as where I am standing, what kind of light is shining on it and so on. But to argue from this to the assertion that the ideas are '*in*' my mind (or God's) is open to question.

Considerations such as these led later philosophers to adopt different strategies to deal with the problem of perception. We shall look at two: **Phenomenalism** and **Scientific realism**.

Phenomenalism

Berkeley's successor Hume rejected any invocation of a deity in whose mind 'ideas' might be contained. For him we have knowledge only of impressions (from which ideas, that is, images and so on, are derived) (see 5.3). We might be tempted to suppose that permanent objects exist, but in the last analysis all we are entitled to claim is that a 'physical' object is a group (a 'congeries') of sense-experiences. The nineteenth century philosopher John Stuart Mill went further by asserting that the material world consists of 'groups of permanent possibilities of sensation'. Such a notion, however, does seem to be rather obscure, and takes us no further in our attempt to understand the nature of external reality. His account is sometimes called 'factual phenomenalism'. In our own century an alternative version of the attempt to reduce objects to 'sensa' (that is, sense-data, impressions, 'ideas') and so on was developed by, in particular, A.J. Ayer [in his *Language, Truth and Logic* – but later to be criticized and discarded in his *Problem of Knowledge*]. The central aim of his 'linguistic phenomenalism' is to provide a translation of *statements* about **material objects** into *statements* about **sensa**. A material object is thus in some sense a **logical construction** from sensory data. When I say that I see a table, I therefore mean that I see certain shapes and colours, feel edges and surfaces, and experience particular smells. (A similar view was held by Russell in some of his later writings.) The advantage of such a theory is that it introduces the possibility of talking about one's experiences of facts in two different ways. So while in everyday conversation we might talk about seeing a table, a switch to the language of sensa would make it possible to fend off any attack by a sceptic questioning the nature or existence of material things. Thus, we could make a statement about our sense-contents which we could regard as certain ('I am seeing a red, shiny, circular patch', for example), without committing ourselves to a more questionable assertion about the nature or existence of a 'material thing' (that is, a tomato). Another advantage would seem to be that the problem of a physical object's permanence could also be avoided. The assertion 'There is a table in the next room' could be translated into a statement such as 'If you went into the next room, you would be aware of a round shape, a flat surface, a brown colour and so on'.

*Comments

You should read carefully what Ayer has to say about phenomenalism in *The Problem of Knowledge*, ch. 3(vi). See also Ryle, *Concept of Mind*, VII(5). We shall make two general points here for you to think about:

(1) The phenomenalist claims that statements about physical or material objects are to be translated into statements about sense-data or sense-contents. However, it is doubtful whether this translation can be completely performed. We may say, for example, that 'I see the table' means 'I see an elliptical, shiny, brown, path': but is this sufficient? Are there not other features of my experience (other sensa) which are equally descriptive? How can I be sure that I have listed sufficient sensa to describe the 'table' experience so as to eliminate ambiguity and secure uniqueness of reference?

(2) Sense-content statements for the phenomenalist seem to be put forward to ensure certainty and to avoid commitment to the postulation of entities such as 'material objects'. But it is an open question whether it is possible to refer to 'sense-contents' without presupposing the existence of publicly-observable objects. (Compare the discussion in 5.2, 5.3 and 5.5 above.) As Ryle says, 'we cannot describe sensations themselves without employing the vocabulary of common objects'. And he goes even further, claiming that the very notion of sensible objects is absurd, because they are not things which can be *observed*. Observation (looking at, listening to and so on) applies properly only to things like trees, men, or gate-posts. It might be said that it is only after we have looked at and identified an object that we come to describe its features or qualities in terms of a sensation language. So far from being translatable from a material object language, a sense-content language is parasitic on it.

Scientific realism

(This theory is associated particularly with J.J.C. Smart.) If you ask a scientist to describe the 'real' table, he will probably talk about molecules of various chemicals as being composed of atoms of chemical elements such as carbon, hydrogen and oxygen. The atoms likewise are made up out of smaller particles (protons, neutrons and electrons). We do not of course observe these particles, or even the larger molecules. What we actually see is the result of light waves falling on and being partially reflected off a surface consisting of millions of molecules bonded together. The phenomenalist would argue that such entities as atoms or electrons are unobservable, and would attempt to 'construct' statements the scientist makes about experimental observation out of statements made about 'particles'. (Such observations statements would of course have to be translated in their turn into statements about 'sense-contents'.) However, given the difficulties associated with any attempt to carry out a phenomenalist reduction, which we referred to in the previous paragraph, scientific realism must be taken seriously. We accept that there are things in the world outside us, and yet it would seem that we cannot penetrate to their 'inner nature' through direct sense-experience (sight, touch). Do not the scientist's experiments give us the knowledge we require? The postulation of atoms and their constituent particles, electromagnetic waves and so on enables us to make verifiable predictions about the appearances of objects, the reactions between chemicals, changes in temperature of things and many other phenomena. Moreover, other experiments involving measurements of various kinds suggest to us that atoms and molecules are bonded together in particular ways or, under specified conditions, move around. And again this makes predictions possible about our everyday experiences, which can be shown to be fulfilled. (To take a simple example: the molecular theory can help us to understand how certain rigid solids when heated turn into liquids which flow.)

*Comments and criticisms

There are two particular difficulties which Scientific Realism would have to contend with:

(1) The account that science offers is changing and, arguably, incomplete. The nature of the world as described by eighteenth century science is in many respects quite different from that postulated by Quantum Theory, for example. We have no reason, however, for supposing that the insights of twentieth century science are the last word; there is much we do not understand about the universe, and it is certainly possible that modern particle theory could undergo radical modifications in the light of new discoveries. We should therefore be wary of grounding our *knowledge* in scientific accounts. A scientific realist might counter by admitting that the scientific account of the world does indeed change, but that in the course of time it approximates ever more closely to the 'truth'. Atoms, for example, used to be no more than theoretical postulates. But today they can actually be seen through powerful microscopes. This is a fair point. However, it is possible that there are limits – not to knowledge as such but to what can be perceived 'objectively'; if some of the findings of modern physics are correct, then we must admit that *sub-atomic* particles cannot and could *never* be observed because they are affected by the very process of observation. Furthermore we should have to be very clear about what criteria are being appealed to when the claim is made that science is approximating more and more closely to the 'truth'.

(2) Some people would claim that there is another danger associated with locating 'reality' uniquely in a scientific world-view: the familiar things of everyday life become in some sense only 'appearances'. As ordinary people we still hanker after the common-sense view. We feel more at home with the familiar world of trees, tables and people, in which we actually live. How far such a view is *philosophically* acceptable is a matter for you to think about in the light of the discussion in this section. But at the very least, it might be said, no account of perception can ignore the claims of our everyday experience.

Transcendental idealism

You will remember from your reading of the discussion in 5.4 that, according to Kant, on account of the structuring of our experience by the sensibility and the understanding, we necessarily perceive the world in a particular way. So rather than our having to conform to the external world, the world of experience conforms to our own faculties. Kant calls this his 'Copernican Revolution'. He sets out his arguments concerning the forms of intuition in the *Transcendental Aesthetic*; while in the *Transcendental Analytic* he examines three issues concerning the forms or categories of understanding: (1) what the basic forms are; (2) why they are needed for experience (this involves his 'deduction' which he argues will justify our use of them); and (3) how they are used. His arguments are complex and demanding. We shall not therefore consider them here. It is sufficient to say that the upshot of Kant's thesis is that he dismisses both 'pure' realism (the view that we experience things-in-themselves, objects as they actually are in the world) and 'subjective' idealism (the theory that external things exist only in or for minds). He calls his own position 'Transcendental Idealism' (or 'Empirical Realism'), according to which we must accept that what we actually experience are phenomena, things as they appear to us under the *a priori* forms of intuition and understanding. We must, however, suppose that there is a 'transcendental object' (Kant designates this as 'X'), that is, a real thing which exists in the world before we experience it and to which our representations can be referred in accordance with 'rules'. After showing how the *a priori* categories can be applied to *sensible* appearances, he argues that because we are conscious of existing in time there must be something permanent underlying the changes of our perceptions and which 'fixes' our own existence in time.

The relevance of this theory to the question of our knowledge of the external world is clear. We do not know 'noumena' – objects as they are in themselves. We perceive things *as experienced entities – phenomena*; that is to say, whatever is there 'outside' us is known to us only through the structuring 'filters' of our sensible and cognitive faculties. And it is within this framework that the conventional distinction between 'real' and 'illusory' has to be accommodated.

*Comments and criticisms

Some mention was made earlier of problems associated with Kant's account of judgements. There are also difficulties with his classification and 'deduction' of the categories. So far as the present section is concerned, there are two other issues that should be mentioned:

(1) If, as Kant holds, space and time are 'forms of intuition' which are as it were built into our experiences by virtue of our mental faculties, it would seem to follow that they do not apply to 'things-in-themselves' (though of course on his premises we cannot know anything about such noumenal entities). At the same time it seems natural and reasonable to suppose that the actual world consists of distinct objects (including ourselves), separated from each other, and constantly undergoing change. Moreover, the scientific world-view is predicated on the assumption that there is such an 'objective' world which behaves as described and predicted by scientific laws. (**Note**: there are some radical dissenters from this position however – see 8.4.) Kant of course wants to avoid the Newtonian view that space is a kind of empty box within which things move around; and his position is close to that of Leibniz, for whom space is the total set of relations between phenomena, that is, perceived modifications of simple substances ('monads'). But it is questionable whether his 'subjectivist' position can be reconciled with our common-sense and scientific views.

(2) Following on from this first criticism is another, which concerns Kant's fundamental distinction between phenomena and noumena. It is generally accepted that there is in fact a serious ambiguity within the *Critique of Pure Reason*. Sometimes he talks of noumena as non-spatial things-in-themselves, which we can know nothing about; the world therefore consists of phenomena *and* noumena [see A 30 and 371]. Elsewhere [A 255, 257] it seems that he does not regard noumena as objects at all. Rather the concept is introduced as a limit to show the impossibility of our going beyond experience; the world consists *only* of phenomena. It is difficult to decide between these two positions. But although Kant himself does not seem to have resolved the issue explicitly, it has been

argued that he tended towards the weaker ('limit') view but found it difficult to shake himself free from the more Berkeleyan view of objects as representations which cannot exist independently of our perceptions. Kant's position is then, roughly, that we perceive a real world but it can be known to us only as it appears to us – under the forms of sensibility and structured by the forms of the understanding. However, the problem remains of scientific laws which apply to the real world and yet are in some sense constituted by ourselves. This problem will become clearer in the discussion of causation in 11.3.

Conclusion

We shall now try to summarize the main points of the general thesis to which we have been led in the course of the preceding discussion. No definitive or indisputable 'theory' of perception is offered; and you should be prepared to consider the following points critically:

(1) As 'ordinary' people we back up our claim to knowledge of the external world by appealing to the evidence of our senses – in particular that of sight: we *see* objects such as trees and tables, cats and dogs. In the absence of a sighting, or where there may be some doubt about the precise identity of something, we *listen* to sounds, *smell* scents and *touch* surfaces. To refer to objects we use a common language, in a 'public' forum or framework. We make statements such as 'the tree is green', 'the sugar tastes sweet'.

(2) The more philosophically-minded person is aware that the actual appearances of publicly-observable objects vary according to circumstances. The tree may *look* blue in the early morning; the stick may *look* bent under water; the water may *feel* warm if your finger is particularly cold but cool if your finger has been on a hot surface; food may *taste* different after a curry. It is then argued that while for most everyday purposes we operate with conventionally acceptable criteria of *normality* (trees are 'green' in daylight, water at 40 degrees Celsius is 'warm'), our 'sense-contents' may vary. We assume that the content of our experience depends on three factors: (a) an external cause (the *material* object), (b) the perceiver himself, and (c) the conditions under which the interaction between the two takes place (light, distance, mood, or physical state of the perceiver and so on). Whether our assumption is tantamount to knowledge must depend on what is publicly acceptable. My friends *know* that I have not seen a *real* pink elephant because they have just seen me finish my tenth whisky! We agree that the stick is not *really* bent because we can measure it in the water. We accept that the star we see is not *actually* 'there' *now*.

(3) The 'material' object postulated in (2) is now handed over to the scientist, who endeavours: (a) to describe its nature or structure in terms of 'models' and 'theories', and (b) to 'explain' how such an object when interacting with the human brain and sense-organs under specified conditions can give rise to the sensory data we call appearances (whether veridical or illusory).

Perhaps generally we can say that Kant is correct when he says we perceive the real world but only as an appearance. It is reasonable to accept that our perception is constrained both by the nature of the objects from which the stimuli impacting on our sense-organs emanate and by the *modus operandi* of those organs themselves. But this does not commit us to a Kantian account of space and time and the categories, which seems to be incompatible with scientific realism [at least in the *Critique of Pure Reason*; some attempt to deal with this problem seems to have been recognized by Kant in his later *Metaphysical Foundations of Natural Science*: but unfortunately this cannot be considered here]. There should be no inconsistency between the claims made in (1), (2) and (3) above; for in our everyday references to things, in our descriptions of the ways in which they appear to us, and in scientific accounts of the world in terms of atoms, waves and so on, we are using different 'levels' or 'areas' of language and explanation, each of which is appropriate to the context and purpose of the description. In each case the claim to knowledge can be admitted: but the conventionally accepted criteria are different. (Explanation and the question of scientific truth will be examined in Ch. 8.)

5.11 The self and others

Reading: Descartes, *Meditations*, II; Hume, *Treatise on Human Nature*, Book IV, Sec. VI; Ryle, *The Concept of Mind*, ch. VI; Ayer, *Language, Truth and Logic*, ch. VII; Sartre, *Existentialism and Humanism* and *Being and Nothingness*, especially Parts II and III

Knowledge of the self

What knowledge can we have of our own self? This cannot be answered without also considering what is meant by the 'self'. The two questions are in fact inseparable: to put forward an account of what the self is presupposes that we have the knowledge to justify that account. We shall start by looking at what may be thought of as the 'ordinary man's' or 'common-sense' view.

This view owes much to the dualism of Descartes. You will remember (see 5.2) that he supposed man to consist of two quasi-substances, mind and body. He discusses the mind in *Meditation* II and refers to the 'unity' of mind and body in *Meditation* VI:

> Nature likewise teaches me by these sensations of pain, hunger, thirst, etc., that I am not only lodged in my body as a pilot in a vessel, but that I am besides so intimately conjoined, and as it were intermixed with it, that my mind and body compose a certain unity.

This sort of philosophical standpoint immediately raises a number of difficulties. (1) If mind and body are different sorts of substances (the latter material, extended in space, explicable in terms of 'mechanical' causes and scientific laws; the former immaterial, having no extension, and to be understood in terms of 'final' causes), then how do we account for their interaction? What is the relationship between them? (2) How are we to understand personal identity? Does it belong to the mind, to the body, or to the 'unity' of both? Discussion about the nature of mind can be left to 11.3, but it is useful to mention here that much post-Cartesian philosophy has been concerned with finding a solution to the dualist theory. (*You should study carefully Descartes' mechanistic account of the interaction between mind and body in the Sixth Meditation.) Thus some rationalist successors of Descartes suggested that God intervenes on each occasion of human action to ensure that events in the mental realm are paralleled by corresponding behaviour in the physical world, or that He 'programmes' individuals so that events in the two realms will coincide (just as two different watches can be set so as always to show the same time). Berkeley, as we have seen, rejected the idea of matter and saw all things (collections of 'ideas') as being 'in' minds or spirits – and ultimately 'in' the mind of God. As for Kant, he rejects the notion of soul except as an Idea (of pure reason), because we cannot argue from a concept to an actual existing unitary thinking substance. The soul cannot be simple, he says, because this attribute can apply only to an object that can be experienced. Nevertheless, he argues that if we are to think of an experience of an object both as being *mine* and a *unity*, there must be not only the 'transcendental object' (see above) but also a *sense* of a unifying 'self' to hold our perceptions together in the one experience (the 'manifold'). He talks of the 'transcendental unity of apperception' which is the source not only of the manifold but of the 'synthetic unity' of objects. So in conclusion he says that so far from the 'I think' being experienced, the self, as the transcendental unity of apperception, is a *presupposition* of all possible experience and cannot be known in itself.

Later 'idealist' philosophers, culminating in Hegel, argued that the Kantian theory was inconsistent and untenable: but whereas they (like the earlier rationalists) 'absorbed' the material world in Mind, other thinkers adopted a 'materialist' account, minds being explained in terms of or 'reduced to' matter. For Ryle, who explicitly sets out to demolish the 'dogma' or 'myth of the Ghost in the Machine', 'mind' and 'body' belong to different logical types. Minds do not 'exist' as bodies do. To talk of a mind is to talk about particular ways in which bodies do or can behave. In ch. I he writes:

> If my argument is successful, there will follow some interesting con-sequences. First the hallowed contrast between Mind and Matter will be dissipated, but dissipated not by either of the equally hallowed absorptions of Mind by Matter or of Matter by Mind, but in quite a different way. For the seeming contrast of the two will be shown to be as illegitimate as would be the contrast of 'she came home in a flood of tears' and 'she came home in a sedan chair'.

Ayer, in *Language, Truth and Logic* (as you might expect from your earlier study of his views on perception), seeks to avoid the problem of how minds relate to bodies by applying his technique of 'linguistic phenomenalism'. As he says in ch. VII:

> It should be clear . . . that there is no philosophical problem concerning the relationship of mind and matter, other than the linguistic problem of defining certain symbols which denote logical constructions in terms of symbols which denote sense-contents. The problems with which philosophers have vexed themselves in the past, concerning the possibility of bridging the 'gulf' between mind and matter in knowledge or in action, are all fictitious problems arising out of the senseless metaphysical conception of mind and matter, or minds and material things, as 'substances'.

We shall now consider the problem of personal identity. This can be put in the form of the question, 'How do I know I am the same person now as I was, say, twenty years ago?' Now of course there is an obvious ambiguity in our use of the word 'same'. Over a period of twenty years we must all of us have changed in many ways. Our hair may be grayer, our skin more wrinkled. We must have had many experiences, some happy, some sad, which in various ways have left their mark on us. Through observation or through reading we have probably deepened our knowledge of other people, of ourselves, or of the world in general. In one sense therefore we are no longer the same person. Indeed there are extreme cases – after brain surgery, or after serious mental illness, perhaps – when it might be particularly apt to talk of someone as being a different person (in the case of schizophrenia we might even talk of two or more 'persons' in one body!). But in a more 'normal' or everyday usage of 'same', we would all accept that despite the changes in our physical appearance and despite our experiences we are in a fundamental sense the same person. How do we justify our claim to *know* this? The criterion most often appealed to is that of **continuity**. This may be considered from two standpoints, which we may describe as the 'external' and the 'internal'. (It is tempting to use the terms 'mental' and 'physical', but we shall avoid these for the time being in view of the difficulty raised above concerning the interaction of mind and body.)

Consider 'external' continuity first. Suppose we look in the mirror each morning after we have got up. The image we see is familiar. We recognize ourselves. There are changes, it is true, but they are subtle and slow. The changes are obvious when we compare an image of ourselves now with that of a photograph taken twenty years earlier – still more so when we look at snaps of ourselves at school or in the pram. Now an objection can be raised here. Have we allowed for the possibility of error? Let us suppose we have a photograph of ourselves aged five but no other? Can we be sure that there have not been radical changes in our appearance since then? Should we not settle for the weaker claim – that we *believe* we are the same person? To answer this we can appeal to the testimony of (i) other people, and (ii) the evidence of our own memories. Thus people who have seen us grow up – parents, friends, teachers and so on – can assure us of our physical continuity; we have lived or worked with them in the same environment for many years. Moreover they have been able to associate a continuity of certain features of character, behaviour and speech with our changing but continuous physical appearances. For our part we can call on our memory images – which constitute our 'internal' continuity. We remember being with those people who provide us with the confirmatory testimony we seek, and we can remember particular occasions in our past history which took place when we were very young. We have of course also to remember who those people are! But it is not only ourselves who appeal to memory images. Our parents and friends must be equally reliant on their own memories when they assure us both of our 'sameness' and of the ways we have changed over the years. This of course raises the whole question of the reliability of memory itself. We do occasionally forget things, but on the whole we tend to take our memory for granted. Indeed, it is arguable that the notion of 'forgetting' presupposes a 'normal' standard of reliability. If memory is ever called in question, if we are uncertain, or if we are called to account, say, in a court of law, we then appeal to documentary evidence such as newspapers, diary entries and so on. But even here do we not presuppose the validity of memory? How otherwise could we know that an entry on a particular day *was* ours? (*You might also consider an even more fundamental question: whether our very use of language itself is not in some sense dependent on memory. How can we be sure that we are using words correctly, or that a term has not changed its meaning?)

Another problem has to be considered. We may well have grounds for claiming to know that we are 'internally' or 'externally' continuous. But how do we account for the continuity of memory images, or of what Ayer calls 'sense-contents'? What is the connecting thread? Is there a 'substantial ego' in which our images and sense-experiences somehow inhere and which we might 'intuit' in the manner of Descartes or Locke? This is rejected by Kant, for whom the idea of personal identity is itself just a representation and may be no more permanent than the thoughts it is supposed to hold together. Ayer too rejects any such '*ego*' or 'self'; such a substance is an entirely unobservable entity. It cannot be revealed in self-consciousness because this involves no more than the ability to remember one's earlier states as corresponding to sense-contents occurring in one's personal history. The existence of a substantive ego, says Ayer, is completely unverifiable. But it does not follow, he argues, that the self is an aggregate of sense-experience – a 'bundle of perceptions', as Hume puts it, between which no 'real connection' can be discerned. Rather, 'the self is reducible to sense-experiences in the sense that to say anything about the self is always to say something about sense-experiences'. And Ayer has made it clear that to refer to an object as a logical construction out of sense-contents is not to say that it is actually constructed out of those sense-contents, or that they are in any way parts of it, but that it is to express 'in a convenient, if somewhat misleading, fashion, the syntactical fact that all sentences referring to it are translatable into sentences referring to them'.

The (approximately Cartesian) view that we have direct knowledge of the self with our minds is also attacked by Ryle. He calls it the theory of 'the twofold Privileged Access'. By this is meant that the mind is: (a) constantly aware that something is happening 'inside' – or on its 'private stage' as Ryle puts it; (b) that it can also scrutinize some of its own states and operations (feelings, thoughts, volitions and so on) by some sort of 'non-sensuous perception'; and that these two 'powers' of awareness and non-sensuous perception (termed respectively 'consciousness' and 'introspection') are exempt from error. (Read Ryle's careful account in ch. VI, (2) and (3), of the different ways 'conscious', 'consciousness', and 'introspection' are actually used in everyday contexts or as technical terms in philosophical theories.) Ryle's main objection to the theory that minds have insight into their own workings through conscious mental 'happenings' is that 'there are no such happenings; there are no occurrences taking place in a second-status world, since there is no such status and no such world . . .'. But he also puts forward other objections which do not depend on rejection of the 'Ghost in the Machine' dogma. The most important are these: (1) To suppose that my being conscious of my mental states is to know them, or the necessary and sufficient ground for knowing them, is 'to abuse the logic and even grammar of the verb "to know" '. (Contrast this with Russell's 'knowledge by acquaintance' of things of the 'inner sense' – see 5.5.) (2) The theory would make it logically impossible for people to be mistaken about their mental states. (3) The theory can lead to an infinite regress. Suppose, for example, we are conscious of inferring a conclusion from premises. According to the theory, could we not ask whether we are conscious of being conscious of inferring – and so on? If so, then either we would have to admit an infinite number of 'layers' of consciousness or deny that the original states (constituting the outermost 'layer') are things we can be conscious of; in which case 'conscious' could no longer be used to define 'mental'.

Ryle goes on [VI, 3] to criticize the notion of introspection. Like Hume and Ayer, he argues that in 'introspection' we are really for the most part *retrospecting*; and this does not disclose any 'occult' happenings or give us a Privileged Access to facts of a special status. What then do we mean by 'self-knowledge' for Ryle? What does the word 'I' actually stand for? His answer [VI, 5 and 6] is that it does not stand for anything; for 'I', like other pronouns, is not a name. Pronouns are, he says, 'index words' which 'can indicate the particular person from whom the noise 'I' (or 'you' etc.), or the written mark "I" issues'. Moreover they are 'elastic'; they can be used in a variety of ways. In some cases 'I' can be replaced by 'my body' (as in 'I was warming myself before the fire'); while in other cases it cannot (for example, in 'I am annoyed'). Likewise in the statements 'I was just beginning to dream' and 'I caught myself just beginning to dream', 'I' is being used with a different logical force. Ryle refers to actions, the descriptions of which involve the 'oblique mention of other actions' (that is, *catching* oneself beginning to dream) as 'higher order actions'. It is in this way that Ryle seeks to account for what he calls 'the systematic elusiveness of 'I' and the 'partial non-parallelism' between the first-person pronoun and 'you' or 'he' [VI, 7]. To concern oneself about oneself is not to refer to or point to an occult 'self'; it is only 'to perform a higher order act, just as it is to concern oneself about anybody else'. Now reference to my own actions is different from my reference to yours because my referring also belongs to the same person referred to by 'I'. But in talking about an action of mine I can no more talk about my 'talking about the actions' than a book review can be a criticism of itself. Explanation of the 'elusive residuum' in terms of higher orders of actions, argues Ryle, removes the 'ultimate mystery'.

It is in the light of this kind of analysis that Ryle's own account of the 'Self' is to be understood. As he says in VI, 4:

> It has been argued from a number of directions that when we speak of a person's mind, we are not speaking of a second theatre of special-status incidents, but of certain ways in which some of the incidents of his one life are ordered. His life is not a double series of events taking place in two different kinds of stuff; it is one concatenation of events, the differences between some and other classes of which largely consist in the applicability or inapplicability to them of logically different types of law-propositions and law-like propositions. Assertions about a person's mind are therefore assertions of special sorts about that person. So questions about the relations between a person and his mind, like those about the relations between a person's body and his mind, are improper questions. They are improper in much the same way as is the question, 'What transactions go on between the House of Commons and the British Constitution?'

Self-knowledge for Ryle is thus knowledge of the various ways in which a *person* behaves, but with so-called 'mental' events being understood in terms of dispositions to behave or in terms of actual publicly-observable behaviour. Continuity, then, for both Ayer and Ryle would therefore seem to be confined to 'external' events or experiences.

*Comments and criticisms

In response to the somewhat similar approach of Ayer and Ryle to the problem of self-knowledge, two particular points should be considered:

(1) Let us suppose that they are both right to reject the Cartesian-type theory that we can 'introspect' or directly 'intuit' the Self. Does it follow that language describing 'inner' experiences *can* or *should* be translated into language referring to sense-experiences (Ayer); or that such 'inner' experiences *can* or *should* be understood in terms of dispositions of external behaviour (Ryle)? It should be noted that Ayer's proposed translation seems to be put forward largely in the interest of convenience. Maybe, he says, the self is not *actually* constructed out of sense-contents: but we can say nothing about it; its existence is unverifiable. However, the notion of verification is itself suspect both in its application and in relation to the theory of meaning (see 11.1). As for Ryle's solution, it is certainly open to question whether his procedure can be consistently carried through, not least because I can modify my behaviour in such a way as to lead others to make false inferences about my 'inner' states. (You might like to think up some examples. Consider also how Ryle might try to answer this objection. See also 5.6 above.)

(2) Ryle's introduction of the 'person' as the proper object of assertions – about both 'bodily' and 'mental' experiences – undoubtedly has merit. A similar position is held by P.F. Strawson. For him a person is

a type of entity such that *both* predicates ascribing states of consciousness *and* predicates ascribing corporeal characteristics, a physical situation etc., are equally applicable to a single individual of that single type.

[*Individuals*, p.104]

But Ryle's account can be accepted independently of his 'dispositional' theory; and this is because his notion of a person is in some respects rather limited. He would seem to leave out of his analysis any appreciation of the person as an *agent*, an autonomous being, or as a being with *moral responsibility*. While the rather simplistic intuitionism of Descartes may be rejected, we can certainly argue that we know ourselves in our *actions*, and from both an 'internal' and 'external' aspect. (Can this approach provide an answer to Ryle's 'infinite' regress' objection?) The possibility of moral choice also raises difficulties for descriptions of persons in terms of dispositions. And what account can be given of unconscious or subconscious activity? (This is another issue we cannot consider further here but which you might like to think about in the light of the above discussion. Some of these topics will be looked at in Chs 11 and 12.)

It does seem then that we can know ourselves in very much the same way as we know external objects. But yet we also seem to be in a fundamental sense more than bodies or special sorts of bodies: we are living organisms which have unique *characters*, that is, we can think, feel, hope, imagine and act in various ways which are definitive of each individual. Might we not go further and suggest that to know ourselves as persons presupposes the network of interrelationships we establish with *other people*? Something like this is proposed by a philosopher to be discussed briefly at the end of this chapter. But first we must say something about our knowledge of others.

Knowledge of others

If Ayer is right that all sense-experiences are private to a single self; that the sense-experiences of another person cannot form part of one's own experience; and that other people *are* 'logical constructions' out of *their* sense-experiences, then it would seem that one cannot have any grounds for believing in the existence of others. But Ayer denies that solipsism is a necessary consequence of his epistemology. Just as we reject Locke's notion of a 'material substratum' as metaphysical and yet can make meaningful assertions about material things, so can we have access to other people's experiences and 'empirical manifestations' without invoking any 'entity' lying 'behind' the sense-experiences in terms of which we define them:

And thus I find that I have as good a reason to believe in the existence of other people as I have to believe in the existence of material things. For in each case my hypothesis is verified by the occurrence in my sense-history of the appropriate series of sense-contents.

In this way Ayer claims to have avoided the difficulties presented by the so-called 'argument by analogy'. According to this, although one cannot observe the existence of other people (because sense-contents belong to one's own personal history), one can nevertheless *infer* their existence with a high degree of probability from one's own experiences. Thus, if I observe in the behaviour of a body a resemblance to my own body's behaviour, I am entitled to argue that the body is related to a 'self' (which I cannot observe) in the same way as my body is related to my own (observable) self. But this argument, says Ayer, is an attempt to answer the *logical* question, 'What good reason have I for believing in the existence of other people?', not the *psychological* question, 'What causes me to believe in the existence of other people?' It might be acceptable if the object 'underlying' the other body *could* be manifested in the observer's experience: but, says Ayer, this is not the case; it is a metaphysical object, and no argument can render probable the assertion that it exists.

What reason have we for supposing, on Ayer's thesis, that the 'others' we observe through the reduction of 'their' sense-experiences to our own are not in fact so many robots? The answer he gives is that we can distinguish between a conscious man and an unconscious machine by applying appropriate tests to their perceptible behaviour. A conscious object will exhibit 'the empirical manifestations of consciousness': a dummy or machine will not. [Compare Ryle's discussion in chs I(3) and II of *The Concept of Mind*.]

In conclusion, Ayer states that while each man's sense-experiences are private to himself, it does not follow that we cannot believe another person's experiences are qualitatively the same as our own. Indeed we have to define the content of another man's experiences in terms of what we can ourselves observe. It is in this sense that Ayer can talk of other people's sensations as being accessible to us. Likewise we have good reason for supposing that other people understand us and that we understand them, because we can observe the effects, which we regard as appropriate, on each other's actions. It follows that we can believe ourselves as conscious beings to inhabit a common world.

*Comments and criticisms

Ayer's solution to the problem of 'other persons' is undoubtedly plausible and is acceptable in so far as it avoids the Cartesian or Lockean commitment to an underlying 'self' lying 'behind' appearances. However, his account is not entirely satisfactory. You might like to consider the following points (compare the criticisms made above of Ayer's phenomenalism as applied to the problem of perception of objects in general):

(1) It can be argued that one mistake Ayer has made is to suppose that because a 'self behind the appearances' is inaccessible – indeed 'metaphysical' or 'fictitious' (because it could never be verified empirically) – the self must therefore be *constructed out of* those appearances. And he has made this mistake because he has accorded logical and epistemological priority to sense-experiences. But if we consider the context in which terms referring to qualities are actually employed, Ayer's position seems less tenable. We do not, for example, use 'red', 'round', 'large'

and so on in isolation; their use presupposes application to existent objects such as trees, tables – and people. Moreover, other terms such as 'happy', 'clever' and 'intelligent' ascribe characteristics specifically to persons. In other words, it is only because we take it for granted that the world is populated with objects (some of which are persons) that we can make proper use of descriptive terms.

(2) Ayer's 'logical constructionism' seems to fail for another reason. Let us suppose that another person is defined in terms of a set of sense-contents. Quite apart from the obvious point that such a definition could never be known, any statement ascribing some quality to that person would appear to be tautological. Consider, for example, the statement, 'John is thin and tall'. Now by 'John' we mean a set of sense-contents $a + b + c + \dots$. But these sense-contents must include 'thin' and 'tall'. So the statement becomes, '$a + b + c + \dots + thin + \dots + tall$ is thin and tall'. Furthermore, it is not clear how terms such as 'happy' or 'intelligent' can be accommodated in Ayer's theory; for there is no one set of observable phenomena which can be said to exhaust the meaning and application of such terms as applied to a particular individual. A similar objection may be made against Ryle's attempt to translate 'mental' descriptions into actual or hypothetical dispositional terms.

Conclusion

It would seem then that we do have good grounds for our claim to know that there are other people and to know something about them (and to know they are not robots). We see them and recognize them as persons. We communicate with them. They give us information about themselves, either explicitly or implicitly by the ways they behave towards us and to others in the public community. It is only when we have this information that we are able to use descriptive language correctly. Of course our experiences are in a trivial sense 'private'. My seeing someone as pale, or my interpretation of that person as being frightened or in pain, is *mine*. Likewise, it is as much a matter of the logic of the term 'pain' as of the fact that we are spatially and temporally separated that I cannot experience *your* pain. But what allows me to refer to paleness, fear, or pain is publicly observable. We do not have to invoke a 'hidden self'. But neither do we have to resort to the subterfuge of phenomenalistic reductionism. The presentations of paleness, fear and so on *are* the ways in which a particular person appears to us in given circumstances.

The self and the other

Before ending this chapter we shall say something about the contribution made to the problem by a thinker who has worked in a radically different tradition from that common to the philosophers we have been considering so far. Jean-Paul Sartre (1905–80) was both an eminent French novelist and per-haps the best-known representative of the philosophical movement known as **existentialism**. However, he was also strongly influenced by the German philosopher Edmund Husserl (1859–1938), the founder of **phenomenology** –

which has been central in the development of twentieth century continental thought. So to understand Sartre we need to look at a few of the principal features of Husserl's philosophy, in particular his concept of **intentionality** and his method of **bracketing**.

Intentionality, as conceived of by Husserl, is supposed to be broadly a characteristic of acts (some being 'physical', others 'mental') in so far as they involve activity and are 'directed' towards and relate to some 'object'. The object may or may not exist: what I see or kick out at, that is, what I 'intend' could be a hallucination (like Macbeth's dagger) – see also 11.3. As for 'bracketing', this is a suspending of belief (Husserl calls it the *epoché*) in the actual existence of the intended object. We then use the object as an imaginative example (he talks of 'free imaginative variation', which involves the adding or subtracting of predicates contained in its description) whereby we can come to intuit the 'essence' or 'general structure' of the intended object and similar objects. Husserl calls this process a transcendental-phenomenological reduction, that is, a 'leading back' to the phenomena themselves. In addition to revealing the essences of objects this method gives us also the certain and indubitable existence of what Husserl calls the 'transcendental ego' or pure consciousness as the foundation of the world of experience.

*Comments

All this seems to have something in common with what Descartes was attempting to do and suggests a kind of epistemological foundationalism. There has, however, been a great deal of debate among Husserl scholars as to whether his philosophy is best interpreted in Cartesian terms. Husserl, at least in his earlier work, said that his thought could be correctly described as Transcendental Idealism (though not in any Berkeleyan sense). But while arguably his account avoids the problem raised by Descartes (for Husserl the transcendental ego is neither a thinking substance in which thoughts inhere nor the stream of thoughts themselves), he came to accept that there were difficulties with his approach which seemed to attribute an independent existence to the transcendent ego as separable from the empirical self. In his later work he came to modify his thesis and redefined the transcendental ego, arguing that it is correlative to what he called the '**life-world**'. Similarly the phenomenal world itself became the correlate of the 'intersubjective community' of individuals instead of being that which exists in a transcendental reduction of a given individual. This lends support to those scholars who think of Husserl more as a common-sense realist. (Perhaps there is something comparable here to Wittgenstein with his notion of a foundational 'scaffolding', as mentioned earlier.)

How then does Sartre respond to Husserl? He is in agreement with the critique (made by both Husserl and phenomenalists) of dualist theories which suppose there to be a 'self' lying 'behind' appearances. But he is equally critical of the 'monism' of thinkers who attempt to reduce (not in the Husserlian sense) the self to appearances or to behaviour. He also utilizes the notion of intentionality. But whereas Husserl 'bracketed' the existence of intended objects and confined himself to an examination of them *qua* mental phenomena and 'essences' (though Husserl did in fact also develop a complex ontology of essences), Sartre explicitly argued that consciousness demands that such objects have 'being'. He refers to them as existing 'in themselves' (*en soi*). But he also says that phenomenological consciousness points back to a 'pre-reflective' consciousness. Here Sartre reinterprets the Cartesian ego: the self is now understood as an *agent*, an *active* being, a being 'for itself' (*pour soi*), which is characterized by its capacity to 'intend' or 'mean'. This relates further to the central tenet of Sartre and other existentialists that 'existence is prior to essence', which is discussed in *Existentialism and Humanism* and more extensively in his major work *Being and Nothingness*. Now conscious being for Sartre is conceived as setting itself off against everything that constitutes the 'world' – things 'in themselves' including its own body and past experiences. This 'setting-off' is thought of as 'negating'; and as a result human consciousness introduces a 'hole', a 'nothingness', or 'non-being' into being-in-itself. There is thus a 'gap' between the *en-soi* and the *pour-soi*. It does not follow from this that Sartre is committed to scepticism so far as the existence of others is concerned. We have referred to the 'intentionality' of being-for-itself. But does this establish the existence of other *minds*? Sartre believes it does – but not through an appeal to any argument by analogy. Rather he invokes the notion of 'inter-subjectivity' based on our experience of our own *feelings*. Thus, when we feel shame, guilt, embarrassment and the like, the existence of others is presupposed: such experiences involve our considering ourselves as being observed and treated as an object by another consciousness – an '*autrui*'. Such an account of other minds is implicit in these remarks in *Existentialism and Humanism*:

> Contrary to the philosophy of Descartes, contrary to that of Kant, when we say 'I think' we are attaining to ourselves in the presence of the other, we are just as certain of the other as we are aware of ourselves. Thus the man who discovers himself directly in the *cogito* also discovers all the others, and discovers them as a condition of his own existence. He recognizes that he cannot be anything (in the sense in which one says one is spiritual, or that one is wicked or jealous) unless others recognize him as such. I cannot obtain any truth whatsoever about myself, except through the mediation of another. The other is indispensable to my existence, and equally so to any knowledge I can have of myself.

Sartre admits there is a major conflict here between the subjective and free self-conscious self and its recognition of itself as an object. This issue was taken up by his friend and colleague Maurice Merleau-Ponty (1908–61). He accepted the Cartesian primacy of the thinking self and also Husserl's *epoché*, but he claimed that the phenomenological reduction led back not to a separated transcendental consciousness or ego but to the 'lived experience' of what he called the 'body-subject'. Rejecting Sartre's sharp dualism of the *pour soi* and *en soi*, he argued that in perception we find ourselves already embodied and active in the 'life-world' which is a domain of intersubjectivity. Knowledge of the self and of the other are thus intimately connected in a 'dialectic of ambiguity', by which he means that knowledge is never complete.

*Merleau-Ponty is a significant figure in French thought whose merits as a philosopher are only now being more widely recognized – not least by many philosophers working in the 'analytic' tradition. His later utilization of a 'structuralist' theory of language raises a serious critical problem concerning the access of the body-subject to the 'other'. Unfortunately limitations of space prohibits an extensive treatment of his work. However, you will find further references to both Merleau-Ponty and Sartre in Chs 11 and 12; and Ch. 11 also contains a short account of structuralism. If you want to study the philosophy of Merleau-Ponty, you are referred to the Reading list below.

QUESTIONS

A. Texts

*1 Explain and examine critically Descartes' method of 'hyperbolic' doubt.

*2 Explain what Descartes means by '*cogito, ergo sum*'. What does it achieve? What are the philosophical difficulties with it?

3 Why is Descartes more certain of himself as a thinking thing than of himself as possessing a body?

4 Discuss the Cartesian criterion of truth.

5 Descartes identified three substances: *res cogitans, res divina* and *res extensa*. How are these substances related? How successful was Descartes' account of their relations? [IB, specimen, 2000]

6 What conclusion does Descartes draw from his discussion of the wax? Is it justified?

7 State, with illustration and critical comment, Descartes' threefold classification of ideas. Which class was the most important for his philosophy?

8 How does Descartes try to establish the existence of the external world?

9 How, on his principles, does Descartes account for the possibility of error?

10 Examine Hume's critique of innate ideas [*Enquiry*, Sec. II].

11 Hume thinks of the mind as passive – a receptor of information provided by the senses. Examine this view critically.

12 'No negation of a fact can involve a contradiction.' Explain what Hume means by this.

13 Explain and examine critically Hume's distinction between 'relations of ideas' and 'matters of fact'.

14 Explain Hume's objections to 'abstract reasonings'.

*15 When discussing the possibility of knowledge of what lies beyond what is given to the senses and memory, Hume emphasizes what we can 'conceive'. Examine why he does so.

16 In what sense is Hume a sceptic? Is his position tenable?

17 Give a critical account of Hume's doctrine of the idea of necessary connection.

18 Does Hume attack or defend the idea of a continuing body?

*19 Russell argues [*Problems*, ch. III] that it is rational to believe that our sense-data are really signs of the existence of something independent of us and our perceptions. Examine this claim.

20 Explain and analyse Russell's distinction between knowledge by acquaintance and knowledge by description.

21 Examine critically Russell's theory of truth.

22 Examine critically Russell's theory of induction.

23 Does Ayer's treatment of the problem of induction lead to scepticism?

24 In what sense, according to Ayer, can analytic propositions give us new knowledge? Examine this claim critically.

25 What reason can Ayer have for believing in the existence of other people? Is it a good one?

26 How, according to Sartre, do I know myself?

B. Problems

27 How would you distinguish ordinary doubt from philosophical doubt? Discuss the merits of the latter. [AEB, 1996]

28 Is it logically possible to doubt everything?

*29 Can a sceptic know that he does not know anything?

30 'The sceptic's problems are insoluble because they are fictitious' [Ayer, *Problem of Knowledge*]. Examine this statement.

31 (a) Identify and briefly illustrate two ways in which beliefs may be justified.
   (b) Outline and illustrate the role of justification in distinguishing between knowledge and true belief.
   (c) Assess the view that knowledge is justified true belief.
[AQA (AEB), specimen, 2001]

*32 Is the claim that all knowledge is relative to the knower tenable?

33 Explain with examples the following sets of distinctions: necessary/contingent; *a priori/a posteriori*; analytic/synthetic.

34 Can a judgement be both synthetic and *a priori*?

35 Discuss critically the claim that the necessity of a 'necessary' proposition lies in a mere linguistic convention, in a determination to use words in a certain way.

36 'A thing cannot be completely green and red all over at the same time.' Can we *know* this?

37 Discuss the strengths and weaknesses of (a) the correspondence theory, (b) the coherence theory of truth.

38 Pragmatism claims that a belief is true if it is useful, and false if it is not. How would you argue against this position?

39 Discuss the claim that truth is what I say it is. [IB, specimen, 2000]

40 Examine the theory that truth is 'idealized rational acceptability'.

41 Can reason alone give us knowledge of reality?

42 What reasons are there for supposing that the world is not as we experience it? [IB, 1987]

43 Our knowledge of things in the world around us is based on inference rather than on direct perception. Can this assertion be justified?

44 Examine phenomenalism considered as a response to scepticism concerning the existence of things we believe ourselves to perceive.

45 (a) Briefly explain the view that our senses only inform us about how things *seem*.

(b) Outline and illustrate two arguments which might be used to support a representative theory of perception.

(c) Assess the case for naïve realism. [AQA (AEB), specimen, 2001]

46 Explain the distinction between primary and secondary qualities. Why was it introduced? Is it tenable?

*47 Examine the philosophical problems arising out of the common-sense assumption that physical objects are actually coloured.

48 Can statements about physical objects be successfully translated into statements about sense-data?

*49 Explain and examine the so-called problem of 'knowing other minds'.

50 Compare and contrast our knowledge of our own pains and our knowledge of other people's pains.

51 How can I know that I am not the only person in the world?

52 What problems are solved by the view that we know other people solely through observing their behaviour?

53 Do I know myself better than I know other people?

54 What problems are involved in arguing *from* our own case *to* the existence of other minds? [AEB, 1997]

55 Can 'knowing that' be assimilated to 'knowing how'? What are the implications for one's knowledge of one's 'self'?

56 'I am the same person now as I was ten years ago.' Examine this statement.

57 Can I know you are not a robot?

58 To what extent can the content of our memory provide us with knowledge of our past? [AEB, 1997]

*Notes/guided answers have been provided for questions **1, 2, 15, 19, 29, 32, 47** and **49** (at end of book).

READING LIST

A. Prescribed texts
Ayer, A.J., *Language, Truth and Logic.* (AEB)
Descartes, R., *Meditations.* (AEB, IB)
Hume, D., *An Enquiry Concerning Human Understanding.* (AEB, IB)
Putnam, H., *Reason, Truth and History.* (IB)
Russell, B., *The Problems of Philosophy.* (AEB)
Sartre, J.-P., *Existentialism and Humanism.* (AEB)

B. Other texts
Ayer, A.J., *The Problem of Knowledge.*
Berkeley, G., *Principles of Human Knowledge; Three Dialogues between Hylas and Philonous.*
Descartes, R., *Discourse on Method.*
Gettier, E.L., 'Is justified true belief knowledge?' (in Griffiths – see below under **4**).
Hume, D., *A Treatise on Human Nature.*

Husserl, E., *The Idea of Phenomenology; Cartesian Meditations.*
James, W., *Pragmatism.*
Kant, I., *Prolegomena; Critique of Pure Reason.*
Locke, J., *Essay Concerning Human Understanding.*
Merleau-Ponty, M., *The Phenomenology of Perception.*
Ryle, G., *The Concept of Mind.*
Sartre, J.-P., *Being and Nothingness.*
Smart, J.J.C., *Philosophy and Scientific Realism.*
Wittgenstein, L., *On Certainty.*

C. Supplementary reading
(If you are a beginner, you are recommended to start with titles marked with an asterisk.)

1. Historical survey
Ayer, A.J., *Philosophy in the Twentieth Century.**
Hamlyn, D.W., *Sensation and Perception.*
Passmore, J.A., *A Hundred Years of Philosophy.*
Scruton, R., *A Short History of Modern Philosophy.**
Warnock, G.J., *English Philosophy since 1900.**

2. General introductory texts
The following cover all or most of the topics dealt with in Ch. 4, and although of
    varying degrees of difficulty should be found helpful by beginners.
Audi, R., *Epistemology.*
Dancy, J., *Introduction to Contemporary Epistemology.*
Hamlyn, D.W., *The Theory of Knowledge.**

3. Books and articles on individual philosophers
Foster, J., *A.J. Ayer*
Berman, D., *George Berkeley: Idealism and the Man.**
Grayling, A.C., *Berkeley: The Central Arguments.*
Urmson, J.O., *Berkeley.**
Warnock, G.J., *Berkeley.**
Kenny, A., *Descartes.**
Sorrell, T., *Descartes.**
Williams, B., *Descartes: The Project of Pure Enquiry.*
Ayer, A.J., *Hume.**
Pears, D.F., *Hume's System.*
Stroud, B., *Hume.*
Bell, D., *Husserl.*
Körner, S., *Kant.**
Scruton, R., *Kant.**
Walker, R.C.S., *Kant.*
O'Connor, D.J., *John Locke.**
Yolton, J., *Locke: An Introduction.*
Dillon, M.C., *Merleau-Ponty's Ontology.*

Priest, S., *Merleau-Ponty.**

Lyons, W., *Gilbert Ryle: An Introduction to his Philosophy.*

Ayer, A.J., *Russell.**

Grayling, A.C., *Russell.**

Sainsbury, R.M., *Russell.*

Danto, A.C., *Sartre.**

Warnock, M., *The Philosophy of Sartre.**

Grayling, A.C., *Wittgenstein.**

Kenny, A., *Wittgenstein.*

4. Other books and essays on particular topics

Austin, J.L., *Sense and Sensibilia.*

Ayer, A.J., *The Foundations of Empirical Knowledge.*

Ayer, A.J., *The Origins of Pragmatism.*

Dancy, J. (ed.), *Perceptual Knowledge.**

Grayling, A.C., *The Refutation of Scepticism.*

Griffiths, A. Phillips (ed.), *Knowledge and Belief.** (Contains the Gettier article.)

Nagel, T., *The View from Nowhere*, Chs I–V.*

Parkinson, G.H.R. (ed.), *The Theory of Meaning.**

Russell, B., *Human Knowledge: Its Scope and Limits.**

Russell, B., 'Pragmatism' (in *Philosophical Essays*).

Strawson, P.F. (ed.), *Philosophical Logic.**

▼ 6 Ethics

6.1 Theories of ethics: introduction

You may well by now be feeling a little 'shell-shocked', so to speak: Chapters 2 to 5 were certainly quite demanding. Moreover you may feel – and with justification – that the chapter on the theory of knowledge was rather abstract and dealt with problems which, although of considerable philosophical interest, are not at the centre of our everyday concerns. I cannot promise that the chapter you are embarking on will prove to be any easier, but the issues we shall be dealing with do differ from epistemological controversies in that they are about matters which vitally concern most of us at some stage of our lives. When we were quite young – perhaps particularly then – we often asked questions like, 'Why shouldn't I do that?', 'Why should I be good?' These are legitimate philosophical questions, that admit of a variety of answers. The answers we received as children were usually rather basic: 'Because, if you are not good/if you do that, you won't get your tea/pocket money', 'Daddy will smack you', 'God will be angry', 'You might have an accident' and so on! Depending on the sophistication of our moral education, we might later have been offered other answers, such as 'You will become a better person', 'You will improve your chances of living harmoniously with others in society', or 'You will be more successful in life'. At a more reflective stage, we may pose deeper questions such as 'What do we mean by calling a person "good"?', 'What *is* the "Good"?', 'Are actions "right" because of their consequences?', 'Are intentions and motives relevant to the "rightness" or "wrongness" of actions?'

Now to keep the discussion on a relatively personal and concrete level it will be sensible if we concentrate on a specific moral issue, say that of killing another human being. Consider this question: 'Have you ever thought about murdering your husband/wife/neighbour/tax inspector/——? (You can fill in the space yourself with an appropriate name!) The answer most of would give is undoubtedly, 'No'; or, if you *have* ever entertained the idea, it was probably little more than a passing fancy. But suppose you were really seriously considering despatching someone you disliked intensely. Even then it is unlikely you would set about making detailed plans, and still less likely you would actually do the deed. Why not? Obviously, for most of us the fear of detection, conviction and punishment would be sufficient deterrent. There is however a moral as well as a legal dimension to the whole issue. Most people would say that murder is wrong. 'Thou shalt do no murder' is, after all, the Fourth Commandment. But this is certainly an over-simplification, if not a simplistic response. We have first to contend with the problem of definition: what is meant by 'murder'? Is it to be equated with 'killing' as such? If so, then a soldier who shoots an 'enemy' in battle is guilty of murder. Certainly some pacifists might take this view. Yet many orthodox Christians argue that, at least in certain specified circumstances, such killing is justified. What then is the moral justification for conscientious objection to military service? In some countries 'judicial execution' is sanctioned as a punishment for various crimes – not only against the state but against religion. Some unorthodox Muslims, for example, believe that it is right to kill 'blasphemers'. And what of suicide, euthanasia and abortion? There are no easy answers, and the answers that are often given do not seem to follow the lines of demarcation between religious people and non-believers. Buddhists would in general regard any kind of killing (including the killing of animals) as unethical. But many Christians, while agreeing about the wrongness of, say, abortion, might disagree over the acceptability of euthanasia.

It is unlikely that we shall *solve* all these problems, but we can try to clarify the issues by (1) critically examining some of the main systems of ethics, and then (2) considering how they might deal with the specific problem of killing. This chapter should therefore give you some idea of practical moral philosophy and it should also be of help to those of you who are required to study set texts for examination purposes. But before we tackle the first 'system' it will perhaps be useful to have a look at some of the important technical terms which are used to classify various kinds of ethical theories:

(1) **Teleological** versus **deontological** theories. This is a fairly clear-cut distinction. Teleological theories (you will remember the reference to teleology in the discussion about Aristotle's philosophy) are characterized by their assumption that the rightness or wrongness of an action depends in some way on its results or consequences. These 'ends' may be of various kinds, and so there are many different teleological theories, Plato's ethics is teleological, the end of human action being 'the Good'. Aristotle took the end to be *eudaimonia*. But other philosophers, for example, Hume and J.S. Mill, have taken pleasure or happiness to be the criterion of morality. Deontological theories, on the other hand, claim that actions are right or wrong 'in themselves', or that they are in accord with a law of some kind (for example, the 'moral law', the law of God, the law of 'nature' and so on). Perhaps the best example of a philosopher who held a deontological theory of ethics is Kant.

(2) **Subjective** and **objective** theories. The subjectivist is rather like Humpty Dumpty who, you may recall, asserted, 'When *I* use a word it means just what I choose it to mean – neither more nor less'. In the same way the subjectivist in ethics believes himself to be the final arbiter of the moral standard. His or her own personal feelings, likes and dislikes are alone held to determine what is right and wrong, good or bad. In contrast, objectivist theories appeal to standards or moral codes which are said to exist independently of individual preferences. A given action remains good whether I like it or not.

(3) **Relativism** and **absolutism**. This distinction overlaps with the previous one to some extent. Subjectivistic ethics are relativistic in that the moral standard

varies with the insights or feelings of each individual. Absolutist ethics which claim, for example, that all men are bound by a universal and unchanging code are likewise objective. It is, however, possible for a theory to be both objective and relativistic. It might be claimed, for example, that the rightness or wrongness of killing somebody is determined by 'society' or an authority of some kind which overrides individual preference, but that whether it is actually right or wrong depends on the particular circumstances. Thus the killing of a murderer or of an enemy in war might be sanctioned, whereas to kill one's neighbour other than in self-defence would be contrary to the moral code of that society.

(4) **Naturalist** and **non-naturalist** theories. Naturalist theories regard moral judgements as 'facts' about the world, and claim that moral words (for example, 'good') can be defined in terms of 'natural' qualities such as 'happiness' or 'pleasure', or such notions as 'being conducive to the survival of the group'. These theories thus assert that there is no clear-cut distinction between factual judgements and evaluative judgements (that is, between an 'is' and 'ought'). Non-naturalist theories either deny that moral words can be defined in terms of natural properties, or, more strongly, that moral words can be defined at all; they are *sui generis*.

There are other distinctions that can be made. Some of these will be referred to in the course of the chapter. And some theories may not fall neatly into any of these classifications. But you may find it helpful to refer back to these brief accounts as you work through the various sections. We shall start by looking at the contribution made to moral philosophy by Hume.

6.2 Hume: sentiment and utility

Reading: *Enquiry into the Principles of Morals*; refer also to the *Treatise*, Book III

When asked about morals many people tend to say that they 'know' what is good and what is bad. This was also essentially the view of the distinguished Cambridge philosopher G.E. Moore (1873–1958), who adopted what may be described as a 'common-sense' view of both ethics and perception. 'Good', Moore argues, cannot be defined, because it is always an open question whether what we take 'good' to be defined in terms of is itself good. Thus, we might say the good is that which leads to happiness: but then we can still ask whether happiness is good. 'Good', he concluded, cannot be analysed in terms of anything else – especially any 'natural' quality. Any attempt to define the term commits what he called the **naturalistic fallacy**. There is a parallel here between Moore's ethics and his account of perception. There can be no doubt, he says, that there is an external world. Things exist. We can see them and touch them. And this is because they are composed of basic 'entities' such as round and yellow with which we are directly acquainted and in terms of which propositions such as

'This is an inkstand' might be analysed. (Compare the discussion of Russell in 5.5. It was in fact Moore himself who introduced the term 'sense-datum'.) Similarly, he claims [in his *Ethics* and *Principia Ethica*] that the term 'good' names a simple 'objective' which, like 'yellow' is unanalysable; and that other ethical terms such as 'right' and 'duty' are to be defined in terms of *it*. Now this raises the question of how exactly we distinguish between good and bad 'wholes'. According to Moore, 'goods' can be directly perceived or **intuited**. But it can then be asked further what the nature of an intuition is. This was an issue which was much debated in the seventeenth and eighteenth centuries. Some philosophers, in parti-cular Richard Price (1723–91), supposed intuition to be a kind of **intellectual** apprehension and as providing direct insight into the rightness or wrongness of actions. (This is to be contrasted with the deductive processes which characterize the ethics of Plato and Aristotle). Opposed to this 'rationalist' intuitionism were philosophers of the 'moral sense' school, for example, the Third Earl of Shaftesbury (1671–1713) and Francis Hutcheson (1694–1746), who thought of moral and aesthetic intuitions as a special sorts of **feelings**. Similar views were held in the twentieth century by H.A. Prichard (1871–1947) and the Aristotelian scholar W.D. Ross (1877–1971). How then can we decide between the two positions? Or, to widen the scope of the discussion, how do we discover the foundations of morals? The contribution to the debate of David Hume is especially important. We shall therefore examine his thesis as presented in the *Enquiry into the Principles of Morals*.

Arguments in favour of both reason and sentiment (that is, feeling) are so plausible, he says, that both may 'concur in almost all moral determinations and conclusions'. He therefore proposes to follow a simple method. This will consist of an analysis of 'that complication of mental qualities, which form what, in common life, we call Personal Merit'. What he intends to do in morals (which is for him an aspect of the wider study of man or human nature) is in fact comparable to what Newton did for physics: to follow the 'experimental method, and deduce general maxims from a comparison of particular instances'. As he says in Sec. 138:

> Men are now cured of their passion for hypotheses and systems in natural philosophy, and will hearken to no arguments but those which are derived from experience. It is full time they should attempt a like reformation in all moral disquisitions; and reject every system of ethics, however subtle or ingenious, which is not founded on fact or observation.

He starts his examination of 'human nature' by identifying the two social virtues, Benevolence and Justice.

By **Benevolence** [Sec. II] Hume means 'natural philanthropy' [184] or 'a feeling for the happiness of mankind and a resentment of their misery' [135]. This affection for humanity is manifested in such qualities as mercy, sociability, generosity and so on [see 139]. In Part II of Sec. II, Hume argues that *part* of the merit of such a person's actions lies in their **utility**, that is, other people derive happiness from them in so far as he offers love or friendship, or provides for those in need. Such utility also explains why such actions are so universally approved. In 143 Hume seems to regard the 'public utility' or 'the true interests of mankind' as the primary means by which we may determine our duty. (You should note his discussion in 143 and 144 of how some actions or life-styles which *appear* at first sight to be praiseworthy or reprehensible may subsequently turn out to deserve the opposite description when experience reveals the true consequences.)

Similar considerations apply to **Justice**, by which he means, roughly, the possession of the goods or property which will ensure an individual's happiness: 'anything which it is lawful for him, and for him alone to use' [158]. But in Part I Sec. III Hume proceeds to show that in the case of this social virtue, utility is the *sole* origin. In support of his claim he points out [145–149] that there could be no place for justice in extreme situations such as either (a) a 'golden age' when mankind lacked for nothing and lived in perfect harmony and tolerance, or (b) a 'state of nature' characterized by want, ignorance and savagery. (*Hume has in mind here not only Hobbes' state of nature where life was 'nasty, brutish and short' but also the view of society put forward by Thrasymachus and his friends in Plato's *Republic*. See Hume's footnote [151] and Ch. 3 of this book.) His conclusion is summarized in 149:

> Thus, the rules of equity or justice depend entirely on the particular state and condition in which men are placed, and owe their origin and existence to that utility, which results to the public from their strict and regular observance.

The ideas of property thus become necessary in a society which operates between extremes; and hence arise the usefulness, merit and moral obligation of justice. To support this account of justice and public utility Hume discusses [Part II of this Sec. and Sec. IV] *particular* laws both within a given state and between nations, and the rules or conventions which hold between individuals in matters of friendship, etiquette and so on. There must even be honour among thieves if their 'pernicious confederacy' is to be maintained. 'Common interest and utility beget infallibly a standard of right and wrong among the parties concerned' [171].

Hume now [Sec. V] raises the important question of *why* we approve of the social virtues on account of their utility. What alternative accounts can be given of the origin of moral distinctions? They cannot all have arisen from education; such descriptions as 'honourable', 'shameful', 'lovely' and 'odious' must have had their source in the 'original constitution of the mind', if they were to be intelligible [173]. Neither could morality be grounded in self-love or private interest; 'the voice of nature and experience seems plainly to oppose the selfish theory' [174]. Moreover, he says, we often praise actions in other places or times which could not be remotely relevant to our self-interest. Sometimes we even approve of the actions of an adversary which could be *contrary* to our interests. Nevertheless, as he shows in Part II, the interest of each individual cannot be divorced from the general interest of the community:

Usefulness is only a tendency to a certain end; and it is a contradiction in terms, that anything pleases as means to an end, where the end in no wise affects us. If usefulness, therefore, be a source of moral sentiment, and if this usefulness be not always considered with a reference to self; it follows, that everything, which contributes to the happiness of society, recommends itself directly to our approbation and good-will.   [178]

Hume's position may still seem a little unclear. He has rejected self-love as the basis of morality but has stressed the interdependence of the individual's self-interest and that of society. And yet we may still approve of the actions of others even when they *conflict* with our interests. How *does* utility relate to the self? Why *does* public utility 'please'? Hume's answer is to appeal to the notion of **sympathy**. What he means by this is explained in the *Treatise on Human Nature* [II, I, Sec. XI] in terms of the association of ideas. But in the *Enquiry* [179–190] he thinks of sympathy as arising directly from a capacity we all possess of putting ourselves, by means of our imagination, in the place of another person and of praising or blaming him for exhibiting qualities which would arouse in us pride or humiliation respectively if we possessed them. In other words, through sympathy we experience the sentiments of humanity and benevolence. A man, says Hume [187], cannot be indifferent to the happiness or misery of his fellow beings. Whatever promotes their happiness is good, what tends to their misery is evil. And we discover from our experience that utility is in all circumstances a source of approval – a 'foundation of the chief part of morals, which has a reference to mankind and our fellow-creatures' [188].

Not surprisingly, Hume argues in Sec. VI that the sentiment of humanity and the moral sentiment are 'originally the same; since, in each particular, even the most minute, they are governed by the same laws, and are moved by the same objects' [193]. Furthermore, the fact that we approve of such qualities as temperance, patience, presence of mind and so on, which serve the possessor alone without claim to any public value, cannot be attributed to any theory of self-love on our part, but supports rather a doctrine of disinterested benevolence which ensures that there is no incompatibility in the community between morality and utility.

In Part II of Sec. VI Hume seeks to support his theory further by reference to our regard for 'bodily endowments' and the 'goods of fortune'. In Sec. VII he examines qualities which appear to be valued for the immediate pleasure they bring to their possessor rather than for their utility: but he argues that, in all such instances, social sympathy operates and that there is therefore no inconsistency with his general theory. Similar considerations apply to qualities 'immediately agreeable to others' [Sec. VIII]. (These sections need not be studied closely. But at this stage you might find it worthwhile to read Appendix II carefully, where Hume sets out more extensive criticisms of the self-love theory in favour of the doctrine of disinterested benevolence; and then Sec. IX in which he summarizes the arguments developed in the *Enquiry*.)

He can now return [Appendix I] to the question raised at the beginning of the *Enquiry*, namely, whether the foundation of morals is to be sought in reason or sentiment. He recognizes that reason has a role to play in assessing the consequences of actions and determining their utility, but he asserts that it is through sentiment that we gain insight into morality itself. In support of his view that reason cannot be the sole source of morals he offers five 'considerations'. (These are summarized briefly here, but you should study his arguments carefully.)

(1) [236–239] Reason, he says, can judge either of matters of fact or of relations (see 6.3 below). But in the case of certain 'crimes', for example, ingratitude, it is the *sentiment* that determines their immorality. Morality cannot consist in the relation of actions to rules; to determine the 'rule of right', reason would have to start from a consideration of those very relations themselves. '**Virtue**' is thus defined as 'whatever mental action or quality gives to a spectator the pleasing sentiment of approbation' (and 'vice' the contrary).

(2) [240–242] There is a distinction in method or procedure between 'speculative' reasoning and moral deliberations. In the former we consider what is known and infer from it something which was previously unknown, whereas in the case of the latter all the objects and their relations must be known so that we base our approbation or blame on the total situation.

(3) [242] Moral beauty can be compared with natural beauty; in our apprehension of both, approval (or disapproval) arises from contemplation of the whole – and through the sentiments rather than by the intellectual faculties.

(4) [243] If morality consisted merely in relations it would apply as much to inanimate objects as it does to moral agents.

(5) [244–245] The *ultimate* ends of human actions can never be accounted for by reason. If you ask someone why he uses exercise he will say it is because he desires health, sickness is painful, and he hates pain. What more is there to be said? There can be no infinite progression: 'something must be desirable on its own account, and because of its immediate accord or agreement with human sentiment and affection'.

The bounds of reason and taste are thus easily ascertained. 'The former gives us knowledge of truth and falsehood: the latter gives the sentiment of beauty and deformity, vice and virtue' [246]. It is only taste that can become a motive for action, in so far as it gives pleasure or pain and therefore happiness or misery. 'Cool and disengaged' reason can do no more than direct the impulse received from appetite or inclination. Hume is thus setting out a more moderate version of the assertion to be found in the *Treatise* (Book II, Part III, Sec. 3):

> We speak not strictly and philosophically, when we talk of the combat of passion and of reason. Reason is, and ought only to be, the slave of the passions, and can never pretend to any other office than to serve and obey them.

*Comment and criticisms

(1) It is important that you should be clear about what Hume claims is the basis of morality. While it is reason which determines what is or is not 'useful', reason is

subordinated to sentiment (feeling) in so far as it is the latter which endows utility with moral worth.

(2) Following on from the first point, it can be argued that Hume's psychological analysis is faulty. He seems to be committed to a 'bifurcation' of the self in the sense that reason and irrational sentiment are treated as distinct and separate elements in man, though they may 'concur in almost all moral determinations and conclusions' [*Enquiry*, 137]. (*You might compare his view of the self with that of Plato – though of course Plato stresses the primacy of reason whereas Hume's position is distinctly anti-intellectualistic.) His ethics is thus lacking in any recognition that ethical decisions might perhaps be better regarded as being made by 'the whole man', an integrated personality in whom reason and the feelings are intimately fused.

(3) Another problem that needs to be examined concerns the two social virtues Hume discusses, namely benevolence and justice. We approve of the former, he says, because it is immediately pleasing and agreeable and not only for its utility. This seems to suggest that it is in part a person's disinterestedness or unselfishness, thus personal qualities, that lie at the basis of morality. Even if a course of action turned out not to be socially 'useful', that action might still be morally approved of. In the case of justice, however, 'public utility is the *sole* origin . . . and reflections on the beneficial consequences of this virtue are the *sole* foundation of its merit' [*Enquiry* 145]. In the *Treatise* [Book 3, II, 2] he also asserts that 'it is only from the selfishness and confined generosity of man, along with the scanty provision nature has made for his wants, that justice derives its origin' – though he makes it clear that he rejects the 'self-love' doctrine and that sympathy with the public interest is the source of moral approval of that virtue. Now given Hume's narrow interpretation of justice in terms of 'property', it can be argued that private and public interest have not been completely reconciled as between the two social virtues. (Do you agree with this? Come back to the question again after you have worked through the rest of this chapter, especially 6.4, and 7.2 and 7.3).

(4) As a corollary to his subordination of reason to sentiment as the means of discovering virtue and vice, Hume had already, earlier in the *Treatise* [III, I, 1], drawn attention to an observation which he thinks may be of 'some importance'. In every system of morality he has encountered he has found that the author has moved imperceptibly from assertions about what 'is' or 'is not' to claims about what 'ought' or 'ought not' be done. (This is sometimes referred to as a move from premises that are essentially 'factual', such as 'This action produces happiness', to 'value judgements' – This is right or good; you ought to do it'.) It seems altogether inconceivable, Hume says, how this new relation can be a deduction from others of a different kind. Hume's point is that in so far as moral distinctions are derived from a 'moral sense' – one's own particular sentiment – they do not involve inferences of reason. The distinction of vice and virtue is founded neither on relations, nor is it perceived by reason. There can therefore be no inference from an 'is' to an 'ought'. However, it has often been suggested that Hume himself commits this fallacy in so far as he endows utility with moral worth and thus

provides a basis for duty. This is another issue you will need to think about (see especially 6.7). There are at least two answers that might be made to this charge. (a) Hume did not in fact reject the move from 'is' to 'ought'. (This claim is difficult to sustain in view of the clear account he gives in the *Treatise*.) (b) Hume does stress the primacy of sentiment as the source of moral judgements. Our perception of duty is thus located in moral feeling and in particular in sympathy; and the question of an *inference* from an 'is' to an 'ought' does not therefore seem to arise. (This answer has more cogency.)

(5) Lastly, you should note that the two strands in Hume's ethics, namely utility and sentiment, were developed, respectively by the 'utilitarian' philosophers of the nineteenth century and the so-called 'emotivists' in our own. But, whereas for Hume the 'feeling of approval' for actions which have pleasant consequences is shared by the majority and thus has an 'objective' aspect, some emotivist theories are necessarily subjectivist. Utilitarianism and emotivism will be discussed later. In the meantime we shall look at the moral philosophy of Kant who rejected both theories.

6.3 Kant and duty

Reading: *The Moral Law: Kant's Groundwork of the Metaphysic of Morals* (trans. and ed., H.J. Paton). This book, first published in 1785, is demanding, but like Aristotle's *Nicomachean Ethics* it is one of the most important contributions to moral philosophy ever written and deserves concentrated effort. Before tackling it, you should read through again the brief summary of Kant's epistemology given in Ch. 5. Page references throughout will be to the numbers given in the margins of Paton's book and corresponding to the second edition of Kant's original text.

You should note first of all what Kant is reacting against. In pages 89–95 he discusses a central distinction between what he calls the **autonomy** and the **heteronomy** of the will. This can be explained in the following way. If I say I ought to do something because I want to gain or achieve something else (for example, tell the truth because I want to maintain my reputation), then I am said to be acting or willing heteronomously and thus, as Kant puts it, in accordance with a **hypothetical** imperative. But if I decide that I should not lie, regardless of any consequences, but simply because I recognize it as my duty to behave in this way, then I am said to be acting autonomously and in accordance with the **categorical** imperative. This distinction lies at the heart of Kant's ethics. He goes on to distinguish further between two kinds of principles based on the assumption of heteronomy: (a) **empirical** principles which are dependent on such notions as moral sense, sympathy, and happiness itself; and (b) **rational** principles, which are grounded in the concept of some form of perfection. Thus he is clearly rejecting both the type of ethics represented by Hume and that constructed by some of his rationalist German predecessors (Aristotle's ethics would also be open to the same criticism). But he does admit [93] that if he had to decide between moral sense and perfection, the latter has the merit of being assessable by pure reason.

We can now go back to the beginning of Kant's book. You will remember that in the *Critique of Pure Reason* he argued that human knowledge must be confined to the world of phenomena – 'things in themselves' are inaccessible – and that what knowledge we have results from the intuition of sensory data under the forms of space and time, which are then structured by *a priori* categories or principles of the understanding. In the *Groundwork* he holds that in the practical realm of ethics there is a similar synthetic *a priori* principle – the **moral law** – which conditions our behaviour. Just as knowledge results from the interplay between the rational activity of the mind and the empirical realm, so here in morals we experience Reason in its practical aspect. His aim in this treatise, he says [in the Preface] is to prepare the way for a Critique of Practical Reason by seeking out and establishing 'the supreme principle of morality'. (His Second Critique was in fact published three years later in 1788.) In chs I and II Kant starts out from our everyday moral consciousness and attempts to lead back (by an 'analytic' argument) to the fundamental principle which he thinks underpins moral judgements. In ch. III he undertakes an examination of reason itself so as to pass to the supreme principle (by means of a 'synthetic' argument) and thence back to our everyday judgements – thereby providing justification for the principle.

Of all the qualities of mind man may possess, says Kant, there is only one which can be called good without qualification, namely a **good will** [p.1]; and it is good intrinsically through its willing alone – not because it can lead to some end such as happiness [p.3]. Indeed if the purpose of nature had been to bring about man's happiness, instinct would have been a surer guide than reason or will [p.5]; reason's search for happiness does not lead to true contentment [p.6]. The true function of reason must therefore be to produce a good-will in itself, and therein lies its proper satisfaction [p.7].

To make this notion of a good will in itself clearer, Kant devotes the next ten pages to an examination of the concept of **duty** which includes it. He firstly [p.9 ff.] distinguishes between actions which are performed *for the sake of duty* and those which are *in accordance with duty*; only the former have intrinsic moral worth. Consider these cases. A shopkeeper does not overcharge his customers. We help someone in distress. Right and proper, you may say, and certainly in accord with duty. However, it may well be that the shopkeeper's action stems from an immediate inclination (for example, 'love' for his customers), or from self-interest (his business will benefit). Likewise our action as the good Samaritan may be done because it gives us pleasure to spread happiness. In neither case, says Kant, does the action have genuine moral worth, because it is not performed *from* duty. He now introduces a second proposition [pp.13–14]. The moral worth of an action done from duty does not lie in the purpose to be attained by it, but depends on what he calls the formal **principle of volition** by which it is determined. From these two general statements Kant derives a third proposition: 'Duty is the necessity to act out of reverence for the law' [p.14]. If we rule out both inclination and the anticipated effects of our actions as irrelevant to the moral worth of our actions, we are left only with the objective idea of **law** and a subjective feeling of **reverence** for it generated from within ourselves. (You should study Kant's footnote [pp.16–17] carefully.)

Kant now [pp.17–20] proceeds to a notion central to his moral philosophy: the **Categorical Imperative**. What kind of law must it be, the thought of which is to determine a will that is to be good absolutely and without qualification? Kant's answer is that it must be a *universal* law; and the principle of action becomes 'I ought never to act except in such a way that I can also will that my maxim should become a universal law'. Suppose, for example, I make a promise but without intending to keep it. It may be prudent (and to determine this, one would have to take account of the probable consequences for oneself of making false promises), but is it right? What would happen if everyone were to act in this way? Clearly, such a law would be self-stultifying – there could be no promises at all – and I could have no reverence for it.

Such an account, Kant concludes, is already implicit in the moral perceptions of the ordinary man. What the philosopher must do is to articulate these perceptions so as to make them more comprehensive and intelligible, thereby enabling the ordinary person to resist the claims of inclination and to reinforce the law of duty [pp.21–24].

In the early sections [pp.25–36] of ch. II Kant stresses: (1) that if morality is to have any truth or objective reference at all it must be valid for all rational beings (human or otherwise); (2) that it must be grounded in pure reason independently of experience (it would be quite mistaken to seek to base it on examples drawn from our experience – even our concept of God as the highest or archetypal good has to be derived from the *Idea* of moral perfection); (3) that ethics must therefore first be established on metaphysics before we seek to popularize it. The most important parts of the chapter, however, are Kant's discussion of imperatives [pp.36–50], and his several formulations of the categorical imperative [pp.50–81].

Make sure you understand what he means by an 'imperative' [pp.37–38]. As rational beings we have the capacity to act in accordance with objective moral principles (we have 'will', that is, 'practical' reason), but in so far as we are imperfectly rational we do not always do so. Objective principles therefore appear to us as 'necessitating', that is as obligatory, as commands. Such commands are expressed in terms of imperatives (characterized by an *'ought'*). Imperatives are thus 'only formulae for expressing the relation of objective laws of willing to the subjective imperfection of the will of this or that rational being – for example, of the human will' [p.39]. In the case of God or any *holy* or perfectly rational good will, imperatives are inapplicable.

Kant's distinction between hypothetical and categorical imperatives, which we referred to above, is now introduced [p.40]. (For a first reading you could well pass over the subsequent discussion, pp.40–50. Just note that he differentiates between several types of hypothetical imperative, and that while such imperatives are 'analytic', the categorical imperative is a 'synthetic *a priori* practical proposition'. We discussed this briefly in ch. 5; Paton deals with it effectively on pp.28 ff.)

The more important issue at this stage is how the *categorical* imperative is actually applied. You will recall the problem, discussed earlier, of whether it can be right to make a promise without intending to keep it. This helps to make clear his main formulation of the categorical imperative: '*Act only on that maxim through which you can at the same time will that it should become universal law*' [p.52]. (Note the alternative and subordinate formulation given in the same section.) Let our maxim (that is, 'subjective principle of action') be 'I may make a promise with false intent'. To test it for moral validity we must ask whether this principle can be willed universally. Kant's answer is that it cannot, because if everybody behaved in this way the notion of 'promising' would break down, would no longer have purchase, as it were. (*What kind of criterion is Kant proposing here? Study carefully the four illustrations he provides [pp.53–57]. Is the same test being applied in each case? This is a point we shall refer to again at the end of the chapter. Note also his rejection of teleology [pp.57–91].)

From pages 64 to 81 Kant introduces three further alternative formulations of the categorical imperative. We must be clear about the connections between them and the first two formulations. When we act it is for some end. Only ends in themselves can be the proper object of morality; and since it is only rational beings that can exist as ends in themselves [Why? – see Sec. 66 and his footnote] the practical imperative can be formulated as: '*Act in such a way that you always treat humanity, whether in your own person or in the person of any other, never simply as a means, but always at the same time as an end*' [pp.66–67]. Further, because we as rational beings are ends in ourselves, we must act in accordance with a universal law which is self-imposed – which is the product of our own will. This gives rise to the fourth formulation of the imperative, namely that we should act so that our will can regard itself as at the same time making universal law through its maxim [pp.69–74]. From this Kant derives his final formula [pp.74–77]. Recognition of the rationality and autonomy we all possess must lead to the concept of a **kingdom of ends**, that is, 'a systematic union of different rational beings under common laws'. This thus provides another test for the morality of legislation. Notice that Kant stresses only three of his formulations in his 'Review' [pp.79–81]: (1) the formula of the Law of Nature (which is concerned with the form or universality of maxims); (2) the formula of the End in itself (which relates to the *matter* or end of the maxim); and (3) the formula of the Kingdom of Ends (which synthesizes both form and matter into a totality). (Note Kant's short discussion of 'dignity' [pp.77–79] and his review of the whole argument [pp.81–87], which is summarized well by Paton.)

The remaining sections [pp.87–96] of the chapter deal with the autonomy and heteronomy of the will, which we discussed above.

In ch. III Kant is concerned to show that a categorical imperative is possible only on the presupposition that rational, willing beings are *free*: 'ought' implies 'can'. This raises a particular difficulty that relates back to the arguments and conclusions of the *Critique of Pure Reason* (see Ch. 5 of this book). As rational free agents how can we at the same time be members of both the 'noumenal' (intelligible) and 'phenomenal' (sensible) worlds? How can freedom and necessity be reconciled? Kant notes further that it is impossible for us to have knowledge of the intelligible world, and that we can explain neither freedom itself nor our 'interest' in moral laws – how an *Idea* (of moral law) can give rise to what is essentially based in moral *feeling*. (We shall not discuss Kant's account further here. The problems of freedom and 'reality' will be examined in Ch. 11 of this book. But note Kant's point that the Idea of an intelligible world, although incomprehensible, is yet unconditionally and *practically* necessary, that is, essential for morality.)

*Comment and criticisms

While it is to Kant's credit that, unlike Hume, he accords a proper place to the 'practical' reason, he is often criticized for having gone to the other extreme. His moral philosophy is formalistic and austere. We may feel it to be contrary to our ordinary notions of what it is to be good that Kant should deny that description to a man acting out of love for his neighbour. But it is of course Kant's declared aim to identify the *formal* element in moral judgements; and it is in consequence of this that he singles out action for the sake of duty as the basis of the good-will. This, however, lays him open to the objection that he has virtually defined goodness in terms of duty. This is certainly questionable; and indeed, as history has shown, many an action has been performed in the name of duty which we regard as distasteful if not evil. Does not moral philosophy first require an objective standard in terms of which our intentions, our actions themselves, or their consequences can be assessed? In the light of these general comments there are three aspects of his ethics which you should consider critically:

(1) Whether or not an action has been done for the sake of duty in a strict sense (and thus can be regarded as emanating from a good will) can be determined, according to Kant, by the application of the categorical imperative. The central difficulty here, however, is whether it *can* be shown that the maxim on which we act *is* universalizable. It is not entirely clear from the many concrete examples Kant examines whether the test is absence of contradiction or, less rigorously, one of 'workability'. The difficulty with this approach is that the criterion seems to vary, depending upon the empirical circumstances of the case. The concept of 'not being able' is insufficiently clear. Have a look again at the many examples Kant discusses, with reference to his three main formulations of the categorical imperative.

(2) It is of course doubtful whether Kant's formalistic criterion allows for special empirical circumstances. But this then gives rise to another difficulty. Suppose according to the categorical imperative it is morally wrong to steal. (If everybody were to steal, then most probably the economic structure of society would break down.) But would not Kant allow that stealing might be permissible to avoid starvation? The imperative could be reformulated to accommodate this qualification: 'It is wrong to steal *unless* one would otherwise starve'. But should not further requirements be imposed, for example: that the hungry person has failed to receive charity from his neighbours; or that the State's provision is inadequate? But what is to count as 'inadequate'? Why can he not receive charity? Has he begged for it? Why can he not work? And so on. The point emerging here is that Kantian formal universality is being transformed into particularity; a general rule into specific instances – and arguably unique ones in so far as no two persons' circumstances are identical. Thus his categorical imperative seems to be

inherently *impractical* as a test of ethical rectitude. This is by no means the end of the matter. But it gives you something to reflect on.

(3) Another criticism relates to the last of Kant's formulations, namely that which refers to the 'kingdom of ends'. Now there is a close link between this concept and that of the perfect good (*summum bonum*). Kant has made it clear that happiness is not the ground of the moral law, but he also claims that the pursuit of virtue, that is, the good, will in due course also lead to happiness. There is not of course a logically necessary connection between the search for virtue and the production of happiness. And indeed as physical objects in the phenomenal world we may in fact achieve neither. It is for this reason that Kant's postulates of immortality and God in the *Critique of Pure Reason* are so relevant to his moral philosophy; for it is only on the assumption that the soul is immortal that we can think in terms of the *possibility* that holiness can be achieved. Moreover, the postulation of God Kant sees as a precondition for the necessary (although *synthetic*) connection between happiness and virtue. Does this mean then that, after all, Kant is really appealing to an absolute Good as the ground of morality prior to that of duty? We can also question whether happiness and virtue can be so sharply separated. (You might compare Aristotle's treatment of 'well-being' here.) If we suppose that the pursuit of virtue will in due course lead to happiness, can we completely disregard the possibility of happiness, albeit in a 'future life', as a motivating factor when we do our 'duty'? Is there not therefore a teleological element in Kant's otherwise deontological ethics? (Compare Hare below, 6.7.) At the very least we can say there is a certain tension between our recognition of duty as revealed through the formalism of the categorical imperative and the anticipation of happiness as implicit in the metaphysical postulate of God.

6.4 Mill's utilitarianism

Reading: J.S. Mill, *Utilitarianism*

Utilitarianism did not originate with John Stuart Mill (1806–73). As you have seen, the doctrine of 'utility' was adhered to by Hume but only in the context of his intuitionism. The utilitarian aspects of his system were subsequently taken over by later thinkers and received what was perhaps their fullest – if somewhat uncritical – exposition by the notable reformer Jeremy Bentham (1748–1832). But it is with Mill that utilitarianism is nowadays particularly identified. His essay was in fact written in answer to criticisms of his father's moral philosophy, which was closely associated with Bentham's system, but with some recognition of its weaknesses in theory and application.

Chapter I is introductory. Mill here sets out his explicitly teleological position:

> All action is for the sake of some end, and rules of action, it seems natural to suppose, must take their whole character and colour from the end to which they are subservient. [para. 2]

But how are these ends to be determined? According to Hume the intuitionist it is through sentiment, a moral sense, that we discover what is right or wrong; reason cannot provide us with a proof. But intuitionism (and he would include the intuitionist element in Hume's ethics here) is rejected by Mill, as is any theory which claims that ultimate principles are known *a priori* [para. 3] [*Consider carefully his criticism of Kant in para. 4. Do you agree with Mill's point that to apply the categorical imperative is no more than to test a rule by reference to the consequences of its universal adoption? Does this show the untenability of Kant's premisses? Compare also the second criticism made in 6.3 above.] Indeed, questions of ultimate ends are not amenable to direct proof at all [para. 5]. Nevertheless he claims that it is possible through the exercise of reason to discover 'considerations . . . equivalent to proof' which enable us to accept or reject the utilitarian theory. But before he examines these considerations he discusses [ch. II] what is meant by utilitarianism and how it has been misunderstood.

Two misconceptions are referred to in the first paragraph: (a) that utility should be opposed to pleasure; (b) that by pleasure is meant voluptuousness. Mill first of all sets out [para. 2] a broadly Benthamite formulation of utilitarianism:

> The creed which accepts as the foundation of morals, Utility, or the Greatest Happiness Principle, holds that actions are right in proportion as they tend to promote happiness, wrong as they tend to produce the reverse of happiness. By happiness is intended pleasure, and the absence of pain; by unhappiness, pain, and the privation of pleasure.

He then devotes paragraphs 3–8 to an analysis of pleasure and what it involves. You should note the following points. Pleasures should be distinguished not only in terms of quantity but with reference to their quality. 'It is quite compatible with the principle of utility to recognize that fact, that some *kinds* of pleasure are more desirable and more valuable than others' [para. 4]. To determine which are the most desirable pleasures we must consult those people who are 'highly endowed' and make the fullest use of their 'higher faculties'. Such people may have experience of suffering and may not easily achieve happiness, yet they may be *content*. 'It is better to be a human being dissatisfied than a pig satisfied; better to be Socrates dissatisfied than a fool satisfied' [para. 6]. If a person should choose the lower pleasure while yet appreciating the intrinsic superiority of the higher, this must be due to infirmity of character. 'It may be questioned whether any one who has remained equally susceptible to both classes of pleasures, ever knowingly and calmly preferred the lower; though many, in all ages, have broken down in an ineffectual attempt to combine both' [para. 7]. (*You might consider here how far Mill's discussion of higher pleasures, the man of 'higher faculties', and of weakness of the will is reminiscent of Plato's treatment of these issues in the *Republic*).

Paragraphs 9 and 10 are important in so far as Mill introduces the wider issue of the individual in the context of society: the utilitarian standard 'is not the agent's own greatest happiness, but the greatest amount of happiness altogether'.

Indeed, he goes further and makes the pursuit of happiness the *standard* of morality [see para. 10].

The rest of the chapter is devoted to Mill's replies to a number of objections. You should find his discussion quite straightforward. Particular note, however, should be taken of the point raised in paragraph 15 concerning self-sacrifice. An individual may well be willing to do without happiness for the sake of something he prizes more: but what of the circumstance in which one sacrifices his own happiness so as to serve that of others? [para. 16]. This can only occur in an imperfect world, says Mill, but the readiness to make such a sacrifice is man's highest virtue. He recognizes the so-called paradox of **hedonism**, that 'the conscious ability to do without happiness gives the best prospect of realising such happiness as is attainable' [para. 16]. And he adds that the sacrifice has value only if it increases or tends to increase the sum total of happiness.

Now let us suppose that an individual does choose to behave in accordance with the moral standard – whatever it may be. Why *should* he? What is its sanction? What is the source of its obligation, its binding force? Why am I bound to promote the general happiness? If my own happiness lies in something else, why may I not give that the preference? Such questions form the content of ch. III and relate particularly to the problem of self-sacrifice. Mill distinguishes between *external* and *internal* sanctions. By external sanctions [para. 3] he means 'the hope of favour and the fear of displeasure, from our fellow-creatures or from the Ruler of the Universe', together with our feelings of sympathy for them or of awe for God. Such sanctions, strengthened by the possibility of reward or punishment, will become available to enforce the utilitarian morality once it is accepted by society. The internal sanction is then identified as a disinterested, subjective feeling in our minds, which arises when we violate our duty; and as such is the essence of Conscience [paras 4 and 5]. Note that for Mill this feeling of moral obligation is not innate but acquired, and susceptible of being 'cultivated in almost any direction' [para. 8]. So what determines the conscience to be used positively? Mill's answer [para. 10] is to appeal to a 'powerful natural sentiment', namely:

> the social feelings of mankind; the desire to be in unity with our fellow creatures, which is already a powerful principle in human nature, and happily one of those which tend to become stronger, even without express inculcation, from the influences of advancing civilisation. The social state is at once so natural, so necessary, and so habitual to man, that, except in some unusual circumstances or by an effort of voluntary abstraction, he never conceives himself otherwise than as a member of a body; and this association is riveted more and more, as mankind are further removed from the state of savage independence.

Mill is clearly an optimist; he believes in progress. As society evolves, its members will increasingly come to recognize the inseparability of their respective interests. (Mill's full account [paras 9 and 10] of the moral and political growth of society and the human mind should be studied carefully and compared with Hume's views on the individual in society. Note, by the way, the point made about freedom and individuality at the end of para. 9; this issue will be taken up when we come to deal with Political Philosophy).

Chapter IV of *Utilitarianism* is concerned with 'proofs' of utilitarian principles, or 'considerations . . . equivalent to proof', as he put it in ch. I. Mill first [para. 2] restates the utilitarian position:

> Questions about ends are . . . questions what things are desirable. The utilitarian doctrine is, that happiness is desirable, and the only thing desirable, as an end; all other things being only desirable as a means to that end.

The first paragraph of his 'proof' is designed to show that happiness is *one* of the ends of morality; and it is an argument which has led to much critical comment:

> The only proof capable of being given that an object is visible, is that people actually see it, the only proof that a sound is audible is that people hear it; and so of the other sources of experience. In like manner, I apprehend, the sole evidence it is possible to produce that anything is desirable, is that people do actually desire it. [para. 3]

The second part of the 'proof', in which he tries to show that it is *only* happiness which is desirable, is developed in paras 4–10. The initial problem is that people often desire other things, for example, virtue. The essence of Mill's argument to counter this is that when people appear to desire virtue disinterestedly, it is ultimately because it is conducive to happiness. Happiness is in reality 'not an abstract idea, but a concrete whole'; it is made up of many elements [para. 6]. Virtue is one of these goods. But while it was not 'naturally and originally' part of the 'end' which we might seek, we have come to feel it as a good in itself as a result of its association with the pleasure it gives rise to [paras 5–7]. Happiness is the only thing which is really desired for its own sake; and this can be backed up, he thinks, by observing ourselves and others. This in effect constitutes a third stage in his 'proof' [para. 10].

The final chapter (V) sets out Mill's views on justice – a concept you have already come across in the sections on Plato, Aristotle and Hume. You should not find his account difficult. In fact Mill seems to have moved little from Hume's position. In the first three paragraphs he argues against the view of justice as being a human instinct; even if it were, it would still need to be 'controlled and enlightened' by reason as other instincts are. So how do we account for the 'subjective mental feeling' of justice? Throughout the next main section of the chapter Mill lists a number of different kinds of unjust action (you can be left to read these for yourself), and by comparing these types he concludes that they appear to have little in common. So he now embarks on a short survey of the history of the concept, its etymology and its relationship with law and the general notion of moral obligation. His conclusion is that justice 'implies something which it is not only right to do, but which some individual person can claim from us as his moral right' [final para., section 2]. Justice thus differs from virtues such as generosity and beneficence, which we are not morally bound to practise towards other individuals. He goes on, in the third section of the chapter, to show that the *sentiments* which give rise to the idea of justice are rooted in 'the impulse of self-defence and the feeling of sympathy' [para. 4, section 3]. His intelligence joined with this power of sympathizing with other human beings enables a man 'to attach himself to the collective idea of his tribe, his country, or mankind, in such a manner that any act hurtful to them raises his instinct of sympathy, and urges him to resistance' [para. 5, section 3]. The sentiment of justice is thus 'the natural feeling of retaliation or vengeance, rendered by intellect and sympathy applicable to those injuries . . . which wound us through, or in common with, society at large' [para. 6, section 3]. Mill makes the social relevance of justice even more explicit in para. 7:

> If [a person] does not feel [resentment] – if he is regarding the act solely as it affects him individually – he is not consciously just; he is not concerning himself about the justice of his action.

And you should note particularly his appropriation of Kant's imperative, 'So act, that thy rule of conduct might be adopted as a law by all rational beings', for his own utilitarian ethics:

> To give any meaning to Kant's principle, the sense put upon it must be, that we ought to shape our conduct by a rule which all rational being might adopt *with benefit to their collective interest.*   [para. 7]

Thus, concludes Mill [para. 8, section 3], 'the idea of justice supposes two things; a rule of conduct, and a sentiment which sanctions the rule'. The first is supposed to be common to mankind, and intended for their good; the second is a desire that offenders against the rule should be punished, but a feeling which derives its morality from the concept of 'intelligent self-interest' and its 'energy of self-assertion' from the human 'capacity of enlarged sympathy'.

The remaining two sections of the chapter are devoted to: (1) an examination of a number of particular cases which arouse disagreement as to what is just and unjust; (2) a discussion of whether there is, in the last analysis, a fundamental difference between justice and social expediency. His answer is summarized with particular clarity in the two final paragraphs of the last section. All cases of justice, he says, are also cases of expediency, but the former covers certain 'social utilities' which are vastly more important, absolute and imperative than any others are as a class, and which are 'guarded by a sentiment not only different in degree, but different in kind'.

*Comments and criticisms

Mill rejects both *a priori* rationalism and intuitionist ethics. His criterion for the rightness or wrongness of actions is the goodness or badness of their consequences; and this is assessed in terms of the amount of pleasure or happiness thereby produced. He is not, however, a 'classical' utilitarian for whom society is seen as an aggregate of individuals each seeking to achieve his own best interests, the result of which would be to bring about 'the greatest happiness of the greatest number'. For Mill, society is essentially 'organic'. Certainly he lays considerable emphasis on personal liberty, but like Aristotle he implicitly argues for a much closer identification between the individual and society. Likewise he takes care to distinguish between different *qualities* of pleasure as well as quantities. Again there is much in common here between Mill and Aristotle's concept of *eudaimonia*. But there are a number of difficulties in his system which need to be looked at carefully:

(1) Has he adequately reconciled private with public interest? Why *should* an individual sacrifice his own welfare for that of the general good? As we have seen, according to Mill, the feeling of moral obligation to others has been so inculcated in us by society that the conflicts which inevitably arise in an imperfect world can be rationalized when we recognize altruism as a genuine moral motive. It must, however, be asked whether this modification of Benthamite utilitarianism is consistent with Mill's concern for liberty. Can he entirely escape the twin dangers of indoctrination and paternalism (as when it is said, 'you will be made to behave in a way conducive to the good of society without regard for yourself', or 'you will be made to behave in a way which will be in your own best interest without regard to your personal wishes')? Come back to this issue again after you have read 7.3.

(2) Mill's point that pleasures differ in quality and that quantity alone must not be the sole measure of 'goodness' is undoubtedly an improvement on that of Bentham. But by what criterion is the value of a pleasure to be judged? The pleasures of the intellect, feelings, imagination and the moral sentiments must be prized more highly that those of mere sensation, he says. And this is because a distinction can be made between happiness and contentment. Mill does not, however, go all the way with Aristotle and introduce the notion of man's proper function or end. The only reason he gives [ch. IV] for advocating the pursuit of the 'higher' pleasures is that most sensitive and sensible people do actually pursue them. Because people do actually desire such pleasures they must be desirable. Some philosophers, especially G.E. Moore, have accused Mill here of circularity and, more generally, have criticized utilitarians for committing the 'naturalistic fallacy' in that they have attempted to derive moral principles from non-moral factual judgements (compare 6.2 above). It is certainly arguable that what Mill actually meant – but did not make sufficiently clear – is that if we want to know what kinds of pleasures are rated highly in our society we should look to see what people (especially those whom we admire and rate highly as human beings) do actually desire. He is not saying that happiness *ought* to be desired; only that as a matter of fact most human beings find it more satisfying to strive for the higher things in life and aspire to the condition of a Socrates, albeit dissatisfied, rather than that of a contented pig. Whether there are alternatives to the utilitarian philosophy itself is of course a different and wider issue which it is the purpose of this chapter to help you to consider.

(3) Note also the connected problems of *determining* (a) the consequences of actions, and (b) the quantification of the happiness they are deemed to bring

about. Try to think of some particular examples. Can we always be sure of what *is* a consequence? What of the long-term as opposed to the immediate consequences? How long should we wait to find out? Or should we argue from the basis of historical precedent. (Note the problem of inductive reasoning referred to in the previous chapter.) As for quantification, can happiness or pleasures be 'measured'? Would it be better for, say, ten people to be very happy or, for twenty people to be moderately happy?

(4) An important disagreement among some commentators concerns the *status* of the principles advocated by Mill. A distinction has been made by, in particular, the influential American political philosopher John Rawls (see 7.3) between **act**-utilitarianism and **rule**-utilitarianism. According to the former, it is the consequences of individual specific actions which should be considered when we are deciding how we should act in a particular situation. Rule-utilitarians, however, argue that it is the conformity or non-conformity of actions to general rules, the consequences of which can be anticipated on the basis of past experience, that should be taken as the criterion for our moral judgements. Take as an example the making of a promise to a friend. The act-utilitarian decides to keep his promise because the long-term effects of breaking it would be harmful to the friend and probably the wider community. But, as pointed out in the third criticism above, the consequences cannot always be readily assessed or guaranteed. Yet we must make decisions *now* as to how we should act in *this* situation. Rule-utilitarianism might seem to be the better guide here in so far as one's decisions are based on rules that over the course of time have proved to be conducive to the general happiness; and indeed the positive consequences of conforming to a rule could even in certain circumstances outweigh any anticipated benefits of acting in a contrary manner on the basis of act-utilitarianism. For example, one might believe it would be better for one's friend in a particular case to *break* the promise, but that in the long run – and in line with a general rule – it would be better for society (and perhaps oneself?) to keep the promise. Nevertheless, the rigid following of rules can lead to inconsistency and to formalism. Moreover it can be objected that each case is unique. (Compare again 6.3 above and see also 7.9.). What is Mill's position? This is not easy to determine; he does not discuss the distinction any more explicitly than Hume does [*Treatise*, Book III, II, 2–4]. He is usually regarded as an act-utilitarian, but his interpretations of Kant [in chs II and V] do provide some support for those who would see him as a rule-utilitarian. (See also his references to rules in ch. II and 'rules of conduct in ch. V.)

Despite the differences between their respective theories of ethics, the philosophers we have looked at so far in this chapter share a commitment to some form of 'objectivism'. For Kant, morality is grounded in an absolute universal law self-imposed by and applicable to all imperfectly rational beings as a categorical imperative. The teleological systems of both Hume and Mill likewise have an objective aspect. According to Hume, actions which give rise to pleasant consequences arouse the sentiment of moral approval in the majority. There is thus a common agreement as to what is approved of. Similarly, for Mill the *principle* of rule-utilitarianism (if we interpret his ethics in this way) is the objective standard applicable universally, even though the actual rules may vary from society to society and thus are ethically relative. The philosophers we shall be examining in the next two sections, however – Friedrich Nietzsche (1844–1900) and Sartre – may both be thought of as having propounded subjectivist theories of ethics. Both, moreover, are noted for their literary styles. In contrast to the measured tones of Hume or Mill, or the heavy academicism of Kant, much of Nietzsche's writing is terse and passionate, replete with metaphor and aphorism. But whereas Nietzsche is clear, Sartre in his major philosophical works (though not in his novels and plays or lesser philosophical essays) is at times notoriously obscure.

6.5 Nietzsche and the 'will to power'

Reading: *On the Genealogy of Morals*; *Beyond Good and Evil*

Friedrich Nietzsche (1844–1900) covered a wide range of subjects; and his views on philosophy, literature, history, religion and so on cannot easily be disentangled and isolated from within his writings. This can be seen particularly in *Beyond Good and Evil*, which consists of a series of aphorisms and short essays. Although this is the AEB set-book, we shall concentrate in this section on *On the Genealogy of Morals* (*GM*), which contains a more systematic presentation of his ethics. With the aid of the following general survey of his philosophy as a whole, you should not find it too difficult to grasp the central themes of *Beyond Good and Evil* (*BG*).

Introduction

Nietzsche rejected all traditional theories of ethics [see *BG*, 186–203]. In his early writings [for example, *The Birth of Tragedy*] he argued that perfection should be understood in aesthetic terms – the being exemplified by the 'creative genius'. It was the function of culture to provide foundations for this; and Nietzsche said that such a culture would have to be one in which the Dionysian and Apollonian attitudes would be unified. The former is 'life-affirming', and represents emotion and excess, the absorption of oneself in the totality of things; the latter epitomizes cool reason, restraint and individuality. What Nietzsche looked for is a higher kind of man who will have the vision to rise above mediocrity, conventional value systems, even asceticism or self-renunciation. This view underlies his critique of idealism, Christianity, the natural sciences, and nation states and ideologies, which he regarded as subordinating the individual to false ideals. It is left to the individual philosopher to articulate this vision and transcend his historical situation.

In his later work [*GM*; *BG*, 24–44, 51, 188, 186–203 and 257–258] Nietzsche traced the emergence of the concept of virtue from the notions of custom, authority and then conscience, and argued for a '**transvaluation of values**' and for an affirmation of the '**will to power**'. His hero is now no longer the creative genius but the '**Superman**' or 'Overman' (*Übermensch*). By this, Nietzsche meant an individual possessed of the highest possible intellect, the greatest physical strength and will, the most perfect culture, who makes or defines his own values [see *Thus Spake Zarathustra*]. This is an ideal at which superior individuals should aim. Nietzsche combined it with the 'myth' of eternal recurrence, which is demanded by what he called 'the principle of conservation of energy'. He regarded the myth as the highest formula of the 'yea-saying' attitude which can be attained. Given an infinite universe, all possible combinations of determinate 'centres of force' would have occurred again and again. An infinite universe would thus seem to be required to avoid any appeal to a transcendent deity. In any case, for Nietzsche such an appeal would have been in vain; for, as the 'Madman' says [*The Joyful Science*, 125], 'God is dead; we have killed him' – and with him all 'objective' knowledge, value and meaning. God must make way for the 'Superman' who will fill with meaning the nihilistic void left by the destruction of religion and metaphysics [*Zarathustra*].

Consistently with his postulation of the will to power, Nietzsche argued the aim of knowledge is mastery. We seek to control, order the flux of Reality or Nature, namely impressions, sensations and Ideas, transform them into concepts or 'Being'. It follows that for him there is no absolute truth, in so far as to know is to interpret or construct Being from Becoming – to adopt a 'perspective'. Truths are fictions which are useful to us in the conduct of our lives. Thus we think of ourselves as a permanent substance, and we suppose the external world consists of enduring and causally connected substances. Perspectives are not only functions of knowledge; instincts too have perspectives. Nietzsche even argued that the categories of reason and fundamental logical principles are fictions and perspectives – by using which the will to power can control the world of Becoming.

The Genealogy of Morals

In the First Essay Nietzsche sets out to discover the origin of morals and in particular the concept of 'good'. Rejecting the attempts of certain 'English psychologists' to derive the notion from the *utility* of unegoistic actions, he shows that goodness as a value was *created* by the aristocrats, the nobility, to differentiate themselves from the 'low-minded, common and plebeian' herd whom they designated as 'bad' [Sec. 1–2]. It is thus *men* who are good or bad in this sense. How then did 'good' come to be applied to actions and assessed in terms of their utility? Nietzsche provides an answer in terms of his concept of *ressentiment* ('resentment'). The masses come to fear the aristocrats, and in opposition to the latter's affirmation of beauty, nobility and fullness of life they come to assert their own system of values:

> The slave revolt in morality begins when *ressentiment* itself becomes creative and gives birth to values: the *ressentiment* of natures that are denied the true reaction, that of deeds, and compensate themselves with an imaginary revenge. While every noble morality develops from a triumphant

affirmation of itself, slave morality from the outset says No to what is 'outside', what is 'different', what is 'not-itself'; and *this* No is its creative deed. This inversion of the value-positing eye – this *need* to direct one's view outward instead of back to oneself – is of the essence of *ressentiment*. In order to exist, slave morality always first needs a hostile external world; it needs, physiologically speaking, external stimuli in order to act at all – its action is fundamentally reaction. [Sec. 10]

Nietzsche thus distinguishes between two 'levels' or kinds of morality: that of the nobles and that of the herd – a 'master-morality' opposed to a 'slave-morality'. The aristocrats see the slaves as 'bad': but for the herd blinded by *ressentiment* the nobles are 'evil' [11]. The term 'good' thus also comes to have a double meaning. In the master-morality, good is strength, authenticity and self-affirmation. In the herd-morality, however, it is identified with meekness, sympathy and humility – as epitomized in particular by Christianity [13–15]. These two sets of opposing values ('good and bad', 'good and evil') have been engaged in a fearful struggle for thousands of years, says Nietzsche [16], and indeed may coexist within the same individual [10]:

One might even say that [the struggle] has risen ever higher and thus become more and more profound and spiritual; so that today there is perhaps no more decisive mark of a '*higher nature*', a more spiritual nature, than that of being divided in this sense and a genuine battleground of these opposed values. [16]

There is no room, according to Nietzsche, for absolute or universal moral systems (such as that of Kant). The herd is welcome to its own set of values – be it grounded in Christianity, utility, or whatever; and it can be left to philosophers to determine the order of rank among values. But for Nietzsche the primary aim must be to rise above herd-morality, beyond Good and Evil, to create a higher value for himself.

The Second Essay is concerned with such notions as 'guilt' and 'bad conscience', which are characteristic of the man of *ressentiment*. In Secs 1–15 Nietzsche examines and criticizes several accounts of how they may have originated. His brilliant analysis of 'punishment' [12–13] is particularly worth looking at (his approach has much in common with that of Wittgenstein in the present century). He argues 'our naïve genealogists of law and morals' have thought that the procedures or customs of punishment were *invented* for the purpose of punishing. In fact the 'meaning' of punishment (he calls it the 'fluid' element) arose very much later in culture than these customs and was projected and interpreted *into* them; and, moreover, 'punishment' does not possess just *one* meaning but 'a whole synthesis of meanings' or utilities – the most essential of which in the popular consciousness is that it is supposed to 'possess the value of awakening the feeling of guilt in the guilty person' [14]. But, on the contrary, argues Nietzsche, punishment does not sting the conscience; among criminals this is rare, rather it makes men hard and cold, it sharpens their feeling of alienation, strengthens their power of resistance. This leads on

[16] to a central notion – that of 'internalization', by which he means the turning inward, the repressing, of human instincts that cannot discharge themselves outwardly. (A comparison with Freud is of interest here, although he interpreted repression in terms of sexuality.) Nietzsche refers particularly to the *instinct for freedom*. Restricted and confined by the narrowness of custom and political power (with its capacity to inflict punishment), man the animal in the course of time turned back on himself that very wildness and freedom he had sought to give full rein to. And it is through this internalization that the bad conscience arises [17]. Nietzsche goes on to argue [22] that in order 'to drive his self-torture to its most gruesome pitch of severity and rigor' man postulates a holy God, who is both Judge and Hangman, before whom he can present himself as guilty, and by whom he will be condemned to an eternity of torment in hell. Herein lies a madness of the will, a sickness in man. (By contrast with what he intends to be a Christian concept of God, Nietzsche says [23] that the Greeks used their gods – 'those reflections of noble and autocratic men, in whom *the animal* in man felt deified' – to ward off the 'bad conscience' and to rejoice in their freedom of soul. Moreover, so far from punishing man for his evil deeds, they nobly took the guilt upon themselves by admitting that he must have been a god who led him astray.)

It is important for an appreciation of Nietzsche's ethics that the bad conscience should not be understood negatively – solely in terms of its initial painfulness and ugliness [18]. It is certainly an illness, but only as pregnancy is an illness [19]:

> For fundamentally it is the same active force that is at work on a grander scale in those artists of violence and organizers who build states, and that here, internally, on a smaller and pettier scale, directed backward, in the 'labyrinth of the breast', to use Goethe's expression, creates for itself a bad conscience and builds negative ideals – namely, the *instinct for freedom* (in my language; the will to power); only here the material upon which the form-giving and ravishing nature of this force vents itself is man himself, his whole ancient animal self – and *not*, as in that greater and more obvious phenomenon, some *other* man, *other* men. This secret self-ravishment, this artists' cruelty, this delight in imposing a form upon oneself as a hard, recalcitrant, suffering material and in burning a will, a critique, a contradiction, a contempt, a No into it, this uncanny, dreadfully joyous labour of a soul voluntarily at odds with itself that makes itself suffer out of joy in making suffer – eventually this entire *active* 'bad conscience' – you will have guessed it – as the womb of all ideal and imaginative phenomena, also brought to light an abundance of strange new beauty and affirmation, and perhaps beauty itself – After all, what would be 'beautiful' if the contradiction had not first become conscious of itself, if the ugly had not first said to itself: 'I am ugly'?

We can now see, after reading the First and Second Essays, that what Nietzsche is looking towards is an affirmation of life, which while it may grow out of the 'bad conscience' yet passes beyond it, transcending the good and evil of 'herd-morality'. This will make it possible for the 'yea-sayer' to create his own values –

necessary if he is ultimately to reach that higher state exemplified by Nietzsche's mythical 'Superior Man' (*Übermensch*) and described poetically in his *Thus Spake Zarathustra*. As he says in *On the Genealogy of Morals* [Second Essay, 24]:

> Some day, in a stronger age than this decaying, self-doubting present, he must yet come to us, the *redeeming* man of great love and contempt, the creative spirit whose compelling strength will not let him rest in any aloofness or any beyond, whose isolation is misunderstood by the people as if it were flight *from* reality – while it is only his absorption, immersion, penetration *into* reality, so that, when he one day emerges again into the light, he may bring home the *redemption* of this reality: its redemption from the curse that the hitherto reigning ideal has laid upon it. This man of the future, who will redeem us not only from the hitherto reigning ideal but also from that which was bound to grow out of it, the great nausea, the will to nothingness, nihilism; this bell-stroke of noon and of the great decision that liberates the will again and restores its goal to the earth and his hope to man; this Antichrist and antinihilist; this victor over God and nothingness – *he must come one day*.

It is in the light of such notions as liberation, victory and affirmation of life that we can understand the oft-quoted Nietzschean phrase 'the will to power'.

Nietzsche's discussion of 'ascetic ideals' in his Third Essay reinforces his central theme. (Space precludes an extensive account, but you should find the main points clear enough.) The human will, he says [1], has 'a horror of a vacuum': it needs a goal, that is a purpose, a sense of meaningfulness in life, and 'it will rather will *nothingness* than *not* will'. In the course of the Essay, Nietzsche shows how the 'great, fruitful, inventive spirits' (particularly philosophers) [8] have sought to achieve this goal through the exercise of poverty, humility, or chastity in their lives and achievements. [Note that he is, however, scathingly critical of 'artists' – see Secs 2–5, 25.] But herein lies paradox. The ascetic ideal, while 'world-denying, hostile to life, suspicious of the senses and freed from sensuality' [10], is inherently self-contradictory. For while the ascetic 'priest' (as Nietzsche terms the incarnate desire of man to be different) is apparently the enemy of life – the denier or 'nay-sayer' – and like the 'bad conscience' epitomizes man's 'sickliness', yet at the same time the priest 'is among the greatest *conserving* and yes-creating forces of life' [13]:

> The No he says to life brings to light, as if by magic, an abundance of tender Yeses; even when he *wounds* himself, this master of destruction, of self-destruction – the very wound itself afterward compels him to *live*.   [13]

(For a fuller account of the 'ascetic priest' and the self-contradictory nature of the ascetic life you should read Section 11.) For all his weaknesses, therefore, such an individual is the spearhead of mankind: he shows the disgruntled, under-privileged and unfortunate herd meaning, salvation, a way forward to a fuller life. What that meaning might be, for what end or why man wills, what he wills with – these questions are subordinate to the central fact that the will itself is saved [28].

*Comments and criticisms

It is not surprising, in the light of his general conclusion, that Nietzsche should have embraced a form of pragmatism in his views on truth and knowledge. The test of truth is its value for life. The desire for knowledge, like the transcending of conventional morality, must be understood as a manifestation of the Will to Power. Nietzsche's moral philosophy is thus clearly opposed to the deontological rationalism of Kant; absolute standards are postulated by philosophers who are horrified by a vacuum. He must equally reject utilitarianism as a valid ethic; pleasure is neither what men seek nor the test of right actions, but is what men experience as their power increases, while pain, viewed negatively, occurs when the Will to Power is blocked or frustrated, but, viewed affirmatively, is the catalyst for further progress, for further 'self-overcoming'.

Necessarily our discussion of Nietzsche's ethics is incomplete. Moreover, the unsystematic and wide-ranging nature of his writings have led to many divergent interpretations of his thought. Criticisms here must therefore be tentative. But we suggest you think about the following two points:

(1) Nietzsche contrasts the self-created values of the 'aristocrats' with herd-morality, as higher is contrasted with lower. But what are these 'revalued' values? How are they to be differentiated from those of the herd? Nietzsche seems to understand them only as the means whereby man is enabled to move ever upwards on the ascending path so that he may eventually achieve the status of the Superior Man. But the Superior Man is described as being 'integrated', 'creative', 'life-affirming' – terms which if they are evaluative at all would seem to presuppose some kind of 'objective' criterion. It is therefore a point for discussion whether our description of Nietzsche as 'subjectivist' is entirely appropriate. Is he not himself after all propounding a universal or absolutist moral system?

(2) Nietzsche's approach in *On the Genealogy of Morals* is broadly psychological. But it is on this basis that he contructs what is essentially a hypothesis to account for the emergence of the 'higher' man and the possibility of the Superior Man. Although not perhaps a central philosophical issue, Nietzsche's interpretation of history and, in particular, of Christianity are open to question and should be looked at critically.

6.6 Sartre and authenticity

Reading: Sartre, *Existentialism and Humanism; Being and Nothingness*, Part III; see also Taylor, *The Ethics of Authenticity*, and de Beauvoir, *The Ethics of Ambiguity*

Sartre's contribution to ethics is bold and uncompromising. He may perhaps be seen as taking Nietzsche's 'individualism' to the ultimate. Unfortunately, the conclusions he comes to in *Existentialism and Humanism* (1946) are inconsistent with his general metaphysics and ontology as set out in his major work *Being and Nothingness* (1943), and he subsequently repudiated them. But, as we shall see, the arguments of *Being and Nothingness* seem to rule out the possibility of ethics at all; and it is in a still later work, the *Critique of Dialectical Reason* (1960) (to be discussed briefly in 7.4), that Sartre claims to have found a way through the impasse. (It is for this reason that if you wish to gain an adequate understanding of Sartre's moral philosophy you should have some acquaintance with all three texts – whether you are working for the 'A' level or the IB examination, or for no examination at all. You will also find it helpful to look back at the brief account of Sartre given in the previous chapter.)

We shall start with the arguments of *Existentialism and Humanism*. Sartre's initial claim [see pp.26–28] is that man does not possess a 'human nature'. People who claim there is a creator usually think of him as a 'supernal artisan' who holds in his mind a universal conception of Man, each individual man being a particular realization of this universal. But, says Sartre, there is no God and therefore no human nature. As for atheistic thinkers who nevertheless adhere to the notion of a human nature common to all men, they assume that 'the essence of man precedes that historic existence which we confront in experience' [27]. For Sartre, however, and for existentialists in general, the converse is the case: existence precedes essence: '. . . man first of all exists, encounters himself, surges up in the world – and defines himself afterwards . . . Man is nothing else but that which he makes of himself' [28]. It is for this reason that people have called existentialism a 'subjectivist' philosophy; and Sartre goes on to suggest [29] that by 'subjectivism' is meant: (a) the freedom of the individual subject, and (b) ('the deeper meaning of existentialism') that 'man cannot pass beyond human subjectivity'. It follows from this that the entire responsibility for our existence is placed directly upon our own shoulders, and further that when we make a choice between one course of action and another we thereby '*affirm the value of that which is chosen*' [my italics]. This latter claim is central to Sartre's ethics. He rejects the **authenticity** of actions which are undertaken in accordance with systems of externally imposed values. To act *is* to endow our actions with value. 'If I regard a certain course of action as good, it is only I who choose to say that it is good and not bad' [31]. To act in accordances with the dictates of a God, the doctrines of Christianity, or the principles of philosophical system is to be guilty of 'bad faith' or '**self-deception**' (*mauvaise foi*). This is an important concept, discussed at length in *Being and Nothingness* [see Part I, ch. 2]. What he means by this is made clear on pp.50–51 of *Existentialism and Humanism*:

> Since we have defined the situation of man as one of free choice, without excuse and without help, any man who takes refuge behind the excuse of his passions, or by inventing some deterministic doctrine, is a self-deceiver. One may object: 'But why should he not deceive himself?' I reply that it is not for me to judge him morally, but I define his self-deception as an error. Here one cannot avoid pronouncing a judgement of truth. The self-deception is evidently a falsehood, because it is a dissimulation of man's complete liberty of commitment.

In other words, to refuse to face up to what Sartre, following Heidegger, calls 'abandonment' (that is, deciding one's being for oneself), to shy away from one's total responsibility for one's actions, to hide behind externally defined values, is to deny that freedom which is the very definition and condition of man: '. . . man is free, man *is* freedom' [34]. 'One can choose anything, but only if it is upon the plane of free commitment' [54]. (You should study the concrete example Sartre discusses on pp.35–39 by way of illustration of his doctrine, namely the story of his young pupil who (in 1940) cannot make up his mind whether he should go to England to fight for the Free French or should stay at home to look after his mother. You are also recommended to read Sartre's four-volume *The Ways of Liberty*, in which his philosophical and ethical theories are worked out through the medium of a novel.)

There is another important claim in *Existentialism and Humanism*, to which reference must be made. When we make a decision and choose a course of action, says Sartre, we commit not only ourselves but humanity as a whole. In legislating for the whole of mankind, the individual man 'cannot escape from the sense of complete responsibility' and consequently experiences 'anguish'. It is not immediately obvious how this assertion of 'universalizability' of decisions and actions can be reconciled with the subjectivity of Sartre's ethics. He attempts to provide support for his view on pp.44–45. The Cartesian '*cogito*', he says, provides us with an absolute truth – one's immediate sense of oneself. But he goes on to affirm that in the 'I think' is contained also knowledge of other people. (His argument has already been quoted in 5.11; you should refer back to it now.) It follows then that:

> the intimate discovery I have of myself is at the same time the revelation of the other as a freedom which confronts mine, and which cannot think or will without doing so either for or against me. Thus, at once, we find ourselves in a world which is, let us say, that of 'inter-subjectivity'. It is in this world that man has to decide what he is and what others are.

Now for Sartre what is characteristic of man is that he is 'self-surpassing'. Although we all find ourselves in different historical situations, we are all constrained by certain limitations – material, social and political. Such limitations are 'objective' (that is, they are met with and recognized everywhere) but in so far as they are *lived* they are 'subjective': man freely determines himself and his existence in relation to them, and in this respect we can identify a common or universal human purpose – self-realization:

> There is no difference between free being – being as self-committal, as existence choosing its essence – and absolute being. And there is no difference whatever between being as an absolute, temporarily localized – that is, localized in history – and universally intelligible being.   [47]

It is on this basis that Sartre feels justified in universalizing his commitment. To take his own example (and indeed an issue he had to face in his own life) – whether to join the Communist party:

A man who belongs to some communist or revolutionary society wills certain concrete ends, which imply the will to freedom, but that freeom is willed in community. We will freedom for freedom's sake, and in and through particular circumstances. And in thus willing freedom, we discover that it depends entirely upon the freedom of others and that the freedom of others depends upon our own. Obviously, freedom as the definition of a man does not depend upon others, but as soon as there is a commitment, I am obliged to will the liberty of others at the same time as mine. I cannot make liberty my aim unless I make that of others equally my aim.   [51–52]

Thus, as he says, 'although the content of morality is variable, a certain form of this morality is universal'. But he goes on to make it clear that he is not thereby adopting a Kantian position. For Kant, 'the formal and the universal suffice for the constitution of a morality', but Sartre argues that 'principles that are too abstract break down when we come to defining action' [52]. In concrete cases there are no criteria by means of which we can judge how best to act. We must 'invest' our own rule or authority; and what matters is whether we do so in the name of freedom. (Study the two cases discussed by Sartre on pp.53–54. Do you agree with his claim that the two opposing moralities are equivalent?)

*Comments and criticisms

(1) Although Sartre has expressly rejected Kantianism as being too abstract, the 'rule' which he invents for himself, which is grounded in the concept of freedom, nevertheless owes something to the German philosopher. And it is here that the inconsistency with the theory developed in *Being and Nothingness* becomes evident; for, as we saw in 5.11 above, he makes it clear in the book that by attributing freedom to the 'Other', he (the 'Other') becomes a threat or an obstacle to us [see *Being and Nothingness*, Part III, especially ch. 3]. Moreover, we can never approach the Other on the basis of equality, where 'the recognition of the Other's freedom would involve the recognition of our freedom':

> The Other is on principle inapprehensible; he flees me when I seek him and possesses me when I flee him. Even if I should want to act according to the precepts of Kantian morality and take the Other's freedom as an unconditioned end, still this freedom would become a transcendence-transcended by the mere fact that I make it my goal. On the other hand, I could act for his benefit only by utilizing the Other-as-object as an instrument in order to realize this freedom. It would be necessary, in fact, that I apprehend the Other in situation as an object-instrument, and my sole power would be then to modify the situation in relation to the Other and the Other in relation to the situation. Thus I am brought to that paradox which is the perilous reef of all liberal politics and which Rousseau has defined in a single world: I must 'force' the Other to be free.
>
> [*Being and Nothingness*, pp.408–409]

(**Note**: Rousseau and this 'paradox' are discussed briefly in 7.3 below.) It seems then that any kind of altruistic or social ethics, whether of the Aristotelian, Kantian, or Utilitarian variety, which might just conceivably be consistent with the premisses of *Existentialism and Humanism*, is clearly ruled out by the pessimistic analysis of human relationships which Sartre supplies in his major work. Nevertheless, Sartre does contemplate a way out. As he says in the footnote to p.412: 'These considerations do not preclude the possibility of an ethics of deliverance and salvation. But this can be achieved only after a radical conversion which we cannot discuss here'. (We shall say something about this 'radical conversion' in 7.4.)

(2) Another possible weakness in the moral philosophy of *Existentialism and Humanism* stems from the 'first principle of existentialism' – its subjectivity. Man commits himself, makes his own choices, without reference to any pre-existent values. But, it can be objected, each situation is unique. If value is created by the commitment to a course of action, might this not lead to an emptying of all meaning from the concept of 'value'? If, on the other hand, Sartre were to say that a particular situation is like another in certain respects and that therefore in the interests of consistency a similar course of action is enjoined upon him, would this not be to introduce an objective criterion by means of which the action is to be judged? To what extent can an arbitrary choice be called a choice at all? This is of course by no means the end of the matter; and you should try to think through the implications of questions such as these.

6.7 Ethics and language

Reading: A.J. Ayer, *Language, Truth and Logic*, ch. VI; R.M. Hare, *Freedom and Reason*

Ayer's 'emotivism'

All the moral philosophers we have looked at so far, whatever fundamental differences there may be between their systems, would agree on at least one important point, namely that when we make moral judgements we are actually *saying* something, that is, moral statements are meaningful – they may be used for communication. This might seem an obvious requirement of language in general. The claim that ethical language is in a strict sense *significant* has, however, been contested by the so-called 'emotivists', of which school of thought Ayer is perhaps the most notable twentieth century proponent.

You will remember that in 5.4 we discussed the distinction between analytic and synthetic propositions. According to Ayer, the latter are all empirical hypotheses. How then can he account for 'judgements of value', which are generally supposed to be synthetic but yet can hardly be thought of as having anything to say about our future sensations? Ayer sets out to show that to the extent that such statements are significant, they are ordinary 'scientific' statements; and in so far as they are not scientific, they are not literally significant but are expressions of emotion and as such neither true nor false.

He first of all divides ethical propositions into four classes: (1) propositions which 'express definitions of ethical terms, or judgements about the legitimacy or possibility of certain definitions'; (2) propositions describing the phenomena of ordinary experience, and their causes; (3) 'exhortations to moral virtue'; (4) actual ethical judgements. Only the first class, he says, can be said to constitute ethical philosophy; the others are either not propositions at all or belong to the sciences of psychology or sociology. And it is to this first category that he will confine his discussion.

Ayer criticizes two kinds of moral philosophers, both of whom have claimed that statements of ethical value can be translated into statements of empirical fact. The 'subjectivist' argues that to call an action right, or a thing good, is to say that it is generally approved. (*It is not clear whom Ayer has in mind here. If it is Hume, then his interpretation is open to question; for, arguably, Hume is not saying that to call action right *is* to say it is generally approved of but that we call it right *because* its pleasant consequences are approved of. We endow actions with moral value. This need not, however, entail translation of ethical statements into factual ones.) A 'utilitarian' (for example, J.S. Mill) defines the rightness of actions, and the goodness of ends, in terms of the pleasure, or happiness, or satisfaction to which they give rise. But Ayer rejects both kinds of naturalism on the grounds that no self-contradiction is involved in the assertion that some actions generally approved of are not right (or things generally approved of are not good), or in the assertion that it is sometimes wrong to perform the action which would actually or probably cause the greatest happiness (or the greatest balance of satisfied over unsatisfied desire). (*But if people approve of them, what can make such actions or consequences 'wrong'? Hume and Mill would want to know what other criterion is being applied here.) Thus the sentence '*x* is good' cannot be equivalent to '*x* is pleasant' or '*x* is desired'. Ayer does not deny that a language could be invented in which all ethical symbols are definable in non-ethical terms, but argues that in *our* language, sentences which contain normative ethical symbols (that is, sentences such as '*x* is wrong' when expressing a general *type* of conduct) are not equivalent to sentences which express empirical propositions of any kind – psychological or otherwise.

Now in rejecting the reducibility of ethical to empirical concepts, Ayer might be thought to have left the way open to 'intuitionist' or 'absolutist' theories of ethics. The difficulty of course with such theories is that they rule out the possibility of proving the validity of any moral judgement; one person's 'intuition' is as acceptable as any other's. There is no criterion by means of which the validity of judgements can be tested. For intuitionists, moral propositions are unverifiable and yet are held to be genuinely synthetic – thus undermining Ayer's main argument. So he must seek for a third view which is neither 'naturalistic' nor 'absolutist'. He agrees with the absolutists that the fundamental ethical concepts are unanalysable, but unlike them he can provide an explanation. They are, he says, 'pseudo-concepts'; in a statement such as 'You acted wrongly in stealing that money' the juxtaposition of 'You acted wrongly' and 'You stole that money' adds nothing to the *factual* content of the latter assertion. What we are doing when we say that stealing money is wrong is no more than to express our moral disapproval of the action. We are saying nothing which could be true or false. Ethical terms, moreover, not only can be used to arouse feeling but also to stimulate action. The 'meanings' of concepts such as 'good', 'duty' and 'ought', when used in an ethical context, are then differentiated in terms of both the feelings they express and the responses they are intended to provoke. It is now clear, Ayer says, why we cannot find a criterion for determining the validity of ethical statements; they have no objective validity at all!

He goes on to explain that his account differs from the 'orthodox subjectivist' theory in so far as the latter maintains that ethical sentences express the speaker's feelings without denying (as against Ayer) that they have genuine propositional status. But Ayer admits that subjectivist theories (his own included) seem to be open to G.E. Moore's objection: if ethical statements were simply about the speaker's feelings, arguments about questions of value would be impossible. In reply, Ayer argues that in such cases the dispute is not about values at all but about questions of fact. We do not say that the person who disagrees with us has the 'wrong' ethical feeling but seek to show he has misjudged the effects of an action, the agent's motive, or other special circumstances. What we have to do is to deploy suitable arguments 'in the hope that we have only to get our opponent to agree with us about the nature of the empirical facts for him to adopt the same moral attitude towards them as we do'. This should be possible, he says, if the disputants in a moral argument share the same 'system of values' (which should be the case if they have been morally 'conditioned' in the same way and live in the same social order). This last point would suggest that ethics, as a branch of knowledge, is for Ayer a social science; and indeed he not only explicitly states this but goes on to assert that Kantian and hedonistic or eudaemonistic theories can both be accounted for in terms respectively of fear of a god's displeasure and fear of society's sanctions in relation to the promotion or otherwise of happiness. Ayer's 'emotivist' theory of ethics is thus seen to be a form of reductionism consistent with his phenomenalistic theory of perception which we discussed in Ch. 5.

*Criticisms

(1) The first and perhaps obvious point about Ayer's theory relates to what has already been said in comments about his account of knowledge (see 5.11): his criterion of meaning is simply incorrect. To talk of a person, a thing, or an action as being good is to say – in a given context of discourse – that it satisfies specific standards (which can be made explicit) to a degree sufficient to justify the use of the term 'good'. It is not thereby denied that such terms as 'good', 'right' and so on also have an evaluative function (this is an issue to be looked at in the next part of this section), but it can be argued that to be evaluated, a person or an object must already possess certain characteristics, the reference to which is in part contained in the meaning of those terms. (Again, this does not commit us to the view that all descriptive terms must be of one kind. 'Red'

may differ from 'large' in its possible functions as much as the latter does from 'good'.)

(2) The most serious objection to the emotivist thesis, however, is that it does seem to make moral argument difficult if not superfluous. As we saw, Ayer clearly anticipated such a criticism and suggests that moral disputes *are* possible but are then arguments about matters of fact and not matters of value. Once we agree about the facts, and provided we share the same 'system of values', there will be no disagreement, he says. But does this not evade the issue? Surely, what we wish to ascertain is whether a *system* of values is possible on the basis of an emotivist theory? And this seems doubtful, for, firstly, feelings are in a very real sense subjective; and, secondly, to reduce moral judgement to two general categories of approval/disapproval is to obscure the wide range of subtle moral distinctions shared by different moral philosophies regardless of their premisses. Is it not possible, on Ayer's own thesis, both that we may agree on the facts that we have similar feelings about an action or person – but for different *reasons*? (As an exercise, you might like to accept Ayer's challenge in the middle of the chapter to construct an imaginary argument and think of some examples.)

(3) A third point worth considering is Ayer's criticism of subjectivist and utilitarian theories. Even granted that this may have some validity – and you should think about this in connection with the discussion in 6.4 – does it follow (a) that moral terms cannot be defined at all, and (b) that therefore an emotivist theory is the only alternative? Ayer argues that a language can be *invented* in which ethical symbols are definable in non-ethical terms, but that such a reduction is inconsistent with the conventions of our own language. Is Ayer's appraisal of these conventions correct?

Hare: prescriptivity and universalizability

Like Ayer, Hare (b. 1919) is concerned initially with the 'language of morals'. (This is in fact the title of his first and particularly influential book. If at all possible you should find time to read it. The main conclusions are however restated in *Freedom and Reason*; and we shall be discussing them in this section.) But whereas Ayer thinks a 'strictly philosophical treatise on ethics' should confine itself to giving an analysis of ethical terms (which in his case leads to their being classified as 'pseudo-concepts'), Hare in his writings on ethics combines detailed analysis of such terms with an extensive examination of moral arguments about concrete issues. Indeed, as he says in the Preface to *Freedom and Reason*: 'The function of moral philosophy – or at any rate the hope with which I study it – is that of helping us to think better about moral questions by exposing the logical structure of the language in which the thought is expressed.'

Hare's primary aim is to reconcile two apparently incompatible kinds of moral philosophy. On the one hand there are theories loosely brought together under the heading of 'subjectivism' (this includes Ayer's 'emotivism'), which in general deny the rationality of morals; and on the other hand 'descriptivist' theories (in particular 'naturalism'), which were developed in order to preserve rationality but at the expense of our freedom to form our own opinions. Hare hopes therefore to be able to resolve the antinomy between 'freedom and reason'. To do this he employs three conclusions drawn from *The Language of Morals*. (1) Moral judgements are a kind of **prescriptive** judgement. (2) Moral judgements are distinguished from other prescriptive judgements (for example, imperatives or commands) in that they are **universalizable**. (3) It is possible for there to be logical relations between prescriptive judgements. If this were not so then moral argument could not be developed. We shall discuss each of these points in turn.

Prescriptivity [Hare, ch. 2]

Before it is explained what Hare means by 'prescriptivity', something must be said about **descriptive meaning**. 'A judgement is descriptive if in it the predicate or predicates are descriptive terms and the mood is indicative'; and what makes such terms descriptive is that their meaning is determined by certain kinds of rules implicit in our discourse, by which he means 'consistency of practice in the use of an expression which is the condition of its intelligibility'. (You should note the similarity between this view and Wittgenstein's account of meaning referred to in 5.2 above.) A descriptive term can thus be misused if in using it one breaks the descriptive rule which attaches it to a certain kind of object (as when we say, for example, that a blue object is red). Now, according to Hare, value-words such as 'right' and 'good' are descriptive expressions just as much as 'red'. He thus differs from philosophers such as Ayer. But he also differs from descriptivists who seek to define value-words *completely* in terms of either 'natural' properties (for example, pleasure) or in terms of non-natural features, that is in terms of other value-words. And this is because he believes that when we use moral terms we are, in addition to describing a person or action, commending or putting him/it forward as a criterion of rectitude, to be imitated by others. In other words, we have added prescriptive meaning to the descriptive term. Thus when we say that someone should be called 'good' (on account of his character or exemplary behaviour), we are not just explaining how the word should be used but we are giving *moral* instruction' which is likely to have an effect on the life of the person who accepts it. As Hare says [2.7]: 'our descriptive-meaning rule has thus turned into a synthetic moral principle'. (It should be noted that, according to Hare, not all moral-judgements are value-judgements – though both kinds are expressed in prescriptive language; and prescriptive language includes moreover singular and universal imperatives.) Sometimes the prescriptive meaning of a word is primary and the descriptive meaning secondary (which allows for changing standards); in other contexts the reverse may be the case (we would indeed use words like 'courageous' or 'industrious' in a purely descriptive sense without any commendatory intention at all) [see also Hare, 10.1].

*Criticism

The issue that you need to think about here is whether Hare's distinction between descriptive and prescriptive meaning can be sustained at all. Consider again a word like 'good'. When I use it to refer to a person, action, or thing I usually mean that the person, action, or thing meets a certain standard or satisfies specifiable conditions. John is good, because his attitudes/intentions/actions are good, that is, he behaves in conformity with certain standards accepted by his society or promoted by his religion; and *War and Peace* is a good book (many critics have drawn attention to its literary quality, readers derive a particular kind of enjoyment from it). Now if we wish we can therefore talk as Hare does about the descriptive meaning of the word 'good' – though it is clear that the kinds of 'properties' exhibited by the person, action, or thing are not 'perceptible' qualities like red, large and so on. But what precisely are we adding to 'good' when we assign prescriptive meaning to it? Hare says we are commending the person or action; we are providing him with moral instruction. There are, however, two difficulties here. (1) The commendation belongs to us, the users of the word, whereas the properties which justify our use of it in its descriptive function are at least in some sense independent of us. Can we ever be sure when a word is being used with this prescriptive meaning? When someone says that a piece of work is good, he means it has reached a certain standard: is he also commending it or expressing his approval? (2) To the extent that such commendation might be applied to any noun or adjective word whatsoever, the question is raised whether prescription can have any *special* role to play in ethics – or at least whether it is sufficiently central to justify Hare's appeal to it as one of the 'rules of moral reasoning' (see below).

Universalizability [Hare, chs 2 and 3]

This is a feature of language which, argues Hare, is shared by both descriptive and moral judgements. Suppose I say of an object that it is red. Now because of the 'rules' of our discourse, we are committed to saying of *any* other thing which is like the first object in the relevant respects that it too possesses the property of being red. Singular descriptive judgements are thus universalizable in the sense that the meaning-rules of the descriptive terms they contain are themselves universal rules which relate to the notion of similarity [2.3]. From what has been said in the preceding paragraph it can be seen that moral judgements must therefore also be universalizable by virtue of their possession of descriptive meaning. If I call something 'good' I am committed also to calling something like it 'good'. The descriptive meaning is universalized; and to it is added the prescriptive meaning. It is this additional element in the meaning of moral terms, says Hare, that can make a difference to their logical behaviour in inferences [2.6]. The question 'Why should this be so?' brings us to a consideration of his third conclusion from *The Language of Morals*.

*Comment

Hare's use of the concept of 'universalizability' is by no means as clear and unambiguous as one would wish. In 3.4 he says that universalism is a logical and not a moral thesis; and he suggests that there are certain affinities between his own position and those of Kant and Sartre in this respect [see Hare, pp.34 and 38]. The parallels are, however, misleading. Certainly Hare, like both Kant and, to a lesser extent, Sartre (in *Existentialism and Humanism*), takes the view that a moral principle applicable to oneself must be taken to apply equally to others in similar circumstances. This is broadly a moral requirement (given that the test, according to Kant, is not always, if at all, a question of self-contradiction [see 6.3]). But Hare also talks of universalizability in a wider and seemingly obvious sense as a feature of all descriptive terms whether moral or not, namely that they must be used consistently in the same way in similar contexts. Thus to the extent his universalism is like Kant's, it is not a matter of logic: to the extent it refers to a logical requirement of language, its affinities with the Kantian thesis are minimal.

Moral judgements and logical relations [Hare, chs 6 and 10]

Concentration on the *language* of morals has – at least until recently – led many philosophers to ignore concrete moral issues. Hare is particularly concerned to bridge the gap and seeks to do so by examining the logic of moral inference. In both *The Language of Morals* and *Freedom and Reason* he frequently affirms his adherence to 'Hume's Law', namely that it is logically impossible to deduce an 'ought' from an 'is', that is, a moral statement from a non-moral statement, a 'value' from a 'fact'. So as to bring ethics to bear on moral problems, 'naturalist' theories, says Hare, have defined moral terms so that the premisses in a moral argument are not morally neutral. Factual premisses could then be made to *entail* (that is, to lead necessarily to) moral conclusions. Hare, however, wishes to maintain that ethical premisses are neutral as between different moral opinions in the sense that ethical theory 'provides only a clarification of the conceptual framework within which moral reasoning takes place' [6.2]. So how then can we move from premisses to conclusions without falling foul of 'Hume's Law'? Hare's solution is to invoke his two notions of prescriptivity and universality as the rules of **moral reasoning**. What we must do in a concrete situation is to decide what we *ought* to do by looking for an action to which we can *commit* ourselves (prescriptivity) but which is also an action we can accept as exemplifying a principle to be prescribed for others in like circumstances (universalizability). If either requirement is not met, the argument must fail. In addition to this logical 'framework' Hare lists three other ingredients which are required if we are to test a moral principle: the **facts of the case**, the inclinations or **interests** of the people involved to reject an evaluative proposition forced upon them by the logic of the argument, and their readiness to use **imagination**. In ch. 6 he provides a very simple example of moral reasoning so as to demonstrate his theory; and in chs 7 and 8 the theory is generalized and developed in much greater detail to take account of moral conflicts. His analysis is acute and valuable. It certainly deserves much greater attention than space will allow here.

In effect his argument is this. If I wish to turn a singular prescription (for example, 'Let me put *A* into prison') into a moral judgement ('I *ought* to put *A* into prison'), I must appeal to a general moral principle ('Anyone who is in my position ought to put his debtor into prison if he does not pay'). If *I* owe someone else (*C*) money, then I am committed (by virtue of the universalizability of 'ought' and the principle) to the moral prescription '*C* ought to put me into prison' *and*, further (by virtue of the prescriptivity of 'ought'), to the singular prescription 'Let *C* put me into prison'. If I am disinclined to accept this, then it would seem that I should have to accept that the prescription 'Let me put *A* into prison' does not hold. Now I can 'escape' from the force of the argument by refusing to accept either the universalizability or the prescriptivity of 'ought'; or by refraining from making a moral judgement at all about some or all of my own or other's actions; or by reinterpreting the facts – by showing that there are morally relevant differences between his case and mine. Alternatively, I might say that if I am determined to put *A* into prison I must override his, and therefore my own, disinclination by appealing to a universal moral principle (for example, the sanctity of contracts) either on utilitarian grounds or because he espouses an ideal, such as that of abstract justice. This leads Hare to go on in the later chapters to discuss: (a) conflicts of interests and desires in 'multilateral' situations and their reconciliation, when he adopts a position close to that of Mill's theory; and (b) the conflicts between individual interests and adherence to ideals by people who pursue them 'fanatically' even when it requires the interests of others – and their own – to be sacrificed.

*Comments and criticism

Our summary of Hare's main arguments is inevitably selective and incomplete, and undoubtedly has not done them full justice. But we have said enough for you to tackle the book yourself and think critically about the assumptions he makes and the conclusions he draws. We have suggested possible weaknesses in his two notions of prescriptivity and universalizability; and this in itself should be sufficient for you to question whether the weight of his thesis can be supported by what seems to be an insecure foundation. You should look in particular at his use of 'ought' statements and his move from moral prescriptions ('*x* ought . . .') to 'Let *x* . . .' statements. It is certainly arguable that these so-called 'singular prescriptions' are no more than disguised (and trivial) affirmations that the drawing of the conclusions of the form '*x* ought . . .' from general principles of the form 'Anyone ought . . .' *are* (as Hare himself notes) logically valid deductions, and that therefore acceptance of the premises must commit one to an acceptance of the conclusions as applying to oneself, not because of the adoption of any notion of *prescriptive* meaning but as a consequence of the nature of formal logic. Note also Hare's affinities with utilitarianism and especially his arguments in ch. 7 against the distinctions between (a) deontological and teleological theories, and (b) act- and rule-utilitarianism (refer back to Chs 6.3 and 6.4 of this book). The more important questions, it may be claimed, are (i) why a specific general principle is adopted at all, and (ii) why, having recognized that it applies to oneself (given that there are not special circumstances which might be legitimized by other qualifying principles), one fails to act in the morally appropriate way. The first has been implicitly examined throughout this chapter, in our discussions of various theories of ethics, and will be referred to again in 6.8. The second is the problem of weakness of the will that we touched on in 3.12 and 4.8, which we shall deal with now.

Weakness of will [Hare, ch. 5]

Can a man who knows, or claims to know (in a strong sense) that an action is wrong, yet nevertheless still perform it, or fail to do something which he knows he ought to do? How can he ignore the dictates of reason? Why does he give in to his passions? We have suggested that neither Plato nor Aristotle really resolved this problem. Does Hare have a solution? It should first of all be noted that he sees the very existence of this problem as providing support for his central distinction between prescriptivism and descriptivism. In a thoroughgoing descriptivist theory there could be no possibility of an 'ought' implying a 'can'. The fact that someone expresses regret or shows remorse when failing to act as he thinks he ought shows that he recognizes the prescriptive force of 'ought'. How then did Plato (or Socrates) and Aristotle, both of whom he regards as descriptivists, deal with the issue? Hare suggests that they tried to deny the problem, Aristotle by invoking the notion of a natural necessity (it is man's nature to seek the good), Socrates by concentrating on personal desires and thereby ignoring the universalizability of value-judgements. Moral 'weakness' is thus a failure of reason. An alternative way of avoiding the problem, he says, is to deny the prescriptiveness of moral principles as applying to ourselves in the particular instance or by watering down the content of 'ought'. Some of these instances are tantamount to hypocrisy. But the typical case of moral weakness is a case of 'ought but can't', which Hare analyses in terms of 'psychological' impossibility. Thus a person (Hare cites the examples of Medea and St Paul) may accept the binding force of the moral judgement but cannot obey it because of a 'recalcitrant lower nature or "flesh" ', or because 'in his whole personality or real self' he ceases to prescribe to himself. Hare therefore concludes that there is no genuine counter-example to the prescriptivist thesis.

*Comment

This is an issue you should think about seriously. Note carefully what Hare is saying: the failure to act on a moral imperative is to be accounted for in terms of a denial or prescriptivity, or of universalizability, or by an appeal to a 'psychological' impossibility. As for the first, this must surely mean that the individual does not recognize the imperative as morally binding, while denial of universalizability may reflect his belief that there are special circumstances which exempt his from acting in a particular situation. Arguably, in neither case should the description 'weak-willed' be applied. In referring to 'psychological impossibility' Hare does not seem to have progressed much further than Plato or Aristotle. The question can still be posed as to *why* the rational person allows his 'recalcitrant lower nature' to dominate? Why is it recalcitrant? To what extent is he still to be held *responsible* for his action or inaction? We do of course recognize cases of severe depression (caused, at least, partially, by chemical imbalance in the brain, or by circumstantial trauma) when a person literally *cannot* act in the appropriate manner. But then generally we do not blame them. Here too, however, it is doubtful whether we should talk of moral weakness or weakness of the will. (We shall consider the issue of 'freedom' further in Ch. 11.) What Hare does not consider is the possibility that one 'ought but *doesn't* rather than 'ought but *can't*. Thus we might imagine a situation in which a person says 'I know I *ought* to do X' (perhaps visiting his mother in hospital) but I don't *want* to do it (perhaps because he *prefers* to take his girl-friend to the pub). He recognizes both the prescriptive nature of the imperative and its universal application, yet he still does not 'do the decent thing'. Why? Maybe he is concerned with short-term happiness (though he knows he will later feel guilty). In more serious situations a person perhaps believes he will escape punishment. This is arguably to take a more realistic view of 'weakness'. Or should we not just say that such people are morally 'bad' rather than weak? (And what should we say of someone who admits to recognizing what he ought to do but simply says he is not going to do it and can give no reason or explanation?) These kinds of considerations do not necessarily undermine Hare's distinction between descriptive and prescriptive aspects of judgements. But let us suppose that an individual's refusal to conform to the moral imperative (because he prefers to do something else) *is* taken as a denial of prescriptivity. His behaviour might then be understood in descriptive terms, 'ought' being defined by reference to the *likely* (but by no means inevitable long-term benefits to himself (as in hedonistic or egoistic theories). This is of course the central point of contention between Hare (and Ayer) and the naturalists. To examine this further we must look again at the so-called 'is-ought' or 'fact-value' distinction.

Facts and values [see especially *Freedom and Reason*, chs 6 and 10]

Is it legitimate to infer from a factual premiss or premisses to a conclusion which is evaluative? Hume is generally credited with having been the first philosopher to suggest that such reasoning is fallacious (see Ch. 6.2 above). His words are worth quoting in full:

> In every system of morality which I have hitherto met with, I have always remarked, that the author proceeds for some time in the ordinary way of reasoning, and establishes the being of a God, or makes observations concerning human affairs; when of a sudden I am surprised to find, that instead of the usual copulations of propositions, *is*, and *is not*, I meet with no proposition that is not connected with an *ought*, or an *ought not*. This change is imperceptible; but is, however, of the last consequence. For as this *ought*, or *ought not*, expresses some new relation or affirmation, it is necessary that it should be observed and explained; and at the same time that a reason should be given, for what seems altogether inconceivable, how this new relation can be a deduction from others, which are entirely different from it.   [*Treatise*, III, I, 1]

A careful reading of this extract might lead one to question whether Hume is in fact criticizing the move from 'is' to 'ought' in such uncompromising terms. Is he not, rather, making the somewhat weaker claim that it *seems* inconceivable that the latter can be deduced from the former, and that a reason needs to be given if the inference *is* possible? Be that as it may, Hare has no doubts. As he says in *The Language of Morals* [2.5; compare *Freedom and Reason*, 2.6 and 6.9]: 'No imperative conclusion can be validly drawn from a set of premises which does not contain at least one imperative'. His basic objection to naturalists who would seek to deny this claim is that naturalism 'makes moral questions depend upon conceptual ones' [10.1]. Some naturalists, for example, see the evaluative content of a moral word as being tied to its descriptive meaning so that the use of the word commits one to making certain evaluations. It may well be, says Hare [10.2], that through the unanimity of people's evaluations, a word has a certain descriptive meaning tied to it. But nobody can be compelled logically to accept this evaluation; he can be compelled to accept only the implications of the descriptive meaning. To reinforce his point Hare goes on to say that as attitudes in society change, a word may lose its evaluative meaning (though 'it is difficult to break away from evaluations which are incapsulated in the very language which we use'), or the conceptual apparatus may change and the word may acquire a new descriptive meaning.

*Comments and criticisms

Hare's argument is persuasive. But does not his admission that both our evaluations and the conceptual apparatus we use can change with circum-stances and context in fact undermine his position? There seems to be no logical or *a priori* reason why a language should not be formulated in which facts and values *are* inseparable and which would therefore license an inference from non-imperative premises to an imperative conclusion. The possibility of this really depends on how one sees language. Do we control language or does language in some sense control us? If we *are* free to change our way of looking at the world and our behaviour in it, then why should we not reconcile naturalism and the quest for, say, happiness or well-being, with both rationality in morals and freedom? I may choose to act in a particular way believing that action to be conducive to my happiness (in some refined sense as defined by, say, Aristotle or Mill). I can preserve universality by recommending to others that a similar course of action in similar circumstances will be likewise conducive to their happiness and thence to the well-being of society as a whole. And, in the recommendation, a degree of prescriptivity is preserved which is not inconsistent with the factual assertion in which the recommendation is grounded. Moreover, it should be remembered that it is Hare himself who argues that the distinction between deontological and teleological theories is a false one.

Space precludes further examination of Hare's important and influential book. Our analysis has undoubtedly not done his thesis full justice; and nothing has been said about the practical examples he discusses, particularly in chs 9–11. But you will be able to explore some of the issues we have raised and consider their application to concrete moral issues as you study the next and final section.

6.8 Practical ethics

If you have worked systematically through this chapter (and the relevant sections of Chapters 3 and 4), you should have a fair understanding of at least the basic assumptions and arguments of some of the great moral philosophers. But before we make a start, something must be said of a difficulty that has no doubt occurred to you. Plato, Aristotle, Kant, Mill, Nietzsche and so on were undoubtedly thinkers of high intelligence and possessed considerable philosophical acumen. But the ethical systems they constructed in such detail and with such moral insight differ radically from each other. They cannot all be correct, you may say. Perhaps none of their theories is correct. How can we tell? Your attention has been drawn to some of the criticisms that can be made about each of them. But there does not seem to be any 'metaethical' criterion to which we can appeal. Perhaps all we can do is to see whether they actually work in practice. It only needs a little reflection to see that all of them *could* in some sense 'work', given an appropriate social framework for them to operate in (even allowing for the philosophical objections we have raised). Systems of moral codes, principles, rules, or laws could perhaps be established which would facilitate the implementation of Aristotle's doctrine of the 'mean', Kant's categorical imperative, or Mill's utilitarianism, as the case may be. Nietzsche would of course have dismissed such conventional morality and would have sought to 'revalue' all values in his quest to become the 'Overman'. If needs be, his moral standards could be imposed on the 'herd' by force. As for Sartre, at least in his *Existentialism and Humanism*, his conclusion would seem to be consistent with any ethical system whatsoever. It is immaterial *how* we decide to live; what matters is our free commitment.

There is also a second difficulty. Britain is a pluralist society in which therefore it is often difficult to achieve a consensus on such controversial issues as capital punishment, abortion, euthanasia and so on. How can the 'ordinary' person hope to come to definite conclusions when professional philosophers disagree about the cogency of ethical premises or the consistency of arguments? Even in more 'monolithic' societies such as, say, China or Ireland, in which there is arguably greater uniformity of opinion on moral issues, as a result perhaps of a shared commitment (for example, to communism or catholicism respectively), there is frequently considerable debate, if not about fundamental principles then at least as to how they are to be applied in particular cases. This lack of agreement, however, can be looked at in a positive light. The adoption of a totally unquestioning attitude is surely an abnegation of our responsibility as rational beings to assess facts, follow through chains of arguments and act appropriately in the light of conclusions.

So what we propose to do now is to subject the problem of killing to careful analysis and at the same time to explore the possibilities of reconciliation between teleological and deontological standpoints. Account needs also to be taken of the role of 'intuition' or 'moral sense', and of the 'fact-value' controversy referred to in 6.7. But there is an important caveat. It might be argued that too much emphasis on theory and debate can lead to inaction. Most of us, on seeing a small child fall into a pond, would take immediate steps to save it from drowning. Our initial response would most probably be regarded as instinctive. We might well be critical of a person who, before acting, sat down to work out whether saving the child would be conducive to the maximization of general happiness, or whether his action would be in accord with one of the formulations of the categorical imperative. But this does not do away with moral philosophy; for it can still be asked on what grounds would such criticism be based. Is instinctive action in some sense better than action that has been carefully thought out? Perhaps it is only in such situations that we are 'true to ourselves', or that our rationality is fully integrated with our feelings so that we are acting as complete persons? These are important and legitimate philosophical questions. Moreover it should not be thought that ethics necessarily leads to a passive attitude when one is confronted by major contemporary issues. When we find ourselves in serious disagreement with others, more often than not we are forced into a critical examination of the underlying principles which inform moral decisions, and which in turn may be grounded in wider social or religious 'world-views'; and we are right to ask of those with whom we are in dispute (and they of us) that acceptance of a commitment to those presuppositions be fully justified. In this way we might expect ideally (and it must be stressed that it *is* an ideal situation to which we as fallible beings aspire) to develop: (1) a better understanding of the complexity of many moral problems and the relationships between ethics, law, politics and religion; (2) more openness and respect for views sincerely held by other people but which differ, often radically, from our own; and (3) greater integrity in our own behaviour.

The taking of human life

It is interesting to note that, contrary to the impression you may have been given so far, throughout the world – in different cultures and societies, past and present – there is a great deal of agreement about morality: we might even say there is a 'basic' moral code common to all human beings. Most people would not hesitate to say that lying, stealing and murder are 'wrong' and should be punished. So, you may ask, what is all the fuss about? Let us confine our attention to **murder**. By murder I mean 'the unlawful premeditated killing of one human being by another' (*Collins English Dictionary*). The most heated discussions are usually about two issues:

(1) The reasons *why* murder is considered to be *morally* unacceptable. (**Note:** the definition just quoted is a *legal* one: as we shall see, law and morality do not always coincide.)
(2) Special circumstances: are capital punishment, abortion, assisted euthanasia and the killing of one's 'enemy' in war morally wrong? (We shall look at these later, and will start by considering the perhaps less controversial examples.)

Why should I not kill my husband/wife/neighbour? Leaving aside any consideration of *legal* restrictions and confining the discussion strictly to the moral dimension, we might say first of all that it is against the will of God (God's 'law'). But how do we know this? Well, the Church tells us it is wrong; or it says so in the *Bible* (or in the *Koran*). One problem here of course is that 'holy books' are not always consistent, or they require interpretation; and different sects interpret the 'Word of God' in a variety of ways. But let us suppose for the sake of argument that there is no ambiguity and that there is a clear-cut injunction (for example, the Fourth Commandment) against murder, if not all forms of killing. Now does this mean that it is wrong to murder someone *because* God says it is, or that God says it is because it *is* wrong? If the former is the case, then this produces a difficulty for the atheist or agnostic. It would be unwise (and uncharitable) to suggest that the non-believer is necessarily less 'good', kind and well-disposed towards his neighbour than a committed Christian, Jew, or Muslim. To follow a moral code need not therefore necessarily commit one to a religious world-view. The believer might argue that nevertheless morality must in the last analysis have a religious basis, though the atheist or agnostic may choose to disregard it. This however misses the point: that moral principles may coincide with the code adhered to by, say, Christians and yet can still be accepted because of their conformity to secular criteria. The question can also be asked *why* in any case God decides that murder should be proscribed. Either we must regard God's decision as arbitrary and irrational (or beyond human understanding), or as being made because 'good' and 'evil' are after all categories intrinsic to the very nature of existence. (Compare Kant's point that our concept of God as the archetypal good must itself be derived from the Idea of moral perfection.) Moreover it hardly needs pointing out that to ground morality so exclusively in religious assumptions is unwise, as it might well be undermined should they ever become discredited. So what secular criterion or criteria can we appeal to in support of the claim that murder is wrong?

If we adopted a Kantian standpoint we should reject murder because as an action it would be in breach of the categorical imperative. To murder someone would be to treat him as a means, not as an end; and we should have to say that the maxim of action is not universalizable, presumably on the grounds that if such killing were licensed it would logically lead to the extinction of the human race. A similar indictment of murder as contrary to morality could also be expected of those who subscribe to a utilitarian ethic such as Mill's. The murder of one's neighbour could hardly be described as conducive to the general happiness of society. Such assessments are however gross oversimplifications; and whether one subscribes to a deontological or teleological theory, some analysis of the background and circumstances of a murder are required if the moral aspects are to be analysed adequately. For murderers, unless they are in some sense genuinely ill (psychopaths, for example), or suffering from stress to a degree which might be held (in law) to exculpate them, usually commit their crimes for a specific reason or reasons. Let us consider a few possibilities. Mr X beats his wife unmercifully. She *could* have left him, called the police, and so on, but chose to put cyanide in his custard. My Y's daughter was killed in a terrorist bomb attack. He shot one of the perpetrators in retaliation. Mr Z's life was ruined when his business was destroyed and his wife taken by a rival whom he therefore stabbed to death. Now in all these cases it is not simply the action of murder as such that we are being asked to treat as a potentially universalizable maxim, but the murder of someone who in some sense has been wronged. The Kantian objection must therefore be modified. The question of human extinction no longer arises, as it is only a small proportion of people who would be eliminated given such a criterion. And it is by no means clearly established that there would be any incoherence or inconsistency in universalizing the maxim that people who have perpetrated certain wrongs in carefully specified circumstances might legitimately be killed. It could also be argued, on Millian lines, that greater happiness of society might ensue if such undesirable citizens were removed. There would however still be two difficulties. Firstly, murders in such circumstances would be instances of individuals taking the law into their own hands, and if not properly organized and controlled might lead to a free-for-all with the consequent breakdown of the social order. Secondly, it is not clear that such a defence could escape the Kantian objection, that to kill even an 'undesirable' would still be to treat him as a means (for example, to achieve personal satisfaction, retribution and so on).

Suppose then we empower a legitimate authority (the monarch, the state, the judiciary) to take on the responsibility for those persons guilty of wife-beating, terrorism, *crimes passionels* and so on). And what if the punishment is death – by hanging, lethal injection, electrocution (to name but some of the methods)? Certainly the killing is *legal*. But some people would argue that it is still *morally* wrong. Murderers might be incarcerated for life, forced to do community work, sent into space, or whatever, but not executed. What is the basis for such a position? One answer is that capital punishment is contrary to the Biblical injunction 'Thou shalt not kill'. But Christians themselves are divided on this issue. Many say that it is the job of the teaching church to interpret the Christian message in the light of revelation, and they assert that it is permissible for a legitimate government to determine what kinds of punishments should be imposed for particular crimes. Others (members of the Society of Friends perhaps, as well as most Buddhists) might argue that the killing of another human being is always morally unacceptable. (Consistently with their principles, they also refuse to participate in wars except in a non-combatant capacity. As against this, Roman Catholic teaching, for example, allows for the killing of the enemy provided the war satisfies a number of conditions to be accounted as 'just'. Whether this can be sustained in this nuclear age is much disputed.) It should also be noted that there are other strong arguments against capital punishment which are not grounded in a religious perspective – not least that there are many well-documented cases of people who have suffered capital punishment but who have subsequently been shown to have been innocent of the crimes for which they were executed. Against this there are those who would say that capital punishment is a better deterrent than, say, life imprisonment, and that it is in the interests of society that a few innocent people should die than that a larger number of murders be committed. This might suggest a utilitarian position? What does Mill have to say? And what is Kant's view?

Perhaps somewhat surprisingly, both philosophers are strongly in favour of the death penalty, but for quite different reasons. Kant argues for capital punishment because he thinks of punishment in general in terms of retribution. Putting a murderer to death is necessary if 'balance' is to be maintained in justice or the moral order. The rightness of the action therefore does not depend on any consequences which might affect the criminal but on whether the agent (the judge, hangman and so on, who receive their commission from the law of society) acts for the sake of duty – out of reverence for the moral law. Although this is consistent with one formulation of the Categorical Imperative, it can be argued that Kant is now no longer treating the guilty individual as an end in himself. Kant would seem to admit this himself. In his *Metaphysic of Morals* he implies that those who break legal and moral contracts are thereby excluded from active citizenship and lose something of their personhood and become akin to 'things' (compare the discussion of Rousseau in 7.2).

Mill on the other hand supports the death penalty *because* of what he sees as the consequences for the criminal. Unlike Kant, he stresses the deterrent and reformist aspects of punishment. Now in view of the serious nature of the crime, it would seem that nothing less than imprisonment for life with hard labour would suffice. But this would undoubtedly bring about a great deal of suffering; and Mill argues that it would be both a greater deterrent to others and more merciful to a murderer (or a thief!) to hang him than to leave him languishing in gaol. This is questionable and raises issues about the nature of short-term consequences for society in general (Mill's case has of course been over-simplified here. You will find his argument in his parliamentary speech reprinted in the collection of articles edited by Singer, listed in the Bibliography.)

There is little doubt that both Kant and Mill stress important aspects of moral judgements. For Kant, actions are right in so far as they conform formally to the objective moral law; the good person acts for the sake of duty, that is, because his action is right and not because it might bring about, say, greater happiness. But whereas Kant emphasizes motives or intentions, Mill sees the consequences of an action as the criterion by which it should be judged. Is there any possibility of reconciliation between these two theories? It certainly seems a little artificial to separate intentions from actions (Mill) and actions from consequences (Kant). Kant does after all appeal to consequences as a *test* for the universalizability of maxims for action ('If everybody acted like this, society would disintegrate, promises would lose their meaning, etc.'). And in Mill's ethics, one's decision whether to perform a specific action or not must take account of what one perceives to be the consequences, and must therefore be assimilated to one's intentions ('I intend to do this because I think it will increase the total sum of happiness'). Let us therefore adopt as a basis on which to make moral judgements the following propositions. (1) The 'goodness' of an intention depends on the 'goodness' of the consequences of the intended action. (2) 'Good' consequences may be supposed to be those which (in some definable sense of 'well-being') contribute to the well-being of the individual and through him the well-being of society. (3) An action derives its 'rightness' from intentions and consequences: thus, a good action is one which is done with good intention to bring about good consequences. Several qualifications must be made here. (3a) If the consequences prove to be in some sense 'bad', the actions which led to them might still be regarded as right in so far as they stem from a good intention. The question can however be raised about the extent of the agent's responsibility for not having foreseen such consequences. (3b) If the intentions are bad, an action might still be regarded as right to the extent that it gives rise to good consequences, but the agent could not then be regarded as praiseworthy.

A further point should be made that Kant, although a 'universalist', cannot avoid particularizing, as each moral situation can be regarded as having its own special features or circumstances; while Mill, to the extent that he can be regarded as a rule-utilitarian, cannot avoid universalizing. In fact both philosophies must come to terms with the dual problem: that generalizations in ethics may fail to address concrete situations, and conversely that too much emphasis on the uniqueness of the particular case can lead one to lose sight of the moral implications. Thus to say simply that X murdered Y and that he should therefore be condemned takes no account of the motives and intentions of the agent, or circumstances and consequences of the deed. A general principle to the effect that killing is wrong (whether because of its breach of the categorical imperative or because such actions have bad consequences) fails to allow for exceptions. At the same time, if one treats the killing as a special case (perhaps the murderer's mother was ill, there were political motives, or the consequences might in the long run prove to be beneficial to society), then consistently one must treat other killings as special cases, and the general principle 'killing is wrong' might in due course fail to have any application at all. Clearly a balance between generality and particularity is required. How this balance is to be achieved and where lines should be drawn (and how 'well-being' or 'beneficial' are to be defined) can in the last analysis be decided only as a result of experience and discussion until a consensus is arrived at by the community at large.

It should be noted that the consensus we have just referred to, although in part a consensus of judgement as to what is to count as 'right' or 'wrong', 'good' or 'bad', must be primarily a consensus of procedure. The arguments we are developing in this section are based on the premiss that ethics is not an absolute or immutable system but a dynamic on-going framework of guiding principles worked out to facilitate the day-to-day relationships and intercourse of human beings in society. It is as it were the oil that reduces friction in the social machinery. Any consensus must however be firm and flexible. It must be sufficiently firm to resist both the 'free-play' of subjectivism and the corrosion of what we may term 'closed value systems', both of which will in due course affect the efficiency of the 'machine'. Let us make clear what this means. If each and every individual were to establish his own code of behaviour independently of his relationships to other people, the notion of morality would cease to have meaning. In at least one sense of the term, 'subjectivism' must rule out ethics altogether; morals can only make sense in the context of shared beliefs. Subjectivism, as used in the writings of certain existentialists, however, is consistent with different systems, and is to be welcomed in so far as such philosophers emphasize freedom and commitment. (Some of the difficulties with this form of subjectivist ethics have already been discussed – see 6.6.) It will of course always be open to an iconoclast or a solitary Nietzsche-like figure to seek his own salvation in his own way. But society must resist any attempt by the individual claiming special insights to impose his vision (very often by force) without subjecting them to appropriate testing procedures and discussions. The threat posed by the often well-organized and vocal interest groups, who also claim special knowledge or moral insight (that is, they subscribe to 'closed value systems' which may be grounded in either a political or a religious ideology), is perhaps more serious. But if the consensus is to be firm it must also be flexible in that it should allow for the coexistence of minorities or individuals who dissent from the moral beliefs of the majority. It is ultimately a problem for legislators to establish what we might call a 'lowest common denominator' framework of rules and principles in which all members of society might operate in optimal harmony.

Let us now attempt to bring together some of the features of this 'consensus', which have been discussed above. It is assumed that members of a society possess the capacity both to reason and to make moral judgements. The guiding principle of the consensus might be: **reasoned intention-in-action as referred to** *probable* **consequences**. The ends to be sought-after might be the maximization of opportunities for personal development as human beings in society and the cultural progress of that society as a whole.

Of course, statements such as these raise a multitude of further difficulties. What is meant by such phrases as 'personal development' and 'cultural progress'? Can 'opportunities' be maximized for all people equally? If *my* opportunities are increased, might this not be at the expense of *yours*? Some of these points will be raised again in Ch. 7. But it must be left to you to think seriously about them after you have completed your study of the book. One aspect in particular of personal development should however be mentioned now, namely, that it should include a growth in understanding of and response to the very consensus which makes that development possible. And it is here perhaps that the notion of 'conscience' might be incorporated into the ethical scheme we are tentatively working out. One difficulty with this concept is that it has tended in the past to have been appropriated by religion and has been interpreted rather narrowly to mean 'the voice of God'. Less literal-minded Christians, however, have accepted the requirement that conscience be 'informed', that is, the human agent should take the fullest account of the moral principles relating to the problem – as 'revealed' by God in the *Bible* or through the teaching Church. Conscience would thus appear to belong to the 'reason' rather than to 'feeling', though we may sometimes refer to conscience as the 'moral sense'. A second problem is that the deliverances of the (rational) conscience vary from society to society. And even within the Christian tradition it has often seemed that God issues different instructions to different people in similar circumstances. For the purpose of our scheme, therefore, we should probably be on safer ground if we thought of conscience as the capacity of a rational individual to recognize and be sensitive to the demands of the 'moral imperative' as articulated by a 'consensus'. It might indeed be regarded as akin to a skill (like typing or playing football) which can be improved and refined through constant training and practice, so that it can become almost instinctive. This kind of approach is not inconsistent with a more narrowly-theological interpretation, but it has the advantage of accommodating the varying perceptions of intuitions to be found in different cultures or indeed within a single culture. It also rules out an extreme individualistic view of conscience, in that the 'inner voice' has to be grounded in a shared and therefore 'objective' moral standard. (There are no doubt difficulties with such a formulation. This is a philosophical issue you can perhaps follow up for yourself.)

Actions which are deemed to promote personal development or social progress are *approved of* and therefore *recommended* as models: conversely, actions which are perceived as retarding progress or as liable to weaken the cohesion of society come to be disapproved of and recommendations are made that they should be avoided. (*It is also left to you to consider whether and how such an approach can facilitate a synthesis of teleological and deontological ethics. Does 'recommendation' satisfy Hare's requirement for prescriptivity? Can universalizability be reconciled with the particularity of 'special' cases? Is the move legitimate from *perception* [of actions as retarding progress] to *disapproval* and *recommendation* [to avoid them]? Look again at what was said in 6.7 about facts and values.)

On the basis of the tentative conclusions we have come to in the course of the preceding discussion, we can now consider other situations which involve the taking of human life, namely, suicide, euthanasia and abortion. As in the cases of capital punishment and pacifism there is considerable disagreement – among religious and non-religious people alike – as to whether such actions are morally acceptable. And there does not seem to be any predictable pattern to people's convictions about such matters. For example, a person may be in favour of capital punishment yet against abortion – or vice versa. So let us look at some of the arguments – we shall consider **suicide** first.

It can be said that, in so far as we are wholly responsible for ourselves, we have the right to determine when our lives should come to an end. We might feel, for example, that if we were suffering extreme pain (as in terminal cancer) suicide might be an understandable and acceptable course of action. People under severe stress brought about by their social or domestic circumstances (they could, for example, be having to contend with sustained physical or psychological abuse by a mentally disturbed or evil-intentioned partner) might also decide that they could put up with their situation no longer and decide to end it all. What objections can be made to this?

Firstly, it could be said that we are all creatures of God and that it is for Him to decide when to take us to His heavenly home. But does God intervene in His creation, deciding that the time has come for this or that individual to 'shuffle off the mortal coil'? (See 9.5.) Can any death – whether from disease, earthquake, or car accident – be thought to be a consequence of God's intention or 'will', rather than the result of natural causation? Or is the natural order itself a manifestation of God's will? But we can suppose ourselves to have free will. Yes, but to commit suicide is to misuse that freedom. On the other hand, if the God in whom we believe is merciful and compassionate, He will not condemn such an action. This kind of discussion would of course have no cogency for an atheist.

Secondly, it might be claimed that to kill oneself is selfish. It would be to run away from one's problems. It fails to take account of the consequences for others (family, friends and so on). In answer to this, it could be argued that if one were considering suicide (as providing final release from excruciating pain, for example), one's relatives would be saddened by one's death whether or not it was brought about by illness or by preemptive suicide. One could discuss it beforehand and make appropriate provision for those likely to be most affected. Indeed the pain of those left behind might paradoxically be lessened through the knowledge that their loved one was in full control of the time of his or her own death. It might be argued further that in many cases an individual could be fully justified in being 'selfish' in so far as suffering may be a consequence of unbearable domestic or social pressures. Any ethical consideration of the feelings of others should rightly be subordinated to the necessity of escaping from the situation. Morality is simply irrelevant here. It might be said that any suicide must in part reflect a failure of partner, family, or friends to be fully aware of the circumstances or to take steps to prevent the tragedy. Accusations of a suicide's selfishness should not therefore be made without full regard for the complexity of human existence and the pressures of contemporary society. At least in most countries, suicide is no longer illegal!

Thirdly, we must allow for the possibility that some suicides could even be regarded as altruistic acts. One's death might save one's family or the wider community from incurring heavy expenditure on medical services. Or if one were suffering from a dangerous and incurable disease, death would prevent it from being passed on to others. Perhaps these are improbable scenarios. But in some cultures (Japan, Ancient Rome) suicide has been looked upon as an act of bravery – particularly if it is committed to help one's friends. (Oates, a member of Scott's ill-fated Antarctic expedition deliberately left his tent and perished in the hope that his colleagues might benefit – though in hindsight we would say that death was inevitable for them all.)

Lastly, you might like to consider how Kant would have applied the categorical imperative to determine the morality of acts of suicide.

Let us now turn to **euthanasia**. We must first make a distinction to clarify what this actually means. If a medical doctor administers a high dosage of a drug (say, diamorphine) with the intention of relieving pain but also in the full knowledge that in all probability the drug will hasten death, it is generally held that this does not constitute 'mercy-killing'. (The underlying principle here is sometimes referred to as the doctrine of **double-effect**.) This is legal in Britain (although in a court of law it may not always be easy to ascertain the doctor's actual *in mente* intention). However, if a drug (say, potassium chloride) were injected – at the request of a terminally ill patient – with the intention of causing him or her to die (and hence bring an end to the suffering), this would be regarded as an instance of euthanasia. It is illegal in Britain, although permitted in, for example, the Netherlands. The issue here is whether it is ethically acceptable (and whether the law should be changed accordingly). Many people say that they would wish their lives to be brought to an end in the event of their suffering irreversible brain damage as a result of an accident, or should they become physically and mentally incapacitated in their old age and therefore a burden to their family and society. Again the possible consequences have to be weighed against each other. From the point of view of the sufferer, and perhaps also of his or her family, euthanasia might well be considered beneficial. Objectors might argue, however, that it would tend to blunt or weaken the moral sensitivities of the society as a whole. Were euthanasia to be legalized – and laws do not always reflect standards of morality – it might also be regarded as the thin end of the wedge. 'Look what happened in Nazi Germany,' they say. The moral acceptability of euthanasia must therefore presuppose that the person whose life is to be terminated has given his or her permission voluntarily. This does of course raise questions as to whether such permission has in fact been given in a specific case, or how it was obtained. And what moral attitude should be adopted towards this issue in the case of people who are incapable of communicating their wishes, such as people who as a result of brain damage are little more than 'cabbages'? Can people who have lost all capacity for rational thought or moral judgement be regarded as 'persons' with 'rights'? This of course relates to the wider context of religion, political philosophy and the philosophy of mind. Is the possession of rights contingent on an ability to contribute in some way to society? It can certainly be argued that a society which is able to show compassion and care for those most handicapped in its midst is in some sense a 'better' society than one which would sanction 'mercy-killing'. It might also be claimed that despite their handicaps, such individuals nevertheless have 'souls' and therefore it would be quite wrong to terminate their lives; to do so would be nothing less than murder.

It is over the question of **abortion** perhaps that the greatest controversy has raged. And certainly the issues do seem to be rather more complex. Let us take the oft-quoted case of a woman who knows that her unborn child will be severely handicapped (she has taken a drug or has had German Measles early in pregnancy, and tests have confirmed the prognosis). She has four children already, her husband is unemployed, and housing conditions are poor. Legally she would be entitled to seek abortion and would have no difficulty in securing one through the National Health Service. But does this make the abortion morally 'right'? Those who say it does not can make out the following sort of case. The unborn child has a 'right' to life. Moreover, human life is sacred. Each one of us has a 'soul' which comes to us from God. To kill the child in the womb, whatever its handicaps, is an affront to the Creator. As in the case of euthanasia – perhaps more so – abortion weakens respect for life. Society should be able to cater for such disabled children regardless of the financial cost. Caring for them is in any case an opportunity for people to show patience and love. Who is to say that the child might not live a happy life and make a contribution to the wider community? (There are many well-documented cases of individuals born, for example, blind, mute and even totally paralysed, who have been able to achieve fulfilment in a variety of ways.) From this standpoint the consequences of abortion would be regarded as 'bad', as would the action itself.

In answer to these objections a number of points can be made. (i) 'Rights' belong to people who are actually members of society and are given to them by society. (This would of course be contested by those who subscribe to various forms of a natural rights theory, especially the view that rights are intrinsic to human beings by virtue of their being God's creatures. And it is because of such differing views that it need not be inconsistent to be in favour of abortion in certain circumstances and yet be opposed to the death penalty for murder; whereas there would appear to be an inconsistency when many of the most vociferous opponents of abortion, on the grounds that human life is sacred, often seem less concerned about capital punishment. Presumably it is argued that the sacredness of a murderer's life must be subordinated to a higher principle in so far as they have broken one of God's commandments.) (ii) The unborn child belongs to the mother; her wishes and desires – her autonomy – must be paramount. Certainly in the earliest weeks of pregnancy the child is not viable, that is, it could not survive outside the womb. (You might note here the relevance of the 'double-effect' principle mentioned above. In some [usually Roman Catholic] societies, while abortion in general is proscribed, a doctor might be permitted – by the state [the Church's view remains equivocal] – to abort an embryo in order to save the life of the mother – it not being his primary intention to kill the child. With today's standards of medical care – at least in Western societies – few doctors have to contend with such a dilemma. But the matter becomes more contentious when extended to abortion of a child conceived as a result of rape, or when the mother is, say, only twelve years old, or to adult mothers whose mental or physical health might be under threat if the pregnancy were allowed to go to full term. You can be left to ponder these possibilities for yourself.) (iii) The sacredness or sanctity, it might be argued, is likewise a human concept. The existence of a Creator is questionable. (iv) As to the existence of a 'soul' in each individual, this of course gives rise to the question of when exactly in the development of the foetus it becomes 'ensouled'. Most speculation about this, however, may be redundant, as what really matters for most opponents of abortion is that termination of pregnancy prevents the embryo from realizing its potential as a human being; and from the biological standpoint (even without the introduction of religious or metaphysical concepts) it can be argued that this potential is present from the earliest moment when the zygote comes into being after the ovum has been fertilized. The philosophical debate can then be concentrated on the issue of balancing the respective claims of the child's 'right to life' (if it is deemed to possess such a right) against the needs and wishes of its mother (and perhaps also the father). (v) One might also refer to the wider claims of society at large. Particularly pertinent is the problem of overpopulation in some Asian and South American countries, when a failure to control births might lead to mass starvation. Abortion is arguably an extreme measure; contraception and sterilization might seem to be more satisfactory alternatives. But for many opponents of abortion such methods are equally unacceptable from the moral point of view. (The potential for life, it might be argued, is implicit in the DNA of egg and spermatozoon even before fertilization occurs.) (vi) Note lastly that some philosophers, following Lord Devlin (see the Reading list) argue that all morality forms a 'seamless web' and that people who deviate from the moral standard in one respect are likely to deviate from the whole. In other words, if one lies and steals, one might be expected to encourage euthanasia, then abortion, and so on. (This is sometimes called the 'slippery slope' argument.) There is really no firm evidence to support this. It is doubtful whether the general behaviour and morality of people as a whole in, say, Britain or the USA have declined in recent years. Certainly attitudes have changed (towards marriage and sex, for example) but, if anything, most people are more caring and concerned for others in 2000 than they were in 1900. As for the matter of respect for life, there likewise does not seem to be any evidence that children (or the elderly) are treated less well in societies in which abortion and euthanasia are permitted than they are in societies in which those practices are illegal. Indeed, given the relative prevalence of paedophilia in Catholic institutions discovered in recent years, the Church's own record in relation to children is perhaps somewhat unedifying.

*General comments

It is probably utopian to suppose there could ever be a final resolution of such controversial issues; proponents and opponents start from different premises and often appeal to different criteria. It would be quite mistaken, however, to conclude that some form of 'moral relativism' is inevitable – a charge increasingly made in recent years. Although moral decisions are made by individuals, they are made in the context of society and, as pointed out above, there is much common ground within and across different societies and cultures. Controversies usually arise over special cases. If you want to engage into a serious philosophical debate about these and other problems of practical ethics, you should take note of the following guidelines:

(1) Be sceptical about the validity of general principles which are alleged to admit of *no* exceptions. Moral issues are usually much more complex than they might seem at first sight.
(2) Several moral principles may in fact be simultaneously applicable to the same situation.
(3) Consider intentions, actions and consequences (actual and foreseeable); each may be taken to have an input into the rightness or wrongness of an action.

You may of course have good reasons for acting (or not acting) in the way you do, and you may wish to recommend to others that they follow a similar course of action. However recognize that they may well be operating within a different framework and may approach moral problems from a different standpoint. A certain minimum of agreement on basic rules of behaviour is obviously necessary for the smooth running of society. What this 'lowest common denominator' should be in a particular community is of course a matter for on-going debate and legislation. Society is not static. Attitudes change; new problems arise as societies develop and technology advances. Beyond this minimum, however, it should be regarded as undesirable for one person's code to be imposed on another individual. We might call failure to acknowledge this the 'fallacy of moral asymmetry' (it is not a fallacy in the strict logical sense of course – see Ch. 2). In the case of abortion, for example, the law does not require a woman to have an abortion if she does not wish it. Opponents of abortion, however, would seek to prevent her from terminating her pregnancy – regardless of the circumstances. Such an attitude can even be manifested in an irrational fanaticism – as when anti-abortionists murder those with whom they disagree! The position we are advocating does not of course mean that one should not seek to influence the majority 'consensus' by reasoned debate, and ultimately to get the law changed if it can be shown that the consequences of a particular practice for the wider community can provide justification for limiting individual autonomy. (Some of the problems arising from conflicts between the individual and society will be examined in the next chapter.)

There are many other practical issues relevant to the interrelationships of human beings which we have not been able to cover, for example, business ethics, feminism and children's rights. Suffice it to say that in general we would advocate that in a mature pluralist democracy, no form of discrimination, whether on grounds of race, gender, or creed, should be regarded as acceptable. This view does of course need to be clarified and defended. This is a job for you! But there are a few other moral issues that should be examined briefly to complete this chapter. These concern: (a) the killing of non-human creatures, and (b) our treatment of 'nature' – our environment (including our own bodies).

Non-human life

Debate about man's treatment of the other creatures who share our planet has become as intense as discussions of human relationships. What right have we to decide their fate? Why should they be killed? People who approach the problem from a religious standpoint are not of one mind. According to the *Bible*, God said 'Let us put [man] in command of the fishes in the sea, and all that flies through the air, and the cattle, and the whole earth, and all the creeping things that move on the earth'. It is an open question, however, whether for Christians and Jews 'domination' is to be taken to imply that we have the right to kill animals. For Buddhists there is less ambiguity, in that the first of the Five Precepts (*pañca-sīla*) enjoins one to promise to abstain from taking life. As it says in the *Dhammapada*, 'Whoever strives only for his own happiness, and in so doing hurts or kills living creatures which also seek for happiness, he shall find no happiness after death'. Most Buddhists, however, do not take this in an absolutist sense and allow for individual and cultural circumstances. So under what conditions might the taking of animal life be considered acceptable? What reasons do we have for killing other creatures? (You might like to think about what Kant and Mill would have said about this issue, in terms of respectively the categorical imperative and the 'happiness' produced.)

(1) Most obviously we kill for food – as indeed most animals themselves have been doing for millions of years. We do not condemn the lion for killing a gazelle, or a bird for catching a worm. So why should it be thought to be morally unacceptable for man to kill a lamb or a fish? A common answer is that we are of a higher order of intelligence and, alone of the myriad species on the planet we follow ethical codes; we do not have the right to treat other animals as means to an end; and in any case we could survive as vegetarians. In reply we might say that there is no cosmic injunction or natural law against our killing animals for food. Some nutritionists might also question whether a solely vegetarian diet is satisfactory. Another point that can be made relates to consistency. On what basis is the objection to killing living things made? If it is simply that life has intrinsic value, then it is difficult to see how even the eating of vegetables can be justified. More reasonably, the concern of those opposed to the killing of animals for food is probably that such creatures are in some sense sentient (see below), and that we are able to empathize with them.

(2) Many organisms are pests: they carry diseases, or they destroy our crops. If we had not controlled them millions of our own species might have died – from malaria, plagues, or starvation. Supporters of animal rights presumably

would say we must take our chances. It is difficult to see how they might be convinced otherwise.

(3) We use some animals for experiments so as to ensure that some of the drugs we use to counter disease are safe, and in many cases the animals die. This is a less 'open and shut' argument. We cannot always be sure that the response of, say, a mouse, to a given drug can be taken as an adequate basis for predicting the response of a human being. Even if the animal's death is not a consequence, quite frequently experiments inflict suffering. One answer to this is that experimentation is the lesser of two evils. Moreover, we should be concerned primarily with the survival of our own species; the 'will' to survive is, after all, deeply engrained in all living organisms. Given the choice of either supporting a ban on all experiments on animals or giving a close relative a chance of life as a result of a new and thoroughly tested drug, most people would opt for the latter (given scientific assurance that the tests can be relied on). This does not mean that we should not as far as possible treat other animals with respect and seek to minimize suffering. But it is a matter of priorities.

(4) Some people kill animals for sport. If the animals end up in the kitchen, and it was the primary intention of the hunter to eat them, this brings us back to (1) above. (This could be regarded as another example of the 'double-effect principle'.) To kill for sport alone, or to satisfy some 'blood-lust' might be regarded as morally reprehensible, but here we encounter another problem: a conflict of rights within a democracy. I might not like what you are doing, but this does not of itself justify my physically preventing you from going about your lawful business. (We have of course frequently seen the lengths to which fanatical anti-sports – and anti-vivisection – groups will go in their attempts to impose their perceived moral position on others.) It is of course open to any objector to seek to get the law changed, as discussed earlier.

Underlying most objections to the killing of animals, or subjection of them to treatment which we suppose to be in our own interests, is the assumption that they have rights, or if they have not, that they should be given rights. Something will be said about *human* rights in the next chapter on Political Philosophy. But a few comments can be made here about other organisms. Why do people feel that animals should have rights? When we say a horse, a cat, or a mouse, for example, has a 'right' we mean (roughly) that they have a claim on us to be treated in a fair or appropriate manner – the right to life, the right not to suffer physical abuse, the right to suitable living conditions, for example What could be the basis for this claim? Where does the 'right' come from? The answers usually given usually include some reference to 'sentience', consciousness', or 'self-consciousness'. But appeal to such qualities is fraught with difficulties. Leaving aside the problem of whether we can know that a particular organism can feel pain, or is aware of itself, it is clear that there would be a certain arbitrariness in according it rights. Mammals, yes, but earthworms probably not, and bacteria (and all vegetable life) definitely not – *pace* those kindly souls who believe trees have feelings and who talk to their marrows – unless one advocates their possession of rights by virtue of living. We might say they thereby have intrinsic value. There is another problem. Many philosophers argue that having rights entails recognizing duties and responsibilities. (That is why people who commit certain crimes are put in prison: they lose their right to liberty.) But animals cannot generally be said to have ethical awareness or moral codes. (There are 'hard cases' of course. The elephant may, it is claimed, have some respect for its own dead. Domestic animals often appear to show loyalty to their owners. But it is doubtful that this is proof of any 'moral sense' of responsibility. It at least remains an open question.) So perhaps the real justification for *granting* rights to animals lies in our recognition of a certain commonality between them and us. First of all we should appreciate that most other species have been around for millions of years before *homo sapiens* appeared on the scene. We share the same planet and often the same food resources. The cells of all living organisms are composed of the same molecules – DNA and proteins. We are all products of the same evolutionary process. And, at a deeper level still, all living things have emerged from the Earth itself and ultimately from stellar dust. So to get a better purchase on this issue of our relationship to other animals, perhaps we should look briefly at the wider perspective and consider our common environment.

Nature and the environment

The debate about our treatment of other creatures is part of a wider debate about our own species and our relationship to our planet – if not the cosmos. It is clear as we move into the Third Millennium not only that technology has made extraordinary progress throughout the twentieth century but that the rate of change is itself increasing. Arguably we are on the verge of major breakthroughs in physics, molecular biology and genetics, and cognitive and neuro-psychology. We must of course remain cautious and sceptical; there have been many such false dawns in the past. What is incontrovertible, however, is that for all the benefits technology has brought to mankind it has also seriously damaged the environment. Few people would today dismiss the dangers: depletion of raw materials, the destruction of the rain forests with potentially devastating effects on climate and food supply, the increase of gaseous emissions which impact an the ozone layer and also are probably causing global warming. Many philosophers are now accordingly taking a serious interest in 'environmental ethics' or 'ecophilosophy'. What should our attitude be towards 'nature' (which of course includes ourselves)?

In so far as we are dependent on the planet Earth for our survival we may say it has **instrumental value** for us. It is this which justifies our claim to have 'rights' over it and its other inhabitants. It is therefore obvious that it is our interest as a species to use its resources more wisely. However, in recent years many writers have launched attacks on what they see as 'anthropocentrism' and 'speciesism' in our attitude towards our planet and other creatures. (Some are explicitly and often vociferously against all technology.) Such 'deep ecologists' reject 'reductionist' and materialist attitudes and argue in favour of 'holistic' approach towards the environment which they suppose to possess **intrinsic value**. While what they have to say should certainly be taken seriously, but there are several objections that can be made, particularly against the more extreme proponents of holism. (a) Even if it were possible to halt technological progress, this would seem to be undesirable, because it would be counter-productive and would probably make the survival of our species less likely. One need only refer here to the contribution it has made to medicine, food development, communications and so on. (Technology also offers the prospect of exploration and even terraforming of local planets within a century or two, which could be beneficial if conditions on Earth do deteriorate.) Of course technology has its downside: Hiroshima and Nagasaki marked the point of no return for the human race. And many people are now concerned about the possible harmful consequences of current advances being made in genetics. How long will it be before Aldous Huxley's *Brave New World* becomes a reality? Nevertheless, it is arguable that in an open, pluralist society, wedded to a market economy there can be no place for total political control of research and censorship of knowledge. Indeed it is this very openness which should ensure that technology is subjected to sufficient on-going scrutiny and operates within guidelines so that new discoveries will, as far as can be envisaged, be beneficial to mankind. (b) Paradoxically many of those who criticize tendencies to anthropocentrism are themselves guilty of anthropomorphism in so far as they attribute 'personal' qualities not only to animals but to the Earth itself – which they regard as in some sense a living organism and call 'Gaia'. This is controversial, but it does seem that in this they are committing a 'category mistake' (see 2.10). (c) By in effect imposing a moral imperative on man to have regard for the environment and other organisms they are already setting us apart. We do not demand of chimpanzees or earthworms that *they* act in responsible ways towards us. If we did we should be doomed to frustration; other animals are not moral beings. It is questionable therefore whether this tacit admission of our uniqueness is consistent with what in many instances seems also to be an 'anthropophobic' attitude and a disproportionate concern for animal 'rights'.

Finally let us ask this key question: Why should we bother? Why should the fate of future generations be of any concern to us today? In the last analysis this is a matter for each individual to decide for himself or herself. Leaving aside all consideration of whether there is an ultimate 'purpose' to our existence, such as might be supposed by religious people, perhaps the best answer that can be given relates to our concern for our immediate families. You are naturally concerned about the well-being of your children and grandchildren – as indeed am I (perhaps this is a biologically grounded imperative), and would be unhappy at the thought that their future might be blighted by disease, hunger, or pollution. You are probably less worried about cousins, and still less interested in the fate of friends and neighbours – though in so far as you have built up a relationship with them over the years you cannot disregard them totally (the idea of belonging to a group, community, or society is clearly central here). Some people profess also to have sympathy (see the discussion of Hume in 6.2) for the plight of complete strangers, who live in far-off lands, and whom they have never met ('they are humans like us'). (But can there be genuine altruism?) So it would seem that as rational and emotional beings we cannot completely dissociate ourselves from generations to come (unless we are totally egoistic), and should have some regard to how we are conducting ourselves now in relation to the environment.

We must end the discussion here and turn to political philosophy. But note that the question 'What is man?' (do we have a 'nature'?) will be examined in Ch. 12.

QUESTIONS

A. Texts

1 What does Hume declare to be the relation between justice and utility? Show briefly how he justifies his contention.

2 'Since Hume admits that only reason can determine what is useful, and since his whole thesis is that the moral is the useful, surely it follows that it is reason which determines what is the moral. How then can he aver that morality rests in sentiment?' Examine this criticism of Hume.

3 Hume says reason is the slave of the passions. Is it?

4 'Hume's doctrine of sympathy amounts to a doctrine of self-love, and is therefore a negation of all morality.' Discuss.

5 What does Kant mean by the statement that duty is the necessity of acting out of reverence for the law?

*6 Examine critically Kant's notion of the Good Will.

7 Examine Kant's distinction between hypothetical and categorical imperatives.

8 State and criticize Kant's successive formulations of the categorical imperative.

9 'For a holy will there are no imperatives.' Explain what this means.

10 What is Kant's answer to the question: 'How is a categorical imperative possible?'

11 What are the limits imposed by Kant on the making of promises? How valid is Kant's view?   [IB, specimen, 2000]

12 How does Mill criticize the 'intuitionist' view of ethics? How far is Mill himself an intuitionist?

13 What, according to Mill, are the sanctions of the utilitarian ethic?

14 Discuss Mill's 'proof' of the principle of utility.

15 How does Mill attempt to prove that justice is a branch of morality?

16 By what criteria does Mill distinguish the different qualities of pleasures?

*17 Is Mill's attempt to establish the General Happiness principle successful?

*18 Explain Nietzsche's thesis that we need a critique of human values.

19 Examine critically Nietzsche's concept of *ressentiment*.

20 Explain and discuss Nietzsche's claim that 'when someone cannot get over "psychological pain", that is not not the fault of their "psyche" but, to speak crudely, that of his belly. A strong and well constituted man digests his experiences.'   [IB, specimen, 2000]

21 Is Nietzsche's philosophy 'subjectivist'?

*22 Examine critically the Sartrean view that man makes his own values.

23 Explain and discuss Sartre's concept of 'self-deception'.

24 Sartre claims [*Existentialism and Humanism*] that man 'in choosing for himself . . . chooses for all men'. Discuss whether this is consistent with the 'subjectivity' of his existentialist ethics.

25 Discuss the consequences for the self of living an inauthentic life, according to Charles Taylor.   [IB, specimen, 2000]

26 Why does Ayer believe that it is not possible to translate ethical terms into empirical terms?

27 Examine critically Ayer's view that when I use the words 'right' and 'wrong' all I am doing is expressing my ethical *feelings*.

28 How does Ayer answer the objection that on his theory it would be impossible to argue about questions of value? Is his answer satisfactory?

B. Problems

29 Why might it be thought that feelings are a better guide to action than reason?

*30 Is being morally good the same thing as following a set of moral rules?

*31 Critically examine the view that moral values are relative.

32 To what extent, if any, is morality a subjective matter? [AEB, 1996]

33 Do the consequences of our actions always determine their goodness?

[IB, specimen, 2000]

34 Discuss the view that I cannot reach a moral decision by myself, but that I always need to discuss a moral problem with others. [IB, specimen, 2000]

35 Examine the distinction between 'act-utilitarianism' and 'rule-utilitarianism'.

36 Can an 'ought' be derived from an 'is'?

*37 Can a clear distinction be made between 'prescriptive' and 'descriptive' meaning?

38 'I know what I ought to do but I am not going to do it.' Examine critically the grounds on which such an assertion might be justified.

39 'If I adopt a rule for myself, I must adopt it for others.' Must this be so?

40 Could a Utilitarian successfully defend capital punishment? Give reasons for your answer. [IB, specimen, 2000]

41 'No man should be put to death, even as an example, if he can be left to live without danger to society' (Rousseau). Discuss.

42 Can voluntary euthanasia be justified? Discuss the philosophical difficulties.

43 Examine the ethical arguments for and against experimentation on animals.

44 Do animals have rights? If so, where do they come from? If not, should they be given them?

45 Under what circumstances, if any, could a strict *deontologist* regard suicide as acceptable? [AEB, 1997]

46 What moral problems are raised in considering whether or not one person should try to prevent another's suicide?

47 On what grounds might it be considered right to sacrifice one's own welfare for the benefit of another person?

48 What arguments might a utilitarian and a deontologist use to *oppose* abortion and how far would you accept these? [AEB, 1996]

49 Does the fact that an unborn child is developing within its mother's body give her the right to determine whether or not it should be aborted?

50 Is the intention to use nuclear weapons or germ warfare as a *deterrent* (a) coherent, (b) morally justifiable?

51 Should I concern myself with the welfare of people in a distant land about whom I know little? Examine the moral considerations.

52 If I am concerned about the well-being of my children and grandchildren, does it follow that I should be equally concerned about the welfare of the fourth and subsequent generations of my descendants? Justify your answer.

53 I may well be concerned about pollution, changes in the weather and the like. But are there any moral grounds why I should feel it incumbent on me to have regard for preserving the environment?

54 I may disagree with, say, genetic engineering, experiments on animals, or abortion. Does this give me the right to engage in direct (physical) action to prevent others from carrying out their intention to pursue such a programme?

55 Explain what is meant by 'fanaticism'. Is it morally coherent?

(See also questions on ethics for Chs 3 and 4. Some of the above questions, especially those referring to 'rights', could well be left until you have studied Ch. 7.)

*Notes/guided answers have been provided for questions **6, 17, 18, 22, 30, 31** and **37** (at end of book).

READING LIST

A. Prescribed texts
Ayer, A.J., *Language, Truth and Logic.* (AEB)
de Beauvoir, S., *The Ethics of Ambiguity.* (IB)
Kant, I., *Groundwork of the Metaphysic of Morals.* (IB)
Nietzsche, F., *Beyond Good and Evil.* (AEB)
Nietzsche, F., *The Genealogy of Morals.* (IB)
Sartre, J.-P., *Existentialism and Humanism.* (AEB)
Taylor, C., *The Ethics of Authenticity.* (IB)

B. Other texts
Hare, R.M., *Freedom and Reason.*
Hare, R.M., *The Language of Morals.*
Hume, D., *Enquiry Concerning the Principles of Morals.*
Kant, I., *Critique of Practical Reason.*
Mill, J.S., *Utilitarianism.*
Sartre, J.-P., *Being and Nothingness.*

C. Supplementary reading
(If you are a beginner, you are recommended to start with titles marked with an asterisk.)

1. Historical background
MacIntyre, A.C., *A Short History of Ethics.**
Warnock, M., *Ethics since 1900.**

2. General introductory texts
Gensler, H.J., *Ethics; A Contemporary Introduction.*
Mackie, J.L., *Ethics: Inventing Right and Wrong.**
Nielsen, K., *Ethics without God.**
Williams, B., *Ethics and the Limits of Philosophy.**
Williams, B., *Morality: An Introduction to Ethics.**

3. Books and articles on individual philosophers

(See also the Book list to Ch. 5.)

Mackie, J.L., *Hume's Moral Theory.**
Acton, H.B., *Kant's Moral Philosophy.**
Britton, K., *Mill.**
Plamenatz, J., *The English Utilitarians.**
Thomas, W., *Mill.**
Danto, A.C., *Nietzsche as Philosopher.**
Hollingdale, R.J., *Nietzsche: The Man and his Philosophy.*
Stern, J.P., *Nietzsche.**
Murdoch, I., *Sartre, Romantic Rationalist.*
Warnock, M., *The Philosophy of Sartre.**
Note also the 'Cambridge Companion to Philosophy' series.

4. Other books and essays

Barrow, R., *Injustice, Inequality and Ethics.**
Broad, C.D., *Five Types of Ethical Theory.*
Devlin, P., *The Enforcement of Morals.**
Feinberg, J. (ed.), *Moral Concepts.**
Foot, P. (ed.), *Theories of Ethics.*
Frankena, W.A., *Ethics.**
Glover, J., *Causing Death and Saving Lives.*
Hart, H.L.A., *Law, Liberty and Morality.**
Hudson, W.D., *Modern Moral Philosophy.*
Mitchell, B., *Law, Morality and Religion in a Secular Society.**
Moore, G.E., *Ethics.**
Murdoch, I., *The Sovereignty of Good.**
Nagel, T., *The View from Nowhere*, chs VIII–XI.
Parfit, D., *Reasons and Persons.*
Singer, P. (ed.), *Applied Ethics.**
Toulmin, S.E., *An Examination of the Place of Reason in Ethics.**

7 Political philosophy

7.1 Introduction

Through your reading of 3.8–3.11 and 4.10 you will already have some idea of what political philosophy is all about. In the present chapter we shall consider a number of important philosophical issues arising out of an analysis of the political and social relationship that may obtain between individuals and societies. Think first of the problem of controlling behaviour. If we all acted with total selfishness, with no regard at all for the effects of our actions on other people, there could be no concept of socially accepted standards. Indeed our behaviour might well become self-defeating in the sense that the actions of other people might actually prevent us from achieving our own aims. Alternatively society would disintegrate into a battlefield on which conflicting factions would engage in an incessant struggle for power. If on the other hand we all agreed on what the 'right' actions were in all circumstances, then perhaps we would live together in a state of perfect harmony.

But of course life is not like that. We have differing conceptions of morality, and modern societies are complex entities. It is the task of governments not only to regulate the economic and social life of the community but also to legislate so as to reconcile conflicting perspectives and ensure that society runs smoothly. This leads to the problem of **authority**. What gives our rulers the right to control the lives of individual citizens? From where do they derive their authority? Why should we obey the state? These matters will be discussed in the next section. If we do submit to a 'higher' authority, to what extent are we relinquishing our liberty? Should the state's role be purely negative – to prevent harm being inflicted on an individual? Or should the state go further and positively encourage individuality and freedom in the sense of 'self-realization' or 'rational self-direction', as Isaiah Berlin puts it in his *Four Essays on Liberty*? The problem of **liberty** will be examined in 7.3. Does 'positive' freedom necessarily entail inequality? Can all citizens be **'equal'** in some absolute sense, or must we rest content with the notion of equality of opportunity? Is this consistent with **justice**? The final section (7.4) will be devoted to an examination of Karl Marx's conception of society.

7.2 Authority and obedience

Reading: Hobbes, *Leviathan*; Locke, *Second Treatise on Civil Government*; Rousseau, *The Social Contract*, Books I–III and *Discourse on the Origin of Inequality*

At some time in our lives most of us find ourselves in a position of having to do what we are told. At school we have to do our exercises. At work we must follow our employer's instructions. In everyday life we have to obey the law – drive on the correct side of the road, 'keep the peace' and so on. What is the basis of the authority which imposes itself on us in such ways? There are two general answers that might be initially given to justify our acquiescence. (1) The authority is regarded as having the appropriate knowledge, experience, or expertise. 'Teacher knows best', it may be said. And recognition of his having authority in this sense would be thought sufficient reason for our following the instructions of our family doctor, for example. In like manner the ruler of a state might be thought to possess the degree of wisdom or virtue necessary to ensure the well-being of all the citizens, and on these grounds would expect them to be obedient to his commands. (2) Rulers of states, however, (and school teachers) are additionally generally thought to be *in* authority; and this notion of authority suggests that they have the *power* of coercion. If we do not do what we are told we are liable to be punished.

An alternative and perhaps more precise distinction can also be made: between **de facto** and **de jure** authority. A person is in authority *de facto* if by virtue of his position or knowledge he is recognized as being entitled to command us to act in some way. It does not follow from this, however, that we have 'given' him this authority. To *grant* someone (a ruler, policeman or football referee, for example) authority presupposes a set of rules, an agreed framework, within which he can exercise it. In this sense we may talk of *de jure* authority. Of course possession of authority *de facto* more often than not is a consequence of being in authority *de jure*. But the reverse does not seem to be the case; we can always ask someone who seeks to exercise authority over us by what right it is claimed. And an acceptable justification cannot always be given. This is a central issue which concerns us in much of what follows.

The two meanings of 'authority' are implicit in the political philosophy of both Plato and Aristotle. The Guardians or Philosopher-Kings of the *Republic* are uniquely endowed with 'reason' and have been given the specific training to rule the 'ideal' society. Likewise the 'middle-class' administrators and members of the judiciary, who take it in turn to rule Aristotle's 'Polity', are qualified to do so by their virtue and experience. Now two points must be noted here. Firstly, neither of these kinds of society is 'democratic' in the sense of the term as generally used today: the majority of inhabitants of Plato's 'ideal' state play no part in choosing who should rule them. Through state-controlled education they are indoctrinated with the metaphysical and ethical principles underlying their society, and thus have no alternative but to accept the authority imposed on them from birth. Secondly, in the Platonic–Aristotelian view of the state, authority is inseparable from a concept of **law** as grounded in a metaphysical theory of human nature or of 'reality'. (It is true that in the *Republic* there is no provision for a 'constitution' in which citizens' rights might be enshrined. In the perfect state there would be no need of laws, for the Guardians are ruled by reason while the other two classes are ruled by the all-wise Guardians. In his later works on political theory [the *Statesman* and the *Laws*] Plato recognized that there are no perfect rulers, and endeavoured to introduce a code of law, embodying the absolute standards in accordance with which he thought society should be regulated.)

With the rise of Christianity the Platonic conception of law is incorporated into a theological framework. God is now the ultimate authority; and in the writings of one of the most influential of early Christian political theorists, St Augustine (354–430), the standard against which the actions of fallen man are to be judged in the social context is divine or eternal law. In his *The City of God* (which you are strongly recommended to read if you have time) Augustine argues for a political structure which interferes with the affairs of the citizen only to the extent necessary to maintain unity and order, each individual being left to work out his own salvation in the light of his conscience – that is, his apprehension of the archetypal eternal law – and with the aid of divine grace.

If Augustine was influenced by Plato, the Aristotelian tradition reappears in the writings of St Thomas Aquinas (1224–74), though he also incorporates Platonic elements in his monumental synthesis. The central notion of man as a *natural* political being is restored. The state is no longer limited to playing a minimalist role in human society but is now regarded as providing the essential context in which man can fulfil himself spiritually as a creature of God. The ideal constitution is an elected monarchy, the ruler exercising his authority with the consent of the governed by virtue of the fact that each man is, like himself, rational and is free to use his own judgement. Aquinas also distinguishes between four kinds of law. The law on the basis of which society is run is termed 'human' law. This is subordinated to 'natural' law which provides the standard for human law but which itself is understood as 'participation in the eternal law by a rational creature' and is 'self-evident' through the exercise of practical reason. The fourth kind of law is 'divine' law which is given to man in revelation.

The social contract

It is possible to argue that in the several systems we have referred to in the preceding paragraphs, *de facto* authority is legitimized in terms of a *de jure* authority which is itself grounded in metaphysical or theological principles, given to us through faith or through the exercise of pure reason. But what if standards are no longer believed to be universal or objective? What support can there be for a claim to the possession of authority *de jure*? Why should an individual feel himself obliged to obey his rulers (other than out of fear of coercion or punishment)? This is a problem which concerned a number of post-medieval philosophers who in different ways appealed to the notion of a 'social contract'.

Hobbes

Thomas Hobbes (1588–1679) may perhaps be described as a sceptical materialist and a psychological egoist. Although our senses may permit us to construct a science of moving bodies, we can have no certain knowledge of what the world outside us is really like. He rejected 'supernatural' accounts of man: human beings are to be understood as working like a machine. Human nature operates on the basis of two principles: desire (stemming from sensations) and reason (by means of which desires are put into effect). The good is 'whatsoever is the object of any man's appetite or desire'; the object of his hate and aversion is evil [*Leviathan*, 24]. There can therefore be no possibility of our knowing any 'objective' moral principles. So Hobbes's political philosophy takes as its starting point the evident desire in all men for security and ultimately self-preservation. Man, he says, is in 'continual fear and danger of violent death'; and it is in response to this that man decided to band together in society – without which life would be 'solitary, poor, nasty, brutish and short' [62]. He is not suggesting that such a state of affairs actually ever existed; the state of nature is a hypothetical one. Rather his point is that unless some agreement is reached, man will relapse into this natural state and anarchy will prevail. (Hobbes was writing with the experience of the Civil War fresh in his memory.) So to overcome the difficulties of moral scepticism and relativism and consequent potential conflicts, rational men agree amongst themselves to surrender all their natural rights (except the right to self-preservation – which is 'inalienable') to a **sovereign** whose subjects they would then become. The sovereign (which could be a single man or a group – and could even take power by conquest) thus acquires *de jure* authority; and in Hobbes's version of the social contract becomes 'that great LEVIATHAN, or rather, to speak more reverently, . . . that mortal God, to which we owe under the immortal God, our peace and defence' [87]. But this Leviathan has absolute power and is 'above the law' in the sense that he determines and enforces the civil law, that is, what is right and wrong. It is only when he fails to secure order within the state (his *raison d'être*) that resistance to this authority can be justified and his power undermined.

Locke

Although he also embraced a social contract theory, Locke diverged markedly from Hobbes in a number of respects:

(1) [chs II–V] He rejected the image of primitive man as being in a condition of brutish hostility concerned solely with his own personal welfare. For Locke, people are naturally social; they are subject to rational laws of nature instituted by God for the proper functioning of His creation. Natural rights, which he identifies as life, liberty, and property, thus have a supernatural basis. [See Sec. 6 of his Treatise.]

(2) [ch. VIII] As in Hobbes's theory, the contract is made between individuals, but for Locke their rights are given up to the **community** ('commonwealth' is his preferred term [ch. X]) and not to a sovereign [Sec. 96]. Indeed an absolute

monarchy (which Hobbes had argued to be the best form of government to secure peace within the state) is inconsistent with civil society; for under such a ruler, who possesses all legislative and executive power within himself, a citizen is denied appeal for any injury suffered [Sec. 90]. Locke's society is also more 'democratic' in the sense that he invokes rule by the majority as a practical necessity. Without it the state would be enfeebled and would not be viable [Sec. 98]. Authority thus lies with the government of the 'commonwealth' and is grounded in the agreement of the majority. As Locke remarked in Sec. 142, the legislature 'must not raise taxes on the property of the people without the consent of the people given by themselves or their deputies' – a remark that was later to be echoed repeatedly during the American Revolution ('no taxation without representation').

(3) [chs IX, XI, XII–XIV] It should be noted that in Locke's versions of the social contract, only those natural rights are surrendered which are necessary for the well-being of the community. As he says, quoting Cicero, '*Salus populi suprema lex*', that is, 'The welfare of the people is the supreme law' [Sec. 158]. The role of the state is to be confined to protecting the individual's life, liberty and property [see, for example, Sec. 131]. Hobbes is of course much more 'absolutist'.

Rousseau

It is with the quixotic French writer and philosopher Jean-Jacques Rousseau (1712–78) that the social contract theory is especially associated. To understand his account of the contract and therefore what he means by authority, we need first of all to look at his notion of 'natural man' which he presented in an early essay, the *Discourse on Inequality* (1755). Two central points should be noted:

(1) (As against Hobbes) 'savage' man is essentially amoral. 'Men in a state of nature, having no moral relations or determinate obligations one with another, could not be either good or bad, virtuous or vicious.' However, this is a preliminary view. Rousseau goes on to stress that primitive man is naturally *virtuous*. For although akin to other animals in that his behaviour is instinctive (and also in not possessing language), natural man manifests two principles 'prior to reason':

> one of them deeply interesting to us in our own welfare and preservation, and the other exciting a natural repugnance at seeing any other sensible being, and particularly any of our own species, suffer pain or death. It is from the agreement and combination which the understanding is in a position to establish between these two principles, without its being necessary to introduce that of sociability, that all the rules of natural right appear to me to be derived – rules which our reason is afterwards obliged to establish on other foundations, when by its successive developments it has been led to suppress nature itself. [Preface]

This 'repugnance' is attributable to compassion; and this is 'a natural feeling, which, by moderating the activity of love of self in each individual, contributes to the preservation of the whole species' [Part I]. He goes on to suggest that natural man, although amoral, was **perfectible**, that is, possessed a capacity for moral and social improvement which could be developed given the right conditions for growth.

(2) The fact that natural man did not fulfil this potential is due, argues Rousseau, to two factors: (a) the idea of private property, and (b) the increasing domination of 'passion' by reason once man is in society. Now (as against Locke) Rousseau suggests that primitive man did not have any possessions: 'the only goods he recognizes in the universe are food, a female and sleep: the only evils he fears are pain and hunger' [Part I]. But in Part II he sets out to show how man became 'civilized' and therefore corrupt as he acquired property and established the 'artificial' institutions of society. As he puts it:

> The first man who, having enclosed a piece of ground, bethought himself of saying 'This is mine,' and found people simple enough to believe him, was the real founder of civil society ... Society and law, which bound new fetters on the poor, and gave new powers to the rich; which irretrievably destroyed natural liberty, eternally fixed the law of property and inequality, converted clever usurpation into unalterable right, and, for the advantage of a few ambitious individuals, subjected all mankind to perpetual labour, slavery, and wretchedness. [paras 1 and 37]

Rousseau's account of man's 'fall from innocence' – from primitive simplicity, through to the invention of tools, development of skills, the foundation of family life, the emergence of language, the introduction of morality, law, and punishment (as *amour propre* came to dominate the natural feeling of 'self-love'), and finally to the full-blown complexity of modern societies with their violence, misery and inequality – is set out with great clarity; and you should experience no difficulty in following it. Of more relevance to the topic of this section is the thesis of his major work, the *Social Contract*, which has a positive aim, namely, to suggest the means by which the human condition might be ameliorated – though he recognized that there could be no return to the hypothetical 'state of nature'.

He starts [Book I, chs i–v] by attempting to show that there is no natural 'sacred right' in social order; any such right must be grounded in conventions. Right can be created neither by force nor by any 'natural authority' of one man over another. It follows then that those who would claim the right to enslave others can, in the last analysis, justify their presumed authority only by appealing to the consent of the slave; and this is absurd. 'The words *slave* and *right* contradict each other, and are mutually exclusive' [I, iv]. As Rousseau says in ch. i, man, although everywhere in chains, is born *free*. 'To renounce liberty is to renounce being a man, to surrender the rights of humanity and even its duties,' [I, iv]. The problem then is how man's intrinsic freedom is to be realized. Rousseau's solution is nothing if not radical. If rights are ultimately to be grounded in political convention, then political structures must be established so as to ensure that freedom of the subject is preserved. And this can be achieved only through the surrender of each and every man not to an *individual* authority but to what Rousseau calls the **general will** (*la volonté générale*). This is the basis of his 'social compact' [I, vi]:

> Each of us puts his person and all his power in common under the supreme direction of the general will, and, in our corporate capacity, we receive each member as an indivisible part of the whole.

This authority (Republic or body politic) is called variously the **State** (when passive), **Sovereign** (when active) and **Power** (when compared with other similar bodies). In so far as they are under the laws of the state the people are called subjects, but they are also citizens in that they share in the 'sovereign authority'. Rousseau's 'body politic' is an 'organic' community. It cannot 'alienate any part of itself'. It cannot 'offend against one of the members without attacking the body', while to attack the body must lead to the resentment of its members [I, vi]. It follows that there can be no place for the manifestation of a particular will or interest in conflict with the common interest; this would be to drive a wedge between the individual as subject and as citizen. He must therefore give up to the corporate body his natural liberty in order to gain civil liberty and thus moral liberty 'which alone makes him master of himself; for the mere impulse of appetite is slavery, while obedience to a law which we prescribe to ourselves is liberty' [I, x]. (*This is an important and controversial feature of Rousseau's theory of the state. You might compare it with the rational man's self-imposition of the categorical imperative in Kant's moral philosophy – see 6.3 – and with the Marxist conception of society discussed in 7.4 below. The issue of liberty will be tackled in the next section.) As Rousseau says in I, vii:

> In order then that the social compact may not be an empty formula, it tacitly includes the undertaking, which alone can give force to the rest, that whoever refuses to obey the general will shall be compelled to do so by the whole body. This means nothing less than that he will be forced to be free; for this is the condition which, by giving each citizen to his country, secures him against all personal dependence. In this lies the key to the working of the political machine; this alone legitimizes civil undertakings, which, without it, would be absurd, tyrannical and liable to the most frightful abuses.

Rousseau's 'general will' as expressed by the Sovereign, that is, the body politic when active, thus has supreme *de jure* authority. Sovereignty is inalienable [II, i], indivisible [II, ii] and infallible – provided citizens can communicate with each other and the general will can make itself known [II, iii]. The 'pluses and minuses' of particular wills can then cancel each other out, so that the general will, which is concerned only with the common interest, 'remains as the sum of the differences'.

The remaining chapters of Book II are concerned mainly with law and legislation. A law, says Rousseau, is an act of the general will made by the whole people for the whole people: it 'unites universality of will with universality of object' [II, vi]. However, it is difficult for a public body to implement a system of legislation because it does not always see the good it wills; individual judgement is not always enlightened. A legislator is therefore necessary, who will occupy an office in the state which is neither magistracy nor sovereignty. He will himself have no personal right of legislation and must submit his decisions to the free vote of the people. But, says Rousseau, he must ultimately have recourse to an authority of a different order, namely God, if he is to constrain without violence those whom human prudence cannot move. 'The great soul of the legislator is the only miracle that can prove his mission' [II, vii]. Such a being will thus unite understanding and will in the social body: the parts will be made to work exactly together and the whole will be 'raised to its highest power' [II, vi].

Throughout Books III and IV Rousseau examines different forms of government. (You should note in particular his view that because the government itself is not sovereign, but merely an agency subject to the dictates of the community as a whole, the general will is as likely to be expressed in a democracy as in a dictatorship.)

*Comments and criticisms

There are clearly both differences and similarities between these various versions of the social contract theory. Note especially the contrast between Hobbes's view of man in the 'primitive' state and that of Rousseau; the accounts given by Locke and Rousseau on property; and compare what all three thinkers have to say about 'nature' and 'rights'. As for the contract theory itself, you might think about the following three points:

(1) According to the theory in its simplest form a contract is made between individuals. Leaving aside any consideration of what man was like in the so-called 'state of nature', it is certainly not easy to ascertain when or how or in what form actual agreements were made. It is for this reason that social contract theories are said to be 'hypothetical'. Thus far they can be useful in providing us with an explanatory framework which can help us to analyse actual societies. Their value in providing an account of the origin of societies must, however, remain doubtful. (You will find a short summary of a modern version of the 'hypothetical' social contract theory at the end of the next section.)

(2) It can be argued that the social contract theory treats the 'individual' as an abstraction, that is, as a separate entity possessing rights who then freely consents to submit himself to the authority of a sovereign individual or government. Some critics have claimed that the attempt to incorporate essentially asocial individuals in the social framework of a contract is to introduce a tension into the theory if not a direct inconsistency.

(3) As we have seen, while the versions of the theory put forward by Hobbes and Locke tend to emphasize individualism as being prior to 'collectivity', Rousseau's society is distinctly 'organicist'. But in his case this gives rise to several particular difficulties. (a) Rousseau's notion of the 'general will' is metaphysical if not incoherent. It can be identified neither with any particular will nor with an

aggregate of individual wills. In practice it turns out to be the collective opinion of an actual grouping within society. (b) Closely connected with the first point is Rousseau's account of freedom. The individual must be compelled to understand that his particular viewpoint is false and that his 'real' will is to be identified with that of the community as a whole, wherein also lies his true freedom. He must be forced to be free. This does seem to be paradoxical, to say the least. (c) These weaknesses in his theory are the more serious in that for Rousseau the individual citizen subordinates himself not only to the law but to the community's conception of morality. Indeed the distinction between the two concepts virtually disappears in Rousseau's scheme. But it remains unclear as to what the moral ideals or standards of the community, as expressed through the general will, can actually be.

7.3 Liberty, equality, justice and community

Reading: Mill, *On Liberty*; Rawls, *A Theory of Justice*, especially ch. 1, Secs 1–4, ch. 2, 11–17, ch. 3, ch. 4, 33–35 and 39–40; see also Arendt, *The Human Condition*, ch. II; Nussbaum, *Poetic Justice*; Taylor, *The Ethics of Authenticity*

Liberty – Mill

An examination of the basis of authority leads on naturally to the question of liberty or freedom (which we touched on in the previous section in our discussion of Rousseau). By this is meant not the so-called 'freedom of the will' (which we shall be considering later in the book) but, as Mill puts it, 'the nature and limits of the power which can be legitimately exercised by society over the individual'. As we indicated in the introduction to the chapter, an initial distinction can be made between 'negative' freedom and 'positive' freedom. The former refers to a notion of liberty where individuals are said to be free to the extent that they are not coerced or constrained by other people. They are able to act in accordance with their own wishes and inclinations without restriction. But to refer to wishes and inclinations is to introduce the notion of choice as between alternatives. People usually act for some purpose, with a view to achieving a goal. Such choice and the deliberation which precedes it constitute the core of freedom in its positive aspect. In this section we shall look at freedom in both these senses and with particular reference to Mill's *On Liberty*, which contains what is perhaps the classical exposition of 'individualism'.

First of all, note Mill's account of liberty as he believes it to have developed in the course of history [ch. I]. In olden times, liberty meant 'protection against the tyranny of the political rulers'. It became necessary to limit the power of such rulers over the community, and this was achieved, says Mill, through: (a) the recognition of political liberties or rights, and (b) 'the establishment of constitutional checks, by which the consent of the community, or of a body of some sort, supposed to represent its interests, was made a necessary condition to some of the more important acts of the governing power'. However, it became clear that the habitual opposition of rulers to the ruled did not cease on the introduction of electoral accountability. What was now needed was that the interest and will of rulers should be identical with the interest and will of the people. 'The nation did not need to be protected against its own will.' But, as Mill points out, the will of the people in practice means the will of the (active) majority – a majority which can and often does coerce, indeed exercise tyranny over, minorities by means of laws, enforceable by punishment, or through the force of public opinion and disapproval of dissentient opinions. (This might be regarded as a criticism of Rousseau.) Such factors as these lead Mill to assert his central principle:

> The sole end for which mankind are warranted, individually or collectively, in interfering with the liberty of action of any of their number, is self-protection. That the only purpose for which power can be rightfully exercised over any member of a civilized community, against his will, is to prevent harm to others . . . Over himself, over his own body and mind, the individual is sovereign.

There are two features of his account, as it develops in the course of his book, which need to be stressed:

(1) 'Liberty of action' is used by Mill in a wide sense to include liberty of thought, feeling and tastes, the freedom to hold, express and publish opinions on all subjects, and the liberty to unite with others – with the limitation that what we do does not harm others. 'No society in which these liberties are not, on the whole, respected, is free, whatever may be its form of government; and none is completely free in which they do not exist absolute and unqualified' [ch. 1]. But as he says in ch. III:

> No one pretends that actions should be as free as opinions. On the contrary, even opinions lose their immunity when the circumstances in which they are expressed are such as to constitute their expression a positive instigation to some mischievous act . . . Acts, of whatever kind, which without justifiable cause, do harm to others, may be, and in the more important cases absolutely require to be, controlled by the unfavourable sentiments, and, when needful, by the active interference of mankind.

(2) His views on individualism. The individual is important in Mill's political philosophy because it is only through his 'spontaneity' and originality that society can be enriched. The free development of individuality is not only one of the leading essentials of well-being but is a co-ordinate and necessary part of all that is designated by the terms civilisation, instruction, education and culture. The expression of individuality is thus a precondition for human progress. And by developing his individuality each person becomes more valuable to himself and thereby is capable of being more valuable to others [ch. III]. It is easy to understand therefore why Mill was so concerned to promote

liberty of thought [ch. II]; for unless individuals are free to pursue truth unhindered by repressive laws or prejudiced conventions, we can never know whether or not an opinion is true and we must remain in the power of those who claim infallibility.

It can thus be seen that Mill starts out by making an eloquent defence of negative freedom, but with his emphasis on individuality in effect also implicitly promotes freedom in its positive aspect. The problem now arises of determining the precise limits to the authority of the state over the individual. This is discussed in ch. IV. Note first the assertion that society is not founded on a contract. Nevertheless he argues that the acceptance of society's protection obligates the individual to observe two conditions, namely (a) that he should not injure those interests of others, which legally or 'by tacit understanding ought to be considered as rights'; and (b) that he should bear his share of 'the labours and sacrifices' incurred in the exercise of this protection. Beyond these conditions the individual should have 'perfect freedom, legal and social, to do the action and stand the consequences'. Mill summarizes his position clearly in paragraph 6:

> What I contend for is, that the inconveniences which are strictly inseparable from the unfavourable judgement of others, are the only ones to which a person should ever be subjected for that portion of his own conduct and character which concerns his own good, but which does not affect the interests of others in their relations with him. Acts injurious to others require a totally different treatment. Encroachment on their rights; infliction on them of any loss or damage not justified by his own rights; falsehood or duplicity in dealing with them; unfair or ungenerous use of advantage over them; even selfish abstinence from defending them against injury – these are fit objects of moral reprobation, and, in grave cases, of moral retribution and punishment.

Thus, if the individual harms another he should be punished or at least reproved. But Mill seems to argue against paternalistic interference with the individual himself – even if it appears that the latter is harming his own interests. (Study carefully the arguments Mill subsequently puts forward in ch. IV against this central thesis and his own replies. The examples he gives, drawn from various periods in history where freedom has been restricted, are also of value for an understanding of his position, as are the 'applications' he discusses in ch. V. Note in particular the two 'maxims' given at the beginning.)

Equality and justice

Although Mill places considerable emphasis on self-development, it seems clear that he is not propounding a doctrine of selfishness; on the contrary, individualism, he argues, is a precondition for the well-being and progress of society. Nevertheless, we can certainly imagine circumstances in which an individual's concern with his own self-realization might tend to degenerate into self-seeking to the detriment of the welfare of others. This might be manifested by the emergence of inequalities in society. Before we develop this point some more distinctions must be made:

(1) In a fairly obvious sense we are all unequal from birth in that we inherit different characteristics. Some people are more intelligent than others, some are good at music while others are tone-deaf. Some people are good athletes, others have poor physical co-ordination or, more tragically, are disabled.

(2) People may be said to be unequal in their upbringing. A child born to a peasant family in the Third World clearly does not start out in life with the advantages of housing, health and education enjoyed by many of us in the affluent West. Such inequalities are clearly relevant to freedom. Can the peasant child be said to have as much freedom as ourselves if his choice is restricted by poor nutrition or sub-standard living conditions?

(3) In a more abstract sense it can be argued that 'political' inequalities exist within society, the implication being that all men were equal in the pre-social 'state of nature'. Despite their differences the several political thinkers referred to in the sections on authority and liberty concur in their acceptance of this view. According to Hobbes men are more or less equal in brutishness and cunning; Locke regards them as equally free under 'natural law'; while for Rousseau men are equal in their autonomy and perfectibility. It is only within society that this equality is lost: for Hobbes and Locke political inequality arises as a result of the partial surrender of their freedom by citizens to an individual sovereign or to a ruling class, but for Rousseau inequality is the necessary concomitant of social conventions which sanction property relationships. Much subsequent political philosophy has therefore been concerned with the problem of balancing 'natural equality' against the demands of society in the context of which, seemingly, individual self-realization has to be sought. This is in effect the problem of justice.

As we have seen, 'justice' is itself an ambiguous term. We shall confine the discussion here to justice in the broadly Aristotelian sense of 'distributive' justice. (Refer back to 4.7. You might also look again at what we said about the conceptions of justice held by Plato and Mill in 3.9 and 6.4 respectively.) Now 'distributive' justice means roughly 'fairness': equals are to be treated equally and unequals unequally in the relevant respects. What are these 'relevant respects'? What criterion should be applied to ensure fair treatment? An arguably simplistic approach would be to say that in so far as all people are citizens in a particular society then not only should they be subject to the same laws but they should have the same income, the same housing, the same education and so on. This approach has the merit of apparently eliminating the inequalities listed under (2) above, and although political inequality between ruler and ruled (point 3) still obtains, every citizen is in this respect unequal to the same extent. However, it can be objected that this criterion fails to take account of the fact that people who are physically or intellectually unequal from birth, that is, in sense (1) above, must have different **needs**. 'Fairness' might then necessitate that people unequal in such respects be treated preferentially – in compensation. The difficulty here is where the line should be drawn. People have different aspirations. Some are more ambitious, or work harder than others. Unless we subscribe to some kind of 'determinist' doctrine (see Ch. 11), we should think of such people as selecting their priorities and choosing their courses of action rationally and freely. Should not they therefore be treated on the basis of **merit**? Should they not be rewarded for hard work and achievement? Moreover 'need' is also a relative term. Certainly a disabled person is 'in need' and in a central sense of justice should be given preferential assistance. But most people who are fortunate not to suffer from physical or mental disability may well have their own special needs; and how is one to decide whether one case is more deserving of 'unequal' treatment than another?

Decisions of this kind must, it would seem, be left to the state. Some people might be expected to treat others fairly on an individual basis, perhaps in accordance with a set of moral principles. But protection of the rights and attention to the needs of all members of the community, consideration of priorities, and resolution of conflicts, are all matters of such complexity that general agreement can normally be effected only through legislation. How far the laws of a community should be grounded in or reflect a particular moral code is of course itself a controversial matter, particularly in a so-called pluralist society (compare 6.8). Reference to the state, however, raises two particular issues concerning (1) the extent of state intervention in private matters, and (2) the degree of participation afforded to individual citizens in the legislative process.

(1) Mill of course wished to restrict state interference to the minimum [see chs IV and V of *On Liberty*]. But, as the poet John Donne wrote, 'No man is an island', and it is not always easy to separate private concerns from the public domain. Certainly Mill was concerned for the welfare of others: that a person's actions should not harm other people was after all the basis for his principle of Liberty. It is however arguable that despite his laudable aim, to root out prejudice and coercion, his vision of society was too optimistic. Emphasis on individualism, on self-regarding action, can all to easily lead to a *laissez-faire* mentality as a result of which the weakest go to the wall unless their rights are recognized and protected by the state. As against this we should be aware of the dangers inherent in what Mill termed 'the tyranny of the majority' – which as often as not means the tyranny against individual liberty of prevailing opinion and feeling. How these extremes are to be avoided, how the claims of the individual to freedom are to be reconciled with the claim of the state to ensure justice for all is a central problem for political philosophy that remains unresolved to this day. The solution, if solution there be, may well be connected with the second of the two issues mentioned above, namely that concerned with participation of the governed in the governing process. It is to Mill's credit that he argued strongly in favour of co-operative societies, decentralization of power and greater participation by the people in local government, and he was an early champion of women's rights.

(2) The problem of participation brings us back again to the question of liberty; for it can be argued that if a society is to be genuinely democratic, in the

literal sense of the word, then citizens must be sufficiently free (that is, from constraint or coercion) to take part in political activity which has a bearing on their own well-being in the community. Not all of us can at the same time be members of parliament or local councillors. But at the very least participation means that the channels of communication between the legislature and the governed must be kept as open as possible. The problem here is that even in Western democracies, which we usually refer to as 'free' societies in contrast to the (until recently) totalitarian 'democracies' of the communist world, there are wide divergencies in the 'quality of life' enjoyed by their citizens. People who earn disproportionately high incomes, often as a direct result of market forces rather than on the basis of merit alone, thereby gain access to better education and health facilities, which in turn may ensure that their participation in the political process is more effective than those who find themselves in less fortunate circumstances. Moreover, it is not surprising that such political power is often exercised to ensure the maintenance of the status quo.

Rawls

To bring this section to an end we shall look briefly at a recent attempt to reconcile liberty, equality and justice made by John Rawls (b. 1921). In his book *A Theory of Justice* (1972) he develops a theory which, as he says, 'seems to offer an alternative systematic account of justice that is superior, or so I argue, to the dominant utilitarianism of [much modern moral philosophy]'.

Rawls' social contract theory – which (as he himself tells us in the Preface) is 'highly Kantian in nature' – is explicitly 'hypothetical'. His aim is to identify and analyse the principles of justice 'that free and rational persons concerned to further their own interests would accept in an initial position of equality as defining the fundamental terms of their association' [Sec. 3]. The principle of justice thus conceived is that of fairness. There are in fact two such principles, and these are given their final statement in Sec. 46:

(1) The first provides that each person's liberties should be maximized – consistent with the provision of equal liberty for every other person. Liberty is thus an essential aspect of Rawls' theory of justice.
(2) According to the second principle, social and economic inequalities are to be arranged so that (a) they benefit everyone, the primary concern being to bring about the greatest benefit for the worst off (subject to what Rawls calls the 'savings principle', which relates to the sharing of the burden of capital accumulation and the raising of the standard of civilization and culture between the generations); and (b) offices and positions are open to all – there should be equality of opportunity.

These principles are qualified by two 'priority' rules:

(1) The first (the priority of liberty) states that the principles of justice are to be ranked in lexical order and that therefore liberty can be restricted only for the sake of liberty. (By **lexical priority** he means that a principle does not come into play until those previous to it are either fully met or do not apply [Sec. 8]). There are two cases:

(a) a less extensive liberty must strengthen the total system of liberty shared by all;

(b) a less than equal liberty must be acceptable to those with the lesser liberty.

(2) According to the second rule (the priority of justice over efficiency and welfare), the second principle of justice is lexically prior to the principle of efficiency and to that of maximizing the sum of advantages; and fair opportunity is prior to the difference principle. (By '**difference principle**' he means that no advantage can be morally acceptable if it does not benefit those members of society who are the most disadvantaged.) As he says:

> All social primary goods – liberty and opportunity, income and wealth, and the bases of self-respect – are to be distributed equally unless an unequal distribution of any or all of these goods is to the advantage of the least favoured.

Again there are two cases:

(a) an equality of opportunity must enhance the opportunities of those with the lesser opportunity;

(b) an excessive rate of saving must on balance mitigate the burden of those bearing the hardship.

What Rawls is asking us to do is to divest ourselves of the preconceptions and expectations we associate with our present status in society, and to use our imagination to put ourselves in the position of the least favoured members of the community. We must distance ourselves – behind what he calls the 'veil of ignorance' – from the advantages we possess in society as it actually is and from our own particular views about the good, so as to ascertain what primary goods are essential for a minimal, tolerable existence. What would we as free and rational persons then choose in this hypothetical situation? What would we regard as the basic requirement necessary if our well-being is to be advanced? The answer given is: a fair share of the social goods. But he makes it clear in his listing of principles and priority rules that the demand for liberty would be expected to take precedence over the quest for material prosperity. In this way, he argues, if the distribution of society's goods is to be made on the basis of a guarantee that the least favoured people in society will enjoy the maximum benefit consistent with the rules of priority, then the natural self-regarding tendencies of the rest of the community will be tempered by altruism.

What if the government fails to implement the contracted principles of justice? Rawls' answer is that resort to civil disobedience may be permissible [Secs 53–59]. His position on such a controversial issue is of interest not least because its radicalism is related to a contract theory in much the same way as the revolutionary founders of the United States were inspired by the contract theorists of the seventeenth and eighteenth centuries. The stirring words of *The Unanimous Declaration of the Thirteen United States of America* (4 July 1776) are well-known:

We hold these truths to be self-evident, that all men are created equal, that they are endowed by their Creator with certain unalienable Rights, that among these are Life, Liberty and the pursuit of Happiness. That to secure these rights, Governments are instituted among Men, deriving their just powers from the consent of the governed. That whenever any Form of Government becomes destructive of these ends, it is the Right of the People to alter or abolish it, and to institute new Government, laying its powers in such form, as to them shall seem most likely to effect their Safety and Happiness.

We are not of course implying that Rawls is preaching revolution. He sees civil disobedience as falling between legal protest on the one side and conscientious refusal and various forms of resistance on the other. He defines it as 'a public, non-violent, conscientious yet political act contrary to law usually done with the aim of bringing about a change in the law or policies of the government' [Sec. 55]. He is not therefore suggesting that it might be legitimate to overthrow a democratically elected government, but he is advocating the right of the individual to disobey the law if the government is perceived as failing to implement the principles of justice (that is, liberty and equality) 'which regulate the constitution and social institutions generally'. He further makes it clear that while the law is broken, yet fidelity to the law is expressed by the public and non-violent nature of the act, and by the willingness of the agent to accept the legal consequences of his disobedience. Moreover, in deciding whether civil disobedience is justified, the citizen must behave responsibly and look to the political principles that underlie the constitution and not to his own personal or party political interests [see Sec. 59]. Note also that, for Rawls, civil disobedience is grounded solely in the shared conception of justice that underlies the political order. This is in contrast to conscientious refusal which, although in time of war may be based on political considerations, is more usually founded on appeals to moral or religious convictions [see Sec. 56].

Rawls' moral and political philosophy has had a considerable impact on 'liberal' intellectual life in America. His thesis, however, has proved to be highly controversial:

(1) It has been objected that it is not possible to hide completely behind the 'veil of ignorance'; we cannot start from an 'empty' position. The concept is formalistic. It would seem to follow that we do not have a 'rational' choice in Rawls' sense; or, if we do, other procedures, for example, risk-taking, might be equally rational.

(2) Rawls regards property as grounding his theory of rights. Some critics, in particular Nozick (see the Reading list at the end of this chapter), argue that the right to property is antecedent to a Rawlsian society by virtue of tacit agreements, contracts and the like; and redistribution would in fact constitute an *injustice*. Moreover, happiness, or freedom, rather than redistribution of property 'goods' could be taken as the proper foundation for justice.

(3) Rawls seems to subordinate liberty to justice. Some critics are not happy with the perceived consequence that citizens might be compelled to act in

accordance with the principles, notwithstanding their acceptance of the social contract.

We now move on to examine some of the ideas of a political thinker whose writings have had a profound influence on the political and social history of the twentieth century in that they became the holy books of communist totalitarianism and world-revolutionaries.

7.4 Marxism and revolution

Reading: Marx and Engels, *The German Ideology, Theses on Feuerbach.* Sartre, *Search for a Method*

Marx

Perhaps the most famous publications of Karl Marx (1818–83) are the *Communist Manifesto* (1848), which he wrote in collaboration with his close friend Friedrich Engels (1820–95), and *Capital*, the first part of which appeared in 1867 (the second and third parts were published by Engels after Marx's death). *The German Ideology*, written in 1845–46 though it was not published until 1932, is important, however, as providing an early account of Marx and Engels' political philosophy. Marx's *Theses on Feuerbach* were composed about the same time.

The German Ideology opens with a sustained attack on a number of left-wing German philosophers usually called the 'Young Hegelians' [see the first section, The Illusions of German Ideology, pp.39–41]. This might seem surprising, for what these thinkers held in common was an adherence to the eighteenth century doctrines of 'liberty, equality and fraternity' which had informed the French and American Revolutions (as discussed in the previous section), and an opposition to the conservative authoritarianism of the Prussian monarchy. There is nothing here Marx could not sympathize with. But what he objected to was the naïvety of Young-Hegelian philosophers, their ignorance of economics, and their 'abstractness' and obsession with theory.

To understand Marx's position on these issues, something must be said briefly about Hegel's idealistic philosophy. Hegel identified the Real (the Totality of all things, the Idea, or the Absolute) with Reason or Universal Spirit. History, he argued, is its self-expression. According to Marx and Engels' interpretation, this Idea 'alienates' or projects itself in unconscious Nature which thus becomes its opposite. After further development it gives rise to man and thereby returns to self-consciousness or Spirit. This is brought about through a 'dialectic' process of successive negations by means of which a thesis generates an antithesis both of which are then subsumed under a higher synthesis.

Now the significant feature of Marx's own position is that he in effect adopted the Hegelian dialectic but rejected the idealism. Reality is identified not with Spirit or the 'Absolute Idea' but with 'material' Nature; and all human thought is to be understood as reflecting the dialectic process of the real as it works in the world and in human history. (You should note here the influence of Feuerbach on Marx. Although Marx is critical of him in many respects, he accepted Feuerbach's arguments against Hegel and also his view that religion arises as a result of man's 'self-alienation'. Note also the role played by Engels in Marx's writings. It has been argued that much of the methodology of 'Marxism' – in particular the application of dialectic to material nature – was the work of Engels [who, ironically, was not philosophically trained as Marx had been].) A further important objection Marx laid against Hegel was that it is not enough to understand the world or (as did Feuerbach and the Young Hegelians) merely to criticize religion, thoughts and ideas; philosophy must result in political and social action. The Young-Hegelian ideologists, he says, when they are 'fighting against "phrases"':

> forget . . . that to these phrases they themselves are only opposing other phrases, and that they are in no way combating the real existing world when they are merely combating the phrases of this world.
>
> [*The German Ideology*, p.41]

And as he says in the oft-quoted statement in his *Theses on Feuerbach* [XI]: 'The philosophers have only *interpreted* the world, in various ways; the point is to *change* it'. How, and into what, the present order of things is to be changed are precisely the questions Marx seeks to answer in *The German Ideology*. In the most general terms we might say that this book embodies a **materialist theory of history** (which includes the notion of 'class-war') underpinned by a **labour theory of value**. But a more detailed examination is required. Most of the main ideas are clearly set out in Part I A (Secs 2–4, pp.45–52]. (You are recommended to devote particularly close attention to these sections, even though Marx develops some of the ideas discussed there later in the book.)

Marx's starting point is not dogma but real individuals grounded in 'natural conditions', who are distinguished from animals in that they produce their means of subsistence and thereby their actual material life. This activity or 'mode of life' *defines* the individual:

> As individuals express their life, so they are. What they are, therefore, coincides with their production, both with *what* they produce and *how* they produce. The nature of individuals thus depends on the material conditions determining their production. [42]

It is important to appreciate that Marx is not propounding an individualist thesis such as was held by Locke or Rousseau. The idea of a pre-contractual 'State of Nature' is for Marx a myth [compare p.49]. Productive forces and hence 'individuals' are from the moment of their first appearance in history *inseparable* from social and political relationships or **intercourse** [*Verkehr* – see p.42] grounded in material activity. The first historical act, he says is the production of the means to satisfy needs such as eating and drinking, a habitation and clothing. Moreover it is this social context that gives rise to and indeed determines language, culture, and consciousness itself:

The production of ideas, of conceptions, of consciousness, is at first directly interwoven with the material activity and the material intercourse of men, the language of real life. Conceiving, thinking, the mental intercourse of men, appear at this stage as the direct efflux of their material behaviour. The same applies to mental productions as expressed in the language of politics, laws, morality, religion, metaphysics, etc. of a people. Men are the producers of their conceptions, ideas, etc. – real, active men, as they are conditioned by a definite development of their productive forces and of the intercourse corresponding to these, up to its furthest forms.　　　　[48]

'Life', he says [p.48] 'is not determined by consciousness, but consciousness by life'. It should be noted that Marx sees himself as thereby avoiding the error of 'abstractionism' which he thinks was committed by both British empiricism and German idealism [pp.47–48].

The initial social relationship is that of the **family** [p.49], and it is in this context that a number of key terms in Marx's analysis are first introduced: **division of labour**, **contradiction**, **alienation** and his account of property and class. From the beginning of history productivity (that is, in labour and procreation) involved man simultaneously in both natural and social relationships which are interdependent:

Consciousness is at first . . . merely consciousness concerning the *immediate* sensuous environment and consciousness of the limited connection with other persons and things outside the individual who is growing self-conscious. At the same time it is consciousness of nature, which first appears to men as a completely alien, all-powerful and unassailable force, with which men's relations are purely animal and by which they are overawed like beasts; it is thus a purely animal consciousness of nature (natural religion) just because nature is as yet hardly modified historically. (We see here immediately: this natural religion or this particular relation of men to nature is determined by the form of society and vice versa. Here, as everywhere, the identity of nature and man appears in such a way that the restricted relation of men to nature determines their restricted relation to one another, and their restricted relation to one another determines men's restricted relation to nature.)　　　　[51]

As the population increased, with a consequent increase of productivity and needs, so does the **division of labour** become more explicit and complex. Grounded originally in the sexual act, in genetic differences, or in chance happenings, division of labour becomes 'truly such from the moment when a division of material and mental labour appears' [51].

Contradictions are introduced between social relations and forces of production; and Marx goes on to assert that this is a necessary process:

The forces of production, the state of society and consciousness can and must come into contradiction with one another, because the *division of labour* implies the possibility, nay the fact that intellectual and material activity – enjoyment and labour, production and consumption – devolve on different individuals, and that the only possibility of their not coming into contradiction lies in the negation in its turn of the division of labour.   [52]

(Implicit here is the 'materialized' Hegelian dialectic referred to above.)

From the concept of division of labour, Marx derives his theory of **property** and **class**. Property arises from the unequal distribution of labour and its products contingent upon the opposition of individual families in society. Indeed division of labour and private property are identical expressions, the former relating to an activity while the latter refers to the product of that activity. Division of labour gives rise also to different **classes** (for example, feudal, urban, aristocracy and bourgeoisie) defined by their several activities, that is, their relation to property and the means of production. Marx's historical analysis of the emergence of classes will not be summarized here; it can easily be followed particularly in Sec. C of *The German Ideology*. But two important points arising from it deserve mention. (1) Class interest and class conflict. The possession of private property leads to antagonism between classes, one of which comes to be the dominant or ruling class. This ruling class, says Marx, controls not only the means of material production but also the ideas of an epoch [64]. In due course – once the contradiction between forces of production and social relations has become apparent – a class struggle ensues which brings about the overthrow of the dominant class, the victors becoming the new ruling class. (2) Civil society and the State. By 'civil society' Marx means the totality of commercial relationships (*Verkehr*), grounded in the forces of production, which exist between individuals:

> Civil society embraces the whole material intercourse of individuals within a definite stage of the development of productive forces. It embraces the whole commercial and industrial life of a given stage and, insofar, transcends the State and the nation, though, on the other hand again, it must assert itself in its foreign relations as nationality, and inwardly must organise itself as State.   [57]

The State for Marx is an abstraction. It is, 'the form in which the individuals of a ruling class assert their common interests, and in which the whole of civil society of an epoch is epitomised' [80]. Again:

> ... all struggles within the State, the struggle between democracy, aristocracy, and monarchy, the struggle for the franchise, etc., etc., are merely the illusory forms in which the real struggles of the different classes are fought out among one another.   [53]

It follows that all common institutions, including the legal system and justice which 'is reduced to the actual laws', are formed through the mediation of the State [80].

Underlying class conflict is '**alienation**' (a key term Marx derived from Hegel). By this he means the feeling or awareness of discord experienced by individuals when they come to recognize a lack of coincidence between their own interest and that of the community. Initially it is man's own activity – the social role into which he is forced as a result of division of labour – which opposes him, but subsequently it is the bureaucratic and political State itself that is the alien power which enslaves him and constitutes a threat to his individuality in the context of family or civil society [see pp.53–56]. The primary aim of political activity must therefore be to eliminate alienation, to achieve a society in which there is no conflict between private and public interest, a society in which men will be really free. Such a society will necessarily be classless, propertyless, a true democracy – in a word, **communist**.

We are now brought to the second of the two questions posed at the beginning of our account: *how* is the communist society to be realized? Marx's answer is through revolution. Now revolution was of course the stock in trade of eighteenth and nineteenth century libertarian movements in Europe and America which appealed to 'Laws of Nature', the 'Rights of Man' and so on (compare 7.3). And it is no coincidence that this should have been followed by an explosion of revolutionary energy in France only thirteen years later which would – in theory – guarantee '*Liberté, Egalité, Fraternité*' to all. But Marx will have nothing to do with such abstractions which he sees as expressions of bourgeois ideology grounded in property relations. [See, for example, what he says about 'Utilitarianism' on pp.109 ff. and compare his discussion of 'Kant and Liberalism' on pp.97 ff.] His ideal is the establishment of the 'revolutionary dictatorship of the proletariat'. This can only be achieved when the bourgeoisie itself is overthrown, the class-system is abolished and the State has withered away, thus producing a real community in which the individual will be able to cultivate his gifts and achieve personal freedom [p.83]:

> Both for the production on a mass scale of this communist consciousness, and for the success of the cause itself, the alteration of men on a mass scale is necessary, an alteration which can only take place in a practical movement, a *revolution*; this revolution is necessary, therefore, not only because the *ruling* class cannot be overthrown in any other way, but also because the class *overthrowing* it can only in a revolution succeed in ridding itself of all the muck of ages and become fitted to found society anew. [94–95; see also pp.82–88]

The communist revolution differs from all previous revolutions, Marx says: it is directed against the *mode* of activity, does away with *labour*, and abolishes classes and thereby class-rule (because the 'class' that carries it through 'is not recognized as a class, and is in itself the expression of the dissolution of all classes, nationalities, etc. within present society' [94]. It is important to note that the revolution must be simultaneously world-wide [Marx gives his reasons on p.56], and that communism is not thought of as an *ideal* but as an actual movement:

> Communism is for us not a *state of affairs* which is to be established, an *ideal* to which reality [will] have to adjust itself. We call communism the *real* movement which abolishes the present state of things. The conditions of this movement result from the premises now in existence.   [56–57]

*Comments and criticisms

First of all you should take note of two general points:

(1) When talking of communism we naturally have in mind a political and social system which we associate with 'totalitarian' regimes such as the former Soviet Union or the People's Republic of China. To refer to such societies by the blanket term 'communism' does however obscure the very real differences which exist between them and which are in part attributable to 'deviant' interpretations or differing implementations of *Marxist* communism. So far as 'interpretations' go, we may distinguish broadly between 'orthodox' Marxists, such as Lenin, Stalin and Mao, who tend to stress the materialist aspects of Marx's writings; and 'revisionists' who tend towards an 'idealist' interpretation. The latter group includes Georg Lukács and his followers, such as the philosophers of the so-called Frankfurt School – Adorno, Horkheimer and Marcuse, who set out to rediscover the more 'humanist', anti-positivist Hegelian Marx, and who rejected the inflexible and uncritical stance of the strict orthodoxy then prevailing in the Soviet Union. Their efforts were facilitated by the belated publication of *The German Ideology* in 1932. More recently the aims of the Frankfurt founders have been revitalized by the work of Jürgen Habermas. (Some discussion of his 'critical theory' will be found in Ch. 12.) Sartre also belongs to the 'revisionists' (see below). (Note that such classifications are rough and ready. In actuality these various writers and activists differ quite considerably from each other in their readings of Marxist theory or in the ways they believe Marxism should be out into practice in the political process.)

(2) We must ensure that we do not judge the philosophical tenability of Marx's political thought on the basis of how acceptable or otherwise we find some contemporary communist regimes (any more than we should criticize Nietzsche's philosophy because of its alleged appropriation by German fascism, or judge the 'truth' of, say, Christianity or Islam by the standards of societies which in the course of history have professed to be informed by the Christian (or Islamic) ethic; there is probably little to choose between the Inquisition and the Ayatollahs, or the KGB). But having said that, it is fair to add that if Marxism either has not been properly implemented, or – as most critics would claim – if it is not seen to be 'working' (that is, as a political or an economic system), then this may at least in part reflect an inherent weakness in the theoretical basis of the system itself.

The following criticisms are relevant:

(a) Marx claimed that 'Marxism' was 'scientific'. But it is certainly not scientific in any conventional sense of the term. It is difficult, for example, to think of Marx's account of Nature as a 'hypothesis' which is open to experimental testing, or as an explanatory model for a particular phenomenon. And this is primarily because his 'theory' is intended to apply to the totality of phenomena, that is to Nature itself. What could then count as falsifying counter-instances? (You will be learning something about the philosophy of science in the next chapter. Note in particular Karl Popper's views (8.3), and his criticisms of Marxism in *Conjectures and Refutations* and *The Open Society and its Enemies*.)

(b) In contrast to Hegelian philosophy, Marx's theory is essentially materialist. This is not to say he denies the existence of mental phenomena, but be does think of material Nature as prior and argues that consciousness and cultural modes or structures such as religion, art, moral systems and philosophy itself originate from and are determined by a substructure which is to be understood in terms of economic or productive forces. This is certainly a bold claim which, to say the least, is questionable (see also 12.5).

(3) Most later interpreters regard the Marxist system as a species of metaphysics. The key concept is obviously the 'dialectic'. Nature is a process which progresses dialectically. There are two principal difficulties. (a) The concept of 'dialectic' is open to the same criticisms made of it in its original Hegelian context: it is a wide-ranging notion, and although relating to material phenomena it is alleged to be grounded in a logic of successive negation and counter-negation. Certainly we may talk of two statements as contradicting each other: but it is less clear how, say, a seed can be negated when it starts to grow into a plant. (b) Following on from the first difficulty, descriptions of the world process (that is, of man in Nature – historical events, the class 'struggle' itself) just do not seem to work without a great deal of artificial forcing of acts into the preformed dialectic mould.

(4) There is a tension between the apparent inevitability of the dialectic process and individual human choice. Marx claims it is the job of philosophy to change the world rather than to understand it. But if the world is going to change anyway in accordance with the dialectic, what role can man play other than to be acquiescent – which is hardly a revolutionary attitude? It is perhaps possible to reconcile these two factors by thinking of man as being active – in dialogue – with Nature, as it were, and as thereby making explicit the dialectic process. Man's activity *is* the dialectic in action (compare the discussion of Sartre's 'Marxism' below).

There are no doubt many other objections that might be made against Marxism as a 'philosophy', but these four points should give you more than enough to work on.

Sartre and Marxism

As mentioned in 6.6, Sartre, although pessimistic at the end of *Being and Nothingness*, thought ethics might be possible given a 'radical conversion'. This proved in due course to be a conversion to Marxism and resulted in a massive tome on political and social philosophy entitled *The Critique of Dialectical Reason*. (The expected book on ethics was never written.) We shall do no more here than to summarize a few of the main ideas. (If you would like to tackle the original text you are recommended to study Sartre's introductory essay, *Question de Méthode* [translated as *Search for a Method*], written to provide the critical foundations for the book as a whole, and which has the advantage of being much easier to read.)

Sartre starts [ch. I of *Search for a Method*] with the view that a philosophy is 'a particular way in which the "rising class" becomes conscious of itself' [pp.3–4]. But it must be more than this; it must be 'simultaneously a totalization of knowledge, a method, a regulative Idea, an offensive weapon, and a community of language' [6]. He sees this 'vision of the world' further as 'an instrument which ferments rotten societies' and as becoming 'the culture and sometimes the nature of a whole class'. Just as in the past the philosophies of Descartes, Locke, Kant, and Hegel have filled this role, so it is now Marxism that Sartre sees as being the dominant philosophy of the present day [7]. However, he is at the same time severely critical of contemporary Marxists. They treat as concrete truths what should be taken as heuristic (guiding) principles or regulative ideas; their method does not derive concepts from experience but is certain of their truth and treats them as constitutive schemata. (The terminology of 'regulative' and 'constitutive' here is Kantian.) The sole purpose of the method is 'to force the events, the persons, or the acts considered into prefabricated moulds' [37]. Moreoover, the 'intellectual' or 'lazy' Marxist interprets history teleologically, in terms of a mechanistic movement towards a moment of final completion, a 'totality'; and thereby subsumes the concrete particular – especially man, whom Sartre sees as free and creative – under the universal. The Marxist is here guilty of 'bad faith', for he is

> bringing two concepts into play at the same time so as to preserve the benefit of a teleological interpretation while concealing the abundant, high-handed use which they make of the explanation by finality. They employ the second concept to make it appear to everyone that there is a mechanistic interpretation of History – ends have disappeared. At the same time they make use of the first so as surreptitiously to transform into real objectives of a human activity the necessary but unforseeable consequences which this activity entails. Hence that tedious vacillation in Marxist explanations. From one sentence to another the historical enterprise is defined implicitly *by goals* (which are only unforeseen results) or reduced to the diffusion of a physical movement across an inert milieu.
>
> [47]

What Sartre wants to do is to get back to what he sees as the Hegelian roots of the original Marx. He wants to put man back into the picture: '. . . it is men whom we judge and not physical forces' [47]. 'This lazy Marxism puts everything into everything, makes real men into the symbols of its myths' [53]. And he seeks a Marxist philosophy which is not a predetermined totality but a continuous totalizing process.

To put concrete man back into history it is necessary to make the historical object 'pass through a process of mediation' [42]: contemporary Marxism 'lacks any hierarchy of mediations which would permit it to grasp the process which produces the person and his product inside a class and within a given society at a given historical moment' [56]. And Sartre sees it as the function of existentialism,

> without being unfaithful to Marxist [i.e., pure] principles, to find mediations which allow the individual concrete – the particular life, the real and dated conflict, the person – to emerge from the background of the *general* contradiction of productive forces and relations of production. [57]

The 'progressive–regressive' method to be employed, the purpose of which is 'to place man in his proper framework', is sketched out mainly in ch. III. By 'regressive', Sartre means that it is concerned with the uncovering of the fundamental structures that link men to each other and to Nature. This is achieved by the making of what he calls 'cross-references'. And it is 'progressive' in that it is a continuous process of 'totalization'. A biography, for example (Sartre examines in detail the writer Flaubert) is progressively determined through an examination of the period, and the period by an examination of the person's life. 'Far from seeking immediately to integrate one into the other, [the method] will hold them separate until the reciprocal involvement comes to pass of itself and puts a temporary end to the research' [135]. Regression is a move back to an original condition: progression is the movement towards the objective result [154]. Moreover the method, Sartre insists, is heuristic and not *a priori* like the 'synthetic progression' of the 'lazy' Marxists; he is concerned to show how the individual actually makes his free choices in the context of his social grouping but at the same time 'transcends' himself within the dialectical historical process. This purposive activity (compare Aristotle) Sartre refers to by the technical term **praxis**. It thus consists of three aspects: (a) the plan or intention (the **project**); (b) the factual or objective situation man seeks to alter; and (c) the 'passing beyond' (*dépassement*) that situation. The objective situation is called the 'practico-inert'. But it is not just a material structure which limits man; it may be a class, or indeed anything produced by him which as an '*en-soi*' is found to be in opposition to the freedom of man himself, the '*pour-soi*', and which thus becomes the source of alienation as expressed in what Sartre calls **need** or scarcity (*besoin*) [91].

The full significance of praxis is revealed in the Conclusions. Marxism, says Sartre,

> appears to be the only possible anthropology which can be at once historical and structural. It is the only one which at the same time takes man in his totality – that is, in terms of the materiality of his condition. [175]

But anthropological disciplines, or the sciences of man – disciplines such as history, sociology, ethnology, and Marxism itself, study the development and relation of human facts but '*do not question themselves about man*' [168]. Intellectual Knowledge is in opposition to Being:

If anthropology is to be an organized whole, it must surmount this contradiction – the origin of which does not reside in a Knowledge but in reality itself – and it must on its own constitute itself as a structural, historical anthropology. [169]

What is needed, therefore, is a process of 'interiorization' or 'internalization' by means of which existence can be reintegrated into Knowledge. It is here that praxis has a role to play [see pp.170–172], for the 'determinations of the person' (that is, those economic and cultural factors which oppose or condition him) are 'themselves sustained, internalized, and lived' by the personal project; and it is in his 'comprehending' of the project that man makes his own reality, 'existentializes' the ideology. 'Comprehension' is described as being both 'immediate existence (since it is produced as the movement of action)' and as 'the foundation of an indirect knowing of existence (since it comprehends the existence of the other)'. And by 'indirect knowing' Sartre means the result of reflection on existence. It is indirect in the sense that it is presupposed by the concepts of anthropology 'without being itself made the object of concepts'. He makes it clear that the process is entirely rational and reproduces the dialectical movement from the 'given' to 'activity'. (Hence his substitution of 'Dialectical Reason' for 'Dialectical Materialism'.) Moreover, 'the demand for an existential foundation for the Marxist theory' is, he says, already contained implicitly in Marx's own Marxism [177]. If Marxism does not reintegrate man into itself as its foundation, it will 'degenerate into a non-human anthropology' [179]. What Sartre seems to be saying is that existentialism and Marxism require each other; existentialism will enliven Marxism and as it does so it will no longer exist as an independent philosophy. The final paragraph of the book contains what is perhaps the clearest statement of his new standpoint:

Thus the autonomy of existential studies results necessarily from the negative qualities of Marxists (and not from Marxism itself.) So long as the doctrine does not recognize its anaemia, so long as it founds its Knowledge upon a dogmatic metaphysics (a dialectic of Nature) instead of seeking its support in the comprehension of the living man, so long as it rejects as irrational those ideologies which wish, as Marx did, to separate being from Knowledge and, in anthropology, to found the knowing of man on human existence, existentialism will follow its own path of study. This means that it will attempt to clarify the givens of Marxist Knowledge by indirect knowing (that is, as we have seen, by words which regressively denote existential structures), and to engender within the framework of Marxism a veritable *comprehensive knowing* which will rediscover man in the social world and which will follow him in his *praxis* – or, if you prefer, in the project which throws him toward the social possibles in terms of a defined situation. Existentialism will appear therefore as a fragment of the system, which has fallen outside of Knowledge. From the day that Marxist thought will have taken on the human dimension (that is, the existential project) as the foundation of anthropological Knowledge, existentialism will no longer have any reason for being. Absorbed, surpassed and conserved by the totalizing movement of philosophy, it will cease to be a particular inquiry and will become the foundation of all inquiry. [181]

*Comments

How far Sartre's thesis represents a genuine and coherent reinterpretation of Marxism is a question best left to Marxist scholars to answer. The initial problem is in any case probably one of understanding what he actually means. Terms such as 'comprehending', 'internalization', 'progressive', 'regressive' and 'indirect knowing' are used in a somewhat idiosyncratic fashion; and no doubt much careful reading of the text will be required if you are to cut through the obscurity and achieve some clarification. The short and admittedly incomplete sketch provided in this section should however provide you with some assistance. As for actual criticisms of Sartre's regenerated Marxism, the main issue is probably that of freedom: can the individual's existential freedom to make himself, to choose his own course of action, be reconciled with his commitment to a Marxist dialectic of inevitability? It can certainly be argued that this conflict between freedom and necessity, which is implicit in the Marxist system, is particularly acute in Sartre's version because of the emphasis he laid on freedom during his 'pure' existentialist period as expressed particularly in *Being and Nothingness*. We shall come back to this problem in Ch. 11.

QUESTIONS

A. Texts

1 Explain Locke's concept of the state of nature and its purpose in his political theory.

2 Explain the role played by consent in Locke's political theory.

*3 Examine critically Locke's theory of the Contract.

4 Discuss the power of the legislature in Locke's political philosophy.

5 Discuss the implications of Locke's strict libertarian views for modern Western political life. [IB, specimen, 2000]

6 Discuss Rousseau's judgement on property in the *Discourse on the Origin of Inequality*.

7 Explain and discuss the distinctions drawn by Rousseau in relation to inequality.

*8 Examine Rousseau's concept of the General Will.

9 Has Rousseau any notion of the rights of the individual?

10 Is Rousseau's argument for the Sovereign in the *Social Contract* libertarian or totalitarian? [IB, specimen, 2000]

11 Why is Mill opposed to the policy of 'coercing' people into prudence or temperance?

*12 Why does Mill emphasize the importance of individuality in *On Liberty*?

13 Mill argues that the law should not interfere in the conduct of an adult's life so long as that behaviour does not cause harm to others. Do you agree with this view? What difficulties might there be in implementing such a principle?

14 According to Mill, democratic tyranny would be far worse than aristocratic or

despotic tyranny. Why did Mill think this? Discuss the measures he advocated to counteract democratic tyranny.

15 Explain and discuss why, according to Mill, we must recognize both freedom of opinion and freedom of expression of opinion. [IB, specimen, 2000]

16 Explain what Marx meant by 'alienation'.

*17 Marx was critical of Feuerbach and the Young Hegelians for just wanting to interpret the world; in his view the philosopher's job was to change it. Discuss this view, and consider whether we should conclude that Marx was therefore not in a strict sense a philosopher.

18 What did Marx and Engels mean by 'ideology'?

19 Examine the distinction Marx makes between the 'State' and a 'real community'.

20 The system of Marx and Engels is generally referred to as 'dialectical materialism'. Examine the concept of 'dialectic' in this context.

21 Examine Marx's concept of 'class-warfare'.

22 Does Sartre's 'humanized' Marxism represent an improvement on 'orthodox' Marxism?

23 Robert Nozick criticized the principle of fairness defined by Rawls as a principle which legitimizes enforcement of the obligations that have arisen under this principle of fairness. Nozick argues that persons engaging in mutually advantageous, co-operative ventures according to rules restrain their liberty in ways necessary to yield the desired results. Is it the case that the principle of fairness limits the liberty of persons as claimed by Nozick? Discuss.

[IB, specimen, 2000]

24 Explain and discuss Martha Nussbaum's view that fairness is only possible if the judge acts as a 'judicious spectator'. [IB, specimen, 2000]

B. Problems

25 Do laws constitute the best way to harmonize individual liberty with public order?

*26 Can there be an unjust law?

27 Is it the case that the only purpose for which power can be rightfully exercised over any member of a civilized community, against his will, is to prevent harm to others?

28 Should the law be used to enforce the moral standards of society? [AEB, 1997]

29 Is submission to authority necessarily an abdication of one's responsibility?

30 Can there be genuine authority exercised in the absence of power?

31 What are the purposes of the state-sanctioned punishment of individuals? Consider the philosophical difficulties associated with each.

32 What are 'natural rights'? Are they sufficient to define the limits of the power of the state over the individual?

33 What are 'unalienable rights'? Where do they come from? What are they grounded in?

34 Compare and contrast positive and negative freedom ('freedom to' and 'freedom from'). [AEB, 1996]

35 Can we justify a model of society that promotes the economic well-being of its citizens at the cost of the democratic values of freedom, equality and fraternity?

[IB, specimen, 2000]

*36 Explain what you understand by civil disobedience and how it might be justified. Could it ever be justified if your country were at war with another state?

*37 Society restricts one's freedom, yet one can be truly free only within a social context. Can this apparent contradiction be resolved?

38 How can positive discrimination be justified? What problems for individuals or for society as whole might ensue as a result?

39 'The well-being of the people is the supreme law.' Discuss.

*Notes/guided answers have been provided for questions **3**, **8**, **12**, **17**, **26**, **36** and **37** (at end of book).

READING LIST

A. Prescribed texts
Arendt, H., *The Human Condition.* (IB)
Locke, J., *Second Treatise on Government.* (IB)
Marx, K. and Engels, F., *The German Ideology.* (AEB)
Mill, J.S., *On Liberty.* (AEB, IB)
Nussbaum, M., *Poetic Justice.* (IB)
Rawls, J., *A Theory of Justice.* (IB)
Rousseau, J.-J., *Discourse on the Origin of Equality; The Social Contract.* (AEB, IB)
Taylor, C., *The Ethics of Authenticity.* (IB)

B. Other texts
Hobbes, T., *Leviathan.*
Marx, K., *Theses on Feuerbach.*
Sartre, J.-P., *Search for a Method.*

C. Supplementary reading
(If you are a beginner, you are recommended to start with titles marked with an asterisk.)

1. Historical background
Plamenatz, J.P., *Man and Society.**
Redhead, B. (ed.), *Political Thought from Plato to NATO.**
Sabine, G.H., *History of Political Theory.*

2. General introductory texts
Raphael, D.D., *Problems of Political Philosophy.**
Wolff, J., *An Introduction to Political Philosophy.*

3. Books and articles on individual philosophers
Marcuse, H., *Reason and Revolution.* (On Hegel.)
Singer, P., *Hegel.**
Peters, R., *Hobbes.**
Tuck, R., *Hobbes.**
Dunn, J., *Locke.**

Berlin, I., *Karl Marx.**
Singer, P., *Marx.**
Sowell, T., *Marxism: Philosophy and Economics.**
Ten, C.L., *Mill on Liberty.*
(For other books on Mill see the Reading list for Ch. 6.)
Barry, B., *The Liberal Theory of Justice.* (On Rawls.)
Grimsley, R., *Jean-Jacques Rousseau.*
Wokler, R., *Rousseau.**

4. Other books and essays
Augustine, *City of God.**
Barrow, R., *Injustice, Inequality and Ethics.**
Berlin, I., *Four Essays on Liberty.**
Mabbott, J.D., *The State and the Citizen.**
Nozick, R., *Anarchy, State, and Utopia.**
Popper, K.R., *Conjectures and Refutations*, chs 15–20.
Popper, K.R., *The Open Society and its Enemies.**
Quinton, A. (ed.), *Political Philosophy.**
See also the books by Devlin, Hart and Mitchell in the Reading list for Ch. 6.*

▪ ▼ 8 The philosophy of science

8.1 Introduction

We live in an age of science; and throughout this century in particular man has made extraordinary progress both in his understanding of the universe and in his use of scientific knowledge to improve the quality of life. All around us we find examples of its benefits: television, aeroplanes, new medicines to conquer disease, computers and the Internet, synthetic materials for clothes and furnishings. There is of course a darker side. We may have reached the Moon and before long will have set foot on Mars: but at the same time we are steadily destroying Mother Earth. Material resources are being used up at an unprecedented rate; the tropical rain forests are disappearing – 50 hectares are being cut down every minute; acid rain is polluting the soil; we are pouring noxious substances into the atmosphere and thereby probably bringing about long-term and perhaps irreversible changes in the world's climate. It would be quite wrong, however, to lay the blame wholly on scientists. The reasons for man's predicament are numerous and broadly political, social and economic. Indeed to a greater or lesser extent we must all accept our share of responsibility; and it is incumbent on each one of us to do what we can to reverse current trends if we have any concern at all for future generations (see 6.8). Moreover, it is not science as such which is on trial so much as the way we use it. So what then *is* science? What is the scientist trying to do? What are his methods? These seemingly straightforward questions do in fact lead to some quite complex philosophical problems.

The word 'science' is derived from the Latin word *scientia* which means 'knowledge' and it is nothing less than knowledge of the whole universe that scientists seek. It is of course necessarily a collective enterprise; no individual nowadays can possibly carry out research on anything but a very narrow front. He can no longer say with Francis Bacon (1561–1626): 'I take all knowledge to be my province' (particularly as the great scientist and essayist included under the heading of knowledge rather more than science as we use the term today). That is why we talk not so much of scientists as of physicists, chemists, biologists and, perhaps, anthropologists; or at a still higher level of specialization, of nuclear physicists, biochemists, neurobiologists and so on. But does this research give them knowledge in the sense of insight into 'reality'? If so, what is this 'reality'? How does a biologist's 'reality' differ from the insight achieved by, say, quantum mechanics? Do different kinds of scientists employ the same methods? What are these methods? What is a scientific theory? How is it tested? These are typical of the very many questions asked by philosophers of science; and we shall be looking at some of them in this chapter.

8.2 Scientific explanation

Reading: Hempel, 'Explanation in Science and History'; Popper, *The Logic of Scientific Discovery*, chs I and X; *Conjectures and Refutations*, Introduction and ch. I

According to a commonly held view of scientific method (which owes much to the writings of Francis Bacon and John Stuart Mill), practising scientists proceed roughly along the following lines. As a result of careful **observation** of the world they may become aware of something to be **explained**. A tentative guess or suggestion, called a **hypothesis**, is then put forward as a possible solution. The hypothesis is then **verified** or **confirmed** by means of appropriate **experiments** and thereby qualifies for the status of a **theory** and provides the backing for scientific **laws**. The essential criterion by which the adequacy of a theory is judged is its power of **prediction**; that is, the extent to which it can enable us to say in advance that certain sorts of events *will* occur if the theory is **true**. Such an account is not only over-simplified but is in fundamental respects thoroughly mistaken and open to philosophical objections. We shall start by considering the idea of explanation. What are explanations? What are they for? What do they achieve? Are there many different types of explanation? How do they 'fit' together? Should we expect them always to be reconciled? What makes a given explanation 'better' than another? What are the criteria of adequacy?

Typically an explanation is offered in response to the question 'Why?' – and, as most of us know, questioning starts very early in life. As children we want to know, for example, why there is flashing and booming during a thunderstorm; why Dad was late home from work one night; why we have to go to bed at 6 o'clock; why we get presents at Christmas; and so on. Children are naturally curious. Moreover they want to feel secure. Answers to such questions, even if in certain respects they are 'incomplete' or even 'wrong', can provide a framework which facilitates a child's physical, intellectual and emotional development as a human beings. It would seem that initially children are easily satisfied. The presents they find at the end of the bed came from Santa Claus. In 'primitive' societies the thunder is a sign that the gods are angry and need to be propitiated. But, in the course of time, man has sought for more sophisticated explanations. These are characterized by a framework within which statements about specific instances or phenomena can be grounded in more general principles. In this section we look specifically at *scientific* explanation.

Traditionally scientific explanations have been supposed to involve both inductive and deductive procedures. You will remember from your reading of 2.9 that there are philosophical difficulties associated with induction. But it was also pointed out there that to deal with these Mill tried to show that inductive arguments were really deductive ones; while Karl Popper argued that scientific procedures do not essentially involve induction at all – thereby avoiding the difficulties. Many other influential twentieth century philosophers of science (such as R. Braithwaite, C.G. Hempel and E. Nagel) have also held a similar view – which is generally called the 'hypothetical-deductive' or '**covering-law**' theory of scientific explanation. According to **Hempel** (1905–97), a statement describing the event to be explained (the 'explanandum') is deduced from an 'explanans', which is a conjunction of a set of general laws with a series of statements describing particular facts. (Because a phenomenon can be accounted for by reference to general laws or theoretical principles, Hempel refers to this model of explanation as 'nomological'.) Thus if we wished to explain *why* a stick looks bent in water, we would show how this statement could be deduced from statements about particular circumstances such as the densities of the air and water on that occasion, and the angle of the stick in relation to the water surface, in accordance with the appropriate laws – in this case the laws of refraction. The uniformities expressed by the general laws can in their turn be subsumed under more inclusive laws and eventually under comprehensive theories (for example, the wave theory of light), which results in both a wider scope of scientific understanding and greater depth in so far as the original empirical laws are seen to hold only within certain limits. It is important to stress that Hempel regards such inferences as *deductive*, for this avoids the charge of circularity. Suppose we want to know why a piece of copper expands when heated (instance I_n). The explanation is that it is an instance of a general law, 'All pieces of copper expand when heated'. Clearly, if we said that this supposedly universal law had been established on the basis of a succession of observations of the behaviour of different pieces of copper, we could hardly be said to have offered an explanation at all, because the generality of the law must have already been established by reference to this instance I_n. Moreover, it is possible that the next occurrence could prove to be a counter-instance: the copper might not expand on heating. Hempel's account seems to avoid this difficulty in so far as the general law is grounded not inductively in a succession of instances but in a framework of more general laws and theories at a 'deeper' level.

Many philosophers who have proposed this model of scientific explanation do however admit that there is a second type which is inductive and thereby probabilistic. Thus Hempel suggests that in such arguments the explanandum (Oi) is expressed in a statement that in a particular instance (i), for example, someone's allergic attack, and outcome (O)-subsidence of the attack – occurs; and that this explanandum is explained by means of two explanans-statements. The first of these (Fi) corresponds to the series of statements describing particular factors (F) in the 'covering-law' model, while the second namely, $P(O,F)$ expresses a law affirming that the statistical probability for the outcome to occur is high when the various factors are realized. Probabilistic explanations are therefore still nomological in Hempel's sense, although not deductive in so far as the conclusions are derived from an only probable premiss.

*Comment and criticism

Hempel's account of explanation is much more sophisticated and extensive than might be thought from the necessarily short summary given here. There is, however, one point – which Hempel himself discusses – that needs to be taken up. So far as the probabilistic type of explanation is concerned, the problem we referred to above concerning the soundness of the foundations on which science is constructed remains unanswered. Explananda must remain probable and not certain, as indeed must the scientific laws from which they are derived. But, it may be asked, are not *all* scientific laws (and therefore explanations) probabilistic, since even the universal laws which constitute the premises of deductive arguments must have been established on the basis of a finite body of evidence. Moreover, it can be questioned whether the distinction between the deductive and probabilistic models of explanation should be maintained at all. In answer to such possible objections Hempel argues that the argument confounds a logical issue with an epistemological one: 'it fails to distinguish properly between the *claim* made by a given law-statement and the *degree of confirmation*, or *probability*, which it possesses on the available evidence'. Universal law-statements (of the simplest kind), he says, assert that *all* elements of an indefinitely large reference class (for example, copper objects) have a certain characteristic (for example being good conductors of electricity); whereas statistical law-statements assert that, in the long run, a specified proportion of the reference class have some specified property. The difference in claim of the two kinds of law is reflected in the difference of form. Now, this is no doubt correct. But the point at issue is whether the *claims* made in each case are justified. Deductive arguments from premises *accepted* as true are impeccable as valid inferences. But if such a universal premiss proves subsequently to admit of exceptions then doubt *may* then be cast on the validity of the inference and the truth of the conclusion – unless the exception can be accommodated by a modification of the general law. All such claims have therefore to be regarded as being made on a provisional basis. This of course must lead on to a further important question: what is the status of theories? In what sense can they be said to be 'true' or 'certain' so as to ground general laws? How are theories related to 'hypotheses'?

(**Note**: Throughout this section, discussion of explanation has been tacitly confined to a consideration of the *natural* sciences – physics, chemistry and, more controversially, biology. Whether some form of covering-law theory has a role to play in the methodology of the *social* sciences, concerned as they are with human motives, choices and actions is a question that has been much debated in recent years. We shall be looking at some of the issues in Ch. 12.)

8.3 Theories, laws and hypotheses

Reading: Toulmin, *The Philosophy of Science*; Popper, *The Logic of Scientific Discovery*, chs IV and VII, and *Conjectures and Refutations*, ch. 3; Kuhn, *The Structure of Scientific Revolutions*

Theories and laws

Some philosophers of science have argued that no clear distinction can be made between these two terms as they are used in the experimental context. Those who seek to uphold such a distinction usually claim that laws are statements containing terms which refer directly to 'observables' or which can be defined by reference to 'operational' procedures, whereas theories contain at least some terms which lack observational reference or operational definability. This seems to be broadly consistent with the contrast made in 'deductive-nomological' accounts of scientific explanation between generality and particularity. Just as an observable phenomenon (for example, a bent stick) can be explained by laws (the laws of refraction), so can laws be explained by more general laws, which are in their turn subsumable under comprehensive theories. There are, however, several difficulties associated with the observability criterion:

(1) The notion of being 'observable' is not always clear-cut. What is observable to one person might not be to another. This might be due to differing cultural presuppositions, or different historical perspectives. (When the Kinetic Theory of gases was first formulated, although it could be checked experimentally, molecules and atoms could not be observed, as sufficiently powerful instruments had not been invented.) However, while this might make the distinction difficult to apply in some instances, it does not break it down completely.

(2) A more serious objection is that in so far as laws are related specifically to observables and experimental procedures, a given law or set of laws might well be operating at various times against a background of different theories. This could give rise to at least two related problems. (a) There might be formal inconsistency between the deductive inferences by means of which experimental law statements are derived from theoretical premises. (b) The deductive link between laws and theories might be broken altogether.

(3) This follows on from the second point: how, it may be asked, can laws which relate to observables and are grounded in experimental procedures be deduced in any case from theoretical statements which (in some instances at least) lack such reference?

These three difficulties must lead to a consideration of the wider question of how theories and laws (that is, observation statements) *are* to be linked. A full discussion of the issue is beyond the scope of this book, but we shall make some mention of three kinds of solution which have been proposed.

(1) **Reductionism**. This approach, associated particularly with P.W. Bridgman (1882–1962) and A. Eddington (1882–1944), has something in common with the reductionist programme of positivism and phenomenalism discussed in 5.10 – and is open to similar objections. According to Bridgman, theoretical concepts are definable in terms of a set of physical or mental 'operations' (and it is for this reason that his version of reductionism is called **operationalism**). Thus, a physical concept such as length is said to be synonymous with the actual physical operations by which length is measured; while a mental concept such as

mathematical continuity is equivalent to the 'mental' operations by which we determine whether a magnitude is continuous. The fundamental difficulty of such a project is that it cannot be completely carried through, as there will always be further observables other than those already identified in an experimental situation. Moreover, it can be argued that with some theories (for example, quantum mechanics and theories of the social sciences) translation is not possible at all. (If you have a scientific background you might like to think about the problems raised by quantum theory.

(2) **Instrumentalism**. According to this view, both theories and lower-level 'laws of nature' are compared to tools in the sense that we can use them to derive one set of observation statements from another. They thus function as rules of inference. **Toulmin**, an English instrumentalist, thinks of theories as analogous to maps. Just as a map transforms and presents a collection of readings in a surveyor's notebook into a clear and orderly pattern, so do the ray-diagrams of geometrical optics present, 'in a logically novel manner', all that is contained in a set of observational statements (and no more than this). Theories of greater generality (for example, the wave theory of light) are thought of as 'maps' exhibiting greater detail (such as physical maps as contrasted with road maps). Which map one uses depends on the kinds of questions asked and the degree of accuracy required of the answers. Now it is fundamental to instrumentalism that both laws of nature and the more general theories, in so far as they are rules, are spoken of as 'holding' under certain circumstances or as 'applicable' in an appropriate context. It is only after the relevant requirements and conditions have been laid down that the question of truth can be considered; for it is the map itself which defines the criteria for the correct use of the term 'true' in that context. The physical map might be 'truer' than the road map in that it provides more detail. As Toulmin says:

> If we are to say anything, we must be prepared to abide by the rules and conventions that govern the terms in which we speak; to adopt these is no submission, nor are they shackles. Only if we are so prepared can we hope to say anything true – or anything untrue.   [*Philosophy of Science*, ch. 4.5]

Many critics have found this position difficult to accept. Theories, they say, must have some descriptive power: they must say something true about the world, otherwise how could we talk of falsifying and rejecting a particular theory in favour of another?

(3) **Models**. Most philosophers of science nowadays accept that models have an important role to play in explanation, though there is disagreement as to what they are or how they function. The notion of a model is in any case ambiguous. Here we shall confine the discussion to what are usually termed 'theoretical models'. Such a model can be regarded as being a 'structure' in terms of which both the 'unobservables' of a theory and the observable experimental operations and data can be accommodated and interpreted. The model incorporates elements from aspects of our experience with which we are already in some sense familiar. What this means should be clear from an example. When scientists talk

of light as being either 'wave-like' or 'particulate' they are using concepts drawn from everyday life. We have all seen waves in the sea and particles of various kinds. Now of course the scientist does not mean that light *is* made up of heaving oceans or ball-bearings travelling through space at an enormous velocity. Rather, he is suggesting that by thinking of light *as if* it shared these features with water or ball-bearings, as the case may be, we can facilitate the articulation of fundamental theoretical concepts, the derivation of empirical laws, and the prediction of certain kinds of events. (In certain situations, for the explanation of specific phenomena, it is found that the wave model is more suitable; to think of light as corpuscular, however, is more appropriate to explanations of other kinds of phenomena.) The relationship between a theoretical model and the 'familiar' experiences which gave rise to it is thus essentially analogical.

Once an analogy has been decided upon and applied to the new context, it is essential that its explanatory potential be explored as fully as possible. Although most analogies prove to be fruitful in this respect, they are invariably limited; and it is to determine these limitations or inadequacies that experiments have to be carried out, usually involving observations, measurements and subsequently deductive (mathematical) procedures. Let us consider another example, the electric current. In general terms, an electric current is today regarded as involving the movement of negatively charged particles (electrons) through a conductor. As a result of their observations of what happens when a simple cell is connected to a suitable response system (in the eighteenth century it was a frog's leg muscle!), the early theoreticians suggested that this might be due to a kind of fluid – on the analogy of water flowing through a pipe. There were a sufficient number of similarities to justify this claim. Water can build up a pressure, and the rate of flow can be varied for a given amount of 'push' by narrowing the bore of the pipe. In the same way one can refer to the electrical 'pressure' and can talk of an increase of resistance if the conductor is made thinner. Thus, although an electric current can indeed be thought of in terms of something 'flowing', the analogy breaks down in a number of respects. The behaviour of electrons is not very much like the behaviour of molecules of water. (Indeed certain phenomena exhibited by water, such as surface tension, expansion and viscosity, are today explained by forces acting between their constituent atoms, which are in turn accounted for in terms of the charges on the nuclei and electrons they are composed of.) These features of water which are not shared by electricity are often referred to as **negative analogies**.

What we have said so far is based on the assumption that there is a distinction between theories and laws. It does not follow, of course, that it is always clear-cut. The physicist and philosopher of science N.R. Campbell (1880–1949) uses the term 'theory' to refer to the total explanatory structure of general principles (axioms and theorems), experimental laws, correspondence rules for connecting the laws with the 'formal' principles, and the analogical models in terms of which the theoretical concepts and empirical data can be interpreted. This is not inconsistent with usage of the term in its narrower connotation. But to say that theories can be distinguished from laws is not to argue for their separability. In fact a case can be made out for saying that experimental laws, empirical data and 'facts' must all be considered as being in some sense 'theory-laden': that is, it is not possible to conceive of them except in the context of a theoretical framework. Likewise it can be argued that theories demand application and interpretation in experimental situations if they are to fulfil their proper function. The semantic distinction would then seem to be of peripheral significance.

This third approach restores an objective reference to theories without reduction, so that theoretical entities can be linked to observables. By the use of models, theories can be given empirical content. Consideration of a theory's 'objectivity' in relation to the empirical aspect must, however, be delayed until we come to the final section of this chapter, where we shall be looking at the question of scientific 'progress'.

Two further important issues are raised by our discussion: (1) How does the practising scientist initially select a model or theory? (2) What criterion or criteria does he appeal to in order to determine its acceptability? These questions will be dealt with now in our examination of hypotheses.

Hypotheses

What are hypotheses? Again, as with laws and theories, there is no clear-cut single answer which would satisfy all philosophers of science without exception. There does, however, seem to be broad support for the view that hypotheses are: (a) general statements put forward to stand as the premises of an explanatory structure, and (b) that they are provisional in the sense that they have not yet been shown to be true and might well be false, in which case of course they could no longer be retained as premises. In other words, hypotheses can be thought of as untested theories or theoretical models. This raises an immediate difficulty: are not theories themselves continually open to revision? How then can a distinction be admitted between theories and hypotheses? A useful approach is to contrast the two notions by comparison with the distinction made in 5.9 between knowledge and belief. You will remember we there concluded that the difference between them might be accounted for in terms of the strength of one's commitment. If I say that I know 'p' to be true, then not only do I believe it but also I am in effect making public my willingness to back up my claim by providing (or indicating how I might provide) appropriate evidence. Similarly, we might say here that a theory is a hypothesis which has withstood appropriate testing procedures. In the same way we might distinguish between 'hypothetical models' and 'theoretical models'. Three questions need now to be considered: (1) How do we come by hypotheses or models in the first place? (2) What kinds of testing procedures are appropriate? (3) What are the criteria by which hypotheses may be judged to be 'successful'?

(1) The question of how a model or theory comes to be selected prior to its being tested does in fact cover two separate issues: (a) the initial 'empirical' stimulus (for example, observations such as the twitching of a frog's muscle when connected to a Voltaic cell); and (b) the 'intellectual' processes that go on in the scientist's head. Why did some eighteenth century scientists make a particular connection between the behaviour of water (which they could see) and an

electric current (which they could not)? Or, why should a phenomenon such as diffraction have encouraged support for a wave theory of light? If one studies many different instances of scientific discoveries, it will be seen that the intellectual processes may be varied. In some cases the link may be made as a result of a rational inductive procedure involving generalization from a succession of cumulative data, or the use of mathematical (deductive) inferences. In other cases a discovery has been made through a 'leap' of intuition or imagination. It may result from carefully directed experimentation, or it may be the product of luck or chance. Most probably both induction and intuition have a role to play.

(2) So far as science is concerned, the procedures employed to test hypotheses make use primarily of experiments. We shall demonstrate what this might involve by considering the example of light referred to above. A stick appears to be bent when it is partially submerged in water. It has also been observed by scientists that in an appropriate experimental situation, light falling on a metal surface causes electrons to be emitted (this is called the 'photoelectric effect'). At one time it was thought that both the corpuscular theory (originally proposed by Newton) and the wave theory of Huyghens could account for the apparent bending of the stick, but it was later shown by simple mathematics that according to the former, light bends away from the normal when passing into a medium in which its velocity is smaller, whereas the wave theory predicts that it will bend towards the normal. It was shown experimentally in 1882 that light passing from air to water (in which it moves more slowly) is in fact refracted towards the normal, thus confirming the prediction of the wave theory. By contrast, it is now accepted that the photoelectric effect can be explained only on the assumption that light is emitted as discrete 'packets' or '*quanta*', that is, that it must be supposed to exhibit corpuscular properties. As before, the explanation and confirmation of the prediction involve experiments, measurement and mathematical procedures.

There are two qualifications in particular which should be mentioned here.

(a) Experimentation is not always possible. In astronomy, for example, the options open to the scientist for altering conditions are severely limited. For most purposes, however, 'controlled' or 'selective' observation has proved to be quite adequate. An excellent example of this is the confirmation of Kepler's three 'Laws of Planetary Motion' by appropriate and precise measurements of the positions of the various planets. (These laws were subsequently shown to be consistent with Newton's Law of Universal Gravitation – which can today be tested experimentally.) Difficulties can also arise in sub-atomic physics where the actual attempts to observe and experiment with particles have an influence on their behaviour. Experiments can however be set up to permit observation and measurement of predicted effects of sub-atomic particles (for example, as recorded on a photographic plate).

(b) The distinguished philosopher Karl **Popper** has argued cogently that the notion of a 'bare' observation from which one moves to theory is absurd. Observation, he says, is always selective:

It needs a chosen object, a definite task, an interest, a point of view, a problem. And its description presupposes a descriptive language, with property words; it presupposes similarity and classification, which in its turn presupposes interests, points of view, and problems.

[*Conjectures and Refutations*, p.46]

Certainly a particular hypothesis or 'conjecture' will have been preceded by observations (for example, the observations that the hypothesis has been designed to explain). But these observations presupposed the adoption of a 'frame of reference', of expectations, or of theories. There is however no danger here of an infinite regress, says Popper [p.47], for if we go back to 'more and more primitive theories and myths we shall in the end find unconscious, *inborn* expectations'. Popper makes it clear that while these are *psychologically* or *genetically a priori*, such 'knowledge' is not *a priori* valid; an inborn expectation may be mistaken. (See also the discussion of 'causation' in 11.3 below.)

(3) The examples just discussed in this section have shown that one criterion by means of which the success or acceptability of a hypothesis can be judged, and as a result of which it may be 'promoted' to the level of a theory, is its **predictive** power. By attributing certain features to light we can make predictions about its behaviour under a given set of conditions. If it proves to exhibit such behaviour, then we have grounds for supposing the hypothesis is correct. There are, however, serious logical difficulties associated with this criterion:

(a) Consider this argument: if Socrates was a great thinker, then Socrates died at a great age; Socrates died at a great age; therefore Socrates was a great thinker. It should not take you long to realize that this is an invalid argument although both statements are true. (If you are doubtful, then make up some examples of your own which follow the same pattern.) Now in view of the fallaciousness of such an inference we have to be careful about arguing to the correctness of a hypothesis/theory on the grounds that a prediction has been confirmed.

(b) **The Paradoxes of Confirmation**. The 'paradoxes' arise out of a conjunction of four 'confirmation criteria' originally set out by the French logician Jean Nicod: (i) 'All *A*s are *B*s' is confirmed by any (*A* and *B*); (ii) 'All *A*s are *B*s' is disconfirmed by any (*A* and non-*B*); (iii) 'All *A*s are *B*s' is neither confirmed nor disconfirmed by any non-*A*; (iv) Whatever confirms one hypothesis in a set of logically equivalent hypotheses confirms the others. Now each of these criteria seems plausible on its own, but there appears to be a 'paradox' when they are taken together. It can be shown, for example, that the statement 'All ravens are black' is logically equivalent to the complex statement 'All things which are (ravens or non-ravens) are (black or non-ravens)'. (Do not worry if you do not see why this is so; to understand the equivalence requires some knowledge of modern logic – see Ch. 2 Part II.) It follows then, according to Nicod's criteria, that anything whatsoever, apart from (ii) (that is, instances of ravens which are non-black), will confirm the statement 'All ravens are black'. But this seems to be rather odd, for it would mean that the statement would be confirmed both by instances of non-ravens (for example, swans) and by any other black thing. It is also inconsistent with (iii). To avoid the inconsistency Hempel denied condition (iii). But we are then still faced with the apparent paradox that 'All ravens are black' is confirmed by an examination of non-ravens (as this statement is logically equivalent to 'All non-black things are not ravens'). Nelson **Goodman** (1906–98) argued that it is condition (iv) that should be rejected. But this does not seem to be satisfactory, as we normally think of logically equivalent statements as being shown to be true or false by the same empirical evidence.

Goodman (in *Fact, Fiction and Forecast*) also suggested another paradox relating to the confirmation of hypotheses, which he called 'the new riddle of induction'. Suppose we put forward the hypothesis 'All emeralds are green' (on the grounds we have observed a large number and have not found any counter-examples). Now consider this definition: For any x, x is 'grue' if and only if *either* x is green and x is at a time < AD 2000, *or* x is blue and x is at a time > AD 2000. On the basis of this, a second hypothesis can be proposed: 'All emeralds are grue', because at the time when this was written (1965) all the observed emeralds were both green and grue. However, these two hypotheses are incompatible in so far as the first claims that after 2000 all emeralds would be green, whereas the second asserts they will be grue, and therefore blue.

There has been a great deal of discussion about both of these paradoxes – most of it being quite technical. Some writers have attempted to get round the paradox by pointing out that while 'green' refers to a quality of emeralds, 'grue' is a 'positional' or spatio-temporal predicate. Goodman answers this by arguing that 'green' and 'grue' can be defined in terms of each other via another definition which incorporates a third term 'bleen'. But we cannot consider this further here. One might also argue that we use the term 'emerald' to refer to a particular kind of precious stone having a unique chemical composition and properties, and so the stones referred to as being grue could not be emeralds at all. This, however, raises philosophical problems concerning meaning, reference and naming. (You will find some useful articles on both the above paradoxes in the volume edited by Nidditch – see the Reading list at the end of the chapter.)

A second criterion by which a hypothesis (and hence theories and laws) may be judged is that of **simplicity**. This is an ambiguous notion. It can be used in an aesthetic sense (for example, of a mathematical proof) to mean something like 'elegance'. Some supporters of inductive accounts of science (see, for example, Reichenbach's pragmatic justification discussed in 2.9) have argued that, by choosing the simplest generalizations from observations to arrive at laws of nature, we can make inductive inferences 'work'. 'Simplest' here can be understood by reference to the analogy of curve construction in mathematics (Cartesian or co-ordinate geometry). Given a number of points we may start by joining them by straight lines. But as the number of points increases we might find that it is possible to draw a curve through them, which, we can predict, will become smoother with still further accumulation of points and will be seen to represent an algebraic relation or 'law'. This notion of simplicity has been criticized by Popper [*The Logic of Scientific Discovery*, p.138] on the grounds that an unlimited number of curves can be drawn through a finite set of points, and that we have no reason for supposing that, say, a linear function is simpler than a quadratic one, or a circular function simpler than an elliptical.

The acceptability of a hypothesis/theory is sometimes judged by its **coherence** with other hypotheses or theories. Thus, if we are presented with two hypotheses which are claimed to account equally well for the facts and both are supported by appropriate experimental data, we accept one rather than the other if it 'fits in' with the broader explanatory framework within which we are already operating. There are obviously a number of problems with this criterion. (i) It involves circularity, since the acceptability of other hypotheses/theories in the general structure must in their turn presuppose a 'fit' with the new hypothesis we are seeking to introduce. (ii) The notion of 'fit' or coherence is obscure. Does it involve logical consistency? If so, then might there not be other hypotheses which are equally consistent in this sense with the general framework, in which case an additional criterion is still required for deciding between them? (iii) Such a view would tend to blur the distinctions between scientific and 'metaphysical' or 'religious' views of the world; a metaphysical hypothesis might be held to be as 'coherent' with other theories in the explanatory system as the 'scientific' one under consideration. (iv) It can be argued that the coherence criterion tends to undermine the notion of scientific truth. (Compare the Coherence Theory of Truth discussed in 5.7. The question of the 'truth' of scientific theories will be looked at in the next section.)

In his influential books *The Logic of Scientific Discovery* and *Conjectures and Refutations*, Karl Popper has worked out an alternative account which purports to deal with the various difficulties associated with these criteria of acceptability which we have been discussing. First of all we should note that Popper in effect starts out from the standpoint of the 'Covering-Law' theory of explanation but rejects the 'probabilistic' version (and 'traditional' view) that hypotheses are confirmed by inductive procedures. According to such a criterion no scientific theory can be conclusively verified. Popper therefore goes on to argue that in fact what is characteristic of scientific method is not a verificational procedure but **falsification**. He thus denies Nicod's confirmatory condition (i) in favour of the disconfirmatory condition (ii). If a hypothesis is proposed, we should, by observation and experiment, seek to discover a counter-instance which will conclusively falsify the hypothesis – given specific and clearly defined conditions. This may not of course lead to a total rejection of the hypothesis, but at the very least we shall be forced to modify it to take account of the counter-instance. It is for this reason that we still use Newton's Laws of Motion when we wish to calculate the distance travelled by an object accelerating at a given rate during a particular period of time, although the Newtonian theory has been superseded by Einstein's Relativity Theory where large distances or very high speeds (approximating to the velocity of light) are concerned, or by Quantum Mechanics as applied to the world of micro-particles; Newton's theory works well enough for everyday purposes within an acceptable degree of approximation.

You should note the following additional points in Popper's account of scientific procedure.

(1) **Falsifiability** is regarded as being a **criterion of demarcation** between science and non-science. Any 'theory' (for example, religious or metaphysical) which is consistent with all possible states of affairs, that is, for which there are no instances which would enable us to determine whether the theory is true or false, cannot be said to be scientifically informative. (It is for this reason that Popper is so critical of the claims made for Marxist Dialectical Materialism to be scientific – see 7.4 above.) This is not to say – as the logical positivists did – that such theories are nonsensical.

(2) Popper also rejects the appeal of some philosophers of science to **probability** as the means whereby the difficulties over induction can be avoided. He distinguishes between 'probability' and 'degree of corroboration'. The probability of a statement is, he says, inversely proportional to 'the content or deductive power of the statement, and thus to its explanatory power'. Thus we can say that the statement 'There will be an earthquake within the next thousand years' has a high probability but has a minimal informative content, and as such is not scientifically interesting. But if we predict that there will be an earthquake in London on 1st January 2000 starting at 6.30, this is much more precise and informative, very much less probable – and therefore testable and scientific.

(3) **Simplicity**. Popper claims that the various epistemological difficulties which arise in connection with this concept can be answered if it be equated with his notion of 'degree of falsifiability' and thereby associated with the 'logical improbability' of a theory. The simplest theories, according to this definition, are those which have the most empirical or informative context and have a high degree of testability. As you have probably realized, Popper's redefinition of 'simplicity' is in effect an alternative formulation of his anti-inductivist methodology; and as he says himself, 'I do not attach the slightest importance to the *word* "simplicity"'.

*Criticisms

(1) One problem with Popper's general approach, according to some practising scientists, is that he does not always describe accurately what they actually do. Indeed it is sometimes unclear whether he is setting out to describe scientific procedure or laying down guidelines for what he believes should be done if scientific investigations are to be successful. But it is probably unfair to single out Popper in this way. Like many other philosophers of science he is concerned to investigate the *logic* of scientific methodology, and it may well be that working scientists in their day-to-day activities adopt a more pragmatic approach by making use of different methods at different times depending on the circumstances (availability of data, nature of the problem under investigation, experimental facilities, even the intellectual and emotional states of the scientists themselves). Despite Popper's emphasis on falsifiability, the practising scientist might still find inductive verificational procedures to be fruitful on occasion.

(2) A more serious objection has been made by T.S. **Kuhn** of Princeton (1922–96) in *The Structure of Scientific Revolutions*. According to Kuhn most theories are

incomplete or inadequate in certain respects: 'no theory ever solves all the puzzles with which it is confronted at a given time; nor are the solutions already achieved often perfect'. Theories give rise to what he calls 'anomalous experiences', that is, failures of data to 'fit' theories. Superficially these might seem to be Popper's 'falsifications', but if they were, says Kuhn, then all theories ought to be rejected at all times. Popper of course does not wish his criterion to be applied in such an uncompromising manner. We must, he says, adopt a suitably critical attitude so that when counter-instances result in the falsification of a hypothesis, we must investigate these instances carefully with a view to constructing a modified version of the hypothesis which will give us better understanding of the exceptions. Some data-theory 'fits' are however more severe, and in such cases, argues Kuhn, Popperians will require some criterion of 'improbability' or 'falsification' which will be open to the same kinds of difficulties probabilistic verification theories have to contend with. Indeed falsification for Kuhn is seen as akin to verification in that it is a process which is separate from the emergence of an anomaly or falsifying instance and leads to a new **paradigm** (see the next section). All historically significant theories fit the fact – but more or less well. It makes more sense, Kuhn says, to consider which of two competing theories (for example, Priestley's as opposed to Lavoisier's theory of burning) fits the facts *better*. And this involves a joint verification–falsification process.

(3) Lastly, it has been claimed by some critics of Popper that despite his rejection of inductivism in science, he in fact tacitly makes use of an inductive procedure in so far as hypotheses appear to be strengthened to the extent that attempts to refute them have failed. However, Popper is not saying that hypotheses thereby become more *probably* true. On the contrary, he appeals to the degree of **'verisimilitude'** of a theory, by which he means the extent to which the theory corresponds to the totality of real facts (as opposed to only some of them). It is doubtful whether the use of the notion of an 'approximation' to the truth involves a commitment to inductive inferences.

You will be in a better position to assess both the relative claims of the Popperian and Kuhnian models and the acceptability of Popper's concept of verisimilitude after you have considered the problems of truth and progress in science.

8.4 Progress and truth

Reading: Kuhn, *The Structure of Scientific Revolutions*; Popper, *Conjectures and Refutations*, ch. 10

Few scientists would want to say that no progress has been made in their discipline since, say, the fifteenth century, however the term 'science' be interpreted. Thus much more is known about the universe today than in the time of Galileo. Many discoveries have been made (in heat, electricity, light and so on). Many puzzles have been solved. But perhaps of more interest to philosophers of science are the mechanisms or patterns of progress, and how progress is to be gauged. For example, it has long been thought (especially by verificationists and inductivists, thought a similar view can also be held by a 'hypothetico-deductivist'), that progress is linear and cumulative. By this is meant that as new theories are introduced and 'confirmed', so they both build on and incorporate the content and explanatory potential of previously held theories. Thus it might be said that Einstein's Theory of Relativity is more 'general', covers more facts, or has greater explanatory capacity than the gravitational theory of his predecessor Newton. Now while this is correct, it does not follow that Newton's insights should be understood as having been simply absorbed by the more embracing Relativity Theory. A number of radical contemporary philosophers of science, including Popper and Kuhn, would be inclined to say that Newton's account was simply false. Newton's laws *seem* to work when applied to falling apples or motor cars accelerating up the M4, but more precise measurement would show that they do not in fact 'fit' the facts.

The statements we have been making here are of course a little vague. A more rigorous analysis is required if we are to achieve a better understanding of what scientific progress involves and how the accounts offerered by Popper and Kuhn actually differ. Popper argues for a systematic subjection of 'bold conjectures' to 'criticism' with a view to their refutation. He sees this as the normal activity of scientists but admits that it may be described as 'revolutionary' (in the sense that as a result of the critical procedure 'dogmatic' theories can be overthrown and progress achieved). By contrast, Kuhn thinks of 'normal science' as being at once a more conservative and ideological activity. Scientists work within a community committed to a shared framework of theory, ideas and presuppositions, that is, 'paradigms' (a term that was first used in this sense by G.C. Lichtenberg in the eighteenth century). Their allotted task is to unravel problems or puzzles within the context of that framework. At particular stages in the history of science, normal scientific activity reaches a crisis, suffers a breakdown, and the community undergoes a shift of vision, or change of paradigm. While such shifts in the ways a scientific community looks at the world may be preceded by an awareness of anomalies such as inadequacies of 'fit' between data and theory, and consequent blurring of the rules of normal science as *ad hoc* 'divergent articulations' or adjustments are made, the switch from one paradigm to another more often seems to be similar to a change of religious commitment. Kuhn himself refers to the 'transfer of allegiance' from one paradigm to another as 'a conversion experience' [Reflections on my Critics', in *Criticism and the Growth of Knowledge*, p.260]. And in *The Structure of Scientific Revolutions* he writes that:

> the new paradigm, or a sufficient hint to permit later articulation, emerges all at once, sometimes in the middle of the night, in the mind of a man deeply immersed in crisis. What the nature of that final stage is – how an individual invents (or finds he has invented) a new way of giving order to data now all assembled – must here remain inscrutable and may be permanently so.   [p.89]

It is not surprising, given such remarks as these, that the procedures described in Kuhn's model have been criticized for being irrational. Objections have also been raised against his ambiguous usage of the term 'paradigm' (Margaret Masterman has identified twenty-one different meanings of the term in his book). However, we are not going to consider these particular issues here but shall concentrate on a more important problem, namely the conflict between 'objectivism' and 'relativism'. To get a better understanding of what is involved let us first of all return to Popper's notion of 'verisimilitude' mentioned in the previous section. A complex formal definition of his concept is provided in sec. 3 of the Addenda to his *Conjectures and Refutations*, but the essentials are clearly set out in ch. 10:

> Assuming that the truth-content and the falsity-content of two theories t_1 and t_2 are comparable, we can say that t_2 is more closely similar to the truth, or corresponds better to the facts, than t_1, if only either (a) the truth-content but not the falsity-content of t_2 exceeds that of t_1, (b) the falsity-content of t_1, but not its truth-content, exceeds that of t_2. [p.235]

Popper here distinguishes between the actual truth or falsity of a statement and the *content*, that is, the class of all its logical consequences. If it is true, then this class can consist only of true statements, but if it is false then the class will always consist of true or false statements. Thus, 'It always rains on Sundays' is false, but its conclusion that it rained last Sunday happens to be true. So whether a statement is true or false, there may be more truth, or less truth, in what it says, according to the number of true statements in the class of its logical consequences. If we assume that the content and truth-content of a theory (a) are measurable, then, says Popper, a measure of the verisimilitude of the theory will be (in simplest terms) $Vs(a) = Ct_T(a) - Ct_F(a)$. Thus, although a theory might be false in that disconfirming instances have been discovered, we can still talk of it as being an approximation to the truth. Newton's theory of dynamics, for example, although refuted can still be regarded as superior to Galileo's because of its greater content or explanatory power:

> Newton's theory continues to explain more facts than did the others; to explain them with greater precision; and to unify the previously uncon- nected problems of celestial and terrestrial mechanics. [p.236]

Now it would seem from these quotations that Popper is committed to the view that there is an unchanging world or 'nature' which our scientific explanations approximate to more and more closely as our conjectures or hypotheses are systematically tested, refuted, or modified, and give rise to 'Objective Knowledge' (the title of another of his books). As was stated in the previous section, Kuhn rejects Popper's falsification procedure. But, more seriously, he rejects Popper's commitment to 'objectivism'. For his part Popper accuses Kuhn of being a relativist, on the grounds that according to Kuhn a paradigm shift involves not only a change in theory so that data will fit but also a change in the actual definitions of such central terms as 'truth' and 'proof', and indeed perhaps 'nature' itself.

Kuhn's position is clearly explained in 'Reflections on my Critics'. He denies that he is a relativist in so far as he believes that 'scientific development is, like biological evolution, unidirectional and irreversible. One scientific theory is not as good as another for doing what scientists normally do'. Within the context of 'normal' science, members of the community agree as to which consequences of a shared theory sustain the test of experiment and are therefore true, and which are false. But if it is correct to call him a relativist this must be in a sense opposed to Popper's claim to be able to compare theories as 'representations of nature, as statements about "what is really out there"':

> Granting that neither theory of a historical pair is true, they nonetheless seek a sense in which the latter is a better approximation to the truth. I believe that nothing of that sort can be found. [p.265]

Kuhn then discusses two reasons for his rejection of this objectivist position. (1) To say, for example, of a field theory 'that it approach[es] more closely to the truth' than an older matter-and-force theory should mean that the ultimate constituents of nature are more like fields than matter and force. But there are difficulties here with language, says Kuhn (it is not clear how 'more like' is to applied), and with the evidence for which conclusions about an ontological limit are to be drawn, which should be not from whole theories but from their empirical consequences. This involves 'a major leap'. (2) Popper's commitment is broadly to an 'objective' truth in Tarski's sense (compare 5.7 above). But, argues Kuhn, Popper takes it for granted that the objective observers understand 'snow is white' or, for example, 'elements combine in constant proportion by weight' in the same way. There is, however, no such neutral language shared by proponents of competing theories adequate to the comparison of such observation reports.

This second objection does in fact constitute the crux of the disagreement between Kuhn and Popper. And Kuhn's view that a change of paradigm necessarily involves changes in the meanings of the descriptive terms used in the paradigms, and therefore our 'world-view' or 'ontology', has received powerful support from several other influential American philosophers, notably P.K. Feyerabend (University of California, Berkeley) and W.V.O. Quine (Harvard). Thus Feyerabend has argued that the meaning of the phrase 'being warm' is different in the context of the kinetic theory, which explains temperature in terms of molecular movement and energy, from what it is in everyday non-scientific discourse. Feyerabend's general approach however, is more sympathetic to Popper than Kuhn. He is critical of the kind of conservatism implicit in Kuhn's concept of 'normal' science, and argues in favour of testing a variety of metaphysical systems as an antidote to dogmatism:

> Metaphysical systems are scientific theories in their most primitive stage. If they *contradict* a well-confirmed point of view, then this indicates their

usefulness as an alternative to this point of view. Alternatives are needed for the purpose of criticism.

['How to be a good empiricist', in Nidditch, *The Philosophy of Science*, p.37]

*Comments

If you are to appreciate fully the important issues discussed in this section and try to resolve the disagreements between Popper and Kuhn, it is essential that you read as much as you can of the primary sources. It is important to note that quotations have been taken from the first edition of *The Structure of Scientific Revolutions*, and that in the second edition Kuhn has modified his standpoint to some extent so as to take account of criticisms. His 'Postscript' in the book should be read carefully in conjunction with his two papers (and the papers of his critics) in *Criticism and the Growth of Knowledge*. You should also read the cited essay by Feyerabend.

The whole issue of objectivism versus relativism in science in fact relates to the wider metaphysical notion of 'reality'. Some of the epistemological problems have already been looked at in Ch. 5. We shall examine the concept further in 11.5.

QUESTIONS

Texts and problems
1 The word 'science' originally meant knowledge. Does such knowledge have to be derived from observational and experimental data which are indubitable?
2 In what sense can scientific theories and laws be said to be 'true'? Is this an acceptable claim?
3 In what way do Popper's views differ from 'traditional' views of science?
4 Examine the distinction between 'falsificationism' and 'verificationism'.
5 'The criterion of the scientific status of a theory is its falsifiability, or refutability' [Karl Popper]. How valid do you think this statement is?

[IB, specimen, 2000]

*6 (a) Describe and illustrate the view that science is paradigmatic.
(b) Assess the implications of this view for falsificationist accounts of science.

[AQA (AEB), specimen, 2001]

7 Giving examples, discuss the statement that 'All observations are theory laden'.

[AEB, 1996]

8 Explain what extrapolation is, giving examples. What assumptions are made when extrapolating points on a curve? Of what value may the process of extrapolation be to progress in science?

[AEB, 1996]

9 Is there progress in science? Discuss this in relation to the concept of 'verisimilitude'.
10 'Science does not really explain events; it only describes them.' Discuss.
*11 Outline and examine critically Hempel's 'Covering Law' model of scientific explanation. (Its supposed application to the social sciences will be considered in 12.4.)
12 Is there such a thing as 'normal' science?

13 What grounds have we for supposing that sub-atomic particles exist?

14 Is the 'simplicity' of a scientific theory any guide to its 'truth'?

15 Examine the role of 'models' in scientific explanations.

(See also the question on induction in Ch. 2 and the questions on causation in Ch. 11.)

*Notes/guided answers have been provided for questions **6** and **11** (at end of book).

READING LIST

A. Principal texts
Kuhn, T.S., *The Structure of Scientific Revolutions*.
Nidditch, P.H. (ed.), *The Philosophy of Science*. (Includes essays by Feyerabend, Goodman and Hempel.)
Popper, K., *The Logic of Scientific Discovery*.
Popper, K.R., *Conjectures and Refutations*.
Toulmin, S.E., *The Philosophy of Science*.

See also:
Ayer, A.J., *Language, Truth and Logic*, ch. V. (AEB)

B. Supplementary reading
(If you are a beginner, you are recommended to start with titles marked with an asterisk.)

1. Historical background
Burtt, E.A., *The Metaphysical Foundations of Modern Science*.
Gillispie, G.C., *The Edge of Objectivity: An Essay in the History of Scientific Ideas*.
Hull, L.W.H., *History and Philosophy of Science*.*

2. Introductory texts
Hempel, C.G., *The Philosophy of Natural Science*.*
Magee, B., *Popper*.*
Medawar, P.B., *Induction and Intuition in Scientific Thought*.*
O'Hear, A., *An Introduction to the Philosophy of Science*.*
Rosenberg, A., *Philosophy of Science: A Contemporary Introduction*.*
Trusted, J., *The Logic of Scientific Inference*.*

3. More advanced books
Braithwaite, R.B., *Scientific Explanation*.
Campbell, N.R., *The Foundations of Science*.
Feyerabend, P., *Against Method*.
Goodman, N., *Fact, Fiction and Forecast*.
Hacking, I. (ed.), *Scientific Revolutions*.
Hanson, N.R., *Patterns of Discovery*.
Hempel, C.G., *Aspects of Scientific Explanation*.

Hesse, M.B., *Models and Analogies in Science.*
Lakatos, I. and Musgrave, A. (eds), *Criticism and the Growth of Knowledge.*
Mackie, J.L., *Truth, Probability and Paradox.*
Nagel, E., *The Structure of Science.*
Newton-Smith, W.H., *The Rationality of Science.*
Popper, K.R., *Objective Knowledge.*
Van Fraassen, B., *The Scientific Image.*
Wisdom, J.O., *Foundations of Inference in Natural Science.*

▣ ⊻ 9 The philosophy of religion

9.1 Introduction

In the previous chapter we examined some of the central concepts and methods of the natural sciences, such as 'explanation', 'hypothesis' and 'theory'. The philosophy of religion is concerned similarly with certain concepts which are fundamental to the religious practices and beliefs of mankind. This brings us at once to the question of definition: what is meant by 'religion' and 'religious'? The major religions of the world differ greatly, and from earliest times there have of course been many other faiths with their own special features. The Babylonians, Egyptians, Greeks and Romans believed, for the most part, in many gods (they were 'polytheists'). Judaism, Christianity, and Islam, however, are 'monotheistic' religions; their adherents believe in one supreme deity. In Hinayana Buddhism the concept of a personal God is absent. In trying to define the 'essence' of religion, various writers have tended to emphasize different aspects or functions. Thus religion may be seen as involving a feeling of dependence on a higher 'power', as providing an ultimate foundation for morality, or as encapsulating the 'truth' about the universe and man's place in it. However, most philosophers today would probably accept that an attempt to find a single definition embracing all religions is likely to be as unsuccessful as the attempt to discover what games as diverse as football, tennis, hurling, chess and patience have in common. A better approach is to identify the characteristics found in different religions but not all of which are exhibited in a particular one. Thus we can discover (a) belief in a supernatural being, (b) rituals, (c) the concept of the 'sacred', (d) prayer, (e) religious feelings such as a sense of mystery or awe, and (f) a 'world-view'. We might note also the grounding of ethics in religious conceptions of the world and the significance of religion as a cohesive force in many societies. (The word 'religion' is probably derived from a Latin word meaning 'to bind'.) In his *Notes towards a Definition of Culture*, T.S. Eliot argued that religion is inseparable from the total culture or 'way of life' of a people; culture being its 'incarnation', as he put it (on Culture see Ch. 12).

It is of course not possible to examine these characteristics in a short chapter. You can learn more about them by reading some of the books listed at the end. We shall instead concentrate on some of the central philosophical issues: the nature of religious language and the 'truth' of religious assertions; what is meant by 'faith'; 'proofs' for the existence of God; and the problem of evil. The reference above to 'world-view' suggests that there is some overlap between religion and metaphysics. Certainly many medieval philosophers took it for granted that there was. This and the problem of 'fatalism' (the view that the future is already 'fixed' and – in this context – that God has foreknowledge of future events) will be discussed briefly in the next chapter. When assessing the claims of religion to provide access to 'Truth' you will also need to bear in mind the conclusions of Ch. 8. Whether there is any serious conflict between religion and the findings of science is, however, still an open question.

9.2 Religious language

Reading: Ayer, *Language, Truth and Logic*, ch. VI; Aquinas, *Summa contra Gentiles*, I, 30–35; *Summa Theologiae*, 1a.13. 1–6, 12; Wittgenstein, *Lectures and Conversations on Religious Belief*

A central feature of most if not all religions is prayer, and this usually consists of an attempt by believers to communicate with a god or gods. Prayers may be directed to a number of ends or meet several needs: worship of the creator, confession of faults, or the petitioning of favours such as the forgiving of sins, healing of the sick and so on. Such communication has been seen by many philosophers to be a problem in so far as it involves the use of everyday concepts applied to what may be thought of as a supernatural being. Thus, in the Christian context God is addressed as 'Father', He is referred to as a 'ruler' of a 'kingdom', as 'making' the world. Moreover, various qualities are attributed to God: goodness, wisdom, perfect love, omniscience and omnipotence. What is the status of such language? *Can* these terms be applied to such a being with the same literal meanings they possess in the everyday context? If not, in what way or ways do they differ in their application?

Positivist philosophers, such as Ayer in his first book, *Language, Truth and Logic*, have argued that religious assertions (like those of ethics) are literally non-sensical because there is no empirical evidence to be found which could count as **verification** of their truth. As he says [p.120]:

> The theist, like the moralist, may believe that his experiences are cognitive experiences, but unless he can formulate his knowledge in propositions that are empirically verifiable, we may be sure that he is deceiving himself.

There are in fact two distinct issues: (a) the verification theory of *meaning* and (b) the verification *principle*. According to (a) the 'meaning' of a proposition is understood in terms of the way it is actually verified, whereas (b) states in effect that if I do not know *how* to verify a proposition then the sentence which expresses it cannot be said to be factually significant. The latter thus makes a stronger claim; for it might be possible for me to use a sentence in a meaningful way (that is, I know how to set about verifying it) and yet for its meaning *not* to be identified with its mode of verification. Ayer, for example, argues, as we have seen, that religious and ethical assertions have emotive meaning but that if they are to be factually meaningful at all we must know how to verify them.

*Comment

What is to *count* as verification? A supernatural being cannot be observed in any ordinary sense of the term. Believing Christians, however, might say that God can be 'observed' through His activity in the universe He has created. They may be thinking here of some kind of 'revelation' through sacred literature (the *Bible*, *Koran*, or *Upanishads*, for example), the 'living' Church, in 'Nature' – as Locke wrote, 'The works of Nature everywhere sufficiently evidence a Deity', or in the moral consciousness: we reach God, said Kant, not only through the starry heavens above but also through the moral law within. How far all this constitutes 'proof' of God's *existence* is a question we shall leave to the next section; and of course one must take account of the objections raised by Popper to verificational procedures in general (see 8.3). But these different approaches do at least open up the possibility that 'verification' might be interpreted less narrowly than the positivists would have us believe. (See further discussion of verification in 11.1.)

Whatever the difficulties associated with verification, need we be limited to the view of meaning as only emotive? Wittgenstein has argued that one should not search for 'meanings' but look at the ways in which language is *used* in a specific context. Religion is a 'Form of Life' and religious language functions in accordance with its own set of conventions and criteria in terms of which alone it can make sense. To understand what the sentence 'God is good' 'means' we must consider its use in the context of the Christian way of life – prayer, ritual, ethical commitment, and of course the whole underlying theology. Problems only arise when we insist on thinking that in such sentences as 'God is love', 'God' and 'love' are functioning in their 'ordinary' or everyday senses. (We should note also that the affirmation of God's perfection and goodness is made also by adherents of the other great monotheisic religions, Judaism and Islam.)

*Comment

A difficulty with this kind of approach is that while different 'Forms of Life' (including non-religious 'forms' such as that of the humanist) might be recognized, the possibility of an 'objective' comparison 'from the outside', as it were, appears to be ruled out, because what might seem to be 'outside' is considered to be merely another 'inside' standpoint (another language 'game') on the same level as its own presuppositions and procedures. Evidence in the scientific sense is held to be inappropriate. If this is so, then it would seem that we must conclude that whatever the status of theological utterances, they are either not factual assertions or are factual in a peculiar sense.

Accepting that religious language is not factual in the usual senses of the term, many philosophers have suggested variously that it is metaphorical, symbolic, or a means by which we can be directed towards what is essentially a mystical experience of the divine. There is, however, yet another approach to the problem, which has been followed by the adherents of quite diverse religious traditions, namely, that statements about God or gods must be understood in **analogical** terms. In its crudest form (as in the religions of ancient Egypt, Babylonia, the Greeks and the Romans, and in early Judaism) this involves no more than an anthropomorphic attribution to the divine of human qualities such as motherhood and fatherhood, power, wisdom and love. A much more sophisticated version was developed by St Thomas Aquinas. Following Aristotle, Aquinas starts out from 'existences' and not from conceptually defined 'essences'. The problem is then how we are to predicate what he calls 'transcendentals' (he identifies six: being, thing, unity, distinction, true and good) of anything which we can say 'It is', and this includes the 'necessary Being', that is, God. Now in the *Summa contra Gentiles* Aquinas argues that when we apply the name of a quality both to God and to a finite being we are not using the name in the same sense (that is, the term is not used **univocally**), but neither are the senses totally different (the term is not being used **equivocally**). Thus to use his own example, we can call *hot* both the Sun itself and the heat generated by the Sun. This exhibits **analogical** use of language. Aquinas in fact distinguishes between what he calls the 'Analogy of **Proportionality**' and the 'Analogy of **Attribution**'. By means of the first we move from a statement about the way in which the qualities of a created being are related to its nature, to a statement about how attributes of uncreated being (God) are related to *its* nature. This thus involves an extrapolation of a relationship from finite to infinite being. The difficulty here, as Aquinas recognizes, is that this does not tell us anything about what God is actually like. So it is necessary to extend the analogy by attributing to God properties experienced in ourselves. Thus we may talk of human wisdom or fatherhood and then apply these terms to the relationship we say obtains between us and Him. This presupposes that there is a relation of causal dependence between creature and creator. (How Aquinas sought to prove this is discussed in the next section.)

*Comments and criticisms

Many objections have been raised against Aquinas's doctrine of analogy:

(1) We may think of God as the cause of a property in his creatures. But it does not follow that we *have* to think of God Himself as possessing that property. (In the language of scholasticism, we may attribute, for example, goodness to God 'virtually' but not 'formally'.)

(2) If this is so, then it would seem to follow that God, as the ultimate cause of all things, must be supposed to possess all conceivable predicates in this 'virtual' sense. Thus He must be not only omnipotent, omniscient and good, but also as the cause of the physical universe, (virtually) heavy, hot, multicoloured and so on. Indeed, He must also be large *and* small, hot *and* cold – and prior to creation there could be nothing with which He could be compared which might allow the use of such predicates as relative terms. It is therefore questionable whether any qualities can be attributed to God at all.

(3) As for the Analogy of Proportionality, it is doubtful whether this can be applied at all, for quite apart from the problems (a) of thinking of God as having

properties and (b) of supposing there to be relations between them and the Creator, it must be asked how the alleged proportionalities between His qualities and nature can be compared with those which are found between our qualities and nature. Even to suppose that there *is* a similarity between the two sets of relationships is to beg the question.

Underlying these – and many other difficulties – is a general point, namely that there is perhaps *no* middle way between univocal and equivocal language. The former leads to anthropomorphism, the latter to meaninglessness: or, if analogical language is given a place, how could it ever be determined that qualities descriptive of material beings existing in space and time are predicable meaningfully of a spiritual non-spatial and non-temporal creator? St Thomas's arguments are of course technical and not easy to follow for the beginner. If you want to follow up these issues you should read the books by Copleston and Kenny referred to in the Reading list at the end of the chapter.

9.3 The existence of God

Reading: Aquinas, *Summa Theologiae*, Ia.2.1–3; *Summa contra Gentiles*, I, 10–13; Descartes, *Meditations*, III, V; Hume, *Enquiry Concerning Human Understanding*, XI; Ayer, *Language, Truth and Logic*, ch. VI; James, *Pragmatism*, III, VIII

That we have and use the concept of an all-powerful, all-knowing, perfectly good and supernatural creator is of course indisputable. Without such a concept no discussion about the meaning and applicability to such a being of terms referring to properties or attributes would make sense. Because we have the concept, however, it does not necessarily follow that God exists. In this section we shall try to give you some understanding of the numerous attempts which have been made by philosophers and theologians over the centuries to prove that He does. Alleged 'proofs' tend to fall into three main groups: (a) rationalist proofs from the concept of God itself; (b) empirical proofs based in some sense on the existence of the world or universe; and (c) 'pragmatic' and moral proofs. But before we consider each of these in turn something needs to be said about the concepts of 'existence' and 'proof'.

First of all you should note that these concepts are closely connected in so far as what is to *count* as a proof for God's existence partly depends on what we *mean* by 'existence'. You will remember that the question of how we are to understand the term arose also when applied to Plato's Forms (3.5). We can also ask a similar question about the 'ontological' status of sub-atomic particles in modern physics. The problem with the existence of God (and perhaps to a lesser extent with Plato's Absolute Form of the Good) is that there do not seem to be any clearly defined and generally accepted procedures, against the background of which 'existence' could be coherently and consistently employed. Tables and chairs, cats and dogs certainly exist in that I can see and touch them. But I do not (and could never) observe electrons or protons. Nevertheless, we can talk meaningfully of their existence either because they play a special role in the hierarchy of scientific explanation (at least according to some accounts – see 8.3), or because we can observe and measure their effects (such as tracks on a photographic plate). Perhaps I can also talk about the existence of images, sensations and concepts; I certainly have them. But there is a difficulty here about the status of concepts. Do they 'exist' in some Platonic sense 'before' or 'apart from' their instantiations in physical things? This has been a much-discussed issue at various times in the history of philosophy. Some thinkers have gone so far as to attribute a 'real' existence to imaginary objects such as unicorns, to mathematical 'entities' such as numbers, or to self-contradictory notions such as a square circle. Can we therefore refer to God as existing in any sense which is not anthropomorphic or does not involve explicit or implicit reference to a space–time–matter framework? If God does exist then it would seem that His 'existence' cannot be understood in the sense in which the term is employed to refer to tables, electrons, images, or even unicorns or numbers; and this is because of the difficulty, discussed in 9.1 above, of referring to Him in language which is neither univocal nor equivocal. Yet the fact is that we do talk of God and, rightly or wrongly, we do attribute qualities to Him. Moreover, only philosophers who embrace some form of positivism are prepared to state dogmatically that such talk is meaningless. We shall come back to the question of existence after we have examined critically the various 'proofs'.

The ontological argument

This (rationalist) argument, originally formulated by St Anselm (c. 1033–1109) in his *Proslogion*, may be summarized as follows:

(a) Even a fool (who 'says in his heart, "There is no God" ' – Psalm 53) must admit that he understands the concept of God as 'something than which nothing greater can be conceived'.
(b) This idea exists at least in our understanding (*in intellecto*).
(c) It cannot exist in the understanding alone, for if we suppose it does then we can conceive it to exist in reality, which is greater.
(d) Therefore, if that than which nothing greater can be conceived exists in the understanding alone, the very being than which nothing greater can be conceived *is* one than which a greater can be conceived; and this is absurd.
(e) So there must exist both in the understanding and in reality a being than which nothing greater can be conceived.   [*Proslogion*, 2]

In *Proslogion*, 3 he offers a slightly different version. A being which cannot be conceived not to exist must be greater than one which *can* be conceived not to exist. It would then be self-contradictory to conceive as non-existing a being than which nothing greater can be conceived. Therefore, there must so truly exist such a being that it cannot even be conceived not to exist.

Anselm then sets out an objection put forward on the fool's behalf by a monk called Gaunilo. If we are to say that the being than which nothing greater can be conceived necessarily exists, then we must first have some evidence of His existence. For otherwise could we not just as well argue that because we can conceive of the existence of the most perfect island it must exist in reality; if it did not it would be less perfect than any known island, and this too would involve a contradiction. In his reply Anselm reiterates that God is a special case in that, unlike islands or any other finite thing, He is a being than which nothing greater can be conceived and must therefore exist in reality:

> For no one who denies or doubts the existence of a being than which a greater is inconceivable denies or doubts that if it did exist, its non-existence, either in reality or in the understanding, would be impossible. For otherwise it would not be a being than which a greater can be conceived. But as to whatever can be conceived, but does not exist: if there were such a thing, its nonexistence, either in reality or in the understanding, would be possible. Therefore if a being than which a greater is inconceivable can even be conceived, it cannot be nonexistent.

Anselm's ontological argument was taken up by Descartes. In the Fifth Meditation he argues that the existence of God can be no more separated from His essence than the idea of a mountain from that of a valley, or the equality of the three angles of a triangle to two right angles, from its essence. But whereas it does not follow that a mountain actually exists because we can conceive a mountain with a valley, in the case of God He cannot be conceived except as existing. And the reason Descartes gives for this is that God possesses all perfections and existence is a perfection.

*Comments

St Thomas Aquinas criticized Anselm's argument on the grounds that the conclusion that God in reality exists just does not follow from the fact that we understand the name 'God' to mean 'that than which a greater cannot be conceived'. Moreover, he says, atheists deny that there is something in reality than which a greater cannot be thought. The most cogent criticism of the ontological argument, however, comes from Kant in the *Critique of Pure Reason*, and is directed against Descartes' version. The proposition 'this or that thing exists' is, he says [B 625–626], either analytic or synthetic (see 5.4). If it is analytic, then the assertion that the thing exists adds nothing to the thought of the thing, or results in a tautological argument. If, however, we maintain 'as every reasonable person must' that the proposition is synthetic, then how can it be claimed that the predicate of existence canot be rejected without contradiction? In fact, continues Kant, ' "Being" or "existence" is not a real predicate at all. When we say "God is" or "There is a God", we attach no new predicate to the concept of God, but only posit the subject in itself with all its predicates, and indeed posit it as being an *object* that stands in relation to my *concept*' [B 626–627]. There is no difference in number between a hundred real thalers (currency) and a hundred possible or imaginary ones. What is at issue is whether they actually exist (which, he says, would affect his financial position very differently), but this cannot be ascertained by any analysis of the concept of a hundred thalers. As Russell has pointed out (*The Philosophy of Logical Atomism*), when I say 'God exists', I am not saying anything about God's attributes, any more than I am about the King of France when I state 'The King of France exists', but am asserting that the concept of God is 'instantiated'.

Much has been written about the ontological argument, and there have been numerous attempts to circumvent these logical objections (most notably by Norman Malcolm). While it is doubtful that any of these attempts has been successful, this particular argument for the existence of God continues to weave a spell over many philosophers and theologians who perhaps are inclined to exaggerate the power of the human intellect.

The cosmological argument

The cosmological argument, and the next two, are empiricist arguments. The cosmological proceeds along the following lines. We apparently see one thing as being caused by another and this in turn by something else prior to it. We then argue that since there cannot be an infinite regress there must be an unconditioned First Cause or God. Both Plato and Aristotle put forward versions of this argument, but it has come to be associated especially with Aquinas and Descartes.

Aquinas presented the argument from three different standpoints (the first three of his so-called 'Five Ways'):

(a) The argument from **motion**. We observe that some things in the world are in motion. Whatever is in motion must have been moved by something else. This cannot go on to infinity; for without a first mover there would be no motion to be imparted from one thing to another.
(b) The argument from **efficient causality**. In the world of sense we find there is an order of efficient causes. If there was no first cause there could be no intermediate or ultimate causes.
(c) The argument from **possibility and necessity**. It is possible for the things in nature to be and not to be, since they are found to be generated and to corrupt. If everything were like this then at one time there could have been nothing in existence, in which case there would be nothing in existence now. There must therefore be something the existence of which is necessary. This necessity is either possessed by the thing itself or caused by another. In the latter case, once again there can be no regress to infinity. There must therefore be a being 'having of itself its own necessity'.

[We have given only summaries of Aquinas's arguments. You can follow them in full in the *Summa Theologiae*, Ia.2.1–3.]

Descartes' version is set out in the Third *Meditation*. Unlike Aquinas, he starts out from the contents of his own consciousness (as of course he must, as he has not yet provided his justification for supposing that the external, physical world really exists). He recognizes that he has the idea of God which is neither 'adventitious' nor 'factitious' but which is 'innate' (see 5.2). Using the terminology of late medieval scholastics, he argues that the cause of an idea must ('it is manifest by the natural light') contain as much reality as the effect, both **formally** or **eminently** and **objectively**. (By 'formally', Descartes means roughly that the cause contains the effect to an equal extent and in the same way or 'mode', as when, for example, the shape of my thumb exists in the impression I make in wax; if the cause contains reality 'eminently' then it possesses *more* 'reality' than the effect. 'Objective' reality is what the idea possesses by virtue of its denotation, that is, the concept of 'thumb'.) He also recognizes his dependence (in respect of both his production and his conservation) on a being external to himself. It follows then, says Descartes, that the idea of an Absolute or Perfect Being (God) must be supremely (objectively) real, and its cause must possess commensurate formal reality. Since Descartes himself is imperfect, the idea of a Perfect Being must also contain more reality 'eminently' than the idea. God must therefore exist, as a thinking thing and possessing 'the idea of all the perfections I attribute to Deity'. Moreover, God must be the cause of the idea in Descartes' mind, for

> though the idea of substance be in my mind owing to this, that I myself am a substance, I should not, however, have the idea of an infinite substance, seeing I am a finite being, unless it were given me by some substance in reality infinite.

Descartes reinforces his conclusion by appealing to what is in effect the 'Second Way' of Aquinas:

> Then it may again be inquired whether this cause owes its origin and existence to itself, or to some other thing. For if it be self-existent, it follows, from what I have before laid down, that this cause is God; for, since it possesses the perfection of self-existence, it must likewise, without doubt, have the power of actually possessing every perfection of which it has the idea – in other words, all the perfections I conceive to belong to God. But if it owe its existence to another cause than itself, then we demand again, for a similar reason, whether this second cause exists of itself or through some other, until step by step we at length arrive at an ultimate cause, which will be God. And it is quite manifest that in this matter there can be no infinite regress of causes, seeing that the question raised respects not so much the cause which once produced me, as that by which I am at this present moment conserved.

*Criticisms

Many objections have been made against the cosmological argument. You might like to think in particular about the following:

(1) The postulation of a 'First Cause' is either self-contradictory or arbitrary. If it is claimed there are no uncaused causes, then how *can* there be a *first* cause? If in reply it is argued that God is a special case, that He is *causa sui*, then we might answer that this is a piece of gratuitous special pleading.

(2) It is claimed that there can be no infinite regress (of motions or causes). It is unclear why not. The assertion of an infinite regress does not seem to involve a contradiction. Why could not the universe have been always in existence? The most recent findings of science (though not of course necessarily the last word) have indicated that the universe did in fact have a definite beginning with the 'Big Bang' some 15,000 million years ago (though estimates vary). A possible alternative scenario is that of the present (expanding) universe as having emerged from the collapse of a previous (contracting) universe, and so on *ad infinitum*. (A somewhat similar concept is found in certain Hindu and Buddhist world-views.) If this were so, then it could certainly be argued that this is no more implausible than the claim that God exists. Some philosophers might say that, while He need not be invoked to account for the 'beginning' of the universe (for on this theory there was not a beginning), God is needed to sustain and conserve the total series of events, or cyclical sequences, albeit infinite, which constitutes it. However, this would seem to suggest that the universe and God are co-eternal. As against this it could be said that if the universe is itself eternal, the concept of a God as creator or sustainer is superfluous. More recent data would seem to indicate that this cyclical hypothesis is probably wrong and that the universe is an 'open' one – forever expanding and never to slow down and contract. So what of the 'Big Bang' hypothesis – that the cosmos originated from what mathematicians call a 'singularity', an infinitesimally small and infinitely dense energy point? This account is not incompatible with there being a God as creator and sustainer of the primordial energy. Some theoretical cosmologists, however, have suggested that the universe could have originated literally out of 'nothing'.

(3) Another objection relates to the alleged causal efficacy of God. Difficulties might seem to be raised by the claim that a transcendent, eternal, immutable spiritual being can bring into existence a material world of change and decay. (There are parallels here with the problem raised by Plato's *chorismos* – see 3.5). Apologists would answer that an omnipotent creator can do anything. The attribution of omnipotence, however, begs the question. One can say only that *if* such an omnipotent being exists then he must possess the power to produce the universe. This does not deal with the objection. If it then be argued that our limited intellect cannot comprehend how God exercises His power, we might query whether that intellect is adequate to devise an infallible proof for His existence.

(4) Is it even coherent to talk of a first cause? If by 'causation' we mean some sort of regularity in or relationship between events, or (with Kant) an *a priori* 'subjective' category, then it is arguable that the concept of a causal agency cannot be applied to a being 'existing' outside of the space-time/matter/energy continuum. (You should come back to this point after you have read the section on causality in 11.4).

(5) Finally, you should note the invalidity of the move from asserting that the *members* of a group of things or events have causes to the claim that there must therefore be a single cause for the *group* as a whole.

Spinoza

A few remarks are pertinent here about the philosophical account of God proposed by Baruch (or Benedict) Spinoza (1632–77) in his *Ethics*, which are relevant particularly to points (2) and (4) above. Spinoza, like Descartes, was a rationalist; his metaphysical system is an attempt to provide an explanation and knowledge of all reality through pure reason. His system is interesting for the way it is set out (Spinoza called it *de more geometrico* – 'in a geometrical manner'): it consists of definitions, axioms and propositions which are allegedly proved through logic. He hoped to show that there can be only one substance, which is infinite, possesses infinite attributes and which exists of necessity – in it existence and essence are identical (so Spinoza thus accepted the ontological argument). This Substance he called 'God or Nature' (*Deus sive Natura*). It can be considered as active or passive. As active it is 'nature naturing' (*natura naturans*), cause-of-itself and cause of its own modes or modifications – roughly the entities composing the universe, including animals and humans. But as 'nature natured' (*natura naturata*) it is passive, the modes considered as caused. Although the One Substance possesses infinite attributes, we human beings, as individual finite modes, can know it only through two, thought and extension. As thus apprehended it may therefore be considered as both mind and body (which of course Descartes had regarded as distinct substances).

Spinoza's system might seem to offer an attractive solution to the kinds of difficulties we have been discussing. The universe *is* God (such a philosophical view is called **pantheism**). It is eternal, uncreated, its own cause: it belongs to its own nature or essence to exist. No further explanation is required. Given this assumption, and Spinoza's proofs that there can be only *one* substance no origin of the universe need be sought. However, the validity of his arguments is questionable. And there are many philosophical problems which his metaphysics, arguably, cannot answer satisfactorily, including the issue of human freedom – given his seemingly deterministic account of Nature as caused; the relationship of individual human minds and bodies to the universal Mind and Body; and the problem of evil. (The latter will be discussed in 9.5; mind and freedom will be looked at in Ch. 11.)

The teleological argument (often called the argument from design)

Suppose you are living on a desert island and one day, while walking along the beach, you find a watch. By examining its parts and the way they are put together, and by observing its working – how its moving hands indicate the passage of time – you would quite reasonably argue that it had been constructed by an intelligent designer. The watch has a function or purpose. In a similar manner, it might be argued that the human eye exhibits 'teleological' order, that is, the way *its* parts fit together and operate suggests that it too has a purpose (compare the discussion of teleology and final causes in 4.2). Thus it must have been produced by an intelligent designer, which is God. This is, in essentials, the argument put forward by the moral philosopher and theologian William Paley (1743–1805); and it too has been found attractive by some Christian philosophers. Aquinas's 'Fifth Way' can be seen to be a version of the teleological argument, though his formulation is weakened by its association with Aristotelian physics. When we look at the world, he writes [*Summa Theologiae*, Ia.3c]:

> we see that things which lack intelligence, such as natural bodies, act for an end, and this is evident from their acting always, or nearly always, in the same way, so as to obtain the best result. Hence it is plain that not fortuitously, but designedly, do they achieve their end. Now whatever lacks intelligence cannot move towards an end, unless it be directed by some being endowed with knowledge; as the arrow is shot to its mark by the archer. Therefore some intelligent being exists by whom all natural things are directed to their end; and this being we call God.

*Criticisms

(1) It can be objected that to think of, say, an eye as an artefact, in the sense that a watch is, is already to apply a distorting model. Certainly an eye has a function just as a watch does. But whereas our knowledge of a watch's purpose is partly tied up with what we know about watchmakers and the importance of time in our culture, we are well able to appreciate what an eye is 'for', how it works, how it is constructed, without making any kind of assumptions about a possible 'designer'. (Moreover, when we describe the operations of the eye we do so in terms quite other than those appropriate to the working of watches, which consist of springs and cogs and so on.)

(2) The second point a follows from the first. Alternative explanations – the Darwinian theory of evolution, for example – can be offered to account for the development and functions of the eye. It might be argued in reply that while such a theory might be considered to explain how certain mutations in an organ could in particular circumstances enhance the chances of survival of the species posessing that organ, it cannot account for the origin of livings things from simpler organisms, or of those simpler organisms from inanimate matter. This is disputable. [You will find it instructive to read Richard Dawkins' *The Blind Watchmaker* or Jacques Monod's *Chance and Necessity* and then, in marked contrast, *The Phenomenon of Man* by Teilhard de Chardin.]

(3) Whatever the acceptability of the argument from particular cases of design, the move from the universe as a whole to a cosmic designer is illegitimate. This is based on the following reasoning. (a) The total universe cannot be described in terms appropriate to parts of it. (b) It is doubtful if any sense can be made of the notion of 'function' or 'purpose' as applied to the universe. An 'orthodox' answer is that God needs a creation so as to express His infinite love. If this is so, then this would tend to support the idea of a universe without beginning or end; otherwise there would have been a 'moment' or moments when God's love was not being expressed – unless we admit the possibility of there being an infinity of temporal universes. (c) From a cursory examination of just our own planet, the universe does not seem always to be particularly pleasant. Are plagues, earthquakes,

floods, starvation, and other apparently meaningless and unpredictable accidents – 'the slings and arrows of outrageous fortune' – to be regarded as evidence of design? The best of all possible worlds, as Leibniz put it?

(4) It could be argued that the notion of 'design' is in any case in some sense subjective: whatever we may think of as designed (apart from our own artefacts) seems so only because we consciously or unconsciously happen to see it in that way. To talk of natural things and events as exhibiting design is to use metaphorical language. To use the language of design to refer to a God could also be regarded as a lapse into anthropomorphism.

(5) Objections can be made against the notion of the 'First Designer' similar to those made above against the concept of the First Cause. Moreover, even if the teleological argument be admitted, it does not prove the existence of the God of the Christians (or indeed of any of the other major monotheistic religions). At the most it points to an impersonal unity such as is affirmed in many Mahayana Buddhist and Hindu religious texts.

(6) It should also be mentioned that both the cosmological and teleological arguments were held by Kant to assume the ontological argument; they presuppose 'that the concept of the highest reality is completely adequate to the concept of absolute necessity of existence' [*Critique of Pure Reason*, B 635]. On that ground alone they are, for Kant, regarded as invalid, though he was sympathetic to what he called the 'physico-teleological' proof. They also commit the fundamental error of all metaphysics in that reason oversteps its legitimate bounds, as shown by his 'antinomies' – pairs of arguments which purport to show that at one and the same time mutually contradictory assertions can be held. Thus the Fourth Antinomy consists of a thesis: 'there belongs to the world either as its part or as its cause, a being that is absolutely necessary'; and an antithesis: 'an absolutely necessary being nowhere exists in the world, nor does it exist outside the world as its cause' [B 481].

(7) A more recent version of the argument from design, the so-called 'Anthropic Principle' might seem to hand the initiative back to religion. According to some modern cosmologists the existence of the universe can no longer be thought of as resulting from mere chance. It is suggested that the fact the universe is as it is and that we are here as conscious beings to understand its workings points to a designer. This is because if the 'fundamental constants' of nature (such as the mass-to-charge ratio of the electron, the strength of the force which binds nuclear particles together, and so on) did not have just the values they in fact possess, then the universe would never have come into existence. The 'fine-tuning' that seems to be implicit here points to the existence of a God who thought it all out. The odds against such a universe coming into existence without a designer are colossal. In reply it has been suggested that our universe may be just one of millions co-existing, each one differing from the others by virtue of a slight adjustment in the values of the fundamental constants. Of course we have no evidence of this, and probably there could never be any. But then have we any *evidence* that our universe was created by God, other than the fact of its existence and our consciousness of it? The Anthropic Principle, moreover, has still to

contend with the other objections raised against the argument from design. And in the last analysis, acceptance of the existence of God is as much an act of faith as is commitment to the many-universes theory.

Many religious people, including some philosophers, are quite prepared to accept that arguments like the three we have been looking at are dubious or cannot establish the existence of the God in which they believe. (This is not to say that such arguments are not taken seriously. The Five Ways of Aquinas are still regarded by many Roman Catholics as providing an adequate *a posteriori* demonstration that God exists. Further discussion is unfortunately not possible here.) They tend therefore to appeal to different types of 'proof'. We shall make a few brief comments about two of these.

The argument from religious experience

Everyday life is for most of us routine and humdrum. But from time to time many people claim to have had 'special' sorts of experiences which they claim variously to be 'uplifting', 'mystical' and 'magical'. The experiences may be visual or auditory, or they may consist in a more general and uncategorizable emotional 'glow' or warmth. The intensity of some of these 'spiritual' experiences is such that those who enjoy them are often led to interpret them in metaphysical or religious terms. They assert that they have encountered the Absolute 'One', the Ultimate Reality, God. Such people are possessed of total conviction; they are in no doubt about the authenticity of their experience and their meeting with God as a Person.

*Comments

How does philosophy respond to this kind of claim? There are three points in particular that should be made:

(1) These kinds of experience are so diverse that generalizations about their significance must be regarded as unwise.

(2) Alternative 'naturalistic' explanations of these experiences are possible, so the onus must be on the believer to justify his or her claims. What kinds of explanations might there be? Perhaps the experiences could be attributed to emotional trauma, or to drugs? Trance-like and 'mystical' states can often be induced by the heightened atmosphere associated with, for example, religious rites or ascetic practices involving fasting for long periods of time. Or they may result from meditation, listening to certain kinds of music, or even auto-suggestion. (You might like to think up more explanations for yourself.)

(3) We have only the claim itself of the individual who has had the experience. While we would not wish to dispute that he or she has had some sort of intense spiritual experience, it is difficult to discover any objective criterion by which the claims to contact with God could be established. It should be noted that it is not being asserted here that none of these experiences is authentic. It is certainly

possible that some indeed are to be understood as direct encounters with a supreme deity. The problem is how to distinguish the genuinely supernatural experience from the natural, or, more frequently, from the spurious. The opportunities for self-deception, albeit unintentional, are legion.

The pragmatic argument

As used by the unphilosophical layman, this argument may perhaps be called the argument of last resort. 'I will admit', he says, 'that all the arguments put forward so far are open to serious objections. I am even prepared to accept, for the purposes of discussion, that what I claim to be experiences of God may have an alternative explanation. But what you cannot deny is that, for me at least, belief in God actually *works*. It gives sense to my life; it helps me in my relationships with other people; it gives me peace of mind. So there must be something in it'. Implicit in this declaration is the view that because the belief is (or seems to be) effective, there must be some 'objective' content or reality to support it. A more sophisticated version of this pragmatic approach is to be found in the writings of William James. His position can be summed up as follows. (a) The positive content of religious experience lies in 'the fact that the conscious person is continuous with a wider self through which saving experiences come'. (b) This wider self, higher reality, or God produces real effects in this world:

> When we commune with it, work is actually done upon our finite personality, for we are turned into new men, and consequences in the way of conduct follow in the natural world upon our regenerative change.

(c) When religious people pass beyond this 'instinctive belief' to make broader assertions of faith (such as, 'God's existence is the guarantee of an ideal order that shall be permanently preserved'), they are bringing into play 'a real hypothesis', which is, however, to be distinguished from a scientific hypothesis:

> A good hypothesis in science must have other properties than those of the phenomenon it is immediately invoked to explain, otherwise it is not prolific enough. God, meaning only what enters into the religious man's experience of union, falls short of being an hypothesis of this more useful order. He needs to enter into wider cosmic relations in order to justify the subject's absolute confidence and peace.

(d) It is not necessary to go further; and indeed James is not committing himself to a specifically Christian deity:

> The practical needs and experience of religion seem to be sufficiently met by the belief that beyond each man and in a fashion continuous with him there exists a larger power which is friendly to him and to his ideals. All that the facts require is that the power should be other and larger than our conscious selves. Anything larger will do, if only it be large enough to trust for the next step. It need not be infinite, it need not be solitary. It might

conceivably even be only a larger and more godlike self, of which the present self would then be but the mutilated expression, and the universe might conceivably be a collection of such selves of different degrees of inclusiveness, with no absolute unity realized in it at all.

(All these quotations are taken from *The Varieties of Religious Experience*, Lecture XX and Postscript.)

In Lecture II of *Pragmatism*, 'What Pragmatism Means', James sums up the importance of pragmatism in religion:

> Pragmatism [is] a mediator and reconciler . . . and, borrowing the word from Papini [an Italian pragmatist, 1881–1956, whom James admired], . . . 'unstiffens' our theories. She has in fact no prejudices whatever, no obstructive dogmas, no rigid canons of what shall count as proof. She is completely genial. She will entertain any hypothesis, she will consider any evidence. It follows that in the religious field she is at a great advantage both over positivistic empiricism, with its anti-theological bias, and over religious rationalism, with its exclusive interest in the remote, the noble, the simple, and the abstract in the way of conception . . .
>
> Her only test of probable truth is what works best in the way of leading us, what fits every part of life's best and combines with the collectivity of experience's demands, nothing being omitted. If theological ideas should do this, if the notion of God, in particular, should prove to do it, how could pragmatism possibly deny God's existence? She could see no meaning in treating as 'not true' a notion that was pragmatically so successful. What other kind of truth could there be, for her, than all this agreement with concrete reality?

*Criticism

You will probably find this approach most refreshing, avoiding as it does the dogmatism usually associated with much institutionalized religion. But in its very strength lie the weaknesses of pragmatism. So far from addressing the philosophical issues raised by empiricism and rationalism, James has in fact by-passed them altogether by redefining 'truth'. (You should refer back to the discussion of the pragmatic theory of truth in 5.7.) Moreover, while his concern for openness and unprejudiced thinking is laudable (and a philosophical virtue!), his emphasis on 'what works best' runs the risk of emptying the concept of 'God' of meaning; for *any* belief in *any* being *or* ideal which can be construed as an expression of the 'higher' self or 'higher' part of the universe would presumably be entirely acceptable if it proves to have what the believer feels to be desirable consequences. And what are to count as 'desirable' consequences raises as many questions as the problem of God's existence does.

We have looked at a number of different 'proofs' that God exists. Limitation of space prevents us from discussing any others (but see 6.3 for a reference to Kant's conception of God as a 'Regulative Idea', which is one version of the **argument**

from morality). Before moving on to the final section, where we shall deal with miracles and the problem of evil, there is one further topic, already referred to, that needs to be examined and which is to some extent connected with the pragmatic view of religious belief, namely, the question of faith.

9.4 Faith

Reading: Aquinas, *Summa contra Gentiles*, I, 3–8; Newman, *Grammar of Assent*; Kierkegaard, *Philosophical Fragments*; Wittgenstein, *Lectures and Conversations on Religious Belief*; Buber, *I and Thou*

In an everyday sense we use the term 'faith' as a synonym for 'trust', 'reliance', or 'confidence' (which is derived from the Latin word for 'faith'). Thus we might say, rightly or wrongly, that we have faith (confidence) in British justice, or that we trust a friend to help us when we are in need. Religious people may refer to God in such terms. 'Faith' does, however, have a meaning with epistemological overtones; and we must consider how it differs from 'knowledge' and 'belief' (see Ch. 5).

The question of faith is discussed by Aquinas in Book II of the *Summa Theologiae*. A clear account of its nature is also given in the *Summa contra Gentiles*, which has been largely followed by Thomists within the Roman Catholic Church. Aquinas distinguishes between truths about God which are accessible to the human reason (for example, that He exists, is one, and so on), and truths about God which exceed the capacity of human reason. This is just as well, he says, for otherwise people who are less intelligent, busy with daily affairs, or just indolent would be cut off from God. Moreover, the quest for God through reason, that is, the study of metaphysics, takes a great deal of time and presupposes arduous training. Reason is also fallible:

> That is why it was necessary that the unshakable certitude and pure truth concerning divine things should be presented to me by way of faith.
>
> [*Summa contra Gentiles*, I, 4(5)]

Now an obvious question that might be raised concerns Aquinas's use of the term 'certitude'. But it should be noted that he is talking of a certitude about 'divine things' which are then 'presented' to us through faith rather than about the certitude of faith itself. In fact if we link up his discussion of faith with his 'Five Ways' we can get a better idea of his general position. What he seems to be saying is that: (a) God's existence can be proved by the exercise of human reason; (b) human reason has its limitations; (c) through careful consideration of the supernatural workings of the deity in the world (such as miracles), and having regard to the authoritative teachings of the Church, we come to assent to divine truth. Thus faith is man's response to God's revelation. But as he makes clear, while we have the choice whether or not to assent to divine truth, our decision is influenced by God's 'grace':

Now, for the minds of moral men to assent to these things is the greatest of miracles, just as it is a manifest work of divine inspiration that, spurning visible things, men should seek only what is invisible. Now, that this has happened neither without preparation nor by chance, but as the result of the disposition of God, is clear from the fact that through many pronouncements of the ancient prophets God had foretold He would do this. The books of these prophets are held in veneration among us Christians, since they give witness to our faith.

[*Summa contra Gentiles*, I, 6(2)]

(This raises the question of human freedom. See 11.4).

In affirming that he holds 'certain' truths by faith Aquinas is thus at the same time willing to provide some justification or backing for them. Faith would therefore seem to have much in common with knowledge – as we discussed in Ch. 5. Such 'truths', however, are not demonstrable in the way that everyday empirical experiences are (today we would include scientific assertions); and Aquinas himself would grant that faith is not knowledge in a strict sense. At the same time to have faith in something (a proposition or a person) involves more than belief; for in the latter one accepts the possibility that one may be wrong.

*Comment

You must be left to consider whether this view of faith as a 'mode of cognition' somewhere between knowledge and belief is tenable. Perhaps the main difficulty is that the evidence a fideist might wish to introduce as backing for his claim does not itself enjoy the kind of *general* support that might be invoked in the case of claims of knowledge of facts such as 'London is the capital of the UK' or '2 + 2 = 4'. Faith presupposes a religious context which is meaningful only to those who claim to have evidence of, say, God's existence and His workings in the world; and these are of course controversial claims.

Although Aquinas's account of faith has been influential and remains of major importance even in our own day, there have been other approaches. Of particular interest is the notion of **commitment**, which has been employed by a number of philosophers coming from quite different traditions.

For John Henry **Newman** (1801–90), a leading figure in the 'Oxford Movement' and convert to Roman Catholicism (he subsequently became a Cardinal of the Church), commitment is implicit in his concept of 'assent' as discussed in his *An Essay in Aid of a Grammar of Assent*. By a careful examination of evidence and use of both formal and informal inference, we must seek to bridge the gap between rules and matters of fact. Reasoning must become 'concrete' whereby each person takes full responsibility for his or her own individual decisions and acts; and this must involve the reaching of a conclusion, the recognition of 'certitude' in relation to the truth of a proposition, and the giving of his 'assent' to it. The 'power of judging and concluding, when it is perfection', Newman calls 'the illative sense'. 'Certitude' differs from 'certainty' – which is a term applicable to propositions themselves in that it involves a personal response (commitment) of the mind to a proposition. Newman further distinguished between 'notional' and 'real' assent. As applied to problems in the philosophy of religion, such as the existence and nature of God, notional assent involves assent to the truth of a proposition, but real assent is a commitment to God as a person with whom one can establish a relationship. The importance of Newman's approach to faith is his insistence that both notional and real assent are required, in our approach respectively to propositional inference and to the concrete realities to which propositions point us. It should be mentioned also that on the question of proof of God's existence Newman looks to the moral conscience of man rather than to the traditional formal arguments we discussed earlier.

Newman's approach to religion has something in common with the 'existentialism' of the Danish thinker Søren **Kierkegaard** (1813–55), in that both grapple with problems of assent and commitment in human relationships with each other and with God. But whereas Newman is concerned to sift and assess 'evidence' calmly and dispassionately, Kierkegaard is critical of systematic philosophy (particularly Hegel's) and is concerned primarily to find a response to feelings such as 'anguish', 'guilt' and 'dread', which are characteristic of the concrete human situation (at least as experienced by Kierkegaard himself). What is central for him is the act of **choice**. Throughout our human existence we must make decisions; and the most important is whether or not to accept Christianity. The supreme act therefore is the 'leap of faith' by which the truth of Christianity is validated.

The notion of existential commitment is of course not unique to Christian philosophers. (Sartre, as we have seen, was an atheist.) Another important religious existentialist was Martin **Buber** (1878–1965), who tackled the problems of faith and commitment from within Judaism. A key distinction he makes is that between two kinds of relationship between persons. The first is the 'I–It' monologue. In such relationships each person objectifies the other, in effect turns himself or herself into a thing enmeshed in a causal network. Such a relationship is thus not genuine. In 'I–Thou' relationships, however, an authentic **dialogue** is established. The 'other' is no longer treated as a discrete 'object' but as a living centre of unique value and choice – through whom all other things in the world are comprehended. Significantly the 'I' itself is transformed when entering into this authentic dialogue. And Buber makes it clear that the 'I–It' and the 'I–Thou' relationships are mutually exclusive; one cannot be both a Thou and an It simultaneously. Herein lies the commitment, akin to Kierkegaard's 'leap': the 'I' no longer withholds part of itself as it does in the 'I–It' relationship, but gives itself up totally and unconditionally to the Thou in an on-going, open, ever self-renewing present existence – the past is over, dead, fixed. The relevance of this thesis to religion for Buber is clear. At the centre of his Judaism is his acknowledgement of a direct 'I–Thou' encounter and communication with God rather than an 'objectivizing' of the self within and by a system of religious dogma.

*Comment

The obvious difficulty with the existentialist notion of choice (unlike Newman's 'assent') is that no criterion is appealed to in order to resolve religious or moral conflicts, or if an appeal were made, one could object that the criterion, whatever it might be, must itself first be chosen. This must therefore lead either to an infinite regress to some kind of objective truth or moral code, or to a restatement of the fundamental arbitrariness of all commitment. For Kierkegaard this commitment must involve what he calls a 'paradox'. Truth is either already within us or it must be communicated to us through a teacher. If the latter then the supreme Truth can be revealed to us only by God himself – and through a human being. It is this which Kierkegaard sees as a paradox surpassing human understanding; and it is in the unconditional embracing of this paradox that the 'objectivity' of God and Christianity is manifested. As Tertullian (c. 160–220) remarked, the Incarnation must be certain because it is impossible. The notions of both paradox and choice, however, never seem to be fully worked out by Kierkegaard, and we must conclude that his account of faith remains flawed. (Compare and contrast the approach to religion and morality of the atheist existentialist Sartre in 6.6 above.)

Both Aquinas and Newman saw no incompatibility between faith and reason, though faith clearly transcends reason. Kierkegaard equivocates on this issue, but he does seem to suggest that reason is of value only to the extent that it allows us to recognize the intrinsic paradox of Christianity which justifies our decision to commit and submit ourselves to revelations of its 'truths'. Buber distinguishes clearly between faith in the sense of a firm belief in statements about religious statements and faith as **trust** (the Hebrew word is *emunah*) – in God's word, as revealed to His people in the Old Testament. As he says in *Between Man and Man*, 'Real faith . . . begins when the dictionary is put down. . . . It is not a *what* at all, it is said into my very life'. To the extent that it avoids the dogmatism (in a non-pejorative sense) of Christianity and grounds transcendence in our (human) experience of relationships Buber's 'faith' is eminently 'reasonable'. For Wittgenstein, however, reason is irrelevant, in the sense that it cannot help us decide between religious belief and unbelief. This is because the believer and the unbeliever are, as it were, living on different planes. Religion constitutes a different 'form of life' from that of, say, science, or of history; and the propositions of religious belief must be judged by the criteria or rules which can be understood only by those already living by them. It is as if one could understand the rules of a game only by playing it, in which case when playing cricket one could not fully understand what it would be like to play chess or patience. It follows therefore that beliefs about God and Christ make sense only to the committed Christian. We are reminded here of St Anselm's, 'I do not seek to understand that I may believe, but I believe in order to understand'.

*Comment

It should be noted that Wittgenstein himself, although baptized into the Roman Catholic Church, was not a Christian, and once remarked of two Catholic philosophers of his acquaintance, 'I could not possibly bring myself to believe all the things they believe'. It can, however, be argued that in his later writings he was concerned to protect 'forms of life' such as religion, ethics and aesthetics from the iconoclastic onslaughts of positivism and to maintain the meaningfulness of each 'form' – according to its own internal logic or criteria (see 11.1). This has an advantage for the believer in that his feelings of awe when confronted with what he sees to be the essential mysteriousness of the universe, his sense of what Rudolf Otto termed the 'numinous', and his response to a deity allegedly transcending the space–time continuum of mundane existence – all this is held to escape the net of scientific analysis and explanation. A difficulty with such a view is that any kind of comparison between different religions would seem to be ruled out; in switching from one belief system to another we should necessarily be exchanging one set of 'rules' for the correct employment of key concepts ('God', 'existence', 'incarnation' and so on) for another set (applicable to, say, 'Buddha', 'karma', 'nirvana' and so on). Attempts to validate fundamental religious 'truths' *historically* (for example, that Christ was crucified and rose again from the dead) must therefore be in a sense irrelevant. A religion has to be accepted on a kind of package deal basis, complete with doctrine, ritual, ethical code and holy books. If you don't like this one – if it doesn't 'work' for you – then try another.

Understandably most Christians and Muslims – indeed adherents of any religion that makes absolutist claims to the 'Truth' – will find this conclusion unsatisfactory. But it does seem unavoidable. Doctrinally the major theistic world religions are at least in part mutually contradictory: both Judaism and Islam, for example, reject the divinity of Jesus Christ. All three faiths do, however, affirm the existence of a Supreme Creator – God, Jahweh, or Allah; and in this respect at least they are afforded some opportunity for reconciliation. Arguably, Buddhism and Hinduism are doctrinally more open in that they regard all world faiths as valid paths to the Truth or the 'One': just as water takes on the shape of its various containers while its essential nature remains unchanged. This is clearly an issue which admits of no easy answers.

9.5 God and the natural order

Reading: Aquinas, *Summa Theologiae*, Ia. 47–49; Hume, *Enquiry concerning Human Understanding*, VIII–XI

Let us leave aside the various difficulties referred to in the previous two sections and accept that God does exist and that the faith of millions is well-founded. In this final section of the chapter we shall look at two of the problems that can arise in supposing that God maintains a relationship with the natural order, with His creation.

Miracles

The word 'miracle' is frequently used in a very general way to refer to a fortunate occurrence for which no immediate explanation is to hand or has been sought.

Thus a person pulled from the wreckage of an aeroplane might afterwards say something like: 'I do not know how I got out; it was a miracle'. Or we might read a headline in a newspaper: 'Five year old's miraculous escape from inferno'. In a strict philosophical and theological sense, however, miracles are, to quote Aquinas, 'things which are done by divine agency beyond the order commonly observed in nature' [*Summa contra Gentiles*, III, 100]. The definition used by Hume is that a miracle is 'a transgression of a law of nature by a particular volition of the Deity, or by the interposition of some invisible agent' [*Enquiry*, Sec. 90]. Many examples of alleged miracles are described in the New Testament (the feeding of the five thousand, for example, or the raising of Lazarus), and of course Christianity itself is grounded in the central claim that God Himself became a man in the person of Jesus, was crucified, and was then resurrected. Hume, however, rejects any argument for the existence of God which appeals to so-called miracles. In so far as they are by definition 'extraordinary' occurrences, and are, in contrast to the 'ordinary' events of our normal experience, improbable his central point is that if we were to accept an event as being miraculous, strong evidence would be required [*Dialogues on Religion*, 113]. This means that the historical evidence adduced in favour of the alleged miraculous event as having occurred would have to outweigh the totality of the evidence available to us – based on our experience – which leads us to suppose that such events could not have happened [*Dialogues on Religion*, 127]. A miracle could be accepted only if it were even more miraculous that the evidence for it was false. Neither can we accept alleged miracles as a basis for religion, because firstly there is a greater probability that stories of miracles have been fabricated; and secondly all religions invoke miracles. But if not all religions are true, then clearly most of the supposed miraculous occurrences must be false. It might be said that men have a natural belief in God. But Hume argues that the evidence does not support this claim. Many primitive societies were animistic or polytheistic – and indeed were often for all intents and purposes atheistic. He dismisses the dogmas and beliefs of Christians as likewise so much superstition. What 'true' religion there is must be concerned with no more than the recognition that any cause of order in the universe 'probably bears some remote analogy to human intelligence'. Only thus far would religious belief seem to be acceptable and God's existence in some limited sense be feasible. Otherwise he is severely critical of religion; it not only leads to fanaticism but also is actually harmful to morality in so far as religious people, he thinks, tend to act for reasons other than for the sake of virtue.

Hume's arguments should be taken seriously, though they are not immune to objections. One obvious point is that it may not be as straightforward as Hume seems to suppose to measure strength of evidence or degrees of probability. We shall not consider his position further here. (You can be left to consider this yourself.) Instead we shall concentrate on three general difficulties which the apologist for miracles must come to terms with:

(1) The above definitions refer to a 'law' or an 'order' of nature. But as we saw in Ch. 8, it is a far from easy matter to pin down precisely what a 'law' is. Both 'law' and 'order' suggest some kind of regularity or sequence, and at the least it would seem that whatever meaning or meanings these terms have should be

understood in the context of explanation as a whole. Now, references to God as transgressing a law or as acting beyond the order imply that this regularity is in some sense broken. Perhaps the best way of understanding this is to look at a specific case – the Incarnation. The 'Virgin' Mary is alleged to have conceived not as a result of the 'natural' process of intercourse with her husband Joseph, but through the direct intervention of the Holy Spirit. It is this single event which constitutes the breach of the law or order of nature; what happened thereafter follows the normal physical and biological processes operating within space and time. It is important to note, however, that if an event is to count as a miracle, then a natural 'order' is presupposed. If an alternative account of science were offered in terms of, say, probabilities, then the logical distinction between what is 'scientific' and what is 'miraculous' might well be seen to disappear. (This will be taken further in 11.3.) But if the distinction be maintained, then another problem has to be considered.

(2) How is a miracle recognized as such? The short answer is: with great difficulty. What are the marks of the Incarnation which might lead us to suppose it *was* a miraculous intervention of God in the world? We have all manner and kinds of 'signs' and 'wonders': the Star of Bethlehem, prophecies, the testimony of Mary herself. But this 'evidence' would hardly stand up in a court of law. Moreover, no good grounds have been adduced to suggest that the standard scientific account of conception is inapplicable to this case. Let us consider another example. A few Irish villagers claim to have seen a statue of the Virgin Mary move. Within days crowds of visitors are flocking to the shrine: the movement of the statue is confirmed again and again. Statues do not move of their own volition. There is no earthquake. It must be a miracle. Subsequent research by psychologists from the local university leads to an alternative naturalistic explanation (which does not, however, in any way weaken the belief of most of the pilgrims – indeed the researchers are accused by many of being atheists). It is significant that in this case the Church has not confirmed the phenomenon as being a miracle. This does, however, raise the fundamental problem of how miraculous occurrences can be distinguished from non-miraculous ones. Is there not always the possibility that a naturalistic explanation might be found? If it be objected that miracles are 'one-off' events, whereas scientific explanation requires repeatability of testable observations in a 'controlled' experimental context, then we might reply that repetition cannot be ruled out. Other cases of 'immaculate' conceptions have been recorded – though this does not in itself eliminate the possibility that *the* immaculate conception was brought about by the causal agency of God.

(3) Another difficulty relates to the seeming arbitrariness of what are claimed to be miracles. Why should God (or the Virgin Mary) select this particular statue in this relatively obscure village? If there is a disaster and a survivor claims that God miraculously saved him on account of his prayer or faith, then what answer can be given to the retort that many of those who perished were practising Christians and no doubt had prayed with equal fervour? Either such claims are unjustified or God is fickle – which seems inconsistent with the Christian conception of His attributes. It should also be noted that 'miraculous' occurrences in other cultures

seem to be manifestations of the deity or deities peculiar to their own religious beliefs and practices; and this again suggests that naturalistic explanations (hallucinations, mass hysteria, individual psychological disturbances, hypnotic states induced by ritual or meditation, and so on) might be more appropriate – unless appeal be made to a supernatural power of which the Christian God, Hindu deities, the 'Tao' and so on are all symbols or manifestations: but such a syncretic approach brings further difficulties, and would in any case be rejected by most Christians.

It should not be concluded from what we have said that miracles are impossible. On the contrary, *given* the Christian concept of an omnipotent God, it is entirely reasonable to expect Him to intervene in His creation when – according to the Biblical story – mankind has turned away from Him. But this brings us back to the issue of faith in revealed 'truths' which are subsequently validated by an authoritative Church. The 'package' of revelation, practices and beliefs hangs together.

The problem of evil

Whether or not miracles genuinely occur is not seen as presenting the religious believer with any serious difficulty. The problem of evil, however, is rather more troublesome and is potentially a greater threat to the stability of faith. To discuss this we must first of all distinguish between 'natural' evil and 'moral' evil.

(1) **Natural evil**. We may suppose ourselves to be in control of our lives. We get up in the morning, go to work, come home again, enjoy our recreations in the evenings or at weekends, and so on. But in reality life is insecure and often unpredictable. Certainly, much that goes wrong – train crashes, gas explosions and wars – can be attributed to our human fallibility. But what of natural disasters such as droughts, plagues, earthquakes and, more improbably, the impacting of a massive meteorite on our planet's surface, which could send us the way of the dinosaurs? We cannot in any real sense be held responsible for such events as these (though perhaps we might have had better contingency plans in place). So is God ultimately responsible? If He is omniscient and omnipotent, why could He not have created a universe in which his creatures would not die of disease, or be crushed under falling rocks? It might be said that if He was to produce a dynamic universe of matter–energy in space–time (in a static universe nothing would happen at all – hardly a coherent option), then necessarily it had to be one in which man and other living organisms would have to contend with danger. Indeed, arguably, had it not been for such natural occurrences – be they the necessary consequences of natural laws or of chance – the evolutionary process would never have given rise to *homo sapiens*. And it is in the manner in which he confronts and attempts to overcome disasters, and to bring relief to the injured, that man shows his moral worth. Leibniz argued that God had created the best of all possible worlds, and that natural disasters could be regarded as God's way of 'testing' his creatures. He was severely criticized for his views by Voltaire in his

poem on the Lisbon earthquake which occurred on All Saints' Day 1755. Voltaire pointed out that the innocent suffered along with the 'guilty'. A further defence offered by the believer would be to claim that, come what may, God does indeed look after those who have faith in Him. He can and does intervene 'miraculously' when we are in peril. In any case we all must die, and what matters is whether we are to be brought into the divine presence in the next life. As to the possibility of miracles, the objection raised earlier remains to be answered, namely, that God's interventions seem to be remarkably arbitrary. And whether there *is* a 'life' after death is a question which is itself a matter of faith.

(2) **Moral evil**. Let us suppose the problem of natural evil can be satisfactorily resolved. The problem of moral evil is far more intractable. By moral evil we are referring roughly to the harm that we human beings inflict on each other. This is real enough; even a cursory look at the history of the past few thousand years suggests that it is endemic in man. The twentieth century alone has seen two world wars, Stalin's pogroms in the former USSR, the Nazi concentration camps where millions of Jews and other peoples were horribly tortured and ultimately met their deaths in the gas chambers, 'ethnic cleansing' in Ruanda and Kosova – the list of atrocities seems endless. And on a less dramatic level we can all cite examples of individual cruelty either from our own experience or from what we read in the newspapers. The problem for the Christian (and no doubt for adherents of other theistic religions) is how a loving God could permit such evils in His world. There are at least two standard answers to this:

(a) In so far as God is love He must have created beings who can respond to that love of their own volition. In other words they must have the freedom to choose or to reject God's laws. To have created robot-like beings who are 'programmed' to respond necessarily to Him would not be adequate to His love. In answer to this, however, it might be said that if God is omnipotent, as He is defined to be by Christians, then surely it is within His capacity to have created beings who would have chosen His way freely. Moreover it can be asked *why* in fact did man 'fall' from grace if he had the moral and intellectual capacity to distinguish good from evil? To attribute his backsliding to the influence of Satan, as described in the Book of *Genesis*, is to by-pass the central issue of weakness of will (see 6.7), and again it can be asked why God did not create beings who would have been able to resist the Devil's temptation. At this point the tendency of many believers is to lapse into agnosticism and to admit that it is not given to us mortals to understand the workings of the divine mind. A further difficulty must be mentioned. God is conceived to be not only omnipotent but also omniscient. He must therefore have known in advance how His creatures would act. He must therefore have had good reason to arrange matters as He did. This leads on to the second answer. (It also raises the further difficulty of 'fatalism' – see 11.4.)

(b) Man's freely chosen decision to follow the path of selfishness and evil must be seen as part of God's plan to maximize the amount of good in His creation. This seems paradoxical, but the point here is that having rejected God, man's return to Him through the sacrifice of God Himself in the person of Christ is all the more satisfying to the Creator and a more authentic manifestation of His love. Within the framework of Christian belief there is a kind of logic here, but to the non-believer it might well seem that God's creatures are in some sense being manipulated, and that God's omniscience and omnipotence do not appear to be fully reconciled.

There is a third approach which may help to resolve the problem – the view presented by Spinoza. His ethics follows from the assumptions and conclusions of his general metaphysics. He does not deny the reality of evil. Like Hobbes, he defines it in terms of our experience of pain, just as the 'good' is understood in terms of pleasure. We call something good because we desire it; we call something bad because we have an aversion to it. The question of God's responsibility does not arise because God *is* Nature, and all that happens within and as part of Nature is necessitated. There are, Spinoza says, no imperfections in Nature: what we regard as evil is but a reflection of our finite, limited point of view. This might seem to be a trite response. But Spinoza's approach is in fact positive and owes something to the Greek Stoics. His ethical ideal is to eliminate pain and seek pleasure, that is, perfection. This involves essentially release from the servitude of passive emotions and conversion of them into active emotions: the elimination of confused ideas and the acquisition of adequate ones. His ethics is therefore fundamentally intellectualistic. The virtuous man is he who, acting under the guidance of reason, seeks self-preservation, though in Spinoza's system this is not inconsistent with a recognition of others as seeking the same end. He calls this 'the intellectual love of God', 'pleasure accompanied by the idea of God as eternal cause'. This love of God he sees as 'our salvation, blessedness or liberty'. It is also the same thing as the love of God for men. Spinoza's ethical ideal seems therefore to be the acquisition of virtue through wisdom, as a result of the attainment by reason of a complete knowledge of Nature *sub specie aeternatis* (under the aspect of eternity). The individual will then be able thereby to achieve a state of imperturbability in the face of all that life brings to his existence.

*Spinoza's account has the advantage that we no longer have to blame God for not making a better world: responsibility for evil lies with ourselves and the circumstances we find ourselves in; and it is up to the individual to overcome it. However, this apparent success has not been achieved without some philosophical cost; for if all that happens in Nature is necessitated, causally determined, what sense can be made of such terms as human 'choice' and 'responsibility'? What control can we be said to have over our actions? Freedom and determinism will be discussed in Ch. 11.

In conclusion it should be stressed that it is not the intention of the writer to belittle religious claims but rather to draw attention to the philosophical difficulties implicit in them. Whether or not you are working for an examination, it is important that you consider such claims and possible objections seriously. Further reading must be regarded as essential; and you are directed to the extensive Reading list that follows.

Texts and problems

*1 In what sense – if at all – can God be said to exist?

2 Is the idea of God unique?

3 How, if at all, can it be shown that the idea of God is nothing but the creation of the human mind?

4 Why did Aquinas reject Anselm's ontological argument? Do you think he was correct to do so?

5 Examine critically Aquinas's arguments for the existence of God from motion and efficient causality.

6 Critically evaluate Descartes' 'causal' argument and his version of the ontological argument.

7 Do you consider the argument from design to be successful? Examine its strengths and weaknesses.

8 'Once the idea of a proof is properly understood, it is immediately apparent that any attempt to prove the existence of God is doomed from the outset.' Discuss this statement with reference to one or more of the classical attempts to prove the existence of God.   [IB, specimen, 2000]

9 Are rational arguments for God's existence conclusive independently of religious faith?   [IB, specimen, 2000]

10 'Religious faith is more than belief but less than knowledge.' Discuss this assertion.

*11 'I know that my redeemer liveth.' How might one know such a thing?

12 (a) Briefly explain what is meant by the view that belief in God is a basic belief.
    (b) Outline Pascal's Wager and explain what it is intended to show.
    (c) Assess the view that faith rather than reason is necessary for religious belief.   [AQA (AEB), specimen, 2001]

13 (a) Briefly explain the problem of evil.
    (b) Outline **one** argument which attempts to explain why God permits natural evil.
    (c) Assess whether the existence of evil invites the conclusion that God does not exist.

[AQA (AEB), specimen, 2001]

14 God is conventionally supposed to be both omniscient and omnipotent. Should we expect Him to intervene or not to intervene in human affairs?

15 'When the divine light pours into the soul, the soul is united with God, as light blends with light. If I am to know God directly, I must become completely He and He I: so that this He and this I become and are one.' Identify, explain and discuss the nature of the religious experience described in this passage.

[IB, specimen, 2000]

16 Is one's having had what may be regarded as a religious experience sufficient as a proof of God's existence?

17 'Suppose, for instance, that the fact, which the testimony endeavours to establish, partakes of the extraordinary and the marvellous; in that case, the evidence, resulting from the testimony, admits of a diminution, greater or less, in proportion as the fact is more or less unusual.' Examine this statement of Hume.

[IB, specimen, 2000]

*18 Would the occurrence of miraculous events prove the existence of God?

19 'Christianity is an exercise in believing the impossible.' Discuss.

20 'In a religious discourse we use such expressions as: "I believe that so and so will happen," and use them differently to the way in which we use them in science' [Wittgenstein]. Do you agree with this view?

21 Commitment is more important than truth. Discuss this assertion with reference to religion.

22 Examine some of the philosophical difficulties associated with religious syncretism.

*Notes/guided answers have been provided for questions **1, 11** and **18** (at end of book).

READING LIST

A. Prescribed texts
Aquinas, St Thomas, *Summa Theologiae.* (IB)
Ayer, A.J., *Language, Truth and Logic.* (AEB)
Buber, M., *I and Thou.* (IB)
Descartes, R., *Meditations.* (AEB, JB)
Hume, D., *Enquiry Concerning Human Understanding.* (AEB, IB)

B. Other texts
Aquinas, St Thomas, *Summa contra Gentiles.*
Buber, M., *Between Man and Man.*
Hume, D., *Dialogues Concerning Natural Religion.*
James, W., *Pragmatism; The Varieties of Religious Experience.*
Kierkegaard, S., *Concluding Unscientific Postscript; Philosophical Fragments.*
Newman, J.H., *An Essay in Aid of a Grammar of Assent.*
Spinoza, B., *Ethics.*
Wittgenstein, L., *Lectures and Conversations on Religious Belief.*

B. Supplementary reading
(If you are a beginner, you are recommended to start with titles marked with an asterisk.)

1. Historical background
Lewis, H.D. and Slater, R.L., *The Study of Religions.**
Smart, N., *The Religious Experience of Mankind.**

2. General introductory texts/books on individual philosophers
Britton, K., *Philosophy and the Meaning of Life.**
Copleston, F.C., *Aquinas.**
Davies, B., *An Introduction to the Philosophy of Religion.**
Gardiner, P., *Kierkegaard.**
Gaskin. J., *The Quest for Eternity: An Outline of the Philosophy of Religion.**
Hick. J., *Philosophy of Religion.**

Kenny, A., *Aquinas.**
Kenny, A., *What is Faith?**
Kolakowski, L., *Religion.**
Lewis, H.D., *Philosophy of Religion.**
Nielsen, K., *An Introduction to the Philosophy of Religion.**
Smart, N., *The Philosophy of Religion.**
Yandell, K.E., *Philosophy of Religion: A Contemporary Introduction.**

3. Other books on general or specific issues
Adams, M.M. and R.M., *The Problem of Evil.**
Davies, P., *God and the New Physics.**
Dawkins, R., *The Blind Watchmaker.**
Ferré, F., *Language, Logic and God.*
Hick, J., *Evil and the God of Love.*
Hick, J., *Faith and Knowledge.*
Kenny, A., *The Five Ways.*
Lewis, H.D., *Our Experience of God.**
Mackie, J.L., *The Miracle of Theism.*
Malcolm, N., 'Anselm's Ontological Argument', in *Knowledge and Certainty.*
Mitchell, B. (ed.), *The Philosophy of Religion.**
Otto, R., *The Idea of the Holy.**
Stace, W.T., *Mysticism and Philosophy.*
Swinburne, R., *The Coherence of Theism.*
Swinburne, R., *The Concept of Miracle.*
Swinburne, R., *The Existence of God.*
Swinburne, R., *Faith and Reason.*
Teilhard de Chardin, P., *The Phenomenon of Man.** (This book could usefully be read in conjunction with P.B. Medawar's critical essay, 'The Phenomenon of Man', in his *The Art of the Soluble.*)

◼ Ṽ 10   The philosophy of art

10.1 Introduction

You do not have to be a scientist to be aware of the contribution science has made to our daily lives. Likewise, although you may not yourself profess belief in a religion or be consciously following the precepts of, say, Christianity, Judaism, or Buddhism, you will probably agree that religion too is pervasive – even in societies where the prevailing orthodoxy is atheism. A similar observation can be made about the arts. One need not be a painter, composer, or poet to appreciate that in one way or another we are influenced by art, music and literature. All around us we see advertisements, we listen to songs on the radio, and we read newspapers. But, you may say, surely this is not what is meant by 'real' art? Michelangelo, Renoir, Constable, Van Gogh, yes; but paintings of Coca-Cola bottles? As for music, surely we cannot refer in the same breath to Beethoven and the Beatles? And how can we possibly compare, say, a 'Mills and Boon' novel to *War and Peace*? This is not to say, of course, that 'pop' or 'mass' art is necessarily worthless. Perhaps it is. But this raises a fundamental problem: is there a criterion of value? Or several criteria? How do we actually judge the 'worth' of a picture, or a piece of music or writing? Is it not all a matter of subjective opinion? *A chacun son goût*, as the French say. As you have no doubt guessed, these are questions which belong to the philosophy of art. And there are many more, relating to the 'purposes' of art, the nature of beauty, the effects of art on individuals and societies, and how the various arts are to be classified. In this chapter we are going to consider just three questions: (1) What is the artist (and we shall use this term in a wide sense to include composers and writers) trying to achieve and why? (2) How do artists realize their aims? (3) How do we judge that they have been successful? Underlying all three questions is the central one: What counts as 'good' art?

10.2 The purpose of art

Reading: Plato, *Republic*, Book X; Aristotle *On the Art of Poetry*; Collingwood, *The Principles of Art*; Langer, *Philosophy in a New Key*, chs VIII and IX

The heading of this section is misleading, for art cannot be said to have just *one* 'purpose'. Different artists often have quite divergent conceptions of what they are doing. So let us consider some of them.

Imitation

The view that art involves some form of imitation originates with the ancient Greeks, in particular with Plato. As you will remember from your study of his *Republic* in Ch. 3, what he means by 'imitation' is closely bound up with his theory of Forms. Of course, in one sense of the term, imitation for Plato is simply one way in which he conceives of the relationship between sense objects and the eternal 'Ideas' (just as 'participation' is another). But in a narrower sense, he thinks of 'works of art' (which he classifies in the *Sophist* under the general heading of things acquired or produced by 'craft' or 'skill' – *techne*) as images (*eikones*) of physical things. They are thus at two removes from the 'real' world of the Forms (compare 3.5). He also refers scathingly to imitative works of art as 'mimetic' depictions of how things appear to us rather than what they are actually like even at the level of the sensory world [see *Republic*, Book X]. In general then Plato does not look to the arts as a means by which we can ascend to true knowledge, although he does qualify this when he argues in other dialogues [for example, the *Symposium* and the *Phaedrus*] that some works of art may be said to exemplify the Idea of Beauty to a greater or lesser extent. The primary 'purpose' of the artist can in fact only be appreciated when the arts are placed at the disposal of the rulers and subordinated to the moral and political requirements of the state.

Aristotle too subscribes to an imitation or representation theory though he confines his discussion on the whole to poetry [his classical work is called *On the Art of Poetry*] and combines it with another theory of art, the 'formalist' theory, which we shall look at shortly. It was the *Ars Poetica* of the Roman poet and critic Horace (65–68 BC) that proved to be particularly influential. In his opinion, 'the experienced poet, as an imitative artist, should look to human life and character for his models, and from them derive a language that is true to life'. He also advocated that aspiring poets should imitate not only nature but the models of their Greek predecessors (especially Homer) – advice that was eagerly adopted by many eighteenth century writers such as Pope and other English Augustans.

*Criticism and comments

Imitation theories do not seem to work consistently or are limited in their application. Certainly there are numerous examples of paintings deemed generally by 'cognoscenti' to be great works of art and which do in an obvious sense imitate their subjects. Thus we can refer to portraits by Reynolds or the landscapes of Constable as being faithful or accurate representations. But what are we to say of the impressionist paintings of, say, Monet? Few would deny them the accolade of greatness: yet to the uninitiated Monet's work might seem to be in certain respects nothing more than distortions of reality. 'Reality' is in fact the key word here. For the impressionists what matters is not a detailed 'photographic' depiction of real things as such, but immediate, fleeting appearances. And of course there have been very many artists who would explicitly deny that their work is intended to be imitative of a 'visible' reality in any sense at all, but who claimed to be penetrating to the subconscious mind (Surrealism) or to be redefining the real (as in Expressionism and Abstractionism).

When we move away from the visual arts, imitation theories seem even more inappropriate. There are a few pieces of music which, it would seem, have been composed deliberately to imitate some event or natural occurrence. Thus Debussy's *La Mer* conveys to the listener something of the sound of waves – as does Mendelssohn's *Fingal's Cave*. We might mention also the storm sequence in Beethoven's *Pastoral Symphony*. Another example of direct imitation is found in Saint-Saëns' *Danse Macabre* suite, which cleverly conveys to us the sound of skeletons dancing. But for the most part this kind of direct copying of sounds is absent in works of the 'great' composers.

The possibilities of imitation are perhaps wider in literature. In poetry the use of such devices as alliteration and onomatopoeia enables the poet to reduplicate sounds made by natural objects such as streams or insects. Tennyson makes use of these techniques with good effect in *Morte d'Arthur* to convey the noise made by the armoured knight, Sir Bedivere, as he strides across the mountains in mid-winter:

> Dry clash'd his harness in the icy caves
> And barren chasms, and all to the left and right
> The bare black cliff clang'd round him, as he based
> His feet on juts of slippery crag that rang
> Sharp-smitten with the dint of armed heels

Much prose fiction may perhaps also be said to be imitative to the extent that it attempts to create and describe complex human situations and relationships 'objectively' and in considerable detail. Classical examples are the tragedies of Shakespeare and nineteenth century 'realist' novels such as Flaubert's *Madame Bovary*. But, as in the case of music and painting, there are so many counter-examples of novels or plays which cannot be fitted easily into such a rigid classification that the imitative theory has to be regarded as being of limited value.

Expression

The written word is not only descriptive; it frequently has the capacity to communicate emotions. And this is a feature it shares with both painting and music. Some philosophers of art have been so impressed by this capacity that they have attempted to work out a theory on the basis that art is an expression of human feeling. This general statement is of course ambiguous. It can mean either that a work of art is that which is the result or product of human feeling, or that it is the means by which feeling is to be expressed and derives its worth in proportion to the degree to which such feeling has been 'objectified'. It is in this second sense that the principal exponents of the theory, the Italian philosopher B. Croce (1866–1952) and the English historian and philosopher R.G. **Collingwood**

(1889–1943), understand art to be 'expression', but only if expression be identified with 'imagination'. In his book *The Principles of Art* Collingwood firstly rejects the identification of art with craft and representation, magic and amusement. After a discussion of the concepts of thinking and feeling he deals with the relationship of imagination with each of them. A theory of language as the imaginative expression of (a) emotion and (b) thought is then followed by his claim that art itself is a form of language. The origin of art, he says, can lie neither in man's physical nature (that is, sensation or its emotions) nor in the intellect (concepts). 'The activity which generates an artistic experience is the activity of consciousness', which 'converts impression into idea, that is, crude sensation into imagination':

> At the level of imaginative experience, the crude emotion of the psychical level is translated into idealized emotion, or the so-called aesthetic emotion, which is thus not an emotion pre-existing to the expression of it, but the emotional charge on the experience of expressing a given emotion, felt as a new colouring which that emotion receives in being expressed. Similarly, the psycho-physical activity on which the given emotion was a charge is converted into a controlled activity of the organism, dominated by the consciousness which controls it, and this activity is language or art. [ch. XII]

Collingwood's theory, which sees art as essentially cathartic in so far as it is a channel for the release of emotion, undoubtedly merits serious attention. It is certainly consistent with Wordsworth's view of poetry as 'the spontaneous overflow of powerful feelings' originating from 'emotion recollected in tranquility' and from the workings of imagination. Imagination for Wordsworth is a 'plastic-power' which can shape and mould sense-impressions into significant forms; it is 'that glorious faculty that higher minds bear with them as their own'. Similarly, Coleridge constructs the term 'esemplastic' (from the Greek words *eis en plattein* – 'to shape into one') to distinguish imagination from 'fancy'. Whereas fancy is but 'a mode of memory emancipated from the order of time and space' and 'must receive all its materials from the law of association' (compare 5.3), imagination (in its 'secondary' signification) 'is essentially *vital*' as opposed to objects which, as objects, are 'fixed and dead':

> It dissolves, diffuses, dissipates, in order to re-create; or where this process is rendered impossible, yet still, at all events, it struggles to idealize and to unify. [*Biographia Literaria*, ch. XIII]

('Primary' imagination for Coleridge is 'the living power and prime agent of all human perception, . . . a repetition in the finite mind of the eternal act of creation in the infinite IAM'. He considers the secondary to differ from it only in degree and in the mode of its operation.)

Parallels are also to be found in the art of van Gogh and the later Expressionists. The function of a painting is now no longer to define the object but to serve as a medium for the expression of the artist's feelings or passions, and as a means by which nature itself can be 'spiritualized'. It is by loving a thing, wrote van Gogh, that one can perceive it better and more accurately. As for music, we might note the feelings aroused in the listener by the later work of Beethoven – especially the last Quartets; or by the compositions of Chopin, Schubert, Sibelius, Mahler and many others.

*Criticisms and comments

An obvious question is whether we can be sure about what is 'going on' inside an artist's head. After all, what we see or hear is the work of art itself, the completed product. Is it not possible that a poem, a painting, or a symphony might have been created 'intellectually' in an 'emotion-free' state of mind? If so, would the composition necessarily be an inferior work of art? Collingwood, quoting Coleridge, says that 'we know a man for a poet by the fact that he makes us poets. We know he is expressing his emotions by the fact that he is enabling us to express ours' [*The Principles of Art*, ch. VI]. But this will not do, for several reasons:

(1) Different people may respond differently to the same work of art. I may be intensely moved by, say, *Boris Godunov*, whereas Mussorgsky's opera may leave others 'cold'.
(2) Despite Collingwood's (and Coleridge's) assertions we cannot be sure, unless the artist has told us, that he experienced some sort of emotional release in the moment of creation or that the emotions engendered by my auditory and visual experiences of the composition 'correspond' to his. And of course this 'gap' or disparity between interpretation and intention is one which many an unwary critic has fallen headlong into.
(3) Perhaps the main difficulty is that Collingwood's emphasis on the creative process (which in any case might well be regarded as a matter for psychology) ignores the role played by the work of art itself. What we would like to know is to what extent (perhaps by means of their structures) the actual paintings, poems, or string quartets contribute to our experience. Collingwood, however, is uncompromising in his rejection of formalist theories:

> Music does not consist of heard noises, paintings do not consist of seen colours, and so forth. Of what, then, do these things consist? Not, clearly, of a 'form', understood as a pattern or a system of relations between the various noises we hear or the various colours we see. Such 'forms' are nothing but the perceived structures of bodily 'works of art', that is to say, 'works of art' falsely so called; and these formalistic theories of art, popular though they have been or are, have no relevance to art proper and will not be further considered in this book. The distinction between form and matter, on which they are based, is a distinction

belonging to the philosophy of craft, and not applicable to the philosophy of art.

The work of art proper is something not seen or heard, but something imagined. [ch. VI]

Form

Because of the evident difficulties associated with both the imitative and expressionist theories, some philosophers have suggested that an adequate theory of art must be based on the notion of 'form'. What does this mean? For Plato, as we have seen, the form of a work of art would be the nonsensible 'archetype' or set of archetypes from which the physical things represented by the work of art would themselves derive their reality. The term is also used by Kant in his *Critique of Judgement*, which we shall say something about in the next section. But 'formalism' as a theory of art is particularly associated with the critics Clive Bell and Roger Fry.

Rejecting both representative and expressionist theories, Bell argued that 'good' art possesses 'significant form'. But he does not provide a detailed analysis of what he means by this beyond defining it in terms of its effect, namely its ability to arouse a specifically *aesthetic* emotion in the sensitive viewer or listener. He does not deny that a painting might be representational or that a piece of music might make the listener feel happy or sad: but he claims that such qualities of the work of art are irrelevant to their aesthetic value. What matters is the way the elements of the composition are arranged and interconnected. And by 'elements' is meant such features of the work as colours, lines, shapes, and the ways they are arranged and fused together in what is in fact a complex 'organic' unity. We can get a better understanding of 'significant form' by referring to the work of the post-Impressionist Cézanne, who, Bell thinks, exemplifies his theory particularly well. By concentrating on the formal construction of his paintings, Cézanne subordinated the particularity and immediacy of objects (trees, bowls of fruit, cups and so on) to geometrical forms and colours which he perceived as revealing an underlying universality or order in nature. It is this potential for revealing the 'universal' that Bell identifies as significant form; and it is for this reason that he is so dismissive of imitation and expression. (A somewhat similar view of formalism in music was put forward by the Austrian critic Eduard Hanslick; and the possibility of applying the theory to literature – which Bell excludes – was investigated by Fry.)

*Comments and criticisms

(1) As with the imitation and expression theories, it may be doubted whether the formalist approach can cope with the variety and range of compositions produced by man in different cultures over a period of thousands of years. Individual painters, musicians, writers, sculptors and so on have started out with different aims and have developed many idiosyncratic techniques. Moreover, it can certainly be argued that 'form' in, say, the visual arts does not correspond completely to the formal features characteristic of the other arts, on account of

the fundamental differences between the media which they make use of. In painting we may be concerned with lines, shadows, contrast and balance of colour. The musician too is interested in balance, contrast and harmony, but as between sounds. Similar considerations probably apply to poetry, but it is a matter for debate whether comparable relationships can be identified in prose other than by analogy. To say that formal criteria are applicable to all works of art simply because they are made of parts which can be related to each other in some way is to make the theory so vague and general as to be virtually useless.

(2) It is doubtful whether 'form' can be totally isolated from content in the way that formalists seem to require. In the visual arts in particular, when we look at painting we are usually aware of it as being a picture *of* something. Cézanne may well have *intended* that his landscapes or still lifes should be the vehicles by means of which 'universality' is conveyed to the observer. But we still see trees or bowls of fruit. And in any case most other artists would claim that they had quite different aims. In music too, the attention we pay to *sounds* may well dominate our recognition of 'formal' aspects. As for literature, 'formal' patterns or structures probably play a relatively minor role in the total aesthetic experience, the primary features being description of character and places, and of course the 'plot'. Aristotle was one of the first critics to set out formalistic requirements, and in his *Poetics* [ch. 7] he argues for the need for plots in drama to be of a reasonable size, the 'parts' to be properly ordered, and for character to be subordinated to the action. But 'universal truth' for him is achieved through the correct imitation rather than through attention to formal aspects such as order and balance.

(3) It can also be argued that formalism cannot be separated from expressionism. This seems to have been recognized by the American philosopher Susanne **Langer** (1895–1985) in her books *Feeling and Form* and *Philosophy in a New Key*. Langer distinguishes between an aesthetic emotion, which is experienced, that is, expressed, by the artist as he labours to create his masterpiece, and the emotional content of the work itself, which can be felt both by artist and beholder as they contemplate the finished painting. The former springs from 'an intellectual triumph, from overcoming barriers of word-bound thought and achieving insight into literally 'unspeakable' realities'. The emotive content of the work, however, is something deeper than any intellectual experience: it is 'more essential, pre-rational, and vital: something of the life-rhythms we share with all growing, hungering, moving and fearing creatures: the ultimate realities themselves, the central facts of our brief, sentient existence' [*Philosophy in a New Key*, ch. IX]. It is the capacity of a work as a whole (and Langer's thesis is applied to all the arts), or of natural objects which an artist might seek to imitate, to bring about this emotional response to content that she identifies with 'significant form' or 'artistic truth'. 'Artistic truth' is, she writes, 'the truth of a symbol to the forms of feeling – nameless forms, but recognizable when they appear in sensuous replica'. Nevertheless, despite the greater philosophical rigour of Langer's arguments as compared with those of Bell and Fry, her notion of 'artistic truth' and the nature of the symbolizing process is not made sufficiently clear. We shall return to this in the next section.

10.3 Beauty and judgement

Reading: Plato, *Symposium*; Collingwood, *Principles of Art*, ch. XIII; Langer, *Philosophy in a New Key*, chs VIII and IX; Ayer, *Language, Truth and Logic*, ch. VI

Throughout the discussion so far we have been seeking at least implicitly to find answers to the first two questions raised at the beginning of the chapter: what is the artist trying to do, and how does he or she set about realizing his or her aims? We must now deal with the third question: how we are to judge whether or not he or she has been successful, and with the fundamental problem of what constitutes 'good' (and 'bad') art. As we might expect, each of the three theories of art so far considered offers its own criterion.

For the representationist, good art is art which successfully imitates its objects. The obvious difficulty here is that an element of subjectivity is unavoidable. Imitation is not to be understood as a one-to-one correspondence of particulars. Different artists will 'perceive' in a diversity of ways what they are endeavouring to represent, thereby reflecting their psychological or cultural preconceptions. How are we to determine that one representation is more successful or 'true to life' than another? In any case, as has already been said, many works of art (including music and literature) do not claim to be imitative and yet can still be described meaningfully as 'good'.

According to Collingwood, the expressionist, a good work of art is an activity in which the agent is successful in expressing a given emotion. Conversely, bad art fails to express that emotion thereby 'corrupting' consciousness (albeit temporarily or partially)

> on the threshold that divides the psychical level of experience from the conscious level. It is the malperformance of the act which converts what is merely psychical (impression) into what is conscious (idea). [ch. XII]

The problem with this kind of criterion is also one of subjectivity. How, it may be asked, can the beholder or listener possibly know whether the artist has or has not been successful in expressing his or her emotion? To say that experienced and sensitive critics are agreed that a given work of art (painting, novel, etc.) *is* good and that therefore its creator must have expressed his or her emotions successfully would be to beg the question. Even if a living artist tells us that he has experienced some kind of catharsis, this can be no guarantee that he will thereby be assured of critical acclaim.

What of formalism? Langer frankly acknowledges the subjective aspect and is content to leave the decisions on the whole to those who have the requisite knowledge and sensitivity:

> To understand the 'idea' in a work of art is therefore more like *having a new experience* than like entertaining a new proposition; and to negotiate this knowledge by acquaintance the work may be adequate *in some degree.*

There are no degrees of literal truth, but artistic truth, which is all significance, expressiveness, articulateness, has degrees; therefore works of art may be good or bad, and each must be judged on our experience of its revelations. Standards of art are set by the expectations of people whom long conversance with a certain mode – music, painting, architecture, or what not – has made both sensitive and exacting; there is no immutable law of artistic adequacy, because significance is always *for* a mind as well as *of* a form.   [ch. IX]

This seems to be a balanced and attractive view, though of course it has to be conceded that judgements as to the adequacy of works of art can still be made by those who do not subscribe to theories which make use of such concepts as 'significant form' or 'artistic symbolizing'. So let us look at another approach to the problem, according to which 'good' works of art can be identified by virtue of their possession of **beauty**. What is beauty? How do we recognize it?

Beauty has been regarded by many philosophers, most notably Plato (in the *Philebus*), as an intrinsic quality of objects (such as geometrical shapes, colours and musical sounds). Unfortunately Plato oscillates between two different accounts of this quality. It is either to be defined in terms of formal features of the object, namely 'measure and symmetry', or it is indefinable. Either way, beauty in sensible things is objectively real in so far as it exemplifies the Ideal or universal Beauty (which he discusses in the *Symposium*). It should be noted also that beauty for Plato is also ultimately a Form of the Good, and that the pleasures that are evoked by our contemplation of beautiful things are 'pure'.

Now if Plato is right, we should not expect there to be disagreement about whether a given work of art is or is not beautiful (provided we leave aside the possibility that a listener may be tone-deaf or an observer blind to 'symmetry'). Yet we do differ greatly in our appreciation and assessment of art, music and literature. Some people have therefore maintained that beauty is indeed 'in the eye of the beholder', or that it is but a capacity possessed by works of art to 'cause' the idea of beauty in us. Some other philosophers, in particular Ayer, and critics (especially I.A. Richards) have argued that the language used about beauty is essentially emotive (compare 6.7). The problem of reconciling subjectivity of response with the presumed universality of aesthetic judgement is one which Kant grappled with in his third Critique, *The Critique of Judgement*, Part I, (It will be useful to check over what you have learned about Kant's theory of knowledge and ethics, as his views of art are an integral part of his philosophical system.) Only a short summary of some of the main ideas will be given here.

When we describe a flower as being red we are, according to Kant, essentially subsuming sensory data under concepts. But in the case of a judgement like 'This flower is beautiful' we are relating what is being perceived to what he calls 'a delight . . . apart from any interest'. This is a 'judgement of taste' (as contrasted with 'judgements of the agreeable'). He goes on to show (in the 'Analytic of the Beautiful') that although such judgements of taste are singular they do have (*a priori*) universal validity, that is, we expect other people to react to the object (the beautiful flower) in the same way as we do. This cannot be proved, for we are not dealing here with concepts; and my taste cannot serve as an adequate ground for another's. So what is the basis for Kant's assertion that judgements of taste are both universal and refer necessarily (but 'synthetically') to aesthetic satisfaction? His 'Transcendental Deduction' is difficult to follow. But again we can grasp the central points by contrast with the 'Deduction' of the first Critique. Empirical knowledge is possible, he says, because the raw data of sense are subsumed under the concepts of the understanding mediated or synthesized by the imagination. In the case of judgements of taste, however, the imagination and understanding are in a state of 'free-play'. This condition is brought about by what he calls the 'purposiveness without purpose', which is characteristic of an aesthetic object in so far as in its wholeness of form or appearance it looks as if it has some sort of function, although it has not. As a result of this 'purposiveness' and 'free-play' we experience a disinterested satisfaction which depends on our awareness of a harmony between the understanding and the imagination. Since it has already been established in the first Critique that our understanding and imagination work together (because we share knowledge), so we are all capable of feeling their 'free-play' and hence of experiencing aesthetic pleasure:

> For, since the delight is not based on any inclination of the Subject (or on any other deliberate interest), but the subject feels himself completely *free* in respect of the liking which he accords to the object, he can find as reason for his delight no personal conditions to which his own subjective self might alone be party. Hence he must regard it as resting on what he may also presuppose in every other person; and therefore he must believe that he has reason for demanding a similar delight from every one.
>
> [*Critique of Judgement*, Sec. 6]

In addition to his examination of 'beauty' Kant also investigates the concept of the '**sublime**' in the third Critique ('Analytic of the Sublime'). Following Edmund Burke [*A Philosophical Inquiry into the Origin of Our Ideas of the Sublime and Beautiful*, 1756], Kant tries to show that our feeling of the sublime is a different kind of satisfaction which arises from our contemplation of the greatness of human reason and our recognition of our moral worth.

In Part II of the *Critique of Judgement* (the 'Critique of Teleological Judgement') Kant seeks to use his analyses of the beautiful and the sublime to reconcile the phenomenal and noumenal worlds of nature and freedom respectively, which he had examined in the first two Critiques. Our experience both of the formal 'purposiveness' we perceive in beauty and of the terrifying formlessness of nature's sublimity underpin our morality and point to a cosmic purpose (compare Kant's ethics, discussed in 6.3).

*The fundamental difficulty with Kant's theory is that in the last analysis it fails to deal satisfactorily with aesthetic disputes. If I see a flower as beautiful, it may well be that, given the validity of Kant's 'Transcendental Deduction', I should expect other people to perceive it in the same way and acknowledge its aesthetic qualities. The fact remains, however, that critics continue to disagree about the merits and demerits of paintings, symphonies and novels. So, to complete this chapter, we shall now look briefly at another standard against which the 'worth' of a work of art is often judged, namely its role or '**function**' in society.

10.4 Art and society

Reading: Collingwood, *Principles of Art*, ch. XIV

Many philosophers and artists, starting with the Greeks, have suggested that the fundamental criterion by which the 'goodness' of works of art should be judged is the contribution they make to society. Certainly, what artists do cannot be seen in isolation from culture as a whole. Art (like ethics, religion and science) is – to use Wittgenstein's phrase again – a 'form of life'. It is akin to a game which is played in accordance with rules, and 'what belongs to a language game is a whole culture' [*Lectures on Aesthetics*, I, Sec. 26]. 'The words we call expressions of aesthetic judgement play a very complicated role, but a very definite role, in what we call a culture of a period' [25]. 'In order to get a clear idea about aesthetic words you have to describe ways of living' [35]. Wittgenstein also suggests that the rules appropriate to, say, music are different from those used in the appreciation of architecture [23]. And there is no doubt that in most civilizations there is a close, even symbiotic, relationship between art, religion, ethics, science and philosophy. It is understandable therefore that the influences of art on a culture and in particular on its social aspects should have been taken seriously. Some writers, Tolstoy for example, have argued that for a work of art to be regarded as such it must communicate feelings of universal brotherhood; it must bind men together. Art is necessarily religious in nature. Many Marxist–Leninist thinkers, however, argue that the function of the artist is to serve the 'revolution', by making explicit the socio-economic 'laws' which determine human culture and by furthering the 'class-struggle'. The artist is thus primarily a propagandist and his work is to be judged on this basis. (Whether art itself can be explained completely in terms of the socio-economic infrastructure is an open question and one which does not seem to have been fully worked out by dialecticians – if the frequent acrimonious debates and ritual purges of artists in, say, the (pre-*Glasnost*) Soviet Union are anything to go by. Consider the experiences of Pasternak and Shostakovitch, for example.) (On Marxism and society, see also Chs 7 and 12.)

*Criticisms

Three points in particular can be made about such an approach to art:

(1) Both the Tolstoyan (religious) and the Marxist (atheistic and dialectical) standpoints effectively brand as 'decadent' or 'bourgeois' many of the works of art which most people for one reason or another would regard as 'great'.

(2) Emphasis on the social impact of art is not inconsistent with appreciation of the aesthetic qualities it may be supposed to possess by virtue of its formal structures.

(3) Similarly the social importance of art should not be allowed to obscure its significance for the individual artist or other individuals who may feel that a particular work in some sense speaks to the 'human condition'. Indeed many English literary critics starting with Matthew Arnold and (some would say) ending with F.R. Leavis assess writing in terms of its ability to generate self-knowledge and 'intense moral seriousness'.

Conclusion

We are faced with the problem of reconciling (a) different critical appraisals of works of art and (b) two apparently opposed views of art – 'art for art's sake' and art as propaganda.

As to the first, it has to be recognized that Wittgenstein's 'rules' for the 'correct' use of aesthetic language can change. Sometimes only a few rules change [compare Wittgenstein, *Lectures on Aesthetics*, I, Sec. 16]. But often the changes are more radical:

> Suppose Lewy has what is called a cultured taste in painting. This is something entirely different to what was called a cultured taste in the fifteenth century. An entirely different game was played. He does something entirely different with it to what a man did then. [29]

A suitable way of dealing with aesthetic disagreements might therefore be to develop a 'consensus' theory similar to that suggested in Ch. 6 on Ethics. The judgements we make about works of art at any particular cultural stage should take into consideration not only their forms and structures, and the techniques of the creator, but also his intentions. (Would we regard a pleasing pattern produced by a chimpanzee let loose with pots of different coloured paints as a work of art? Perhaps this is why we have reservations about 'action' painting.) It may well be that in the light of such considerations sensitive and experienced critics come to articulate the artistic standards of a culture. This is not, however, to argue in favour of élitism or an 'aristocracy' of taste. Each of us can make use of his or her own judgement, and through informed discussion can seek to reinforce, refine, modify, or even to change the consensus radically – as indeed some 'great' artists themselves have done. One need only mention Picasso in painting, Joyce in literature and Stravinsky in music. But it may well be that despite changes in the 'rules' – or in our interpretation of them – there is a certain lowest common denominator of taste in aesthetics (as there could also be in ethics in relation to the 'rightness' of actions and the 'goodness' of intentions and consequences) which can be identified in different cultures and cultural stages.

The second problem is more controversial. Certainly account should be taken of the social consequences of the arts. Does this mean that censorship can be justified? Plato had no doubts about this. But there is a powerful tradition particularly in Britain that the freedom of the artist to express himself through his chosen medium should be infringed as little as possible. How can the respective claims of the individual and society be reconciled? First of all, it has to be said that censorship of 'bad' art would not seem to be justified on *aesthetic* grounds. If it *can* be shown that the consequences of a particular work are likely to be 'bad' for society, then whatever objections are raised should be based on *moral* and *legal* considerations. Is the work liable to offend public decency? Is it blasphemous? Is it likely to encourage crime? And so on. The problems here concern definitions and the assessment of probabilities. What are meant by 'liable' and 'likely'? Who is to say? An eminent critic, or 'the man on the Clapham omnibus'? Should a utilitarian criterion be adopted? If but one person finds a work of art offensive, should that be regarded as sufficient justification for restricting the artist's freedom to publish (and others to enjoy his composition)? Probably what is required in any 'civilized' society is a reasonable balance. The artist should recognize that the creating and exhibiting of a work of art is at least potentially a publicly observable act. He should therefore paint, write, or compose his music responsibly and with integrity, aware of the wider implications. Likewise those with moral/religious axes to grind should think of issues such as freedom of the artist and the value of such freedom to society as a whole or to an individual committed to a different set of ideals or principles. Indeed it can be argued that in the last analysis the responsibility of the artist, writer – and philosopher – should be to the individual, and that this must outweigh his obligation to reflect or support any political or religious ideology which lays claim to 'Absolute Truth'. For without the individual's freedom to examine, choose, accept, or reject, 'commitment' is worthless. If mankind is to survive there can be no room for fanatics who would as soon shoot a writer as allow him to express a view inconsistent with their beliefs. Art, like other manifestations of the human spirit – religion, ethics, and science – must be given room to breathe and develop.

As you will appreciate, there are many problems in the philosophy of art we have not been able to investigate here; and those we have studied have been examined only cursorily. But it is hoped that this chapter has helped you to find your way round yet another part of the philosophical landscape. We shall return in Ch. 12 – under the heading of 'hermeneutics' – to consider further the question of an artist's intentions and also whether there can be said to be an 'objective truth' in a work of art.

QUESTIONS

Texts and problems

*1 'The artist's representation is . . . a long way removed from truth' [*Republic*, 598]. Discuss what Plato means by this.

2 'The only poetry that should be allowed in a state is hymns to the gods and paeans in praise of good men' [*Republic*, 607]. Examine Plato's assertion critically.

3 How does Aristotle's concept of 'imitation' differ from Plato's?

4 What does Aristotle mean by 'catharsis'? Discuss the implications for aesthetics.

5 Discuss some of the difficulties inherent in mimetic theories of art.

6 Art is the imaginative expression of emotion, according to Collingwood. Examine this claim.

7 Is it possible to separate our evaluation of a work of art from our knowledge of the artist's intentions? (See also 12.5)

*8 'Music does not consist of heard noises, paintings do not consist of seen colours, and so forth' [Collingwood]. Do you agree?

9 Examine the concept of 'significant form' as used by Bell, Fry and Langer.

10 For a work of art to be called good it must be beautiful. Examine this assertion.

11 Given that the 'beautiful is that which pleases universally without requiring explanation', why do we need to be educated in art to appreciate it fully?

[IB, specimen, 2000]

12 Why does Kant think we are all capable of experiencing aesthetic pleasure?

13 Examine Kant's concept of 'purposiveness' to the extent that it is relevant to his theory of aesthetics.

14 Are judgements of taste universal, as Kant maintains?

15 The function of art is to instruct not to please. Discuss.

16 'The purpose of aesthetic criticism is not so much to give knowledge as to communicate emotion' [Ayer]. Discuss.

17 In order to get a clear idea about aesthetic words you have to describe ways of living' [Wittgenstein]. Investigate the meaning and implications of this assertion.

18 While many people engage in artistic pursuits in the course of their daily lives (decorating their houses, dancing, playing music, etc.), they are often uninterested in the Fine Arts, finding them too hard to understand. Discuss the artistic process in our lives. [IB, specimen, 2000]

19 How might one set about distinguishing qualitatively, and in terms of 'value', between, say, a song by Schubert and the winning entry in the Eurovision song contest?

20 Discuss the justification in a pluralist democratic society for banning a work of art on the grounds of (a) blasphemy, (b) sedition, and (c) obscenity.

21 'Art [in the theatre] – the image, not the fact – cannot degrade and corrupt, though it certainly upsets and disturbs.' Do you agree?

*22 'Science is abstract, life is concrete, literature bridges the gap.' Discuss with examples.

23 Do you agree with Sartre's view that an ethical choice may be compared to the construction of a work of art?

*Notes/guided answers have been provided for questions 1, 8 and 22 (at end of book).

READING LIST

A. Principal texts

Aristotle, *On the Art of Poetry.*
Collingwood, R.G., *The Principles of Art.*
Kant, I., *The Critique of Judgement.*
Langer, S.K., *Philosophy in a New Key.*
Plato, *Republic, Phaedrus, Symposium.*
Wittgenstein, L., *Lectures and Conversations on Aesthetics.*

See also the prescribed text: Ayer, *Language, Truth and Logic.* (AEB)

C. Supplementary reading
(If you are a beginner, you are recommended to start with titles marked with an asterisk.)

1. Historical background
Beardsley. M.C., *Aesthetics from Classical Greece to the Present.**
Read, H., *The Meaning of Art.**

2. General introductory texts
Carroll, N., *Philosophy of Art: A Contemporary Introduction.**
Danto, A.C., *The Transfiguration of the Commonplace: a Philosophy of Art.**
Sheppard, A., *Aesthetics: An Introduction to the Philosophy of Art.**

3. Other books and essays
(This is a somewhat arbitrary but representative list.)
Abrams, M.H., *The Mirror and the Lamp: Romantic Theory and the Cultural Tradition.*
Bell, C., *Art.*
Burke, E., *A Philosophical Inquiry into the Origin of our Ideas of the Sublime and Beautiful.*
Coleridge, S.T., *Biographia Literaria.*
Fischer, E., *The Necessity of Art: a Marxist Approach.**
Fry, R., *Transformations.*
Fry, R., *Vision and Design.*
Gadamer, H.-G., *The Relevance of the Beautiful and Other Essays.*
Gombrich, E.H., *Art and Illusion.**
Hanslick, E., *The Beautiful in Music.*
Hegel, G.W.F., *Aesthetics: Lectures on the Philosophy of Art.*
Langer, S.K., *Feeling and Form.*
Leavis, F.R., *The Common Pursuit.*
Leavis, F.R., *The Great Tradition.*
Osborne, H. (ed.), *Aesthetics.**
Richards, I.A., *Principles of Literary Criticism.*
Schiller, J.C.F., *Letters on the Aesthetic Education of Man.*
Scruton, R., *Art and Imagination.*
Scruton, R., *The Aesthetic Understanding.*
Tolstoy, L., *What is Art?**
Wollheim, R., *Art and its Objects.**

For commentaries on the philosophies of Plato, Aristotle, Kant, Hegel, and Wittgenstein, see the Reading lists for Chs 3–5.

▾ 11 Metaphysics

11.1 What is metaphysics?

Reading: Kant, *Critique of Pure Reason*, Preface and Introduction, (or *Prolegomena*); Ayer, *Language, Truth and Logic*, especially chs I and II; Wittgenstein, *Tractatus Logico-Philosophicus*; *Blue Book*; *Philosophical Investigations*; Popper, *Conjectures and Refutations*, chs 7, 8 and 11

You will remember that a few brief comments were made about metaphysics at the beginning of the book. The purpose of this chapter is to examine a number of central metaphysical issues. But first we shall sketch out some of the differing views about the nature of metaphysics as a branch of philosophy and consider several influential criticisms.

It is not easy to pin down exactly what metaphysics is; so-called metaphysical issues are inextricably linked with problems of epistemology and philosophical logic. But it might fairly be said that while epistemology is about the nature of knowledge and how we have knowledge, metaphysics is concerned rather with what there *is*, or with what we refer to by such all-embracing terms as 'reality', 'existence' and 'being'. This suggests a second feature said by some philosophers to characterize metaphysical thinking, namely a concern with generality or comprehensiveness. While individual sciences, such as physics or biology, and 'human' sciences like history and sociology are concerned with particular and partial investigations into the world, metaphysics, it is said, seeks to articulate and describe the cosmos in its totality. Judged by these broad criteria, Plato was indisputably a metaphysical philosopher, as was Aristotle (who was the first to use the term – see Ch. 4). St Thomas Aquinas was the greatest metaphysician of the medieval period. Building on the foundations laid by Plato and Aristotle, he was concerned not only to reconcile Christian theology with philosophical speculation, but also to analyse such concepts as existence and essence, substance, universals and particulars. In the 'modern' era, Descartes, Leibniz, Hegel, Bradley and Whitehead (who analyses nature in terms of 'processes', 'events', or 'occasions') may be cited as metaphysicians of the first rank. The climate of thought during much of the twentieth century, particularly in Britain, has, however, been largely inimical to metaphysical thinking as a result of the influence of logical positivism and, more recently, so-called linguistic analysis. We shall consider each of these shortly. But first of all some reference must be made to **Kant's** attempted rejection of metaphysics.

In 5.10 we gave a brief outline of Kant's transcendental idealism. We shall not attempt to provide a fuller account here. Quite apart from considerations of space, his *Critique of Pure Reason* will be found quite demanding for the beginner. But it is important to understand the impact that Kant's philosophy made on traditional metaphysical thinking. The essential feature of traditional metaphysics (which for Kant meant particularly the philosophy of Wolff, a disciple of Leibniz) is its concern with a supposed 'reality' that transcends experience and which is alleged to be accessible only to pure reason. It was this characteristic in particular which Kant objected to. As he wrote in the Preface to the First Edition of the *Critique*:

> The perplexity into which [human reason] . . . falls is not due to any fault of its own. It begins with principles which it has no option save to employ in the course of experience, and which this experience at the same time abundantly justifies it in using. Rising with their aid (since it is determined to this also by its own nature) to ever higher, ever more remote, conditions, it soon becomes aware that in this way – the questions never ceasing – its work must always remain incomplete; and it therefore finds itself compelled to resort to principles which overstep all possible empirical employment, and which yet seem so unobjectionable that even ordinary consciousness readily accepts them. But by this procedure human reason precipitates itself into darkness and contradictions; and while it may indeed conjecture that these must be in some way due to concealed errors, it is not in a position to be able to detect them. For since the principles of which it is making use transcend the limits of experience, they are no longer subject to any empirical test. The battle-field of these endless controversies is called metaphysics.   [A viii]

It is Kant's primary aim in the *Critique* to investigate the proper use and limits of reason and as a result to reject the dogmatic claims of metaphysics in a strict sense (that is, the 'metaphysics of speculative reason'). By contrast, both mathematics and natural science are 'possible' and constitute knowledge in so far as they are both grounded in a union of the senses and the understanding, and contain synthetic *a priori* judgements as principles. Nevertheless metaphysics is possible 'as natural disposition':

> For human reason, without being moved merely by the idle desire for extent and variety of knowledge, proceeds impetuously, driven on by an inward need, to questions such as cannot be answered by any empirical employment of reason, or by principles thence derived. Thus in all men, as soon as their reason has become ripe for speculation, there has always existed and will always continue to exist some kind of metaphysics.   [B 21]

(The 'questions' Kant refers to here relate of course to the 'Ideas' of God, freedom and immortality.)

Kant's objections to metaphysical speculation are echoed by **Ayer's** remark in *Language, Truth and Logic*: 'Surely from empirical premises nothing whatsoever concerning the properties, or even the existence, of anything super-empirical can legitimately be inferred' [ch. I]. But the grounds for the logical positivists' criticism of metaphysical claims lie in their doctrines of linguistic 'meaning' and verification:

> The metaphysician . . . does not intend to write nonsense. He lapses into it through being deceived by grammar, or through committing errors of reasoning, such as that which leads to the view that the sensible world is unreal.
>
> One cannot overthrow a system of transcendent metaphysics merely by criticising the way in which it comes into being. What is required is rather a criticism of the nature of the actual statements which comprise it.
>
> [Ayer, ch. I]

And it was the hope of positivists such as Ayer that metaphysical statements might be reformulated by translation into empirical (scientific) statements.

We have already said something about Ayer's 'principle of verification' in 9.2. It is important to note here that since the initial publication of *Language, Truth and Logic*, which, as Ayer himself admits in the second edition, was 'in every sense a young man's book' and 'written with more passion than most philosophers allow themselves to show', his views have undergone some change. In the first edition, a statement is 'weakly' verifiable and therefore meaningful if 'some possible sense-experience would be relevant to the determination of its truth or falsehood'. Recognizing the vagueness of such a criterion and the 'liberality' of a subsequent formulation (in that it 'allows meaning to any statement whatsoever'), Ayer finally proposes that for a (non-analytic) statement to be literally meaningful it should be either directly or indirectly verifiable. A statement is said to be directly verifiable if 'it is either itself an observation-statement, or is such that in conjunction with one or more observation-statements it entails at least one observation-statement which is not deducible from these other premises alone [*Language, Truth and Logic*, Introduction].

*Comments and criticisms

You will of course need to read the introduction to the second edition if you are to understand fully his new formulation of the verification principle and the reasons for his having modified his original position. But it is clear that he remains unsympathetic to traditional metaphysics. So what response can be made to Ayer's use of the criterion of verifiability as a 'methodological principle'?

(1) It should be pointed out first of all that the principle has been criticized by Popper on the grounds that no finite series of observations could ever establish the truth of a hypothesis beyond doubt. Ayer, however, argues [ch. I] that a hypothesis cannot be conclusively confuted (that is, falsified). You can follow up this dispute yourself (see the discussion of Popper's methodology in 8.3 above). So far as the metaphysician is concerned, of course, it matters little whether the 'criterion of demarcation' between science and metaphysics is one of verification or falsification.

(2) One major difficulty with Ayer's verification principle is that the notion of an 'observation-statement' is not as clear as one would wish. He indicates that the truth of such a statement is grounded in the occurrence of some 'sense-content'; and this is defined as an immediate datum of 'outer' or of ' "introspective" sensation'. But, as we have seen (5.10) there are difficulties in Ayer's phenomenalism both in connection with (a) his proposed translation of sentences about 'material objects' and 'minds' into sentences about sense-contents, and (b) the 'privacy' of sense-contents. And it should also be noted that phenomenalist or sense-datum theories are themselves not free of metaphysical assumptions. (This is a point you might like to think about for yourself.)

(3) A second difficulty is that much more than metaphysics seems to be excluded by Ayer's criterion. Take, for example, a statement such as 'happiness is its own reward'. It is arguable that this statement cannot easily be regarded as an observation-statement or that it entails one in conjunction with other such observation-statements. This is not to say of course that human language is not in the last analysis closely linked to what we experience through our senses. But this would not be sufficient for Ayer; for if there is such a connection then all words of the language, including 'metaphysical' terms, could be said to originate from 'observations', though at varying degrees of removal from them (which perhaps might correspond to their relative levels of abstractness).

(4) Statements like 'happiness is its own reward' are clearly meaningful in some sense of the term. So what is their status if the verificationist's translation into observation-statements cannot be easily effected – if at all? Ayer (in the second edition) does grant that 'it is indeed open to anyone to adopt a different criterion of meaning and so to produce an alternative definition which may very well correspond to one of the ways in which the word "meaning" is commonly used'. He doubts though that statements satisfying a different criterion would be capable of being understood in the sense in which we understand scientific or common-sense statements. But what *are* 'common-sense' statements? Is not 'God is good' just as much a common-sense statement as 'happiness is its own reward'? Or, if 'common sense' *can* be defined more narrowly to exclude religious, aesthetic, or more general 'metaphysical' statements (and this might seem to be a rather arbitrary procedure), Ayer does not seem to be denying that such statements might still be understood. Of course statements like 'God is good', 'material objects exist', 'human beings have minds' and so on are probably not scientific: it may be they are not 'common-sensical'. But does it follow that they are *non*-sense? Ayer himself seems to recognize that metaphysicians are unlikely to yield to the claims of the verification principle when he suggests that it needs to be supported by detailed analyses of particular metaphysical arguments if metaphysics is to be effectively eliminated.

Wittgenstein's approach to metaphysics has been equally significant. In his *Tractatus* he suggested that propositions or sentences are in some analogical sense *pictures* of reality, that is, of 'states-of-affairs' in the world. 'Behind' propositions are thoughts which 'contain' the possibility of states-of-affairs.

'Elementary' propositions (of which other propositions are 'truth-functional' complexes) are made up of names which denote simple 'objects' in the world. [There are similarities here between Wittgenstein's thesis and that of Russell (his supervisor at Cambridge) in the latter's 'Logical Atomism': but whereas Russell seeks to identify simple or basic objects as seemingly unanalysable properties or 'sense-data' such as yellow, Wittgenstein fails to identify simples, though he regards them as *a priori* necessary to set out the limits and presuppositions of language (just as Kant was trying to show the limits of reason). Ethics, metaphysics, the 'mystical' are inexpressible: they are 'beyond' the world; they are 'transcendental' (compare Kant's 'noumenal'). Wittgenstein does not dismiss metaphysics as nonsense; things do exist about which we can say nothing. But they are non-sensical, for whatever *can* be said must be expressed in propositions which 'picture' the facts which are *in* and constitute the world. [The *Tractatus* is an extraordinarily complex book, which, despite its logical structure, clarity and perceptive insights, is full of cryptic utterances about language and its relationship to thought and the world. At some stage in your studies you will find it well worth the effort to study the book in depth. Some knowledge of it will in any case be essential if you are to appreciate the significance of Wittgenstein's later writings, especially the *Philosophical Investigations*. The extremely short account given here, however, should enable you at least to investigate the parallels and differences between Wittgenstein's early philosophy and the views of the logical positivists with whom he (and Popper) had regular discussions and who were influenced by the *Tractatus*.]

Not long after the publication of the *Tractatus* Wittgenstein gave up philosophy – thinking that all problems had been solved! However, in 1929 he started to write and teach again, and gradually retracted much of what he had previously written – though there are continuities in his work. His new ideas were circulated in dictated lecture notes of 1933–34 [*The Blue Book*]. These, together with a draft of a possible book [*The Brown Book*], were in due course absorbed into a more extensive and deeper presentation of his thought, later published as *Philosophical Investigations*. As against his position in the *Tractatus*, he now argued that there is not just one universal form of language; and he rejected his earlier view that words have meaning or 'sense' because they are 'pictures' of reality. Rather, language must be seen as being used in a variety of ways, and meaning consists in *use*. Metaphysical puzzles arise, he says, from a *misuse* of language (see also 2.10 and 5.6). What does he mean by this? The characteristic of a metaphysical question, he says, is 'that we express an unclarity about the grammar of words in the *form* of a scientific question' [*Blue Book*]. More generally, metaphysical utterances use ordinary forms of language in odd ways. Suppose I ask, 'How do we know chairs exist?' In reply someone might say, 'Look, use your eyes; you can touch them'. But if I asked whether numbers exist, or 'God exists, it would seem that I was expecting some sort of empirical evidence or criterion. But in our 'ordinary', everyday language do we ever use 'exist' in this sense as applicable to numbers or God? To refer to such 'entities' as if they were objects like chairs, which we can see and feel, is to misuse language. 'Philosophical problems arise when language goes *on holiday*' [*Investigations*,

Sec. 381]. Traditional philosophical problems arise because 'when language is looked at, what is looked at is a form of words and not the use made by the form of words' [*Lectures and Conversations*, I, 5].

'The essential thing about metaphysics: it obliterates the distinction between factual and conceptual investigations' [*Zettel*, Sec. 458]. What the philosopher must do therefore if his intelligence is not to be bewitched by means of language [*Investigations*, Sec. 109] is to look at the ways words are used in ordinary discourse:

> When philosophers use a word – 'knowledge', 'being', 'object', 'I', 'proposition', 'name' – and try to grasp the *essence* of the thing, one must always ask oneself: is the word ever actually used in this way in the language which is its original home? – What *we* do is to bring words back from their metaphysical to their everyday use. [*Investigations*, Sec. 116]

We must 'show the fly the way out of the fly-bottle' [309]. It should be stressed though that although metaphysics for Wittgenstein is 'nonsense', in that it is produced by trying to express by the use of language what ought to be embodied in the grammar, he is not *anti*-metaphysical (any more than he was in the *Tractatus*). Philosophical problems, he says, 'have the character of *depth*. They are deep disquietudes; their roots are as deep in us as the forms of our language and their significance is as great as the importance of our language' [*Investigations*, 111]. Consider the question 'Are sense-data the material of which the universe is made?' There is an objection, Wittgenstein says, to saying that a 'grammatical' movement has been made. 'What you have primarily discovered is a new way of looking at things. As if you had invested a new way of painting; or, again, a new metre, or a new kind of song' [401]. The comparison here with art or poetry is significant. Wittgenstein sees it as entirely desirable to try to talk about art, religion, ethics – and metaphysics: what he criticizes is when ordinary language is used out of its proper context for the purpose. This of course raises the fundamental problem: is language ever anything other than 'ordinary' – can we ever escape the rules of our grammar (that is, our concepts)? This is a question which has been taken up particularly by P.F. **Strawson**, Ryle's successor at Oxford.

As was mentioned at the beginning of this book, Strawson has distinguished between 'descriptive' and 'revisionary' metaphysics [*Individuals*, Introduction]. Descriptive metaphysics, which is represented by such philosophers as Aristotle and Kant, is concerned 'to lay bare the most general features of our conceptual structure'. It is similar in intention to logical or conceptual analysis (such as Wittgenstein's) which relies on a close examination of the actual use of word but it is wider in scope and digs more deeply. 'Ordinary language' philosophies tend to 'assume, and not to expose, those general elements of structure which the metaphysician wants revealed'. Revisionary metaphysicians such as Descartes, Leibniz and Berkeley, on the other hand, seek 'to produce a better structure' of our thought about the world. But it is Strawson's argument that revisionary metaphysics is at the service of descriptive metaphysics; for however much we change our concepts 'there is a massive central core of human thinking which has no history – or none recorded in histories of thought; there are categories and concepts which, in their most fundamental character, change not at all'.

11.2 Existence and reality

Reading: Russell, *Problems of Philosophy*, ch. IX; Searle, *Mind, Language and Society*, ch. 1; Feyerabend, *Farewell to Reason*; Putnam, *Reason, Truth and History*, chs 3 and 5; see also 'Other texts' in the Reading list for this chapter.

Let us leave for the time being these critiques of metaphysics and consider how some metaphysical problems have been treated by a variety of philosophers. We start by making a number of distinctions to help you to get your bearings, as it were.

First of all we must distinguish three closely connected but different questions. (1) What kinds of things exist? This is a question about **ontology**. (2) What kinds of significant assertions can we make about supposedly existent things? This a question about **semantics**. (3) How can we *know* what does or does not exist? This is an **epistemological** question. The second and third questions have already been to some extent dealt with. You should note, for example, the brief examination of Russell's Theory of Descriptions (2.10); Plato's treatment of predication (3.6); and our investigation of knowledge and belief with reference to 'facts', material objects, phenomena and sense-data, minds (Ch. 5 *passim*), sub-atomic particles (Chs 5 and 8) and God (Ch. 9).

The second important set of distinctions allows us to construct a kind of framework within which all the above issues can be usefully considered. Philosophers from Greek times down to the present day may be regarded (more or less) as **realists** or **antirealists**. Realism in turn may be subdivided into what may be loosely termed **strong** and **weak** varieties.

Strong realists agree that there is a world 'out there' – we might call it 'Nature'; and it is the job of the philosopher to attain, comprehend, describe, explain, or 'mirror' it, to attain the ultimate or absolute Truth about it. Strong realism aspires to an ideal of perfect knowledge, the one true descriptive and explanatory system. Particularly characteristic of the eighteenth century Enlightenment thinkers it is nevertheless a view common to many philosophers from earliest times, even though they may have differed greatly in their assumptions and methods. Plato, Aristotle, Aquinas, rationalists such as Descartes and Spinoza, and 'moderate' empiricists such as Locke, may all be regarded as strong realists, arguing as they do that we can have knowledge of or insight into it through pure reason or through reason grounded in sense-experience. Even idealists such as Berkeley and Hegel do not dispute that there is a real and knowable world, though they think of it as intrinsically mental – the manifestation of God or 'Spirit/Mind' (*Geist*). Kant (a 'critical idealist' or 'empirical realist') is somewhat ambivalent – depending on what 'spin' one puts on his words in the *Critique of Pure Reason*. If we regard the 'noumenon' as an actual 'thing in itself', it is real but unknowable: our knowledge is then confined to phenomena. If, however, the noumenon is considered to be but a negative or limiting concept, then the phenomenal world *is* the real world but one which can be known only as structured through the forms of intuition and understanding. On the basis of this latter interpretation Kant may perhaps be seen as a forerunner of weak realism (sometimes called 'internal realism' or 'perspectivism'). This is the thesis that there is indeed a real world but it can be known only from a particular perspective – from within a particular conceptual scheme or cultural world-view, or coloured by our environment and education. There may well be an 'absolute' or 'objective' standpoint – God's point of view, we may say, but this is inaccessible to the human observer and thinker. We cannot get outside, as it were, to view this world, including ourselves, as it 'really' is. Some such view as this (and again philosophers often differ greatly from each other) seems to be held by Wittgenstein, Strawson, Quine, Putnam, T. Nagel and Searle. The debate between strong and weak realism has been quite intense in recent years – and it is not confined to philosophers working in the 'analytic' tradition. The dispute between two significant 'Continental' philosophers, Gadamer and Habermas, may also be not unfairly interpreted as exemplifying that between weak and strong realism respectively. (See Ch. 12.)

What of antirealism? Here too there are different kinds. Sceptical empiricists such as Hume argue that while we have a natural belief in the existence of an external world, judged by philosophical standards such a belief is false; there is no way this natural belief could be verified, and we can therefore have no knowledge of a 'real' world. Other philosophers have come to adopt an antirealist position from different directions – from philosophical logic (Dummett, for example), from the natural sciences (Feyerabend), or from linguistics (Derrida). While again there are marked differences between these various thinkers, the common theme is that in some sense we make our own realities; the idea of a world composed of ultimate entities, substances and essences, which can be known, whether completely or partially, whether from one or different points of view, is untenable. There is no ultimate or absolute 'Truth', no Holy Grail of metaphysical speculation. There is only an infinite variety of relative conceptual or linguistic schemes. Derrida says there is no reference outside the text (*hors texte*). Richard Rorty has described philosophy as but another kind of 'conversation' in our cultural life, its function being to analyse different forms of discourse and cultural practices so as to achieve 'better' ways of talking and acting.

In this section we shall look first at realist answers to the first of the three questions listed above and consider their treatment of such traditional concepts as substance and universals, and then 'being' itself. After that we shall consider the claims of antirealism, with particular reference to the second question, before dealing with 'weak' realism as perhaps a middle way.

*Note: It cannot be emphasized too strongly that the terms we have been using ('realism', 'antirealism', 'strong' and 'weak') should be regarded as nothing more than convenient pegs on which to hang our discussion. Many philosophers would quite legitimately want to argue that philosopher *A* is not a realist in some sense, or philosopher *B* is a weak rather than a strong realist; or even that such descriptions are inherently misleading. Obviously to deal with such objections would require a book in itself. The important thing is to look at what each philosopher's assumptions and arguments are rather than worry too much about the 'label'.

Substance

Like many technical terms 'substance' has acquired a variety of meanings in the history of philosophy. As we saw in Ch. 4, Aristotle (in his *Categories*) used it to refer to: (a) 'individual' things (for example, man or horse) consisting of matter and form, and which are neither predicable of a subject nor present in it – these individuals are *primary* substances; and (b) *secondary* substances which are variously species of primary substances or the genera of species. However, in his *Metaphysics* it is 'species forms' which are proposed as being substantial in some primary sense. There is much debate among scholars as to whether and how these positions can be reconciled, but there is a broad consensus that he seems to be suggesting that it is the 'form' which actually makes a 'bit' of matter into an individual thing and is thus primary substance in a metaphysical sense, the composite of form and matter being primary substance in some everyday or scientific sense. Aristotle's account of substance led to a great deal of discussion throughout the middle ages and stimulated much of the philosophical debate between rationalists and empiricists from the time of Descartes; and indeed it has continued to this day. Let us look at what Locke had to say about substance. (Look back first at the discussion in 5.10.)

Locke distinguished between 'nominal essence' and 'real essence'. Consider a number of instances of gold. In each case we perceive (for Locke 'have ideas of') such properties or (secondary) qualities as yellow, malleable and so on. By considering these instances we can form the complex abstract idea of a common essence which characterizes this particular 'natural kind' of thing (gold). This is its **nominal essence**. He argues further that we must suppose there to be an internal structure or constitution which supports and indeed provides a scientific explanation of these qualities which give rise to our ideas. This unperceived constitution is the **real essence** of the gold. What then of 'substance'? In our common speech we may talk of gold as a substance, but by this we are more correctly referring to the real essence, and this gives us the idea of *particular* substance. As he says [*Essay*, II, xxiii, 1]: '. . . not imagining how these simple ideas can exist by themselves, we accustom ourselves to suppose some *substratum* wherein they do subsist, and from which they do result; which therefore we call "substance" '; 'Everything in which there resides immediacy, as in a subject, or by means of which there exists anything that we perceive, i.e., any property, quality, or attribute, of which we have a real idea, is called a Substance' [*Arguments Demonstrating the Existence of God*, Definition V]. However, Locke also has the abstract idea of substance *in general*. This he understands as the pure substratum of *all* properties – primary qualities and the 'powers' in them which he says are the cause of our ideas of secondary qualities. The obvious difficulty is that 'substance' in this sense seems to be a rather empty concept if all we can say about it is that it is 'something' in which attributes inhere. And Locke frankly acknowledges this:

> And thus here, as in all other cases where we use words without having clear and distinct ideas, we talk like children who, being questioned what such a thing is which they know not, readily give this satisfactory answer – that it is something which in truth signifies no more, when so used, either by children or men, but that they know not what; and that the thing they pretend to know and talk of is what they have no distinct idea of at all, and so are perfectly ignorant of it and in the dark. [*Essay*, II, xxiii, 2]

In so far as he also says [I, iii, 9] that we cannot get such an idea as pure substance from sensation or reflection Locke seems to be admitting that reference to it is inconsistent with his own empiricist theory of knowledge (see 5.3 and 5.10). He was certainly criticized for his agnosticism by Leibniz, for whom simple substances ('monads') were regarded as 'real unities', 'having no parts' and above all as possessed of activity or inner force: 'substance is a being capable of action'. It is arguable, however, that to talk of substances as active still fails to provide us with any information about their character or 'essence'. It was also pointed out by Hume that we have no *knowledge* of substances other than their 'simple ideas' or attributes. But then we are in danger of falling into the trap of circularity. For if we say that 'the apple is sweet', we would seem to mean no more than that 'this object which consists of properties $a + b + c + \ldots +$ sweetness is sweet'.

Closely associated with the problem of substance is that of **identity**. If the world is made up of substantial entities of some kind or other, we have to consider not only their nature but also how to account for their apparent continuity or 'perdurance' in space and time. There are difficulties here for both Lockean and Humean approaches. If an object is identified in terms of a collection of properties (Hume referred to them as 'bundles of perceptions'), then presumably it must become a different individual should it lose one or more of them, or acquire new ones? This certainly conflicts with our ordinary views of continuity and change. But what *does* continue? Locke's notion of a 'substratum' is equally unsatisfactory. For him it has to be a 'pure' and immutable entity devoid of any properties because it has been introduced solely as a support for them. If we allow that the substratum itself might change as the individual's attributes change, would we not then have to seek a further *sub*-substratum for the substratal changes to inhere in, and so on. Thus the concept of a substantial substratum is either empty or leads to an infinite regress. Moreover, we would still not have solved the central problem of identity. When does a tadpole become a frog, or a seed a plant? If different properties are supported by the same substratum, are not the changes only cosmetic, as it were? If the substratum itself changes, then (leaving aside the possibility of regress) at what point do we say a *new* substance has come into being? We seem to be back with collections of properties. And this in turn raises a further question: are some properties more 'essential' than others? Could a tadpole be yellow and ten metres long?

The problem of identity is now merging into a number of issues which have been long pondered by 'analytic' philosophers since early in the twentieth century. You will remember the brief discussion in 2.10 about Frege's distinction between 'sense' and 'reference'. He argued that the statement 'Phosphorus is [that is, is identical to] Hesperus' is not a tautology, because the names can be replaced by definite descriptions which give them their meaning ('the morning star' and 'the evening star' respectively), which 'fix' the reference, and this happens to be the same entity, namely the planet Venus. Of course a given object may have a variety of descriptions associated with it, many of which are personal or subjective to different people. But Frege said that there are some descriptions which are 'public' and grounded in our rule-guided language. The problem of course is again how we distinguish the 'private' from the 'public' descriptions, particularly if we allow for change – as we must. More recently Strawson and Searle, among other philosophers, have worked out a 'cluster' of descriptions theory, which owes something to Frege's original insights. However, the problem with this is that it is not clear how one is to distinguish between those descriptions in the cluster which are *definitive* of the name that refers to the object and those which are about contingent or accidental attributes. The work of Saul Kripke (and of Putnam, whose views are similar) turns this whole issue on its head. Rejecting any kind of cluster theory he introduces the notion of names as 'rigid designators'. Names have no meaning or sense; they only have reference, and sense does not determine reference. Kripke allows that they may be initially fixed by a description, but the link to a particular object or 'natural kind' (gold, or an individual person, for example) is then maintained by a 'causal chain'. A name continues to apply to the same object in all 'possible worlds'. So 'gold' would still refer to a chemical element of atomic number 79 even if a sample subsequently were found which was non-malleable and green. Consider another example. Suppose we say 'Aristotle' refers to some individual, with a particular kind of 'internal structure' or 'essence', who was born in Stagira, was taught by Plato and so on. One or other of these descriptions may fix the reference of the name, but although it happens to be the case that the individual Aristotle went on to become the teacher of Alexander the Great the name 'Aristotle would still have denoted that same individual even if he had, say, not taught Alexander but had become tutor to the emperor of China.

*Comment and criticisms

Kripke's and Putnam's causal reference theory is convincing. It avoids the possible logical contradiction that might seem to arise if the name of a particular individual is tied to a particular set of descriptors and continues to be used despite changing descriptions. But the theory has its own difficulties. One consequence is that it allows for the introduction of *a posteriori* yet necessary truths and also truths which are contingent and *a priori*; and this is, not surprisingly, highly contentious. (Look back to 5.4 for the classifications of Hume and Kant.) There are also difficulties associated with the introduction of the idea of 'possible worlds' and with modal logic. We shall not consider these rather technical matters here. However, there are other objections. What kinds of 'internal structures' are deemed to be essential? Are the names we use to refer to elements of those structures also rigid designators, in which case we presumably must accept that different descriptors *could* apply? How than could they function as *essential* structures of individuals or natural kinds? Do we not have here too the possibility of infinite regress? Another problem relates to freedom of choice. 'Aristotle' designates a particular individual rigidly by virtue of his inner structure or essence. How then *could* be have become, say, tutor to the Emperor of China, rather than tutor of Alexander the Great while remaining the *same* individual? Firstly it should be noted that the notion of 'sameness' is ambiguous. Kripke would argue that it is the same Aristotle referred to (in virtue of causal continuity) even though different descriptors now apply. But then the introduction of the notion of causal continuity might seem to suggest some form of determinism. (How we explain freedom and reconcile it with our genetic composition ['nature'] and the social and environmental influences on us in our early years['nurture'] is another metaphysical problem to be looked at later.)

Universals

What other kinds of entities might be supposed to populate the universe? Many philosophers from Plato onwards have suggested universals. These have been traditionally associated with the *predicates* in descriptive sentences of the '*S* is *P*' form (whereas 'substance' has been linked with *subjects*). Universals might refer to properties ('*X* is sweet', '*Y* is wise') or to relations ('*A* is bigger than *B*', '*C* is father of *D*'). (See Ch. 2.)

With regard to universals both Plato and Aristotle were **realists**. (Be careful again of this term. Note that a philosopher who is a 'realist' in the sense discussed earlier does not have to hold a realist view of universals.) Plato, you will recall, regarded at least some general terms as denoting Forms or real essences which can be apprehended only through the power of the intellect. They are therefore objects of thought and in some sense independent of mind, though what their actual status was believed to be by Plato is still a matter of controversy (see 3.5 and 3.6, and refer also to 5.5 for Russell's account in *Problems*). Aristotle certainly criticized any account of universals which suggested they 'existed' apart from individual things in some kind of transcendent realm, and he argued that while they are objects of thought (as Plato had claimed) they can exist concretely only *in* things. Aristotle also disagreed with Plato about which terms might be held to relate to universals, denying, for example, that there is a universal 'Goodness'. But these differences apart, both Aristotle and Plato thought of universals as central in the quest for definitions and thus knowledge. For Plato, to grasp a universal 'Form' of a thing is to explain what and why it is. Remember, however, that Plato's view as to which kinds of general concept – individual objects, attributes – could actually be said to 'have' or point to Forms varied from book to book.) For Aristotle too (see 4.4), universals as 'first causes', 'necessary definitions', intuitable by *nous* are the ultimate basis for knowledge and explanation – though we may start from our sense-experience.

The Aristotelian realist theory was taken up and modified in the Medieval period by St Thomas Aquinas, who referred to it (following the Arabic philosopher Ibn Sina, or Avicenna (980–1037) as a theory of **universalia in rebus** ('universals in things') as contrasted with the **universalia ante res** ('universals prior to objects') doctrine of Plato (and St Augustine). The importance of Aquinas' contribution to the problem of universals in fact lies in his attempt to reconcile these two opposing traditions. Although he agrees with Aristotle's view that different members of the same species (say, apples) contain within themselves the same individual 'essence' or universal, he also subscribes to a theological version of Platonism, namely that the totality of universals exist in and are identical with God's mind as ideal models and are therefore *ante res*. In fact he goes further and, following Avicenna's interpretation of Aristotle, argues that the 'active' intellect (compare 4.5) 'illumines' and abstracts the universal element implicit in the image of an object as given to us through our senses, impresses it on the 'passive' intellect, and thus produces the universal **concept** (which Avicenna called the universal **post rem** ['after the thing']).

Conceptualism. It would be wrong to think of this theory as an alternative to realism as such, for conceptualists do not deny the *reality* of universals but rather think of them as general concepts (or, in some versions, as images) which are *post res* as just discussed. And as empiricists they differ from St Thomas in the accounts they give of how we generate these universal concepts. Both Locke and Berkeley, for example, appeal to the notions of **resemblance** and **representation**. Thus:

> The mind makes the particular ideas, received from particular objects, to become general; which is done by considering them as they are in the mind, such appearances separate from all other existence, and the circumstances of real existence, as time, place, or any other concomitant ideas. This is called 'abstraction', whereby, ideas taken from particular beings become general representatives of all of the same kind; and their names, general names, applicable to whatever exists conformable to such abstract ideas. Such precise, naked appearances in the mind . . . the understanding lays up (with names commonly annexed to them) as the standards to rank real existences into sorts, as they agree with these patterns, and to denominate them accordingly. Thus, the same colour being observed today in chalk or snow, which the mind yesterday received from milk, it considers that appearance alone, makes it a representative of all of that kind, and having given it the name 'whiteness', it by that sound signifies the same quality wheresoever to be imagined or met with; and thus universals, whether ideas or terms, are made.   [Locke, *Essay*, II, xi, 9]

While, for Berkeley, '. . . an idea, which considered in itself is particular, becomes general by being made to represent or stand for all other particular ideas of the *same sort*' [*Principles of Human Knowledge*, Introduction, XII].

It should be noted here that Berkeley's positive thesis is actually presented in the context of a sustained criticism of Locke for his **abstractionist** account. Elsewhere in the *Essay* [see, for example, III, ii, 6–9] Locke had maintained that given a group of similar individual things (for example, men or triangles) the mind arrives at the general idea by leaving out of the compound idea of the group what is particular to each member but retaining what is common. But how, asks Berkeley [*Principles*, Introduction, XV], could one 'frame an idea of a triangle which was neither equilateral, nor scalenon, nor equicrural'? It is only that particular triangle, he says, which equally stands for and represents all rectilinear triangles whatsoever that can be said to be universal. How fair Berkeley's criticism is of Locke is debatable. Locke's terminology is, however, notoriously ambiguous: 'idea' is used variously to refer to a mental or psychological concept and to an image. It would certainly be difficult to understand what an *image* might be like which has not particular characteristics.

Resemblance is also invoked by Hume [*Treatise*, I, i, 7], who, while following Berkeley, closely links the notion with his own doctrine of 'association' (see 5.3). When we have a particular idea we are able to associate it with others of a similar type on account of a mental capacity or predisposition which has been acquired through earlier habitual associations – mediated by the same general *word* we apply to each experience of the idea. (*This appeal to a general term as the means by which particular ideas are universalized is to be contrasted with Berkeley's position, according to which 'a word becomes general by being made the sign, not of an *abstract* general idea, but of several particular ideas of the same sort, any one of which it indifferently suggests to the mind' [*Principles*, Introd., XI]. Compare Locke: 'Words become general by being made the signs of general ideas' [*Essay*, III, iii, 6]).

Nominalism. According to this view universals do not 'really' exist; what two objects, which we believe to have some property in common, for example, redness, actually share is nothing other than the term 'red'. This is, however, an extreme version of the theory, held especially by William of Ockham (*c.* 1285–1349). A more moderate form of the doctrine was espoused by Hobbes, for whom the denial of universality consisted in the assertion that all named things are 'singular and individual'. But it is on account of the 'similitude in some quality, or other accident' [*Leviathan*, III, 21] that one universal name is imposed on a given class of things. And as he says in his *De Corpore* that 'names are signs not of things, but of our cogitations' [I, 17], it would seem that his nominalism approximates to the conceptualism of Hume which also appeals to resemblances between objects.

*Comments

As we have seen, moderate nominalism is hardly distinguishable from a variety of conceptualism. As to the more extreme theory, it is difficult to see how this could have ever got off the ground. If there is nothing in common between the qualities in different things, to which the general name is applied (or which are included in the same concept denoted by the name), what is the justification for using the *same* general name? At the very least it must be an arbitrary one. Moreover, it is doubtful whether language could function at all on such a basis, for each person might well be appealing to a different criterion of usage.

Conceptualist accounts seem to be more acceptable, but in so far as general concepts presuppose common or similar elements in different things it is not certain that the problem of universality has been satisfactorily resolved. If we say that two tomatoes are both red, are we not affirming that there is such a thing as redness? The argument here is really about what we mean by 'thing' or 'is/exists'. So let us return to a moderate realist view such as Aristotle's. Is there anything wrong with this? If by saying that the two tomatoes both exhibit redness we mean no more than that they are both of the same colour then our statement is innocuous, and it is unnecessary to introduce the language of 'universals' at all which seems to do no more than obscure the issue. (Whether the colour 'exists' *in* the actual tomatoes or 'in' our minds – as 'sense-data', for example – is another matter of course, which we looked at in 5.10.) The realist account, however, is rather more dubious if – as Aristotle and Plato claim – the appeal to universals helps us *explain* the nature of objects. To say a tomato is red because it 'shares in' the universal redness does not tell us anything more than what we know already, namely that it is red! A further difficulty with realist theories is that in the case of certain sorts of descriptive qualities things do not come 'ready made' with them, as it were; rather it is we who decide which descriptions are appropriate in the circumstances. Thus, a lump of wood may be described as a lump of wood, a chair, or a work of art (perhaps a piece of sculpture depicting an animal). A realist theory could not easily accommodate the notion of different 'universals' ('chairness', 'animality') being present 'in' the object simultaneously and seemingly dependent on the observer for their 'existence'.

It has been suggested by Strawson in his article 'Universals' that conceptualism and (naturalist) realism are in fact two contrasting theories between which no reconciliation is possible, as there is no impartial standpoint from which they may be judged. This is something you might like to think about. Do you agree with him? Compare his approach here with the similar approach he makes to the problem of freedom and necessity – see 11.5. What *does* it mean to say that redness 'exists' (a) in thought, and (b) in things?

There are two further important general points that need to be made about the problems of both substances and universals:

(1) At the heart of these metaphysical disputes lies an erroneous view of meaning. In our ordinary discourse words like 'apple' or 'red' are used to refer to perceivable objects and qualities. It has been assumed either tacitly or explicitly by some philosophers (for example, Plato and early Russell) that words acquire their meaning by virtue of this denotation. This has resulted in a philosophical wild-goose chase for the 'real' or 'existing' denotata allegedly corresponding to other names such as 'matter' or 'redness', as if they were analogous to physical objects. Indeed the search for 'meanings' can itself be thought to exemplify the same error – as if there were 'things' called meanings floating around in a kind of metaphysical space waiting to be attached to words. Wittgenstein has argued that to avoid this kind of error one should look at the actual ways in which these words are used in our ordinary language [see *Philosophical Investigations*, Secs 116, 124, and compare Ryle's notion of the category mistake which we looked at in 5.6]. He

is also critical of the view that there need necessarily be certain resemblances common to all usages of a word which might underpin the appeal to 'universals'. Thus, talking of the word 'game' he writes:

> Don't say: 'There *must* be something common, or they would not be called "games" ' – but *look* and *see* whether there is anything common to all. For if you look at them you will not see something which is common to *all*, but similarities, relationships, and a whole series of them at that. To repeat: don't think, but look! Look for example at board-games, with their multifarious relationships. Now pass to card-games; here you find many correspondences with the first group, but many common features drop out, and others appear. When we pass next to ball-games, much that is common is retained, but much is lost. Are they all 'amusing'? Compare chess with noughts and crosses. Or is there always winning and losing, or competition between players? Think of patience. In ball-games there is winning and losing; but when a child throws his ball at the wall and catches it again, this feature has disappeared. Look at the parts played by skill and luck; and at the difference between skill in chess and skill in tennis. Think now of games like ring-a-ring-a-roses; here is the element of amusement, but how many other characteristic features have disappeared! . . .
>
> And the result of this examination is: we see a complicated network of similarities overlapping and criss-crossing; sometimes overall similarities, sometimes similarities of detail.   [*Philosophical Investigations*, Sec. 66]

You might also note Berkeley's attack on Locke, who claimed that words have signification by virtue of the fact that they 'stand for ' ideas, that is, concepts or possibly images; and that the purpose of language is to communicate our ideas. 'Whereas, in truth', wrote Berkeley [*Principles*, Introd., XVIII], 'there is no such thing as one precise and definite signification annexed to any general name, they all signifying indifferently a great number of particular ideas'. Moreover he points out [XX] that language has *many* ends; it is not just for the communication of thought (compare Wittgenstein, *Philosophical Investigations*, Sec. 23).

(2) We have discussed the concepts of substance and universal with reference to, respectively, the subject and predicate which are characteristic of the traditional logical formulation of sentences. However, it should be obvious to you that this identification is not rigid. We might talk of a chair as a substance (as in 'the chair is brown'). What was a subject now seems itself to be predicated of a different subject. This of course brings us back to Aristotle's distinctions between primary and secondary substance and between genera and species, with all their attendant difficulties. An alternative approach is provided by Strawson in *Individuals*. The subject–predicate form can be preserved provided we interpret subject-expressions as referring to *particulars* and as being 'complete', whereas predicate-expressions are not 'complete'. By 'particulars' he means 'individuals' in a broad sense such as 'historical occurrences, material objects, people and their shadows'. Qualities, properties, numbers and species, however, are not. As

for the notion of (in)completeness, a subject-expression is complete in the sense that it 'presents a fact in its own right'; while a predicate-expression is incomplete to the extent that it does not [*Individuals*, p.187]. Thus, if I say 'Socrates' or 'that person there 'is wise I presuppose that there is an individual there who can be identified in relation to the space–time system by the use of appropriate descriptions (appearance, position and so on). The subject-expression can therefore lead to an affirmation of a fact. By contrast a predicate-expression ('is wise') on its own cannot do this [see Strawson, *Individuals*, pp.186, 232]. Strawson makes it clear that the use of a subject-term does not commit us to the actual *existence* of the denotatum (as in the case of 'The man-in-the-moon lives on cheese'). Here we have an expression which apparently refers but does not in fact do so, in which case the proposition is simply false. (Contrast this with Russell's Theory of Descriptions; see 2.10). Or:

> We can see it simply as operating in a different realm of discourse, the realm of myth, fiction or fancy rather than that of fact. In these realms, within limits which we lift and impose in various ways, we can presuppose existences and allocate truth-values as we choose.   [*Individuals*, p.228]

Being

We now turn to the controversial figure of Martin **Heidegger** (1889–1976) – controversial both as a thinker and as a human being. He has been regarded by many critics, particularly those in the logical positivist and analytical traditions, as a charlatan, the writer of dense, almost unreadable, indeed nonsensical tomes. By others he has been lauded as the greatest philosopher of the twentieth century. He has also been strongly criticized for his support of National Socialism in the nineteen thirties and forties and for his failure to condemn the persecution of the Jews by the Third Reich. However, our concern here is with Heidegger the philosopher; and certainly as such he has exerted a profound influence not only on other philosophers, including Sartre, Merleau-Ponty, Gadamer, Habermas and Derrida but also on workers in the fields of literature, theology and psychology. He cannot therefore be ignored. Notwithstanding the seeming impenetrability of *Being and Time* and his other writings, they should be studied as far as possible with an open mind; the issues he grappled with throughout his life are genuine philosophical *aporia* (problems), and how he sought to solve them should be examined seriously.

Heidegger's central concern was with the concept of **Being** – the true significance of which, he argued, man from the time of the Presocratics onwards has lost hold of. All attempts by earlier ontologists to give an account of being in terms of substances and categories, matter, noumena, 'transcendental egos', phenomena and so on have, in his opinion, all failed. A further objection to this 'metaphysics of presence' is that such philosophizing is inherently theoretical and assumes there is some ultimate 'objectivity' which can be accessed. This is not to say that Heidegger is adopting an antirealist position, but rather what is real is revealed in man's *practical* engagement with the world. This is his concern in Part I, Division 1 of *Being and Time*.

While critical of Husserl's theoretical stance, Heidegger uses the phenome-nological method himself to uncover the underlying structure of human existence. The starting point must be **Dasein**. This term means 'being here/there', 'being situated', or 'being-in-the-world'; and Heidegger introduced it to refer to us humans as beings who experience themselves in the every-day situation as being 'thrown' into the world – as already belonging to a 'lived' world. This cultural and historical world conditions us and hides phenomena which Heidegger thinks of as constituting an implicit 'pre-theoretical' sense, a 'primordial understanding' of our situation as personal agents in this world He argues further that we manifest our human 'existentiality' in realizing our anticipated possibilities – thereby reaching Being.

As Dasein we can be said not only to be 'thrown' into the world and limited by its 'facticity', but also as able to 'take a stand' (in forming our projects), and as articulating in discourse (usually through language) the intelligibility of things in the world. This can be made clearer by considering a concrete example Heidegger himself used to illustrate what he means and what is involved in the concept of Dasein. Consider someone using a hammer in his or her workshop. When engaging in this activity what he or she is attending to is not the hammer, nails, wood and their various properties but rather the practical project – the process considered as leading to an end having a purpose, fulfilling a function. Heidegger here distinguishes between what he calls 'present-to-handedness' (*Vorhandenheit*) and 'ready-to-handedness' (*Zuhandenheit*). Objects consi-dered as present-to-hand are in a sense abstractions from their practical use, particularly when they are treated as physical objects for scientific investigation and explanation. In our everyday engagement with the world, however, objects are ready-to-hand, are being used, appropriated for projects; and this for Heidegger constitutes primacy – present-to-handedness being secondary or derivative. In this utilization lies what he calls the world's 'worldhood' (*Weltlichkeit*) – a holistic network of functional relationships. He regards this worldhood as the primary object of intentionality – in terms of which alone theoretical and practical intentionality, in the Husserlian sense, can be understood.

This example is important because it draws attention to the possibilities of Dasein and points to the significance for Heidegger of the relationship between self and the world. Dasein is understood as acting as a 'clearing' through which entities in the world can reveal themselves (can 'stand forth'). It is thus the instrument through which Being itself emerges from concealment into presence.

In the course of his *magnum opus* Heidegger introduces a number of technical terms – 'interpretation', 'care', 'fallenness', 'anxiety' (*Angst*), 'conscience', 'guilt' and 'destiny'. Most of these, together with his concern with death as a threat and as terminating the possibilities of Dasein (its projects and choices), and his lengthy analysis [in Part I, Division 2 of *Being and Time*] of authentic and inauthentic temporality of Dasein seem to emphasize the existential aspects of his thought. But he himself rejected this interpretation. He had intended to write a third Division to be devoted to the presentation of a fundamental ontology of Being, but the book ends with a number of unresolved questions concerning the relation of Being to Time. Dasein has been presented as disclosing Being. But Heidegger concludes by asking how this disclosure is possible. Do we have to go back to the primordial constitution-of-being of that Dasein? Furthermore, there are problems with temporality. If the existential-ontological constitution of Dasein's totality is grounded in temporality, how are we to interpret this 'ec-statical' (that is, 'outside of itself') projection of being, this mode of 'temporalizing of temporality'? Can we get from primordial time to the meaning of Being? 'Does time itself manifest itself as the horizon of Being?', he asks. There are other problems too. Can the unity of Being be reconciled with the plurality of Dasein? Is Heidegger's account of finitude, the inevitable culmination of life in death, consistent with his assumption that the individual can be fully realized only when he ceases to be real, that is when he ceases to be? And perhaps the key problem is how Being in itself is to be understood, that is, considered apart from its revelation through the engaged agency of Dasein. Can this question be considered at all?

Unfortunately, Division 3 never appeared. And neither did Part II of *Being and Time*, which was to have been an exploration of the basic features of a phenomenal 'de-struction' of the history of ontology – the problematic of temporality being the clue. By 'de-struction' Heidegger means, negatively, that the ontological tradition from the ancient Greek philosophers down to Hegel, as it is treated nowadays, must be shaken off, loosened up, but with the positive aim of 'dissolving' the concealment or forgetting of being which he supposed that tradition to have brought about. (The 'de-struction' of Kant was partly fulfilled in his important 1929 book *Kant and the Problem of Metaphysics*, but this made little or no contribution to the exposition of the fundamental ontology of time and being which the unwritten Division 3 of Part I was to have provided. It would seem that Heidegger had come to realize that such an ontology might not be attainable.)

From 1930 onwards there appears to have been a 'turn' (*Kehre*) or change of direction in his thinking – though he stressed that his new approach was but a reorientation, with a different emphasis on the still central concept of Being as presence. His general approach is indicated in his *Introduction to Metaphysics* (1935), which is concerned primarily with answering the 'fundamental question of metaphysics' – Why does anything [any 'essent'] exist? Obviously only a few general themes can be indicated here. His initial concern is to determine what is meant by 'essents', indeed, what the essence of Being is; how to get beyond the 'blunted, indefinite meaning of the word'. He starts with the Greek philosophers who, he says, identified the essent with *phusis* or nature. He interprets this as a special kind of process inherent in Being itself, whereby essents become observable. It is an emergence from the hidden. Heidegger attempts to show in due course this concept became restricted and Being came to be forgotten. What he seeks to do is to restore the centrality of Being and man's 'being-there' – which he associates with the need to recover the Western world's spiritual destiny from the technological and nihilistic forces threatening it in his own day. Heidegger explicitly says he is not now attempting to establish a traditional ontology in which the question of being means an enquiry into being as such, or the defining of the transcendental in terms of Dasein. He is concerned not with 'the existential ec-static temporality of the human being-there' but rather with Being as the subjective consciousness of the human essent.

An examination of essents, be they tools, vehicles, mountains, Bach's fugues, Hölderlin's hymns or the Earth itself – for the purposes of which he makes use of some highly questionable etymology of Greek terms and quotations – shows that while 'being' is a universal name, the name itself and what it names are unique. The 'is' discloses itself to us in many ways. The world in its many inflections relates to Being quite differently from the way that all other nouns and verbs relate to the essents expressed in them. But despite the seeming impossibility of identifying a universal generic meaning common to the many modes of 'is' as species there is, Heidegger says, a single determinate trait. This directs our contemplation of Being to a definite unifying and determining horizon of understanding and thus contains the meaning within the realms of actuality and presence, permanence and duration, abiding and occurrence. So if we are to preserve the historical importance of the question 'How does it stand with Being?' we must reflect on the source of our hidden history and will thereby 'hold to the discourse of being'. Accordingly Heidegger embarks [ch. 4] on an investigation of how Being has come to be limited in its relations with Becoming, Appearance, Thinking and 'the Ought'.

*Comment

Many commentators see Heidegger's later speculations as becoming ever more bizarre. But it is fair to say that what we find in *An Introduction to Metaphysics* through to his last writings is a move from the subjectivity or centrality of Dasein as the agent for the revelation of Being towards the view that man is used by Being for its 'safekeeping'; man is conceived as the 'shepherd of Being'. There is a central paradox in that to the extent man seeks to uncover Being – for example, through speculation, present-to-handedness, Being becomes concealed: 'Being conceals itself through emerging-into-presence'. This ties in with his earlier critique of the theoretical stance and of real presences. But more significantly is his account of the role of language. Language is now no longer regarded as a tool or instrument by means of which Dasein can engage with and thereby understand the multifarious modes of Being. Rather language itself is, as he puts it (in his *Letter on Humanism*), 'the house of Being and it is by dwelling [there] that man ek-sists'; language speaks to man. We can perhaps say that language is in a sense ontologically prior to Dasein. We also find Heidegger appealing to a philosophical poetry. As he says in the *Introduction to Metaphysics*, 'Language is the primordial poetry in which a people speaks Being' [p.144], and in particular he looks to the writings of Hölderlin to restore this pristine relationship to Being. In his *On the Way to Language* (1957) he introduces the concept of 'the Fourfold' (*das Geviert*). By this somewhat mythical notion he seems to be referring to the cosmos as an 'interplay' between earth, sky, man and the gods, and which constitutes the 'saying' of Being to man – through 'poetic language, as it were.

All this must seem to be exceedingly obscure. One longs for the clarity to be found in the writings of such philosophers as Ayer, Ryle and Searle. Perhaps

Heidegger's tortuous prose and his idiosyncratic terminology are inseparable from his passionate concern with the human condition and its destiny – the style is the man. However, there is a certain thread of continuity in his developing philosophy, which should be stressed and can serve to round off this inadequate account of his thought. This relates to the concept of temporality. Shortly after *Being and Time* had been published, Heidegger introduced a distinction between the temporality of Dasein (*Zeitlichkeit*) and the temporality of Being (*Temporalität*). Unfortunately his account of the latter and its relation to Dasein is incomplete and not worked out systematically; and it is unclear how it fits in with other distinctions already made in *Being and Time* between temporal and atemporal realms of Being. He subdivides the temporal realm into two modes, Nature and History; the atemporal realm into the extra-temporal and the supra-temporal. But in what sense is being extra- or supra-temporal? Is he referring here to some kind of Husserlian realm of essence? And how can Dasein belong to both categories of history (*qua* person) and Nature? Can Dasein confront Nature 'in itself', that is, prior to both its 'present-to-handedness' and 'ready-to-handedness'? Is this what is implicit in the concept of the 'Fourfold' and to be achieved through the poetic? Is there a suggestion here of a mystical strain in Heidegger's last years – a pointing to atemporal Being beyond all understanding?

If you are brave enough to venture further into the realm of Heideggerian philosophy, you will find some helpful commentaries listed in the Reading list at the end of this chapter.

Reality and language: the flight from realism

You will have gathered from your reading of this section so far that a concern with language is central in the work of most major twentieth century philosophers; and this is as true for many continental thinkers as it is for philosophers in the 'anglophone' analytic tradition. (Rorty, in his essay 'Wittgenstein, Heidegger, and the reification of language', argues plausibly that the thought of the early (*Tractatus*) Wittgenstein has much in common with the post-*Kehre* Heidegger, and vice versa: but you must consider this for yourself.) What is important for our present discussion is the relevance of language to the problem of realism. And it has been widely accepted that the antirealist positions adopted by some contemporary philosophers can be seen as a kind of neo-Kantianism translated into linguistic terms.

Firstly, consider again the 'strong' interpretation of Kant's critical philosophy. Noumenal reality is placed beyond our grasp: it is the world in itself and unknowable. We are left instead with a phenomenal world of 'representations', which for Kant of course are intuited under the forms of sensibility and structured by the forms of the understanding; and it is these forms that are the source of synthetic *a priori* knowledge. However, this, together with the notion of 'things-in-themselves', is rejected by empiricist and logical positivist philosophers. What matters to them is what we are actually 'given' in our experience; for it is sense-data which both serve as a foundation for knowledge and the basis for the method of verification, which offers a criterion for the meaningfulness of the statements we use. As you saw earlier with Ayer, it has become but a matter of convenience or utility whether we use a sense-datum language or a material-object language. There is no way we can get 'outside' to check that data do in fact represent or copy 'real' objects.

The antirealist implications of verificationism are shown clearly in the work of Michael **Dummett** (b. 1925). Many philosophers have argued that to understand a proposition, to know what it means, is to know what its 'truth-conditions' are, that is, what makes it true. However, Dummett rejects the view that truth is implicitly understood (in correspondence theories, for example). And instead of searching for 'transcendent' truth-conditions he argues for a verificationist-pragmatic approach to meaning. 'Truth' is to be understood in terms of 'verification-conditions', which justify our acceptance of truth-conditions. (In logic and mathematics, for example, verification-conditions relate to our ability to recognize that there are proofs for statements.) However, the problem is that while truth-conditions are sometimes explicit, there are many situations in which we do not – and indeed could not know what those conditions are (particularly with reference to past or future events, or, in the case of subjunctives, counter-factual conditionals). They are 'verification-transcendent'. As a consequence Dummett argues that 'bivalence' must be abandoned, that is, the view that every proposition is either true or false; for otherwise we are committed to a notion of transcendent truth.

Despite the tendency to antirealism of logical positivism and verificationist philosophies they are in general committed to the concept of progress in the natural sciences. Even this, however, is rejected by Thomas Kuhn and Paul Feyerabend (though Kuhn seems to have mellowed somewhat in his more recent work). As mentioned in 8.4, they argue that technical terms may have different meanings and reference at different times and in the context of different theories. As a result there is no meeting point between scientists belonging to different cultures or committed to different 'paradigms'. This is often called the 'incommensurabilty' thesis. It is then concluded that there can be no absolute or objective truth towards which science can progress – even asymptotically in the way that, say, Popper suggests.

*Comments and criticisms

Because of the technicalities involved we shall not comment further on Dummett's antirealism. As for Feyerabend, one can reply by arguing that although some terms may change their meaning and indeed their reference in the course of time, it does not follow that communication breaks down utterly. Certainly the emergence of a new theory may enable us to look at a phenomenon in a new way, and may give us a different explanation. But how could this be recognized if we did not already have some access to and grasp of what the previous theorists were attempting to say? In other words, is not some translatability between different theories or paradigms a *sine qua non* for understanding the changes in content and scope of the later as compared with the earlier explanatory mode? It is also arguable that in the course of time scientific theories have indeed become better and 'truer' as they have come to be grounded in more comprehensive or wide-ranging principles which in some real sense have allowed us to explain phenomena more completely. If our understanding of biology or gravity were still Aristotelian it is doubtful if we could have landed on the Moon or cracked the genetic code. These necessarily few comments are of course unfair to Feyerabend. You are directed to his *Against Method* for an entertaining account of his arguments and his replies to critics.

Let us return to the issue of 'structuring'. Many thinkers are happy to accept that our experience is in some sense structured but – as against Kant – they argue that there is not just one mode of structuring intrinsic to our human powers. Rather, experience, and indeed our conceptual apparatus, is itself determined by the language we use. This view has arisen largely as a result of a particular view of language developed in Europe by the Swiss linguist Ferdinand de Saussure (1857–1913) and in America by Franz Boas (1858–1942) and Edward Sapir (1884–1939). This is the theory of **structuralism**; and it has given rise to a particular variety of relativistic antirealism.

The central thesis proposed by de Saussure is that language must exist in some sense prior to its instantiation in individual speech-situations or, to use today's terminology, speech-acts. Language is regarded as possessing meaning in itself, as it were, rather than as the intentional object of mental acts or of psychological 'contents'. This thesis is implicit in de Saussure's distinction between '*langue*' and '*parole*'. '*Langue*' refers to the total structure of 'signs', that is, meanings and words, which *parole*, as a set of individual speech-acts (be they English, Chinese, or any other language), instantiates. Furthermore de Saussure argues in favour of a holistic approach to language. The meaning of a given word or term – considered as a 'sign' – is to be understood relationally. When I say, for example, that an object is red, this entails it is not green, blue and so on. What is signified is not some underlying non-linguistic 'essence'. Signification consists rather in the role played by the written or spoken word in the total structure of system elements or 'signifiers'. De Saussure thereby emphasizes synchronicity rather than diachronicity: co-temporal relationships rather than concern with the origins and growth of language through time.

The significance of this kind of approach can be seen particularly clearly in the writings of the American linguist Benjamin Lee Whorf. His hypothesis is, roughly, that the concepts we use – Whorf refers to 'cryptotypes' or 'categories of semantic organization' – are determined by our language, and that therefore as we switch from one language to another so will our 'world-view' change. His thesis thus seems to be even more wide-ranging than Feyerabend's:

> The forms of a person's thoughts are controlled by inexorable laws of pattern of which he is unconscious. These patterns are the unperceived intricate systematizations of his own language . . . And every language is a vast pattern-system, different from others, in which are culturally ordained the forms and categories by which the personality not only communicates, but also analyzes nature, notices or neglects types of relationship and phenomena, channels his reasoning, and builds the house of his consciousness.   [*Language, Thought, and Reality*, p.252]

Whorf came to this conclusion as a result of his field research into the language of the Hopi Indians. He claimed, for example, that the Hopi verb lacks tenses and that the Hopi do not need to use terms that refer to space or time as such. Spatial and temporal terms are

> recast into expressions of extension, operation, and cyclical process provided they refer to the solid objective realm. They are recast into expressions of subjectivity if they refer to the subjective realm – the future, the psychic-mental, the mythical period, and the invisibly distant and conjectural generally. [p.64]

The general consensus of linguists and philosophers who have investigated this problem, however, is that the hypothesis does not stand up to close examination. All human beings seem to be endowed with much the same physiological and mental apparatus for responding to and talking about the world; and there seems to be no convincing evidence to suppose that we do not all work with the same kinds of 'hard-core' concepts (material objects, persons, space, time, number and so on) regardless of the language we use. The Whorfian hypothesis does however carry some credibility if it is interpreted in a weaker sense to refer to the reflection of cultural idiosyncrasies, particularly of a practical nature, in the grammar and vocabulary of a given language. Eskimo contains a large number of words meaning 'snow', each emphasizing a special aspect. Some Australian Aborigine languages are alleged to have no number words above 'three'. Likewise, it is probably true to say that certain words have 'emotional' overtones (think of the significance of '*Heimat*' for Germans) or make complete sense only in the context of the culture in which they are grounded (for example, words which refer to customs, religious rites, codes of honour, and so on).

A more extreme position – we might call it 'strong antirealism' is held by another controversial philosopher, the 'post-structuralist' Jacques **Derrida** (b. 1931), who is discussed here not so much for the quality of his thinking (again critics disagree about this) as for the sheer boldness and inconoclastic nature of his claims. Like Heidegger, Derrida has been both revered and reviled, derided and, it would seem, almost deified by his many acolytes who are increasingly found occupying key vantage points on the intellectual scene, from which they launch their assaults on traditionalists, humanists, realists and all those who still believe philosophy has an important contribution to make to human life and culture.

Derrida's concern – one might even regard it as an obsession – is with what he calls the 'logocentrism' of Western philosophy. By this he means a 'realist' view that through philosophy, conceptual analysis and system-building, the philosopher can gain access to, grasp, intuit a 'reality' which is signified, pointed to, described by language as signifier. As we have already seen, this reality has been referred to in a multitude of ways by different philosophers: Plato's Forms or Ideas, substances (Aristotle and others), Husserl's essences, truth, the self, Being and God. Following Heidegger, Derrida talks of the 'metaphysics of presence'. A corollary of this realism is a set of characteristic polarizations or oppositions which, in his view, have brought about paradoxes and contradictions.

Such oppositions include appearance–reality (obviously), logos–mythos, intelligible–sensible, nature–culture, mind–body, self–other, intuition–signification, and even speech as against writing. Derrida sees it as his task to expose the sterility of this whole enterprise which, until the twentieth century, has seemed to be an unquestioned assumption of the Western philosophical tradition. Western philosophy, he says, has to be 'deconstructed'. This term has something in common with Heidegger's *Destruktion* but Derrida is more radical, and he also regards Heidegger himself as having fallen under the spell of the metaphysics of presence. By means of deconstruction Derrida questions and sees himself as undermining these traditional assumptions and categories, and thereby, if not actually bringing philosophy to an end, at least showing it to be a futile activity, though one to which those of us who are prepared to think at all are perhaps condemned to engage in.

By 'deconstruction' Derrida means an activity – it would be inconsistent with Derrida's general tenets to call it a method – which is grounded in a distinction he makes between the 'essential' and the 'inessential', and it applies to every opposition. The inessential (for example, mythos, the sensible and writing) is what appears to be marginal, that is, excluded by the essential pole of a binary opposition (logos, the intelligible and speech). However, inessential characteristics turn out paradoxically also to be features of the essential. He calls this the 'logic of the supplement'. To make this clear we shall look at the opposition between writing and speech. Derrida argues that the intellectual tradition of the West has been characterized not only by logocentrism but also by 'phonocentrism', that is, the subordination of the written word to living speech. This was, he points out, emphasized particularly by Plato [*Phaedrus*] who regarded writing as a kind of alienation from speech and prey to abuse and misunderstanding in that meaning has been distanced from its original living source. Paradoxically, Derrida adds, writing is needed to preserve meaning in absence of speech and the 'presence' in it. He claims that these opposing good and bad aspects are articulated in the double meaning of the word *Pharmakon* used by Plato: 'poison' as well as 'cure'. Derrida argues that if we examine a text with this in mind we shall discover this and similar oppositions, as well as other problems and tensions. These will become apparent if we attend to the seemingly inessential features of the text – metaphors, footnotes, rhetorical devices and the like. In so far as these inessentials are the means whereby these inherent tensions and contradictions can be identified and resolution achieved they become essential; and it is this that constitutes the logic of the supplement.

Arguably, the structuralists may not have denied that language *as a whole* has in some sense or other the characteristic of being 'about' a world. This view of language is rejected by Derrida. He agrees with structuralism that signs are used in an arbitrary way to mark differences and thereby to carry meanings. However, he maintains that it: (1) has succumbed to the logocentrist prejudice, and (2) has preserved the primacy of speech over writing – which Saussure, like Plato, regarded as potentially dangerous. To deal with these errors and to develop his own radical position Derrida argues that there is a fundamental ambiguity in the term 'difference'. In French 'to differ' is *différer* but it can also mean 'to defer'; and this notion of deferring becomes central to Derrida's deconstructionalist thesis.

Meaning for Saussure and the structuralists lies in the 'differential' structures, not in the putative 'presences'. But Derrida goes further. In so far as words carry meaning only in relation to other words, for its meaning to be manifested each word has to be connected to another. This must of course therefore be a never-ending process. A meaning is forever beyond capture, as it were, for we always need another word to articulate a given word's meaning. Alternatively we can say that to understand the meaning of a given word we need to grasp or apprehend the linguistic system or network in its totality – a task which is clearly impossible from within. It is in this respect that Derrida says the text defers the meaning, puts it off. He therefore introduces the term *différance* (spelt with an 'a' rather than an 'e') to designate this concept of deferral.

He argues further that these supplementary features of writing are essential characteristics of speech as well as of writing – speech also being inseparable from context. But it does not follow that speech should now be seen as subordinate to writing, that is, the reverse of the Platonic view. Rather, according to Derrida, implicit in both speech and writing there is what he terms *arché-écriture* ('arche-writing'). This cannot be defined in any objective sense. He means by it that which does not allow itself to be reduced to presence. More-over, that by means of which the difference is manifested through language signifies a difference which lies neither in a subjective self-presence nor in a transcendental objective presence. Put differently (no pun – though Derrida would welcome it as such), it is itself a kind of transcendental condition for the functioning of the differentiating system of signs in such a way that meaning is always deferred. We might think of it as the core concept of his new non-logocentric linguistics – which he calls 'grammatology'. This is not an objective scientific linguistics. (Such objectivity would drag us back into oppositions and contradictions because objectivity implies presence, yet science requires repetition and hence temporal differentiation and deferral, which would undermine the notion of presence.) Rather, grammatology – which is in effect Derrida's own, and for him the only possible philosophy – is manifested or realized in the deconstruction process: this is its proper role.

*Comments and criticism

It may seem that disproportionate space has been devoted to Derrida. If this is so then it is because, in the author's view, he epitomizes – indeed is instrumental in bringing about – what might be called an 'anything goes' mentality in philosophy and cultural life generally. There are two points to be made here:

(1) Quite obviously a major casualty of his attacks is any theory of interpretation which supposes there to be a 'truth' in a text, work of art, culture and the like (see the discussion of Gadamer in Ch. 12 below). For Derrida, deconstruction must give rise to a multitude of textual interpretations, all of equal validity – or invalidity; for no criterion can be appealed to in terms of which they might be scaled other than perhaps unquantifiable pleasure or aesthetic satisfaction. There are also implications for ethics and politics. There can be no absolute values if by such we mean entities akin to metaphysical presences. Nor can

'political codes and terminologies' be immune; and the consequences for such a position would seem to be either anarchy or a *laisser-faire* conservative acceptance of the status quo, on the grounds that one can have no reason to choose between one ideological position and another. However, given his own record as a champion of radical causes ranging from anti-apartheid movements to feminism, it might be argued that such positions can be accommodated within a deconstructionist framework which by its nature demands a total openness, infinite deferring and rejection of doctrinal rigidities: but this clearly is a matter for debate. The important issue is perhaps whether the whole enterprise is tenable. This leads on to the second point.

(2) Derrida says there is no reference beyond or outside language. This implies that sense is subordinated to reference (the view held also by Kripke and Putnam). At the same time his position seems to be that reference is confined to the interrelationships of signs. Clearly he does not mean there is only language. Derrida himself is not a collection of words which sleeps in a linguistic bed and eats words at mealtimes (this would give a new slant to the phrase 'I hope he eats his own words'). A more reasonable interpretation of his writings suggests that he does indeed accept the everyday view that language is about things but that his concern is constantly to warn against the dangers of logocentrism – which is, as he says, inescapable but which we constantly revisit. At the same time his position is clearly an antirealist one. And what we now need to do is to look at alternatives which would seem to be attempting to avoid the 'metaphysics of presence, or the 'mirror of nature' assumptions of 'traditional' realists, while yet avoiding the radically extreme cul-de-sac which Derrida (and other philosophers, such as Rorty) seem to be pushing philosophy into. So let us now consider some of these.

One way of responding to extreme antirealism is to ask again the question: What kinds of things *do* exist? According to **Strawson** [*Individuals*], while we may indulge ourselves in 'revisionary' metaphysics, in the last analysis it must be subservient to 'descriptive' metaphysics which alone can help us to understand the actual structure of our thought about the world. As we have seen, he claims there is a 'massive central core of human thinking' which he hopes to lay bare; this is the primary function of philosophy. The basic particulars of this conceptual structure are material objects and persons, while qualities, relations, states, processes and species 'seem relatively poorly entrenched', as reference to a material object is presupposed if they are to be identified. Presumably minds, Platonic 'essences' and God are all relegated to the 'realm of myth, fiction, or fancy'. What of the status of, say, the sub-atomic particles of physics? Strawson calls these 'theoretical constructs'. They are unobservable, but in so far as we do make identifying references to them this can only be through reference to 'those grosser, observable bodies' which are composed of them. They thus constitute another class of the poorly entrenched particulars which belong to the descriptive metaphysician's conceptual scheme. Given Strawson's general position, it should be clear that it should not be necessary for philosophers either to resort to reductionist procedures (such as Ayer's), which for the most part cannot be carried through, to replace sentences referring to non-particulars by sentences which involve particulars, or to seek to construct the 'ideal' language which purports to give us the 'true' picture of 'reality [see Wittgenstein's *Tractatus* and Russell's 'Logical Atomism'].

The eminent American philosopher W.V.O. **Quine** (b. 1908) offers a quite different approach. Like Whorf he accepts that 'radical translation' between different languages is not possible. But this is not because each language by virtue of its vocabulary or syntax in some way determines a world-view but because of 'indeterminacy of correlation' [see *Word and Object*]. Quine thinks of language as a set of dispositions to respond to socially observable stimuli. So to ascertain whether a native uttering the word 'gavagai' in his language means the same as that which we mean when we refer to a rabbit, we must compare the stimulus conditions. But the problem here, he argues, is that we can never demonstrate complete synonymity. (Note that he is not saying that the meanings are incommensurable.) It may be that 'gavagai' is used by the native to refer to 'mere stages, or brief segments' of rabbits. And we cannot ask the native: 'Is there the same correlation between our respective responses to the terms "the same" and "that"'. We can of course attempt to compile a list of native words by 'segmenting heard utterances into conveniently short recurrent parts' and equate them hypothetically to English words and phrases. Quine calls these lists 'analytical hypotheses'. (The native 'words' – and of course the English ones – are required to carry sentences which are 'stimulus-analytic', that is, sentences to which a subject would assent after every stimulation, within the modulus.) But, says Quine:

> there can be no doubt that rival systems of analytical hypotheses can fit the totality of speech behaviour to perfection, and can fit the totality of dispositions to speech behaviour as well, and still specify mutually incompatible translations of countless sentences insusceptible of independent control.   [p.72]

Understandably, Quine's approach to ontology differs from both Russell's and Strawson's. He rejects the possibility of a single 'ideal' logical language underlying grammatical forms. But he is also dismissive of the emphasis on ordinary language and its alleged central core of concepts. And he criticizes Strawson's distinction between descriptive and revisionary metaphysics and Wittgenstein's sharp separation of philosophy and science. Instead he proposes the notion of 'semantic ascent', that is, the move from talking in certain terms to talking about them, and the criterion of 'systematic efficacy'. We certainly start out from our 'ordinary' language, but we are not tied to it. We *can* revise it, restructure it, adding or dispensing with certain concepts to suit our requirements as we move up from descriptions of our everyday experiences to those of the natural sciences, and then on to the more abstract levels of mathematics, logic and finally ontology. So it follows that what 'exists', what is 'real', depends on our 'ontic commitment': the degree of generality and abstraction we are prepared to allow in our conceptual scheme. The philosopher's job is not then to operate from 'outside' with a view to disclosing some supposed hard core of conceptual categories but rather to moderate, to simplify the categories of his own conceptual scheme – categories which differ from those of zoologists, physicists, mathematicians and so on only in breadth:

> The philosopher's task differs from the others . . . in detail; but in no such drastic way as those suppose who imagine for the philosopher a vantage point outside the conceptual scheme that he takes in charge. There is no such cosmic exile. He cannot study and revise the fundamental conceptual scheme of science and common sense without having some conceptual scheme, whether the same or another no less in need of philosophical scrutiny, in which to work. He can scrutinize and improve the system from within, appealing to coherence and simplicity; but this is the theoretician's method generally. He has recourse to semantic ascent, but so has the scientist. And if the theoretical scientist in his remote ways is bound to save the eventual connections with nonverbal stimulation, the philosopher in his remoter way is bound to save them too. True, no experiment may be expected to settle an ontological issue; but this is only because such issues are connected with surface irritations in such multifarious ways, through such a maze of intervening theory.
>
> [Quine, *Word and Object*, pp.275–276]

*Comment

How should we characterize Strawson and Quine? Strawson's methods – to lay bare 'core concepts' – have a distinctly Kantian flavour, but they lead to a realist conclusion – the affirmation of material objects and persons as basic particulars. And indeed, although in his own study of Kant [*The Bounds of Sense*] he argues for the strong interpretation of the critical philosophy, his own 'descriptive metaphysics' is much more in line with the weak thesis: the phenomenal world is the real world, and we are in direct contact with it, even though the way we experience is governed by the actual structure of our thought expressed through language. Quine's 'ontological relativity' is of course bound by no such restriction. Our ontic commitment is a pragmatic matter. But this does not mean that he is advocating a 'free for all' philosophy. What is at issue is how best to describe the world so as to suit our purposes; and we are free to revise our concepts as we wish. Nevertheless, the real world of physical objects is the starting point for the philosopher as it is for the scientist. As he says: 'our ordinary language of physical things is about as basic as language gets' [p.3]. The problem is that there are philosophers who 'treat ordinary language as sacrosanct'.

Another contribution to the debate is that of **Putnam**. Indeed, his 'internal realism' – which can also be regarded as neo-Kantian on the weak interpretation [see especially pp.60–64 of *Reason, Truth and History*] – arguably offers one of the most satisfactory solutions. (See also the account of 'substance' earlier in this chapter and his theory of truth discussed in 5.7.) He says metaphysical realism is unacceptable because it uses a theory of reference which is based on a 'God's eye point of view' of the way language relates to the world. We cannot achieve an absolute comparison of our system of concepts with reality. But this does not mean that he is committed to relativism – which denies there are any absolute standards of truth or rationality. On the contrary, he rejects relativism because it fails to distinguish between the correctness of a belief and its seeming to be correct. He proposes instead that while remaining within a conceptual system we can consider the ways in which our beliefs, judgements and principles relate to and reinforce one another with a view to achieving a partial comprehension of reality. Rationality, although grounded in language and culture, nevertheless has a regulative aspect which enables us to criticize our traditions and provides the basis for the employment of such concepts as justification, truth and warranted assertibility within the context of a given culture.

It is clear then that for Putnam, while we cannot transcend the limits of our conceptual schemes, it is through them that our access to the real world is articulated. Certainly there are many alternative culturally bound schemes. But it is not the case that terms employed in different cultural contexts are incommensurable; if they were, no translation of any language would be possible, and 'we would have no grounds for regarding [other organisms] as thinkers, speakers, or even persons' [*Reason, Truth and History*, p.114]. And conceptual schemes are open to critical assessment:

> What makes a statement, or a whole system of statements – a theory or conceptual scheme – rationally acceptable is, in large part, its coherence and fit; coherence of 'theoretical or less experiential beliefs' with one another and with more experiential beliefs, and also coherence of experiential beliefs with theoretical beliefs. Our conceptions of coherence and acceptability are ... deeply interwoven with our psychology. They depend on our biology and our culture; they are by no means 'value-free'. But they *are* our conceptions, and they are conceptions of something real. They define a kind of objectivity, *objectivity for us*, even if it is not the metaphysical objectivity of the God's Eye view. Objectivity and rationality humanly speaking are what we have; they are better than nothing. [pp.55–56]

Arguably, Putnam's internal realism offers a viable alternative to the theses of Strawson and Quine. Debate will no doubt continue. But let us now move on to investigate that which, it is generally supposed, makes it possible for us to acquire some understanding of 'reality', namely the mind.

11.3 Mind

Reading: Descartes, *Meditations*, II and VI; Ryle, *The Concept of Mind*; Putnam, *Reason, Truth and History*, ch. 4; Searle, *Minds, Brains and Science*; *Mind, Language and Society*, chs 2–4; Freud, *Outline of Psychoanalysis*

You will probably find it useful to start by checking through again the main points made in 5.11. But note that whereas we were concerned there mainly with the problem of *knowledge* – how we can know ourselves and others – in this section we are going to deal with such questions as: 'What is the *nature* of the mind?' and 'How is it related to the body?' They are considered to be metaphysical to the extent that science either has not or, perhaps, cannot provide adequate answers.

It can scarcely be denied that we have bodies; we can see and touch them – though some philosophers, for example, Plato and Bradley, will argue about their status – perhaps they are but appearances or only semi-real? But in what sense can we talk of our having minds? If they 'exist' at all, it is doubtful that we can describe them in terms of any of the five senses. So what are they? What are their characteristics? As we have already discussed, Descartes tried to show that mind is an individual **substance** possessing its own special properties and entirely distinct from the body to which, however, it is conjoined by the fiat of an omnipotent creator. It would not be too much of an exaggeration to say that most subsequent 'theories' of mind can be seen as attempts to deal with the difficulties raised by this essentially **dualistic** position of Descartes. But before looking at these let us set out some of the criteria which have been proposed for distinguishing minds (or, to use the terminology preferred by many modern writers, mental *states*, *processes*, or *events*) from bodies, or non-mental states.

Consciousness. This is a criterion adopted by Descartes himself. States of mind are states of thinking or consciousness. But he is using the term 'consciousness' in a wide sense; a 'thinking thing' is, he says, one that doubts, understands, affirms, denies, wills, refuses, that imagines also, and perceives.

Privacy. It is sometimes claimed that mental states are characterized by the fact that they are private to the possessor; he is said to have 'privileged access'. Thus: I alone am aware of my own pain; I can keep my thoughts to myself; and so on.

Intentionality. You will remember reference was made to this concept in 5.11. It first appeared in medieval scholasticism but it was adopted and developed by the Austrian psychologist and philosopher Franz Brentano (1838–1917) before being taken over by Husserl, Sartre and others. Essentially 'intentionality' (the philosophers of the Middle Ages called it 'the intentional inexistence of an object') is used to refer to a feature alleged to be possessed by mental states, namely that they are *directed* towards an object which may or may not 'really' exist. Thus, even if there is no such thing as a unicorn, in thinking about a unicorn we are thinking about something, which is accorded some sort of ontological status. This feature was held by Brentano to be exclusively characteristic of mental phenomena: 'No physical phenomenon manifests anything similar. Consequently, we can define mental phenomena by saying they are such phenomena as include an object intentionally within themselves'.

*Comments and criticisms

Each of these suggestions has some merit, but they are all open to difficulties:

(1) Descartes' identification of the mental with 'thought' or 'consciousness' fails for a number of reasons. (a) As Bernard Williams has pointed out, we may often notice something and 'take it in' without actually being aware of it. It may be much later that our perceptions are brought to consciousness. (b) Closely connected with (a), unconscious activity could not, on Descartes' criterion, be regarded as mental. Moreover, does the mind cease to exist when we are asleep? (c) It would be incorrect to regard desires, hopes, beliefs and so on as properties of bodies: yet we may be said to have them without being always conscious of them. Descartes cannot account for tendencies, capacities, or dispositions.

(2) It is a truism to say you cannot have my experiences. But it is doubtful whether this provides an adequate criterion for distinguishing between the mental and the non-mental. Through our overt bodily behaviour, or through the medium of a shared language we are able to communicate these 'inner' experiences to each other. Indeed, it is arguable that at least a rudimentary language is a prerequisite for us to be able to reflect to ourselves about our own thoughts and sensations.

(3) Intentionality is perhaps the most promising candidate. It has, however, been objected that while such a criterion can cope with mental states that are associated with beliefs, hopes and so on (which may be thought of as involving a proposition – 'I believe *that* . . .', for example), it fails in the case of, say, pain. Pain is not something of which we can say correctly that we are aware. But what exactly does having a pain or being in pain involve? If you stick a pin into me, I shall instantly react by moving away from the stimulus. This is an instinctive response, a survival mechanism refined in the course of animal evolution. But a fraction of time after my skin has been pierced (if not simultaneously) an unpleasant sensation reveals itself: pain, we may say, forces itself into my consciousness. It is difficult to understand why we should not talk of there being a mental state which is characterized by some sort of object-directedness – which, in this case, can be located at the point of impact of the pin.

Even if these three suggested criteria are inadequate, many philosophers would not wish to deny the existence of mental states or, more controversially, of minds. Let us therefore move on to consider some of the implications of this position.

Dualism

Let us suppose with Descartes that there *are* minds and bodies. There are two questions in particular that have been frequently posed and which, it is argued, such a theory must answer if it is to be taken seriously: (a) Where is the mind? and (b) How does it relate to the body? As 'ordinary' non-philosophical people we should probably want to say that if we 'have' a mind at all it must in some sense be located in the brain rather than being diffused throughout the whole body, thought it can affect any part of it. This no doubt reflects our tendency to associate seeing, hearing, thinking and imagining with something going on in our head. But as we saw in Ch. 5, many philosophers (most notably Ryle) have objected that this ascription of spatial properties to mind is radically misconceived and casts doubt on the whole dualistic enterprise. Descartes, of course, thought of the mind and body as radically different kinds of substances. The mind, for him, is spiritual and *lacking* extension. But in his *Passions of the Soul* [Art. XXX] he did talk in terms of the 'soul' as having a general influence throughout the body ('the body is united to all the portions of the soul conjointly') and suggested only that it is in the brain (more specifically the pineal gland – though he adduces no good reason for this view) 'that it exercises its functions more particularly than in all the others'. Likewise in the *Meditations* [VI] he writes that the soul is lodged in the body not just like a pilot in a ship but 'intimately conjoined' with it so that mind and body form a 'certain unity'. This must lead on to the tricky problem of interaction. How *can* an essentially non-spatial substance connect with and influence physically extended matter? That there does seem to be some sort of connection is an assumption we usually take for granted in our everyday lives. We 'will' our arm to reach out for the glass of whisky. We feel pain when we walk into a lamp-post. Our 'mental' attitude can affect our performance in a competitive race. Likewise our physical condition can affect our mental proficiency. Then there are the more esoteric stories we may read about of yogin who are said to be able to levitate or walk on red-hot coals through the exercise of mental powers. But to refer to such phenomena is not to offer a solution to the problem of interaction. A number of 'theories' have of course been put forward by philosophers from time to time. For example, according to the **occasionalists** (such as Malebranche, 1638–1715), God intervenes on each occasion I choose to act. I decide to lift up a book; God provides the causal link between my (mental) 'willing' and the (physical) movement of my arm. Leibniz (1646–1716), however, argued that God is involved but once, namely at the moment he created the universe, when he arranged for the two chains of events, the mental and physical, to act in perfect harmony. Thus there is a constant correlation between the two series of events. This theory is called **parallelism**. (We shall not discuss these suggestions further, though they are both open to serious objections. You might like to work out some of these for yourself. And they are not of course the only theories.)

If we leave aside the problem of interaction, dualism has yet another hurdle to overcome – the question of personal identity. This has already been examined to some extent in Ch. 5. So all we shall do here is to make the further point that on dualist assumptions it does not seem to be *necessary* that physical identity (presupposing that an adequate criterion can be decided upon) should be accompanied by a specific series of mental states – particularly as 'minds' are supposed to be non-spatial. How could we be certain that any given succession of mental states constituted just *one* mind? Could we not conceive of the possibility that two (or even more) minds inhabit a single body simultaneously? Perhaps a particular mind can appropriate some or all of the mental states of another mind? These speculations seem a little bizarre, but it is worth mentioning that recent psychological experiments involving brain bisection lend some credence to such possibilities by indicating that the two sides of the brain may function in some sense independently of each other. Two minds occupying different hemispheres? This does seem to be a consequence of dualism.

Monism

In order to avoid these difficulties of 'mind–body' interaction, some philosophers have argued against dualism by proposing a monistic solution. There are in fact a number of different types of monism:

(1) The rationalist Spinoza (see also 9.3) rejected Descartes' view that minds and bodies were substances and argued '*de more geometrico*', that is, in the manner of a geometrical proof, from axioms to conclusions, that there is only *one* infinite (that is, unlimited) substance, of which the mental and the physical are but 'modes' or aspects conceived respectively under the 'attributes' of thought and extension. (Spinoza claimed that the one substance must consist of an infinite number of attributes, but that we are able to conceive of it only under two.) Individual human bodies and minds are thus part of the same infinite substance (which Spinoza also identifies with 'God or Nature', the cause of itself (*causa sui*); and whatever happens within this substance is necessarily (logically and empirically) manifested under the various attributes. The problem of how mind and body can interact is thus by-passed since they are in effect the same thing looked at from different points of view. This is not to say that Spinoza's account cannot be criticized. The notions of attribute and mode are not altogether devoid of ambiguity, and the question can still be asked how the one point of view relates to the other. A more serious objection to Spinoza's metaphysical monism, however, concerns the problems of freedom to be discussed in 11.5.

(2) **Idealism**. Idealist philosophers generally seek to 'absorb' or assimilate the physical to the mental. Thus, for Berkeley there is no 'matter'; 'physical' objects exist only as 'ideas' in the minds of perceivers (ultimately God) – see 5.10. For Hegel the universe as a whole is Absolute Mind or Spirit (*Geist*) manifesting itself as Nature. The emergence of each individual 'mind' from unconsciousness through to perception and self-consciousness is therefore an instantiation of the historical and dialectical process whereby the universal Mind comes to know itself.

(3) **'Materialism/reductionism'**. We use these terms to cover a number of theories, all of which attempt in various ways to 'eliminate' the mental altogether. Logical positivists, for example, attempted to translate sentences about human 'mental' processes (beliefs, feelings and so on) into sentences about physical behaviour, and thence into the language of natural science (that is, physics). This is closely connected with linguistic phenomenalism in epistemology (see the discussion of Ayer in 5.10). Ryle, on the other hand, with his philosophical behaviourism, sought to explain away 'ghostly' workings of a mind by referring them to dispositions and publicly observable behaviour. (Read again the account of his arguments in 5.6 and 5.11.) A more recent theory is the **identity** theory, sometimes called 'central state materialism', espoused particularly by Smart (compare 5.10). According to this view, mental states are identical with brain states: the terms 'mental states' and 'brain states', which have different *senses* but *refer* to the same phenomenon. Given enough scientific knowledge we should be able to correlate them. A more extreme version of the theory, eliminative materialism, has as its aim the rejection of our everyday and

misleading ways of speaking about our mental life in terms of beliefs, hopes and so on (they refer to all this as 'folk psychology'), in favour of a thorough-going scientific vocabulary.

*Criticism

Many philosophers argue that these kinds of approaches to the concept of mind (the accounts of which have necessarily been over-simplified here) fail to avoid the problems of reduction, and do not address adequately the characteristics of mental states, in particular the facts of self-consciousness, privacy and intentionality. (Ryle himself later came to accept that the subjectivity of 'inner' life had neither been eliminated nor satisfactorily accounted for.) Moreover, as for the supposed identity, how could correlations between mental and brain states ever be determined? What would count as a correlation? Do certain *sorts* of mental states correspond to certain kinds of brain states in specific cerebral locations?

(4) **Anomalous monism**. This is a materialist but non-reductive theory of mind developed by the American philosopher Donald **Davidson** (b. 1917). He distinguishes between mental and physical events but argues that different kinds of constitutive principles operate in each case. The physical realm is a closed system, physical events being explainable in terms of strict scientific and deterministic laws. The mental realm, the distinguishing feature of which is intentionality, is, however, open, in that explanations of human action must meet the criterion of rationality. A reason, he says, is a rational cause (of behaviour). And reasons, as well as intentions, and coherence in attitudes and behaviour, are prerequisities for people to be treated as persons and self-determining agents. Now there cannot be any precise psycho-physical laws, because when we try to understand and explain human action by taking account of the wider (holistic) context of beliefs and motives, we necessarily impose these conditions of rationality, consistency and the like; and these correlate only roughly with the physical realm. At the same time Davidson wants to maintain that mental events are still physical in that they originate in brain processes. So while his theory is monistic (and materialistic), mental events considered at the level of belief and desire are anomalous.

(5) Many recent philosophers have come to the conclusion that a solution is likely to be found only if the issues are looked at freshly from new perspectives. A short account will be given of some of these:

Functionalism. This theory is associated particularly with J. Fodor and **Putnam**. The mind is thought of as akin to a computer 'software' program which is processed by the 'hardware' of the brain, though it is possible that mental life might be instantiated in other hardware structures, such as computers themselves or silicon-based organisms, for example. The kind of mental state a person has in a given situation is determined by the function the brain state performs. This, however, can be consistent with the activity of different brain states (many physically distinguishable brain states can have the same function:

for example, bringing about a response to pain). Nevertheless Putnam later saw that functionalism does not work. We cannot, he says [*Reason and Representation*], individuate concepts and beliefs without reference to the environment. What makes a mental state into a particular kind, such as pain, or a belief that something is the case, is to be located in the network of functional connections that link the behaviour of the organism to the environment. It is our descriptions of these interconnections that are articulated in the language of the mental. The problem is that to ascribe meaning to someone's 'representations', or to interpret someone's language ('thought-signs') must proceed simultaneously with the ascription of beliefs and desires to that person. But it is extremely difficult to determine that two expressions are synonymous. We can therefore never, in practice, make the other's beliefs and desires come out the same as ours. Put differently, this means that while the existence of mental states might be compatible with a range of physical systems or structures, they cannot be *identified* with functional, physical-chemical, or computationally characterized states, though they may be emergent from and 'supervenient' on them. A given mental state can be realized in different computational machines but cannot be identified with any particular one.

Biological naturalism. Searle is of the opinion that if progress is to be made in philosophy of mind we must break away from the 'antique and obsolete vocabulary of "mental" and "physical", "mind" and "body"' and look for an alternative to dualism and materialism – both of which he thinks rest on false assumptions. Accordingly he argues that the mind is a biological phenomenon, the most essential feature of which is consciousness. But the primary evolutionary role of the mind is to relate us in certain ways to the environment, especially to other people. The relationship of one's subjective states to the rest of the world is intentionality. Searle's principal thesis therefore is that consciousness and intentionality can be 'naturalized', that is, can be shown to be part of the natural world. These phenomena occur in and emerge from the brain just as digestion is a biological process that occurs in the stomach, or as the molecular structure of water produces its liquidity – a 'higher-level' feature. But this does not commit him to materialism because of the first-person ontology of consciousness which cannot be eliminated by reduction to physical processes. Neither is this a dualist position; for consciousness is a biological process caused by lower-level neuronal processes in the brain.

It is worth noting here that somewhat similar views were developed by the phenomenologist **Merleau-Ponty** (see also 5.11). His initial concern was to overcome discontinuities, especially to bridge the gap between nature and consciousness. We gain access to the world through perception, but for him this is not a mere reflection on passively received sensory data. The world we encounter in perception, what is revealed by 'transcendental reduction' is a 'lived experience' – Merleau-Ponty introduces the concept of the **'body-subject'**. The body is much more than just an entity to be treated as an inert object whose behaviour is to be explained exhaustively in terms of science as a 'second order expression of the world'. (He thus explicitly rejects the claims of behaviourism and reductionist naturalism.) Rather the body must be seen also as a conscious 'subject', exhibiting intentionality, and actively situated in the constantly changing perceptual milieu – the presupposition for all conceptual thinking, rationality, value and existence. In his early work, *The Structure of Behaviour*, Merleau-Ponty rejected behaviourist theories and argued that we are organisms who appear to exhibit goal-seeking activity. He accepted that bodily behaviour as such is a proper object of scientific study in causal terms, but he denied that mental activity can be identified with physical behaviour of the organism or with a network of reflexes, conditioned or otherwise. Science, he said, abstracts from the wholeness and purposiveness of living organisms. Instead he postulated a hierarchy of qualitatively different levels of conceptualization in the structures of things. The lowest or physical level is that at which the organism may be said to be the least 'purposive'. Its response to the environment is explicable in causal or mechanistic terms. But at the vital, that is, biological level such responses have to be understood with reference to the organism's structures and needs. At the highest, mental or human level the organism confers 'meaning' on the environment. This dialectical relationship gives rise to holistic, spatial patterns. No level can be reduced to the lower level; the levels are as it were cumulative. Thus we might say, for example, that while we can analyse ourselves in terms of atoms and molecules – relating to the laws and theories of physics and chemistry, the activity of complex molecules is describable by reference to the laws of biology. As for the highest level, we appeal here to the fulfilment of purposes and needs. Explanation involves reasons rather than (physical) causes. There is no inconsistency between the sets of explanations, and there is no reduction of biology to physics and chemistry, or of human activity to biology. The lower levels do, however, contribute to the higher levels. According to Merleau-Ponty, meaning must therefore already have been conferred at a pre-conscious level of subjectivity. With his theory of cumulative structures he hoped to avoid both materialism and mentalism. You will probably agree that Merleau-Ponty's general thesis is very much in line with the arguments and conclusions Searle sets out in chs 2–4 of his book.

*Comment

It is clear that while there is much common ground between Davidson, (the later) Putnam and Searle (and Merleau-Ponty) there are also differences. Searle obviously wants to distance himself from materialism (which Davidson's anomalous monism seems to be grounded in). Moreover he takes up a position of externalist realism (as against Putnam's 'internal' realism) – though he is quite happy to indulge in conceptual revision to avoid, as he says, the Scylla of dualism and the Charybdis of materialism. It is of course the case that despite the best endeavours of such thinkers as these, the problem of how the highest 'level' – the ontological subjectivity of consciousness – emerges from and relates to the lower biological and mechanistic levels remains unsolved. William Lyons, in his introduction to *Modern Philosophy of Mind*, believes that philosophy of mind is on the verge of producing something approaching a definitive account, 'but it will be a complex and sophisticated account. In our ordinary discourse we will probably still speak as if minds were ghostly drivers of our bodily machines'. As against this Colin McGinn, in the same volume, argues that the mystery will never be resolved, because 'we are cut off by our very cognitive constitution from achieving a conception of that natural property of the brain (or of consciousness) that accounts for the psychophysical link'. You are encouraged to read and think about this challenging essay. Whether or not we should be pessimistic about the outcome, the view held here is that if there is to be any progress it must relate closely to an adequate theory of causation. But before we tackle this next metaphysical problem we shall look briefly at three other controversial topics relevant to the philosophy of mind: immortality, the unconscious and artificial intelligence.

Immortality

Dualists have in general subscribed to the view that the mind, soul, or some aspect of consciousness survives the dissolution of the body at death. (Refer back to the discussion of Plato's arguments in 3.7.) Descartes' commitment to immortality follows necessarily from his claim that mind and body are distinct and separable substances. As he wrote in Part V of his *Discourse on Method*:

> There is [no error] that is more powerful in leading feeble minds astray from the straight path of virtue than the supposition that the soul of the brutes is of the same nature with our own; and consequently that after this life we have nothing to hope for or fear, more than flies or ants; in place of which, when we know how far they differ we much better comprehend the reasons which establish that the soul is of a nature wholly independent of the body, and that consequently it is not liable to die with the latter; and finally, because no other causes are observed capable of destroying it, we are naturally led thence to judge that it is immortal.

(*Compare 5.11. You should note also Kant's view, mentioned in 6.3, that immortality cannot be proved but should be accepted as a 'postulate' of the practical reason. How you deal with this depends on whether you accept Kant's apparent assumption that an *approximation* to perfection presupposes survival of rational personality beyond physical death.)

*Comments

The problem is clearly more acute for most non-dualistic theories of mind. It is difficult to understand what place there could be in a materialist view for the notion of a disembodied consciousness. The survival of consciousness would also seem to be ruled out on behaviourist premises. (Compare Ryle's criticisms of the Cartesian 'myth' discussed in 5.11.) As we saw in 4.5, Aristotle, starting out from an 'organicist' view of man, also grappled unsuccessfully with the problem of the separability of the 'active intellect'. But it is doubtful that he was ever committed to the doctrine of an immortal incorporeal substance such as had been proposed by Plato, despite the interpretation put on the *De Anima* by Aquinas (for whom the survival of an immaterial soul was a theological necessity).

There can be little doubt that the concept of immortality is a particularly difficult one for philosophers to come to terms with. Any theory that suggests that soul or mind is an entity of some kind which is either created by God or comes into existence as a result of the neurobiological processes of the brain has to deal with the problem of interaction. Moreover, this could not possibly establish immortality as a fact; the mind might at the most be brain dependent. It is difficult also to conceive of what kind of state a disembodied soul might be in, or what activity it could enjoy. If its existence is to be understood in any spatial or temporal sense, then we might suppose that science will in due course be able to provide an appropriate explanation (along with other allegedly psychic phenomena such as telepathy, psychokinesis and ghosts). Otherwise we must remain agnostic or accept immortality as an act of faith. For those who believe in a God, the existence of an immaterial personality would not be regarded as impossible.

The unconscious

The notion of an 'unconscious' part of the human mind has been entertained off and on for many hundreds of years. But it is usually associated particularly with the work of the eminent Viennese psychiatrist Sigmund Freud (1856–1939). It is a commonplace that a great deal goes on 'in our head' without our being aware of it. We might wake up in the morning to find a mathematical problem solved which we had been thinking hard about the night before. We forget names, and then find suddenly that they come back to us again. And most of us have had experience of often embarrassing slips of the tongue or pen, spoonerisms, absent-minded mislaying of personal items and so on. All such errors were termed '*Fehlleistungen*' (translated as 'parapraxes') by Freud, who regarded them as providing evidence for unconscious mental activity. Freud's theory is, however, concerned particularly with dream experiences, which he saw as overt responses to impulses repressed deep down in the psyche. It is of course well-known that it was by means of hypnosis and the interpretation and analysis of dreams that Freud sought to gain access to the higher level of the unconscious (the 'preconscious') and liberate his patients from their neuroses.

*Comments

As in the case of immortality, your response to the concept of the unconscious will be coloured by your approach to the mind–body problem in general. The doctrine has come under attack from both behaviourists and existentialists of the Sartrean kind, for whom 'man makes himself', there being no prior human 'nature' conscious or unconscious (compare 6.6). It is important to note though that Freud himself thought of his hypothesis of unconscious mental processes as being thoroughly scientific. As he said in a Lecture given in 1917:

We can challenge anyone in the world to give a more correct scientific account of this state of affairs [Freud is referring here to the actions of a man following an instruction given when he was under hypnosis], and if he does we will gladly renounce our hypothesis of unconscious mental processes. Till that happens, however, we will hold fast to the hypothesis; and if someone objects that the unconscious is nothing real in a scientific sense, is a makeshift, *une façon de parler*, we can only shrug our shoulders resignedly and dismiss what he says as unintelligible, something not real, which produces effects of such tangible reality as an obsessional action!

[*Introductory Lectures*, 18, p.318]

This assertion that the unconscious is a scientific hypothesis raises wider issues about the status of explanations of human behaviour (see the next chapter), and about human intentionality and freedom (see 11.5). It can certainly be argued with plausibility that while unconscious impulses or instincts limit or modify the scope of human 'plasticity', their existence is not inconsistent with a theory of self-determinism. Searle sees Freud's theory as simply an addition to the 'common-sense conception of mental states' which he (Searle) has been advocating. On his theory, behaviour (that is, action) both contains and is caused by internal mental states (beliefs, desires, hopes, fears and so on). Such states can indeed be unconscious, but an unconscious state is mental 'only in virtue of its capacity in principle to produce a conscious mental state' [*Mind, Language and Society*, p.76]. It still has its intentionality but it is no longer conscious [p.65]. An unconscious state may of course be inaccessible because of brain damage or repression [p.76]. And, as he says [*Minds, Brains and Science*, 4]: 'We're often resistant to admitting to having certain intentional states because we're ashamed of them or for some other reason'.

Artificial intelligence

Can computers think? In principle there seems to be no major reason why, with the advance of technology, machines constructed by human beings should not in some sense think or even show emotion. But in what 'sense'? What can be meant here by 'think' and 'feel'? And what kind of machine? If by thinking and feeling we mean the kinds of things that human beings do, and if by machine we mean a digital computer, then, according to Searle, the answer is very definitely 'no'. His arguments are summarized in *Minds, Brains and Science*, 2. The principal point he makes against 'AI partisans' is that they seem to reject the view that the mind is a natural biological phenomenon and instead regard it as formally specifiable. The mind–brain relationship is conceived of as analogous to the relationship between a program and the 'hardware' of the computer system. It should therefore be feasible, they say, given a sufficiently complex program and the appropriate microchip connections, to duplicate thoughts and feelings. Against this Searle says that the definability of a computer program in terms of formal or syntactical structures is totally inadequate to account for minds which have *semantic* contents. In support of his own thesis Searle has devised a 'thought-experiment' which involves the manipulation of Chinese symbols by a person locked up in a room. Rules in English for the correct use of the symbols are provided, and, unknown to the operator, incoming symbols are designated 'questions' by people outside the room while symbols passed out are called 'answers'. The behaviour of the symbol user would be in all respects similar to a native Chinese speaker, but he could not be said to *understand* Chinese. He possesses the syntax but lacks the semantics.

Searle also makes the further point that as the computational properties of brains are not enough to explain its functioning to produce mental processes, so still less could non-biological computers be thought capable of simulating such processes. If we *were* to build an artefact which had mental states, then it would have to possess causal powers equivalent to those of the human brain.

*Comments

It is difficult (given his premises) to disagree with Searle's rejection of AI. Certainly we might conceive of the possibility (say, in a hundred years' time) of constructing an artefact out of protein molecules so that it is virtually indistinguishable from a human being. Well, then of course we should expect it to be able to think; it would be a surrogate human, says Searle. But even if we were able to construct an artefact in some other way, to simulate mental processes it would have to be able to do much more than just implement a syntactical program. To give an analogy, aircraft can be built to fly like birds. In some native tongues they might be referred to as 'silver birds'. But few people would suppose that what goes on inside the 'nerve-centre' of the aircraft (note the metaphor) duplicates the mental capacity of a biological bird (which is considerably less than that of a human being).

11.4 Causation

Reading: Hume, *Enquiry concerning Human Understanding*, IV and VI; Kant, *Critique of Pure Reason* (or *Prolegomena*); Searle, *Minds, Brains and Science*, 4; *Mind, Language and Society*, chs 2 and 4

When we see two billiard balls colliding and moving off again in different directions, or when we suffer a bang on the head from a falling apple, we are inclined to use the language of causation to describe what has occurred. The white ball *caused* the red ball to move, we say. Or, the force of gravity caused the apple to fall, and the impact caused me to experience pain. What is meant by 'caused' here? What are 'causes'? Now it is very easy to fall into the trap of assigning entities of some kind as the 'denotata' of nouns in our language. We talk of causes, so it would seem there must *be* such 'things'. but careful philosophical analysis shows that such an approach is often fundamentally mistaken. Certainly philosophers of a rationalist or idealist persuasion have tended to think in terms of 'real' or 'substantial' causes which in some sense 'necessarily' connect objects.

(Compare the discussion of Plato's 'Forms' in 3.5.) Aristotle (see 4.2) distinguished four kinds of cause. His terminology was used by scholastic philosophers in the middle ages and subsequently partially adopted by Descartes for his cosmological argument (see 9.3). Empiricists, however, have tended towards an antirealist account of causation. We shall examine four theories:

(1) The **regularity** theory. This is a common view, which some philosophers, especially Ayer [see, for example, *Language, Truth and Logic*, ch. 2], have attributed to **Hume**. Hume, you may remember (5.3) argued against suggestions that there are 'powers' in things to bring about changes in objects (or at least that we could have knowledge of such 'powers': he does at times talk of 'secret connections' in nature). He also denied there is any kind of necessary connection between our ideas or objects or events – statements about these being 'matters of fact' and not 'relations of ideas'. The fact that we claim to 'perceive' such connections or have a belief in 'causes' is, he says, attributable to our imagination subsequent to the perception of regularities in nature. We experience pain each time we put our hand in the fire; so we imagine there is a necessary causal connection. Now, the regularity theory states that an object C (the 'cause') causes an object E (the 'effect') if and only if things of the same type as C are 'constantly conjoined' by things of the same type as E. This notion of constant conjunction require some analysis. It could mean (a) that whenever a C occurs it is followed by an E. This is called a **sufficient condition**. The trouble with this interpretation is that it seems to be inadequate unless applied in a context of wider conditions. Thus, we may say that rain causes the seed to germinate, but there are many instances when, despite plenty of rain, a shoot fails to appear. This could well be because other conditions (warmth, oxygen) are absent, or because the seed is diseased, or even because it has received too much water. Or it could mean that E will not occur unless there is also a C. In this case C is said to be a **necessary condition** for E. But this is too restrictive. A window can be broken in many ways – by the boy next door, by the supersonic bang of an aircraft and so on. It might be argued that in both cases the glass is hit by something (a stone, sound waves) and that therefore the necessary condition is an impact by moving matter. Some philosophers argue that each of these situations should be regarded as a *different* event requiring its own necessary condition. (Try to think up further examples and counter-examples.) An alternative approach would be to combine the two notions of necessary and sufficient conditions into a single condition. But this leads to another problem. Does C cause E or E cause C? The usual answer given is that it depends on which comes first. There are situations however, in which events might be said to be simultaneous. (When a cricket ball lands on your head, you head is dented at the same time instant – and perhaps the ball is temporarily deformed as well, though probably not to the same extent!) It might be possible to redefine the conditions in terms of such notions as passivity and direction. (The crash was caused by the moving train hitting the stationary buffers. But might we not want to say that it was the nails that someone had left on the road that burst the tyre and caused the bus to crash?)

The most serious objection to any regularity theory, however, is that it fails to distinguish between cases in which we feel there is a genuine 'causal' connection, and conjunctions of events which we think of as mere coincidences. Thus if I walk under a ladder three times and on each occasion am hit on the head by a brick, is my walking under the ladder a cause? If not, why not? Why then should one billiard ball be said to cause another one to move? An obvious answer is that in the second case the connection is constant whereas in the first it is not; walk under the ladder again (unless there is someone on it who is deliberately trying to drop a brick on your head). This suggestion of course brings us back to the problem of induction discussed in 2.9. Will the movement of the first billiard ball always be followed by the movement of the second? Another answer might be that the second ball would not have moved without the impact of the first one, but the brick would have fallen even if I had not walked under the ladder (we assume once again that there is nobody on the ladder possessed with evil intent); and this can be tested quite easily by standing still and watching to see what happens. But does this entirely solve the problem? Can we be sure: (a) if it does *not* fall then this can be accounted for by the supervention of some other (perhaps unknown) cause, or (b) that the brick's falling is *not* attributable to some other cause. (These examples, which make use of what are called '**counterfactual conditional**' statements, are perhaps a little artificial – you might think them far-fetched – but they do give some idea of how the discussion of the regularity theory might proceed. No doubt you will be able to make up and analyse more examples of your own. The logic of counterfactuals unfortunately cannot be dealt with in this book, but see Sosa and Tooley in the Reading list at the end of the chapter.

*Comment

It can also be questioned whether Ayer's interpretation of Hume as providing a regularity theory of causation is in any case correct. Certainly several statements Hume makes in the *Enquiry* [Sec. 60] (compare 5.3 above) do not seem to be consistent with each other. Thus, he writes:

> Similar objects are always conjoined with similar. Of this we have experience. Suitably to this experience, therefore, we may define a cause to be *an object, followed by another, and where all the objects similar to the first are followed by objects similar to the second.* Or in other words *where, if the first object had not been, the second never had existed.*

and

> The appearance of a cause always conveys the mind, by a customary transition, to the idea of the effect. Of this also we have experience. We may, therefore, suitably to this experience, form another definition of cause, and call it, *an object followed by another, and whose appearance always conveys the thought to that other.*

Now, it is clear that according to the first 'definition' an event B is caused by an event A if all As are always followed by Bs; and there cannot be an occurrence of a *B* without the prior occurrence of an *A*. The second 'definition', however, refers causation to our thoughts or beliefs about a conjunction of events. This seems to commit Hume to a 'subjectivist' view of what is to count as a cause; for we can certainly conceive of the possibility of regularities which we do not ourselves actually perceive, in which case we should not be able to talk of a causal connection. It is possible that Hume – despite his use of the word 'definition' – was really offering no more than an account of how we come to have the idea of a causal relation. This interpretation receives some backing from the summary he provides in Sec. 61 (which you can read through for yourself). If so, then Ayer's attribution to Hume of a regularity theory of causation itself would seem to be incorrect. (In the light of our discussion about the regularity theory you should also consider whether the two statements made by Hume in his first 'definition' are mutually consistent.)

(2) A quite different account of causation was put forward by **Kant** in his *Critique of Pure Reason*. (Look back at the summary of his epistemology in 5.4.) According to Kant, causality is but one of numerous *a priori* 'categories' or 'forms of the understanding' and which, because of the nature of our mental apparatus, constrains us to perceive the cause–effect relationship between events as necessary in so far as they are organized by or conform to that category. Whether or not Kant's doctrine of the categories is itself tenable is open to question, but even if we do regard it as providing a correct interpretation of human experience and knowledge, it is open to an objection already referred to in the discussion about regularity, namely that it cannot distinguish between 'genuine' causal connections and mere coincidence. How could we know that a given series or conjunction of events is *not* subject to the *a priori* imposition of the category of causation? Another difficulty is that a formal category which is grounded in the structures of human understanding is yet supposed to be applicable to and operate within a supposedly 'real' scientific account of nature. Put more simply: why should the way we ('subjectively') experience the world reflect how it 'really' works ('objectively')? This seems to be a problem on both the 'strong' and the 'weak' interpretations discussed earlier; and Kant was certainly aware of it himself (and attempted to resolve this conflict in his *Metaphysical Foundations of Natural Science*).

(3) Mention should also be made of what might be regarded as a linguistic version of Kant's theory. To think of the world in causal terms is, according to **Wittgenstein**, a consequence of a 'convention', that is of an argument to play a 'language game' in accordance with a certain set of rules. A child who gets burned when it puts its hand into the fire or its finger into the electric socket would be said not to know the meaning of the word 'cause'; it does not know the rules for its correct use. This approach has some merit, but it can be objected that examination of the rules of linguistic usage, while undoubtedly having important practical consequences, does not of itself address the central issues. *Why* is the word 'cause' thought to be appropriate in such circumstances? Does it relate to regularities, necessary and sufficient conditions, the way in which we perceive the world, or can some other explanation be provided? Can the rules of the 'game'

be changed to accommodate a different way of looking at the problem? Can we play a new 'game'?

(4) An important recent contribution to the problem has been made by **Searle**. The key notion here is **Intentional agency**. In our daily lives we think of ourselves as bringing about changes both in our own bodies and on the world outside. As children we acquire our most basic concept from experience of objects pushing against others and from our own pushing and pulling. Later we become aware that our own *conscious* efforts can produce changes [*Mind, Language and Society*, p.59]. As Stuart Hampshire says in his *Thought and Action*:

> The categories of causal explanation have . . . their roots within our own experience of ourselves as agents . . .
>
> A human being's action is essentially constituted of means towards an end; it is a bringing about of some result with a view to some result. 'With a view to', or 'in order to', are unavoidable idioms in giving the sense of the notion of an action, the arrow of agency passing through the present and pointing forward in time. We are always looking at the present situation as arising from the immediate past by some agency, and as passing into some other situation by some force or agency that is operative now.
>
> [*Thought and Action*, p.73]

Searle claims further [in *Intentionality*, pp.123–124] that in many cases of 'Intentional (or mental) causations' we directly experience the relationship '*C* causes *E*'. [See also *Mind, Language and Society*, pp.104–105.] The difference between this account and the standard (that is, according to Searle, the Humean) theory is that in the case of the latter, one never has an experience of causation, whereas for Searle when we act on (and perceive) the world we have 'self-referential' states, and 'the relationship of causation is part of the *content*, not the object, of these experiences'. In other words, when, for example, we raise an arm, part of the Intentional content of the experience of acting is our awareness of the fact that it is that very experience which is making the arm go up. Searle then goes on to make a more radical move. He accepts that the world contains discoverable causal regularities, but he denies that there is any problem in supposing that there are causes in the world independent of our experiences (a problem which worried Hume) because what the agent 'ascribes in the case of observation is something he has experienced in the case of manipulation' [p.129]. I may not *experience* the causal relation which exists when a vase falls to the ground and breaks, but it is the same relation as the one I do experience when I smash it myself with a stone. Furthermore it is only by trial and error that I can discover whether the attempt to smash the vase is successful or not, and to be able to make this distinction we have to *presume* that there is some degree of regularity in the world. This presumption is part of a 'Background' which Searle defines as 'a set of nonrepresentational mental capacities that enable all representing to take place' [p.143]. It is for this reason that we can apply the causal relation to events (such as the vase falling under gravity) which lack intentional input, so to speak. Intentional causation and regularity, according to Searle, are therefore not two different kinds of causation. There is only one kind, which he calls 'efficient causation', Intentional causation being a subclass in which the causal relations involve Intentional states [p.135]. Searle thus sees himself both as answering Hume's empiricist scepticism and as finding an alternative to Kant's theory of cause as an *a priori* concept.

*Comment

Searle's thesis in *Intentionality* is much more detailed than the summary he provides in his other books, or indeed than the account we have presented here; and in it he deals convincingly with many objections that might be put forward against his theory. If you have time and the determination to work through this influential book in its entirety you will find the experience to be philosophically most rewarding. This is not to say that he has brought the debate to an end; there are certainly aspects of his approach that need to be looked at carefully. One issue in particular concerns the distinction between Intentional and non-Intentional causation. Now it is a central plank of his interpretation that causation should not be understood in terms of 'regularities, covering laws or constant conjunctions' [*Minds, Brains and Science,* 4] but as one subclass of efficient causation, Intentional causation being the other. It is, however, arguable that in relation to wider issues of consciousness, freedom and explanation, the fundamental problem of accounting for the transition from lower to higher 'levels' remains unresolved. What is required is a means of reconciling two assumptions or claims: (1) the apparent fundamental differences between, say, my hitting a ball or causing a vase to break and the way that the Sun 'makes' plants grow; and (2) the claims that consciousness, Intentionality, human agency can be 'naturalized', and that causation is 'real' and can account both for regularities in nature and for our own agency in bringing about changes in the world. Whether reconciliation *is* possible is a question which has exercised the minds of many philosophers from at least Kant onwards down to Gadamer and Ricoeur in the present day. As a contribution to the debate another approach to causation will now be considered.

There are of course observable regularities in the world and we do look for them in our daily lives with greater or lesser degrees of attentiveness. The search for regularity or repetition is also central to scientific methodology, which in part involves the bringing of discrete data under general principles and laws and the articulating of patterns or unified structures. We can accept also, with Hampshire and Searle, that the human agent can be taken as the starting point in so far as our experience of change in the world and our own control over it gives us some purchase on the concept of cause. Nevertheless, to talk of the Sun as a power which causes plants to grow or the Earth as the agent which makes objects fall towards it is to describe regularly occurring events in metaphorical terms. Many supposedly less 'advanced' societies than our own – and we may assume this was widespread in prehistoric communities – often think of natural things such as trees, rivers, stones and stars as being imbued with 'spirits' which have influence on them and objects in general. We are not of course committed to such a crude animism; and it would be a travesty of the truth to ascribe such beliefs to practising scientists. However, the notion of an object's possessing a capacity to cause another to change in some way continues to play a central role in explanation. What we must do therefore is to 'demythologize' it – by searching for what, at a deeper 'level', may be supposed to be a feature common both to human agency and naturally occurring events. (As Lyons writes, referring to Davidson's anomalous monism: 'The right level for strict causal laws is the micro-level of physics and so of physical events' [p.lviii].)

Consider as a working definition of causation: *For any two (subatomic) 'fundamental' particles A and B, A is said to cause B if and only if a force is mediated between them.* We may suppose the causal relation to be *de re* necessary in that it is a manifestation of the essential properties of the particles, including the quantum particles which mediate the force. (This definition also has the advantage of resolving an issue which has been much debated recently – whether the causal relation is to be understood as linking events or objects; for it is generally held that fundamental particles can be regarded both as spatio-temporal 'objects' and as 'happenings' or events – concentrations of energy.)

Now a core assumption of the theory is that while causation has been defined at this primitive level, the notion of cause at the macro-levels of more complex entities (inorganic molecules, proteins, DNA and higher organisms) is to be understood in terms of and 'transferred' from the activity of particles and their associated energy fields. (Note that 'transference', which derives from Latin, has much the same connotation as the Greek 'metaphor'.) How might we describe this process of 'transference'? There is an initial difficulty. Fundamental particles (electrons, for example) are characterized by indeterminacy: they appear and disappear spontaneously for no apparent reason. Physicists talk of their existence in terms of probability wave equations. However, the key factor for our purposes here is that the behaviour of each individual particle in a complex tends to be cancelled out by the behaviour of others; and arising from the totality of interactions is what we might call a 'fixed' sequence or pattern – an event which can be described in terms of the standard 'deterministic' laws of physics. At a higher level the random movements of atoms in a gas cancel out in such a way that the behaviour of the resultant mass as a whole can be measured and accurately predicted with reference to, say, the kinetic theory and the gas laws, or in the case of a liquid with reference to viscosity, surface tension and so on. Likewise properties such as density or colour can be thought of as resulting from an 'averaging out' (some philosophers of science talk of 'summing over') of particle movement and bonding. Similar considerations apply to the chance mutations which occur as a consequence of particle behaviour at the micro-level, or as an effect of natural irradiation. After a cancelling out of 'chance' events the properties of the resultant organic molecules can be accommodated within the 'strict' laws of biochemistry. As Jacques Monod has shown, both chance and necessity have roles to play in the emergence of complexity from primitive particles to sentient organisms. And, as we know, a great deal that happens in the universe is remarkably stable and predictable. Statistically, of course, there is a very small probability that, for example, a liquid *could* suddenly change its properties. Changes in the structure of atomic nuclei and in the numbers of orbiting electrons *might* bring about a 'miraculous' conversion of water into wine. That this does not seem ever to have occurred – perhaps the wedding feast at Cana was a special case? – is no doubt a matter of some regret to many of us. However, unpredictable and 'contrary to nature' changes might not always work to our advantage. Chaos would ensue if railway lines suddenly dematerialized, or if the Sun stopped and reversed its direction. But it has been calculated that the odds against the molecules of, say, a marble statue all moving in the same direction at a given moment, or of a cow jumping over the Moon, are so large that the number could not be written down in the length of time which measures the age of the universe so far! (See R. Dawkins, *The Blind Watchmaker*, pp.160–161 and the discussion of 'miracles' in 9.4.)

*Criticisms

As you might expect, there are many objections that can be made against this theory (our account of which necessarily has been over-simplified and abbreviated). We shall consider three:

(1) Empiricists would of course say that we can have no knowledge of such a causal relation or indeed of the fundamental particles as 'relata'. However, the assumption that sub-atomic particles, forces and fields exist is not dependent on their observability but rather on the role they play in the wider context of scientific theory. Certainly an empirical aspect is preserved to the extent that appropriate or relevant observations, which might be expected if such particles and forces are operational at the micro-level, may have to be looked for and identified. But this is to say that the supposition of their existence is justified by their explanatory power over a whole range of phenomena in the natural sciences – and indeed in the biological sciences also. Moreover, as we have shown earlier, the radical empiricist position is itself flawed.

(2) Is not the thesis invalidated in so far as it is based on contemporary scientific knowledge? Given historical precedents such as the replacement of the phlogiston theory of combustion by Lavoisier's oxygen theory, or the assimilation of Newtonian physics into the more embracing and arguably 'truer' Einsteinian explanatory framework, we might reasonably suppose that our present explanation of phenomena in terms of particles and fields could be replaced by a 'better' theory. (See 8.4.) Moreover, the origin of quarks, electrons and so on itself remains a mystery. Did they emerge from a 'Big Bang' – the result of a 'quantum fluctuation' as some cosmologists believe? What if something even more fundamental than particles and fields were to be discovered? Would this not undermine our *ad hoc* definition of causation? The answer is 'no'. To deal with the second issue first, to pose a question about the origin of 'fundamental' particles and fields is not inconsistent with the adoption of the definition presented above. The relation of causation has been analysed in terms of two relata and the mediating force, whereas any ultimate origin (God, point source of infinite density, for example) of particles, space and time (and hence the cosmos as a whole) is construed as a single 'entity'. Thus it is inappropriate (a category

mistake?) to call it a first *cause*. Moreover, the view of modern theoreticians is that particles emerge by chance, randomly from a force field (they talk of virtual particles); and here too it is questionable whether the concept of cause is applicable to what have already been described as chance occurrences. As to the possibility that a new scientific theory or explanatory framework might in time be developed, this cannot of course be ruled out. Quantum theory has proved to be in some sense more fundamental than Dalton's atomic theory. Perhaps an even more fundamental theory may emerge which will not only reconcile quantum theory with the theory of relativity (physicists refer to this as 'GUT' – the Grand Unified Theory) but will also invoke 'entities' or structures at a level even below that of quarks. This is of course speculative. (The most promising candidate at the moment is the 'superstring', a vibrating loop of energy one billionth the size of an atom!). But any modification or even replacement of quantum theory would not present any serious difficulty to our analysis of causation; for we should need only to redefine the relation in terms of the new and more 'fundamental' entities and then to show how the quantum level emerges from them. (Note that although the theory being presented here is 'realist' it can be assimilated into an 'internal' realist framework such as that proposed by Putnam.)

(3) The most serious objection perhaps concerns the concept of human freedom. Firstly, how – if at all – can our everyday feeling or supposition that we are in some sense free to choose and act be reconciled with the indeterminacy which seems to be a characteristic of events at the quantum level? Secondly, how can the determinism which seems to be implicit in the concept of scientific law and its associated concepts of regularity and predictability be understood as emerging from this same quantum level, and how can human freedom be reconciled with *this*? Thirdly, what kinds of 'bridging' relationships can be envisaged which might facilitate and account for the transition from the quantum level to higher levels (physical, chemical, biological, psychological, and perhaps even social)? How, in other words, can we (following Searle) accommodate human freedom within a naturalistic framework which will avoid both a crude materialistic reductionism and 'spiritualistic' dualist accounts of human behaviour?

11.5 Freedom and responsibility

Reading: Aristotle, *Nicomachean Ethics* – see 4.8 above; Aquinas, *Summa Theologiae*, Ia, 83–85 and 103; Descartes, *Meditations*, IV; Hume, *Enquiry concerning Human Understanding*, VIII; Kant, *Critique of Pure Reason* (or *Prolegomena*), *Groundwork of the Metaphysic of Morals*; Sartre, *Existentialism and Humanism*, *Being and Nothingness*, Part IV; Searle, *Minds, Brains and Science*, 6; *Mind, Language and Society*, ch. 4

Determinism

The problem of freedom is closely linked with that of causation, and it is associated with a similar conflict between our fundamental intuitions about ourselves and what the natural sciences seem to reveal about the world – or at least some aspects of it. We have already talked about freedom in the sense of political and social liberty in Ch. 7. Our concern here is with 'freedom' in a narrower, metaphysical sense. The issue can be presented simply in the following terms. (A clear statement of the problem is to be found in Hume's *Enquiry*, VIII, 'Of Liberty and Necessity', which you should study carefully.) In my day-to-day affairs I believe that I have some degree of choice and control over my actions. I can decide whether to write another paragraph or go to the pub. Are my actions (and decisions) 'caused'? If they are, then the causes are either 'psychological' (my actions are caused by 'volitions' or 'acts of will', motives, desires and so on) or 'bio-physical' (I think and do what I do because of my character, which was formed when I was very young and over which therefore I had no control, or because of my genetic make-up, which in its turn is explicable in terms of molecular bondings, and such-like). My decisions and actions would thus seem to be 'necessitated': my behaviour is **determined**. If, however, I argue that my actions are not caused then I cannot really be said to be responsible for them. So we appear to be led to a 'Catch-22' situation, that either our actions are our own but we cannot help but perform them, or they are not 'ours', in which case we cannot be held responsible for them. The relevance of this conclusion to ethics is obvious. (You will recall the discussions of moral responsibility in 3.12, 4.8 and 6.7.) How different philosophers have attempted to deal with this dilemma depends very much on the position they adopt with regard to the mind–body problem. Let us consider some of the possible solutions which have been proposed:

(1) **Monist materialism (Hobbes).** Although Hobbes wholeheartedly embraced a 'scientific' view of man and sought to explain all psychological activity in terms of modifications of matter in the brain, he maintained both that human action could still be regarded as voluntary and that we should be held responsible for our behaviour. But he avoided being impaled on one horn of the dilemma only by defining human freedom in somewhat negative terms. Liberty, he said, is the 'absence of all the impediments to action that are not contained in the nature and intrinsical quality of the agent' [*Of Liberty and Necessity*]. Our actions may be caused by our inner 'desires' or 'aversions', but they remain *our* actions and are voluntary in so far as they are manifestations of our intrinsic nature and we are not compelled by external forces to act in such and such a way.

(2) **Cartesian Dualism.** For a materialist such as Hobbes there is no distinction between psychological and physical determinism. In the philosophy of Descartes, however, physical determinism has to be reconciled with an uncompromising commitment to 'inner' freedom. The body, being material and extended, is subject to the mechanical laws of physics: but will (that is, the mind in one of its many aspects) is unlimited in its freedom. And if we are to be held responsible for the evil we commit it is the fault not of the power of willing as such – which according to Descartes is received from God – but from our failure to contain our will within the bounds imposed upon us by our understanding:

Whence then come my errors? They come from the sole fact that, since my will is much more ample and extensive in its range than the understanding, I do not restrain it within the same limits but extend it even to things I do not understand; and as the will is of itself indifferent to those things it very easily falls into error and sin and chooses the false for the true and the bad for the good . . .

If I abstain from giving my judgement on something when I do not conceive it with sufficient clarity and distinctness, it is evident that I act rightly and am not at all deceived: but if I resolve to deny or affirm, then I do not make a right use of my free will; and if I affirm what is not true, it is clear that I deceive myself. Moreover, even though I judge according to the truth, this comes about only by chance and do not escape the blame for misusing my free will; for the natural light teaches us that the knowledge of the understanding ought always precede the determination of the will.

[*Meditation*, IV]

Descartes' account is thus intellectualist; the will must in some sense be subordinated to the understanding, and both intellectual error and moral error are both attributed to the alleged fact that the will is 'more ample than the understanding'. But by subscribing to the view that the will is intrinsically unlimited in itself Descartes is also committed to what might be called an *indeterminist* account of freedom. If so, then this can lead to the criticism that human choices must be arbitrary or random.

(3) **Hume**. Like Hobbes, Hume argued both that our actions are caused (by our desires or motives) and that this is consistent with our responsibility for them. Indeed, he said, it is only because our actions *are* caused, that is, spring from our own character, that we can be said to be responsible for them at all. Freedom, however, is not defined by Hume as the absence of external constraints, but in terms of being determined by one's own motives, it is also important to note Hume's analysis of 'causation'. Causes 'necessitate' or 'determine' their effects, and this is true also of human actions. But 'necessitation' being interpreted in terms of constant conjunctions or regularities rather than of compulsion, a door is left open for freedom and responsibility.

(4) **Kant and 'practical' freedom**. You will remember from the discussions in Chs 5 and 6 and in 11.4 of this chapter that Kant thought of causality as a 'category' of the understanding applicable only to the phenomenal realm. Freedom belongs to the noumenal world and is a presupposition – a 'regulative idea' – of the categorical imperative. As Kant put it, 'ought implies can'. It is by stressing that the idea of freedom, or autonomy of the will, is a *practical* assumption and not a theoretical one that Kant seeks to resolve the antinomy of freedom and necessity. (Note the implicit assumption that the noumenal realm is 'real and not merely a negative concept: this is consistent with the 'strong' interpretation referred to earlier.)

(5) **Sartre**. At the end of Ch. 5 we referred to Sartre's recognition of a conflict between the individual's intuition of himself as totally free (in the sense of being able to *choose* to 'make himself', to 'fill the gap', between the *en-soi* and the *pour-soi*) and his recognition of himself as an 'object' for the 'Other' (*autrui*). How can this conflict be resolved? Sartre's initial solution is to seek to restore his freedom by in turn 'possessing' the Other. What he means by this is made clear in *Being and Nothingness*, Part III, ch. 3, I, where he takes as an illustration the relationship between lovers considered from the psychological aspect. Sartre has to conclude, however, that though his freedom be reaffirmed, the fundamental conflict between the self and the Other can never be terminated. In seeking to appropriate the freedom of his beloved the lover will either treat her as an automaton or as a being whose love for him is the consequence of free commitment. Both alternatives, Sartre says, are unsatisfactory. Clearly the lover does not wish to be loved by a person whom he has enslaved. Neither does he wish to be loved by someone who does not desire him for himself but because of her 'pure loyalty to a sworn oath'. If he adopts the first alternative it will lead ultimately to sadism. If he adopts the second and allows himself to become an 'object' for the beloved, this will result in masochism. But in both cases his freedom is affirmed – and if he does become 'Being-for-the-Other' this will give rise to the further problem of frustration, in so far as by virtue of his free choice he *cannot* in fact be just an object. He could of course remain indifferent to the beloved, observing her behaviour without involvement. But from the point of view of the relationship this would be equally unsatisfactory. (Note that his argument in *Being and Nothingness* is long and somewhat repetitive. You will need to study it with care and patience. Insight into Sartre's philosophical approach can also be gained from a reading of his novels.)

The implications of this pessimistic conclusion for Sartre's ethics have already been discussed (6.6 and 7.4). But what of Sartre's attitude to the question of freedom as such? Is his theory not open equally to the criticisms which can be made of Descartes' account, namely that freedom is equivalent to indeterminacy and that it is therefore arbitrary? For, at least in *Existentialism and Humanism*, Sartre seems to have argued that to commit oneself to a particular course of action in a given set of circumstances *because* that course has been described as being 'right' (by society, or a religious code, for example) is to be guilty of 'bad faith' and is to *deny* one's freedom. So he would appear to be advocating a policy of commitment without motive. This is, however, not Sartre's view. In *Being and Nothingness*, IV, ch. 1 he argues (as mentioned above in 5.11) that conscious being is able to conceive of an as-yet-non-existent future. Through this intentionality of being-for-itself (*pour-soi*), the world, that is, being-in-itself (*en-soi*), is 'negated' or 'set-off' from it. His awareness of the need to eliminate this 'nothingness' or 'non-being', that is, to fill the 'gap', *itself* constitutes the motive for action. Sartre makes it clear that it is not a 'factual state' (the political and economic structure of society, the psychological 'state' and so on) that can be a motive (*motif*) but the recognition that the state of affairs must be changed. 'The motive [*mobile*] is understood only by the end; that is, by the non-existent. It is therefore in itself a *négatité*. There can be a free-for-itself only as engaged in a resisting world. Outside of this engagement the notions of freedom, of determinism, of necessity lose all meaning.' But neither can the factual state 'determine consciousness to apprehend it as a *négatité* or as a lack'. Sartre is thus denying that there is any external determining *cause* of our actions; actions are intentional and are inner-directed. Our motives (*mobiles*, not *motifs*) are thus the only genuine causes and are grounded in the freedom of human conscious-ness, being-for-itself, to think about its situation in terms of negativity and contemplate the possibility of changing it. Freedom is thus a pre-condition for all human action in that it *belongs* to action itself. It would seem to follow then that for Sartre, while actions might be said to be arbitrary as considered from the standpoint of their factual content, they are not indeterminate, in that they are motivated by the conscious recognition of the need to fill the 'gap' between the *en-soi* and the *pour-soi*, between the (absent) future and the present, or between possibility and actuality. As he says: 'freedom is actually one with the being of the For-itself; human reality is free to the exact extent that it has to be its own nothingness' [*Being and Nothingness*, III, 1, I]. The agent himself *is* the sole determinant.

*Criticisms and comments

Just as the different approaches of various philosophers to the problem of freedom are influenced by the kinds of theories of mind to which they subscribe, so are they open to objections appropriate to those theories.

Dualists, for example, have to deal with the problem of how mind and body can be said to interact. This leads to several associated difficulties for the problem of freedom. How is a mind or 'will' free while the body in which it is apparently 'lodged' is causally determined and subject to the laws of science? Or, if the mind be conceived of as psychologically determined, how can this be reconciled with bio-physical determinism of the body? Some philosophers, most notably Ryle and Hampshire, have been strongly critical of the vocabulary of 'willing', 'volition', 'desire' and so on, as used by Descartes, as if they were internal 'episodes' separate from or prior to bodily actions [see *The Concept of Mind*, ch. III].

As for **Hume**, his analysis of causation and necessity makes room for responsibility in so far as it seems to rule out compulsion. But this same analysis leads to difficulties for the concept of personal identity which seems to be a prerequisite for responsibility (compare 5.11).

Kant's 'solution' is important in that it underpins ethics. 'Ought' implies 'can'. But it has to be admitted that a certain tension remains between the sensible and the intelligible worlds to both of which man at the same time belongs. According to Strawson [*Freedom and Resentment*] the view of man as a physical object whose behaviour can be explained scientifically in terms of the notions of cause and necessity is indeed incompatible with his being regarded as a morally responsible person, though both standpoints can be adopted on different occasions or applicable to different people. Both accounts, he says, reflect fundamental aspects of our nature. Moreover, there is no third vantage point from which we might attempt to decide between them. There is therefore no reason why we should deny either. (Do you find a satisfactory solution?) Note that the two incompatible accounts are not like different theories in science (say, the wave theory versus the corpuscular theory), for the latter, although explaining different phenomena, are as it were on the same 'level' and can be tested by the same kinds of experimental methods. Thus there seems to be a fundamental opposition between thinking of ourselves as both physically determined and morally free.

Sartre in effect seeks to preserve freedom by denying any causative role to being-in-itself. Obviously we are born with a specific physical make-up, and we are brought up in a particular family or society. But at all times, he insists, it is we ourselves who choose what we are and what we are to become. We are responsible totally for our character. [Study the examples he gives throughout Part III of *Being and Nothingness*, particularly his discussion and rejection of Freud's psychoanalytic determinism in ch. 1. Do you think this would satisfy the determinist? Could he not argue that our actual *acceptance* (or non-acceptance) of our circumstances might itself be influenced (if not 'determined') by genetic or unconscious factors?]

Perhaps the problem could be tackled more successfully if we started out from 'naturalistic monism' rather than from a dualist standpoint? It must not of course be a materialist monism (for example, of the Hobbesian variety), because this would seem definitely to land us back into a determinism which does not sit too well with the concept of personal responsibility. There are also problems with Spinoza's monism. Although, arguably, he solves the Cartesian mind–body problem, his thesis requires him to attribute a mental aspect to every individual particle and complex of matter in the universe – a position scientifically unacceptable today. Moreover, his commitment to determinism is perhaps more serious than Hobbes's in that metaphysical causation is assimiliated to *logical* necessity. So let us return to the accounts offered by Searle and Hampshire (and note also Merleau-Ponty's important concept of the 'body-subject'), which point to the centrality of intention, intentionality and consciousness to the concept of free agency – which itself is taken to be a fundamental datum. As Searle says:

> . . . evolution has given us a form of experience of voluntary action where the experience of freedom – that is to say, the experience of the sense of alternative possibilities – is built into the very structure of conscious, voluntary, intentional human behaviour. For that reason, I believe, neither this discussion nor any other will ever convince us that our behaviour is unfree. [*Minds, Brains and Science*, 6]

But even for Searle the problem remains of reconciling what seems to be an in-built determinism with this presumption of freedom. He distinguishes between 'bottom-up' and' top-down' causation. The former involves explanation of surface features of a phenomenon (such as the liquidity of water) in terms of the behaviour of micro-particles (in this case molecules). The relation of mind to the brain is, he says, an example of such a relation. In 'top-down' causation, however, a mental event causes a physical event: a person's intention to raise his arm produces the release of the neuro-transmitter acetylcholine at the end-plate of motor-neurons, and he thereby raises his arm [*Minds, Brains and Science*, 6]. Such cases work because the top level and bottom level go together: 'the mental events are grounded in the neurophysiology to start with'. The conclusion Searle draws from this is that so long as we accept the bottom-up conception of physical explanation then 'psychological facts about ourselves . . . are entirely causally explicable in terms of, and entirely realised in systems of, elements at the fundamental micro-physical level. Our conception of physical reality simply does not allow for radical freedom' [*Minds, Brains and Science*, 6]. In *Mind, Language and Society* [p.107] he draws attention to the 'gap' between the causes of our decisions in the form of beliefs and desires and the actual decisions, and the gap between decisions and performances of actions. These gaps (which we call the freedom of the will) arise because 'the intentionalistic causes of behaviour are not sufficient to determine the behaviour' (except in such pathological cases as addiction, obsession, overwhelming passion). So: 'It remains an unsolved problem in philosophy how there can be freedom of the will, given that there are no corresponding gaps in the brain'.

In the last analysis, Searle (like Sartre) therefore relies on his fundamental intuition or consciousness of himself as a freely acting and intentional individual who, in appropriate circumstances, could have done something different from what he did do. But, as he himself admits, he finds himself in much the situation as Hume did when he returned to the everyday world after a session of philosophizing in his study. Is there then no way out of this dilemma? How do mental events, which are grounded in neurophysiology, yet in some way 'escape' from that grounding and allow for free choice?

Clearly we need a theory which will accommodate both continuity and qualitative difference, that is to say, which will recognize that our general activity is indeed grounded in successive neuro-physiological, biochemical, and micro-physical levels or 'cumulative structures' (Merleau-Ponty) while at the same time providing a framework which will enable us to bridge Searle's 'gaps'. The basis of a possible theory has already been roughly outlined above. The question now is how such notions as spontaneity, chance, necessity and determinism can be reconciled in their application to human desires, motives, freedom, choice and of course responsibility.

Firstly let us note the similarities between ourselves and the rest of the animal kingdom. No doubt as a consequence of evolutionary adaptation, we possess in-built mechanisms which enable us to respond rapidly to the environmental stimuli we receive through our sense organs and process by means of our brain. And a great deal of our activity caused by such stimuli we do not have to think about at all. This is often loosely termed instinctive behaviour. Similarly we do not have to concern ourselves with the day-to-day workings of, say, our heart; it functions under the control of the autonomic nervous system. This is clearly advantageous in so far as we are, as it were, thereby released to attend to other matters. Life would be much more complicated, and our survival prospects more uncertain, if we had regularly to 'will' our heart to continue beating or had to remember to breathe every so often. Now all this can also be said of other organisms. But it is instructive to contrast human behaviour with that of so-called 'lower' animals. Show a fly the way out of a room through a hole in the wall a thousand times. Invariably it will continue to buzz around in frustration (though it presumably does not know it is frustrated) – unless it finds the way out by pure 'chance'. Humans and other mammals, however, by virtue of more complex brains possess a greater degree of 'plasticity', learning power and self-control; and we have the capacity to channel our instincts and to direct our sensory organs to specific features of the environment. We are agents in a more fundamental sense than flies, earthworms, or amoeba are. (The concept of action will be discussed in the next chapter.) What role does consciousness play here? And how does it relate to freedom? A useful way of answering these questions is to consider a particular scenario.

Suppose your partner or one of your children is seriously injured in an accident at home and you have to get him or her to the emergency unit at the local hospital with the minimum of delay. You do not have to deliberate about what to do. It is as if there is a database of possible strategies stored in your brain, which have been gathered over the many years since you were quite small. Likewise you can call on a repertoire of skills and capacities which will facilitate the implementation of your decision, such as your ability to drive the car, knowledge of the best route to the hospital and so on, all of which have been learned. Perhaps we can refer to these strategies and capacities as being in the 'subconscious' level of the brain. There are also other bits of information you will need to draw on as you set off on your journey, for example, the rules of the road and possible consequences if you break them. Suppose now you find the traffic lights set at red. You are presented with a dilemma: break the lights and risk possible prosecution, or wait and risk the life of your partner or child. Of course, you will know that in practice the circumstances would be regarded as mitigating and it is unlikely that even if you were prosecuted you would receive anything more than a warning as punishment. However, it is a 'grey area'. Can you be sure the condition of your partner or child *is* life-threatening? What if your going through the red light itself caused injury to another driver or pedestrian? Clearly there are moral issues here. But the point of the example is to suggest that: (1) all these factors are stored in the brain, and (2) that the new series of events relating to the journey and its consequences are *themselves* put into the brain's 'database' so that these in turn can be drawn upon when alternative courses of action present themselves in future situations. Thus we have a kind of 'feed-back' phenomenon. The brain (that is, ourselves) has to be regarded as engaged in an on-going dynamic interaction with the environment and as constantly choosing in the light of new chance encounters. Its (our) experiences are thereby 'channelled' into storage to modify the available sets of strategies. The brain is neither 'single tracked', predetermined to respond rigidly and invariably to given kinds of stimuli come what may, nor is it fickle, indeterminate, its responses (as manifested in actions) totally unpredictable. Brains are in fact *self-determining* organs. Cerebral consciousness can be regarded as a powerful means whereby: (1) new data can be assessed and moderated, and projects proposed and developed, before being stored in the 'subconscious'; and (2) stored data and strategies can be brought out of storage and articulated when needed to meet the contingencies of novel situations. It is pertinent to note that it has been discovered by some researchers that changes in the brain occur up to half a second *before* a subject mentally decides that he intends to make a movement! (See the important discussion of this in J.Z. Young's *Philosophy and the Brain*. This excellent book by a world renowned biologist should be regarded as essential reading if you want to get some background about the workings of the brain and its implications for ethics and some of the issues we are discussing here.) Obviously if a particular situation is for the most part one we have encountered on a previous occasion, the brain can initiate a suitable plan of action without any thought being involved. (Once we have learned to walk or talk we do not need constantly to work out what to do to get ourselves down to the local shop to ask for a loaf of bread: it just 'happens' – see the next chapter.)

Knowing what kind of person someone is (as judged by background, moral convictions, previous behaviour and so on) makes it possible for us to predict with some degree of accuracy how he or she will behave in a given situation. How is this compatible with the concept of freedom of choice? There is really no serious problem about this. Predictability is not and cannot be absolute. Each one of us is unique: we differ in our genetic endowment, education and socialization. (Twins may have the same genome, but the environments in which they are nurtured, although usually similar, are not identical – not least because of different spatio-temporal circumstances.) Furthermore the situations in which decisions are made and actions taken are infinitely various; and these situations themselves modify our individual 'databases' as our brain interacts dynamically with the environment. There is no sense therefore in the idea that we could have a God-like knowledge of a person's make-up and situation which would enable us to say for certain how he or she *will* act. Nevertheless it is equally mistaken to suppose that all predictions will turn out to be false. If social life is to be possible we have to assume that people will act in broadly similar ways in given situations consistently with their 'characters' and circumstances. Moreover it is arguable that individuals whose behaviour is (more or less) completely predictable are usually suffering from, say, neuroses, phobias and the like which reduce the flexibility of their responses to novel circumstances and their ability to create strategies or projects. At the other extreme are those individuals whose behaviour is arbitrary and totally *un*predictable – often people who are overwhelmed by their emotions. Significantly we describe both sorts of individuals as 'out of control' and 'irrational'.

What then of moral responsibility and weakness of will (see 3.12, 4.8 and 6.7)? It is often difficult to determine the extent of the limitations within which we operate. Nevertheless, that approximate lines can be and are drawn is implied by the vocabulary of mental illness we use and which is recognized in law; and it is generally accepted that people suffering from certain kinds of pathological conditions are deemed not to be responsible for their actions. (It may of course still be legitimate to ask, at least in some cases, whether such individuals should not bear some responsibility for succumbing to such states in the first place: but this is a matter for psychiatry and sociology.) Now, let us leave aside 'extreme' cases and concentrate on the majority – so-called 'normal' people who are content to be held morally and legally accountable for their actions. How is it that they (and presumably the writer of this book and you the reader can be included in this majority) so often and in full knowledge fail to act 'rightly'? Firstly it should be noted that frequently when we accuse somebody of being weak-willed we are accusing him or her of not doing what *we* regard as the right thing in the circumstances. But there are situations about which there is common agreement regardless of the moral theory being adopted (such as that of Aristotle, Kant, Hume, Mill and so on). Consider this example. Week in and week out a man spends his wages on himself (drink, betting, or whatever) without regard to the needs of his family. Why? One possibility is that he (his brain) makes a distinction (consciously or subconsciously) between short-term gratification and long-term satisfaction. Perhaps he says to himself: 'I'll spend a few more pounds now; I know there'll be a row at home later'. Perhaps, like Mr Micawber, he thinks something will 'turn up'. Now suppose the anticipated row does break out. This becomes a new datum to be recorded in the brain's 'database', and note will be taken of this the next time he feels like having a few more drinks or bets. As a result it is less likely that he will give in to his immediate desires. If he does, it is probable that the intensity of the next inevitable row will this time 'tip' the decision-making mechanisms of the brain into a new mode so that, other factors or circumstances being equal, he will on the next occasion after that resist the temptations of the pub or betting shop. Strategies have been modified in favour of his own longer-term interests. Indeed he perhaps comes to recognize the coincidence of his *self*-interest with the welfare of his dependants; he comes to see what is *really* good for him. It is possible of course that a person will continue to be weak-willed. The best explanation is that such a person is operating within a framework of conviction that more probable short-term gain for self is always preferable to less probable longer-term benefits to others or even to himself. Judged by our 'normal' standards such behaviour may well be regarded as irrational and anti-social; and it may border on the pathological when in some strong sense he *cannot* change. In such an eventuality it is unlikely that the threat of sanctions will deter or that reforming will be a viable option.

We have moved back into the realms of ethics and political philosophy. So let us summarize briefly by saying that what has been suggested here is that the problem of freedom appears insoluble only because we are looking for a solution in the wrong way or in the wrong place. We must in fact do what Searle himself advocates: engage in some conceptual revision. We must think of the notions of freedom and choice as intrinsically bound up with a 'homeostatic' interaction between the brain and the environment, and with an on-going matching by the consciousness of possible and actual consequences of action. These results are themselves constantly being fed back to the subconscious levels of the brain, thereby modifying its stored strategies for further action as new situations arise which demand its attention. There is no real 'gap'; to be conscious *is* to be free. (It is left to you to consider possible objections to this kind of approach.)

Fatalism

Fatalism is a wider thesis than determinism in that it supposes that the future is somehow 'fixed'. It can be summed up by the assertion 'What is going to happen *will* happen'. To bring this chapter to an end, two arguments for what might seem to be a somewhat surprising claim will now be examined.

The argument from future truth

(A version of this argument was first proposed by Aristotle in ch. 9 of his *De Interpretatione*. There is, however, considerable dispute about how he deals with it.) In its essentials the thesis states: (a) that it is either true or false that I shall be going to Oxford tomorrow, and (b) that whatever I may do or not do will not prevent me from going to Oxford if it is true that I shall, or from not going if it is not true. *Prima facie* the argument appears valid. But it does seem to be quite contrary to our common-sense belief that we have some control over our own future. So either we must be mistaken and everything is predetermined, or there must be something wrong with the thesis.

*Comments

(1) The argument is peculiar in that whichever of the two disjuncts (that is, 'it is true that . . .' or 'it is false that . . .') is true we should have no way of testing it, because *either* outcome is consistent with the claim made that that outcome is inevitable.

(2) Some philosophers have suggested that the argument itself can never get off the ground because statements about the future cannot be said to be true or false (compare the discussion in 5.7).

(3) Suppose we accept that it is possible to talk meaningfully of true or false statements about future events. Need we accept the conclusion that the future is therefore beyond our control? Surely not; for our own decisions and actions, freely taken, themselves belong to the series of contributory events leading up to the ultimate realization of the truth or falsity of the original statement. So far as we ourselves are concerned, it is no more than a logically trivial point (a tautology) that whatever will happen *will* happen. But there is a second form of the argument which relates to an issue already mentioned in Ch. 9, which we shall now look at briefly.

The argument from God's foreknowledge

As self-determining beings, we may believe that we have the capacity to make an input into a series of circumstances culminating in a future event – even though in some 'logical' sense the future will be what it will be. The fatalist, however, still wants to insist that the inevitability of the future event (that I shall go to Oxford tomorrow, or that I shall not) is more than a tautology. To God, 'existing' neither in space nor time, the totality of past, present and future events is known eternally. Thus everything, including my 'freely-chosen' actions themselves, is predetermined; which seems to make my freedom an illusion.

*Comments

Two answers might be made to this new challenge:

(1) God's foreknowledge or omniscience could be of such a kind and capacity as to be consistent with the exercise of human freedom. This is an 'orthodox'

theological response. (It does of course raise other issues, already discussed, such as why God, 'knowing' in advance what would happen in his universe, did not create one with rather less suffering in it.)

(2) A more radical solution would be to limit God's omniscience to the present and to the past. (Whether this would detract from His alleged omnipotence is yet another question.) But if the future of His creation is undetermined even for God, we would have to adjust our concept of God and suppose Him to be engaged in games of chance or trial and error, and therefore in a very real sense committed to experience the suffering of his creatures as their choices enter into and modify the world process. The only other alternative would be to deny the existence of a transcendental 'personal' God altogether.

QUESTIONS

A. Texts

1 Does Aristotle's account of human action deal satisfactorily with the problem of weakness of will?

2 Explain and discuss Aquinas's account of the faculties of the soul.

[IB, specimen, 2000]

3 Explain and discuss Aquinas's view that the soul is incorruptible.

4 Expound and discuss Aquinas's arguments for free-will in man.

*5 Given the distinctions Descartes made between the nature of mind and the nature of body, how did he attempt to account for their interaction? Do you think his account was satisfactory?

6 Why did Hume assert that 'any volume; of divinity or school metaphysics . . . can contain nothing but sophistry and illusion'? Do you accept his suggestion that it should therefore be committed to the flames?

7 Examine critically Hume's account of the origin of 'general ideas'.

*8 Examine critically Hume's account of causality. Note in particular his two 'definitions'.

9 Explain Hume's reasons for concluding that 'the conjunction between motives and voluntary actions is as regular and uniform as that between the cause and effect in any part of nature'. To what extent does Hume succeed in reconciling this conclusion with freedom of action?

10 Examine Kant's claim that causation is an *a priori* category.

11 Kant distinguishes between a metaphysics of 'speculative reason' and a metaphysics as a 'natural disposition'. Discuss why he makes this distinction.

12 Kant states (in the *Metaphysics of Morals*) that freedom cannot be 'explained'. Why does he say this? Consider whether his own solution to the free-will–determinism problem is satisfactory.

13 Sartre says (in *Being and Nothingness*) that 'the indispensable and fundamental condition of all action is the freedom of the acting being'. Is his account of freedom compatible with his distinction between the *en-soi* and the *pour-soi*?

14 Examine critically Ayer's 'criterion of verifiability'.

15 Has Ayer 'eliminated' metaphysics?

*16 Do you think Ayer is correct when he claims that what makes the 'appearances'

appearances of the same thing is not 'their relationship to an entity other than themselves, but their relationship to one another.'

17 Discuss Russell's account of universals and how they differ from other things.

18 'It would seem that knowledge concerning the universe is not to be obtained by metaphysics.' Examine critically Russell's claim.

19 'The essential thing about metaphysics: it obliterates the distinction between facts.' Examine critically what Wittgenstein means.

20 Wittgenstein claims that 'philosophy is a fight against the fascination which forms exert over us'. Examine this claim. [IB, specimen, 2000]

21 'Freud's theory of the unconscious and repression may be a useful assumption for the practice of psychotherapy, but in the last analysis it can never be justified philosophically.' Discuss.

22 How does Feyerabend respond to critics of relativism and how successful is his response?

23 Putnam rejects the assertion that we could only be brains in vats. Is his rejection justified? [IB, specimen, 2000]

B. Problems

24 Could it ever make sense to attribute personality to a machine?

*25 What difficulties are there in the idea of a disembodied mental existence?

26 Is it logically coherent to talk about 'unconscious desires'?

27 (a) Describe and illustrate three features of mental states which are held to distinguish them from physical states.
(b) Assess how, if mind and body are taken to be different substances or to have different properties, mental events could cause physical events.
[AQA (AEB), specimen, 2001]

28 On what grounds can mind and body be regarded as distinct and separate entities?

29 'The mind is the brain.' Give a critical account of the identity theory.
[AEB, 1996]

30 Describe and critically assess functionalism as a theory of the relation of mind and body. [AEB, 1997]

31 Can behaviourism provide an adequate account of mental life?

32 Are all mental states necessarily 'directed' towards some object?

33 Is the concept of an uncaused event self-contradictory?

34 'The categories of causal explanation ... have their roots within our own experience of ourselves as agents' (Hampshire). Discuss.

35 How might one distinguish between a caused event and a coincidence?

36 Must a cause always be prior to its effect?

37 If my decision was scientifically predictable, could it be said to have been made freely?

*38 'I could not help it.' Examine some of the grounds that might be proposed to justify this assertion.

39 If an action is caused, does this mean that the agent is not responsible for its consequences?

40 'There is no point in worrying about the future; we can do nothing about it.' Consider the philosophical implications of such a view.

41 If God knows in advance what I shall do, does this mean I shall not be acting of my own free-will?

*42 Is it the case that reason alone gives us knowledge of reality?

43 Examine the strengths and weaknesses of nominalism.

44 Can realist and conceptualist theories of universals be reconciled?

45 Can we dispense with the notion of substance?

46 Can a philosophical system 'mirror' nature?

47 'There can be many different conceptual schemes, but they are all about the same reality.' Examine this claim.

48 Explain and examine the distinction between 'descriptive' and 'revisionary' metaphysics.

49 In what sense can beings be said to possess Being?

50 'We do not speak language; rather language speaks us.' Critically examine the implications of this Heideggerian assertion for the view that language must be 'about' the world.

51 Is reason limited by the language we use?

52 If from birth I had acquired different language from the one I am using now, would I now necessarily be looking at and understanding the world differently – using different categories perhaps?

*Notes/guided answers have been provided for questions **5**, **8**, **16**, **25**, **38** and **42** (at end of book).

READING LIST

A. Prescribed texts
Aquinas, St Thomas, *Summa Theologiae*, I. (IB)
Ayer, A.J., *Language, Truth and Logic.* (AEB)
Descartes, R., *Meditations.* (AEB, IB)
Feyerabend, P., *Farewell to Reason.* (IB)
Freud, S., *Outline of Psychoanalysis.* (IB)
Hume, D., *Essay concerning Human Understanding.* (AEB, IB)
Putnam, H., *Reason, Truth and History.* (IB)
Russell, B., *The Problems of Philosophy.* (AEB)
Sartre, J.-P., *Existentialism and Humanism.* (AEB)
Wittgenstein, L., *The Blue and Brown Books.* (IB)

B. Other texts
Hampshire, S., *Thought and Action.*
Heidegger, M., *An Introduction to Metaphysics.*
Kant, I., *Critique of Pure Reason.*
Kant, I., *Prolegomena to any Future Metaphysics.*
Popper, K.R., *Conjectures and Refutations.*
Putnam, H., *Reason and Representation.*
Quine, W.V.O., *Word and Object.*
Searle, J.R., *Minds, Brains and Science.*
Searle, J.R., *Mind, Language and Society.*
Strawson, P.F., *Individuals.*

Wittgenstein, L., *Philosophical Investigations.*
Wittgenstein, L., *Tractatus Logico-Philosophicus.*

Reference to the following major works (of varying degrees of difficulty!), all of which are in different ways relevant to the several metaphysical problems discussed in this chapter, will also be found valuable: Aristotle, *Metaphysics*; Berkeley, G., *Principles of Human Knowledge*; Bradley, F.H., *Appearance and Reality*; Hegel, G.W.F., *The Phenomenology of Mind*; Heidegger, M., *Being and Time, Kant and the Problem of Metaphysics*; Leibniz, G.W., *Monadology, Discourse on Metaphysics*; Locke, J., *An Essay Concerning Human Understanding*; Merleau-Ponty, M., *The Phenomenology of Perception*; Plato, *Republic*; Russell, B., *Human Knowledge, The Philosophy of Logical Atomism*; Spinoza, B., *Ethics*; Whitehead, A.N., *Process and Reality.*

C. Supplementary reading
(If you are a beginner, you are recommended to start with titles marked with an asterisk.)

1. Historical background
See the texts listed in the Reading lists for Chs 3 and 5, and also the following:
Knowles, D., *The Evolution of Medieval Thought.**
Passmore, J., *A Hundred Years of Philosophy.**
Ryle, G. (ed.), *The Revolution in Philosophy.**

2. Books on individual philosophers
See the Reading lists for Chs 3–9 and also the following:
Inwood, M., *Heidegger.**
Polt, R., *Heidegger: An Introduction.*
Steiner, G., *Heidegger.**
Ross, G., MacDonald, *Leibniz.**
Pears, D., *Bertrand Russell and the British Tradition in Philosophy.**
Hampshire, S., *Spinoza.**
Anscombe, G.E.M., *An Introduction to Wittgenstein's 'Tractatus'.**
Hacker, P.M.S., *Insight and Illusion: Wittgenstein on Philosophy and the Metaphysics of Experience.*

3. General introductory texts on metaphysics in general
Hamlyn, D.W., *Metaphysics.**
Loux, M.J., *Metaphysics: A Contemporary Introduction.**
Pears, D. (ed.), *The Nature of Metaphysics.**
Quinton, A., *The Nature of Things.**

4. Books on particular metaphysical problems
Reality and existence
Kripke, S., *Naming and Necessity.*
Moore, A.W. (ed.), *Meaning and Reference.*
Price, H.H., *Thinking and Experience.*

Putnam, H., *Mind, Language and Reality.**
Quine, W.V.O., *From a Logical Point of View.**
Rorty, R., *Philosophy and the Mirror of Nature.*
Searle, J.R., *Speech Acts.*
Strawson, P.F., *Individuals.*
Strawson, P.F. (ed.), *Philosophical Logic.**
Whorf, B.L., *Language, Thought and Reality.**

Mind

Anscombe, G.E.M., *Intention.*
Blakemore, C., *Mechanisms of the Mind.**
Boden, M., *Artificial Intelligence and Natural Man.*
Boden, M. (ed.), *The Philosophy of Artificial Intelligence.*
Davidson, D., *Essays on Actions and Events.*
Dennett, D.C., *Consciousness Explained.**
Glover, J. (ed.), *The Philosophy of Mind.**
Hell, J., *Philosophy of Mind: A Contemporary Introduction.**
Johnson-Laird, P.N., *The Computer and the Mind.**
Lyons, W. (ed.), *Modern Philosophy of Mind.** (Excellent anthology.)
McGinn, C., *The Character of Mind.**
Nagel, T., *The View from Nowhere*, ch. III.*
Parfit, D., *Reasons and Persons.*
Pinker, S., *How the Mind Works.**
Scruton, R., *Art and Imagination: An Introduction to the Philosophy of Mind.*
Searle, J.R., *Intentionality.*
Searle, J.R., *The Rediscovery of the Mind.**
Teichmann, J., *The Mind and the Soul.**

Causation

Ayer, A.J., *Foundations of Empirical Knowledge.**
Ayer, A.J., *The Problem of Knowledge.**
Bunge, M., *Causality.*
Mackie, J.L., *The Cement of the Universe.*
Nagel, E., *The Structure of Science.*
Sosa, E. and Tooley, M. (eds), *Causation and Conditionals.**
Trusted, J., *The Structure of Scientific Inference.**

Freedom and responsibility

Ayer, A.J., 'Freedom and Necessity', in *Philosophical Essays.**
Hampshire, S., *Freedom of the Will.*
Melden, A.I., *Free Action.**
Nagel, T., *The View from Nowhere*, ch. VII.*
Ricoeur, P., *Freedom and Nature.*
Sorabji, R., *Necessity, Cause and Blame.*
Strawson, P.F., *Freedom and Resentment.*
Trusted, J., *Free Will and Responsibility.**
Watson, G. (ed.), *Free Will.**

⊠ 12 Man, society and culture

12.1 Introduction: philosophical anthropology

In the preceding chapters we have covered many different fields of philosophy – the theory of knowledge, ethics, political philosophy, the philosophy of science and so on. But nothing has been said about science, religion, art, or indeed philosophy itself as aspects or 'modes' of **culture**. Neither has there been any examination of the creator of culture, namely, ourselves! What is man? He is clearly a product of Nature but yet in some sense seems to transcend it in the cultural dimension. What is meant by 'culture'? Why and how did it come into being at some (unknown) period in human prehistory? How do the many 'modes' and 'structures' (that is, economic, social and political) interrelate? What are the mechanisms of cultural change? Is there progress in culture? Is there a common culture underlying particular cultures? These and many other similar questions are the concern of a branch of philosophy usually called **Philosophical Anthropology** (a subdivision of which is 'cultural philosophical anthropology' or more simply the 'philosophy of culture'). It is a field of philosophy that has tended to be neglected by professional philosophers belonging to the so-called 'analytic' or 'linguistic' tradition. Most of the groundwork was done by such nineteenth and twentieth century German thinkers as Dilthey, Scheler, Plessner, Gehlen and Cassirer, all of whom regarded the philosophical study of man as occupying an important position within philosophy as a whole. (More recently important contributions have been made by Gadamer, Habermas and Ricoeur.) As Scheler observed: 'In a certain sense, all the central questions of philosophy can be reduced to the question of man and his position and metaphysical situation within the totality of Being, the world, and God'. And Kant wrote in a series of lectures on logic:

The field of philosophy as pertaining to world citizenship can be reduced to the following questions:
1 What can I know?
2 What should I do?
3 What may I hope?
4 What is man?
Basically, all these can be classified under anthropology, since the first three are related to the last.

Quite obviously we cannot deal with all these questions about man and culture; a separate and lengthy book would be required. Nevertheless we shall make some attempt in this chapter to tackle some of the key issues. But firstly something more should be said about philosophical anthropology.

Philosophical anthropologists are not of course all of one type; within this field of philosophy (as in all others) there is a considerable variety of interests and emphases. There are, however, certain assumptions and attitudes shared by different practitioners which justify their being so described:

Attitude to science. It might well be said that the findings of modern science, especially evolutionary biology, genetics and palaeontology, as well as social anthropology, already provide us with a substantial body of knowledge about man and culture. Most philosophical anthropologists would not dispute this. But they would argue: (a) that science cannot give us a complete or final understanding of ourselves, and (b) that it is in certain respects seen to be destructive of human autonomy. Underlying this assessment is their identification of causal explanation as a primary characteristic of scientific methodology. Whatever the correct analysis of causation may be (see 11.4), human behaviour should not be accounted for exclusively in causal terms. It is taken as axiomatic that we have the capacity to make free choices and that when we do our actions are not predetermined by our biological or physico-chemical 'make-up' (though some philosophical anthropologists would not deny that such factors may influence our behaviour). Rather we act as **cultural** beings operating within a framework of knowledge and values which we ourselves have created and which we continuously subject to modification as we grow in self-knowledge.

Synthesis. To the extent that scientific methods and the scientific world-view are not rejected out of hand but are recognized as the means by which nature (including man as a bio-physical object but not as the creator of culture) is explained, philosophical anthropologists see themselves as having an important role to play in reconciling the contrasting standpoints of natural science with the 'human' and cultural sciences. To some extent therefore philosophical anthropology adopts an 'overview' and seeks to integrate and synthesize all knowledge. It thereby overlaps with a traditional view of metaphysics but differs from it by virtue of the central place accorded to man.

Philosophical standpoint. Philosophical anthropologists are united in a third respect, namely in their rejection of a philosophy which has become deeply rooted in Western culture – Cartesian dualism and its rationalist foundations. By contrast, philosophical anthropology sees man not as split into a material body and an immaterial soul or mind but as an active, self-determining and creative *unity*.

Methods

There are two characteristics of the 'methodology' or philosophical techniques employed by most philosophical anthropologists: **understanding** (*Das Verstehen*) and **phenomenological** 'bracketing, contributed respectively by Dilthey

(1833–1911) and Scheler (1874–1928) (who was influenced by Husserl). 'Understanding' is not being used here in its everyday sense. For Dilthey it involves the grasping or apprehending of the 'meaning' (*Bedeutung*), that is, the unity of relationships which exist within and between the processes of the individual mind or of a group of individuals, which are expressed through gestures or utterances. As he says:

> In understanding we start from the system of the whole, which is given to us as a living reality, to make the particular intelligible to ourselves in terms of it. It is the fact that we live in the consciousness of the system of the whole which enables us to understand a particular statement, a particular gesture, or a particular action . . . Understanding is our name for the process in which mental life comes to be known through expressions of it which are given to the senses.
>
> [Quoted from Hodges, *Dilthey*, pp.22–21]

In philosophical anthropology this method of understanding is preceded by a descriptive and interpretative ('phenomenological') process which involves a presuppositionless examination and analysis of an individual's actions and relationships with others, the structures of his experiences, and the fundamental 'modes' of culture. This approach is said to be applicable to the 'human' or 'cultural' sciences as opposed to the causal and nomological explanatory methods of the natural sciences, which treat man and his cultural life as objects, as abstractions.

Now whether or not the 'phenomenological' method together with 'understanding' do lead to a revelation of immediately intuited 'meanings' or 'essences' is a topic for considerable debate which cannot be entered into here. It will be sufficient for our purposes to consider some of the possible limitations of scientific explanation (see Ch. 8), as applied to aspects of human behaviour, which might be thought to justify the use by philosophical anthropologists of alternative methodologies. We shall start with a brief look at the 'nature' of man and then move on to examine the concept of action and the methodological status of the 'human sciences'.

12.2 Man

Reading: Aquinas, *Summa Theologiae*, Ia, Quest. 75–88; Marx and Engels, *The German Ideology*; Sartre, *Existentialism and Humanism*; Ortega y Gasset, *Essays Toward a Philosophy of History*; Arendt, *The Human Condition*

What are the essential attributes of man? What is 'human nature'? Numerous thinkers at various times have sought to identify some feature or features of ourselves which, it is alleged, makes us different from all other living things – in more than obvious respects such as our appearance. For Aristotle we are both rational and social beings. Our rationality is affirmed also by philosophers who have adopted the Judaeo–Christian world-view (especially Aquinas). We are seen as creatures of God, 'made in His image', possessed of a soul, but since the 'Fall' our human nature has been corrupt and we have been unable to realize our potential without divine assistance. With the advent of Freud, human rationality, now identified with the *ego*, was supposed to be under threat from the dark subconscious forces of instinct (the *id*) – most notably (or notoriously) the sexual instinct. According to the Marxist (materialist) model, man is a producer (*homo faber*), a labourer and a maker and user of tools by means of which he controls and modifies his environment; and whatever 'nature' he may possess it is inseparable from his activity as a *social* being. By contrast Cassirer sees man as the animal with a symbol-making capacity which enables him to create his own 'ideal world'.

There is probably an element of truth in some or all of these views, though whether they describe *uniquely* human characteristics is debatable. Some higher mammals such as apes seem to possess a capacity for reasoning and problem solving, and even to make use of some sort of language to communicate (though there is much dispute about how these supposed linguistic skills should be understood). Many non-human animals can also make and use tools. But most theologians would probably deny that they have souls. Their opinion, however, must be based on faith as there does not seem to be any empirical method for deciding this issue one way or another. In any case the attribution of such an entity even to man raises many philosophical issues.

Many philosophers deny that man has a nature at all. As we saw in Chapter 6.6, Sartre says that man 'first of all exists, encounters himself, surges up in the world – and defines himself afterwards'. A similar view was held by the Spanish philosopher José **Ortega y Gasset** (1883–1955):

> . . . man has no nature. Man is not his body, which is a thing, nor his soul, psyche, conscience, or spirit, which is also a thing. Man is no thing, but a drama – his life, a pure and universal happening which happens to each one of us and in which each one in his turn is but a happening
> [*Toward a Philosophy of History*, pp.199–200]
> . . . man is the entity that makes itself. [201]

Hannah **Arendt** (1906–1975) too says [*The Human Condition*, pp.10–11] that the problem of human nature seems unanswerable in both its individual psychological sense and its general philosophical sense. To determine and define a natural essence for ourselves in the way that we do for the things surrounding us would be like jumping over our own shadows, and if there were such an essence only a god could know it:

> The perplexity is that the modes of human cognition applicable to things with 'natural' qualities, including ourselves to the limited extent that we are specimens of the most highly developed species of organic life, fail us when we raise the question: And *who* are we?

Arendt and Ortega y Gasset are also in close agreement in their positive accounts of man. Ortega says that while other beings 'coincide' with their objective conditions – with their nature or circumstance – man is different from, and alien to, his circumstance. In his actions he modifies and reforms nature, creating in it objects which had not previously existed. These are technical acts which are exclusively human [94–95]. 'The mission of technology consists in releasing man for the task of being himself' [118]. By this he means that through his 'technical acts' man is enabled to carry out his 'project of existence'. An existent man is engaged in an on-going process to achieve this project which he aspires to. Each man's self *is* this project, existence being the process of what is the aspiration to be this or that [112–113]. So man is 'an entity that has to act in order to be; its being presupposes action' [116]. Ortega accepts that many other animals may possess an ability for manufacturing tools, but it is man's imagination and memory which distinguish him from, say, chimpanzees, and which 'give completely dissimilar structures to their respective existences' [136–137]. Action is also a key concept for Arendt [*The Human Condition*, pp.7–9] – the third of three fundamental human activities. The first is labour, which corresponds to the biological process of the human body. The human condition of labour is life itself, and assures the life of both the individual and the species. The second is work. This corresponds to what she calls the 'unnaturalness' of human existence, in that work provides an 'artificial' world of things. The human condition of work is 'worldliness'. Work and its artefacts provide a degree of permanence to a futile and ephemeral human existence. Action is the only activity that goes on directly between humans without the mediation of things or matter. It corresponds to the human condition of plurality – which Arendt regards as *the* condition of all political (that is, social) life of man. Action is concerned with 'natality', initiation and beginnings. It creates the condition for 'remembrance', that is, history. Arendt stresses the dynamic interrelationship of man and things. We are conditioned beings. Not only must we cope with the conditions of life itself, but we constantly make our own conditions: 'Whatever enters the human world of its own accord or is drawn into it by human effort becomes part of the human condition'. This is reminiscent of Ortega's remark in an earlier work: 'I am I and my circumstances'. And as he says in *Toward a Philosophy of History*: 'Living in the world, man finds that the world surrounds him as an intricate net woven of both facilities and difficulties' [110].

While Ortega stresses man as the 'technician', and Arendt talks of labour and work, it is clear that both would accept that our actions are directed towards the realization of 'projects', 'aspirations' which are not confined to ensuring our survival or securing our material well-being. We are of course the only species able to ask questions about ourselves and our existence, to create art and music, to understand quantum mechanics, or, for that matter, to study philosophy. We are, in a word, uniquely the *cultural* animal. Such a definition, however, still leaves unanswered the question what it is about man that made it possible for him to become 'cultural'. *Why* is it that chimpanzees, cats, or caterpillars have not been able to match this evolutionary achievement? The problem here is that attempts to identify some culture-producing 'essence' run the risk of falling into circularity, for references to, say, rationality or symbolism already presuppose a cultural framework from which such terms take their reference. So in what follows we shall not be looking for a human 'nature' as such but rather we shall concentrate on our human *capacity* to produce, extend and utilize culture as the dimension in which we exist and realize ourselves. And to do this we shall build on some of the tentative conclusions we came to in the previous chapter. Thus we shall assume we are free, that is, self-determining *agents*. Arendt argues, correctly, that action is intimately related to speech, and that it is in our words and deeds that we reveal or disclose ourselves. What we *are*, we may say, we come to know through what we *do*. As Ernst Cassirer writes in his *An Essay on Man*:

> . . . if there is any definition of the nature or 'essence' of man, this definition can only be understood as a functional one. We cannot define man by an inherent principle which constitutes his metaphysical essence – nor can we define him by any inborn faculty or instinct that may be ascertained by empirical observation. Man's outstanding characteristic, his distinguishing mark, is not his metaphysical or physical nature – but his work.
> [p.67]

This 'work' for Cassirer is the use of 'symbolic forms' as the foundation of culture. We shall therefore need to examine the relationships between culture and language. But first we shall explore a little further the concept of action.

12.3 Action

Reading: Searle *Minds, Brains and Science*, 4

(1) **The nature of actions.** An agent acts. But what is an action? A number of distinctions need to be made here:

(a) Actions do not have to be identified with physical movements. I may be said to be snoring when asleep, but this would not normally be called an action – although I *am* 'doing something. By contrast, I can be said to be 'acting' (admittedly in an attenuated sense) even though there may be no overt physical signs to indicate this. I may, for example, be thinking or looking (at or for something). It may in fact be unclear what I am doing unless I reveal my intentions. If you see me at my desk with a book in front of me you may reasonably assume that I am reading. But this appearance is consistent with a number of different actions. I may indeed be said to be doing no more than reading the book. But there are other descriptions of my 'action'. I might be looking something up (or finding something out), exercising my eyes, or rehearsing my part for a play – practising acting as somebody reading a book! Of course the actual physical circumstances are similar in all these cases, and this might encourage some people to say that the action is the same. This would be so if we separated my intentions from what is actually observed, but the physical activity should not then be properly called an action (as in the case of my snoring). It should also be noted that we are not necessarily referring here to *prior* intentions which precede the physical event, as there are many occasions when I intend to do something but end up doing something different; my intentions are not realized. What *makes* each action (reading, or rehearsing for a play) different is the 'intention in action' (to use Searle's phrase), this being a manifestation of 'intentionality', as are also believing, hoping, perceiving and so on.

(b) Actions are not necessarily simple single events. When we walk down the road or type a letter, for example, a great deal is happening. One leg moves in front of the other, our arms swing by our sides; different fingers move variously on the keyboard while our eyes follow notes by our side or text on the screen. But this suggests another problem. We have talked of actions in terms of intentions and intentionality or 'directedness'. We may decide to walk to the shop or type a letter, and the movements of our limbs, as contributory elements in the overall complex action, may well be supposed to be directed towards the fulfilment of some end (the buying of a newspaper, or the completion of a chapter of a book). But clearly we do not consciously decide to place one foot at a particular point on the pavement, or to press with a given finger on the key marked 'A'. Are these then not actions? Perhaps the best way to answer this is to say that the components of the total sequence of events constituting our action or project are learned patterns of behaviour. When we first attempt to acquire a skill we do indeed start with basic movements of fingers, arms and legs: we intentionally direct a given finger to move in the appropriate manner best calculated to bring about the depression of the key. But with practice the movements of our fingers become, as it were, automatic and spontaneous: we 'see' the words on the screen *and* fingers respond. We act 'without thinking', that is, not at the self-conscious level. Of course a great deal is going on in the brain. Perhaps we can talk here of being in 'autopilot' mode. However, all this is possible only because activities were intended actions in the early stages of our learning. The benefits (as measured by efficiency, time-saving, and so on) of our not having to think at every moment about how the walking or typing is to be implemented are obvious. There is a parallel here to what is going on inside us and not under our conscious control – the movement of our diaphragm when we breathe, or the pumping of blood around the body by the heart (referred to in the previous chapter), though of course, in so far as these activities are not generally learned, they differ from the kinds of 'automatic' skills we have been discussing. Nevertheless, our breathing can be consciously controlled, and indeed some yogin claim to be able to control their heart rate and body temperature as a result of years of practice and concentration techniques. It is easier of course to control our fingers on the keyboard: we – our brain, as the control centre of our total organism – can stop when we and/or it want(s) to. This leads to a third distinction – between voluntary and involuntary action.

(c) My actions can be called voluntary in the sense that I want to perform them with some specific end or purpose in view. This does not mean that an action cannot be involuntary; and this is because 'involuntary' is ambiguous. Suppose I bump into somebody. This may be intentional in the sense that I want to bump into him or her and carry through my intention (perhaps I am doing the 'hands, knees and bumps-a-daisy' at a dance). But if I am walking along a busy street looking in the shop-windows, or simply day-dreaming, I might bump into someone inadvertently. Is this an action? Not in our strict sense, though I could well be told to watch what I am doing or where I am going. Consider now the (unlikely) situation in which I am told to bump into someone and that dire consequences will result if I do not (perhaps there is a gun at my head). I comply and therefore act. But this is certainly involuntary in the sense that it was against my (real) will or wishes – though I *could* have done otherwise. Does this mean that in the first example (unintentional bumping in the street) I *couldn't* help it? Well, yes and no. Given the fact that I was not keeping my eyes open, or was not thinking where I was going, or was drunk, then it was inevitable that travelling in such and such a direction and with a given speed I would make contact with the unfortunate pedestrian. But I can still be held culpable for my thoughtlessness or carelessness.

It is because of considerations such as these that the analyses of actions in terms of ascription of responsibility which have been proposed by some philosophers are not adequate. There could also be situations in which one acts and yet the responsibility for the action is said to be somebody else's. Oliver Twist certainly picked the gentleman's pocket, but the real culprit was Fagin. Oliver was responsible only in the sense that it was he who acted. This is not to say though that responsibility in this latter sense is entirely trivial, for to refer to oneself as acting or having acted seems to involve a recognition that one is in control. The capacity for action may therefore be thought to be something which evolves in the early stages of our lives. Babies initially do not act; they respond to stimuli, or behave instinctively. When we are older much of what we do is still instinctive, but we do then have a much greater control over our behaviour, unless we are physically incapacitated or suffering from various kinds of mental disorder. (Note that the latter raises other sorts of difficulties. A 'madman' may run amok and may seem to be out of control. We can still refer to his 'actions', but might exonerate him on the grounds that his intentions or purposes are grounded in a distorted perception of reality. This would be justified perhaps if the individual were psychotic: but we would probably be less sympathetic if he were suffering from a neurosis. This raises the fundamental question whether 'compulsive' behaviour is controllable. Does such behaviour cease to be compulsive if we *know* we are 'doing' it? Compare the discussion in 11.5.)

(2) **The explanation of actions.** We have given some indication of the nature of actions, or how they are to be described. A more important problem is how they are to be *explained*. And here there is a divergence of opinion among philosophers. Some writers (especially Hempel, D. Davidson and A. MacIntyre) argue that actions are *caused* just as, say, the hitting of a brick on a window causes it to break, though they would include as causes of actions such mental features as desires, wishes and wants. Other thinkers, however (for example, G.E.M. Anscombe, Hampshire and Searle), deny that actions can ever be wholly explained causally: rather we should talk of giving **reasons**. Such a view stems

partly from a recognition of the difficulties to be found in attempts to resolve the free-will–determinism problem, and perhaps also from a concern that analyses of human behaviour in terms of causal categories might tend to 'reduce' man to the status of inanimate objects or at least to limit or restrict his autonomy in some sense. Can we say that one or other of these alternative views is wrong?

Consider once again my snoring when asleep. It certainly seems reasonable to say that my snoring was caused by such factors as the position of my head or throat, or blockage of nasal passages (this is not to say that this is a complete or correct 'scientific' explanation). But suppose I am awake, sitting in an arm-chair, and make a snoring noise. Why do I do this? On one level it can still be said that the noise was caused by vibrations in the throat. But such an explanation fails to take account of my intentions and motives. If asked to explain, I could say that I wanted to amuse my grandchild, annoy my great-aunt, clear my throat, test the acoustics of the sitting-room, and so on. Now it might be argued that such intentions are just as much causes as are the various physiological facts adduced earlier. But does this not involve us in an infinite regress, for we can always ask what caused the intentions? This kind of difficulty cannot arise if we think of *ourselves* as causal agents. Certainly we have desires, needs, wishes and hopes: but these are not causes but the relevant factors we take account of when forming our intentions and making up our minds how we should act; and as such they are *reasons* for actions.

In defence of this approach to the question it has been suggested (for example, by Hart) that reason-based actions have about them something of the characteristic of particularity, whereas events explainable in causal terms are subsumed under general laws or principles. Something more will be said about this in the next section, but it can be remarked here that while it is certainly the case that many of our actions conform to observable tendencies which may be said to have 'law-like' features, it must also be noted that in so far as they *are* our actions, performed in the light of assessments of intentions, purposes, likely consequences and so on, the possibility of an unexpected choice being made must always be allowed for. As against this, it might be said that there can likewise be exceptions to causal laws. This is of course true, but it is of the essence of the scientific method to try to accommodate such exceptions by modifying the laws or replacing the relevant theory by another which has greater explanatory potential. In the case of human actions it is always open to the individual to be perverse.

Should we conclude then that unless we adopt some kind of reductionist position, explanations of human action in terms of reasons are *sui generis* and stand alone seemingly irreconcilable with causal accounts of what is going on inside our bodies? How then do we account for the transition from conscious learning processes, which involve intended, intentional and chosen actions, to 'autopilot' activities – 'behind the scenes', as it were – which happen without our conscious control? This is of course Searle's 'gap' in another guise; and you will remember that a possible way of overcoming it was sketched out in the previous chapter. You will need to consider this again in the next section, which is concerned with the wider issue of what kinds of methodology are appropriate for explanations of human behaviour.

12.4 The human sciences

Reading: Hempel, 'Explanation in Science and History'; Searle, *Minds, Brains and Science*, 5, *Mind, Language and Society*, ch. 5

Few philosophers would dispute the explanatory power of the covering law model (8.2) and its successful application to the physical sciences (that is, physics and chemistry). There is, however, much disagreement about the attempt by some advocates of the model, in the interests of 'unified science', to extend its application not only to biology and psychology but further to the so-called 'human' sciences such as history and sociology, and by implication to 'culturology'. This is the aim of Hempel, who argues that an empirical historical phenomenon or event presupposes both particular facts and general principles (which might be, for example, economic, socio-cultural, or psychological) and is connected to them in such a way as to conform to either the deductive-nomological model or the probabilistic version. At first sight this seems innocuous enough. But there are serious objections to such an enterprise. Thus it might be claimed that to force the human sciences into this single explanatory mould is to run the risk of 'reducing' history to psychology (and perhaps psychology in turn to biology and then physics), thereby assimilating 'free' human actions to deterministic causal chains. Reduction here should not be confused with reductionism as referred to in Ch. 5, which seeks to *define*, say, a physical or material object solely in terms of sensations or sense-data. Reduction in the context of scientific explanation involves relating phenomena inferentially to concepts and principles at a different 'level'; and few reductionists in *this* sense would now suggest that, for example, the activity of a living cell can be explained totally (if at all) in terms of the sub-atomic particles of which its constituent protein molecules are composed. That there is a logical connection between the various 'levels' (for example, via 'correspondence rules'), however, remains a matter for concern to some philosophers interested in human behaviour; for it should then still be possible in principle to relate social phenomena such as wars and revolutions systematically to molecular movements in the same way that caloric inputs can be related to fat deposits (Searle's example). What kind of answer can be given to this (weaker) form of reductionism?

*Discussion of Hempel's thesis

In his article 'Explanation in Science and History', Hempel discusses two kinds of explanation supposedly used by historians and which, it has been claimed, do not conform to the covering law model. The first of these, 'genetic explanation' (also examined by Nagel), will not be considered here. The second, however, which has been proposed by W. Dray (to whom, incidentally, is attributed the phrase 'covering law model'), appeals to 'motivating reasons' and is therefore clearly relevant to our discussion of actions in the previous section. Dray's thesis is that the aim of this kind of explanation is 'to show that what was done was the thing to have done for the reasons given, rather than merely the thing that is done on such occasions, perhaps in accordance with certain laws'. Dray goes on to refer to a 'principle of action' which involves an appraisal of the appropriateness of the action, which is made by the agent in the light of the circumstances, the end he wishes to attain, and so on. Hempel summarizes Dray's model of explanation in this way:

A was in a situation of type C
In a situation of type C, the appropriate thing to do is X.

He then argues: (1) that this explanans fails to provide good grounds for believing or asserting that the explanandum did in fact occur, and (2) that it is unclear how the second statement (which expresses a valuational principle) in conjunction with the first (empirical) statement can permit any inference concerning empirical matters (such as A's action) which could not be drawn from the first sentence alone. Now the first objection can be readily dismissed. It is surely *presupposed* that A *did* in fact do X in so far as a putative explanation is being put forward (just as if in a particular context I said 'the chair is very old', it would generally be supposed that there is a chair to which I am referring). As to the second objection, it can be argued that Hempel's formulation of Dray's explanans is misleading; for surely what Dray is suggesting is that A *has decided that* in a situation of type C, the appropriate thing *for him* to do is X. It is the agent himself who after making his appraisal of all the relevant facts makes up his mind whether to act or not and can then provide a rationale if asked why he so acted. This may well involve some reference to ethics: indeed in many everyday situations it would be most surprising if we did not cite the wish to follow moral principles as at least part of our reason for acting in a particular way in appropriate circumstances. Worried by Dray's apparent reliance on normative principles, Hempel suggests that to explain why A did in fact do X we should instead invoke descriptive statements relating to A's dispositions and rationality:

(a) A was in a situation of type C
(b) A was disposed to act rationally
(c) Any person who is disposed to act rationally will, when in a situation of type C, invariably (with high probability) do X.

Such a pattern of explanans does of course conform very neatly to Hempel's probabilistic version of the covering law model, but it fails to provide a complete explanation of A's action. Certainly we may admit the truth of both (a) and (b) in a particular context. (We may have reservations though about the term 'disposed'. Hempel's subsequent discussion is strongly suggestive of behaviourist tendencies. This is a point you might follow up if you read his article.) And it may well be a matter of statistical significance that rational people usually behave in a predictable manner in certain kinds of situation. But: (1) This fails to give an account of *why* a particular rational individual actually performs the action X. It is certainly not the case that he does X *because* any rational person in a similar situation does it ('with high probability'). (2) The covering law model cannot cope with exceptions without either emptying the concept of explanation of all meaning or of rendering human behaviour as inevitable and totally predictable.

For let us suppose that to accommodate an exception (*A* does *not do X*, contrary to all expectation) we redefine 'situation' in (a) and (c) by listing numerous restrictions or qualifications (*A* is a person of a certain age, height and background; the action is specific: he is, say, signing a document relating to a particular event; and so on). Ultimately we shall reach a degree of specificity which would rule out any general reference to other people, in which case (c) could no longer be used in the explanans. Or if (c) were allowed, we should be saying no more than *A* did *X* because he was *A*. There is of course a place for causal and general (nomological) explanations of human behaviour. But as was pointed out in the previous section, it remains open to the individual (provided various conditions are satisfied, such as rationality, self-control, not being under the influence of drugs or 'E'-additives in food) to change his or her mind.

The more general claim made by some philosophers, that the methods of the natural sciences are equally valid when applied to the human sciences, is rebutted by Searle [*Reith Lecture*, 5]. The central point of his argument is that there can be no systematic correlation or 'bridge principles' (roughly what we referred to earlier as 'rules of correspondence') between the natural sciences and the phenomena of the social and psychological sciences. Social phenomena, he says, are to a large extent physically 'open-ended' categories, in so far as they are defined in terms of the psychological attitudes people adopt towards them. Thus there are no fundamental principles by means of which we can stipulate what is to count as money, a marriage ceremony, or a trade union, and so on. Categorization requires thoughts, desires and hopes, and these various aspects of intentionality are constitutive of the phenomena themselves. So, for example, 'in order to get married or buy property, you and other people have to think that that's what you are doing'. It is for this reason that there can be no bridge principles between phenomena described in social terms and the same phenomena described in physical terms. Likewise, there is a lack of correlation between phenomena described respectively in mental and neurophysiological terms, because 'there is an indefinite range of stimulus conditions for any given social concept'. It follows from Searle's account that 'sciences' such as economics and sociology 'cannot be free of history or context'. The significance of context is a central concern of 'hermeneutic' philosophers, who also reject attempts to assimilate the human sciences to models appropriate to the natural sciences. An important figure in this movement is Hans-Georg **Gadamer** (b. 1900 – and at the time of writing still going strong!). An outline of his philosophy is given in the next section.

12.5 Hermeneutics and critical theory

Reading: No specific reading is required for this section. However, if you feel up to tackling some of the key texts try Gadamer, *Truth and Method*; Habermas, *Knowledge and Human Interests*; and Ricoeur, *Hermeneutics and the Human Sciences*. But you may find them hard-going! (Arendt's *The Human Condition* is also particularly relevant to many of Habermas's themes.)

Hermeneutics

Hermeneutics (the word is derived from the Greek *hermeneuein*, to interpret, perhaps cognate with 'Hermes', the messenger of the gods) is a systematic investigation of interpretation. It grew out of the work of, particularly, Schleiermacher and Dilthey in the nineteenth century. The central claim of hermeneutic philosophers is that the human sciences (*Geisteswissenschaften*) are not essentially concerned to *explain* human behaviour – explanation being appropriate rather to the natural sciences (*Naturwissenschaften*). Instead the aim of the human sciences should be to *understand* – motives, intentions, choices of ourselves and other people. The significance of Gadamer lies in his expansion of the concept, with particularly emphasis on the rootedness of human beings in history and cultural contexts. This is usually referred to as man's **historicity**. Furthermore, the process of coming to understand human activity is regarded as comparable to the interpretation of a text or work of art. How is this to be achieved?

Gadamer is critical of what he sees as the limitations of both Dilthey and Heidegger (see 11.2). According to Dilthey (following Schleiermacher), the interpreter should aim at empathetic insight into the mind of the author of the work of art and a reconstruction of the cultural world in which it was created, thereby achieving an objective understanding of its objective 'truth' or meaning. Heidegger (criticizing Husserl) rejected the possibility of an objective interpretation, because: (a) for him understanding is inseparable from the 'life-world', which presupposes a 'foreknowledge', that is, a prior awareness of situations into which human being-in-the-world (*Dasein*) is thrown, and (b) in any case understanding is essentially practical – being a function of human action. Dilthey's methodological hermeneutic (which Gadamer criticizes as Cartesian) thus gives way to an 'ontological hermeneutical circle' characterized by a developing dialectical relationship between increasing foreknowledge and existential understanding of the world and Dasein's engagement with it. Now, hermeneutics for Gadamer is more than merely a set of techniques for interpreting texts. It is concerned with the deeper issue of how human understanding is possible. It has something in common with Aristotle's concept of practical deliberation (*phronesis*) – to be identified neither with *episteme* nor *techne*; and it is also concerned with the relevance of this to man's having free choice or purpose (*prohairesis*), and with the individual's quest for excellence (*Bildung*) in the community. He accepts that there is no absolute 'objective' interpretation of a text or work of art (or indeed of a whole culture), to be discovered by some Enlightenment form of reason, but he also rejects individual relativism and 'intersubjective verification' whereby the insights of each individual or group are guaranteed equal validity or authenticity. However, he argues that although self-consciousness is bound by its immersion in its own socio-cultural situation it is possible for foreknowledge to transcend it. It is in this respect that he parts company with Heidegger. How can an interpretation be neither 'objective' nor 'relative'? Is there not a contradiction here? Gadamer would deny this. His aim in *Truth and Method* is to show that the primordial experiences transmitted through history and art cannot be grasped from the point of view of these forms of consciousness; there is no 'pure' starting point without presuppositions. We find ourselves embedded in a world in a particular place and time, born into a given society, influenced even by the landscape; we possess our own specific thoughts and moods, engage in our own activities. He refers to this as 'effective historical consciousness' – reflecting the fact that we are grounded in history, whether as authors of texts, readers, or interpreters; and he sees us as being thereby constrained by the presuppositions and prejudices (that is, pre-judgements) of our cultural and individual contexts. This is implicit in his use of the key term 'horizon' – the limits of which, according to him, can be transcended.

What makes this transcendence possible is language. Rejecting Heidegger's view (in *Being and Time*) of language as a 'tool', Gadamer sees it as the medium in which we operate, through which we understand. We cannot extricate ourselves from language to come into direct contact with the 'reality' that language is in some sense about. But through an interpreter's 'dialogue' with a text, painting, or other cultural product he can both separate it from its horizons (the author's personal experiences, or the cultural context of the work) and transcend his own horizons. Gadamer argues that as the dialogue progresses, a '**fusion of horizons**' can be achieved and approximation to the ideal meaning attained. Moreover, although our effective history necessarily prevents us from overcoming our prejudices, it is only through them that we can approach our horizons because an effective history *constitutes* those prejudices. The progressive dialogue leading to the fusion of horizons is essentially dialectical in nature; But Gadamer does not follow Hegel's ontology/metaphysics – a dialectic of the Mind or Spirit working itself through the world and consciousness, and culminating in the Absolute and total self-realization. Gadamer's dialectic, which faciltiates openness and transcendence, remains within language. The 'meaning' or truth of the text should not therefore be understood in either rationalist or speculative idealist terms.

Gadamer stresses that hermeneutics, unlike the natural sciences, is not concerned with any explanation of nature but rather with the question 'how is understanding possible' as presented to the totality of human experience of the world and man's conduct of life. It is characterized by a 'forward–backward' movement operating within the 'hermeneutical circle'. This is a circle of whole and part: parts give us a sense of the whole, and to understand the significance of the parts we need to have an apprehension of the whole. But the whole is never fully realizable in terms of parts: we are offered only new fusions, new insights, achieved only within the constraints of history and effective historical consciousness, and the 'resistance' of texts. It is essentially on on-going adventure; and, Gadamer claims that to the extent that it is successful it will bring about a growth in inner awareness, self-understanding and an understanding of the human condition. As for the natural, empirical sciences, Gadamer makes it clear that he is not seeking to question their methodology or functions within their own terms of reference, or even that they may be employed in the social sciences. But he seems to argue that despite their aspiration to certainty, even the natural sciences are not immune from our culturally related assumptions, prejudices and distortions. (Compare the ideas of Feyerabend and Kuhn referred to in 8.4 and 11.2.)

Critical theory

While for Gadamer both explanation in the natural sciences and understanding in the human sciences are dependent on and constrained by our pre-judgements, which reflect the cultural and historical contexts we are situated in, he still seems to accord different roles or functions to the corresponding methodologies of the two kinds of sciences. We turn now to the important contributions made to the debate by Jürgen **Habermas** (b. 1929). Habermas is the leading representative of the programme of social and political philosophy developed in the nineteen thirties by the so-called Frankfurt school of thinkers. His writings are numerous, complex and wide-ranging. We shall therefore concentrate here only on those features which are relevant to the issue of methodology and his debate with Gadamer concerning rationality and truth.

In his early writings (especially *Knowledge and Human Interests*), Habermas identifies three kinds of sciences and claims that corresponding to each is a characteristic form of knowledge relating to a particular human 'interest':

(1) Empirical-analytic sciences. Our interest here is technical control or domination of nature, and to realize our goals we engage in 'purposive' rational, practical action. This corresponds to Marx's concept of work or labour as manifested in the historical-material context as modes of production developing dialectically. Habermas calls purposive rationality 'instrumental' if it involves a search for the means to bring about the relevant ends, and 'strategic' if we take into consideration alternative courses of action on the basis of some arbitrary set of values. He regards natural science as being accommodated within this framework as a regular cumulative process. But he rejects 'realist' or 'objectivist' accounts in so far as methodology is subordinated to our 'interest' in control.

(2) Historical-hermeneutic cultural sciences. Our knowledge-constitutive interest in these sciences is not technical control but communication. Action is not labour but interaction with other humans. This involves 'substantive' rationality, by which Habermas means a concern with the actual validity, or correctness of the norms or values which, as a consequence of consensus of agreement, are binding on the group. Such sciences are superior to the empirical-analytic sciences in that they provide a framework for the understanding of ourselves and of human individual and group relationships – and also of the natural sciences in so far as they have to be practised in a communal context.

(3) Critical-interpretive sciences. Just as the hypothetico-deductive methodology of the natural sciences, according to Habermas, is not universally valid and cannot provide us with complete or total knowledge, so do the historical-hermeneutical sciences have their limitations. Because hermeneutical understanding involves only a 'surface' interpretation of texts, these sciences

cannot uncover what he calls 'false consciousness' which is associated with ideologies. To liberate individuals from their domination, and to promote self-reflection and self-discovery, critical-interpretive sciences are required. The knowledge-constitutive interest here is thus seen as 'emancipatory'. Habermas seeks therefore for a critical social science which will reveal the inherent causal repressive mechanisms, the forces and hidden motivations which are implicit in ideologies (for example, 'positivistic' Marxism and technocratic scientific methodology) and power groupings, all of which 'distort communication'. (Interestingly, but controversially, Habermas appeals to Freudian psychoanalysis as a methodological paradigm of this process of 'reconstruction'.) In this way we can hope to achieve a true and rational consensus. Philosophy is considered by Habermas as playing a key role here. It not only must continue to exercise its traditional function as a 'guardian of reason' but also can 'mediate' between the various spheres of culture which comprise the 'life-world' – natural sciences, arts, law, ethics and so on. Philosophy itself thus becomes a human science making its own special contribution as a 'placeholder' – keeping open questions closed off by other methodologies and ideologies. (You can now see the relevance of Habermas's work to 'critical thinking' – see Ch. 2 above.)

Habermas does not wish to separate theory and practice (and in this respect he sees the Marxist integration of reason into the processes of human self-formation and development through social labour as marking an improvement on the assumptions of the Enlightenment). And to accommodate both, a new epistemological foundation is required. As you will probably have gathered from the discussion so far, Habermas's account of knowledge and indeed his critical theory in general is essentially pragmatic: he rejects any quest for 'ultimate' foundations or a 'first philosophy'. (For this reason his philosophy has often been referred to as a 'transcendental pragmatism'.) Central to this is what he later calls his 'theory of communicative competence' and his 'discourse ethics'. Drawing on analytic philosophy, in particular, the work of Austin and Searle on speech acts (see 2.12 and Searle, *Mind, Language and Society*, ch. 6), he sets out in his 'pragmatics of language' to reconstruct the presuppositions of communication and to understand the universal validity claims of utterances – which in the event of disputes can be examined at the 'meta-communicative' levels of theoretical and practical discourse. In essence, Habermas argues that when we engage in discourse there are a number of requirements that must be satisfied if there is to be communicative competence. Expressions must be comprehensive; propositional content must be true; the speaker has to express his intentions truthfully; and the utterances selected by the user have to be right, that is, correct in the context of existing norms and values. We can then expect intersubjec-tive agreement about the validity claims implicit in ordinary linguistic communication and also about the expectations we have of each other's behaviour, in accordance with the fundamental ideal and regulative norms of truth, freedom, and justice. Given: (a) the elimination of external constraints, so that all participants in a dialogue have the same opportunity to apply speech-acts, and (b) that conditions are obtained in which rational motivation is allowed to determine the conclusions of discourse – we have what Habermas terms the 'ideal speech situation'. This will then facilitate the individual's freedom in action and discourse, and allow for revision or replacement of linguistic systems and the theoretical reformulation of the fundamental ideals.

*Comment

This affirmation of a close interrelatedness of speech and action and their relevance to human autonomy has its parallels in the work of Arendt – who may well have had a direct influence on Habermas's thought. You should read in particular her chapter on Action in *The Human Condition*. You might consider also similarity between Habermas's account of rationality and the regulative norm of truth with Putnam's notion of truth as idealized rational acceptability (5.7).

In his most recent work Habermas attempts a more thorough working out of the connections between our knowledge-constitutive interests and theoretical and practical discourse so that multiple translations can be effected between the two realms of linguistic assertions and action-related experiences respectively. In this way purposive-rational action (to which the empirical sciences apply) can be related to statements about natural events and things, and communicative action (the hermeneutical sciences) can be related to statements about persons and their utterances. We cannot deal with this further here. But something should be said of his response to Gadamer.

In his review of *Truth and Method* he criticized Gadamer for being too ready to submit to the authority of tradition and also argued that his notion of interpretive horizons is methodologically limited. Habermas claims that a self-reflective methodology can be developed which will enable prejudices to be overcome and which will provide the basis for a (pragmatically) objective social science. As against this, Gadamer argues that Habermas is resorting to a traditional and unattainable 'objectivism'. Prejudices cannot be avoided or eliminated; and indeed the claims of psychotherapy and social theory are not themselves free from pre-understandings, effective historical consciousness, which moreover may vary within different cultural milieus. The debate has continued. It should be noted, though, that in recent work Habermas and Gadamer seem to have come closer together on this matter.

Ricoeur

The debate between Habermas and Gadamer has more recently been taken up by Paul **Ricoeur** (b. 1913), who argues that the critique of ideology and the hermeneutics of tradition are interdependent. As we have seen, Gadamer's view is that this ontology of tradition – our pre-understandings, prejudices, effective historical consciousness – limits possible meanings. Habermas, however, aspiring to the ideal finality of emancipation, argues that these constraints can be transcended. Now, understanding involves mediation between the interpreter's immediate and emerging horizons, and this in turn requires the interpreter to 'distance' himself from the text. According to Ricoeur this is to adopt a stance of critical self-understanding similar to that proposed in Habermas's critique of ideology. At the same time he thinks that the critique of ideology cannot be separated from tradition. The ideals of emancipation and undistorted communication go back beyond the Enlightenment to the Greeks, the Hebrews and to the New Testament. Therefore, according to Ricoeur, there is no incompatibility between Gadamer and Habermas; indeed they complement each other, are mutually dependent. Moreover, each becomes ideological when they are artificially separated.

Ricoeur's contribution here illustrates the general reconciliatory nature of much of his philosophizing. (As with other continental philosophers we have discussed, his range of thought and the multiplicity of his writings prohibit a comprehensive treatment in this book.) In his earlier work he was concerned particularly with a 'descriptive phenomenology' which would resolve the seeming oppositions between 'movement' and action, and between freedom of the will and those features of human nature which appear to constrict or condition our willing. 'A common subjectivity' – grounded in the Cartesian *cogito* 'recovered from naturalism' – is the basis for what the descriptive method reveals as 'the reciprocity of the involuntary and the voluntary' [*Freedom and Nature*, Introduction 1]. In his later writings he (like Habermas) drew on analytic philosophy to develop a new 'meta-linguistic' hermeneutic, which would interpret descriptions by attributing to them specific functions, so as to complement the structuralist approach to language, which is concerned with categorizing phenomena and analysing the ways they combine in closed systems. This forms the basis for his attempt to resolve the dichotomy between description and explanation – between the human sciences and the natural sciences.

Central to his approach is his distinction between discourse and dialogue. Discourse is written text, dialogue spoken and heard. Ricoeur says that discourse is detached from the circumstances which produced it: the speech acts, the intentions of the speaker have been left behind, the person addressed can be anyone, and there are no ostensive references. In these respects it differs from dialogue. Ricoeur now argues that similar characteristics may be identified in actions in so far as they can be detached from the agent and can be repeated – leaving their marks or records in the world. Underlying these distinctions is his view that as soon as objective meaning has been detached from the author's subjective intentions, a multitude or 'plurivocity' of possible interpretations is opened up – interpretations which reveal the significance of an action or text as a function of the world-views of both hearer/reader/observer and speaker/author/agent. Central to his attempt to reconcile explanation and understanding is Ricoeur's notion of the 'hermeneutic arc'. This refers to an integration of two hermeneutical moves or directions – from existential understanding to explanation and from explanation back to understanding.

In the first move, guesses are made. This is similar to the forming of hypotheses based on analogies, metaphors and the like. What these hypothetical guesses must accomplish is the provision of sense for terms and readings for texts, and the situation of parts and wholes in classificatory schemes or hierarchies, thus allowing a range of interpretations. The guesses are subjectively validated by means of rational argument comparable to the legal debate that takes place in court procedures. But this is not the same as empirical verification. Guesses which do not admit of confirmability or which are self-confirmed (compare the problem of verification in, say, Freudian, psychoanalysis) are eliminated in a manner based on Popper's concept of falsifiability – the criteria in Ricoeur's methodology being internal incoherence and relative implausibility.

As for the reverse move, Ricoeur makes a distinction between subjective and structuralist approaches in relation to what he sees as the referential function of a text. The subjectivist approach involves a gradual construction of the world behind the text but presupposes the 'pre-understanding' of the interpreter – which can never be fully transcended, though a kind of asymptotic approximation can be achieved. The structuralist approach, on the other hand, suspends reference to the world behind the text and concentrates on identifying and classifying the parts within the text and their interconnections. Two levels can be identified here: (1) there is the naïve surface meaning (the narrative of the myth, for example), but (2) what understanding needs is a depth semantics. This is what the text (in the wide sense) is 'about' as a non-ostensive reference and which passes beyond the author's intentions. For understanding to be achieved an affinity between the reader and this aboutness is required, by means of which subjectivity and objectivity are intimately related. As Ricoeur concludes, understanding is entirely mediated by the whole of the explanatory procedures which precede it and accompany it.

*Comments and conclusion

It has to be recognized that Ricoeur deals with the human versus the natural sciences issue explicitly at the level of language, more particularly in terms of textual *interpretation*. And although it can be claimed that he has achieved a measure of reconciliation between them as regards their methods and structures, from the standpoint of the problems we discussed in Ch. 12 we must regret that he has moved away from his earlier psychological and phenomenological consideration of freedom and causation, the voluntary and the involuntary; for these remain at the heart of the debate between *understanding* and explanation, which characterize the respective kinds of sciences. We might note also that Ricoeur takes Freudian psychoanalysis as illustrating paradigmatically the interdependence of explanation and interpretation. Not only is it a matter of debate as to whether such techniques do in fact contribute to a better understanding of the motives and forces underlying and informing our supposedly free actions, but it is also questionable whether Freudian methods should be called 'scientific' and thus whether genuine 'explanations' have been provided.

A similar complaint can be made about Habermas's contribution. His 'transcendental pragmatic' approach and his emphasis on the interdependence of action and speech are impressive features of his critical social theory and the human sciences in general, as is his concern with the critical-interpretive sciences and with the role of philosophy as mediator between cultural modes and as 'guardian' of reason. Nevertheless, given that we human beings and the natural environment have a common origin, a holistic view requires that human rational motivation and decision making be accommodated to causation without sacrificing autonomy. When I express myself in speech and action I do so freely, remaining open to the world. Yet much is 'going on' inside me which is not under my immediate control. Descriptions in terms of motives, reasons and choices and explanations in terms of 'lower-level' causes are no doubt articulated within different methodological frameworks. But however much common 'surface' features can be identified by reference to shared discourse, or validated pragmatically through action, a full account of the dynamic interplay between man and the environment should include some reference to the continuity that must be assumed to exist between the progressively more complex 'levels' that constitute our being. It is clear that there is still much work to be done by philosophers and scientists – be they of the 'human' or 'natural' varieties – if a satisfactory account is to be achieved.

12.6 Culture and language

Reading: As in previous sections of this chapter, no specific reading is required. However, should you wish to study this topic in greater depth you will find it helpful to study Cassirer's *An Essay on Man* and Harris's *Cultural Materialism*, which are written from opposing standpoints.

'Culture' has been described (in *The Times*, 10 April 1964) as 'a word with one of the widest ranges of use and misuse in the English language'. In its most general sense it refers to the totality of what man is and does, and as such is the proper concern of a branch of philosophy referred to somewhat longwindedly as 'cultural philosophical anthropology', but better termed 'the philosophy of culture' or perhaps even 'metaculture'. Other problems philosophers of culture are interested in include the origin of culture; the interrelationships of the numerous cultural 'modes' (myth, art, technology, religion and the sciences) and 'structures' (the family, society, politics, the law, religious ceremonies and so on); cultural relativism (epistemological and ethical); the connections between culture and civilization; and whether there is 'progress' in culture. To deal with even one of these adequately would require a separate book. Our aim here is to make only a number of general points about the nature and origin of culture, so as to bring our discussion of man and society to a conclusion.

Of many types of theories which have been proposed to explain how culture emerged, perhaps some two million years ago or even earlier, three in particular deserve some mention.

Materialist theories

The foundations for such theories were laid down particularly by **Marx** and **Engels**:

The mode of production in material life determines the general character of the social, political, and spiritual processes of life. It is not the consciousness of men that determines their existence, but on the contrary, their social existences determines their consciousness.

[*Critique of Political Economy*, see also the quotation in 7.4 from p.48 of *The German Ideology*]

A contemporary 'orthodox' account of 'anthropogenesis' and the emergence of culture in terms of Engel's theory of 'labour' is provided by V.P. Alexeev, a Corresponding Member of the USSR Academy of Sciences. In his book, *The Origin of the Human Race*, he writes:

By culture I understand here all the results of human activity, irrespective of whether they are found embodied in relics of material culture or in the spiritual sphere. From that point of view the first steps in tool use or labour had already given rise to culture, and the tool itself, even the most primitive, is an object of culture. The rise of culture is thus inseparable from the origin of hominids and the very beginning of labour. [139]

This kind of approach but without the trappings of dialectics is particularly well exemplified in the cultural materialism of Marvin Harris, who defines the central principle of his theory as follows:

The etic behavioural modes of production and reproduction probabilistically determine the etic behavioural domestic and political economy, which in turn probabilistically determine the behavioural and mental emic superstructures. For brevity's sake, this principle can be referred to as the principle of infrastructural determinism.

[*Cultural Materialism*, p.56]

(The words 'etic' and 'emic' are technical terms used by some anthropologists to designate particular senses of 'objective' and 'subjective'. There is no need for you to concern yourself with them here.)

Functionalist theories

Perhaps the most influential theory of this kind was developed by the social anthropologist Bronisław **Malinowski** (1884–1942), who argued that the purpose of culture, in an institutional context, is to provide primarily for the biological needs of individuals, and then secondarily for their social and spiritual needs. The main points of the thesis are summarized in his *A Scientific Theory of Culture*:

The theory of culture must take its stand on biological fact . . . In the first place, it is clear that the satisfaction of the organic or basic needs of man and of the race is a minimum set of conditions imposed on each culture.

The problems set by man's nutritive, reproductive, and hygienic needs must be solved. They are solved by the construction of a new, secondary, or artificial environment. This environment, which is neither more nor less than culture itself, has to be permanently reproduced, maintained, and managed . . .

We shall attempt to show that a theory can be developed in which the basic needs and their cultural satisfaction can be linked up with the derivation of new cultural needs; that these new needs impose upon man and society a secondary type of determinism. We shall be able to distinguish between instrumental imperatives – arising out of such types of activity as economic, normative, educational and political – and integrative imperatives. Here we shall list knowledge, religion and magic. Artistic and recreational activities we shall be able to relate directly to certain physiological characteristics of the human organism, and also to show their influence and dependence upon modes of concerted action, magical, industrial and religious belief. [pp.36–38]

By means of his functional and institutional analysis Malinowski then defines culture as:

an integral composed of partly autonomous, partly coordinated institutions. It is integrated on a series of principles such as the community of blood through procreation; the contiguity in space related to coopera-tion; the specialization in activities; and last but not least, the use of power in political organization. [A Scientific Theory of Culture, p.40]

and thinks of its origins as:

the concurrent integration of several lines of development: the ability to recognize instrumental objects, the appreciation of their technical efficiency, and their value, that is, their place in the purposive sequence, and the formation of social bonds, and the appearance of symbolism.
[A Scientific Theory of Culture, p.136]

*Criticism

The theories of both Harris and Malinowski are regarded by their authors as being 'scientific' in that they involve the subsumption of empirical data under general laws. Indeed it is their stated intention that this should be so. Thus, for Harris:

Cultural materialism shares with other scientific strategies and episte-mology which seeks to restrict fields of inquiry to events, entities, and relationships that are knowable by means of explicit, logico-empirical, inductive-deductive, quantifiable public procedures or 'operations' subject to replication by independent observers. [Cultural Materialism, p.27]

Malinowski of course is primarily an anthropologist, and it is no doubt legitimate to employ scientific methods in field work. However, he seems to go beyond this when he states:

> The real meeting-ground of all branches of anthropology is the scientific study of culture . . . Not merely anthropology, but the Study of Man in general, comprising all the social sciences, all the new psychologically or sociologically oriented disciplines, may and must cooperate in the building of a common scientific basis, which perforce will have to be identical for all the diverse pursuits of humanism.
>
> [*A Scientific Theory of Culture*, pp.4 and 6]

His thesis is also explicitly reductionist (in the 'weak' or methodological sense):

> We can thus see, first and foremost, that derived needs have the same stringency as biological needs, and that this stringency is due to the fact that they are always instrumentally related to the wants of the organism. We also see how and where they come into the structure of human organized behaviour. We see, finally, that even such highly derived activities as learning and research, art and religion, law and ethics, related as they are with organized performance, with technology, and with accuracy of communication, are also definitely related although by several removes, to the necessity of human beings to survive, to retain health and a normal state of organic efficiency.   [*A Scientific Theory of Culture*, pp.124–125]

There is little doubt then that both Harris and Malinowski would subscribe to the covering law theory of Hempel and Nagel and would wish to apply it, at least in the probabilistic version, to the human sciences in general. (Note Harris's explicit use of the word 'probabilistically' in the quotation above from page 56. It should be mentioned also that Nagel, in *The Structure of Science*, ch. 14, sees no difficulty in acccommodating teleological concepts such as 'end' and 'purpose', which Malinowski employs, to the covering law model, though he is critical of the ambiguity of the term 'function' and is dubious about 'the cognitive value of functional explanations modelled on teleological explanations in physiology'.) This is not to say of course that the two theories have anything in common other than this commitment to the scientific method and a recognition that human culture 'as a whole' emerged as a result of a natural selection process. But culture is not homogenous; it is made up of many individual cultures. Cultural materialists therefore reject the more extreme versions of biological theories (such as sociobiology) which attempt to reduce cultural traits to a multitude of different genes [compare Harris, ch. 5]. And as another cultural materialist, L.A. White, has said, while culture as such would be different if man were biologically different, the basic factor within a culture, which 'determines, in a general way at least, the form and content of the social, philosophic, and sentimental sectors' is technology – a position which is in line with Harris's emphasis on 'production' or 'labour' [see his *The Evolution of Culture*, pp.19 and 213]. Malinowski, of course, regards technology as subordinate to basic human biological needs; and he is also critical of Marxist positions.

From the standpoint of what was said in Ch. 5, both cultural materialism and biological functionalism are suspect. The primary objection to them is that, whatever merit there may be in the use of scientific procedures for the study of human behaviour in an institutional context, man's 'inner' life – his freedom, autonomy and intentionality – cannot be captured by any 'scientific' theory of culture. And it is for this reason that we now turn to a different approach to the nature and origin of culture.

Idealist theories

Advocates of the two kinds of theory discussed so far see the more 'spiritual' aspects of human life (that is, religion, art and thought itself) as being in some sense grounded in or derived from either technology or biology, which are thus accorded a place of primacy in the concept of culture. By contrast, what Harris has loosely called 'cognitive idealist' theories stress the centrality of language or symbols even to the extent, in some cases, of thinking of culture as a medium which has come into existence between man and the word, to the virtual exclusion of his physical environment. This is particularly apparent in the philosophy of Ernst **Cassirer** (1874–1945). The emphasis on symbolism is, however, important. So let us start with Cassirer's account. The ability to symbolize is, he writes [*An Essay on Man*, pp.24–25]:

> a new characteristic which appears to be the distinctive mark of human life . . . Man has, as it were, discovered a new method of adapting himself to the environment. Between the receptor system and the effector system, which are to be found in all animal species, we find in man a third link which we may describe as the *symbolic system*. This new equilibrium transforms the whole of human life. As compared with the other animals man lives not merely in a broader reality; he lives, so to speak, in a new *dimension* of reality. There is an unmistakable difference between organic reactions and human responses. In the first case a direct and immediate answer is given to an outward stimulus; in the second case the answer is delayed. It is interrupted and retarded by a slow and complicated process of thought.

He then goes on to give a somewhat Kantian interpretation of his symbolic universe. Man has to adopt the conditions of his own life. 'He has so enveloped himself in linguistic forms, in artistic images, in mythical symbols, or religious rites that he cannot see or know anything except by the interposition of the artificial medium' [p.25].

This according of a central role to symbolizing is of course not confined to those who have adopted an 'idealistic' approach to culture. Malinowski [*A Scientific Theory of Culture*, p.132] grants that 'symbolism is an essential ingredient of all organized behaviour' and that it must have come into being 'with the earliest appearance of cultural behaviour'. But he maintains that it can be submitted to observation and theoretical analysis in terms of objective facts to the same extent that material artefacts, the behaviour of groups and the forms of customs can be observed or defined. The importance of 'symboling' is also acknowledged by L.A. White in *The Evolution of Culture*:

> By *culture* we mean an extrasomatic, temporal continuum of things and events dependent upon symboling ... no other species has or has had culture. In the course of the evolution of primates man appeared when the ability to symbol had been developed and became capable of expression. We thus defined man in terms of the ability to symbol and the consequent ability to produce culture. [p.3]

Nevertheless, the contrast between on the one hand the approaches of materialism and biological functionalism and on the other that of 'cultural idealism' remains marked. The former think of culture in terms of behavioural responses or adaptations to the physical environment. The latter tend to define culture more narrowly and as transcending material considerations. As the anthropologist D. Schneider puts it, culture consists in the 'system of symbols and meanings embedded in the normative system but which is a quite distinct aspect of it' [quoted from Harris, pp.281–282].

It can now be seen that an adequate theory of culture must avoid the kind of fragmentation of cultural unity that Cassirer's strategy seems to lead to, and should seek to integrate all aspects of the cultural environment, that is, the physical, the social and the 'spiritual'. But at the same time it must be wary of the determinism and reductionism which seem to be implicit in the 'scientific' theories of anthropologists such as Harris and Malinowski. So, to complete this chapter, let us try to bring together some of the ideas discussed in earlier sections with a view to constructing the outlines of such a theory.

It would probably be accepted by most philosophers of culture: (1) that culture in some sense meets human needs, and (2) that these needs may be divided into (a) primary (biological) needs of the organism, and (b) secondary (social and 'psychological') needs. These assertions need some unpacking. We shall consider these needs in turn.

The activity of all organisms is obviously geared to achieving homoeostatic equilibrium with the environment, and to reproduction – these 'ends' being, it would appear, genetically grounded. The evolutionary development of sensory organs and of organs which facilitate movement can be seen as promoting survival, by enabling organisms to seek out food and to avoid the predatory attentions of other living things. With the emergence of social co-operation between members of a particular species, the possibilities of survival were further enhanced. This is seen in the behaviour of insects such as ants and bees, and more especially that of mammals. We can perhaps think of the basic biological instincts or drives as now being channelled and manifested through the 'higher-level' social medium or structure. Moreover socialization itself can thus be regarded as a need.

From the point of view of our discussion in this section the most significant evolutionary development is that of consciousness, thought and language. And there are a number of key questions to be answered. (1) In what way is human language unique? (2) How and why did language originate? (3) How does culture relate to language and nature? All these are complex and controversial issues. So again only a brief outline can be provided here:

(1) Much recent research has suggested that, for example, chimpanzees appear to possess a capacity, not for speech as such (on account of different physiological factors), but for communication. That they communicate with each other in the wild by means of specific calls is not in dispute. But more is being claimed here, in that, it is supposed that they can communicate with man and members of their own species by using a variety of gestures based on a human deaf-and-dumb language. What might be said about this? Firstly, it should be noted that even if chimpanzees do have some potential for gestural communication, this ability has been effected through the intervention of man. Whatever similarities there may be between other higher primates and ourselves (for example, the use of tools, sociability) chimpanzees do not exhibit such a capacity in the natural state. Moreover chimpanzees do not ask questions about the existence of God, do not have law-courts in their communities, and do not grapple with the complexities of quantum theory. A second point concerns language and understanding. Suppose we define language in a general sense as referring to visual or auditory responses to appropriate stimuli in an appropriate context. A parrot could then be said to be using language when it says 'Pretty Polly'. However, few people would claim that the parrot *knows* what it is saying or that it is *intending* to communicate. Twitterings, moos and grunts all fall into the same category. At the same time, when we hear a dog bark or a cat miaowing it would not be unreasonable to suppose there is some sort of elementary thinking going on. The dog 'knows' how to round up the sheep; the cat 'knows' how to 'persuade' its owner to open the tin of cat food. As for chimpanzees, it may be said that they can think in the sense that they can devise problem-solving strategies (how to get the banana by pilling up boxes underneath it), and can also respond to stimuli in a consistent and structured manner. Some researchers would of course say that this behaviour is the culmination of a process of trial and error; no 'conscious' thinking has occurred. The crucial difference, however, between apes and *Homo sapiens* is that our thinking processes are articulated in a 'full-blown' symbolic language. This raises another problem: the nature of the relationship between thought and language – can they be separated?

Much of the evidence for the claim that thinking and language are separable comes from the pioneering work of the Russian psychologist Lev Vygotsky (1896–1934). In his book *Thought and Language* [see especially ch. 4] he shows that a pre-linguistic stage can be discerned in the development of thought and a pre-intellectual state in the development of speech. In our ancestral primates these stages followed independent lines, and have continued to do so in present-day anthropoid species. But with the emergence of man the lines met and thought became verbal, and speech rational. A similar convergence is recapitulated in children at about the age of two, thus initiating a new form of behaviour. Arguments in favour of pre-linguistic conceptualization and the view that language is not to be identified with thinking have been presented also by neuroscientists such as Edelman and Pinker. The philosopher H.H. Price, in his *Thinking and Experience*, likewise suggested that our thinking 'overflows' the symbols it utilizes, that is, much of our thinking is not always explicitly articulated in language. This view, however, has been criticized by most 'analytic' philosophers, who argue that thought is fundamentally linguistic, in so far as thought involves meanings, and meanings can be expressed only in a language the rules for meaningful use of which are 'fixed' in a public context. This debate continues. Moreover attempts to resolve the issue are complicated by the ambiguity of the term 'concept'. Many philosophers have supposed that to have a concept of a thing is to have or to be in contact with some 'entity' – a Platonic Form, an 'abstract' idea, an 'essence'. Such a view has been criticized particularly by 'linguistic' philosophers on the grounds that it supposes all words other than logical connectives to be regarded as names which have meaning by virtue of denotation (see Ch. 2). As against this they argue that to have a concept is in some sense to know how to use a word correctly and how to apply it in appropriate circumstances (see the discussion of Wittgenstein in Ch. 11). If this is so then clearly it must follow that there can be no pre-linguistic conceptualization. However, we are not obliged to define 'concept' in this way; the word itself has a variety of uses in language. It is often used to refer to the ability to pick out or identify that which we suppose the concept to be 'about'. A view something like this is held by Edelman, whose theory of 'Neural Darwinism' makes a significant scientific contribution to the debate about mind and language.

Edelman distinguishes between perceptual and conceptual categorization. By perceptual categorization he means 'the selective discrimination of an object or event from other objects or events for adaptive purposes' [87]. It operates on signals from the outside world but is non-conscious and can be carried out even by automata. Together with memory it can then make learning possible (provided appropriate connections have been established which are mediated by parts of the brain other than those responsible for categorization). Conceptual categorization, on the other hand, is characterized by the ability to grasp abstract and general relational properties. It depends on perceptual categorization and memory, but works from within the brain and treats the activities of portions of global mappings as its substrate. The two forms of categorization together give rise to what Edelman calls correlated 'scenes' or 'images' in 'primary consciousness'. In animals such images can be to some extent regenerated by memory, but there is no reference to a 'symbolic' memory. Animals thus cannot break free from the remembered present. This can occur only in 'higher-order' and intentional consciousness, which involves the ability 'to construct a socially based selfhood, to model the world in terms of the past and future, and to be directly aware' [125], that is, both of one's experiences of the world and of one's being aware. This is perhaps what Susan Langer refers to as the 'symbolic transformation of experience'. The key features of Edelman's thesis then are that a rich conceptual memory faculty, and especially a memory capable of recategorizing phonemes and their syntactical ordering, was a precondition for the emergence of higher-order consciousness, and that the concept of a self–non-self interaction had to emerge prior to true speech – which he sees as unique to *Homo sapiens*. [For a detailed account of the scientific basis of

Edelman's theory you will need to read his trilogy or the more accessible account presented in *Bright Air, Brilliant Mind.*

(2) How and why then did true language emerge? Clearly, as Edelman points out, certain physiological changes were required – evolution of the vocal tract, special cerebral cortical regions which link acoustic, motor and conceptual areas of the brain by re-entrant connections – which provide a system for the transition from presyntactical gestures to a simple ordering of nouns and verbs and thereafter the more sophisticated sensori-motor ordering which is the basis for true syntax. But what more was needed? If full justice is to be done to our awareness of ourselves as autonomous, self-determining agents – and consciousness has a role to play here (as we argued in the previous chapter) – then behaviourist theories must be regarded as inadequate. The American professor of linguistics Noam Chomsky agrees with this, arguing that we are born with an innate capacity to acquire grammatical rules – a 'language acquisition device' – which is genetically based. Similarly Pinker argues for a 'language instinct' much as a spider may be said to have an instinct for spinning its web. However, both stress the infinite creativity of language and therefore accept that no genetic determinism is involved. Even Harris accepts this and criticizes socio-biologists for overlooking the 'semantic universality' of language; for although:

> The human capacity to communicate by means of a 'semantic symbol language' does involve a genetically programmed predisposition to acquire such a language . . . *Homo sapiens* has a unique genetically based capacity to override genetic determinisms by acquiring, storing, and transmitting gene-free repertoires of social responses.
>
> [*Cultural Materialism,* pp.132–133]

Nevertheless, although Chomsky and Pinker agree that language and thought are not to be identified, Edelman rejects the notion of a 'language acquisition device' on the grounds that, as shown by recent research, children are able to learn language because they can first make sense of things and what people do. The implication is that this must have been the case before our hominid ancestors came to convert symbolic memory into true language. We can suppose this to be correct, but yet we might argue that something is still missing from the theory. Yet there are intriguing hints in Edelman's account as to how this lacuna might be filled. We have already referred to his conclusion that a model of self–non-self interaction is probably required prior to true speech. He goes on [p.136] to say that the self, developed through social and linguistic interactions, gives rise to a world that *requires* [his italics] naming and intending:

> This world reflects inner events that are recalled, and imagined events, as well as outside events that are perceptually experienced. Tragedy becomes possible – the loss of the self by death or mental disorder, the remembrance of unassuageable pain. By the same token, a high drama of creation and endless imagination occurs.

On the basis of this it is reasonable to suppose that emotion probably played a major role in effecting the integration of pre-linguistic thought with pre-rational utterances and the translation of private symbols from 'within' the individual to the 'public' shared experience of the social community. Let us explore this possibility by engaging in some – not too fanciful – speculation. (We might call this the **psycholinguistic** theory.) Consider an ancestor living at sometime between, say, 4 million (*Australopithecus africanus*) and 200,000 (*Homo habilis*) years ago. (There is understandably much disagreement among archaeologists, palaeontologists, biologists and others about the period when true language might first have appeared. Much depends on such matters as the emergence of the vocal tract, Broca's and Wernicke's areas in the cerebral cortex, tool-making and the like. But for our purposes here the date is not important.) We can imagine that he (or she, or even a group; for it is probable that linguistic capacities developed in many early hominids simultaneously and in different locations) at some point acquired a dim awareness that his perceptual experience related to something external, 'other' than himself, and correspondingly that he was a 'self' like others in his group but 'other' than them. (This is a primary instance of Edelman's 'self–non-self interaction'.) This would in due course have developed into more sophisticated conceptual spatial categorization – of up and down, in front of and behind, near and far, for example. Similarly he would have become fully conscious of change and temporality – before, now, and after, quick and slow. Natural rhythms such as the rising and setting of the Sun, the passage of the seasons, the day-to-day changing of the weather, all of which would have been of importance in the fight for survival, would no doubt have contributed to this. We can assume he would have felt both 'alienated' from yet part of his immediate surroundings, which he would have regarded equally as threatening and yet as the source of food and shelter. Indeed we can imagine him experiencing what might be termed a 'psychic shock'; and this could well have been the catalyst which projected inner conscious symbolic thought into externality, communicated perhaps by gestures and vocal utterances.

But how? Consider a simple action such as picking a berry off a bush. There is clearly a biological imperative operating here. Now, we might say a chimpanzee 'chooses' this rather than that berry, and although the animal no doubt perceives the fruit, is aware of it (primary consciousness), it seems unlikely that it can reflect on what it is doing in the sense that it can be aware of itself as engaged in the act of foraging. In the case of our hypothetical ancestor the biological imperative is also operative: he is motivated by the biological desire for food. However, additionally there is a 'psychological' need – to overcome 'alienation'. Initially this need would have manifested itself as a 'feeling', 'urge', or 'impulse'; it could not have been consciously articulated. How then might it have been overcome, and what has this to do with language? We can argue that the 'directedness' (intentionality) of his consciousness towards the external object was translated into action – the movement of his arm, the grasping of the berry. Suppose further that a sound was spontaneously uttered, as the manifestation or concomitant of his emotional satisfaction in picking the berry. Not only would this have been recorded in his symbolic memory, but it would now have been accompanied by memories both of the sound as a private phoneme and of his sense of control of an aspect of the environment. Furthermore we can suppose that other members of the group, even if they themselves had not reached this stage, could in due course have associated the heard sound with the observed action. Sounds became endowed with significance: private symbolism became a public shared language. The sound may have taken on the function of a name – of the berry, or food, or the action, perhaps also in due course referring to some such conceptual notion as control or dominance, though over a period of no doubt thousands of years other sounds would have been needed to express these multifarious references, and would have enlarged the group's vocabulary as syntax became more complex.

If this scenario is in any way correct, the consequences for our ancestral hominid would have been profound. To name a thing would have been regarded as controlling or dominating it. Naming would probably also have strengthened social bonding. Anxieties could be made explicit, shared and exorcized, perhaps through magical or religious rites. (These 'powers' of language can be seen even today in many cultures: ritual incantations are supposed to guarantee a successful crop, spells are cast, enemies are vanquished.) Strategies could be discussed, skills refined and new techniques created. More importantly, man's new-found knowledge and experience could be accurately communicated to future generations.

(3) Finally we come to the third question – the relationship of culture to language and nature. The answer is already implicit in the discussion of the previous two questions, and it turns on a fundamental ambiguity in the term 'culture'. There is no reason why we should not talk of 'pre-linguistic' hominid culture – in much the same way as we refer to the culture of other primates, or even of insects. The term refers here to 'way of life', social structure and so on. But when we talk of man as *the* cultural animal, we are referring to ourselves and our ancestors after the 'breakthrough' from internal conceptualization to public expression of a shared 'true' language. Culture and language are both necessary and sufficient prerequisites for each other's existence. The possession of language has enabled our species to 'enculturalize' both our biological and social needs: it channels and moderates them, makes them explicit in consciousness, gives us some degree of control over them and enables us to pass on acquired experience in dealing with them to later generations. There is then no conflict or incompatibility between culture and nature. Culture has grown 'naturally' out of nature: yet it transcends nature and 'loops back' on it to transform it.

There are many other problems that deserve to be discussed. What are the numerous modes and structures of human culture? How exactly do they satisfy our 'needs'. A comprehensive theory of culture would also have to consider such matters as cultural change, progress and standards, and the relationship of culture to civilization. These issues will not be tackled here.

*Comments

The 'psycholinguistic' account of culture is of course highly speculative. Now that you have got this far in your study of philosophy you will, I hope, have acquired a fair understanding of a large number of philosophical problems and have sharpened up your analytical skills. It can therefore be left for you to cast a critical eye over the previous section. However, your might find a few general comments useful to round off the chapter.

The thesis is obviously questionable on the grounds that we do not actually *know* why language and culture appeared. If we see someone running along the road and want to know why, we have probably observed what he did just before and what happened afterwards; we can also ask him, and he can tell us (we cannot be sure of course that he will tell the truth). In the case of language and culture, we can make observations of artefacts unearthed by palaeontologists, and we can study historical documents to build up a picture of past cultures, and anthropologists and ethologists can study present-day cultures. Similarly we can carry out psychological investigations of the development of concepts in children or chimpanzees. But we cannot ask ancestral man why he started to symbolize or make use of gestures and grunts.

In reply we can say that the data provided by these various kinds of scientists do constitute evidence which can be regarded as acceptable within the context of the type of explanatory models we are concerned with in our study of culture. Theories may not be 'testable' as they are in, say, physics or chemistry, but we can appeal to such criteria as coherence and simplicity (compare Quine and Popper). We can also say that, for example, the 'psycholinguistic' theory gives us an understanding of ourselves which is both fruitful and intellectually satisfying. What constitutes 'satisfaction' is of course itself a concept that needs to be looked at. And there is an interesting paradox here, in that we are applying to a general theory of culture the same test that we might wish to apply to constituent cultural modes, such as myth, religion, perhaps even natural sciences and philosophy, namely, that they give satisfaction to the extent that they meet human 'needs'.

Finally, it can be said that this theory avoids the extremes of reductionist material or socio-biological accounts of culture and idealist views (including Cassirer's neo-Kantian 'theory of symbolic forms'). Neuro-biological complexity may well be a precondition for the evolutionary development of symboling, consciousness and language, all of which are implicit in our capacity for choice and self-determination, but neither this nor environmental factors fully account for human culture. In a very real sense, man (in Sartre's phrase) 'surges up' and shapes himself. It is perhaps something like this that Pinker is thinking of when he writes:

> ... nothing in culture makes sense except in the light of psychology. Evolution created psychology; and that is how it explains culture. The most important relic of early humans is the modern mind.
>
> [*How the Mind Works*, p.210]

Texts and problems

1 Can actions be determined?

2 Discuss the view that in the last analysis a human person is an ensemble of forces.

3 The human person is a prisoner of his genes. Do you agree?

*4 Can it ever be appropriate to compare human beings to machines?

5 'Man is a masterpiece of creation, if only because no amount of determinism can prevent him from believing that he acts as a free being' (Lichtenberg). Discuss.

6 Is giving a reason the same as giving a cause?

7 '... social behaviour is to be understood as *rule-following*, and not as *causally regular* behaviour.' Are the social sciences (the sciences of social behaviour) fundamentally different from the natural (physical) sciences? [AEB, 1996]

8 (a) Describe and illustrate how the study of social phenomena may be different from the study of natural phenomena.

(b) Assess whether the claim that 'all knowledge is human' makes it impossible to distinguish natural science from social science on grounds of objectivity.

[AQA (AEB), specimen, 2001]

9 How are problems associated with the concept of action relevant to the debate about the methodological status of the social sciences?

*10 Can 'explanations' in the social sciences be assimilated within the framework of the 'covering law' model? (See also question **9** in Ch. 8.)

11 Do you think that psychoanalysis should be regarded as a science, as a mature theory which states universal laws concerning the functioning of the unconscious?

12 'The vocation of man is the mastery and possession of nature.' Discuss this claim.

13 Discuss the assertion made in the statement: 'The *animal laborans* ... remains the servant of nature and the earth; only *homo faber* conducts himself as lord and master of the earth' (Arendt). [IB, specimen, 2000]

14 To what extent is work a means of achieving social integration and recognitions?

[IB, specimen, 2000]

15 By what criteria can we make a distinction between work that alienates and work that fulfils? [IB, specimen, 2000]

16 'Without "It" man cannot live. But he who lives with "It" alone is not a man.' Discuss this statement of Buber critically. [IB, specimen, 2000]

17 Assess the importance of the difference between 'physical reason' and 'historical reason' in Ortega y Gasset's view of history. [IB, specimen, 2000]

18 'Human beings cannot be alienated in a modern society because modern society is their own production.' Discuss this statement. [IB, specimen, 2000]

19 Discuss the view that a certain use of language can allow any of us to avoid recognizing personhood and can allow us to deny humanity.

[IB, specimen, 2000]

20 Is contemporary secular humanism the natural outcome of history or is it just a temporary phenomenon within one culture?

*21 What philosophical difficulties are raised by the distinction between 'nature' and 'culture'?

22 Is cultural plurality an obstacle to the unity of the human race?
[IB, specimen, 2000]

23 What would justify keeping cultural patterns inherited from the past alive instead of conducting our lives as if we had no cultural past?

24 'In order to fully understand a particular culture, it is always necessary to learn its language.' Discuss this assertion. [IB, specimen, 2000]

25 What distinguishes that which is natural from that which is artificial?

26 Is the value of a civilization a function of its technological achievements?

27 Do ideologies threaten our essential humanity or are they emancipatory?

28 Does interpretation of a text reveal its truth?

29 There can be no interpretation without prejudice. Discuss critically.

*30 Can 'horizons' be 'fused'?

31 'Man is born to suffer.' Examine the philosophical implications of this statement.

*Notes/guided answers have been provided for questions **4, 10, 21** and **30** (at end of book).

READING LIST

A. Prescribed texts
Aquinas, *Summa Theologiae*. (IB)
Arendt, H., *The Human Condition*. (IB)
Marx, K. and Engels, F., *The German Ideology*. (AEB)
Ortega y Gasset, J., *History as a System*. (IB)
Sartre, J.-P., *Existentialism and Humanism*. (AEB)

B. Other texts
Gadamer, H.-G., *Truth and Method*. (On Gadamer, see Warnke, G., *Gadamer: Hermeneutics, Tradition and Reason*.)
Habermas, J., *Knowledge and Human Interests*.
Habermas, J., *The Habermas Reader*, (ed. W. Outhwaite). (On Habermas, see Thompson, J.B., *Critical Hermeneutics: A Study in the Thought of Paul Ricoeur and Jürgen Habermas*.)
Hempel, C.G., 'Explanation in Science and History', in P.H. Nidditch (ed.), *The Philosophy of Science*.
Ricoeur, P., *Hermeneutics and the Human Sciences*, (ed. J.B. Thompson). (On Ricoeur, see Thompson, *Critical Hermeneutics* – above.)
Searle, J.R., *Minds, Brains and Science*.
Searle, J.R., *Mind, Language and Society*.

See also these major works:
Dilthey, W., *Introduction to the Human Sciences*.
Gehlen, A., *Man, His Nature and Situation in the World*.
Merleau-Ponty, M., *Consciousness and the Acquisition of Language*.
Merleau-Ponty, M., *The Structure of Behaviour*.
Scheler, M., *The Place of Man in the Cosmos*.

C. Supplementary reading
(You are recommended to start with titles marked with an asterisk.)

1. General/historical background
Collingwood, R.G., *The Idea of Nature.**
Wachterhauser, B. (ed.), *Hermeneutics and Modern Philosophy.*
Young, J.Z., *An Introduction to the Study of Man.**

2. Books on topics raised throughout the chapter
(See also the Reading list for Ch. 8.)
Alexeev, A.P., *The Origin of the Human Race.**
Apel, K.-O., *Understanding and Explanation.*
Cassirer, E., *An Essay on Man.**
Chomsky, N., *Language and Mind.*
Chomsky, N., *Reflections on Language.**
Davidson, D., *Essays on Actions and Events.*
Dawkins, R., *The Blind Watchmaker.**
Dawkins, R., *The Selfish Gene.**
Edelman, G., *Bright Air, Brilliant Fire: On the Matter of the Mind.**
Edelman, G., *The Remembered Present.*
Hampshire, S., *Thought and Action.*
Harris, M., *Cultural Materialism.**
Kenny, A., *Action, Emotion and Will.*
Langer, S., *Philosophical Sketches.**
Linden, E., *Apes, Men and Language.**
Lorenz, K., *Behind the Mirror.**
Malinowski, B., *A Scientific Theory of Culture.**
Mead, G.H., *Selected Writings.*
Midgley, M., *Beast and Man.**
Monod, J., *Chance and Necessity.**
Pinker, S., *How the Mind Works.**
Pinker, S., *The Language Instinct.**
Ryan, A. (ed.), *The Philosophy of Social Explanation.**
Searle, J.R., *Intentionality.*
Searle, J.R., *Speech Acts.*
Searle, J.R. (ed.), *The Philosophy of Language.**
Taylor, C., *The Explanation of Behaviour.*
Teilhard de Chardin, P., *The Phenomenon of Man.**
Vygotsky, L., *Thought and Language.**
White, A.R. (ed.), *The Philosophy of Action.**
White, L.A., *The Evolution of Culture.*
Wilson, E.O., *Consilience: The Unity of Human Knowledge.**
Wilson, E.O., *On Human Nature.**
Winch, P., *The Idea of a Social Science.**
Young, J.Z., *Philosophy and the Brain.**

▼ **13** Oriental philosophy

It would be quite mistaken to suppose that philosophy is a uniquely occidental enterprise; both India and China can boast of a tradition of philosophical speculation which can be traced back at least to the time of the Presocratics in Ancient Greece. Moreover it would be unacceptably arrogant if we were to regard 'our' philosophers as in any sense superior to their Eastern counterparts. The Indian thinkers Nāgārjuna (second century AD), Dharmakīrti (seventh century) and Śaṁkara (eighth century), in particular, bear comparison with Plato and Aristotle. And in China the influence of K'ung Fu-tzu (Confucius) and Lao Tzu, both of whom flourished in the sixth century BC, continues to be felt even today – although it is true to say that the former was concerned primarily with social and ethical matters, while the philosophy of the latter was essentially concerned with achieving a mystical union of man with the *Tao* (the 'Way' – sometimes transliterated as *Dao*), rather than with either the metaphysical or the critical thinking which characterizes Western and also much of Indian philosophy. Mention should also be made of the contribution of Arabian philosophers during the Middle Ages. But in so far as their primary concern was to reconcile Islamic theology with classical Greek thought, they are probably best regarded as belonging to the Western rather than to any Eastern philosophical tradition. In this final chapter we shall therefore do no more than look briefly at some of the key features of Indian and Chinese philosophy. A proper treatment would of course require a book to be devoted to each culture.

13.1 Early Indian philosophy

Reading: Hiriyanna, *Essentials of Indian Philosophy*, chs I–II

Throughout its long history, Indian philosophy has for the most part been closely integrated with Hinduism. In the first period, dating from as early as 1200 BC, thought about life and the universe was expressed through a collection of sacred texts or 'Mantras', that is, religious songs, called the *Rigveda*. In the earliest of these hymns, certain natural objects or forces are regarded as individual gods or powers (Agni is the god of fire, for example): but in due course they came to be thought of as different manifestations of one Supreme Being, both creator of and active in the world, and sustainer of cosmic order. Together with this movement towards monotheism we also find increasing emphasis on the notion of an impersonal first cause – the *Tat Ekam* ('That One').

Philosophical speculation became more prominent in the *Upaniṣads* – 'secret doctrines', which were written between the fifth and second century BC. In these writings we find two key conceptions stressed: (1) that the universe is one, the manifestation of a primary eternal and absolute principle referred to as Brahman, and (2) that man has an inner 'essence', the *ātman*. While it is not fully clear how the ātman should be understood, these two conceptions are generally held in the *Upaniṣads* to be intimately connected. (A common saying is 'I am Brahman'.) Nevertheless, much of subsequent Indian philosophy is concerned with examining the apparent ambiguity of the relationship. Some thinkers argued that only Brahman is real, the world being but an appearance. Some supposed the self to be identical with Brahman and the world as a manifestation of it (and thus only relatively real). For other philosophers Brahman is both immanent in the world (as multiplicity of individuals and souls) and transcendent (as unity). The kind of knowledge we can have of Brahman will similarly vary with the kind of interpretation we adopt. That knowledge is ultimately possible, however, is implicit in the doctrine of transmigration (*saṃsāra*). Already in the Vedas the soul was held to be immortal. Now in the *Upaniṣads* it is said that the soul will be reborn – depending on our deeds in this life (the doctrine of *karma*). The soul can overcome ignorance and achieve a state of enlightenment or 'release' from the cycle of birth and death (*mokṣa*) through different forms of *yogas*: study with the help of a teacher (*guru*), action, or devotion (*bhakti*). This process is paralleled at the cosmic level, for Brahman can be regarded not only as self-existent, the source of the universe, but also as the self-evolving universe itself – endlessly engaged in a cycle of creation and dissolution. These Brahmanist doctrines (with a more personalist or theistic emphasis) are wonderfully expressed in the *Bhagavad-Gītā* ('Song of the Lord'), which forms Book VI of the monumental epic the *Mahābhārata* and is perhaps the most important Hindu religious text. The poem tells of the conversation between Prince Arjuna and the incarnated god Krishna before a great battle. Arjuna is concerned about having to fight his friends, but Krishna advises him to do his duty as a warrior. There is, he says, no incompatibility between such action and meditation and renunciation of the world; both constitute devotion to God.

It is usual to divide later philosophical developments into two groups: the orthodox Vedic schools and the unorthodox non-Vedic systems. The latter include: (1) the Cārvāka sceptical and materialist school, which rejected traditional religious beliefs, asserting that all knowledge should be grounded in sense-experience; (2) the philosophy of the religion known as Jainism; and (3) Buddhism. We shall consider only the last: but before we do so we shall sketch out some of the *leitmotifs* of the first period of Chinese philosophy.

13.2 Early Chinese philosophy

Reading: Creel, chs I–IX; Confucius, *The Analects*; Lao Tzu, *Tao Te Ching*

While early Indian philosophy was firmly rooted in Hindu religious ideas and practices, Chinese philosophy was initially essentially secular, being largely confined to a consideration of man and his social conduct. Chinese society during the 4th and 3rd centuries BC is notable for its political chaos and constant warfare between states. And it is in this context that the writings of **Confucius** (551–479 BC) are seen to be significant. The *Analects* (or Discourses) is primarily a statement of his moral and political philosophy. The central concept is that of *jen* (or *ren*), which can mean 'humanity', 'goodness', or 'love'. It can be expressed in terms of the polarities of conscientiousness (*chung*), or being true to oneself, and altruism (*shu*). He explains these respectively as establishing one's own character and establishing the character of others [6.28]; and he refers to them as the 'one thread' running through his doctrines [4.15]. As Wing-Tsit Chan points out [p.27], this teaching can be seen as the positive side of Confucius's **golden rule**: 'Do not do to others what you do not want them to do to you' [15.23]. The man of *jen* is the perfect man, the man of benevolence, the 'perfect gentleman' or 'superior man' (*chün-tzu*), who possesses the virtues of righteousness, integrity, propriety (for example, as ritual, *li*) and filial piety. Implicit here are such characteristics as moderation, balance and self-control – the 'golden mean'. It is important also to note that both action and knowledge are emphasized in Confucius's doctrine. The superior man's acts reflect the 'Mandate of Heaven' (*T'ien-ming*), or of the Supreme Being, whose Moral Law is the **Way** (*Dao*). But in Confucius's humanism the concern is with the here and now and not with any consequences that might be incurred after our death by our behaviour: 'It is man that can make the Way great, and not the Way that can make man great' [15.28]. It follows that these ideals should be accepted by rulers if they are to govern wisely and have regard to the well-being of their subjects [for example, 14.45]. A central requirement is that names should be 'rectified' [13.3], that is, they should be correctly applied. For this to happen there must be general agreement on usage – concerning the precise social role to be occupied by different ranks of individuals in the hierarchy. And this presupposes a capacity to interpret *li* correctly (which will of course be possessed by the man of 'humanity'). Implicit also in Confucius's account is the assumption that names must be consonant with actions and must match the actuality of circumstances.

Confucius seemed to accept that men were naturally good and perfectible through study, and he also accepted without question the hierarchical feudal society of his day. These issues were debated and developed by his later disciples. But it was with the philosophy of **Taoism** that we find a distinct change in emphasis from man as a social being to man as an individual. In the *Tao Te Ching* (or *Dao De Jing*) (*Classic of the Way and its Virtue*) **Lao Tzu** advocates that the individual should aim not at following the conventional social standards of society but to achieving harmony, perhaps even a kind of mystical union with the Way. The *Tao* here does not refer to a moral standard or system but to Nature as the underlying pattern of the cosmos: 'Man models himself after Earth. Earth models itself after heaven. Heaven models itself after Tao. And Tao models itself after Nature' [25]. Indeed in the opening lines of the book it is made clear that the eternal *Tao* is, paradoxically, unnameable, indefinable and indescribable. How then is one to follow the Way and become a man of 'superior virtue'? Again there is an element of paradox in the teaching. Lao Tzu exhorts us to empty ourselves of all knowledge, doctrines, proprieties, even one's 'humanity' – Confucianism is clearly the target here [see especially 36–38]. Moreover, to act is to take no action [2, 10, 43 etc.]. This notion of non-action (*wu-wei*) does not mean that one should sit, hermit-like literally doing nothing, but rather that one should let things be and not strain after achievement; one should not act contrary to Nature and one's own inner nature; action should be spontaneous as Nature itself is. Lao Tzu thus advocates a way of life close to Nature, and this is best achieved in an agricultural society which will be free from hierarchies, conformism and artificiality.

Much of the subsequent debate among later Chinese philosophers turned on matters of interpretation of the writings of Confucius and Lao Tzu, though there were also disagreements about human nature and the relationship of individual to society. The Confucian philosopher Hsün Tzu (b. *c.* 300 BC), for example, supposed human beings to be thoroughly evil (as against the positive and optimistic views of another important Confucian, Mencius – *c.* 372–289 BC), and he therefore argued in favour of strict governmental controls – just as 'crooked wood must be steamed and forced to conform to a straight edge'. However, with the relaxation of this 'legalism' during the Han dynasty from the second century onwards, a more eclectic approach to philosophy developed. Confucianism came to be blended with the Taoist ideal of harmony and with two other doctrines, the *yin–yang* and the 'Five elements', which had emerged in the fourth century BC. The *yin* and *yang* were regarded as complementary cosmic principles under which everything could be classified. Thus female, heaven and fire are *yin*, while male, earth and water are *yang*. Both categories are needed if cosmic harmony is to be maintained, though they may change from one to the other, as does winter into summer, for example. The five 'elements' were held to be wood, fire, earth, metal and water; and the philosophers claimed to have identified numerous other correlations with them – five directions, five seasons, five colours and so on. Much philosophical discussion was concerned with the sequential changing of these elements into each other. (Compare the treatment of these ideas by the Presocratics.)

13.3 Buddhist philosophy

Reading: Hiriyanna, ch. 3; Chan, ch. X

India

Buddhism is the name of the religion founded by Siddhārtha Gotama, who was born in India in 563 BC. He came to be called Buddha (The Enlightened One) on account of the illumination he claimed to have attained after many years of searching. Early Buddhism is generally regarded as having developed out of the Upanishadic teachings. The essential features of the doctrine is that by following the so-called 'Noble Eightfold Path', the individual – regardless of social standing – could hope to achieve enlightenment, the state of *Nirvana*, or supreme moral perfection, and escape from the cycle of reincarnation. This Path can be understood as relating to the 'Four Noble Truths': (1) the truth of suffering, (2) the causes of suffering, (3) the ending of suffering, and (4) how this cessation is to be achieved – for which the Eightfold Path is the means. The eight components of the Path are: (1) right understanding, (2) right thought, (3) right speech, (4) right action, (5) right livelihood, (6) right effort, (7) right mindfulness, and (8) right concentration.

After Buddha's death a number of 'schools' of Buddhist belief gradually developed. Initially the most important was Theravāda Buddhism (later to be called *Hīnayāna*, or 'Lesser Vehicle', by followers of the Mahāyāna, that is, 'Greater Vehicle' school). The Theravadas were conservative and claimed to be true to the traditional teachings of the Buddha. Arguably this school is of less philosophical importance than the Mahāyāna, though it did develop a complex psychological analysis of human existence in terms of three categories of aspects or features (*dharmas*) – five 'components', which were then incorporated into twelve 'bases', and these in turn into eighteen perceptual 'elements'. By seeking to control these the seeker of salvation might hope to break the karmic chain and attain Nirvana. However, the existence of a continuous soul or of personal identity is rejected.

Mahāyāna Buddhism, by contrast, is more radical and less traditional. The Buddha is regarded as a manifestation of a divine being rather than just an enlightened human being, and indeed not unique; it is claimed that there are many other 'Boddhisattvas' who are able to postpone their entrance into the final state of bliss so as to transfer 'merit' to others. However, our concern here is with the significant contribution that the various schools of Mahāyāna Buddhism made to Indian and Chinese philosophy, and in particular the Mādhyamika school founded by **Nāgārjuna**. There are three issues that deserve comment here:

(1) The self. While the earlier Buddhists had rejected the idea of a continuous and putatively unifying self, they accepted that the components or aspects of existence were real. (A comparison with Hume might be made here.) The Mahāyāna philosophers, however, rejected even this possibility, principally on the grounds that if there is nothing to unify the elements then they cannot be said to exist.

(2) This conclusion has profound ontological implications. If things do not exist, then what are we to say about the universe in general? According to Nāgārjuna, the world we experience is phenomenal, dependent on our cognitive structures and thus unreal. This is expressed in the concept of the **Void** or emptiness (*śūnyatā*). Nevertheless a distinction can still be made between the phenomenal world and that 'Reality' which we attempt vainly to categorize. This is the Absolute, empty in the sense of being beyond all description and distinction, and which can be the legitimate object of mystical contemplation on account of its very emptiness. Nāgārjuna's attempt to find a middle way (this is the meaning of 'Mādhyamika') between the relatively real or unreal phenomenal world and the 'real' Absolute Void was the focal point for subsequent debate. (See Murti's book on Buddhism, listed at the end of this chapter, for an interesting discussion of the similarities between this doctrine and Kant's philosophy.) Followers of another Mādhyamika school, the Vijñānavādins, for example, argued that the

external world is a complete illusion, only the mind itself being real. Enlightenment is achieved when this is recognized.

(3) Causation. Nāgārjuna is critical of all theories of causation – whether they assert the identity of cause and effect or suppose they are distinct – principally on the grounds that the concept of relation (internal and external respectively) involves a contradiction. Clearly there is a problem here in that we assume the existence of causal connections in our everyday lives, and indeed it is a cardinal point of Buddhist teaching that to break the cycle of rebirth we must attend to the causes and consequences of our actions. However, it seems to have been Nāgārjuna's opinion that from the standpoint of the Void, such teaching is not strictly true. As in the case of the concept of self we are misled by our ordinary language. (Compare here the views of Wittgenstein and many other twentieth century Western analytic philosophers.)

China

Although Buddhism eventually declined throughout most of India, both the Theravāda and Mahāyāna traditions spread to other parts of Asia. It was brought to Tibet in AD 747 by the monk Padmasambhava, but it had spread to China perhaps some 600 years earlier and in due course gave rise to a synthesis with both Taoist and Confucian elements. Two schools of thought became particularly influential: the T'ien-t'ai school of 'perfect harmony' and Ch'an Buddhism (*Dhyāna* is the Sanskrit word for 'meditation'), generally known by its Japanese form 'Zen'. According to the former, the phenomenal world is made up of manifestations of the Mind of Pure Nature. These phenomenal things have only temporary existence and are divided into ten realms extending from Buddhas through spirits, humans, animals and evil beings. Each of these groups is said to possess ten 'characters of thusness', such as nature, substance and energy; and each of these admits of further composition – living being, space and 'aggregates', for example, matter, sensation and thought. This gives rise to a complement of three thousand 'worlds', each one of which is the manifestation of Mind in its totality. Unlike the T'ien-t'ai, Ch'an Buddhism eschews both doctrine and religious practices, and instead appeals to spontaneity and direct insight (demonstrating the influence of Taoism). The aim is to achieve a state of 'no-mind' (*wu-hsin*) or 'no-thought' (*wu-nien*): to act rather than to be 'paralysed' by theorizing and logic-chopping. Insight cannot be learned; *wanting* to achieve it will lead to failure. The aim of the teacher must be to bring the student to a state of receptiveness so that his mind, as it were, just 'lets itself go'. To this end the master will often pose seemingly paradoxical questions or give apparently irrelevant responses to his students' queries – or even strike them a sharp blow! In time the students will 'see' that it is the spontaneity and naturalness of the response rather than its content that shows the way. In the two main Japanese schools, Soto Zen and Rinzai Zen, to achieve enlightenment (*satori*) the emphasis is respectively on 'sitting quietly, doing nothing' and on special kinds of problems (*koan*, in Chinese *Kung-an*) for mediation. (See Watts's *The Way of Zen*.)

*Comment

The primary concern of early Chinese philosophy was with human conduct and the relationship of the individual to the social order and to the 'Way' (understood respectively by Confucians and Taoists as the 'moral standard' or as the 'pattern of the cosmos'). Accordingly there was little metaphysical speculation; it was seen as either irrelevant or inadequate, even futile. Buddhism too was initially a set of ethical codes rather than a philosophical system. However, as we have seen, it did in due course give rise to a great deal of metaphysical thinking, often of a high order. There is clearly something paradoxical about this. Most Buddhist philosophers talk of impermanence, and deny the existence of a continuous substantial self or *ego*: there is only a stream of sensations, feelings and consciousness. Truth lies beyond any rational analysis, so cannot be categorized. It can only be apprehended though total 'detachment' from all philosophical conceptualization. The principal difficulty for non-Buddhist commentators, and indeed many Buddhists, is how to reconcile this kind of approach with the acceptance of a moral self and personal responsibility, causation, reincarnation and the notion of *karma*. It is doubtful whether there has yet been any satisfactory proposal which might bring about the resolution of this problem.

13.4 Indian philosophy: the Vedic schools

Reading: Hiriyanna, chs IV–VIII

From the first century BC onwards eight orthodox Vedic schools of philosophy gradually made their appearance. Only a short summary of the principal tenets of each can be given here, but you will find excellent accounts in Hiriyanna's book.

Nyāya and Vaiśeṣika

Although these schools probably developed independently, by about the fifth century AD they had begun to associate and eventually coalesced. They are therefore generally treated together as teaching one synthesized doctrine. Both make full use of logic and dialectic (*nyāya* means 'argument' or 'enquiry') and are concerned particularly with epistemological problems. Their standpoint is both realist and pluralist. The world consists of a multiplicity of objects which exist independent of our perception. Nine 'substances' (*dravya*) are distinguished: four types of atoms (earth, air, fire and water), an 'ether' (*ākāsa*), space, time, the 'self' and the 'inner organ' (*manas*) of the self. Additionally there are supposed to be six positive 'categories': substance, quality (including relation) (*guṇa*), motion or agency (*karma*), inherence (*samavāya*), particularity (*viśeṣa*) and universality (*sāmānya*); and the negative category of 'non-existence'. The objects of the world are built out of the atoms – which 'inhere' in the wholes; they are thus more than a mere aggregation. The *guṇas* are peculiar to certain classes of things, for example, many objects have weight. The self, in conjunction with its *manas* and sensory input, is the source of all psychic life – knowledge, feeling and volition. The philosophers of this school argue further that objects are directly known, error arising when the perceiver passes illegitimately beyond what is given: when something is presented as being other than how it actually is. Four methods of validation (*pramāṇas*) are accepted: perception, inference, verbal testimony and comparison. As to the origin of the cosmos, thinkers of this school regard God (*Śiva*) as both its creator and architect. He is infinitely powerful and wise, and can be said to possess knowledge, love and bliss in full measure. Cosmological and teleological arguments are invoked to prove his existence. God is the originator of motion. Indeed it is held that all movements are brought about by sentient agents, no physical object being able to move by itself. In their account of causation the atomists argued that, while cause and effect are non-identical, causes inhere in effects, but a given cause can produce a variety of effects. Inductive techniques were therefore developed to discover the laws of nature. The goal of life is to achieve the state of freedom (*mokṣa*) from pain (and pleasure). Success will be contingent on the degrees of merit (*dharma*) and demerit accumulated in the course of one's life through one's actions (*karma*). Through detachment and meditation on ultimate truth, the self can avoid being reborn into another physical body and will cease to be affected by its eternal *manas*.

Sāṁkhya–Yoga

These two doctrines are also generally treated together, Yoga being essentially a meditational discipline which utilizes the Sāṁkhya metaphysic. In this system, matter and spirit are both regarded as real. It is supposed that there is a unitary material Nature (*prakṛti*) which is in a constant state of cyclical change. However, no creator God is admitted in the Yoga doctrine. God (Īśvara) as a perfect Soul (*Puruṣa*), co-eternal with Nature, is postulated as 'prompting' the evolutionary process. Otherwise this Soul is but one of the infinite number of Puruṣas which evolve from Nature. The possibility that something could have emerged out of nothing is rejected, as is the possibility that nothing could have come from something. Accordingly, Sāṁkhya adopted the identity theory of causation (*satkāryavāda*): effects are supposed to pre-exist in causes and causes to post-exist in effects. Prakṛti has three constituents or 'strands': *sattvas* or *tejas* (the pure or bright), *rajas* (the active or forceful) and *tamas* (the resistant or massive). When these internal forces are in equilibrium the cosmos is organized, but the tensions between them give rise to a period of dissolution during which individual substances (*buddhi*) come into being. These are the 'intellects' of the numerous souls. In due course the process is reversed. Dominated by the *sattvas*, the 'internal organ' or mind (the *buddhi* together with the *manas*), by means of sensory and motor organs, facilitates the manifestation by each individual object of the soul's mental life. The *tamas* aspect of Nature gives rise to the material realm, fundamental to which are the five 'subtle' elements (which are at once substantial and qualitative), and these produce 'gross' elements and thence material things. The cosmos is thus understood in dualist terms. Prakṛti is complex, material, the 'agent', while Puruṣa is simple, static, sentient – the 'enjoyer'. An individual Puruṣa is immortal and works, through Nature, but Prakṛti and Puruṣa are thought of as acting as one (and as constituting the empirical self). However, it is not adequately explained how they do so. The existence of Puruṣa is supposed to be provable by reference firstly to the assumption that Spirit is the principle or final cause for the sake of which Nature evolves, and secondly to the discovery in man of a spiritual 'instinct' for self-perfection or 'escape' from Prakṛti. As for knowledge, which is validated through three *pramāṇas* – perception, inference and verbal testimony – philosophers of this school held some form of representationalist theory. But while it is held that the world can be known objectively in that there is some common agreement among all individuals, there is a subjective aspect in so far as each person's knowledge is conditioned by his past life and character. The individual's knowledge is thus incomplete, error arising through concentration on the part rather than the whole. Truth lies in totality and completeness. Each person's aim therefore is to give greater dominance of *sattva* over *rajas* and *tamas*, to 'purify' the 'inner organ'. By seeing through Prakṛti and recognizing its distinctness from Puruṣa he can hope to achieve enlightenment and freedom even within this life, as a consequence of which when he dies his individual Puruṣa as pure spirit will become fully emancipated from material Nature.

Pūrva–Mīmāṁsā

Although the 'Vedic' schools discussed so far are considered as 'orthodox', there has been much debate about their precise relationship to the Vedas and Upanishads. The Pūrva–Mīmāṁsā, however, is firmly grounded in Vedic teachings, the Pūrva deriving from the early Vedas, the Mīmāṁsā from the Upanishads. The primary concern of its advocates was to interpret the scriptures and determine the purpose of the revelation supposed to be implicit in them. This led to a development of interest in the nature and logic of language, words coming to be regarded as possessing 'power'. In its general philosophy the system was realist and also accepted the plurality of souls and funda-mental material entities. As against the Nyāya–Vaiśeṣika teaching, only five categories were accepted (substance, quality, action, universal and 'non-existence'). There are also differences between the two schools concerning the number and characteristics of substances. But they accepted the same qualities as the Nyāya–Vaiśeṣika philosophers with the omission of dharma and adharma. A key concept was that of 'identity-in-difference' (*tādātmya*), exemplified in a variety of dyadic relationships: substance and attribute, universal and particular, whole and part, and knowledge and the self. The teaching about the last is also significant. The self is known both as subject and object, self-consciousness being implied in consciousness but known inferentially. Knowledge of objects, however, is direct; they rejected the representationalist theory. Knowledge is seen as an activity of the self rather than as a quality, and the self is said to be changed in the knowing process. Six pramāṇas are invoked: perception, inference, verbal testimony, comparison, presumption and non-apprehension. The problem of a possible infinite regress in the application of validation procedures is avoided by the adoption of a view of knowledge as intrinsically valid. Error is attributed to such extraneous factors as defective senses and contradiction; truth can be seen when these are eliminated. According to followers of this system there is no creator God; there is no distinction between a supreme self and other individual selves. Indeed the existence of an all-powerful, benevolent God would be incompatible with the existence of evil. The universe is held to have no beginning and no end, and it is non-cyclical. While the survival of the soul and the doctrine of karma are accepted, there was dispute among two divisions of the school about the utilization of the dharma concept. It is agreed that the Veda determines what dharma is, but while some thinkers argued that its attraction lies in some consequence such as attaining 'heaven', others said that dharma ought to be followed for its own sake, for its intrinsic goodness. (Compare Kant's ethics.) It was only in the latest stage of development of the philosophy of this school that the doctrine of mokṣa was adopted.

Vedānta

The Vedānta philosophy ostensibly brings together the various Hindu sacred literatures, especially the Vedas and Upanishads, and much later the Bhagavadgītā together with the Vedānta Sūtra, and synthesizes the various orthodox doctrines. Hiryanna says that it is 'looked upon as the most perfect expression of Indian thought'. Nevertheless many of the conflicts apparent in the earlier philosophies had not been fully resolved, and consequently several schools of Vedānta developed – though they were in broad agreement in their teaching about practical matters.

The **Advaita** ('non-dualist') school is associated particularly with the philosopher **Śaṁkara** (c. AD 788–820). The physical world is regarded as but an appearance. This is attributed to a principle or 'power' called *Māyā* – a term which can therefore be used of the phenomenal world itself. This world is not unreal (*asat*) – neither non-existent nor 'void'; for it *is* something, namely, appearance. Nevertheless it is not fully real (*sat*) because it is not the thing it is an appearance of. (To give an analogy: we may see a rope as a serpent; the serpent is the appearance, but there is no actual serpent there to be seen.) So what is this 'thing' that appears as the world? For the Advaitins it is *Brahman*. This is not to be understood in any personal theistic sense; Brahman is devoid of qualities (*nirguṇa-brahman*). It is 'not this, not that' (*neti, neti*). It is the highest being. For Śaṁkara Brahman is also *Ātman*, the universal Self, which is knowledge, existence and bliss. But it is non-personal (so the problem of reconciling the existence of evil with an omnipotent and benevolent God does not arise). Nevertheless we may think of a latent or potential diversity in Brahman, which is manifested in Maya – Brahman becoming, as it were, 'lower' and 'qualified'. This is called *saguṇa-brahman* (and in human logical categories is personified as Īśvara). Brahman and Māyā can thus be seen as both cause and effect: Brahman, as unity is Prakṛti, and is the explanation and 'cause' of Māyā, but as manifested diversity is the effect; similarly Māyā is a unity and the cause of the incessantly changing diversity which is made manifest in the phenomenal world and hides the unity from us. Strictly speaking, however, Brahman for the Advaitins transcends causal relationships – which belong only to the phenomenal realm. Brahman as 'cause' is really the ground of all that exists; while the world as effect is only 'apparently' so. The universe is non-cyclical and has no beginning or end. The possibility of our having knowledge of what is 'real' and 'unreal' is accounted for in terms of the self (*ātman*). The self as ego (*jīva*) is an 'agent' self and includes both a 'transcendental' or 'pure' consciousness and an 'empirical *ego*'. The former is intrinsically unknowable (indeed 'self-consciousness' is a contradiction in terms), though Saṁkara says its existence cannot be doubted, for it is a precondition for doubting. The Advaitins refer to it as the *sākṣin* ('witness'). The empirical *ego* seems to arise through contact of the pure self with the non-self (*avidyā*) in its two aspects – the 'internal organ' and the physical body. Our changing and often erroneous knowledge arises from our confusing the self and the non-self. According to the non-dualist teaching, individual *egos* are identical with each other and with qualified Brahman or Ātman – in the same way that (to use an example we have referred to earlier) the Morning Star is identical with the Evening Star (the reference is the same but the descriptive phrases have different senses or connotations). But the point that the Advaitins make is that this identity is obscured as a result of the diversification of Brahman as it 'descends' into the phenomenal realm of Māyā (and as the self too is 'dragged down' and disguised by its adjuncts). It follows that the aim of human existence must be to develop right knowledge (*jñāna*) so as to recognize the oneness of the pure *ego* with the universal Self and thereby attain self-realization or freedom (*mokṣa*). This requires study, reflection and meditation. In their account of knowledge the philosophers of this school accepted the representationalist theory. Error arises when we take illusory experiences to be veridical (though these latter, strictly speaking, are but appearances of Brahman). How then are they to be distinguished? The Advaitins appealed to coherence – as a criterion of truth, not a definition; for all experience is in some sense 'about' something objective. 'Ultimate' truth can only be found in the totality of all coherent systems. (Compare the discussion in Ch. 12 about 'weak realism'.)

Viśiṣṭādvaita (qualified non-dualism) is another influential attempt to interpret and systematize the scriptures. The most important commentator of this Vedanta school was **Rāmānuja** (eleventh century). According to him a clear distinction should be made between God on the one hand and both unconscious matter and animate selves on the other. Brahman is a personal being and has qualities – is not undifferentiated. The world is not an appearance of Brahman, yet together with selves is to be regarded as Brahman's 'body'. Rāmānuja argues that there are only two categories of entities: substances and non-substances. There are six substances, especially God, the world (*prakṛti*), and self (*jīva*). The non-substances include five sensory qualities, three *guṇas* (*sattva*, *rajas* and *tamas*), as well as *karma* and causal power (*śakti*), both of which he thinks of as attributes. The relation of God to the world is thus of one substance (a spiritual one) to another. Knowledge for Rāmānuja has to be of that which is determinate. It is always true, but there are degrees of truth. And he accepts only three *pramaṇas*: perception, inference and verbal testimony. Man is dependent on God and controlled by him. Man's purpose is to serve God. He can never become God, but it belongs to man's essential nature to intuit him; and this is fully achieved in the state of release from the body. To bring this about the paths of 'surrender' (*prapatti*) and 'devotion' (*bhakti*) are to be followed, the latter through attention to duty (*karma-yoga*), meditation on the self (*jñāna-yoga*) and meditation on God (*bhakti-yoga*).

The **Dvaita** (dualist) school. The principal thinker associated with this school was **Madhva** (1197–1276). His system is realist, pluralist and theistic. Ten categories are accepted: substance, quality, action, universal, the whole, potentiality, similarity, non-existence and two others, which may be called 'that which specifies' and 'that which is specified'. Of twenty substances the three principal ones are God, *Prakṛti*, and selves (souls). God, who for Madhva (as for Rāmānuja) is identified with Viṣṇu, is both transcendent and immanent in the world; and he is also said to have a 'supernatural body'. Prakṛti and the multiplicity of selves are subordinate to God and dependent on him. Of particular interest is the Dvaitins' attempt to synthesize previous accounts of causation. According to them it is to be understood in terms of the concept of *śakti* (power or energy). Consider the bringing about of a change in a (second) substance by another (first) substance. The second can be understood as an actualization of energy implicit in the first and as such the effect is the partial cause of its manifestation. But the second substance can also be distinguished from the actualizing power itself: and in this respect cause and effect are non-identical. Both cause and the effect are therefore simultaneously 'existent' and 'non-existent' – but considered from different aspects. Prakṛti, as the ground or source of the universe, produces the three *guṇas* – *sattva*, *rajas* and *tamas*; and these in turn give rise to the intellect, the 'self-principle', the 'internal organ', the sensory organs and the five elements. A key feature of the Dvaita philosophy is the notion of 'fundamental difference' (*Bheda*). These differences obtain between God and individual souls, God and the material world, between the individuals themselves, those selves and matter, and between individual material substances – though these differences are not incompatible with the dependence of some entities on others. Individual selves are unique. In material bodies they suffer as a consequence of past *karma*, but in themselves they are characterized by bliss. As for the other categories, those of specificity are also peculiar to Madhva's system. That which specifies (*viśeṣa*) in effect characterizes what makes a thing that which it is. Knowledge is initiated by the individual self but it is regarded as a mode of the internal organ. Knowledge is always of the real: but this includes appearances, dreams and the like. Thus we can have knowledge of the unreal even though such objects do not exist. Truth is understood as correspondence with reality. According to Madhva, valid knowledge (of facts) is primary, but we can also have mediate, secondary knowledge through the three *pramāṇas* – perception, inference and verbal testimony. Seven senses, including *manas* and the 'witness' or transcendent consciousness, are distinguished. The ultimate purpose of existence, according to the Dvaitins, is worship of God, which can be achieved through devotion to him and thereby detachment and knowledge, as well as attention to duty and ritual. The soul continues after death in the state of 'release' in accordance with the divine will and by virtue of his grace. There can, however, be no direct approach to God; a mediator is required.

*Final comments

(1) **Critique.** No critical assessment of Indian philosophy will be attempted here, not least because only a superficial and incomplete survey has been provided. However, it should be clear to you that the key issues are: the relationship of God to the world and individual souls; the analysis of causation; the nature of knowledge and the source of error; and questions concerning the soul itself – its reincarnation and ultimate release. Detailed analysis of the grounds for disagreement between the principal schools would of course be required. The source book in Indian Philosophy given in the Reading list below can be strongly recommended as a starting-point.

(2) **The contemporary scene.** Oriental philosophy in its central concerns has remained largely unchanged from the twelfth century down to the present day. In India, debate continues about how the Vedic writings should be interpreted and about the acceptability of the numerous metaphysical systems which grew up around them; while, in China, Confucianism, Taoism and Buddhism still retain some influence in philosophical circles. Nevertheless the impact of Western thought from the nineteenth century onwards has been considerable. Many scholars in India (and Japan) were influenced by German Idealism. In China the most significant import has been Marxism – of the 'orthodox' Leninist variety. Attention has also been paid throughout Asia to pragmatism, phenomenology and existentialism. (There has been much interest recently in suggested affinities between oriental traditions and the philosophy of Heidegger!) The writings of both Habermas and Gadamer are being read; and there is also increasing recognition of the significance of linguistic or 'analytic' philosophy. But even if we disregard contacts with contemporary occidental philosophy, the coincidental parallels between aspects of particularly the Indian systems and the philosophies of such diverse thinkers as Aristotle, many of the medieval scholastics, Descartes and Kant are often remarkable and remain relatively unexplored. There is good reason to suppose that the next few decades of the third millennium will see still greater collaboration between thinkers from East and West to their mutual benefit and to the benefit of philosophy as a whole.

QUESTIONS

Texts and problems

1 Explain and discuss the following quotation from Confucius:'If a man is not human (*jen*), what has he to do with ceremonies (*li*)? If he is not human, what has he to do with music?' [IB, specimen, 2000]

2 Although in Confucius's ethics *jen* can be understood as the supreme general virtue, he is less clear as to how the individual is to achieve it, the emphasis in his teachings being on convention, social roles and ritual. Discuss.

3 Explain and discuss what Lao Tzu meant when he incites us to get rid of teachers and wise men. [IB, specimen, 2000]

*4 Explain and examine critically the Daoist concept of 'non-action' (*wu-wei*).

5 Compare and contrast the uses made of the concept of 'the Way' by Confucius and Lao Tzu respectively.

6 Do you think the attempt made by philosophers of the Mādhyamika school to find a middle way between the 'unreal' phenomenal world and the 'real' Void was successful?

7 Examine the concept of *manas* ('internal organ' or 'mind') as understood by Vedic philosophers. How does it relate to the concept of the *ātman* (soul)?

8 According to the Nyāya–Vaiśeṣika school, cause and effect are non-identical, but the Sāṁkhya philosophers argued in favour of the view that they are identical. Comment on their treatments of this concept.

*9 Consider whether the Dvaita account of causation constitutes a successful synthesis of the theories proposed by the Nyāya–Vaiśeṣika and Sāṁkhya schools.

10 Can Nāgārjuna's philosophical rejection of the notions of a continuous personal self and of all theories of causation be reconciled with Buddhist teaching about personal responsibility and rebirth?

11 Explain and examine the concept of 'identity-in-difference' of the Pūrva–Mimāṁsā school.

12 Examine the treatment by the Advaitins of the relationship between Brahman and Maya.

13 Compare and contrast the views on knowledge and truth held by the Advaitins and the Dvaitins.

14 Discuss the concept of *mokṣa* as employed by the three principal schools of the Vedanta philosophy.

*15 Compare and contrast the meaning of transmigration in Buddhism and Hinduism. [IB, specimen, 2000]

*Notes/guided answers have been provided for questions **4, 9** and **15** (at end of book).

READING LIST

A. Prescribed texts
Confucius, *Analects*. (IB)
Lao Tzu, *Tao Te Ching*. (IB)

Comprehensive selections from key texts in Indian and Chinese philosophy are to be found in:
Radhakrishnan, S. and Moore, C.A., *A Source Book in Indian Philosophy*.
Chan, W.-T., *A Source Book in Chinese Philosophy*.

B. Other texts
Creel, H.G., *Chinese Thought from Confucius to Mao Tse-Tung*.
Hiriyanna, M., *Essentials of Indian Philosophy*.

C. Supplementary reading

Hiriyanna, M., *Outlines of Indian Philosophy.*

Murti, T.R.V., *The Central Philosophy of Buddhism.* (Quite demanding for the beginner but an outstanding contribution.)

Smart, N., *The Religious Experience of Mankind.*

Watts, A.W., *The Way of Zen.* (Excellent on background.)

Yu-Lan, Fung, *A History of Chinese Philosophy* (2 volumes).

◼ ⌵   Glossary

Note: The following descriptions and definitions are intended to provide you with no more than a rough guide to usage. A more complete and unambiguous understanding of their meanings can be obtained only by a study of the relevant sections of this book and of primary sources.

Alienation: for **Hegel** (an Idealist), the process whereby the products of mind (for example, Nature as emanating from the Absolute Idea of 'God', or physical objects, ideas and so on as created by finite mind, that is, man) become 'set off' against their originator as a consequence of their 'objectification'. According to **Marx** (a Materialist), man also alienates *himself* in so far as he fails to realize himself as an 'agent' and allows himself to be dependent on or exploited by his environment, even though it may in some respects be his own product. (See also *dialectics*.)

Analytic: (as applied to statements or propositions) true by virtue of meaning alone and without reference to empirical content. (See also *synthetic*.)

a posteriori: that which is known through inductive procedures, or knowledge which is grounded in empirical data for its validation.

a priori: that which is known to be true by logical deduction from general principles, or independently of our experience of it and not requiring empirical validation.

Behaviourism: (in philosophy) the thesis that 'mental' states are neither 'internal' nor 'private'; whatever there is to know about the 'mind' can be fully understood and explained in terms of publically observable overt physical behaviour. (**Ryle** is in some respects a behaviourist.)

Categorical imperative: for **Kant**, an unconditional moral principle that lays down that duty or obligation must be the only criterion for assessing human actions. Actions performed for the sake of some other end ('hypothetical' imperatives), although they may be deemed to bring about 'good' consequences, cannot for that reason be accorded the status of 'moral' or 'right'.

Categories: for **Aristotle** 'classes' or 'modes of being' in terms of which Aristotle claimed particular things (for example, man, horse) could be specified (thus: substance, quantity, place and so on – he distinguished ten such categories); for **Kant** formal *a priori* (qv) concepts of the understanding through which 'representations' (that is, raw data of sense 'intuited' under the 'forms' of space and time) are organized and unified in judgement (for example, cause, unity, reality – Kant claims to be able to deduce twelve). **Ryle** introduced the notion of a **category-mistake**: this occurs when a term belonging to one kind of category is used in a context to which a different kind of category is appropriate, and is the cause of philosophical errors.

Causal theory: theory of perception according to which there are 'real' objects in the world which are the cause of our perceptions, though it does not follow that we can necessarily say anything about those objects. (For example, in *Problems of Philosophy*.) (See also *representative theory*.)

Conceptualism: in metaphysics, the theory that 'universals' (qv) or what is common to objects denoted by a general term exist but only as concepts, thoughts, or on some accounts, images ('resemblance' theory). (For example, **Locke**, **Berkeley** and, to some extent, **Hume**) (See also *realism* and *nominalism*.)

Cosmology: subdivision of metaphysics dealing with the nature and origin of the universe. **Cosmological argument**, or 'first cause' argument: argument purporting to establish the existence of God on the grounds that there cannot be an infinite regress of causes, and that a First Cause, an 'uncaused causer' or a 'cause-of-itself' is therefore required to underpin the contingency of the world. (**Plato, Aristotle, Aquinas, Descartes** *et al.*)

Covering-law model: in the philosophy of science a theory of explanation according to which a statement describing the event to be explained (the *explanandum*) is deemed to be deducible from the *explanans* – the conjunction of a set of laws and a series of statements describing particular facts. (Especially **Hempel**)

Critical theory: a social and political philosophy associated particularly with **Habermas**. Utilizing a neo-Marxist framework and drawing on the theory of speech-acts, he developed a critique of repressive ideology and a theory of communicative action underpinned by a new concept of rationality, truth, freedom and justice being regarded as regulative norms.

Deduction: a process of reasoning involving logically necessary inferences from a general premiss or set of premisses to a conclusion.

Deontology: a subdivision of ethics concerned with moral obligation or duty. **Deontological theories** of ethics define the rightness of actions in terms of duty (for example, **Kant**). (See also *categorical imperative*.)

Determinism: the view that whatever we think or do is not only caused but is also the inevitable consequence of antecedent circumstances or causes beyond our control (for example, the movement of atoms, the behaviour of genes, social pressures).

Dialectic(s): for **Plato** a process of argument or disputation by means of which truth is alleged to be elicited; for **Hegel** a process of reasoning and a historical process which involves the progressive 'negation' of one statement or event (the thesis) by another (the antithesis), both being subsequently subsumed into a 'higher' synthesis.

Dialectical materialism: theory of **Marx** and **Engels** that 'mind', man, society and nature are ultimately dependent on and explicable in terms of a material infrastructure and are subject to a dialectical process of change.

Dualism: the view that the world, including man, is constituted out of two different kinds of 'stuff' or substances, for example, mind and matter. (Especially **Descartes**)

Empiricism: the thesis that all knowledge is derived from sense-experience (and that logically necessary truths can provide no information about the world). (For example **Mill** and **Russell, Ayer**); most 'empiricists' usually combine in their philosophies elements of rationalism (**Aristotle, Aquinas, Locke**) or idealism (**Berkeley**). (See also *rationalism*.)

Entelechy: for **Aristotle** what is actual rather than potential, or actuality itself; for **Leibniz** simple substances or 'monads' which contain within themselves a principle of perfection.

Epistemology: branch of philosophy concerned with the nature, scope and justification of knowledge.

Ethics: branch of philosophy concerned with questions about the value of human conduct, for example, the rightness or wrongness of actions, the nature of 'goodness', the justification of moral rules or principles.

Existentialism: nineteenth/twentieth century philosophical movement that stresses the priority of 'existence' over 'essence' and emphasizes the absolute freedom and responsibility of the individual for making himself, his values and his world-view (for example **Kierkegaard**), often combined with phenomenological analysis (see *phenomenology* and *phenomenolism*) (**Sartre, Heidegger**).

Fatalism: the view that the future is predetermined and that whatever 'choices' we make cannot affect an inevitable outcome.

Functionalism: in the philosophy of mind the view that the mind is to be understood as analogous to a computer 'software' program, processed by the 'hardware' of the brain. (**Fodor** and **Putnam** – though the latter rejected the theory in his later writings.)

Hermeneutics: the systematic investigation of interpretation – of texts, culture modes in general; debate centres on such issues as whether 'pre-judgements' can be eliminated and an 'objective truth' attained through 'understanding' (*Verstehen*). (Especially **Gadamer**)

Idealism: the view that reality is mental and that external objects exist only in thought – as ideas in a mind (for example, **Hegel, Bradley**). An idealist standpoint is compatible with both rationalism (**Plato, Leibniz, Hegel**) and empiricism (**Berkeley**). According to **Transcendental idealism** (**Kant**), the world can be experienced not 'in itself' but only as an appearance structured by our cognitive faculties (through forms of intuition and understanding – the 'categories').

Ideas: one of the most ambiguous terms in the philosophical vocabulary. For **Plato**, Ideas are immutable and eternal self-subsistent realities apprehended through reason or intelligence. For **Aquinas**, they are archetypal patterns in the mind of God. In the seventeenth century the term was variously used to refer to all mental images without regard to their origin (**Descartes, Leibniz**). **Locke, Berkeley** and **Hume** subsequently distinguished between 'abstract' ideas (concepts) and 'concrete' ideas (percepts). The latter were later subdivided by **Hume** into impressions and ideas, and by **Berkeley** into ideas of sense and ideas of imagination. Note also **Kant's** use of 'Idea' to refer to concepts of Reason (God, Freedom, Immortality) which may be used 'regulatively' but cannot be applied to experience.

Induction: a reasoning process usually from empirically testable premisses to a general conclusion which may in some respects contain more information than was to be found in the premisses together, or makes that information more explicit. (Compare *deduction*.)

Instrumentalism: in the philosophy of science, the view that the function of theories and ideas is analogous to that of tools, in that they are used to relate sets of observation statements to each other without consideration of whether the theories are 'true'. (For example **Toulmin**) (See also *pragmatism*.)

Intentionality: in the philosophy of mind, this terms refers to the alleged capacity of 'minds' or 'mental states' to direct themselves towards objects whether or not they exist. (**Husserl**, **Sartre** *et al.*)

Intuitionism: in ethics, the theory that we can have direct insight into what is good or bad, either through a 'moral sense' (for example, **Shaftesbury**) or through the reason (for example, **Price**, **Moore**).

Karma ('action'): in Hindu and Buddhist philosophies, the term refers to a causal 'law' or 'force' which determines a person's moral condition in present and future reincarnations according to the nature of his past deeds.

Logical positivism: movement associated with a group of philosophers in Vienna in the 1930s who argued that meaningful propositions must either be analytic (qv) or empirically verifiable (the 'verifiability principle'); most members also claimed that the meaning of a proposition *is* its method of verification ('verification theory'). The 'Vienna Circle' was to some extent influenced by Wittgenstein. (**Ayer** was a member; Popper also attended meetings though did not subscribe to the positivist view of meaning.)

Materialism: theory that denies the existence of mind or mental states, or claims that 'consciousness' can be fully accounted for in terms of material laws and processes. (**Hobbes**, **Marx**, for example) (See also *idealism*.)

Metaphysics: branch of philosophy concerned with the most general questions about 'ultimate' reality and what kinds of things exist, for example, substances, universals; and the nature of mind, matter, time causation and so on. (Throughout the history of philosophy it has usually been difficult to separate metaphysical issues from problems of epistemology.)

Mokṣa: in Hindu thought the state of 'enlightenment' in which one achieves 'release' or freedom from the cycle of rebirth, achieved variously through ritual, good deeds, or contemplative meditation. (In Buddhism it is termed 'Nirvana'.)

Monism: the view that the world, including man, is constituted of one kind of 'stuff', perhaps mental (**Berkeley**, **Hegel**) or material (**Hobbes**). (See also *dualism*.)

Naturalism: in ethics, the theory that moral judgements are judgements about facts or qualities in the world, for example, pleasure or happiness. The **Naturalistic Fallacy** (**Moore**) is alleged to be committed when attempts are made to define, for example, 'goodness' in terms of a natural property, or indeed any property ('goodness' for Moore being an essentially indefinable, simple non-natural property). In the philosophy of mind (biological) naturalism is a theory in which the mind is considered to be part of the world of nature, a product of biological evolution. (**Searle**)

Nominalism: in metaphysics the theory that 'universals' (qv) have no real existence even as concepts; all that objects denoted by a general term have in common is the name. (**William of Ockham** and **Hobbes**; compare also **Quine**) (See also *conceptualism* and *realism*.)

Noumenon (pl. *noumena*): (**Kant**) the thing-in-itself, the real nature of a thing essentially unperceivable and unknowable. (See also *phenomenon*.)

Ontological argument (**Anselm, Descartes**): argument purporting to establish the existence of God on the grounds that God as 'the most perfect being' must contain all perfections and could not therefore be the most perfect being if it lacked existence. Alternatively: to conceive of something as existing is to conceive of something greater than if it did not exist; the thought of a being than which nothing greater can be conceived therefore entails that such a being exists in reality.

Ontology: a subdivision of metaphysics, concerned with the nature of being or with a consideration of what kinds of things actually exist. The other subdivisions are usually taken to be cosmology and psychology (qqv) (**Heidegger, Quine**)

Operationalism: in the philosophy of science, the view that scientific concepts are to be defined in terms of the experimental procedures which can be used to validate them. (For example, **Bridgman**)

Phenomenalism: the view that so-called 'material' objects are in fact nothing other than collections of phenomena (ideas, sensa, impressions) (**Berkeley, Hume**), actual or possible (**Mill**). According to linguistic phenomenalism (**Ayer**), statements about material objects can be translated into statements about 'sense-contents' or 'sense-date' (qv).

Phenomenology: philosophical movement that stresses the analysis and interpretation of the structure of conscious experience and human relationships, without consideration of any scientific or metaphysical presuppositions about the nature and existence of the mind and external reality. (Especially **Husserl**)

Phenomenon (pl. *phenomena*): that which is perceived or experienced; for **Kant** that which appears to the consciousness – as opposed to the 'real' thing-in-itself. (See also *noumenon*.)

Pragmatism: a theory of meaning, truth, knowledge, or value which takes as its criterion the success of practical consequences. (Especially **Peirce** and **James**)

Praxis: particularly in **Sartre's** modified Marxism (*Critique of Dialectical Reason*), purposeful human activity. The concept brings together with the Marxian dialectic Sartre's notion of 'project' (*Being and Nothingness*), that is, a programme for action whereby the 'for-itself' chooses and makes its own being or condition.

Psychology: originally a subdivision of metaphysics and dealing with the nature of the mind, but now either an experimental science or a legitimate field of study for philosophy ('philosophical psychology' and 'philosophy of mind').

Rationalism: the view that it is through the exercise of pure reason (by direct insight or by means of logically necessary deductive arguments), and not from sense experience, that knowledge of first principles or truths about the world is to be acquired. (**Descartes, Spinoza**) Often combined with idealist tendencies (**Plato, Leibniz**)

Realism: in epistemology, the view that the world exists exactly as we perceive it ('naïve' realism); or that the fundamental particles of modern physics are real and that it is out of them that objects we perceive in the world are constructed ('scientific' realism). A realist theory of perception is compatible with phenomenalism (qv), analysis of material objects in terms of 'sensa' (compare **Berkeley**). In metaphysics, 'realism' refers to the theory that 'universals' (qv) have a real existence: '*before* things' (**Plato**), '*in* things' (**Aristotle**). (See also *conceptualism* and *nominalism*.) **Antirealism** is the view that we make our own realities: any philosophy which claims to 'mirror' the actual world and that we can know such 'presences' as ideas, essences, substances, Being and the like is untenable. (**Derrida, Dummett, Feyerabend, Rorty**)

Reductionism: in a strong sense, the thesis that, for example, 'minds', material and animate bodies can be completely analysed (often scientifically) in terms of simpler parts (thus 'man is nothing more than a complex organization of atoms'); in a weaker sense, the view that scientific theories on one 'level' (usually about 'unobservables') can be connected to theories on another 'level' (which make use of theoretical concepts) by means of 'correspondence rules' or 'bridging' statements.

Representative theory: theory of perception according to which at least some of the qualities of material objects are 're-presented' or copied in our sensory experience but are not identical with it. Thus, for **Locke**, our 'ideas' of 'primary' qualities resemble those qualities themselves, but our ideas of 'secondary' qualities, while produced by material objects, do not resemble any quality possessed by them. (Perhaps also later **Russell**, for example *Human Knowledge*.) (See also *causal theory*.)

Scepticism: in a weak sense this refers to a general critical attitude towards accepted beliefs. In a strong sense of the term a sceptic is a person who denies that knowledge is possible (though this position is held by different philosophers with various degrees of commitment). Originally a philosophical movement in ancient Greece. (**Pyrrho**; also **Descartes** – for his method – and **Hume**)

Sense-datum (pl. *data*): what is immediately and directly given to us through the senses (for example, patches of colour, smells) without reference to possible causes (such as 'material objects'). Compared (especially **Moore** and **Russell**; **Berkeley's** 'ideas' and **Hume's** 'impressions').

Structuralism: a theory in linguistics which maintains that words signify not by referring to some putative 'objective' reality but by virtue of their relationship to other 'signifiers' in the total structure of elements constituting the language system. A more radical 'post-structuralism' was developed by **Derrida**. (See also *antirealism*.)

Substance: this term has been used in different ways by various philosophers since Greek times, but in general it refers to the 'essence' of a thing – what makes it what it is, in which its qualities, attributes, or 'accidents' inhere.

Syllogism: the standard form of deductive inference in 'traditional' or Aristotelian logic whereby a conclusion is derived from two premisses, a major and a minor.

Synthetic: (as applied to statements or propositions) true by virtue of reference to empirical data rather than through an analysis of the meanings of constituent terms. (See also *analytic*.)

Teleology: (in ethics and metaphysics) the study of final causes, ends, or purposes, and of purposive or functional activities. **Teleological argument**: an argument from the alleged presence of design or order in the world purporting to establish the existence of an intelligent designer, that is, God. (**Aristotle, Aquinas**)

Universals: what general terms (for example, 'cat', 'whiteness') are alleged to stand for. There has been much disagreement among philosophers both about the ontological status of universals and the precise scope of the term's application. (See *conceptualism, realism, nominalism*.)

Utilitarianism: theory of ethics according to which the rightness or wrongness of actions is to be assessed in terms of the 'goodness' or badness' of their consequences, as measured by, say, the amount, quality, or distribution of happiness engendered. (Especially **J.S. Mill**)

Vedānta: an Indian philosophy claiming to synthesize previous 'orthodox' Vedic philosophical systems and grounded in the sacred Hindu scriptures. There are three principal schools – Advaita (**Śaṁkara**), Viśiṣṭādvaita (**Rāmānuja**) and Dvaita (**Madhva**).

▌▾ Guided answers

Note: These 'guided' answers are entirely the responsibility of the author and have not been provided by any of the examination boards. They are not intended to be definitive or even complete; alternative approaches are of course possible. But they should give you some idea of how to tackle philosophical questions in the examination room. Nevertheless, you should treat the notes critically.

Chapter 2

Question 2

(c) can be represented as (i) 'All things which glitter are gold' (S a P), or (ii) 'No non-gold things are things which glitter' (P e S). Taking (c) as the basis for inference, we may state the logical relations between the propositions as follows:

(c) (i) S a P
   (ii) P e S contrapositive of S a P
(a) S o P contradictory of S a P
(b) P a S superaltern of the converse of S a P
(d) S e P obverse of S a P, or converse of P e S

Note that (b) is a singular proposition which can be regarded as a universal affirmative. Note also that 'gold' is a singular term in all the propositions. However, in traditional logic this does not affect their form.

Question 3

To preserve the syllogistic structure we should have to reformulate the argument in some such way as this:

Major: Some arguments are combinations of propositions involving more than three terms (P i M);
Minor: No combinations of propositions involving more than 3 terms are syllogisms (M e S);
Conclusion: Some syllogisms are not arguments (S o P).

This is a syllogism of Figure 4, Mood *IEO*. A Venn Diagram will show it is invalid (it commits the fallacy of Illicit Minor); there is therefore no specific Mood name.

Note that the conclusion is actually false, and the minor premiss in effect constitutes the definition of a syllogism.

Question 4

Axioms

(1) The middle term must be distributed in at least one of the premisses.
(2) A term distributed in the conclusion must be distributed in its corresponding premiss.
(3) At least one premiss must be affirmative; a syllogism containing two negative premisses.
(4) If one premiss is negative the conclusion must be negative.
(5) The major premiss of a Figure I or a Figure II syllogism cannot be particular.

[Figure I
Assume the minor is affirmative. Its predicate (*M*) is therefore undistributed. *M* must therefore be distributed in the major premiss (Axiom 1). *M* is the subject of the major premiss. Hence the major premiss must be universal, that is, cannot be particular.

Figure II
To avoid an undistributed middle (Axiom 1) one premiss must be negative, Therefore the conclusion must be negative (Axiom 4) and its predicate distributed (Axiom 2). Hence the major premiss must be universal.]
So the question is relevant only to syllogisms in Figures III or IV.

Figure III
If the major premiss is particular, the middle term must be undistributed. *M* must therefore be distributed in the minor premiss (Axiom 1), that is, the minor is an *A* or an *E* proposition. *A* is already affirmative. If the minor is *E*, the conclusion must be negative (Axiom 4), and *P* is therefore distributed in the conclusion and hence in the major premiss (Axiom 2). The major is therefore negative, and the minor must be affirmative (Axiom 3). QED

Figure IV
If the major premiss is particular, *P* is undistributed in that premiss and therefore also in the conclusion (Axiom 2). So the conclusion must be affirmative. Therefore no premiss can be negative (Axioms 4 and 5), that is, the minor must be affirmative. QED

Question 5

(a) contingent; (b) tautology; (c) contingent; (d) inconsistent (all lines give a 'false').

Question 7

(a) Using the symbols *R* ('scientists are **Right**'), *A* ('there is an **Alternative** explanation'), *D* ('**Different** phenomena have been observed'), *S* ('this would suggest a more complex Situation . . .'), *E* ('this would have been indicated . . . in the Experimental data'), we have the premises:

1. $R \rightarrow (D \rightarrow A)$
2. $A \rightarrow S$
3. $(A \rightarrow E) \,\&\, {-}E$

from which the conclusion $D \rightarrow {-}R$ can be derived:

4. $A \rightarrow E$	3, Simp.
5. $-E \,\&\, (A \rightarrow E)$	3, Comp.
6. $-E$	5, Simp.
7. $-A$	4, 6, MT
8. $(R \,\&\, D) \rightarrow A$	1, Exp.
9. $-(R \,\&\, D)$	7, 8, MT
10. $-R \vee -D$	9, DeM
11. $-D \vee -R$	10, Com.
12. $D \rightarrow -R$	11, MI QED

(b) $(x) (Fx) \vee (x) (Gx) \vdash (x) (Fx \vee Gx)$

1	(1)	$(x) (Fx) \vee (x) (Gx)$	A
2	(2)	$(x) (Fx)$	A
2	(3)	Fa	2, UE
2	(4)	$Fa \vee Ga$	3, vI (Add.)
2	(5)	$(x) (Fx \vee Gx)$	4, UI
6	(6)	$(x) Gx$	A
6	(7)	Ga	6, UE
6	(8)	$Fa \vee Ga$	7, vI (Add.)
6	(9)	$(x) (Fx \vee Gx)$	8, UI
1	(10)	$(x) (Fx \vee Gx)$	1, 2, 5, 6, 9, vE QED

Notes: '$\vdash$' is often referred to as the 'assertion' sign (we assert the conclusion on the basis of the assumptions); the numbers on the LHS indicate the assumptions utilized in support of a conclusion; 'vE' is a rule of derivation called v-elimination: given *A* or *B* and a proof of *C* from either *A* or *B* (as assumptions), *C* can be derived as a conclusion.

Question 8

How you answer this really depends on how much of a sceptic you are.

(1) Briefly explain what induction means or involves.
(2) Discuss how it 'works' – give examples.
(3) You should now examine what is meant by 'justification' and consider whether or not the fact that induction 'works' is itself an adequate justification. Look at various accounts of 'pragmatic' justification.
(4) Many philosophers would argue that 'justification' must involve more than this. You should therefore discuss critically the difficulties associated with attempts to justify induction (a) deductively, (b) inductively. Can either of

these approaches be linked with a more pragmatic justification? (By all means refer to the views of, say, Hume, Ayer, Braithwaite and Strawson.)

Question 9

There are many, including Accident, *Ignoratio Elenchi, ad Hominem* and *ad Populum, ad Verecundiam*. Note also the use of similes and poetic devices such as alliteration, and the generally emotional tone of the address – all designed to convince the audience regardless of the logic of the argument. (The 'core beliefs' may of course be true, but what is at issue here is whether they can be justified logically by the arguments presented by the speaker.)

Chapter 3

Question 3

This question refers to Socrates' debate with Polus in the *Gorgias*. The principal claim Socrates makes, and which you should examine, is that the wrongdoer will inevitably be miserable because either (a) he will be punished, or (b) even if he escapes the law on Earth he will suffer in the After-life, as his soul will have become corrupted. (The 'myth' at the end of the dialogue can be compared with the 'Myth of Er' in the *Republic*.)

A major point to be considered is whether the 'soul' can in some sense be corrupted. Discuss also the notion of suffering in an After-life, which assumption Socrates' argument is heavily dependent on. (Note that the weightier metaphysical issues are not worked out in the *Gorgias*, this being left to the *Republic* and Plato's later dialogues.)

Question 4

Start by summarizing Socrates' debate with Callicles in the *Gorgias*. Note Socrates' claim that virtue and pleasure do not coincide – man's proper end being the former alone. You should mention the distinction taken up by Callicles between 'conventional' and 'natural' justice, and Socrates' demand that Callicles define his terms. If you feel like widening the scope of your essay, discuss some of the arguments proposed by Socrates in answer to Thrasymachus (the *Republic*) in relation to self-interest, the mind's 'proper function' and the consequences of injustice for society.

Two points in particular might be singled out for criticism: (a) the notion of justice as the mind's peculiar virtue, and indeed the view that the mind does not have a proper function (note Plato's special usage of 'justice' in relation to the tripartite soul); (b) the actual experience of tyrants (there have been plenty of these in the course of human history!). What were their motives? Were they genuinely 'happy'? What kinds of societies did they engender?

Note: It is possible to reject both totalitarian tyrannies and Plato's 'ideal state' and underlying metaphysics, in favour of the more individualist position from which most of us start in the Western liberal democratic tradition. You could come back to this question after you have studied Ch. 7.

Question 8

You should experience little difficulty with the first part of the question. The importance of the simile lies in the distinctions Plato makes between: (a) 'appearance' and 'reality', and (b) knowledge and belief. Discuss the objects above and below the 'line', relating them respectively to these distinctions. You can then examine his view that knowledge is of immutable reality whereas belief is of 'semi-real' things belonging to the world of change.

Critical points to be considered: (a) Is the interpretation of the line as illustrating a progression consistent with the view that knowledge and belief are two distinct states of mind? (b) (more advanced) The status of the mathematical ideas: they are neither Forms nor objects of sense. Are they therefore 'known'? Is the relationship between them and the Forms analogous to the relationship between 'images' and objects of perception?

Question 11

Start with a definition of what Socrates/Plato means by 'wisdom'. It is the virtue appropriate to the rulers, and it is compared to the 'rational' element in the soul which controls the other parts. The link between soul and state is Justice – manifested when each part of the soul (or each stratum of society) performs its own task correctly. So to know the Truth entails 'right' action.

You can now consider the issue critically. Discuss in particular: (a) whether knowledge of Truth necessarily involves knowledge of the Good; (b) whether there is any inconsistency between knowing what is right (presupposing this is possible) and yet failing to act correctly or wisely; and (c) the general question of the adequacy of the soul-state analogy.

Chapter 4

Question 1

It would be useful first to clarify what Aristotle means by 'happiness' (*eudaimonia*). Stress his view that it is to be measured over a life as a whole, and that account should be taken of 'quality' not just 'quantity'. Say something also about Aristotle's view of man as a rational animal and that 'end' involves the exercising of the capacity to reason.

Comments: (a) *Is* this man's proper function or end? What justifies Aristotle's claim? (b) Is true happiness achievable in this way thus to be considered as the supreme end? Some philosophers would argue that man's 'end' is, for example, to obey the moral law. (Contemplation can lead to self-centredness, withdrawal from the world, anti-social tendencies and so on. How might Aristotle respond?)

Question 4

Start by making it clear that a mean for Aristotle is 'relative' not 'absolute', and illustrate the distinction with a concrete (for example, mathematical) example. You can then consider some of the applications discussed in the *Nicomachean Ethics*.

In your discussion, set out any positive aspects of his doctrine and indicate where you think it breaks down (again refer to examples). Particular attention should then be paid to distributive justice as a mean between greater and less inequality (a 'geometrical' proportionality), and to corrective justice described in terms of 'loss' and 'gain' ('arithmetic'). Is this consistent with Aristotle's claim that just behaviour is a mean between doing injustice and suffering it?

Chapter 5

Question 1

Explain what is meant by 'hyperbolic'. Make it clear that doubting for Descartes was elevated into a method so that a sure foundation for knowledge might be discovered – a 'bottom line' so to speak. List the kinds of things he believed he *could* doubt.

You should then consider whether his systematic procedure holds up in the face of a number of difficulties. Is the introduction of an 'evil genie' consistent with hyperbolic doubt? Identify assumptions Descartes is unknowingly making in the course of articulating his doubts. *Hint*: Think about language and memory (compare also Question 30).

Question 2

The first part should be relatively straightforward. Even if everything is false, in the act of thinking (willing, perceiving and so on) his existence as a thinking thing is affirmed. (You should of course sketch out the main lines of Descartes' argument.)

There are many difficulties that the '*cogito*' argument would have to contend with. Consider its status: is it genuinely an inference, or is it perhaps rather an expression of an intuition? Does it really establish what Descartes claims for it? Note the problems which are raised by it: personal identity; the veridicality of memory; the issue of privacy and the use of a language which in some sense is 'public'; and the possibility of thoughts without a thinker. Some or all of these should be examined critically in your answer.

Question 15

(1) You might start by considering what kind of knowledge Hume is thinking of here, namely knowledge which is achieved by inference from cause to effect. Strictly speaking, this is a move from one true belief to another.

(2) Examine the notion of 'conceiving' as an activity of the imagination. (Note the distinction between fiction and belief.) Outline how, according to Hume, we move by 'force of custom' from a memory or sense impression to the apprehension of an object usually conjoined to it.

(3) You can then deal with the question of Hume's emphasis on conceiving, with particular reference to his avoidance of extreme scepticism. Conception makes true belief possible and is the basis of it. But note that it must be controlled; otherwise it becomes self-destructive.

Two key points for criticism here are: (a) whether it is genuine knowledge that can be achieved in this way, and (b) whether this epistemological claim is consistent with Hume's premises.

Question 19

Essentially what you are being asked to do is to justify the reasonableness of this belief about sense-data. So start by setting out the main points of Russell's causal theory, referring to what he says about inference and correspondence. Mention, for example, the elliptical coin or the table.

Now go on to the critical part of your answer. (a) What is actually meant by a 'sense-datum'? Consider problems of interpretation. Are sense-data mental, or are they perhaps in the surfaces of things? Perhaps they are really identical with things (phenomenalism)? (b) How you deal with (a) will determine your approach to the issue of sense-data as 'signs'. How are they signs? Do they point beyond themselves? Are they representations? But once we isolate sense-data from things we cannot 'pass beyond'; or 'know'; so this makes reasonableness questionable. Are Russell's 'good reasons' adequate (to suppose there are correspondences between spatial relations of physical objects and sense-data)? (c) The problem of privacy. If sense-data *are* 'private' experiences, then is it not *un*reasonable (or at least superfluous) to regard them as *pointers* to an external world, because externality is actually presupposed in the language we use to refer to them? In other words we do have direct acquaintance with things independent of us after all. (This is a more sophisticated objection.)

Question 29

This question seems paradoxical. A good way of dealing with it is to start distinguishing between different senses of 'know' (for example, 'thinks/believes, or 'certain/sure about'). Distinguish also between 'ordinary' doubt and 'philosophical' doubt. You can now develop an argument.

(1) It is reasonable to suppose that we can know or 'believe' that we are liable to error. We have after all been mistaken in the past about many things. Perhaps we can even know this (strong sense – 'be sure about'). We can appeal to criteria, evidence, frames of reference and so on which act as 'anchor' points or tests and enable us to distinguish 'truth' from 'error'.

(2) But can we genuinely know that we cannot know *anything*? If 'know' is taken in the stronger sense (to 'be sure about'), then the claim would seem to be self-

contradictory. Can the sceptic perhaps then know ('believe') that he does not know (is 'sure about') anything? Is such a claim coherent? Is it not inconsistent with various assumptions (for example, that memory is reliable, that not only the sceptic exists but also others whom he is trying to convince), or with his use of language (does he not have to know how to apply the term 'know' correctly in order to make his claim)?

Question 32

A useful approach would be to consider both the pros and the cons. Start by listing the kinds of things that we might be supposed to know (relatively or otherwise).

(1) Pros: (a) argument from illusion; (b) different cultural perspectives imposing different conceptual frameworks; (c) alleged privacy of experience.

(2) Cons: (a) illusions can be explained adequately in conventional or scientific terms; (b) cultural perspectives are not of central importance; perception may be supposed to have a common biological basis, and cultural relativism can be overcome through intertranslatability of concepts; (c) experiences are certainly 'private' in that I cannot (in a trivial or logical sense) have yours, but they can be communicated through a 'public' vehicle of language.

You might end by considering a stronger claim that *all* knowledge (including my knowledge or language, memories and so on) is relative to me. Is such a position tenable? Is this not rather like trying to lift oneself up by one's own shoelaces?

Question 47

Devote some space to interpretation of the question. Start from the common-sense position: by 'physical objects' is meant things like grass, stone and tables; 'real' means in themselves, apart from their being perceived: grass *is* green.

Difficulties: (a) If an object is to remain, say, red, apart from our perception of it, how can we account for changing appearance in different perceptual situations (light, angle, different perceivers)? Perhaps there is a standard or paradigm colour and deviations can be explained scientifically? (b) Is not a colour experience in fact inseparable from the process of perception? To talk of a 'real' colour is therefore contradictory. An answer to this would be that perception does not occur in a void, as it were; perception has to be of objects in space and time, in a given light, from a particular vantage point. (c) Reference to a 'real' colour is incompatible with scientific accounts formulated in terms of atoms, the absorption and emission of light of varying wavelengths and so on. But is not a scientific explanation only one way of looking at the world? Our normal 'conventional' way of describing things as 'really' red is entirely acceptable for 'everyday' purposes; it is up to us to decide when (and why) a different explanation is more useful or appropriate.

Question 49

Knowledge has often been thought to involve direct acquaintance (as in perception or knowledge of a person or place). Other 'minds' (thoughts and feelings and so on) are therefore cut off from us; they are private.

Some possible answers to this view: (a) The implied dualism is untenable or raises too many difficulties. (b) The other person can tell us what he is thinking or feeling. (c) We can know something about someone else's mental life by analogy with our own 'inner' experiences and corresponding 'outward' behaviour. (Behaviour can of course be disguised, but usually we know when and why a person is acting or hiding his true thoughts or feelings.) (d) Knowledge does not have to be by 'acquaintance'; we can have descriptive knowledge, while Ryle seeks to translate knowledge 'that' into knowledge 'how'. (e) You might refer also to Sartre's discussion of the Self and the Other.

Chapter 6

Question 6

As in other questions of this type, first of all make clear what Kant *means* by 'Good Will'. The will is good in itself because it is comprehended under the notion of duty – accessible through reason. The good will acts *for the sake of* duty not *from* duty (or inclination, or, still less, from self-interest; consequences are irrelevant).

Difficulties: (a) The problem of a *definition* of 'goodness' in terms of duty. (b) The problem of formalism/aridity of Kant's approach. (c) The 'test' of the categorical imperative (universalization of maxims) does not always work. (d) Kant's deontology can of course be attacked from a different ethical standpoint (such as utilitarianism). It does not seem to fit in either with the 'ordinary' man's conception of motives and intentions. It is important to look at the specific examples discussed by Kant. Think up others of your own. (See also Question 30.)

Question 17

(1) Summarize Mill's three stages of 'proof': (a) happiness is one end of morality; it is desirable; (b) only happiness is desirable; (c) it is the only thing desired for its own sake.

(2) Now examine whether he is successful. (a) Discuss the question of the validity of the move from 'people desire it' to 'it is desirable' (compare 'see' → 'visible', and consider G.E. Moore's criticisms. Does 'desirable' entail obligation?). (b) Is it the case that *only* happiness is desirable, and that virtue is sought because it leads to happiness? These are contentious points. (c) Is happiness desired for its own sake? What does Mill mean by 'happiness'? You might compare Mill with Aristotle here.

Question 18

(1) Present your discussion in terms of: (a) Nietzsche's rejection of 'herd' values (and universal moral systems), and (b) his quest to transcend them to achieve the higher values of the Superior Man.

(2) Clearly your attitude to his demand for such a critique must stand or fall with: (a) your acceptance or otherwise of this concept of the Superior Man; (b) the tenability of a 'revalued value'. What is the basis for values as applied to such a being? Is an objective criterion presupposed after all?

Question 22

(1) Explain what Sartre means by this. Show how it follows from the alleged priority of existence over essence, and from Sartre's assertion of 'absolute' freedom and 'authentic' choice as contrasted with 'bad faith'. Illustrate with concrete examples.

(2) At least two criticisms might be mentioned. (a) Morality, on such a view, becomes thoroughly subjective and relativistic. (b) Nobody can be criticized for their 'moral' choice provided it is 'authentic'. Do (a) and (b) together render the concept of value meaningless/empty?

Question 30

A possible response:

(1) It might be if applied to someone who is in some sense morally immature – perhaps a child (compare learning to play a game, or acquiring a skill such as cycling). Discuss this.

(2) But there are a number of difficulties if the criterion is applied to rational/responsible adults. (a) Rules tend to be rigid or inflexible – though special cases can be admitted and modified, or secondary rules introduced to cover new situations. (b) Rules can lead to formalism/aridity. Many people would argue that a place must be found for feelings and instincts; morality should relate to the whole person. (c) Perhaps the main problem is that rules tend to ignore intentions/motives/consequences. The test of moral goodness should not relate to actions in themselves as conforming to a rule. Rules can of course be framed to take account of intentions and consequences; but then the notion of a rule may be difficult to apply because of a multitude of modifications and qualifications. Discuss these issues with examples, and think of cases where we might say a person is good even when he breaks a 'rule'. Think how we use 'morally good' in relevant contexts.

Question 31

(1) Note first the ambiguity of 'relative' – as applied: (a) to a person, (b) to a society, culture, or religion.

(2) You can now develop a possible defence. (a) Different societies or religions may approach a moral issue from particular standpoints (give examples). Hence individual views may differ. (Could this lead to extreme subjectivism?) (b) Individual circumstances are unique. Therefore even 'objective/universal' principles might be held to apply differently.

(3) Problems or counter-arguments. Three connected points might be proposed. (a) Objective principles may underlie even apparently divergent value systems. (b) The possibility of dialogue between individuals from different cultures – the search for reconciliation could undermine relativist claims. (c) Social/cultural differences can be exaggerated. (Again give examples).

Question 37

Tackle this question by referring to examples of words such as 'red' (descriptive) and 'good' (prescriptive or commendatory). *Prima facie* a distinction can be maintained. But, as against this, you could consider the view that to call something red is not only to refer to or describe a colour-quality but also: (a) to commend usage to other people, and (b) to express approval/disapproval ('Nature red in tooth and claw', 'He is a "red" ', for example). Likewise 'good', while commendatory, may also be used to describe a (non-natural) quality. (Hare distinguishes between primary and secondary usages.)

The question for you to deal with is whether difficulties in applying the distinction or in knowing which 'meaning' is applicable in particular cases constitute sufficient grounds for us to maintain that the distinction itself is not 'clear'.

Chapter 7

Question 3

(1) Summarize the main points of Locke's theory. Mention in particular the surrender of *some* 'natural rights' to the community, and the role played by the majority in his proposed society. You might also indicate briefly the main differences between his conception and those of Hobbes and Rousseau.

(2) As for a critical examination, there are many points you might follow up. (a) Locke both emphasizes reason and suggests a supernatural basis for natural rights. But rights (life, liberty and property) tend to be assumed. Why does he propose these particular rights? (b) The giving up of rights raises the question of consent in a complex democracy. (c) Discuss the limited role of the state. Is there danger of a *laissez-faire* situation which might result in the weakest members not being protected or not enjoying the benefits of society? But note also that Locke's theory arguably also influenced revolutionary movements in France and America. (d) The ambiguity of the 'well-being' of the community. What *is* necessary for this? (e) (a more technical point) Locke seems to suggest a contrast

between (i) individuals and community and (ii) a contract between a community and government. This might be looked at.

Question 8

(1) Firstly, discuss why Rousseau argues that each citizen must surrender himself or herself to the 'general will' rather than to individual authority.

(2) Then examine what is actually meant by this 'general will' and how it works. (Distinguish between its different aspects of modes – state, sovereign, power.)

(3) Now consider possible difficulties. Here are some suggestions. (a) In the 'organic' state individuality (arguably) is submerged. Is this a good or bad thing? (b) The notion of the 'general will' is obscure or metaphysical. Is it to be identified with a particular individual, an aggregate, or a group? (c) A major problem: the individual *has* to identify himself with the general will to discover 'real' will and to find 'true' freedom. This raises the issue of liberty (compare Hegel and Marx). (d) On Rousseau's account, law and morality would seem to be conflated, and it is not clear what the standards of the community actually are as expressed thought the 'general will'.

Question 12

The central feature of *On Liberty* is Mill's concern with freedom and thought and discussion; and it is perhaps in the light of this that he regards individuality as so important. Individuality results from self-development. Explain what development of the personality involves. (Mention also circumstances which Mill recognises as justifying constraint on the individual.) Discuss the dangers to society which he sees as resulting from uniformity of personality (note the 'tyranny of the majority' or public opinion). So this question is really about the nature of a 'democratic' society. You do not of course have to agree with Mill. If you don't, then give your reasons. If you do, try to answer possible objections.

Question 17

You will no doubt recognize this quotation from Marx's *Theses* which contains his most explicit criticisms of Feuerbach.

(1) Summarize the main arguments, noting and clarifying Marx's contrasts between contemplative and active, subjectivity and objectivity, in relation to idealism and materialism. Refer also to his claim that Feuerbach's 'abstract individual' and the 'religious sentiment' are produced by and are inseparable from society.

(2) Make it clear what philosophy 'as we know it' involves.

(3) Does this mean the end of philosophy as we know it? Clearly, if the Marxist 'revolution' were ever successful, then according to Marx philosophy would

disappear. But you need to consider two central questions. (a) To make explicit and account for the 'errors' of traditional philosophical systems, would not the Marxist 'philosopher' have to employ concepts (for example, 'truth', 'knowledge') and techniques akin to those we normally regard as characterizing philosophy, even if only to redefine them? (b) What of the status of the Marxist 'philosophy' itself? Marx himself rejected the idea of such a philosophy as self-contradictory. Nevertheless, many later thinkers have sought to articulate a Marxist philosophy, with varying degrees of success; and it certainly seems a legitimate exercise to trace the development of the Marxist dialectic from Hegel's system. It is worth mentioning that the tension between 'idealist' and 'materialist' tendencies in Marx's system does not seem to have been satisfactorily overcome. Consider whether this suggests an inherent instability in the philosophical foundations of Marxism which would not be eliminated even if the 'revolution' were at some future date successful.

Question 26

How you tackle this partly depends on your conception of 'justice'. (a) Is justice itself a legal concept or a moral one? If it is the former, then clearly there cannot be an unjust law: what is 'right' or 'just' is defined by legislators. (b) However, it can be argued that justice is grounded in a wider context ('natural' law, morality, religious principles and so on) and that therefore a law could conflict with 'higher' standards – unless there is complete coincidence between the two. (You might consider here whether it is the job of the law simply to regulate society, or whether it should cover every possible facet of human behaviour.)

Examine both approaches, (a) and (b), and centre your discussion around concrete examples of conflicts (for example, homosexuality, or private versus public 'rights').

Question 36

A definition should include reference to a recognition by the person engaging in civil disobedience that there is an accepted framework of law and punishment, and to the importance of non-violence. In support of your justification you should discuss the relevance of conscience, sincerely held beliefs (what is it to be sincere?), and the possibility of moral codes of conduct which transcend the law as it stands (compare the last 'guided' answer). Give examples. By all means refer to, say, Rawls, but be aware of possible criticisms.

As for the acceptability of civil disobedience in a war situation, you could consider the possibility that the individual's stance is motivated by the belief that the war is unjust or immoral. Consider here appeals to supposedly 'higher' moral principles. Would this justify what others might regard as treason? Would this apply to any war? A particular war? Are there any special circumstances? What are the obligations of citizens? Is conformity even more important when the state itself is under threat? Reference to concrete examples is particularly useful in answers to this kind of question. (Consider World Wars I and II, Vietnam and so on.)

Question 37

(1) You might start in fairly general terms by considering what being in a society involves. Is man a 'social' being (compare Aristotle)? Note the relevance of law and rules. Can we talk of being free other than in a social context?

(2) Now distinguish between 'negative' and 'positive' freedom (Berlin). Explain what each kind of freedom means.

(3) Can either of these forms of freedom be extended without limit? What effects might this extension have on the viability of society as a whole?

(4) It should be clear that in any society there are certain things we *cannot* do (logically? practically?). Give examples and explain why not. But within these constraints (note, which vary from society to society), degrees of negative and positive freedom are possible. So only the existence of *unlimited* freedom would seem to lead to a contradiction.

Chapter 8

Question 6

This is a wide-ranging question. Start by explaining what paradigms are in science – refer to Kuhn's general thesis. Some mention of 'normal' science would be useful. Discuss also how the mounting up of difficulties, anomalies and intransigent facts which appear not to be explainable within the paradigm leads eventually to its overthrow (a 'revolution') and its replacement by a new one. (Concrete examples: the displacing of the Phlogiston theory by Lavoisier's Oxygen theory, or the assimilation of Newtonian mechanics within a broader Einsteinian framework.)

As to falsification, discuss Popper's thesis: hypotheses/conjectures are set up to be refuted. He is committed to some sort of 'objectivist' view of science and understands progress in terms of 'verisimilitude'. Clearly there seems to be a conflict between this approach and the paradigm model, in so far as those who adopt the latter are concerned with accommodating facts within a framework rather than with falsification. It is arguable also that those who accept the paradigm model are committed to some kind of non-objectivist or even anti-realist view of scientific truth and progress. Consider in what ways a new paradigm might be said to be 'better' rather than 'truer' (as against Popper's position).

Question 11

Outline Hempel's model (compare also Popper) – give an example (say, the expansion of metal when heated). Then consider a number of key difficulties. (i) Some deductions from general laws, which satisfy the requirements of the model *formally*, may not be regarded as genuine explanations. Do we need to redefine 'explanation'? Or might new evidence show that the supposed anomalous structures *are* explanatory after all? (ii) Show how Hempel attempts to accommodate probabilistic explanations within his covering-law framework. Any problems with this? (iii) Perhaps the most contentious feature of the model is its supposed application to the social sciences. Arguably the latter appeal to motives and reasons rather than 'causes', and that therefore the covering-law model may be inappropriate. Indicate some of the difficulties and again give a concrete example. (Read the discussion in 12.4 and note question **10**.)

Chapter 9

Question 1

Here are some possible approaches to this question.

(1) Is the term 'existence' as applied to God univocal or equivocal? (Problem: how can we know?) Does God exist in the way that electrons, trees and people do, or (if they do) as universals, the unconscious and so on?

(2) God cannot be perceived (unless God = the world as in, for example, Spinoza's philosophy). There is therefore a problem not only of proof but also in the attribution of qualities such as omniscience and love. Are these consistent with His existence? (Note the problem of evil.)

(3) Can 'existence' be redefined in terms of one's feelings or as 'the ultimate source of morality'? Would this be consistent with the concept of the Christian God? Or perhaps 'existence' can be applied only to what is created: it cannot be applied to the Creator?

(4) You could also consider the implicit assumption of the ontological argument that 'existence' is a predicate, and Kant's rejection of this view.

Question 11

I know that I am alive. I know that my cat is alive, or that the rose bush in the garden is living. Discuss the various criteria that enable us to justify such claims and why they cannot be applied to the 'redeemer'.

According to orthodox Christian doctrine, Christ (= God) died, was resurrected, and 'is seated at the right hand of the Father Almighty'. The issue to be examined there is how one can 'know' that Christ is alive (again). Clearly we must look for other criteria, for example His influence on the life of the believer, religious feeling and so on. (Problem: subjectivity and non-universality.) Consider also the function of such an affirmation in the 'total way of life' (Wittgenstein). 'Knowledge' may therefore have to be understood in a fideistic and pragmatic sense: belief in Christ as a living spirit 'works'. This needs to be examined critically.

Question 18

The principal difficulty concerns definition (note the rather loose everyday usage of the term). If a miracle is a 'one-off' event which transcends the laws of nature, how can we know/test this claim? We have to consider the possibility that a (scientific, naturalistic) explanation may be forthcoming at some time in the future, or that a repetition might occur. Consider also the objection that miracles might be thought to indicate selective or arbitrary choice on the part of God. What kind of God would the existence of miracles therefore tend to 'prove'?

Against this, it might be worthwhile to anticipate counter-arguments of believers, for example, that the recognition of an event as being miraculous presupposes faith or a framework of belief (in which case the use of miracles to 'prove' God's existence would seem to be circular?).

Chapter 10

Question 1

Refer to the analogy of the line and to Plato's discussion in Book X of the *Republic*. The central point is that artefacts are copies of 'copies'. (Note the dependence of his views on art on his metaphysics.) You should also say something about the more sympathetic approach developed in the *Symposium* and the *Phaedrus* where imitation is related to the Idea of Beauty. But here too Plato talks of degrees of representation.

In support of a general criticism of Plato you might consider whether art can in fact give an insight into 'truth' (this really requires a discussion of 'truth'; and a sustained attack on his metaphysics and epistemology beyond the scope of the question). Refer to specific examples from painting (and perhaps also from poetry and music).

Question 8

This is really a question about how a work of art is to be judged. If you subscribe to a representationalist or formalist theory, then you would probably be able to set about assessing the aesthetic worth or success of the work independently of what the artist had intended – even if by his own publicly declared criterion his composition might be thought to be a failure. (This is not of course to minimize the difficulties associated with artistic judgement by reference to 'imitation', 'form' and 'beauty'). If, however, you maintain a work of art should itself be regarded as the actual objectification or physical manifestation of the artist's intention (feelings, imagination and so on), then clearly the question becomes more problematic. (a) How could we know his intentions other than through his work (in which case a comparison would not be possible)? (b) The criterion of 'success' would seem to be entirely subjective. (Such difficulties in fact point to a weakness in 'expressionist' theories of art.) You might round off your answer with an examination of the view that evaluation necessarily requires some 'objective', that is publicly agreed, standards (though these may have to reached through constant discussion, comparison and revision until a 'consensus' is achieved – albeit temporary).

Question 22

This is a wide-ranging question and somewhat open-ended. To deal with it satisfactorily a student would ideally need to be quite well acquainted with different theories of literary criticism. Clear definition is essential.

(1) Start by considering what 'abstract' and 'concrete' mean and whether it is correct to apply these terms respectively to 'science' and 'life'. Science certainly deals with theories, hypotheses, models and so on, yet it is grounded in facts, observable and measurable data. Life is about people, events, relationships, actions and choices, all of which may be supposed to be 'concrete', but much of our activity is mediated through language which in its general aspect may be supposed to deal with abstractions.

(2) Now what does literature do? The first problem here is that 'literature' is a blanket term: it covers everything from the *Bible* to *The Sun* newspaper. But confining yourself to the 'classics', investigate whether there are common features. This is controversial and dubious. Perhaps we may think of literature as describing and relating ideas to people and events (factually or imaginatively). You will have to decide whether (at least the 'best' literature) 'bridges the gap' between concreteness and abstractness. In giving examples you will probably find it more helpful to refer particularly to novels (Note: especially *War and Peace* or works by Dostoievsky, Dickens, Hesse and others).

Chapter 11

Question 5

Part (a): Discuss the relevant attributes (the mind is non-spatial, the body has extension, is explicable in terms of mechanical causes). Then go on to say something about Descartes' claim that the mind is 'more easily known' than the body, and that his existence as a thinking being is indubitable (whereas the existence of the body can be doubted).

Part (b): Mention Descartes' view that the mind and body are intimately joined (not like a pilot in a ship). Outline his proposed solution relating to the pineal gland. You can then follow this up with criticisms of his position. How *can* a non-spatial substance interact mechanically with a substance having extension? (You might find it useful to refer briefly to the alternatives proposed by Malebranche and Leibniz to the extent that they draw attention to the difficulties in Descartes' 'solution'.)

Question 8

(1) The two definitions (a 'philosophical relation' and a 'natural relation') are given in para. 60 of the *Enquiry concerning Human Understanding*. Outline these and consider the differences of meaning between the two. Note that there are many regularities which we do not perceive and which would not therefore satisfy the second definition (if there is no perception, there can be no

'conveyance' of an appearance to an idea of an effect). Arguably Hume was not offering a definition at all but examining how the mind comes to have a belief in causation.

(2) Say something about the limitations imposed by his empiricism. As causes and effects relate to experience (impressions and ideas), we cannot go beyond to real 'powers' or 'forces'. We 'feel' connections and transfer this feeling to objects: but this is only a belief (note the role of the imagination).

(3) Finally you might consider the merits/demerits of Hume's position. On the plus side you can mention that it avoids the invoking of magic or supernatural powers. Negatively, it leads to ('attenuated') scepticism, uncertainty, unpredictability, connections being contingent. (But how serious an objection is this?) Moreover, the fact that we an have no further idea of cause may make it difficult for us to distinguish between genuine 'causal' connections and coincidences. (But note the counter-factual conditional in the first 'definition': some philosophers have argued recently that this can provide a basis for the distinction.)

Question 16

Ayer's rejection of a substance/material substratum (as in Locke) might well seem to be acceptable (compare Berkeley) because of the difficulty of *knowing* the relationship between attributes and substance. But is his solution really satisfactory? You might consider the following problems. (a) What criterion of sameness is Ayer offering? Is it spatial–temporal continuity, regular conjunction, or a pattern of some other kind? (b) (following on from (a)) What does he mean by 'relationship'? Will any kind of relationship do to justify the identification of an object as a 'thing'? A tree is a thing. Is a forest a thing? But perhaps to say there is a relationship *is* to say no more than that the collection of appearances constitutes a thing (in which case the introduction of the notion of relationship becomes superfluous). (c) Appearances change. Is some 'substantial' basis therefore required after all? (Compare Kant.) Or is our decision as to whether a thing has continuity or has changed into something else a matter of arbitrary convention? (d) Translatability. Might not a thing have an infinite number of attributes? If so there would seem to be at least a practical difficulty in identifying a thing with its appearances.

Question 25

Starting from the basis of a monist theory, the hypothesis would seem to be incoherent; the notion of being disembodied implies dualism. So on what grounds can the hypothesis be ruled out? Two issues in particular might be discussed. (1) Mind depends on body for its functioning, for example through the brain or nervous system (for perceiving, thinking and willing). Can we accept the possibility of a state of permanent unconsciousness? (2) Could mind be conceived to exist in a non-spatial, non-temporal condition? Are not the attributes of space and time supplied by bodies?

As against this it might be argued that there is no logical impossibility in the concept of a disembodied mental life. Such life might consist of memories in a God-like state – instantaneously coexisting. But would it still be difficult to regard such memories as non-spatial?

Question 38

There are various grounds which might be proposed to justify this claim.

(1) External compulsion (for example, breaking a valuable object because you were pushed by somebody else). Is this really *your* action? Note that in some cases you might be responsible for being in a given state (for example, drunkenness, or lack of forethought) and could therefore be held to be culpable.

(2) Genetic factors: one is 'made' like that. It could be objected that all actions are subject to the same constraint, in which case the distinction between 'free' and 'unfree' might seem difficult to maintain.

(3) Psychological factors: neuroses, compulsions, upbringing, role of the unconscious and so on. Objections here might relate to the theoretical assumptions made, the problem of testing or verifying the claims, or the difficulty in drawing lines (though pragmatic distinctions grounded in psycho-therapeutic practice could be admissible).

(4) Emotions – anger, whims and so on. Again the question can be raised about the degree of control we have over our own actions.

As general points, note the distinctions that can be made between moral, legal and psychological criteria for justification, and the need to consider each case in the context of the person's life history and life-style as a whole.

Question 42

(1) Note the implications of the question: it expresses a standard rationalist view. What we are given through the senses is not 'real' in any fundamental sense. All experience is 'illusory'. It is only through 'pure' reason – clear and distinct ideas, innate ideas, intellect, dialectic and so on – that we can gain access to the 'reality' lying behind, beyond, our perceptions. (Note also the ambiguity in the question. It can mean reason 'on its own' can give us knowledge of reality, that is, without the help of, say, sense-experience; or only reason can give us knowledge, that is, the senses can give us *no* knowledge of reality at all. It is probably simpler to concentrate on the former interpretation.)

(2) There are many points you might make in your discussion. (a) Reason on its own is formal. If it passes beyond the senses it is either uninformative (because tautological) or there is no way of verifying/testing its 'insights' – except in terms perhaps of 'coherence'. (b) The statement flies in the face of ordinary 'common sense'. We do have knowledge of things and people; they are genuinely real. (c) Science built on sense experience gives us reality (and this is not incompatible with everyday descriptions of the world). (d) Metaphysical 'reality', although

unsubstantiated, perhaps can be accommodated in a heuristic/pragmatic framework. But at the very least we need sense perception as a starting point for reason to reflect on, make deductions from (compare and contrast Plato and Aristotle).

Chapter 12

Question 4

Make the general point that many explanations of human behaviour often employ analogies (the heart has been compared to a pump, the brain to a telephone exchange). Discuss behaviourist, physicalist/materialist views; these are legitimate within limits: identify and examine these limits. Consider what humans are/can do more than machines (there are of course different views about this – but refer to such notions as mind/soul, freedom, agency, intentionality and morality). Explanations in terms of the natural sciences (appropriate to a machine) are inadequate or inappropriate when applied to man. Something might also be said about the chemical composition and organization of human bodies (carbon based, proteins, DNA and so on). To what extent are these features definitive? 'Thought experiment': suppose one day a machine were made which looked like and behaved just like a human being. How might we set about distinguishing between the genuine human and its copy?

Question 10

(1) Firstly set out a general view of scientific method (the covering-law model).

(2) Social sciences (psychology, history and so on) are about people/groups of people. People are agents – they choose, act, can change their minds. (Define 'actions': refer to intentionality, end-seeking and freedom.) Prediction is therefore problematic. Moreover they can actually change in response to experimental testing procedures. Hence it may be difficult to fit the social sciences into the covering-law frameworks.

(3) It might be argued that prediction is still possible (statistically). Yes, but it is a contingent matter that many/most people act in characteristic ways in specific circumstances. There is always the possibility of unaccountable exceptions (contrast 'laws' in the natural sciences).

Question 21

'Nature' and 'culture' are both 'blanket' terms – vague and wide-ranging. Some attempt at definition will, however, obviously be required. As to the question itself, here is one possible approach. What is natural is open to analysis by the (natural) sciences. So the question arises whether 'culture' (meaning art, religion, science and so on) is to be seen as: (a) grounded in/reducible to/explainable in terms of economic forces, physics, or even biology; or (b) whether it should be regarded as *sui generis*, as 'transcending' nature. It is of course possible to think of culture as an extension of nature and yet as still subject to only its own appropriate explanatory models. This might raise the issue of how the various 'levels' of explanation relate to each other.

A narrower approach might involve concentrating on the issue of language or symbolism. If culture is regarded as inseparable from or even definable in terms of this, then a discussion would be required about what language is and whether it can be accounted for in biological terms.

It would be useful to relate your answer to the opposing positions of 'materialism' (for example, Marx and Harris) and 'idealism' (for example, Cassirer and Schneider).

Question 30

This question to some extent overlaps with **28** and **29**. There are a number of issues that might be looked at. Consider Gadamer's views: (i) that prejudice (pre-judgement) cannot be eliminated – indeed that it is a precondition for the possibility of interpretation; and that therefore (ii) it is not possible to 'get into the mind' of a creator of, say, a work of art to determine the intention behind it. The truth of a work of art or a text lies in that work or text itself but cannot be isolated from either the cultural context in which it was created or from the cultural 'baggage' of the interpreter. It is in this sense that a fusion of the two 'horizons' must be sought. Consider how this is to be effected. Can it ever be complete? You should also consider Habermas's response – that prejudice is eliminable and through rationality an 'objective' truth attainable. (If you are interested in this topic you will need to read widely, particularly as the antagonists have more recently achieved some accommodation. Note also Ricoeur's contribution to the debate.)

Chapter 13

Question 4

Start by making clear the – perhaps obvious – point that *wu-wei* does not mean literally doing nothing; this would be tantamount to being dead. The key point is that non-action involves being in accord with the *Dao* (a few comments on this would be useful); and that this is to be achieved when one 'empties' oneself of all knowledge, doctrines and preconceptions, and learns to respond to situations spontaneously, 'naturally', in accordance with one's own inner impulses. This should not be confused with impulsiveness, that is, rash behaviour. (Some reference to Zen techniques – which owe something to Daoism – would not go amiss.) Of course there might seem to be an element of paradox in all this. A further issue worth considering is whether the assumption is justified that when one has developed this capacity for 'non-action' one *is* in accord with the *Dao*: what is the metaphysical basis for this?

Question 9

Summarize the Sāṁkhya thesis – that effects must pre-exist in causes and causes 'post-exist' in effects (the 'identity' theory). You might also mention the metaphysical assumptions that underpin this view, namely, that Nature is conceived as a unitary principle underlying the observable world, and that nothing can come from something (nor something from nothing). Then consider the objections of the atomist Nyāya–Vaiśeṣika school (they reject the idea of a presupposed power or energy, and they argue that the identity theory abolishes the distinction between various types of causation). Set out the key points of their own non-identity theory (causation understood in terms of the conjunction of properties constituting eternal or permanent substances – the effects). Now examine whether these two doctrines are effectively synthesized by the Dvaitins. Note the centrality of the concept of 'energy' or 'power' and its actualization or transformation. A clear account of this is needed. Does this suggest an evolutionary and teleological view (are there parallels with Aristotle)? A key issue for critical discussion is the 'two-predicate' theory which they appeal to support the claim that cause can both be identical and non-identical with effect. Does it? (A good answer will necessarily require you to have studied more than just the relevant section of Ch. 13.)

Question 15

You might start by noting that the doctrine of transmigration in both Hinduism and Buddhism presupposes some continuity between stages or lives, not least because it is held that the condition we find ourselves in is determined by the nature of our deeds in previous existences (*karma*). In Hinduism there is generally some explicit appeal to a personal 'soul' which passes from body to body. An account could be given here of some of the general arguments proposed in support of this view. But note that different philosophical schools offer different theories. A more serious difficulty is presented by Buddhism, in that the existence of such a personal soul is denied altogether. So what continues or migrates? You should examine their view that there is continuity of mental states which can become associated with different sets of physical states. Is this an acceptable position? Might it not seem to rule out the possibility of memory of a previous incarnation? (What firm evidence is there anyway that we can remember our past lives? If we cannot, does this suggest that the concept of *karma* can in fact have no relevance to our present moral conduct?) Finally, you might consider some of the other general objections to the doctrine of transmigration. Is it compatible with modern science? In the case of Hinduism we have the problem of how the 'soul' relates to the body. And even in Buddhism some account has to be given of how mental states are to be distinguished from physical ones, and how 'continuity' is effected. (This brings us back of course to the difficulties of causation.)

Should you wish develop your philosophical skills further you are recommended to join the The Royal Institute of Philosophy. Members receive the quarterly publication *Philosophy*, which contains essays on a wide range of topics, and also book reviews. For further information your should write to:

The Secretary
Royal Institute of Philosophy
14 Gordon Square
London WC1H 0AG

If you are intending to study externally for the London University B.A. in Philosophy, you may be interested in the author's comprehensive distance learning programme. For a Prospectus please write to:

Dr A.W. Harrison-Barbet
West Cork Tutorial Centre
14 Connolly Street
Bandon
Co. Cork
Republic of Ireland

e-mail: **hbarbet@eircom.net**

■ ⊻ Bibliography

Please note: (1) The inclusion of a title in this Bibliography should not be taken to imply that the book is currently in print. (2) Many of the titles listed below are available in other editions. (3) In the majority of entries the references are to the first date of publication; new editions may, however, have been issued subsequently. (4) This Bibliography should not be regarded as in any sense definitive or complete; necessarily there is an element of arbitrariness in the selection.

Abrams, M.H., *The Mirror and the Lamp: Romantic Theory and the Cultural Tradition* (New York: Oxford University Press, 1953).

Ackrill, J.L., *Aristotle the Philosopher* (Oxford: University Press, 1981).

Acton, H.B., *Kant's Moral Philosophy* (London: Macmillan, 1970).

Adams, M.M. and R.M., *The Problem of Evil* (Oxford: University Press, 1990; Past Masters).

Alexeev, A.P., *The Origin of the Human Race*, trans. H. Campbell Creighton (Moscow: Progress Publishers, 1986).

Allen, D.J., *The Philosophy of Aristotle*, 2nd edition (Oxford: University Press, 1970).

Allen, R.E. (ed.), *Studies in Plato's Metaphysics* (London: Routledge, 1965).

Annas, J., *An Introduction to Plato's 'Republic'* (Oxford: University Press, 1981).

Anscombe, G.E.M., *Intention*, 2nd edition (Oxford: Blackwell, 1963, 2000).

Anscombe, G.E.M., *An Introduction to Wittgenstein's 'Tractatus'*, 3rd edition (London: Hutchinson, 1967).

Apel, K.-O., *Understanding and Explanation: A Transcendental-Pragmatic Perspective*, trans. by Georgia Warnke (Cambridge MA and London: MIT Press, 1984).

Aquinas, St Thomas, *Summa contra Gentiles*, Book I: God, translated as 'On the Truth of the Catholic Faith' with introduction and notes by A.C. Pegis (New York: Doubleday, 1965).

Aquinas, St Thomas, (prescribed text) *Summa Theologiae*, Book I: Concerning Man, trans. by T. Sutton (London: Eyre & Spottiswood, 1970).

Arendt, H., (prescribed text) *The Human Condition* (1958), 2nd edition with introduction by M. Canovan (Chicago and London: Chicago University Press, 1998).

Armstrong, A.H., *An Introduction to Ancient Philosophy*, 3rd edition (London: Methuen, 1957).

Aristotle, (prescribed text) *Nicomachean Ethics*, trans. by J.A.K. Thomson and revised by H. Tredennick (Harmondsworth: Penguin, 1976). This and his other dialogues are available in various editions published by Dent (Everyman) or Penguin. See in particular H. Lawson-Tancred's translation and edition of *De Anima* ('On the Soul') (Harmondsworth: Penguin, 1986). There is a convenient one-volume abridged collection containing the Oxford translations of most of his main writings: *The Basic Works of Aristotle*, edited by R. McKeon (New York: Random House, 1941). Perhaps even more useful is J.L. Ackrill (ed.), *A New Aristotle Reader* (Oxford: Clarendon Press, 1987).

Audi, R., *Epistemology: A Contemporary Introduction to the Theory of Knowledge* (London: Routledge, 1997).

Augustine, St, *the City of God* (413/27) (Harmondsworth: Penguin, 1972).

Austin, J.L., *Sense and Sensibilia*, reconstructed by G.J. Warnock (Oxford: University Press, 1962).

Ayer, A.J., *The Foundations of Empirical Knowledge* (London: Macmillan, 1940).

Ayer, A.J., *The Problem of Knowledge* (Harmondsworth: Penguin, 1956).

Ayer, A.J., *Philosophical Essays* (London: Macmillan, 1959).

Ayer, A.J., *The Origins of Pragmatism* (London: Macmillan, 1968).

Ayer, A.J., (prescribed text) *Language, Truth and Logic*, 2nd edition (London: Gollancz, 1946; Harmondsworth: Penguin, 1971).

Ayer, A.J., *Russell* (London: Collins, 1972; Fontana Modern Masters).

Ayer, A.J., *Hume* (Oxford: University Press, 1980; Past Masters).

Ayer, A.J., *Philosophy in the Twentieth Century* (London: Weidenfeld & Nicolson, 1982; Unwin Paperbacks, 1984).

Barnes, J., *Aristotle* (Oxford: University Press, 1982; Past Masters).

Barnes, J. (ed.), *The Cambridge Companion to Aristotle* (Cambridge: University Press, 1995).

Barnes, J., Sorabji, R. and Schofield, M. (eds), *Articles on Aristotle* (London: Duckworth, 1979).

Barrow, R., *Injustice, Inequality and Ethics* (Brighton: Wheatsheaf, 1982).

Barry, B., *The Liberal Theory of Justice* (1974) (Oxford: University Press, 1996).

Beardsley, M.C., *Aesthetics from Classical Greece to the Present* (Tuscaloosa: University of Alabama Press, 1975).

Beauvoir, S. de, (prescribed text) *The Ethics of Ambiguity* (Secaucus NJ: Citadel Press, 1980).

Bell, C., *Art* (1914), reprint, ed. J.B. Bullen (Oxford: University Press, 1987).

Bell, D., *Husserl* (London: Routledge, 1989; Arguments of the Philosophers).

Berkeley, G., *Treatise Concerning the Principles of Human Knowledge* (1710); *Three Dialogues between Hylas and Philonous* (1713). Many editions; see particularly *Philosophical Works*, ed. M.R. Ayers (London: Dent, 1975; Everyman); and ed. D. Berman, *Berkeley* (Little Rock, AR: Phoenix, 1997).

Berlin, I., *Four Essays on Liberty* (Oxford: University Press, 1969).

Berlin, I., *Karl Marx* (Oxford: University Press, 1978).

Berman, D., *George Berkeley: Idealism and the Man* (Oxford: University Press, 1996).

Blakemore, C., *Mechanisms of the Mind* (Cambridge: University Press, 1977).

Boden, M. (ed.), *The Philosophy of Artificial Intelligence* (Oxford: University Press, 1980).

Boden, M., *Artificial Intelligence and Natural Man*, 2nd edition (Cambridge MA and London: MIT Press, 1987).

Bradley, F.H., *Appearance and Reality: a Metaphysical Essay* (1897) (Oxford: University Press, 1969).

Braithwaite, R.B., *Scientific Explanation* (Cambridge: University Press, 1953).

Britton, K., *John Stuart Mill* (Harmondsworth: Penguin, 1953).

Britton, K., *Philosophy and the Meaning of Life* (Cambridge: University Press, 1971).

Broad, C.D., *Five Types of Ethical Theory* (London: Routledge, 1930).

Buber, M., (prescribed text) *I and Thou* (1923), revised edition (Edinburgh: Clark, 1958).

Buber, M., *Between Man and Man* (1947) (London: Collins, 1961; Fontana Library).

Bunge, M., *Causality: The Place of the Causal Principle in Modern Science* (Cambridge MA: Harvard University Press, 1959).

Burke, E., *A Philosophical Inquiry into the Origin of our Idea of the Sublime and Beautiful* (1756) (Harmondsworth: Penguin, 1998).

Burnet, J., *Greek Philosophy: Thales to Plato* (1914) (London: Macmillan, 1981).

Burtt, E.A., *The Metaphysical Foundations of Modern Science*, 2nd edition (London: Routledge, 1932).

Campbell, N.R., *The Foundations of Science* (New York: Dover, 1957).

Carroll, N., *Philosophy of Art: A Contemporary Introduction* (London: Routledge, 1999).

Cassirer, E., *An Essay on Man: An Introduction to the Philosophy of Human Culture* (New Haven CT: Yale University Press, 1944).

Chan, W.-T., *A Source Book in Chinese Philosophy* (Princeton NJ: University Press, 1963).

Chomsky, N., *Language and Mind* (New York: Harcourt Brace Jovanovich, 1972).

Coleridge, S.T., *Biographia Literaria* (1817), revised edition (London: Dent, 1967; Everyman).

Collingwood, R.G., *The Principles of Art* (1938) (Oxford: University Press, 1974).

Collingwood, R.G., *The Idea of Nature* (Oxford: University Press, 1945).

Confucius, (prescribed text) *Analects*, trans. D.C. Lau (Harmondsworth: Penguin, 1979); many other editions.

Copleston, F.C., *Aquinas* (Harmondsworth: Penguin, 1955).

Copleston, F.C., *A History of Philosophy*, 9 vols, reissued in 3 vols (New York: Doubleday, 1985).

Creel, H.G., *Chinese Thought from Confucius to Mao Tse-Tung* (Chicago: University Press, 1953).

Crombie, I.M., *An Examination of Plato's Doctrines*, 2 vols (London: Routledge, 1962/63).

Dancy, J., *Introduction to Contemporary Epistemology* (Oxford: Blackwell, 1985).

Dancy, J. (ed.), *Perceptual Knowledge* (Oxford: University Press, 1988; Oxford Readings).

Danto, A.C., *Nietzsche as Philosopher* (New York: Macmillan, 1965).

Danto, A.C., *Sartre* (London: Collins, 1975; Fontana Modern Masters).

Danto, A.C., *The Transfiguration of the Commonplace: a Philosophy of Art* (Cambridge MA: Harvard University Press, 1981).

Davidson, D., *Essays on Actions and Events* (Oxford: Clarendon Press, 1980).

Davies, B., *An Introduction to the Philosophy of Religion*, 2nd edition (Oxford: University Press, 1982, 1993).

Davies, P., *God and the New Physics* (Harmondsworth: Penguin, 1984).

Dawkins, R., *The Selfish Gene* (Oxford: University Press, 1986).

Dawkins, R., *The Blind Watchmaker* (Harmondsworth: Penguin, 1988).

Dennett, D.C., *Consciousness Explained* (Harmondsworth: Penguin, 1993).

Descartes, R., (prescribed text) *Meditations* (1641), also *Discourse on Method* (1637), trans. E.S. Haldane and G.R.T. Ross, Vol. I (Cambridge: University Press, 1969). There are numerous other editions of Descartes' writings – Dent, Penguin, for example. A good one-volume abridged edition of his works is that edited by J. Cottingham (Cambridge: University Press, 1988).

Devlin, P., *The Enforcement of Morals* (Oxford: University Press, 1965).

Dillon, M.C., *Merleau-Ponty's Ontology*, 2nd edition (Evanston IL: Northwestern University Press, 1997).

Dilthey, W., *Introduction to the Human Sciences* (1883), trans. R.J. Betzanos (Detroit MI: Wayne State University Press, 1988).

Dunn, J., *Locke* (Oxford: University Press, 1984; Past Masters).

Edelman, G., I. *The Remembered Present: A Biological Theory of Consciousness* (Part III of a trilogy) (New York: Basic Books, 1989).

Edelman, G., *Bright Air, Brilliant Fire: On the Matter of the Mind* (Harmondsworth: Penguin, 1994).

Evans, J.D.G., *Aristotle* (Brighton: Harvester, 1986; Philosophers in Context).

Feinberg, J. (ed.), *Moral Concepts* (Oxford: University Press, 1969; Oxford Readings).

Ferré, F., *Language, Logic and God* (New York: Harper & Rowe, 1961).

Feyerabend, P., *Against Method*, revised edition (New York and London: Verso, 1988).

Feyerabend, P., (prescribed text) *Farewell to Reason* (London and New York: Verso, 1988).

Field, G.C., *Plato* (London: Oxford University Press, 1949).

Fischer, E., *The Necessity of Art: A Marxist Approach*, trans. A. Bostock (Harmondsworth: Penguin, 1963).

Foot, P., *Theories of Ethics* (Oxford: University Press, 1967; Oxford Readings).

Foster, J., *A. J. Ayer* (London: Routledge, 1985; Arguments of the Philosophers).

Frankena, W.A., *Ethics*, 2nd edition (Englewood Cliffs NJ: Prentice-Hall, 1973).

Frankfort, H., Frankfort, H.A., Wilson, J.A. and Jacobson, Th., *Before Philosophy* (Chicago IL: University Press, 1946; Harmondsworth: Penguin, 1949).

Freud, S., (prescribed text) *An Outline of Psychoanalysis* (1938), trans. J. Strachey (London: Hogarth Press, 1969).

Fry, R., *Vision and Design* (1920) (New York: Dover, Penguin, 1999).

Gadamer, H.-G., *Truth and Method* (1960), 2nd revised edition, trans. J. Weinsheimer and D.G. Marshall (New York: Continuum, 1989).

Gadamer, H.-G., *The Relevance of the Beautiful and Other Essays*, ed. R. Bernasconi (Cambridge: University Press, 1986).

Gaskin, J., *The Quest for Eternity: An Outline of the Philosophy of Religion* (Harmondsworth: Penguin, 1984).

Gehlen, A., *Man, His Nature and Situation in the World* (1940), English trans. (New York: Columbia University Press, 1988).

Gensler, H.J., *Ethics: A Contemporary Introduction* (London: Routledge, 1998).

Gillispie, G.C., *The Edge of Objectivity: An Essay in the History of Scientific Ideas* (Princeton NJ: University Press, 1960).

Glover, J. (ed.), *The Philosophy of Mind* (Oxford: University Press, 1976; Oxford Readings).

Glover, J., *Causing Death and Saving Lives* (Harmondsworth: Penguin, 1977).

Goodman, N., *Fact, Fiction and Forecast* (1954) (Cambridge MA: Harvard University Press, 1982).

Gombrich, E.H., *Art and Illusion* (London: Phaidon, 1960).

Gosling, J.C.B., *Plato* (London: Routledge, 1973; Arguments of the Philosophers).

Grayling, A.C., *Introduction to Philosophical Logic* (1982), new edition (Oxford: Blackwell, 1997).

Grayling, A.C., *Berkeley: The Central Arguments* (London: Duckworth, 1986).

Grayling, A.C., *The Refutation of Scepticism* (London: Duckworth, 1988).

Grayling, A.C., *Wittgenstein* (Oxford: University Press, 1988; Past Masters).

Grayling, A.C., *Russell* (Oxford: University Press, 1991; Past Masters).

Griffiths, A. Phillips (ed.), *Knowledge and Belief* (Oxford: University Press, 1976; Oxford Readings).

Grimsley, R., *Jean-Jacques Rousseau* (Brighton: Harvester, 1983).

Guthrie, W.K.C., *Greek Philosophers from Thales to Aristotle* (London: Methuen, 1950).

Haack, S., *Philosophy of Logics* (Cambridge: University Press, 1978).

Habermas, J., *Knowledge and Human Interests* (1968), trans. J.J. Shapiro (Oxford: Polity Press, 1987).

Habermas, J., selections from his writings – *The Habermas Reader*, ed. W. Outhwaite (Oxford: Polity Press, 1996).

Hacker, P.M.S., *Insight and Illusion: Wittgenstein on Philosophy and the Metaphysics of Experience*, revised edition (Oxford: University Press, 1986).

Hacking, I. (ed.), *Scientific Revolutions* (Oxford: University Press, 1982; Oxford Readings).

Hamlyn, D.W., *Sensation and Perception* (London: Routledge, 1961).

Hamlyn, D.W., *The Theory of Knowledge* (London: Macmillan, 1971).

Hamlyn, D.W., *Metaphysics* (Cambridge: University Press, 1984).

Hamlyn, D.W., *A History of Western Philosophy* (Harmondsworth: Penguin, 1987).

Hampshire, S., *Spinoza* (1951) (Harmondsworth: Penguin, 1976).

Hampshire, S., *Thought and Action* (1960), 2nd edition (London: Chatto and Windus, 1982).

Hampshire, S., *Freedom of the Will* (London: Chatto and Windus, 1965).

Hanslick, E., *The Beautiful in Music* (1854), trans. G. Cohen (Indianapolis IN and New York: Bobbs-Merrill, 1957).

Hanson, N.R., *Patterns of Discovery* (Cambridge: University Press, 1965).

Hardie, W.F.R., *Aristotle's Ethical Theory*, 2nd edition (Oxford: University Press, 1980).

Hare, R.M., *The Language of Morals*, revised edition (Oxford: University Press, 1961).

Hare, R.M., *Freedom and Reason* (Oxford: University Press, 1965).

Hare, R.M., *Plato* (Oxford: University Press, 1982; Past Masters).

Harris, M., *Cultural Materialism: The Struggle for a Science of Culture* (New York: Random House, 1979).

Hart, H.L.A., *Law, Liberty and Morality* (Oxford: University Press, 1963).

Hegel, G.W.F., *The Phenomenology of Mind* (1807), trans. A.V. Miller (Oxford: University Press, 1977).

Hegel, G.W.F., *Aesthetics: Lectures on the Philosophy of Art* (1820–29); trans. B. Bosanquet as *Introductory Lectures on Aesthetics* (Harmondsworth: Penguin, 1993).

Heidegger, M., *Being and Time* (1926), trans. J. Macquarrie and E. Robinson (Oxford: Blackwell, 1962).

Heidegger, M., *Kant and the Problem of Metaphysics* (1929), trans. J.S. Churchill (Bloomington: Indiana University Press, 1962).

Heidegger, M., *An Introduction to Metaphysics* (1953), trans. R. Manheim (New York: Anchor Books, 1961).

Heil, J., *Philosophy of Mind: A Contemporary Introduction* (London: Routledge, 1998).

Hempel, C.G., *Aspects of Scientific Explanation* (New York: Collier-Macmillan, 1965).

Hempel, C.G., *The Philosophy of Natural Science* (Englewood Cliffs NJ: Prentice-Hall, 1966).

Hesse, M.B., *Models and Analogies in Science* (Indiana: Notre Dame University Press, 1962).

Hick, J., *Philosophy of Religion* (1963), 3rd edition (Englewood Cliffs NJ: Prentice-Hall, 1983).

Hick, J., *Evil and the God of Love* (London: Macmillan, 1966).

Hick, J., *Faith and Knowledge* (New York: Cornell University Press, 1967).

Hiriyanna, M., *Outlines of Indian Philosophy* (1932) (Delhi: Banarsidass, 1993).

Hiriyanna, M., *Essentials of Indian Philosophy* (1949) (London: Unwin, 1978).

Hobbes, T., *Leviathan* (1651), edited with introduction by C.B. Macpherson (Harmondsworth: Penguin, 1985); many other editions available.

Hodges, W., *Logic* (Harmondsworth: Penguin, 1977).

Hollingdale, R.J., *Nietzsche: The Man and his Philosophy* (London: Routledge, 1973).

Hudson, W.D., *Modern Moral Philosophy*, 2nd edition (London: Macmillan, 1983).

Hull, L.W.H., *History and Philosophy of Science: An Introduction* (London: Longmans, 1959).

Hume, D., *A Treatise on Human Nature* (1739/40), ed. L.A. Selby-Bigge, 2nd edition, revised with notes by P.H. Nidditch (Oxford: University Press, 1978); many other editions.

Hume, D., (prescribed text) *An Enquiry concerning Human Understanding* (1748; 1777), ed. L.A. Selby-Bigge, 3rd edition, revised with notes by P.H. Nidditch

(Oxford: University Press, 1975). Also includes *An Enquiry concerning the Principles of Morals* (1751).

Hume, D., *Dialogues Concerning Natural Religion* (1779), ed. with introduction by H.D. Aitken (New York: Hafner, 1948); other editions available.

Husserl, E., *The Idea of Phenomenology*, trans. and ed. W.P. Alston and G. Nakhnikian (The Hague: Nijhoff, 1970); and *Cartesian Meditations: An Introduction to Phenomenology*, trans. D. Cairns (The Hague: Nijhoff, 1969).

Inwood, M., *Heidegger* (Oxford: University Press, 1997; Past Masters).

Irwin, T., *Plato's Moral Theory* (Oxford: University Press, 1977).

James, W., *Pragmatism* (1907), introduction by A.J. Ayer (Cambridge MA and London: Harvard University Press, 1975); several other editions.

James, W., *The Varieties of Religious Experience: A Study in Human Nature* (1902) (Harmondsworth: Penguin, 1993).

Johnson-Laird, P.N., *The Computer and the Mind* (Cambridge MA: Harvard University Press, and London: Collins/Fontana, 1993).

Kant, I., *Critique of Pure Reason* (1781; 2nd edition 1787), trans. N. Kemp Smith (London: Macmillan, 1933 and subsequent reprints).

Kant, I., (prescribed text) *Groundwork of the Metaphysics of Morals* (1785; 2nd edition 1786), trans. with notes by H.J. Paton (London: Hutchinson, 1948).

Kant, I., *Prolegomena to any Future Metaphysics* (1787), trans. L.W. Beck (Indianapolis: Bobbs-Merrill, 1950); also translations by Lucas and Ellington.

Kant, I., *Critique of Practical Reason* (1788), trans. with introduction L.W. Beck (Indianapolis: Bobbs-Merrill, 1956).

Kant, I., *Critique of Judgement* (1790), trans. J.C. Meredith (Oxford: Clarendon Press, 1978); other translations available.

Kenny, A., *Action, Emotion and Will* (London: Routledge, 1963).

Kenny, A., *Descartes: A Study of his Philosophy* (New York: Random House, 1968).

Kenny, A., *The Five Ways* (London: Routledge, 1969).

Kenny, A., *Wittgenstein* (Harmondsworth: Penguin, 1975).

Kenny, A., *Aquinas* (Oxford: University Press, 1980; Past Masters).

Kenny, A., *What is Faith? Essays in the Philosophy of Religion* (Oxford: University Press, 1992).

Kierkegaard, S., *Philosophical Fragments* (1844), 2nd edition, trans. D.F. Swenson, revised H.V. Hong, introduction N. Thulstrup (Princeton NJ: University Press, 1962).

Kierkegaard, S., *Concluding Scientific Postscript* (1846), trans. D.F. Swenson and W. Lowrie, introduction and notes W. Lowrie (Princeton NJ: University Press, 1941, 1969).

Knowles, D., *The Evolution of Medieval Thought* (London: Longmans, 1962).

Kolakowski, L., *Religion* (London; Collins, 1982; Fontana Masterguides).

Körner, S., *Kant* (Harmondsworth: Penguin, 1970).

Kraut, R. (ed.), *The Cambridge Companion to Plato* (Cambridge: University Press, 1992).

Kripke, S., *Naming and Necessity*, revised edition (Oxford: Blackwell, 1980).

Kuhn, T.S., *The Structure of Scientific Revolutions* (1962), 2nd enlarged edition (Chicago IL: University Press, 1970).

Lakatos, I. and Musgrave, A. (eds), *Criticism and the Growth of Knowledge* (Cambridge: University Press, 1970).

Langer, S.K., *Feeling and Form: a Theory of Art developed from 'Philosophy in a New Key'* (London: Routledge, 1953).

Langer, S.K., *Philosophical Sketches* (Baltimore MD: Johns Hopkins Press/Mentor, 1964).

Langer, S.K., *Philosophy in a New Key*, 3rd edition (Cambridge MA: Harvard University Press, 1977).

Lao Tzu, (prescribed text) *Tao Te Ching* trans. D.C. Lau (Harmondsworth: Penguin, 1963); many other translations.

Lear, J., *Aristotle: The Desire to Understand* (Cambridge: University Press, 1988).

Leavis, F.R., *The Great Tradition* (1948) (Harmondsworth: Penguin, 1962).

Leavis, F.R., *The Common Pursuit* (1952) (Harmondsworth: Penguin, 1962; London: Hogarth Press, 1984).

Leibniz, G.W. von, *Monadology* (1714) in *Philosophical Writings*, trans. M. Morris and G.H.R. Parkinson (London: Dent, 1973; Everyman's Library).

Leibniz, G.W. von, *Discourse on Metaphysics* (posthumously 1846), trans. P.G. Lucas and L. Grant (Manchester: University Press, 1961). (This, together with the *Monadology*, is also included in *Philosophical Writings*, trans. Ariew and Garbner – Indianapolis IN: Bobbs-Merrill, 1989).

Lemmon, E.J., *Beginning Logic* (Sunbury-on-Thames: Nelson, 1971).

Lewis, H.D., *Our Experience of God* (London: Allen & Unwin, 1959; Collins/Fontana, 1970).

Lewis, H.D., *Philosophy of Religion* (London: English Universities Press, 1965).

Lewis, H.D. and Slater, R.L., *An Introduction to the Philosophy of Religion* (New York: Watts, 1966; Harmondsworth: Penguin, 1969).

Linden, E., *Apes, Men and Language* (New York: Dutton, 1975; Harmondsworth: Penguin, 1976).

Locke, J., *An Essay Concerning Human Understanding* (1690), edited and abridged with introduction by A.D. Woozley (London: Collins/Fontana, 1964); or *The Locke Reader*, ed., with introduction and commentary, J. Yolton (Cambridge: University Press, 1977).

Locke, J., (prescribed text) *Second Essay on Human Government* (1690), in *Two Treatises of Government*, ed. P. Laslett (Cambridge; University Press, 1967); also in *Social Contract: Essays by Locke, Hume and Rousseau*, ed. E. Barker (London: University Press, 1947).

Lorenz, K., *Behind the Mirror*, trans. R. Taylor (London: Methuen, 1977).

Loux, M.J., *Metaphysics: A Contemporary Introduction* (London: Routledge, 1997).

Lycan, W., *Philosophy of Language: A Contemporary Introduction* (London: Routledge, 1999).

Lyons, W., *Gilbert Ryle: An Introduction to his Philosophy* (Brighton: Harvester, 1980).

Lyons, W. (ed.), *Modern Philosophy of Mind* (London: Dent, 1995; Everyman's Library).

Mabbott, J.D., *The State and the Citizen*, 2nd edition (London: Hutchinson, 1967).

MacIntyre, A.C., *A Short History of Ethics* (London: Routledge, 1967).

Mackie, J.L., *Truth, Probability and Paradox* (Oxford: University Press, 1973).

Mackie, J.L., *The Cement of the Universe* (Oxford: University Press, 1974).

Mackie, J.L., *Ethics: Investigating Right and Wrong* (Harmondsworth: Penguin, 1977).

Mackie, J.L., *Hume's Moral Theory* (London: Routledge, 1980).

Mackie, J.L., *The Miracle of Theism: Arguments for and Against the Existence of God* (Oxford: University Press, 1982).

Magee, B., *Popper* (London: Collins, 1973; Fontana Modern Masters).

Malcolm, N., *Knowledge and Certainty* (New York: Cornell University Press, 1963).

Malinowski, B., *A Scientific Theory of Culture* (North Carolina: University Press, 1944; Oxford: University Press, 1960).

Marcuse, H., *Reason and Revolution* (New York: Humanities Press, 1954).

Marx, K. and Engels, F., (prescribed text) *The German Ideology* (1846) (including Marx, *Theses on Feuerbach*, 1888), trans. and introduction C.J. Arthur (London: Lawrence & Wishart, 1970).

McGinn, C., *The Character of Mind* (Oxford: University Press, 1982).

McKirahan, R.D., *Philosophy before Socrates* (Indianapolis IN: Hackett, 1994).

Mead, G.H., *Selected Writings*, ed. A.J. Reck (Chicago IL: University Press, 1964).

Medawar, P., *Induction and Intuition in Scientific Thought* (London: Methuen, 1969).

Medawar, P., *The Art of the Soluble* (Harmondsworth: Penguin, 1969).

Melden, A.I., *Free Action* (London: Routledge, 1961).

Merleau-Ponty, M., *The Phenomenology of Perception*, trans. C. Smith (London: Routledge, 1955).

Merleau-Ponty, M., *Consciousness and the Acquisition of Language*, trans. H.J. Silverman (Evanston IL: Northwestern University Press, 1973).

Midgley, M., *Beast and Man: The Roots of Human Nature*, new edition (London: Routledge, 1991).

Mill, J.S., (prescribed text) *On Liberty* (1859), ed. M. Warnock (London: Collins/Fontana); or ed. H. Himmelfarb (Harmondsworth: Penguin, 1982).

Mill. J.S., *Utilitarianism* (1861), ed. M. Warnock (London: Collins/Fontana, 1962); other editions available.

Mitchell, B., *Law, Morality and Religion in a Secular Society* (Oxford: University Press, 1970).

Mitchell, B. (ed.), *The Philosophy of Religion* (Oxford: University Press, 1971; Oxford Readings).

Monod, J., *Chance and Necessity: An Essay on the Natural Philosophy of Human Biology*, trans. A. Wainhouse (London: Collins/Fontana, 1974).

Moore, A.W. (ed.), *Meaning and Reference* (Oxford: University Press, 1993; Oxford Readings).

Moore, G.E., *Ethics* (1912), 2nd edition (Oxford: University Press, 1966).

Moravcsik, J.M.E. (ed.), *Aristotle* (London: Macmillan, 1968; Modern Studies in Philosophy).

Murdoch, I., *Sartre, Romantic Rationalist* (1953) (London: Collins/Fontana, 1967).

Murdoch, I., *The Sovereignty of the Good* (London: Routledge, 1970).

Murti, T.R.V., *The Central Philosophy of Buddhism*, 2nd edition (London: Allen & Unwin, 1960).

Nagel, E., *The Structure of Science: Problems in the Logic of Scientific Explanation* (London: Routledge, 1961).

Nagel, T., *The View from Nowhere* (Oxford: University Press, 1986).

Newman, J.H., *An Essay in Aid of a Grammar of Assent* (1870), introduction by E. Gilson (New York: Doubleday, 1955).

Newton-Smith, W.H., *The Rationality of Science* (London: Routledge, 1981).

Nidditich, P.H. (ed.), *The Philosophy of Science* (Oxford: University Press, 1968; Oxford Readings).

Nielsen, K., *Ethics without God* (London: Pemberton, 1973).

Nielsen, K., *An Introduction to the Philosophy of Religion* (London: Macmillan, 1982).

Nietzsche, F., (prescribed text) *Beyond Good and Evil* (1886), trans., with introduction and commentary, R.J. Hollingdale (Harmondsworth: Penguin, 1973).

Nietzsche, F., (prescribed text) *On the Genealogy of Morals* (1887), trans. W. Kaufmann and R.J. Hollingdale, ed. with commentary by W. Kaufman (New York: Random House, 1969); also *Basic Writings of Nietzsche*, trans. and ed. W. Kaufmann (New York: Modern Library, 1992).

Nozick, R., *Anarchy, State, and Utopia* (Oxford: Blackwell, 1975).

Nussbaum, M., (prescribed text) *Poetic Justice* (Boston MA: Beacon Press, 1997).

O'Connor, D.J. (ed.), *A Critical History of Western Philosophy* (New York: Collier-Macmillan, 1964).

O'Connor, D.J., *John Locke* (Harmondsworth: Penguin, 1952; reprint New York, 1967).

O'Hear, A., *An Introduction to the Philosophy of Science* (Oxford: University Press, 1989).

Ortega y Gasset, J., (prescribed text) *History as a System and other Essays toward a Philosophy of History* (1941), trans. H. Weyl, with an afterword by J.W. Miller (New York and London: Norton, 1962).

Osborne, H. (ed.), *Aesthetics* (Oxford: University Press, 1973; Oxford Readings).

Otto, R., *The Idea of the Holy*, trans. J.W. Harvey (London: Oxford University Press, 1959; Harmondsworth: Penguin, 1959).

Parfit, D., *Reasons and Persons* (Oxford: University Press, 1984).

Parkinson, G.H.R. (ed.), *The Theory of Meaning* (Oxford: University Press, 1968; Oxford Readings).

Passmore, J.A., *A Hundred Years of Philosophy*, 2nd revised edition (Harmondsworth: Penguin, 1968); supplement: *Recent Philosophy* (London: Duckworth, 1985).

Pears, D.F. (ed.), *The Nature of Metaphysics* (London: Macmillan, 1957).

Pears, D.F., *Bertrand Russell and the British Tradition in Philosophy* (London: Collins, 1967).

Pears, D.F., *Wittgenstein* (London: Collins, 1971; Fontana Modern Masters).

Pears, D.F., *Hume's System* (Oxford: University Press, 1990).

Peters, R., *Hobbes* (Harmondsworth: Penguin, 1956).

Pinker, S., *The Language Instinct: The New Science of Language and Mind* (Harmondswroth: Penguin, 1994).

Pinker, S., *How the Mind Works* (Harmondsworth: Penguin, 1997).

Plamenatz, J., *The English Utilitarians*, 2nd edition (Oxford: Blackwell, 1958).

Plato, (prescribed text) *Republic*, trans. with introduction R. Waterfield (Oxford: University Press, 1994; World's Classics). Plato's other dialogues are all available in editions published by Dent (Everyman) or Penguin, or in the one volume edition of Hamilton and Cairns (Princeton NJ: University Press, 1961).

Polt, R., *Heidegger: An Introduction* (London: UCL Press, 1999).

Popper, K.R., *The Logic of Scientific Discovery* (1934), revised edition (London: Hutchinson, 1972).

Popper, K.R., *The Open Society and its Enemies* (1943), 2 vols, new edition in 1 vol. (London: Routledge, 2000).

Popper, K.R., *Conjectures and Refutations: The Growth of Scientific Knowledge* (1963), 4th revised edition (London: Routledge, 1972).

Popper, K.R., *Objective Knowledge: An Evolutionary Approach* (1972), revised edition (Oxford: University Press, 1979).

Price, H.H., *Thinking and Experience*, 2nd edition (London: Hutchinson, 1969).

Priest, S., *Merleau-Ponty* (London: Routledge, 1998).

Putnam, H., *Mind, Language and Reality: Philosophical Papers*, Vol. 2 (Cambridge: University Press, 1975).

Putnam, H., (prescribed text) *Reason, Truth and History* (Cambridge: University Press, 1981).

Putnam, H., *Reason and Representation* (Cambridge MA: MIT Press, 1991).

Quine, W.V.O., *From a Logical Point of View: Logico-Philosophical Essays* (1953), revised 2nd edition (New York: Harper & Rowe, 1963).

Quine, W.V.O., *Word and Object* (Cambridge, MA: MIT Press, 1960).

Quinton, A. (ed.), *Political Philosophy* (Oxford: University Press, 1967; Oxford Readings).

Quinton, A., *The Nature of Things* (London: Routledge, 1973).

Radhakrishnan, S. and Moore, C.A., *A Source Book in Indian Philosophy* (Princeton NJ: University Press, 1973).

Raphael, D.D., *Problems of Political Philosophy*, revised edition (London: Macmillan, 1976).

Rawls, J., (prescribed text) *A Theory of Justice* (Oxford: University Press, 1972).

Read, H., *The Meaning of Art* (1931) (Harmondsworth: Penguin, 1949).

Redhead, B. (ed.) *Political Thought from Plato to NATO* (London: BBC, 1984).

Richards, I.A., *The Principles of Literary* Criticism (1924) (London: Routledge, 1960).

Richards, I.A., *The Philosophy of Rhetoric* (1936) (Oxford: University Press, 1971).

Ricoeur, P., *Freedom and Nature*, trans. with introduction E.V. Kohák (Evanston IL: Northwestern University, 1966).

Ricoeur, P., *Hermeneutics and the Human Sciences: Essays on language, action and interpretation*, trans. and ed. J.B. Thompson (Cambridge: University Press, 1981).

Ricoeur, P., *The Rule of Metaphor: Multi-disciplinary studies of the creation of meaning in language*, trans. R. Czerny, K. McLaughlin and J. Costello (London: Routledge, 1986).

Rorty, R., *Philosophy and the Mirror of Nature* (Oxford: Blackwell, 1980).

Rosenberg, A., *Philosophy of Science: A Contemporary Introduction* (London: Routledge, 1999).

Ross, G. MacDonald, *Leibniz* (Oxford: University Press, 1984; Past Masters).

Ross, W.D., *Aristotle*, new revised edition, with introduction, J.L. Ackrill (London: Routledge, 1995).

Rousseau, J.-J., (prescribed texts) *The Social Contract* (1752) and *Discourse on the Origin of Equality* (1754), trans. and introduction G.D.H. Cole, revised J.H. Brumfitt and J.C. Hall (London: Dent, 1973; Everyman's Library).

Russell, B., *Philosophical Essays* (1910), revised edition (London: Allen & Unwin, 1966).

Russell, B., (prescribed text) *The Problems of Philosophy* (1912), new edition (Oxford: University Press, 1959).

Russell, B., *The Philosophy of Logical Atomism* (1918), ed. and introduction D. Pears (London: Collins/Fontana, 1972).

Russell, B., *History of Western Philosophy and its Connection with Political and Social Circumstances from the Earliest Times to the Present Day* (1946), 2nd edition (London: Allen & Unwin, 1961).

Russell, B., *Human Knowledge: Its Scope and Limits* (London: Allen & Unwin, 1948).

Ryan, A. (ed.), *The Philosophy of Social Explanation* (Oxford: University Press, 1973; Oxford Readings).

Ryle, G., *The Concept of Mind* (1949) (Harmondsworth: Penguin, 1963).

Ryle, G., *Dilemmas* (Cambridge: University Press, 1954).

Ryle, G. (ed.), *The Revolution in Philosophy* (London: Macmillan, 1956).

Sabine, G.H., *History of Political Theory* (London: Harrap, 1937).

Sainsbury, R.M., *Russell* (London: Routledge, 1979; Arguments of the Philosophers).

Sartre, J.-P., *Being and Nothingness: An Essay on Phenomenological Ontology* (1943), trans. H.E. Barnes, introduction M. Warnock (London: Methuen, 1969).

Sartre, J.-P., (prescribed text) *Existentialism and Humanism* (1946), trans. and introduction P. Mairet (London: Methuen, 1948); there are other editions.

Sartre, J.-P., *Search for a Method* (1960), trans. and introduction H.E. Barnes (New York: Random House).

Scheler, M., *The Place of Man in the Cosmos* (1928), trans. and introduction H. Meyerhoff (New York: Noonday, 1961).

Schiller, J.C.F., *Letters on the Aesthetic Education of Man* (1793–95), trans. E. Wilkinson and L.A. Willoughby (Oxford: University Press, 1989).

Scruton, R., *Art and Imagination: A Study in the Philosophy of Mind* (1974), revised edition (Indiana: St Augustine's Press, 1997).

Scruton, R., *A Short History of Modern Philosophy from Descartes to Wittgenstein* (London: Routledge, 1981; Ark Paperbacks, 1984).

Scruton, R., *The Aesthetic Understanding: Essays in the Philosophy of Art and Culture* (1983), revised edition (Indiana: St Augustine's Press, 1998).

Scruton, R., *Kant* (Oxford: University Press, 1984; Past Masters).

Searle, J.R., *Speech Acts* (Cambridge: University Press, 1969).

Searle, J.R. (ed.), *The Philosophy of Language* (Oxford: University Press, 1971).

Searle, J.R., *Intentionality An Essay in the Philosophy of Mind* (Cambridge: University Press, 1983).

Searle, J.R., *Minds, Brains and Science* (Reith Lectures, 1984) (Harmondsworth: Penguin, 1989).

Searle, J.R., *The Rediscovery of the Mind* (Cambridge MA: MIT Press, 1992).

Searle, J.R., *Mind, Language and Society* (New York: Basic Books, 1998).

Sheppard, A., *Aesthetics: An Introduction to the Philosophy of Art* (Oxford: University Press, 1987).

Singer, P., *Marx* (Oxford: University Press, 1980; Past Masters).

Singer, P., *Hegel* (Oxford: University Press, 1983; Past Masters).

Singer, P. (ed.), *Applied Ethics* (Oxford: University Press, 1986; Oxford Readings).

Smart, J.J.C., *Philosophy and Scientific Realism* (London: Routledge, 1963).

Smart, N., *The Religious Experience of Mankind* (London: Collins/Fontana, 1971).

Sorabji, R., *Necessity, Cause and Blame: Perspectives on Aristotle's Theory* (London: Duckworth, 1980).

Sorrell, T., *Descartes* (Oxford: University Press, 1987; Past Masters).

Sosa, E. and Tooley, M. (eds), *Causation and Conditional* (Oxford: University Press, 1993; Oxford Readings).

Sowell, T., *Marxism: Philosophy and Economics* (London: Unwin, 1986).

Spinoza, B., *Ethics* (1677), trans. G.H.R. Parkinson (London: Dent, 1989; Everyman's Library.

Stace, W.T., *Mysticism and Philosophy* (London: Macmillan, 1961).

Steiner, G., *Heidegger; The Influence and Dissemination of his Thought* (London: Collins, 1978; Fontana Modern Masters).

Stern, J.P., *Nietzsche* (London: Collins, 1978; Fontana Modern Masters).

Strawson, P.F., *Introduction to Logical Theory* (1952) (London: Methuen, 1974).

Strawson, P.F., *Individuals: An Essay in Descriptive Metaphysics* (London: Methuen, 1964).

Strawson, P.F. (ed.), *Philosophical Logic* (Oxford: University Press, 1967; Oxford Readings).

Strawson, P.F., *Freedom and Resentment* (London: Methuen, 1974).

Stroud, B., *Hume* (London: Routledge, 1977; Arguments of the Philosophers).

Swinburne, R., *The Concept of Miracle* (London: Macmillan, 1971).

Swinburne, R., (ed.), *The Justification of Induction* (Oxford: University Press, 1974).

Swinburne, R., *The Coherence of Theism* (Oxford: University Press, 1977).

Swinburne, R., *The Existence of God* (Oxford: University Press, 1979).

Swinburne, R., *Faith and Reason* (Oxford: University Press, 1981).

Taylor, C., *The Explanation of Behaviour* (London: Routledge, 1964).

Taylor, C., (prescribed text) *The Ethics of Authenticity* (Cambridge MA: Harvard University Press, 1992).

Teichmann, J., *The Mind and the Soul: An Introduction to the Philosophy of Mind* (London: Routledge, 1974).

Teilhard de Chardin, P., *The Phenomenon of Man*, trans. B. Wall, introduction Sir Julian Huxley (London: Collins, 1959).

Ten, C.L., *Mill on Liberty* (Oxford: University Press, 1980).

Thomas, W., *Mill* (Oxford: University Press, 1985; Past Masters).

Thompson, J.B., *Critical Hermeneutics: A Study in the Thought of Paul Ricoeur and Jürgen Habermas* (Cambridge: University Press, 1981).

Tolstoy, L., *What is Art?*, trans. A. Maude (London: Scott, 1898).

Toulmin, S.E., *An Examination of the Place of Reason in Ethics* (Cambridge: University Press, 1950).

Toulmin, S.E., *The Philosophy of Science* (London: Hutchinson, 1953).

Toulmin, S.E., *The Uses of Argument* (Cambridge: University Press, 1958).

Trusted, J., *The Logic of Scientific Inference* (London: Macmillan, 1979).

Trusted, J., *Free Will and Responsibility* (Oxford: University Press, 1984).

Tuck, R., *Hobbes* (Oxford: University Press, 1989; Past Masters).

Urmson, J.O., *Berkeley* (Oxford: University Press, 1982; Past Masters).

Van Fraassen, B., *The Scientific Image* (Oxford: University Press, 1980).

Vlastos, G. (ed.), *Platonic Studies*, Vol. I, *Metaphysics and Epistemology*; Vol. II, *Ethics, Politics, and Philosophy of Art and Religion* (New York: Doubleday, 1971).

Vygotsky, L.S., *Thought and Language* (1934), revised edition, trans. and ed. A. Kozulin (Cambridge MA: MIT Press, 1986).

Wachterhauser, B.R. (ed.), *Hermeneutics and Modern Philosophy* (New York: SUNY Press, 1986).

Walker, R.C.S., *Kant* (London: Routledge, 1978; Arguments of the Philosophers).

Warnke, G., *Gadamer: Hermeneutics, Tradition and Reason* (Cambridge: Polity Press, 1987).

Warnock, G.J., *English Philosophy since 1900*, 2nd edition (Oxford: University Press, 1969).

Warnock, G.J., *Berkeley* (1953); reprint with additions (Oxford: Blackwell, 1982).

Warnock, M., *The Philosophy of Sartre* (London: Hutchinson, 1965).

Warnock, M., *Ethics since 1900*, 3rd edition (Oxford: University Press, 1968).

Watson, G. (ed.), *Free Will* (Oxford: University Press, 1982; Oxford Readings).

Watts, A.W., *The Way of Zen* (Harmondsworth: Penguin, 1962).

White, A.R. (ed.), *The Philosophy of Action* (Oxford: University Press, 1968; Oxford Readings).

White, L.A., *The Evolution of Culture* (New York: McGraw-Hill, 1959).

Whitehead, A.N., *Process and Reality* (1929), corrected edition D.R. Griffin and D.W. Sherburne (New York: The Free Press/Macmillan, 1979).

Whorf, B.L., *Language, Thought and Reality*, ed. and introduction J.B. Carroll (Cambridge MA: MIT Press, 1956).

Williams, B., *Morality: An Introduction to Ethics* (1972), reissue (Cambridge: University Press, 1976).

Williams, B., *Descartes: The Project of Pure Enquiry* (Harmondsworth: Penguin, 1978).

Willams, B. *Ethics and the Limits of Philosophy* (London: Collins/Fontana, 1985).

Wilson, E.O., *On Human Nature* (1978) (Harmondsworth: Penguin, 1995).

Wilson, E.O., *Consilience: The Unity of Human Knowledge* (New York: Random House, 1998).

Winch, P., *The Idea of a Social Science* (London: Routledge, 1958).

Wisdom J.O., *Foundations of Inference in Natural Science* (London: Methuen, 1952).

Wittgenstein, L., *Tractatus Logico-Philosophicus* (1921), revised edition trans. D.F. Pears and B.F. McGuinness, introduction B. Russell (London: Routledge, 1961, 1974).

Wittgenstein, L., (prescribed text) *The Blue and Brown Books* (1933–34) (Oxford: Blackwell, 1958).

Wittgenstein, L., *Lectures and Conversations on Aesthetics, Psychology and Religious Belief* (1938) ed. C. Barrett (Oxford: Blackwell, 1966).

Wittgenstein, L. *On Certainty* (1949–51), ed. G.G.M. Anscombe and G.H. von Wright, trans. D. Paul and G.E.M. Anscombe (Oxford: Blackwell, 1960).

Wittgenstein, L., *Philosophical Investigations* (1958), 3rd edition, trans. G.E.M. Anscombe (Oxford: Blackwell, 1967).

Wokler, R., *Rousseau* (Oxford: University Press, 1990; Past Masters).

Wolff, J., A*n Introduction to Political Philosophy* (Oxford: University Press, 1996).

Wollheim, R., *Art and its Objects*, 2nd edition (Cambridge: University Press, 1980).

Yandell, K.E., *Philosophy of Religion: A Contemporary Introduction* (London: Routledge, 1998).

Yolton, J., *Locke: an Introduction* (Oxford: Blackwell, 1980).

Young, J.Z., *An Introduction to the Study of Man* (Oxford: University Press, 1971).

Young, J.Z., *Philosophy and the Brain* (Oxford: University Press, 1988).

Yu-Lan, Fung, *A History of Chinese Philosophy*, trans. D. Bodde, 2 vols (Princeton NJ: University Press, 1952–53).

*Note also there are many other books – on philosophers or fields of philosophy – in the 'Cambridge Companion', 'Arguments of the Philosophers' and 'Oxford Readings' series but not listed above, and which you will find to be of great assistance in your further study of philosophy.

Index of names

A

Adorno, T. 266
Alexeev, V.P. 423
Anaxagoras 56
Anaximander 55
Anaximines 55
Anscombe, G.E.M. 410
Anselm, St 300–1, 314, 456
Aquinas, St Thomas 247, 298–9, 302, 303, 306, 308, 310, 311–12, 314, 316, 339, 345, 350, 351, 377, 406, 453, 454, 458
Arendt, H. 406–7, 419
Aristotle 2, 11, 12, 32, 45, 58, 93–118, 123, 134, 186, 203, 222, 246, 256, 269, 302, 325, 330, 339, 344, 345, 347, 350, 351, 353, 362, 376, 380, 397, 405, 415, 449, 453, 457, 458
Arnold, M. 335
Atomists 4, 56, 161
Augustine, St 5, 247, 351
Austin, J.L. 5, 44, 46, 148, 418
Avicenna (Ibn Sina) 351
Ayer, A.J. 1, 123, 132, 134–5, 137, 138, 156, 159, 164, 170–2, 175–6, 296, 332, 340–1, 359, 365, 372, 380, 381–2, 454, 455, 456

B

Bacon, F. 149, 275, 276
Beethoven, L. van 326, 328
Bell, C. 329, 330
Bentham, J. 198, 203
Berkeley, G. 1, 2, 162–3, 168, 170, 344, 345, 351–2, 354, 372, 453, 455, 456, 457
Berlin, I. 245
Boas, F. 361
Boole, G. 29
Boyle, R. 161
Bracken, H. 162
Bradley, F.H. 1, 149, 150, 339, 369, 454
Braithwaite, R.B. 38, 277
Brentano, F. 369
Bridgman, P.W. 279, 456
Buber, M. 313
Buddha (Siddhārtha Gotama) 440–1
Burke, E. 333
Burnet, J. 58

C

Campbell, N.R. 281
Cassirer, E. 406, 407, 408, 426–7, 433
Cézanne, P. 329, 330
Chomsky, N. 430
Cicero 249
Coleridge, S.T. 327, 328
Collingwood, R.G. 326–8, 331
Confucius 439, 440
Constable, J. 325
Croce, B. 326

D

Dalton, J. 4, 387
Darwin, C. 50, 306
Davidson, D. 152, 373, 375, 410
Dawkins, R. 386
Debussy, C. 326
Derrida, J. 346, 362–5, 457
Descartes, R. 2, 123, 124–8, 134, 140, 143, 144, 145, 161, 178, 301, 302–3, 339, 344, 345, 369, 370–1, 376, 388–9, 390, 391, 449, 453, 456, 457
Devlin, P. 235
Dewey, J. 153, 154
Dilthey, W. 405–6, 415
Dray, W. 412–13
Dummett, M. 346, 360, 457

E

Eddington, A.S. 279
Edelman, G.M. 429–30, 431
Einstein, A. 286, 289, 386
Eliot, T.S. 295
Empedocles 66
Engels, F. 261–2, 422–3, 453
Epicurus 4
Eudoxus 116

F

Feuerbach, L.A. 261–2
Feyerabend, P.K. 39, 291, 346, 360–1, 457
Flaubert, G. 269, 326
Fodor, J. 373, 454
Frege, G. 18, 349
Freud, S. 208, 377–8, 392, 406, 418, 421
Fry, R. 329, 330

◪ Index of subjects

A

Abortion   234–5

Absolute, the   62, 68–71, 153, 261, 308, 372, 416, 441, 452 (*see also* Mind, Monism, Realism)

Abstract ideas   *see* Ideas

Abstractionism (art)   326

Action   Ch. 12.3, 3, 5, 73, 108, 112 ff., 175, 356, 373, 378, 382, 384, 388–96 *passim*, 407–8, 412–14, 417–19, 420, 421, 453

  goodness/rightness of   *see* Ch. 6 (Ethics) *passim*

  karma (Indian philosophy)   438, 443, 444, 446, 447, 448, 455

  wu-wei ('non-action')   440

Actuality and potentiality (Aristotle)   99, 101, 104

Advaita   *see* Indian philosophy – Vedānta

Aesthetics   *see* Art

Agent/agency   *see* Action

Alienation   261, 263, 265, 269, 431, 452

Altruism   200, 203, 214, 233, 240, 259 (*see also* Benevolence)

Analogy   25, 36, 176, 281, 298–9 (*see also* Models)

Analysis – linguistic   *see* Language

Analytic–synthetic propositions   21, 135–8, 301, 452, 457 (*see also* Knowledge – *a priori–a posteriori*)

Anguish (existential)   212, 313, 356

Animals   36, 406, 427–8, 431

  rights   237–9

Anthropic principle   307

Anthropology – philosophical   Ch. 12, 269–70 (*see also* Man)

Appearance (and illusion) (Indian philosophy – *māyā*)   441, 442, 446, 447; (Plato)   Ch. 3 *passim*, esp. 3.5; (other)   160, 167–9

a priori–a posteriori   *see* Knowledge

Arguments   *see* Deduction, Induction, Syllogism

Art(s) (and aesthetics)   Ch. 10, 83, 112, 267, 315 (*see also* Beauty, Expression, Feeling, Form)

Artificial intelligence   378–9

Association of ideas   *see* Ideas

Ātman   *see* Self

Atoms/Atomic Theory   4, 56, 165, 166

Authenticity (Sartre)   Ch. 6.6 *passim*

Authority   Ch. 7.2, 245

Autonomy and heteronomy (Kant)   Ch. 6.3 (*see also* Freedom)

B

Beauty   Ch. 10.3, 58, 62, 68, 83, 98, 191

Behaviourism   145–8, 172–5, 374–5, 377, 413, 452 (*see also* Dispositions, Reduction)

Being   *see* Ontology

Belief (Plato)   Ch. 3.5 *passim*, 62, 63–4, 66–7; (Hume)   130, 132; (Russell)   Ch. 5.5 *passim*; (other)   101, 123, 146, 148, 156–7

  suspension of (*epoche* and 'bracketing' – Husserl)   124, 178, 179, 404

Benevolence   81, 188, 190, 192

Bhakti (devotion)   438, 448

Brahman   *see* God – Indian philosophy

Buddhism/Buddhist philosophy   228, 237, 295, 304, 307, 315, 440

  Mādhyamika   441–2

  T'ien-t'ai   442

  Zen/ch'an   442

C

Categorical imperative   *see* Imperatives

Categories/types (Aristotle)   97, 99, 452; (Indian philosophy)   443, 445, 447, 448; (Kant)   135, 166, 382, 452, 454; (other)   367, 429

Category mistake (Ryle)   43, 145, 170, 240, 353, 452 (*see also* Language – analysis)

Causal theory   *see* Perception

Causation/cause and effect   Ch. 11.4; (Hume)   37, 129–30, 133, 379–82; (Indian philosophy)   442, 443, 444, 446, 447, 448; (Kant)   136, 382; (other)   55, 302–4, 305, 404, 411

Empiricism/experience (*continued*)
296; (Berkeley) 162–3; (Hume) Ch.
5.3; (Kant) Ch. 5.4 *passim*; (Locke)
161–2; (Plato) Ch. 3.5 *passim*; (Russell)
Ch. 5.5, 160–1; (Ryle) 172–4 *passim*;
(other) 1, 126, 134, 263, 454 (*see also*
Knowledge, Perception, Sensa)
Ends (ethics) *see* Teleology
Enlightenment (Indian philosophy) *see*
Soul
Entailment (logic) *see* Implication
Entelechy 102–4, 454
Environment 11, 239–40
Epistemology *see* Knowledge
Epoche see Belief
Equality 245; (Mill) 255–8; (Rawls) 258–
60
Essence/essentiality 4, 99, 161, 178, 179,
305, 347, 348–50, 352, 357, 363, 405, 454,
457
Ethics (Aristotle) Ch. 4.6; (Ayer) 214–17;
(Hare) 217–24; (Hume) Ch. 6.2;
(Kant) Ch. 6.3; (Mill) Ch. 6.4;
(Nietzsche) Ch. 6.5; (Sartre) Ch. 6.6;
(other) 5, 10, 49, 56–7, 58, 315, 334, 454
Buddhist ethics 440–1
'discourse ethics' (Habermas) 418–19
(*see also* Evil, Good, Responsibility,
Virtue)
and language (Ayer) 214–17; (Hare)
217–20 (*see also* Fact and value)
practical/applied ethics Ch. 6.8
Eudaimonia ('well-being') *see* Happiness
Euthanasia 233–4
Evil 5, 207, 318–20, 388 (*see also* Good)
Evolution 50, 306, 393, 427, 430, 433
Existence Ch. 11.2, 62, 70, 98, 179, 211,
298, 299, 305, 343, 353, 366 (*see also*
Essence, Ontology, Realism)
of God *see* God
Existential import 31–2
Existentialism/existentiality (Sartre) Ch.
6.6, 269–70, 377, 390–1; (other) 2, 3,
177, 313, 356, 449, 454
Experience
moral *see* Feeling – moral
religious and mystical 308–9, 343, 439
(*see also* God)
sense *see* Empiricism
Experiment 276, 279, 281, 283, 286
Explanation (Aristotle) 95–6, 100 (*see also*
Action, Causation, Hermeneutics,
Methodology, Understanding)
human sciences/action Ch. 12.4, 410–
11, 415, 420, 421, 424–5, 433

natural sciences Ch. 8.2, 317–18, 373,
375, 424–5
Expression/expressionism (art) 326–8, 331

F
Fact and value 187, 192–3, 220–1, 222, 223–
4 (*see also* Naturalism)
Facts (Russell) Ch. 5.5 *passim*, 150–2;
(other) 37, 129
Faith Ch. 9.4, Ch. 9.5, 1, 5
'bad faith' (Sartre) 211–12, 268, 390
Fallacies Ch. 2.4 *passim*, Ch. 2.13, 23
naturalistic fallacy *see* Naturalism –
naturalistic fallacy
Falsification/falsifiability 280, 286, 341, 421
Fatalism 396–8, 454 (*see also* Determinism)
Feeling
art 188, 326–8, 329, 331
moral/social (Hume) Ch. 6.2; (other)
188, 196, 199, 200, 202, 431, 455
religious 295, 315
Figures *see* Syllogism
Form
art 328–30, 331
logic/grammar Ch. 2.10, 13, 20, 23–4
metaphysics (Aristotle) 95, 99–100, 101,
102, 103, 347, 350; (Plato) Ch. 3.5,
Ch. 3.6, 58, 97–8, 100, 102, 123, 325, 350,
454; (Kant) 135, 136, 166, 452, 454 (*see
also* Definition, Intuition, Matter,
Universals)
Formalism (art) *see* Form
Freedom/free-will/self-determinism
metaphysical Ch. 11.5; (Descartes)
388–9, 391; (Hobbes) 388; (Hume)
389; (Kant) 389, 391; (Sartre) 211–12,
271, 390–1, 392; (Searle) 392–3; (other)
5, 196, 208, 305, 333, 340, 350, 378, 387,
394, 397, 404, 411, 420, 422, 426, 430,
453, 454 (*see also* Causation,
Determinism, Necessity)
political (Habermas) 418–19, 420; (Mill)
203, 253–5; (Rawls) 258–61; (other)
245, 250–1
Function *see* Teleology
Functionalism
anthropology 423–6
mind 373–4, 454

G
God/prime mover/first cause Ch. 9
passim, 4, 71, 83, 103, 153–4, 163, 170,
195, 198, 200, 206, 208, 211, 227, 232,
234, 252, 305, 340, 345, 372, 386–7, 397–
8, 406, 454

arguments for God's existence   Ch. 9.3,
    126
    cosmological   302–4, 307, 444, 453
    moral   198, 310, 313
    ontological   300–2, 305, 307, 456
    pragmatic   309–10
    religious experience   308–9
    teleological   305–8, 444, 458
Indian philosophy   437, 438, 446–7,
    448
Good   Ch. 6 *passim*; (Aristotle)   Ch. 4.6,
    Ch. 4.9; (Hare)   218 ff.; (Hobbes)   248;
    (Hume)   Ch. 6.2 *passim*; (Kant)   194,
    198; (Mill)   Ch. 6.4 *passim*; (Nietzsche)
    Ch. 6.5 *passim*; (Plato)   Ch. 3.6, 83, 84,
    85, 299, 332; (Sartre)   Ch. 6.6 *passim*;
    (other)   156–7, 187, 229, 320, 455
Grammar ('logical')   *see* Language – rules

H

Happiness (Aristotle)   Ch. 4.6, Ch. 4.9;
    (Hume)   191–3; (Kant)   194, 198;
    (Mill)   Ch. 6.4 *passim*, 229; (Plato)
    Ch. 3.12; (other)   224, 237 (*see also*
    Pleasure)
Hermeneutics   3, 46, 414–18, 419, 421,
    454
Hinduism   304, 307, 315, 318, 437
History/historicity (and constraints)   212,
    262, 268, 356, 415–16, 419
Hypothesis   276, 282–8, 309, 341 (*see also*
    Explanation, Methodology)
Hypothetical imperative   *see* Imperatives

I

Idealism   1, 56, 149, 162, 166, 170, 178, 262,
    263, 372, 449, 454
    cultural idealism   426–7
Idealist theory (perception)   *see*
    Perception
Ideas (Berkeley)   162–3, 454; (Descartes)
    Ch. 5.2, 454; (Hume)   Ch. 5.3, 454;
    (Locke)   161–2, 340, 454; (Plato)   *see*
    Form (*see also* Concepts, Sensa,
    Universals)
    abstract   351, 454
    association (Hume)   129, 352
    clear and distinct (Descartes)   126, 127
    innate   *see* Knowledge
    'regulative' 'Ideas' (Kant)   196–7, 340,
    454
    relations between (Hume)   129 (*see also*
    Logic)
Identity
    logical/metaphysical   348–9

personal   171–4, 371, 391, 441 (*see also*
    Self)
Identity theory/central state materialism
    (mind)   372
Ideology   418, 419–20, 453 (*see also*
    Marxism)
Illusion   *see* Appearance
Images/imagination   101, 125, 126, 220,
    283, 327, 333, 380
Imitation   68, 325, 331
Immortality   *see* Soul
Imperatives (Kant)   Ch. 6.3, 199, 202, 227,
    229–30, 251, 389, 452 (*see also*
    Prescriptivity)
Implication (logic)   13, 19, 20, 22, 26
Impressions (sensory)   *see* Sensa
Indeterminism   385, 387, 389, 390 (*see also*
    Determinism, Freedom, Necessity)
Indian philosophy   Ch. 13.1, Ch. 13.4, 440–3
    Nyāya–Vaiśeṣika   443–4
    Pūrva–Mīmāṃsā   445–6
    Sāṁkhya–Yoga   444–5
    Vedānta   446–9
Individualism (Mill)   Ch. 7.3 *passim*;
    (Nietzsche)   Ch. 6.5 *passim*; (other)
    336, 439
Induction/inductive method   Ch. 2.9, 11,
    58, 133, 134, 141, 276, 277, 283, 286, 287,
    288, 444, 455
    Goodman's 'riddle'   285
Inference   Ch. 2.3, Ch. 2.4, Ch. 2.5
    passim, 13, 34 (*see also* Deduction,
    Methodology)
    rules of inference   25–6, 28–9
Instinct   130, 208, 226, 406, 410, 427 (*see
    also* Unconscious)
Instrumentalism (science)   280, 455
Intellect   104, 351, 376
Intelligence (artificial)   378–9
Intension   *see* Meaning
Intention   46, 47, 96, 109, 147, 148, 194–5,
    229, 335, 373, 383, 392–3, 408–9, 418
Intentionality   178, 179, 356, 369, 370,
    374, 375, 378, 383, 384, 390, 392, 409,
    414, 431, 455
Interpretation   *see* Hermeneutics
Introspection   125, 173, 174 (*see also*
    Consciousness, Self)
Intuition(ism)
    epistemology   124, 125, 129, 134, 136,
    140, 144, 166–7, 178, 363
    ethics   188, 199, 202, 215, 455 (*see also*
    Feeling)
    science   283
Islam   186, 226, 227, 295, 297, 315, 437

Is-ought arguments   *see* Fact and value,
  Naturalism – naturalistic fallacy
Īśvara   see God – Indian philosophy

J

Judaism   295, 297, 298, 313, 315
Judgement
  aesthetics   Ch. 10.3 *passim*
  epistemology (Kant)   135–6; (Plato)   64,
    66, 70; (Russell)   Ch. 5.5 *passim*, 152
  ethics   Ch. 6 *passim*; (Ayer)   214–17;
    (Hare)   217–21; (Kant)   194–7
Justice
  cosmic   55
  moral/political (Aristotle)   Ch. 4.7;
    (Hume)   189, 192; (Mill)   201–2, 255–
    8; (Plato/Socrates)   Ch. 3.8, Ch. 3.9, 58,
    59, 62; (Rawls)   258–61; (other)   245,
    256, 418 (*see also* Virtue)

K

Karma   see Action
Knowledge (*see also* Belief, Certainty,
    Scepticism) (Aristotle)   Ch. 3.5, 62,
    63–7, 69; (Descartes)   Ch. 5.2; (Hume)
    Ch. 5.3; (Kant)   Ch. 5.4; (Russell)
    Ch. 5.5; (Ryle)   145–8
  a priori–a posteriori   102, 129, 134, 135,
    137–9, 141, 332, 340, 349, 359, 452
  control of nature   206
  dispositional theory   145–8
  external world   Ch. 5.10
  innate   64–5, 101, 126, 128, 129, 134,
    302
  justification   Chs 5.1–5.6 and 5.8 *passim*;
    (in Indian philosophy)   444, 445, 447,
    448
  limits   2, 136
  of others   175–7, 212
  performatory theory   148
  scientific   Ch. 8.4 *passim*, 1, 165–6,
  self   Ch. 5.2, Ch. 5.11, 59, 139–40, 145–8,
    212

L

Labour   262–4, 407, 417, 418, 423, 425
Language
  analysis (Russell, Wittgenstein)
    ('ideal'/'logically perfect' language)   2,
    12, 21–3, 31–2, 33, 41–4, 343, 366;
    ('ordinary' language/conceptual
    revision)   Ch. 2.10, Ch. 2.11, 2, 3, 6, 46,
    169, 173, 343–4, 353–4, 366, 367, 396,
    442, 449
  and culture   432–3
  and ethics (Ayer and Hare)   Ch. 6.7, 418

  origin and nature   250, 262, 366, 406,
    408, 426–7, 428–33
  private/public   41–2, 128, 132, 143 (*see
    also* rules – below)
  and reality/Being (Derrida)   363–5;
    (Gadamer)   416; (Heidegger)   358–9;
    (other)   359–62 (*see also* Realism)
  reduction   164–5, 341, 342, 360, 365
  religious   Ch. 9.2
  rules and language 'games'/'forms of life'
    297, 314, 334, 335, 344, 349, 353–4, 382–
    3, 429
  and thought/concepts   428–32
  translation   361–2, 366–7
  and truth/value standards   418–19 (*see
    also* Hermeneutics)
Law(s)
  moral (Kant)   194–6, 229, 297
  'natural'   247, 248, 256, 265, 316–17
  scientific   Ch. 8.3, 38, 276, 277–8, 373,
    384, 387, 411, 424
  social/political   57, 118, 246–7, 249, 251,
    254, 257–8, 260
Liberty   *see* Freedom – political
'Life-world' (Husserl)   *see* Community
Literature   Ch. 10 *passim*, 46, 83, 415–16,
    420–1
Logic (*see also* Class, Deduction, Induction,
    Language, Proposition, Relations)
  Aristotelian (logic of terms)   Chs 2.2 to
    2.4
  formal   Chs 2.2 to 2.8
  informal   Chs 2.9 to 2.11, 35
  'laws of thought'   138, 141, 142
  modal   32, 349
  symbolic ('modern')   Chs 2.5 to 2.8

M

Man   Ch. 12.2, 45, 57, 103, 107, 119, 188,
    211, 248, 268–70; (Chinese/Indian
    philosophy)   439, 441 (*see also*
    Anthropology – philosophical)
  the 'human condition'   3, 250, 313, 335,
    359, 407, 416
Marxism   Ch. 7.4, 2, 3, 49, 251, 334, 406,
    417, 418, 449; (Sartre's)   267–71 (*see
    also* Ideology)
Material object   161–8 *passim*, 175, 348–9,
    365 (*see also* Substance)
Materialism   56, 248, 388, 455
  central state   *see* Mind
  dialectical (Marx)   Ch. 7.5, 3, 287, 422–3,
    453
Mathematics   56, 63, 64, 84, 129, 134, 136,
    138, 142, 283, 285, 300, 360 (*see also*
    Deduction, Logic)

Matter (Aristotle)   95, 98–100, 347 (*see also*
   Form)
Māyā   see Appearance
Mean/moderation (Aristotle)   108–10;
   (Confucius)   439
Meaning (logic and language)   22–3
   causal reference theory   349
   denotation and 'picturing' theory   41–2,
      43, 343, 353, 429
   naming   349, 432 (*see also* Nominalism)
   phenomenology   375, 404, 405, 420–1
      (*see also* Hermeneutics, Understanding)
   structuralism   361, 363–4, 365
   truth-conditions   360
   'use' theory   41, 343, 353, 429
   verification theory   296, 455
Memory   75, 127, 140, 141, 171–2
Mental states   *see* Mind
Metaphysics (Aristotle)   Ch. 4.3; (Ayer)
      340–2; (Hume)   131, 132; (Kant)
      135, 136, 307, 340; (Wittgenstein)
      342–4; (other)   Ch. 11, 1, 295,
      455
   descriptive and revisionary (Strawson)
      2, 344–5, 365, 366
Methodology (*see also* Causation,
   Explanation, Science)
   Mill's methods   37 (*see also* Induction)
   phenomenological   179, 356
Mind (*see also* the Absolute, Self)   Ch. 11.3
      passim, 5, 56, 416, 442, 455, 457
   knowledge of (Aristotle)   Ch. 4.5;
      (Berkeley)   162; (Descartes)   170, 369,
      370–2; (Merleau-Ponty)   179–80;
      (Plato)   Ch. 3.7; (Ryle)   145–8
   mental states   369–74 *passim*, 378, 454
      (*see also* Belief, Desire)
Miracles   315–18, 319, 386
Modal logic   *see* Logic
Models (scientific)   281–2 (*see also* Analogy)
Mokṣa   see Soul – enlightenment
Monism (and the 'One')   55, 68, 71, 308,
      372, 395, 437, 438, 455
   anomalous   373
   materialistic   388, 392
   naturalistic   392
   the one and the many   55, 56, 70, 95
Moods   *see* Syllogism
Morality   *see* Ethics
Motion   *see* Change
Motives   5, 96, 108–9, 113, 147, 229, 388,
      389, 390–1, 410, 412, 422 (*see also*
      Causation – causes and reasons, Desire)
Murder   226–8
Mysticism   *see* Experience – religious
Mythology   55, 363

N

Naïve realism theory   *see* Perception
Names   *see* Meaning, Reference
Naturalism
   biological   374–5, 455 (*see also*
      Explanation)
   ethics   187, 215, 217, 224
   naturalistic fallacy   187, 203, 455 (*see also*
      Fact and value)
Nature (Aristotle)   Ch. 4.2; (Indian
      philosophy – *prakṛti*)   444–8 *passim*;
      (Spinoza)   305, 320, 372; (other)   4,
      239–40, 261, 263, 267, 363
   laws of   *see* Law(s)
   'state of nature' (Hobbes)   248–50, 256,
      262
   uniformity   38 (*see also* Methodology,
      Science)
Necessity
   logical   20, 22, 32, 134, 138, 142, 392
   metaphysical   71, 100, 302, 307, 320, 382,
      385, 389 (*see also* Chance, Modal logic)
Needs (human)   256–7, 269, 375, 423–6,
      427, 431, 432, 433
Nirvana   see Soul – enlightenment
Nominalism   352–3, 455
Noumena-phenomena (Kant)   135, 167,
      194, 196, 333, 342, 345–6, 359, 389, 456
Nyāya–Vaiśeṣika   *see* Indian philosophy

O

Objectivity   *see* Realism, Truth
Obligation   *see* Deontology
Observation (science)   276, 279, 280, 284
   observation statements   341–2
Occasionalism   170
One, the   *see* Absolute, Monism, Realism
One and many   *see* Monism
Ontological argument   *see* God –
   arguments for existence
Ontology (and being) (Heidegger – *Dasein*)
      355–9; (other)   56, 71, 97, 345, 366–7,
      456 (*see also* Absolute, God, Realism)
Operationalism   279–80, 456
Opinion   *see* Belief
Opposition, square of (logic)   15, 32

P

Pacifism   186, 232, 260
Pantheism   307 (*see also* God)
Paradigm   289–91, 360 (*see also* Analogy,
   Models)
Parallelism (mind-body)   371
Perception (Aristotle)   101, 102, 103; (Ayer)
      164–5; (Berkeley)   162–3; (Descartes)
      127, 128; (Hume)   128–9; (Kant)   166–

Perception (*continued*)
7; (Locke) 161–2; (Plato) 64, 66, 75;
(Russell) 139–40, 160–1; (other) 57,
187, 374 (*see also* Experience – sense,
Knowledge, Sensa)
causal theory 160–1, 457
idealist theory 162–3
naïve realism 160, 457
phenomenalism 164–5
representative theory 161–2, 351, 445;
(Indian philosophy) 457
scientific realism 165–6, 457
transcendental idealism 166–7
Perfectibility 250, 256
Performatives 46, 148, 155
Person *see* Self
Phenomena-noumena *see* Noumena-
phenomena
Phenomenalism 164–5, 456
linguistic (Ayer) 164, 171, 174, 177, 216,
342, 372, 456
Phenomenology 2, 3, 177, 356, 374–5, 404–
5, 420, 421, 449, 454, 456
Physical object *see* Material object
Pleasure (Aristotle) Ch. 4.9; (Mill) Ch. 6.4
passim; (other) 68, 72, 87, 88, 89, 190,
333
Political philosophy (Aristotle) Ch. 4.10;
(Hobbes) 248; (Locke) 248–9; (Marx)
Ch. 7.4; (Mill) Ch. 7.3; (Plato) Ch.
3.4, Ch. 3.10, Ch. 3.11; (Rawls) 258–60;
(Rousseau) 249–52; (Sartre) 267–71
(*see also* Society, the State)
Positivism (incl. logical positivism) (Ayer)
Ch. 5.4, Ch. 5.11 *passim*, 341, 359;
(other) 279, 287, 296, 300, 315, 360,
372, 455 (*see also* Meaning – verification
theory)
Possibility
logic 32
metaphysics 302
Potentiality *see* Actuality and potentiality
Pragmatic argument *see* God – arguments
for existence
Pragmatism (James) 153–4, 449;
(Nietzsche) Ch. 6.5 *passim*; (other)
59, 360, 367, 422, 449 (*see also* Truth,
Utilitarianism)
'transcendental pragmatism' (Habermas)
418, 421
Prakṛti (Indian philosophy) *see* Nature
Pramāṇas (validation methods – Indian
philosophy) *see* Knowledge –
justification
Praxis/project (Sartre) 269–70, 456

Predicate logic *see* Proposition – logic of
propositional functions
Predication *see* Subject-predicate
Prediction 38, 276, 284, 395 (*see also*
Confirmation, Covering law theory)
Prescriptivity (Hare) 217, 218, 220–4 *passim*
Principles (*see also* Rules)
first (cosmic) principles/'elements' 55–6,
71, 95, 123, 134, 350; (Chinese and Indian
philosophy) 440, 443, 444, 445 (*see also*
Causation – causes and reasons)
scientific Ch. 8 *passim*, 411, 412–14 (*see
also* Law(s))
Privacy Ch. 5.11 *passim*, 369, 370 (*see also*
Language – private)
Probability 38, 130, 132, 277–8, 287, 316
Progress (science) *see* Truth –
verisimilitude
Proposition Ch. 2.2 (*see also* Terms)
logic of propositional functions (predicate
logic) Ch. 2.6
logic of propositions (truth-functional
logic) Ch. 2.5
propositions and 'picturing'
(Wittgenstein) 342–3
quality 14
quantity/quantification 14, 28–9
relations between Ch. 2.3
Psychology 4, 5, 215, 456 (*see also* Mind,
Self, Soul)
Punishment 200, 207–8, 250
capital 228–9
Purpose *see* Causation – causes and
reasons, Teleology
Puruṣa (Indian philosophy) *see* Soul
Pūrva–Mīmāṁsā *see* Indian philosophy

Q
Qualities Ch. 11.5 *passim*, 4, 97, 140, 298,
299–300, (*see also* Categories, Subject-
predicate)
primary and secondary 161–2, 347, 457
quality (logic) *see* Proposition
Quantity *see* Proposition

R
Rationalism 1, 126, 134, 202, 305, 454, 456
(*see also* Reason)
Realism/the 'Real' (*see also* Absolute, God,
Metaphysics, Ontology) (Indian
philosophy) Ch. 11.2, 443, 445, 448;
(Plato) Ch. 3.5; (other) 1, 5, 55, 151,
153, 155, 157, 165, 166–9, 275, 325,
342–5, 350, 355, 359, 365–8, 441, 457
'antirealism' 206, 345, 346, 360–8, 457

internal (Putnam)   367–8

naïve   *see* Perception

Reason (Aristotle)   Ch. 4.3, Ch. 4.5 *passim*,
    111, 112, 415; (Descartes)   Ch. 5.2, 128;
    (Kant)   Ch. 6.3, 340, 343, 376; (other)
    3, 368, 373, 375, 417–19, 422, 453 (*see
    also* Metaphysics, Rationalism,
    Understanding)

normative rationality theory (Putnam)
    155–6

reason versus passion (Hume)   191–2

Reduction(ism)

'behavioural'/'epistemological'
    (perception, mind) (Ayer, Ryle)   146–7,
    172–4, 372–3, 411, 412 (*see also*
    Phenomenalism)

ethics   216

'scientific' (culture/biology)   425, 456,
    457 (*see also* Covering law theory,
    Operationalism)

transcendental (phenomenology)   2, 178,
    374 (*see also* Belief – suspension of)

Redundancy theory   *see* Truth

Reference   41–2, 143, 343, 349, 353, 355,
    360, 365, 447 (*see also* Meaning)

Regularity   380–2, 389 (*see also* Law(s) –
    scientific)

Reincarnation   *see* Soul

Relations   37, 134, 140

logic of   Ch. 2.8

Relativism   57, 155, 290, 346, 367, 368, 415

ethics   59, 186–7, 205, 236, 248

Religion   262, 263, 334, 426

philosophy of   Ch. 9

ren/jen (Chinese philosophy)   *see* Man

Representative theory   *see* Perception

Resentment (Nietzsche)   206–7

Responsibility (Aristotle)   Ch. 4.8; (Sartre)
    211–12; (other)   175, 222, 229, 239, 320,
    388, 391, 395, 410, 443, 454 (*see also*
    Will/volition – weakness)

Revolution

political   265, 334

scientific   289

Rhetoric   Ch. 2.12, 11

Rights   234, 235, 248, 250, 255, 265

animal   36, 237–9

Rules

aesthetics   330, 334

ethics (Hare)   220–1; (Kant)   193–9
    passim; (Mill, Rawls)   204; (other)
    248, 253

language   *see* Language – rules and
    language games

logic   Chs 2.2 to 2.8 *passim*, 206 (*see also*
    logic – Laws of thought)

S

Sāṁkhya–Yoga   *see* Indian philosophy

Saṁsāra   *see* Soul – reincarnation/
    transmigration

Scepticism (Descartes – methodological)
    Ch. 5.2; (other)   124, 135, 136, 164, 457

Science

natural   1, 4, 5, 11, 162, 165–7, 404, 416,
    417–18

philosophy of   Ch. 8

social/human   Ch. 12.4, 404, 405, 417–18,
    421 (*see also* Critical theory,
    Explanation, Hermeneutics, Knowledge,
    Methodology)

Scientific realism   *see* Perception

Self (Descartes)   125–7, 169–72; (Hume)
    192; (Indian philosophy – *ātman*,
    manas)   438–48 *passim*; (Kant)   170;
    (Ryle)   172–5; (Sartre)   179–80 (*see
    also* Knowledge, Soul)

self and other   177–80, 313, 363, 390, 430,
    431 (*see also* Community)

solipsism   175

Sensa (impressions, sensations, sense data,
    sensibilia)   Ch. 5.3 *passim*, 37, 132,
    134, 135, 139–40, 142, 147, 161, 162–3,
    164, 176, 188, 342, 343, 359, 457 (*see also*
    Empiricism, Ideas, Perception,
    Qualities)

Sense   *see* Meaning

moral   *see* Feeling

Sentiment   *see* Feeling

Simplicity (in explanation)   285–6, 287, 433

Śiva   *see* God – Indian philosophy

Social contract   *see* Contract

Social sciences   *see* Science

Society (Hobbes)   248; (Locke)   248–9;
    (Mill)   Ch. 7.3 *passim*, 203; (Marx)
    262–5; (Plato)   Ch. 3.9, Ch. 3.10,
    Ch. 3.11; (Rawls)   258–60; (Rousseau)
    249–52; (Sartre)   267–71; (other)   Ch.
    12 *passim*, 203, 231–2, 234, 240, 247

Soul (Aristotle)   Ch. 4.5; (Indian philosophy
    – *ātman*, *puruṣa*)   438, 441, 444, 445,
    446, 448; (Plato)   Ch. 3.7, 88; (other)
    170, 371 (*see also* Mind, Self)

'enlightenment'/'release'   438, 440, 442,
    444, 445, 447, 449, 455

immortality   64–5, 73–5, 198, 340, 376–7

reincarnation/transmigration   56, 74,
    438, 440, 442, 443

Space and time (Kant)   135–6; (other)
    166, 452

temporality (Heidegger)   357, 359

void (*śūnyatā* – Indian philosophy)   441

Speech-acts (Austin, Searle)   46, 361, 418, 420, 421, 422, 453 (*see also* Action, Ethics, Language)
speech/discourse (Derrida)   363–4
State, the (Aristotle)   Ch. 4.10; (Marx) 264–5; (Mill)   255, 257; (Plato)   Ch. 3.9, Ch. 3.10; (Rousseau)   251–2 (*see also* Society)
Structuralism   180, 361, 364, 420, 457
    post-structuralism (Derrida)   362–5, 457
Subjectivism (*see also* Realism, Truth)
    art and hermeneutics   331, 332, 415, 419
    ethics   186, 205, 210, 211–14, 215–16, 217
    metaphysics and science   290–1, 382
Subject-predicate   65, 66, 70, 98, 135, 136, 301, 350, 452, 457 (*see also* Analytic-synthetic, propositions)
Sublime, the   333 (*see also* Beauty)
Substance (Aristotle)   Ch. 4.3, 103, 347, 354; (Indian philosophy)   443, 444, 445, 447, 448; (other)   4, 95, 170, 347–8, 372, 457
Suicide   232–3
Śūnyatā   *see* Space and time – void
Syllogism   Ch. 2.4, 11, 34–5, 51, 457
Symbols   406, 426–33 *passim*
Sympathy   190, 192, 202, 207, 249
Synthetic propositions   *see* Analytic-synthetic propositions

T

Taoism   318, 439–40, 442
Taste (aesthetic)   191, 332–3
Tautology   20, 21, 301, 397
Teleological argument   *see* God – arguments for existence
Teleology (and purpose)   69, 95, 96, 106, 107, 186, 196, 198, 221, 268, 305–8, 333, 375, 425, 458 (*see also* Causation – causes and reasons)
Terms   *see* Logic, Syllogism
Theory (science)   276, 278–82, 386, 457 (*see also* Covering law theory, Methodology, Reductionism)
Translation   361–2, 366 (*see also* Language, Meaning, Reductionism)
Truth   Ch. 5.7, Ch. 5.8, 1, 3, 10, 13, 39, 46, 47, 59, 83, 84, 123, 141, 144, 280, 310, 345, 349, 360, 364, 397, 443, 445, 446, 447, 448, 454
    artistic   330, 332, 336 (*see also* Hermeneutics)
    coherence theory   143, 149–50, 153, 157, 159, 286, 445, 447
    correspondence theory   150–2, 153, 156, 157, 448

normative rationality theory   155–6, 158, 419
    pragmatic theory   153–4, 157–8, 206
    redundancy theory   154–5 (*see also* Performatives)
    semantic theory   152–3
    truth-functions   *see* Proposition – logic of
    verification   153, 154, 172, 174, 176, 215, 276, 288, 296–7, 341, 359–60, 421, 455 (*see also* Falsification, Knowledge – justification)
    verisimilitude (Popper)   288, 289–91
    warranted assertibility   154, 155

U

Unconscious, the   370, 377–8, 406
Understanding
    Verstand (Kant)   135, 194
    Verstehen (Dilthey, Gadamer)   404–5, 415, 416, 420, 421, 454
Universalizability (Hare)   219–24 *passim*; (Kant)   Ch. 6.3, 229; (Sartre)   212
Universals   58, 65, 66, 97, 100, 101, 102, 137, 139, 140, 142, 350–5, 455–6, 457, 458 (*see also* Concepts, Form)
Utilitarianism (Hume – 'utility')   Ch. 6.2; (Mill)   Ch. 6.4, 193, 215, 227; (Rawls) 258–60; (other)   210, 458
    act/rule   204–5, 221

V

Validity/invalidity   13, 17–18, 22, 23–7 *passim*, 34–5, 36
Value/moral worth   195, 205–10 *passim*, 211, 262 (*see also* Ethics, Fact and value, Rules – ethics)
Vedānta   *see* Indian philosophy
Virtue (Plato)   Ch. 3.12, 59
    cardinal virtues (Plato)   80–2
    and happiness (Aristotle)   Ch. 4.6, 117; (Kant)   198; (Mill)   Ch. 6.4 *passim*
    intellectual and moral (Aristotle) Ch. 4.7
    natural (Rousseau)   249–50
    social (Hume)   191
    virtue and justice (Aristotle)   Ch. 4.7 (*see also* Justice)
    Viśiṣādvaita   *see* Indian philosophy – Vedānta

W

Warrant (reasoning)   40–1 (*see also* Confirmation, Inference, Knowledge – justification, Truth)
Well-being (Aristotle)   *see* Happiness